THE GROWTH OF
SOCIOLOGICAL THEORY

THE GROWTH OF SOCIOLOGICAL THEORY

Human Nature, Knowledge, and Social Change

DAVID L. WESTBY

The Pennsylvania State University

Prentice Hall, Englewood Cliffs, New Jersey 07632

Library of Congress Cataloging-in-Publication Data

WESTBY, DAVID L.
    The growth of sociological theory : human nature, knowledge, and
social change / David L. Westby.
        p.   cm.
    Includes bibliographical references and index.
    ISBN 0-13-365867-8
    1. Sociology—History.   2. Sociologists—Biography.   3. Social
change.   I. Title.
    HM19.W38   1991   90-43502
    301'.01—dc20

Editorial/production supervision: *Edith Riker/Bea Marcks*
Cover design: *20/20 Services*
Prepress buyer: *Debra Kesar*
Manufacturing buyer: *Mary Ann Gloriande*

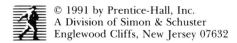 © 1991 by Prentice-Hall, Inc.
A Division of Simon & Schuster
Englewood Cliffs, New Jersey 07632

Printed in the United States of America

10 9 8 7 6 5 4 3 2 1

ISBN   0-13-365867-8

Prentice-Hall International (UK) Limited, *London*
Prentice-Hall of Australia Pty. Limited, *Sydney*
Prentice-Hall Canada Inc., *Toronto*
Prentice-Hall Hispanoamericana, S.A., *Mexico*
Prentice-Hall of India Private Limited, *New Delhi*
Prentice-Hall of Japan, Inc., *Tokyo*
Simon & Schuster Asia Pte. Ltd., *Singapore*
Editora Prentice-Hall do Brasil, Ltda., *Rio de Janeiro*

for Doris,
at last

CONTENTS

Preface   xiii

Acknowledgments   xv

1 Introduction   1

   Three Problematics   3

I THE ENLIGHTENMENT AND THE BEGINNINGS OF SOCIOLOGY

2 The Idea of Progress and the Perfectability of the Human Race   6

   Preface to Part I   7
   Anticipating the Great Transformation: The Idea of Progress   7
   The Two Aspects of the Idea of Progress   11

3 The Philosophical Anthropologies of the Enlightenment and the Idea of the Social   17

   The Enlightenment Rejection of the Christian View of Human
     Nature   19

Hobbes's Philosophical Anthropology   23
The First Dilemma: The Uniformity of Human Nature and the
    Diversity of Human Behavior and Custom   25

The Second Dilemma: The Problem of Evil and the Doctrines of
    Original Nature   31
Rousseau   37
Conclusion   50

4 Knowledge and Human Science   51

Natural Law, Metaphysics, and Scientific Empiricism   54
Natural Law, Metaphysics, and the Ideal of Freedom   64
Conclusion: Knowledge, Human Nature, and Social Change   70

5 The Scottish Moralists   73

The Scots' Concepts of Personal and Societal Relations   75
The Scots' Theory of Progress and the Liberal Market Society   81
Conclusion   94

6 Christian Social Philosophy and the Conservative Impulse   96

Augustine   97
Vico   101
Herder   109
The Reactionary Conservatives   118
Conclusion   124

II THE SOCIOLOGIES OF THE NINETEENTH
    CENTURY

7 Auguste Comte Sociology and the Enlightenment Vision   126

Preface to Part II   126
Saint-Simon   128
Auguste Comte   129
The Theory of Social Statics: Compte's Resolution of the Dilemma
    of the Doctrines of Progress and the Fixity of Human Nature   131
Comte's Theory of Social Dynamics: Science and the Law of the
    Three Stages   134
The Doctrine of the Hierarchy of the Sciences: Comte's Resolution
    of the Dilemma of the Nature of a Human Science and the
    Problem of Human Nature   138
Theory and Practice   143

8 Herbert Spencer and Evolutionary Sociology   146

   The Problem of Human Nature   148
   Spencer's Theory of Sociological Knowledge   154
   Societal Evolution   156
   Conclusion: Spencer, the Problematics, and the Enlightenment   166

9 Backgrounds of Marx: Hegel and the Young Hegelians,
   Materialism, Feuerbach, and Marx's Critique   169

   Hegel   170
   The Materialists   179
   The Theory of Alienation: Hegel, Feuerbach, and Marx   181

10 Marx and Engels: Historical Materialism and the Sociology
   of Capitalist Society   188

   Introduction   188
   Marx and Engels   191
   Marx's Philosophical Anthropology   193
   Dynamics of Change: Historical Materialism and Theory
      of Capitalist Society   196
   The Labor Theory of Value: Use Value and Exchange Value 205
   The Theory of Exploitation   209
   Marx's Sociology of Capitalist Society   217
   Workplace and Society   218
   The State   222
   Classes and Class Consciousness   224
   Marx's Theory of Social Knowledge   229
   Conclusion   234

III   SOCIOLOGY AT THE TURN OF THE CENTURY: THE CRISIS OF
      LIBERALISM AND THE RECONSTRUCTION OF SOCIOLOGY

11 Emile Durkheim I: Philosophical Anthropology
   and the Rules for Sociology   236

   Preface to Part III   236
   Durkheim's Life and Career   240
   Durkheim's Philosophical Anthropology   242
   The Division of Labor   248
   The Rules   262
   Conclusion: Causality and the Domain of Social Facts   279

12 Emile Durkheim II: The Substantive Sociologies
(a) Individualism, Occupational Groups, and the State:
Durkheim's Political Sociology
(b) The Sociology of Religion and the Foundations of
Knowledge   282

Individualism and the Cult of the Individual   283
Occupational Groups   286
The State in Industrial Society   291
Suicide   294
The Sociology of Religion and the Foundations of Knowledge   303
Science, Religion, and Society   313
Conclusion   316

13 Max Weber I: Philosophical Anthropology and the Methodology of the Historical and Social Sciences   318

The Life, the Work, and the Times   318
The Intellectual Setting: The Historicist Movement   321
Weber's Philosophical Anthroplogy   323
The Methodological Foundations   332
Interpretation and Critique of Weber's Theory of Social Action 352

14 Max Weber II: Weber's Conceptual Scheme and Historical Sociology   365

Weber's Theory of Historical Development   365
The Core Problem of Weber's Sociology: Economic Ethics and the
Origins of Salvation Religion   368
The Medieval City   387
The Protestant Ethic and the Spirit of Capitalism   396
Weber's Theory of Rationalization and the Rationalization of the
West: Rationalization in the Social Orders   404
Weber's General Theory of Rationalization   435
Conclusion: Critique and Reprise   440

15 Seminal Contributions in Early Twentieth Century Sociology in the U. S.:   443
(1) Cooley and Mead   443
(2) Thomas and Znaniecki   443

G. H. Mead: Interaction and the Self   445
Social Interactionism: Mead's Philosophical Anthropology   446
Mead's Theory of the Self and Social Interaction   451
Mead and Pragmatism: The Theory of Knowledge and Progress   457

**The Polish Peasant in Europe and America: Theoretical and
Empirical Synthesis in American Sociology**   461
The Polish Peasant: Context and Critique   480
Conclusion   485

16 Conclusion   486

Sociology After 1920   486

Bibliography   491

Index   513

PREFACE

This book is predicated on the assumption that there is always a place for restudies and reinterpretations of the histories of the disciplines, perhaps especially the social science disciplines. It has long been commonplace that the past is for every present always something newly constructed and should, therefore, have something new to say to that present. I want this book to speak to our present, and I hope that the fact that the narrative concludes *circa* 1920 with the account of the seminal turn-of-the-century social theorists, will not prove to be an obstacle to this. In any case, this is as it is: time, space, and the enormous scope and complexity of the materials themselves have forced a momentary suspension of the historical account in a book perhaps already too long. I do intend that the future will see the project brought to an up-to-date conclusion.

Over the years I have come to understand more clearly the seventeenth and eighteenth centuries' influences on our discipline, influences typically given only cursory attention in histories of sociological theory. In this volume I attempt to redress this lacuna by situating and interpreting the first century (roughly 1820–1920) of sociology's development in this context. Such a project must necessarily ignore much, some mention of which should be made if only to anticipate objections.

The growing body of empirically-minded, but theoretically generally disinterested, sociological workers appearing on the scene around 1840 and thereafter will scarcely be mentioned in these pages. The best of these, such as Le Play in France, Booth in England, and Dubois in the US, are not unimportant, but they contributed little to what, with perhaps unwarranted disciplinary arrogance or narrowness, we consider theoretical advance.

Excluded also, for the most part, are the anthropologists, who profession-alized their discipline a generation before sociology, and who did have some influence on important sociologists like Spencer, Durkheim and Weber. Great sociologically-inclined thinkers like Tocqueville, Freud, and Nietzsche, of course, have left their mark on sociology, and such influences will be noted, but they cannot be the central focus of a study such as this, if only because it would be impossible to do justice to the works of such mighty minds within the confines of this project. Finally, I hold to a minimum, an inexcusable minimum some will think, the treatment given a number of important sociological theorists in favor of concentrating on the more or less acknowl-edged masters. In this category fall Tarde and Le Bon in France, Tönnies, Simmel, Ratznhofer, Gumplowicz, and Oppenheimer, and perhaps Husserl as well, in the German-speaking lands; Hobhouse in England, de Greef in Belgium, Westermarck in Finland, Pareto in Italy, Ward, Sumner, and Giddings in the U.S.; and the most remarkable of Russian thinkers, the anarchist Prince Kropotkin. But what I intend here is a study of how certain problematics appearing in the intellectual life of the Enlightenment have influenced the directions of sociological development, not a general survey of sociological ideas.

   One reason for the length of this book has to do with what I take to be fundamental presuppositions and ideas that define the trajectory of sociological theorizing. Sociology being an empirical discipline, it follows, I think, that the empirical work of the great theorists should not be given short shrift or relegated to secondary or remote status, even in a theory book. Much of the importance of all great sociological theorists lies in the manner in which their ideas come to life in their (or in some instances, perhaps others') empirical work. The importance of the empirical dimension increases as we approach the present; the chapters on the turn-of-the-century theorists therefore come to bulge with accounts, interpretations and critiques of their theories as these relate to their empirical work. The reader is asked to bear with the author in what may in some instances be overly prolix disquisitions.

   Finally, it should be said at the outset that, in focusing on the flow of ideas, this project bears the burden of the defect of treating sociology of knowledge issues only sketchily and unsystematically. This is not because these are unimportant, but simply because, once again, to attempt this would inevitably overburden the project. Ideas are not, of course, autonomous from social structure and culture, but neither are they, nor can they be, merely determined by factors defined in terms of these categories. This project is inescapably one-sided, but I view this less as a flaw than as a matter of interest and emphasis.

ACKNOWLEDGMENTS

During the course of writing this book various colleagues, students, and reviewers read the manuscript either in part or in its entirety. For the resulting helpful comments and criticisms I especially wish to thank Janet Newton, Ed Walsh, Charles Bolton, Frank Hearn, Mary Waters, Kevin Ross, and four anonymous reviewers. Norbert Wiley, as always, has been an inspiration to me, and three decades of association, I am quite certain, have left their mark on me and this book. Several years of continuing discussions with David Maines, Mari Molseed, and Scott Camp, I hope and think, have helped to improve the book's quality. All errors, misconceptions, dead-end arguments, and failures of nerve are, of course, my own.

I would like to express my appreciation to several editors at Prentice Hall, particularly Nancy Roberts, for their patience and perseverance through the various phases of the preparation of the manuscript. Frank Clemente and Roland Pellegrin, present and past heads of the department of sociology at Penn State, provided much needed and much appreciated resources over the course of several years. Debi Welsby, Sheri Miller, and Betsy Will bore the brunt of the typing, and I want to thank them for their tireless endurance and inner fortitude in bearing with me in what must have been experienced as a near-interminable succession of unreasonable requests and demands. To my wife Doris goes my appreciation for taking on the thankless and particularly difficult task of typing the bibliography. I am indebted to Craig Gibson for his careful and competent work preparing the name index.

1

INTRODUCTION

The human sciences, even in their present adolescent state, stand as one of the nobler achievements in history. Yet the tentative stirrings of self-understanding that they represent, and the humane future they have always seemed to promise, have never seemed more fragile. For like all other human activities, the social processes of knowledge production are nested in, and inevitably must come to terms with, the political and economic realities of society, as well as the conditions of their own internal organization. The sources of bias are everywhere for they inhere in all experience; the struggles for power reach into all corners of social existence; and much if not most social knowledge itself possesses the potential, inherently disturbing to most, of profoundly challenging the received wisdom. The wonder is not that the human sciences have failed to transform the globe, or even to have approximated the power of their natural science brethren, but, rather, that they continue to exist at all.

   This surprising array of developments—the emergence and growth of the social sciences—has always been of special interest to its practitioners and apprentices. Psychologists, economists, political scientists, anthropologists, and, perhaps above all, sociologists, have always been preoccupied with their origins, their reasons for being, their paths to the present. In this volume I shall be going over ground trodden by earlier chroniclers, but with some different footwork. Certainly, there is little justification for just another historical *account*. In the following pages I develop an interpretation of the emergence of sociology from its presociological origins up to the twentieth century from a different viewpoint, namely, that the great innovations in sociological thought have occurred because of the existence of incongruities

1

and tensions between concrete versions of three "problematics" to be described shortly; and further, that these problematics remained pertinent for the work of the first generation of academic sociologists around the turn of the century, and even for understanding the drift and direction of the discipline today. This is to say that the fundamental questions that exercised the thinkers who brought our discipline into being—the issues at the roots— are still with us.

The concept of "problematic" is central to the task of this work. Abrams's definition grasps *part* of the sense intended here:

> A rudimentary organization of a field of phenomena which yields problems for investigation. The organization occurs on the basis of some more or less explicitly theoretical presuppositions . . .
>
> (Abrams, 1982, xv)

This definition borrows from Althusser (Althusser, 1971) and is intended to direct attention to the broader contexts within which the disciplines are organized. It points to the presuppositional aspects of inquiry distinct from those designated by such terms as *theory, paradigm, conceptual scheme,* and *domain assumption.*

However, for present purposes, it is necessary to modify this concept in two ways. First, I wish to give it an interpretation broader than the context of an existing or developed discipline, and to extend it to *predisciplinary* conditions. The meaning of this will be obvious in the chapters to come; here, it is necessary only to make the banal observation that although sociology did not exist in the eighteenth century, or at any rate scarcely existed, the idea of a problematic may nevertheless be fruitfully applied to the protosociological work of some of the thinkers of the period.

Second, to the principle that the problematic "yields problems for investigation", we append the notion that it does so to one degree or another because of inconsistencies, contradictions, or antinomies that attend the "propositions" themselves, perhaps especially in the predisciplinary condition. Again, the concrete sense of this will come clear in the chapters following.

As an intellectual enterprise, sociology was powerfully conditioned by the directions taken in the intellectual work of thinkers working within three problematics, all emerging from the advancing scientific revolution of the preceding two centuries. These were specifically: (1) the revolutionary idea of progress as a *natural* organizing principle of the human condition, set against theological and static doctrines; (2) the idea of a fixed human nature challenged by notions centering on its malleability, and (3) the astonishing notion, again opposed to received doctrine, that human action could be understood scientifically, and that this understanding could be the basis for an emancipatory practice.

The problematics of human nature, social change, and the possibilities of a science of human social life in the late seventeenth and eighteenth centuries, then, came to constitute *rudimentary* organizations of certain "fields of phenomena" yielding "problems for investigation." The specific forms these problems came to assume derived from or were constituted out of dilemmas and antinomies in the received theologies and philosophies, aspects of the worldviews of this and the preceding period, mainly medieval Catholicism.

Sociology took shape originally (and began to separate itself with some degree of distinctiveness from other types of social analysis) through a dramatic recasting of the assumptions about the social world contained in the medieval Christian worldview. The breakdown of that order—politically, socially, economically—was the massive condition of the appearance of the social sciences in general. It is not assumed that there was any particular *immanent* reason why specific conceptions within these emerging problematics should have been brought together as the first versions of sociology. However, the fact is that—in this interpretation—they were decisive for the development of the discipline. In this analysis, I trace the interlacing of the various concrete formulations of each and attempt to show that they have influenced the emergence of sociology as we know it.

THREE PROBLEMATICS

Social Change: The Great Transformation

Beginning in the West, sometime during the fourteenth century, the massive societal upheaval that Karl Polanyi has called "The Great Transformation" (26) now engulfs the world, and through the forces it has unleashed threatens the very survival of the race. It is, of course, not in the least surprising that this movement has been accompanied by a most varied array of attempts at comprehension and interpretation. Initially mostly religious in nature, these intellectual movements have only relatively recently assumed their secular or "naturalistic" form.

But even among secularized intellectuals, social change as a master problematic would never have been possible within the received antiquarianism that dominated intellectual life well up into the eighteenth century. Until this time intellectual culture had venerated the past and invested antiquity with an authority that precluded anything like a science of society. The decisive shift may be seen in philosophers like Descartes, who wrote that "men must cut themselves off from preconceived notions of past authority"; and Fontenelle, who in *The Dialogues of the Dead* (Fontenelle, 1949) argued that natural philosophy (meaning natural science) and mathematics were disciplines that were able to perfect themselves gradually, but must continue to do so. Descartes and Fontenelle stood with the "moderns" in the seventeenth and eighteenth centuries' debate between "moderns" and "ancients?"

During the course of the eighteenth century, this attitude became quite firmly established, in progressive circles at least, and begins to appear in the thought of thinkers like Condorcet as systematized history of the advancing perfectibility of humankind. Antiquity was now seen as no more than the starting point for a series of epochs leading up to the present, a present typically understood as a transitional stage leading to a new and revolutionary future. The conception of change as progress invaded all important European intellectual cultures: Hegel and his followers in Prussia;

the philosophes and others in France; liberals of various sorts, like John Locke in England, and Tom Paine in the American colonies. The ideology of change as progress was to be decisive for the historic path of sociology. This will be the topic of Chapter 2.

Philosophical Anthropology and the Problem of Human Nature

By "philosophical anthropology" I mean a set of questions regarding the nature of "human nature" in relation to society. Philosophical, religious, and social scientific conceptual systems may all be thought of as possessing, in varying degrees of explicitness, such a framework of understanding. A philosophical anthropology provides answers to at least three questions:

1. In what sense do members of the human species possess a common "original" or presocial nature?
2. What implications does this have for social life (i.e., can the nature of social life be analyzed on the bases of such assumptions)?
3. What ethical implications (i.e., prescriptions for proper conduct or social organization) arise out of the first two considerations?

In the presociological period of the eighteenth century, several forms of more or less secularized philosophical anthropology appears in European intellectual life. These included: (1) the liberalism running from Hobbes through Locke and Mandeville, to classical political economy and the utilitarianism, up to its greatest nineteenth century sociological form, the work of Herbert Spencer, later labeled the theory of "possessive individualism" by McPherson; (2) a basically conservative view, heavily influenced by Christian theology and practice and the theory of the Fall, as represented among French conservative thinkers such as Bonald and Maistre; and (3) a "sociable" conception of man's nature, best represented in the Scottish school of Smith, Ferguson, Hume, and others, and among deists such as Shaftesbury.

Although different in substance, the liberal and conservative views have in common the assumption that an understanding of social life (including politics and economics) requires grounding in characterizations of original nature and proceed, usually deductively (Hobbes is here the exemplar), to an analysis of social life. The "sociable" view is best thought of as an early tentative movement toward a more specifically sociological form of understanding that never quite succeeded in shaking off original nature assumptions. The "original nature *causes* social level" formula underlying so much of eighteenth century social thought has had a profound and lasting effect on the nature of our discipline.

To the foregoing it is necessary to append a disclaimer. Nothing here is to be understood as a rejection of the idea of human nature *as such*, or even its place in present or future sociology. All that is claimed is that in the earlier stages of sociology's development the practice of employing conceptions of original nature as explanations of social phenomena was a domain assumption constituting a major obstacle to the eventual instantiation of a discipline conceived of in nonreductionist fashion. This holds independently of the *substance* of original nature concepts, i.e., whether it is the faculty of reason, or the impulses of self-preservation, of hunger, sex, maternity, and so on, or even the more questionable "social instinct" or "social feeling," or some combination of these, that is (or that are) held to constitute basic human nature. We take up these issues in Chapter 3.

The Possibilities of Social Knowledge

Throughout the medieval period, human knowledge was assumed to be either a manifestation of eternal truth, or, as in Aquinas's understanding of Aristotle's logic, to be deducible from it. All knowledge was seen as a unity since all of nature was the creation of God. By and large, the process of knowing was itself generally unproblematic: it can fairly be said that the middle ages produced no epistemology. Furthermore, it was an implicit corollary of Christian revealed truth that what was already known was far more important than what might be known in the future. The overwhelmingly significant future event, of course, was the second coming, which all Christians *knew* would occur.

The notion that the methods of the natural sciences might legitimately be applied to the social world is essentially an eighteenth century innovation that reaches an early fruition in the work of Saint-Simon and his student, Auguste Comte. From Comte there is a direct line running through the nineteenth century to Durkheim and others. But even before Comte, it was being argued that social phenomena were lawlike, and in particular, that there were natural laws underlying the movement of history. It was this connection, between the new idea that social phenomena were somehow subject to natural laws on the one hand, and on the other, that these laws were historical and developmental (and being laws, "necessary" in their working) that lay at the root of Comte's claims for the scientific status of sociology. The problematic of a human science is the focus of Chapter 4.

Early sociology emerged as a partly unintended consequence of changes of direction and innovations in thought that can be framed in terms' of the three problematics. This set the mold for the growth of sociology for decades to come, and its imprint remains on the discipline. This book, organized in three sections, is an analysis of some of the critical moments in the history of the discipline. In the first section, the three problematics and their interrelations are discussed in terms of their implications and consequences for the early emergence of sociology. This is a period roughly between the late seventeenth century and 1815. The second section focuses on a few seminal nineteenth century thinkers—mainly Comte, Spencer, Marx and Engels and some of their forerunners—to epitomize the ways in which the earlier Enlightenment and anti-Enlightenment ideas were transformed in the intellectual whirlwind of evolution. The third section deals mainly with the postevolutionary path-breaking sociologies of Durkheim, Weber, and the major American pragmatists, the seminal innovators of the turn-of-the-century period.

2

THE IDEA OF PROGRESS AND THE PERFECTIBILITY OF THE HUMAN RACE

PREFACE TO PART I

It is sometimes implied, if only by their omission, that eighteenth-century intellectual developments were, for the most part, a mistaken rationalism for which later sociological thought provided a corrective. But Enlightenment thought was a stage of early sociology apart from which the sociologies proper of the nineteenth century could in no way have been what they were. This was so, first of all, because the very way of thinking about sociology was an Enlightenment (and post-Enlightenment) bequeathal framed by what I shall call the problematics of social change, human nature, and knowledge. In Chapters Two through Four these are dealt with in turn, with emphasis on their interrelationships.

In Chapter Five it will be shown that the Scottish school of moral philosophy went a good distance in the direction of formulating an early sociology around these themes, in the form of analyses of the nature of social interaction and the emerging capitalist societies. In Chapter Six the profound influence of the Christian worldview in the partially secularized thought of Vico and Herder prior to the revolution, and in its reactionary postrevolutionary form, as this appears in the work of thinkers like de Maistre and de Bonald, is brought into focus.

In this and the following two chapters, I shall analyze the nature of and interrelationships among the conceptions of social change, philosophical anthropologies, and theories of knowledge worked out by Enlightenment intellectuals. The tangled interplay of ideas framed by the three problematics became the theoretical staging ground from which the Enlightenment laid its mark on early sociology. Critical to the process was the fact that contradictions were present both *within* and *between* them, and it is in the manner in which these were managed intellectually that early sociology began to take shape.

ANTICIPATING THE GREAT TRANSFORMATION: THE IDEA OF PROGRESS

The major sociological systems of the nineteenth century, running from Comte through Spencer up to Durkheim and Weber, were all constructed in the context of an understanding that Western society, if not the entire world, was in some sense fundamentally progressive in its movement. Nothing is more fundamental to Comte's sociology than the idea that Europe (and ultimately "humanity") was moving away from Catholicism, feudalism, traditional kingships, and above all, the political struggles in the train of the revolution, in the direction of a social order that would be founded on a rational science and its practical applications. A specific conception of progress as a transformation of "mind" frames Comte's entire sociology. Spencer's sociology of a generation or so later likewise places everything within a progressive evolutionary movement. For Marx the economics of capital accumulation and the sociology of class conflict are made comprehensible in terms of the dialectic, a progressive principle of social change.

The work of these thinkers will be treated in some detail later. I mention them here to underscore the importance to nineteenth century thought of an idea they had little part in creating. Now, the sense or meaning of progress as comprehended by many of the intellectuals and the educated of the eighteenth century was of something larger than an idea; it was becoming more like the "ethos" of the times, as it has long since been for us. When today we contend over whether this or that practice or reform is progressive, we are thinking and acting within a problematic that came to life mainly in the thought and writings of that rather diverse group of thinkers in the eighteenth century generally referred to as the philosophes.[1] We must now ask, Just what did these philosophers, scientists, and others mean by progress?

Central to the idea was the presumption of the power of ideas to move and to transform any social and political formulations held to be obsolete, anachronistic, or repressive. Cassirer (1955) expresses this as the power of ideas to *dissolve* society. In its first relatively systematic secular form, Turgot attributed to the mind a quality, and to human moral action a

---

[1] The French word *philosophe* translates literally into English as "philosopher," yet no English word quite renders the French meaning. Some of the major figures were Voltaire, Diderot, D'Alembert, Turgot, and Rousseau in France; Kant, Herder, and Lessing in Germany; Hume, Smith, and Ferguson in Scotland; and Benjamin Franklin in the United States. In employing the designation as an international type, rather than its narrower application to French intellectuals, I follow Gay's usage (Gay, 1969, vol. 1, 10ff.)

potential scarcely imagined before this time.[2] The precocious Turgot, in his Latin *Discours* delivered to the Sorbonne in 1750 at the age of 23, advanced the rudiments of a theory of progress which placed the mind, along with the passions, at center stage of history, thereby launching the idea of human perfectability which was to become the ideological centerpiece of the liberal thought of the following two centuries.

Turgot held that

> ... all the ages are linked together by a chain of causes and effects which unite the existing state of the world with all that has gone before. The manifold signs of speech and writing, in giving to men the means of insuring the possession of their ideas and of communicating them to others, have made a common treasure-trove of all individual knowledge, which one generation bequeaths to the next, an heritage constantly augmented by the discoveries of each age; and mankind, viewed from its origin, appears to the eyes of a philosopher as one vast whole which itself, like each individual, has its infancy and its growth (cited in Teggart, 1949, 115).

Elsewhere, Turgot (1929) even formulated a three-stage theory of intellectual progress that anticipates Comte's theological, metaphysical, and scientific ages. The significance of Turgot's work is that it advances the idea of causal connections in history, and most particularly, the significance of the contacts of different cultures as the incubating conditions for social and cultural change.[3]

The late Enlightenment philosopher, the Marquis de Condorcet, worked out a more detailed scheme through which mankind has supposedly advanced. His *Sketch for a Historical Picture of the Progress of the Human Mind* may reasonably be considered the first actual *theory* of progress, in which the specific nature of the transformation is worked out in all major institutional sphere. He divided the past into ten epochs, as follows:

1. Hunters and fishers.
2. Shepherds.
3. Agriculturalists.
4. The Golden Age of ancient Greece (an age of the flourishing of science and philosophy).
5. From Alexander to the fall of the Roman Empire.
6. From the end of the Roman Empire up to the Crusades.
7. From the Crusades up to the invention of the printing press.
8. From the invention of the printing press up to attacks on the authority of men like Luther, Bacon, and Descartes.
9. From Descartes to the French Republic, a period during which the ideals of reason and freedom were becoming established.
10. The future, in which this trend will continue.

---

[2] For general discussion of the idea of progress, see Brinton (1953), Bury (1955), Cassirer (1955), Gay (1969), and Todd (1918).

[3] For a discussion of and emphasis on this point see Becker and Barnes, 1961, 1, 411–415, and 2, 470–473. For good general discussion of Turgot, see Manuel (1962), Chapter 1.

Condorcet held that this sequence reveals a movement toward perfection that will culminate in complete material security and equality, international peace, and individual liberty for everyone.

> How consoling for the philosopher who laments the errors, the crimes, the injustices which still pollute the earth and of which he is often the victim is this view of the human race, emancipated from its shackles, released from the empire of fate and from that of the enemies of its progress, advancing with a firm and sure step along the path of truth, virtue and happiness! It is the contemplation of this prospect that rewards him for all his efforts to assist the progress of reason and the defense of liberty. He dares to regard these strivings as part of the eternal chain of human destiny; and in this persuasion he is filled with the true delight of virtue and the pleasure of having done some lasting good which fate can never destroy by a sinister stroke of revenge, by calling back the reign of slavery and prejudice. Such contemplation is for him an asylum in which the memory of his persecutors cannot pursue him; there he lives in thought with man restored to his natural rights and dignity, forgets man tormented and corrupted by greed, fear or envy; there he lives with his peers in an Elysium created by reason and graced by the purest pleasures known to the love of mankind. (Condorcet, 1955, 201–202)

A late Enlightenment thinker, Condorcet stands as a transitional figure between the essentially philosophical approach of the Enlightenment and the more explicitly sociological thought of the nineteenth century. His listing of changes that must be instituted if progress is to continue included the establishment of equality for all within all nations, later a central socialist and anarchist tenet, but hardly one of the earlier philosophes. The relatively modern and sociological character of Condorcet's analysis of inequality may be seen, for example, in the manner in which he distinguished between different dimensions of inequality: Those of wealth, of income, and of education must be clearly separated and dealt with through specific reforms appropriate to each. Condorcet even anticipated the modern argument in developmental theory, that late-developing nations can bypass certain stages that the early developing ones, of necessity, had to pass through. He anticipated Veblen's "penalty of taking the lead" in his forecast of an "imminent decadence" of Eastern religions, accompanied or followed by a progress more rapid than that of the West, since much of it could simply be taken over from the West.

Historically oriented theorizing of this sort is distinctly modern in character. The significance of the past, in Turgot's stages or Condorcet's progression, lies in the fact that, if studied properly, (that is, scientifically, or in the empirical spirit), the past will reveal the principles of the progress of the human mind. Such knowledge will make it possible to master not only nature, but human nature as well. This view of the world required a reversal of the attitude toward the past that had prevailed prior to the seventeenth century—the veneration of the ancients and of antiquity—although the philosophes owed much to antiquity and celebrated, even imitated, many of the ancients.[4]

Even while recognizing the immense significance of the ascendence of the idea of progress in the eighteenth century, it must be recognized that Enlightenment optimism was anything but a cheery Panglossism. An *un-qualified* faith in progress became to a much greater extent the ruling idea of nineteenth century thinkers like Comte and Spencer. Gay writes of the philosophes' "grim belief in progress." Hardly any of the thinkers of the time, including Turgot, thought that progress was or would ever be a linear movement in history, or that it would be achieved by anything other than protracted struggle. Kant theorized that progress itself occurs only because of the struggle rooted in human nature.

> Man wishes concord; but nature knows better what is good for his species; and she will have discord. He wishes to live comfortably and pleasantly; but nature wills that, turning from idleness and inactive contentment, he shall throw himself into toil and suffering even in order to find out remedies against them, and to extricate his life prudently from them again (cited in Becker and Barnes, 1961, 2, 484).

It was not only Rousseau who observed that, while humankind may be perfectible in principle, the species is everywhere observed to be corrupt (the immense implications of which for the philosophical anthropology of the nineteenth century will be taken up later). Voltaire's *Candide*, sardonically subtitled "Optimism," is a *refusal* of despair in the face of the most terrible of worldly evils.

It is perhaps obvious that one essential condition for an ideology of progress is belief in the continuing existence of evil. If the future is to be an advance beyond the present, the present must evidently contain a significant component of evil, to which one may not and should not be resigned. Indeed, the religious conception of the universe that preceded the Enlightenment identified evil as a *necessary* component of the nature of things, necessary for its ultimate *perfection*.

> If all partial evils are required by the universal good, and if the universe is and always has been perfectly good, we cannot expect that any of the partial

---

[4] Like virtually every other important modern idea, the roots of progress can be found in the Greeks. In this regard Aristotle's doctrine of the distinction between the domains of law and chance was absolutely fundamental. Along with the several spheres of nature, human social life was included in the former. The *Politics* is a *scientific* treatise seeking to elucidate the laws of *development* (i.e., teleological processes) governing human *communities*. This doctrine, both in Aristotle's own writings and in those influenced by him for more than *two millenia* (meaning practically everyone in the tiny intellectual worlds prior to the Renaissance), tended to formulate the generalized *theory* of explanation as an inquiry to discovery the *accidental factors* (in the domain of chance) that obstructed developmental change from its lawlike course. Thucidides, for example, frames his study of the Peloponnesian war in this fashion. The emergence of modern evolutionary theory in the seventeenth and eighteenth centuries required that this conception be abandoned, and supplemented by an explanatory paradigm in which the focus falls on the central process of change (i.e., progress) itself, in terms of supposed stages of advance (see Bock, 1978 and 1956).

evils will disappear. Logically, thorough-going optimism is equivalent to the doctrine of the Conservation of evil, metaphysical, moral, and physical; the sum of imperfection in the parts must remain constant, since it is in the realization of just that sum that the perfection of the whole consists (Lovejoy, 1936, 245).

The philosophes broke with this doctrine, of necessity, as Lovejoy says, by "temporalizing" the received static conception of the order of things. But to seriously imagine a future in which evil was significantly reduced demanded a great leap of faith. Not only its obvious persistence, but the power of the doctrines that justified it and found it necessary for the larger perfection, were massive intellectual and moral obstacles.

THE TWO ASPECTS OF THE IDEA OF PROGRESS

The philosophes envisaged the future as the progressive embodiment of reason manifested in "human establishments," as the Scots might have put it. But this conception of the future as progress of the mind was a hydra-headed one. On the one hand stands the idea of a covert agency that somehow manifests itself in human affairs, a metaphysic that displaces providence. Cassirer observes that during the course of the eighteenth century, the idea of reason began to acquire the sense of a *force* working in history, supplanting the older, seventeenth century idea of a static pattern in nature.

> The eighteenth century conception of history is less a finished form with clear outlines than a force exerting its influence in all directions, . . .pervading . . . progressively all the fields of knowledge (Cassirer, 1951, 198–199).

This notion was characteristically formulated as secularized natural law. The perspicacious Scot Dugald Steward held that mankind must be understood in terms of its place within a larger design, wherein "superintending wisdom . . . adapts the fin of the fish to the water and the wing of the bird to the air . . ." (Schneider, 1967, 93). Voltaire was a believer in a natural moral law and studied history to reveal "the progress of the human spirit" that resided beneath the incredible diversity of manners and customs. He engaged in his extensive historical work to display the richness and diversity of human culture, on the one hand, but on the other, to help achieve something even more fundamental—reveal the underlying force of reason in human nature.

Indeed, enlightened thought may be said to have held in common the idea of history as a scheme in which mind becomes increasingly conscious of itself. Could not the potential power of the human mind, a power proved by its grasp of the secrets of the physical world in the work of the great Newton and others, be turned on itself to reveal the secrets of what was assumed to be a constant human nature, and ultimately use this knowledge to transform the world? This was a dream by no means original to the eighteenth century. Francis Bacon had long since insisted on "a total reconstruction" of knowledge in the service of practical ends—the control of nature for human benefit. But now, in an increasingly secularized climate, the daring idea of the possibility of mastery, not only over physical nature, but human nature as well, was becoming the practical, even the essential, meaning of progress (Bacon, 1886).

It should be noted in passing that nineteenth century theorists of progress, in one sense at least, had an advantage over the earlier thinkers on whose ideas they were building. The French and industrial revolutions set in motion concrete political and economic forces in the form of actual social movements the like of which the eighteenth century could have scarce imagined. Just as socialist thinkers formulated their ideas in terms of the actualities of a burgeoning urban proletariat, liberals could link progress specifically to an increasingly powerful productive class of industrial enter-prisers. The practical absence of such potent agencies of change in prere-volutionary Europe probably had the effect, for some time at least, of restricting the sense of the driving force of progress to such abstract or disembodied conceptions as the "growth of reason," science or more broadly, an emerging "public opinion" (as literacy began to spread) possessing the quality of "reason" derived from natural rights conceptions. With no obvious agency immediately at hand, it was perhaps only too easy to imagine the future as the work of an abstracted reason.

Progressive eighteenth century thought, of course, has often been represented as a reflection of the interests of the rising bourgeoisie, especially by Marxists. And there is doubtless a good deal of truth in this. But despite the generally high repute of business in the eyes of some of the philosophes[5] and a somewhat Aristotelian view of businessmen as "middle class" and therefore the great stabilizer of society, none of them—not even Adam Smith—ever designated businessmen as a class as the historic force that would bring an emancipated future. The idea of a class as a dynamic or progressive force in history is a nineteenth century innovation. Even the most progressive among the late Enlightenment thinkers typically portrayed class relations as repressive and backward. Adam Ferguson, in some ways the most sociological of Enlightenment minds, writes:

> In every commercial state, notwithstanding any pretension to equal rights, the exaltation of a few must depress the many . . . We think that the extreme

---

[5] There was, of course, much diversity in all of this. Regarding commerce, Diderot announces that "the businessman is a soul of bronze to whom the life of his fellow man means nothing, whose aim is to starve a whole country for the sake of getting a good price for his wares" (letter to Madame de Meux, quoted in Gay, 1969, 2, 402). In England there was a debate between Dr. Johnson and Malachi Postelthwayt regarding whether or not a trader could be a gentleman. Voltaire's "other" view is revealed in the *Philosophical Dictionary*, under the entry "glory."

"The Chinese was a man of letters and a merchant, which two professions ought not to be incompatible, but which have become so among us, thanks to the extreme regard which is paid to money, and the little concern which mankind has ever shown, or will ever show, for merit."

See also the discussion of Mandeville in Chapter 3.

meanness of some classes must arise chiefly from the defect of knowledge, and of liberal education (Ferguson, 1767, 285).

Essentially the same can be said of that handmaiden of industrial progress, technology. Raymond Aron says of Montesquieu, for instance, that he "was far from grasping the implications of the technological discoveries for the transformation of society as a whole" (Aron, 1965, 33). Gay's *The Enlightenment*, a standard and highly regarded English language history of ideas of the period, contains not a single index reference to technology.[6]

The fact that the great transformation to an emancipated future was to be, first of all, one of the mind, meant that the role of intellectuals, i.e., the philosophes themselves, would be of central importance. Indeed, the Enlightenment may be thought of as a kind of reincarnation of that fusion of knowledge and power imagined by the Greeks as the fundamental precondition of the kind of human community necessary for living the good life. Philosophers would have the ear of monarchs ("enlightened" despots like Frederick and Catherine), would create and sustain educational enterprise and generally propagandize the values and substance of science.

Belief in progress as a more or less covert agency working in history, whether identified as "reason" or some other entity, stands in contrast with a more voluntaristic, practical, action-oriented understanding; an understanding evident in the practical actions of many of the philosophes themselves. Especially in his later years, Voltaire was continuously *engagé*. Condorcet was not only involved in the revolution but probably executed by the concrete embodiment of the force he celebrated as progressive.[7] Rousseau was a constant thorn in the side of the authorities, and was forced to live for long periods on the run, while Diderot was imprisoned for his opinions. Turgot, while serving as an official of the state under Louis XVI, tried to put Enlightenment tenets into action, especially in his six edicts of 1776, and was idolized by contemporaries such as Voltaire and Condorcet.

More importantly, an activist, voluntaristic conception of the mind appears on the theoretical plane as well. The eighteenth century was a time during which earlier forms of rationalism were reinterpreted in ways that justified the autonomous political activity of individuals—in some respects a broadening of the religious individualism of the preceding century and a half. Much of the faith in progress was rooted precisely in this conception of the human mind as fitting people for action, for effecting monumental

---

[6] It should be remembered that most of the philosophes were well-to-do, many of them aristocrats, and that they tended to share the still powerful aristocratic disdain of manual labor. Even so, one must be extremely careful about such generalizations. Turgot, for example, thought that progress occurred through four distinct spheres of creativity, of which technology, along with science, morality, and the arts, was one. *Les arts mechaniques* are by no means overlooked in the great *Encyclopédie* of Diderot and D'Alembert.

[7] Condorcet has been arrested by the Jacobins in March of 1794, and was found dead in his cell the following morning. It has always been widely believed that his death was not suicide, the official Jacobin announcement, partly because he was, in fact, under sentence of death.

changes if given free reign to do so. Although the seventeenth century conception of the mind as a passive receptacle remained enormously influential throughout the eighteenth century, the tendency among many of those following was increasingly to modify it in activist, if still somewhat essentialist, directions. Adam Ferguson, in his *Essay*, writes that

> (Man) is in some measure the artificer of his own frame, as well as his fortune, and is destined, from the first age of history, to invent and contrive (1767, 9).

Turgot, in Manuel's judgment, located the spring of progress in our fundamental need to innovate:

> There is for Turgot a basic drive in human nature to innovate, to vast novelty, to bring into being new combinations of sensations (Manuel, 1962, 18).

Although his work was not well-known or recognized as important until much later, the Italian philosopher Giambattista Vico, in his *New Science*, first published in 1725 (see Chapter 6), advanced a theory of history rooted in human agency.

> The first indubitable principle . . . is that this world of nations has certainly been made by men and its guise must therefore be found within the modifications of our own human mind (Vico, 1948, 349).

The passivity associated with this formulation was somewhat of a problem for later thinkers who were increasingly impelled to action. One of the ways in which this was accomplished was through a powerful recasting of the relation of the passions to the mind. In general, the Enlightenment moved in the direction of according a positive valence to the passions, which in one way or another were assigned an important role in progress itself by such diverse thinkers as Turgot, Kant, Diderot, and Hume.[8]

Voltaire objected to Locke's contention that there were no innate ideas, not only because this doctrine was incompatible with a belief in a fundamental and constant human nature, but because the *tabula rasa* seemed to leave no place for a mind active in remaking society. Cassirer says of Voltaire that in his *Essay on Manners* the concept of the mind has acquired an enormously expanded scope (specifically in comparison with Montesquieu, but, clearly by implication, in contrast to prior conceptions as well).

> It comprises the entire process of inner life, the sum total of the transformations through which humanity must pass before it can arrive at knowledge

---

[8] One very important modality through which this occurred, as Hirschman has convincingly shown, was through the introduction of the category of interest (long confined to the political sphere) into the economic sphere, accompanied by a positive sanctification of its consequences there. In Adam Smith's *Wealth of Nations*, for instance, the attachment of our interest to objective ends seems to sublimate and channel the not-so-moral sentiments, or passions, into actions that redound to the collective good. (See Hawthorne, 1977.)

and consciousness of itself. The real purpose of the *Essay on Manners* is to reveal the gradual progress of mankind toward this goal and the obstacles which must be overcome before it can be reached (Cassirer, 1955, 218).

The implication of this doctrine, which grew in power as the century ran on, was, of course, the necessity for transforming those institutions that held the mind in thrall. In particular, this meant emancipation from "superstitution," or traditional religion.[9] Enlightenment itself presupposed the elimination of superstition, which is why so much of Voltaire's literary effort was directed against received religion, Catholicism in particular. Indeed his popular reputation rested more on these attacks on any other aspect of his prodigious work. At a somewhat different level, Hume's *Dialogues Concerning Natural Religion* is probably the most devastating refutation of the *rational* ground of religious belief ever written.

In this connection, it seems that the philosophes' conception of progress was actually a particularization of a more general cyclical theory, in which the Golden Age of Greece and Rome is seen as an early Enlightenment in which the fetters of early tribal religions have been thrown off, permitting a flourishing intellectual culture (an idea developed later by Comte). The medieval period is a retrogression resulting from the triumph and resulting universal sway of the church (in particular, see Gay, 1969, 1, Chap. 1). The mind once again becomes a prisoner of superstition. The earlier achievements of humanists like Erasmus and Pompanozzi, even Rabelais and Cellini, are seen as an early beginning or preparation for the Enlightenment. The teleological drive of historical forces on the one hand, and the idea of mind as the agent of the human personality capable of transforming the world, on the other, became the poles between which much of the electricity of sociological innovation drew its spark.

The double sense of progress as a force in history and as social practice has its modern secular origin in the thought of the Enlightenment. The sociologists of the nineteenth century would set their tasks within the framework of this problematic of change as progress, and the intricacies of its relations with the problematics of human nature and social knowledge: The dilemmas and contradictions among them would be the leaven of enormously innovative social thought.

The reader has perhaps noticed that this discussion has already touched on the questions of human nature and of the possibility of social knowledge. It is important to emphasize that these three problematics, although of necessity discussed separately, at critical points interpenetrate.

---

[9] I refer to "traditional religion," since many of the philosophes, including Voltaire, were deists, or held to one or another form of non-Christian or personal religion. The story is told of Voltaire, who, upon observing the magnificence of the sunrise, fell to his knees crying, "I believe, I believe, O God!"; then, after rising and brushing himself off, announced, "But as for *monsieur* the son or *madame* his mother, that's a different story" (Gay, 1969, 1, 122). Although the philosophes generally imagined themselves as executing a fundamental break with Christianity, it is clear in hindsight that there were powerful continuities. Turgot, for example, delivered both of his *discourses* at the Catholic Sorbonne, arguing that Christianity following the fall of Rome had been the moving power in the progress of the race. See Crane Brinton, "The Enlightenment and the Christian Tradition," in his *The Shaping of the Modern Mind* (1953), 133–144.

Progress means the manifesting of human nature. But what is this nature? Furthermore, on what grounds can we claim knowledge of it? And what is the point of such knowledge, if not to apply it for the benefit of mankind? It is to these further questions, implied already in our discussion of progress, that we now turn.

3

THE PHILOSOPHICAL ANTHROPOLOGIES OF THE ENLIGHTENMENT AND THE IDEA OF THE SOCIAL

Sociology as a more or less scientific discipline emerged historically as part of the modernizing of Western societies. Its very existence presupposes a conception of the social as an ontic domain clearly distinguishable from biological and psychological realities, from history as a particularizing narrative, from philosophy understood as an at least partially nonempirical discipline, and of course, from any and all nonempirical religious or philosophic frameworks of explanation. (To these might be added, in more recent times, the sister disciplines of economics and political science, and somewhat more doubtfully, anthropology).

The task of conceptualizing the domain of the social bears with it that of defining the nature of the human individual and therefore the nature of the relation between them, for societies in their most irreducible sense are groupings of individuals. The theorization of this relation, in so far as it is carried out at a general level, to reiterate what was stated in Chapter 1, I shall take the liberty of calling "philosophical anthropology" (although in doing so I may be open to a charge of working some small violence on the conventional understanding of this term).

Although the cultures of preliterate prehistorical societies may be said to contain notions of human nature and the meaning of collective life, it is only with the appearance of the first civilizations, particularly those along the Nile and the Tigris and Euphrates, that such speculation was raised to the level of systematic thought, by the priesthoods of these societies. And it is only with the Greeks that systematic speculation was lifted from its religious context, thus creating the beginnings of secularized philosophy and science.

The nature of the individual appears as problematic in both Greek and early Judeo-Christian cultures, thereby becoming a principal object of systematic thought. Throughout Western history this fact has profoundly conditioned both thought and action, and done so from a variety of standpoints: ethical, religious, political, economic, social. The echoes of Aristotle's definition of "man" as a political animal with a capacity for reason, for instance, may be found reverberating down through history and reappearing in thinkers such as Bodin in the sixteenth century and Grotius in the seventeenth, then in Montesquieu and Ferguson a century later. In a variety of ways Aristotle's seminal thought influenced the early protosociology of the eighteenth century. One such influence was mentioned briefly in the preceding chapter (see f.n. 4). Of broader and perhaps more profound significance was Augustine's interpretation of the Paulinian understanding of the soul and its bondage to the original sin. This, at any rate, was certainly the critical touchstone against which eighteenth century progressive social thinkers forged their idea of human nature, an important link in the creation of sociology.

Broadly considered, the emergence of sociological thinking in the eighteenth and nineteenth centuries was powerfully conditioned by Western individualism, in action and thought. It meant that conceptions of society, or more abstractly put, of the social as an ontic domain, were framed by what I shall call the individual-society polarity. As I said earlier, such a formulation is perhaps present in all Western attempts to *theorize* what it means to speak of the social. But the individualism of Western thought, especially after the Renaissance and Reformation, lent a very distinctive energy and content to these efforts.

Prior to the appearance of sociology, speculation and analysis of social matters tended, on the one hand, to be collapsed within political thought, as in many social contract theories, and on the other, derived from and thus explained by various qualities imputed to "human nature." (The combination of these two restrictions is perhaps seen most clearly in Hobbes, whose work we shall discuss later.) The first has been remarked upon and analyzed many times over in works on the history of social thought. Although this issue will not be ignored, the emphasis here will be on the second, for this has not received the attention it deserves commensurate with its importance. During the classical and medieval periods, and on into the modern period, theorization of the social domain, in so far as it was even detached from religion, was in various ways reductionist, that is, explained by reference to qualities imputed to individuals conceived of variously, whether biologically, psychologically, spiritually, ethically, or in any other sense.

The fundamental conditions of distinctively sociological analysis are (at least) two: (1) conceptualization of a domain of human activity that is, *in principle*, independent of all others, e.g., the physical, the biological, the psychological, etc.; and (2) setting forth of some canon of explanation within this domain; that is, explanation of social phenomena by their (hopefully demonstrable) relationships to other such phenomena (and not, for example, as the outcomes of the play of psychological forces). This does not mean that, say, human physiology or geographic factors such as terrain or climate do not impose boundary or limiting conditions on at least some sociocultural phenomena. But here it will be assumed that a "discipline" explaining its constitutive phenomena through the effects of phenomena of other domains is, in principle, no discipline at all.[1]

Modern sociological conceptions emerged only gradually from a limited set of ways of theorizing the individual-society polarity, ways that took as their starting points one or another conception of human nature and its relation to the social plane. The discussion here will center on the interplay of two critical distinctions, conceived of as polar conceptions. The first of these derives directly from the preceding discussion. Is the social reality at bottom reducible to the level of the individual (however conceived), or is it a reality *sui generis*? The second has to do with the way in which "human nature" is conceived: Is it *uniform* and *unchanging*, or is it *variable* and *malleable*? The issue to be examined in this chapter is how it was that a nascent human science, grappling with alternative conceptions of *human nature* during the period of the Enlightenment, moved in the direction of a conception of a distinctively social domain or at least prepared the ground for its eventual scientific conceptualization.

To this end I shall proceed first, by discussing the sense in which Enlightenment philosophical anthropology was a reaction against and challenge to traditional Christian belief. Following this I will describe the inner dynamic of the movement from original nature explanations of social phenomena to "environmentalism," thence to the rudiments of the idea of the social, a movement driven by two kinds of tension: the first, between the doctrine of a constant and uniform human nature and the growing experience and appreciation of human diversity; the second, between the rejection of the Christian doctrine of the Fall and consequent corrupted nature of the species, and the obvious persistence of evil in the world. Finally, I will show the working of these ideas in the thought of two important thinkers of the time, Godwin and Rousseau.

THE ENLIGHTENMENT REJECTION OF THE CHRISTIAN VIEW OF HUMAN NATURE

Generally speaking, the Enlightenment philosophers challenged the Christian view of humankind with one in which the human race was removed entirely from the framework of religious definition and placed in the *natural* order of things. It is important to distinguish between two aspects of this shift. In substance, or content, the Enlightenment progressives were unequivocal in

---

[1] Western thought has persistently theorized these domains in terms of hierarchy, or level, as Lovejoy (1936) in his concept of "the great chain of being," has shown. This has both Christian and Greek elements, the latter formed in the terms of the tree of Porphyry (Cohen and Nagel, 1934, 246; Wiley, 1988). The idea of levels of reality raises the fundamental question of distinguishing between the nature of the inner space of any given level and its relations with those "above" and "below." Conventionally, we think of, or define, a level as a space within which some type (or types) of determinate relations (e.g., causal, functional, meaningful, etc.) describe the objects constituting the level. Relations with other levels may be "emergent," i.e., not specifiable in the language describing determinate relations within the level, or bounded by conditions imposing limitations on the level in question. The development and differentiation of the branches of knowledge have histories that can be described in terms of levels and redefinitions of level.

rejecting Christian doctrine, yet at the same time were disinclined to relinquish the domain assumption that *presocial* characteristics of human nature constitute the realm in which understanding of human social behavior should be sought.

Significant challenges to the Augustinian doctrine of original sin, of course, had occurred prior to the Enlightenment. Generally, however, these had been framed by a common acceptance of Christianity. Even the Renaissance humanists, who were of very great importance for Enlightenment social thought, for the most part did not repudiate Christianity (or religion in general) in principle, although the momentous challenges to Christianity set in motion during the Renaissance would evolve into a variety of quasi-religious religions, e.g., deism, "natural religion," Unitarianism, etc., thence into critiques even of these, such as Hume's *Dialogues*, as well as the doctrines of agnosticism and atheism, in what has seemed to so many for two centuries to be an irreversible shift from a God-centered to a human-centered world.

As the Christian conception of human nature was challenged and repudiated, what was placed in its stead? The task of the Enlightenment, writes Cassirer, was nothing less formidable than "to formulate a new concept of the human being and (trace) it various meanings, its applications and modifications" (Cassirer, 1951, 228). In this regard, he observes that the eighteenth century replaced religion with physiology, a shift epitomized in the works of thinkers such as Holbach, La Mettrie, and Diderot. In *L'homme machine* (*Man the Machine*), La Mettrie formulated what was surely one of the most extreme versions of this. Consciousness, which most thinkers after Descartes had regarded as an activity of an immaterial substance, becomes fully explicable as an aspect of the physical organization of the body (La Mettrie, 1960). Holbach, probably the most thoroughgoing materialist of the time, in his *La systeme de la nature*, reduced all activity to mechanical principles, matter, and motion, consciousness itself being a property of the brain and nervous system (Holbach, 1966). Such reductionist systems, with Newtonian physics or Lockean psychology as models, were typical of·the period.

Schemes such as these were constructed and employed as weapons in the struggle against Christianity, especially against the Christian revealed doctrine of an immaterial soul and related tenets. Christianity *separated* mankind from nature through the doctrine of the soul; Enlightenment thinkers formulated *their* theories of human nature on the basis of a rejection of this separation. Locke had already observed that only slight differences separated mankind from the animals, and the latter from the plant world. La Mettrie argued that the differences between what were regarded as "higher" and "lower" forms of life were merely a matter of degree, not of kind, and had to do with differences in complexity of structure (1960). Even a vague form of the idea of evolution was in the air. De Maillet apparently thought that later species may have developed out of earlier, now-extinct ones and suggested that this process could be studied through the science of geology (Fuller, 1938, 238). Robinet argued that neither animal nor vegetable species as they existed today were as God had originally created them (Lovejoy, 1936, 269–283). Others, including the philosopher Maupertuis (1974) and the natural historian Buffon (1971), advanced similar ideas.[2]

In becoming increasingly oriented to the human domain, the Enlightenment extended and modified the idea of reason inherited from the rationalist philosophers—Descartes, Spinoza, Leibnitz—of the seventeenth century. Eighteenth century progressive thought proceeded more in the empirical spirit of Bacon than of Descartes. Enlightenment philosophers understood reason as a broader, richer, more critical—and much more problematic—principle than it had been for the rationalists. For one thing, they were often skeptical of the powers of deduction *as such* to reveal anything about the real world and, powerfully influenced by Newton, preferred to construe reason as constituent of or underlying the empirical procedures of science. But beyond this, many of them—Voltaire, Holbach, Helvetius, and Rousseau—read into reason a powerful *critical* capacity, a capacity that could serve the social function of attacking and exposing the evils of existing institutions and practices. Although a capacity possessed by all, reason throughout most of history has effectively been denied expression and growth through perpetuation of false belief, mainly religious belief, an idea reflected in the following passage from Hume:

> Those who judge of things by their natural unprejudiced reason, without the delusive glosses of superstition of false religion, will reject celibacy, fasting, penance, mortification, self-denial, humility, silence, solitude, and the whole train of monkish virtues (Hume, 1939, 297–298).

The implications of reason in all of these aspects were clearly revolutionary. If reason is possessed by all, by what right do sacred or secular authorities exercise control of the thoughts and actions of others? If the mind possesses such heretofore unimagined powers of inquiry and understanding, should it not be charged with the work of revealing (today we might say "unmasking") and delegitimizing the repressiveness of traditional institutions? And beyond this, if the power of reason is best exemplified by the scientific advances of the time, must it not be equal to the stupendous task of remaking the world into a wonder garden serving human needs? The answer to this last question was a somewhat qualified yes, but with the proviso that, to achieve such an unheard of and grandiose end, reason would have to be turned on humankind itself—to reveal, for the first time, the true

---

[2] Along with the differences, this tendency reveals the continuing influence of Pope's "great chain of being" (Pope).

> Vast chain of being! From which God began,
> natures ethereal, human, angel, man,
> beast, bird, fish, insect, what no eye can see,
> from thee to nothing.

Lovejoy analyzed the idea into three constitutive principles: (1) plentitude, or "the thesis that the universe is *plenum formarum* in which the range of conceivable diversity of *kinds* of living things that is exemplified" (52); (2) continuity, or "shading-off of the properties of one class into those of the next . . ." (1936); and (3) gradation, or hierarchy, "the arrangement of all things in a single order of excellence," (59) "each higher order possessing all the powers of those below it on the scale" (58–59). A superb expression of this is found in Kames (1774).

nature of human nature. In a malevolent and evil world this would clearly be its heaviest task.

The Enlightenment challenged received Christian doctrine in yet another way. In the Christian doctrine of salvation, the basic distinction was that between the saved and the damned. Just who was or was not one or the other was, at the time, a debate ranging from radical universalists at one extreme to narrow sectarians at the other. Enlightenment thought rejected as irrelevant this entire controversy and its underlying assumptions, especially the doctrine of the Fall. But holding that human activity could be reason-guided toward humane ends implied the rejection of the Augustinian unfreedom of the soul in its slavery to the passions.

As a kind of corollary of this, some of the Enlightenment thinkers effected at least a partial moral rehabilitation of the passions. Despite considerable ambivalence regarding the consequences of human emotions, there was a tendency to attribute to them—sometimes, as we shall see, through the device of irony—beneficial or socially useful effects (as in the philosophy of Bernard Mandeville, to be discussed later), as well as in the radical reconstructions of Christian theology undertaken by thinkers such as Shaftesbury, Diderot, or Hutcheson (for a general discussion, see Cassirer, 1951, 102–108). Regarding sexuality, for instance, Gay remarks that:

> The *philosophes* moralized sexuality in a double sense, by endowing lust with moral purity and attempting to purify lust by an appeal to its own inner logic (Gay, 1966, 2, 205).

This positive valence placed on the passions was one of the important factors involved in the movement toward a distinct conception of the social domain, since it encouraged the reassignment of the source of evil from human nature to the functioning of social institutions.

Despite their rejection of doctrinal elements of Christianity, the Enlightenment thinkers nevertheless tended to remain wedded to the formal idea of a constant and unchanging human nature and the reflection or manifestation of this in the social order. This was itself a Christian legacy, but already by the seventeenth century appears in secular dress as well, especially in the work of that most unsociological of political philosophers, Thomas Hobbes. It is useful to go back to Hobbes in examining this domain assumption because it is in his work that the paradigm of the post-Christian relation between presocial human nature and the social order was most rigorously and clearly formulated, and because of his considerable influence (in Cassirer's estimation, "a powerful and lasting influence" [Cassirer, 1951, 19]), despite the fact that later Enlightenment thinkers generally found his philosophy repugnant because of its emphasis on the fundamentally egocentric, and therefore violent nature of human nature and the authoritarian order that he deduced from this.[3] But even while rejecting Hobbes's substantive doctrines, they tended to retain the *form* of explanation in which

---

[3] See for example, Montesquieu's critical comments in *Spirit of the Laws* (Montesquieu, 1966, Book 1).

presocial characteristics of human nature were held accountable for social life.

HOBBES'S PHILOSOPHICAL ANTHROPOLOGY

Hobbes was born at Malmesbury in 1588, the son of a poor country parson, after a term of about seven months. It was said that his premature arrival was precipitated by his mother's fright at the approach of the Spanish Armada. He studied at Oxford and afterward traveled on the Continent where he became acquainted with many important intellectuals, including Galileo. From the perspective of the deposed Stuarts, in exile in Paris, the views expressed by Hobbes in *Leviathan*, his most important work, published in 1651, were decidedly iconoclastic, since they could be interpreted as justifying the usurpation and rule of Cromwell. After the Stuarts had been restored, however, Hobbes regained their favor, and even became friendly with Charles II. He continued to write until his death in 1679.

Hobbes's system is a completely unified one, in which the "great chain of being" stretches from its grounding in geometry, through physics and ethics to politics, the constituent categories of nature.[4] *Geometry* deals with the relations of motion to space; *physics* with the transfer of motion and its effects of bodies on one another; *ethics* with conscious processes; *politics* with the effects of minds on one another. The identical laws apply in all four subdivisions: Ethics is conceived of as a geometry of consciousness, politics as a physics of the social world.

The subject matter of philosophy, for Hobbes, is comprised of bodies and their motions. Space and time are material, being attenuated "phantasms" of bodies in motion. Motion results from the impact of one body on another. We use the terms *cause* and *effect* to indicate the passing of motion from one body to another.

These ideas are applied systematically to the sphere of ethics. The fact that some bodies possess consciousness in no way implies a break in nature. The fundamental categories of consciousness are interpreted by Hobbes as forms of those applied to physical nature. Our bodies endure innumerable collisions in consequence of all bodies being in motion. The collisions result in what we call sensation. As sensations fade, our recollections of them, analogous to phantasms of physical bodies in motion, remain as memory, which Hobbes thinks of as "a decaying sense." Images, simple or complex, persist, and may be "reinforced" by further collisions; older images may be revived by fresh stimuli, and complex "associations" may arise in the mind. It seems natural enough to Hobbes that, given all this, the race should be naturally inquisitive. We desire to represent these processes to ourselves; science and philosophy are the result.

The willful aspects of experience result from the impingement on the body of external impressions. The body responds to the impacts with what Hobbes terms *endeavors*, of which there are two types. If the stimulus

---

[4] The following discussions are drawn from materials in *De corpore* and *Leviathan*.

is pleasurable, it leads us to move toward it; such an endeavor is called appetite or love. If it is painful, we move away; this is hate or aversion. These movements are either voluntary or involuntary. The former may be quite complex, incorporating both pleasurable and painful elements. If an alternation of appetites and aversions occurs, we *deliberate*, and up to the point of actual response, or action, feel *free* in our vacillation. Our ultimate response is an act of will.

The theory of ethics is immediately relevant for the study of politics because, through it, we learn that everyone is set in motion by a desire for self-preservation and self-expansion. This is the human analogue to the tendency for everything to continue in its original line or direction. Hobbes understands this innate tendency toward self-preservation and self-expansion as a universal desire for power. Politics is the universal expression of this desire as it is employed in the furthering of one's *interests*. The functioning of the mind in this self-interested activity is characterized by Hobbes as purely calculative. Indeed, human thought itself is defined as calculation. (One might ask, "Including Hobbes's works?")

If everyone is inevitably engaged in pursuing his or her interests, the resulting collisions can best be described as a *bellum omnium contra omnes*— a "war of all against all." This condition, however, becomes intolerable, resulting in a collective agreement, or *contract*, in which individuals acquiesce in the restriction of their "natural" freedom. By this act, movement from the "state of nature," in which all experience total freedom as a natural right, to the condition of civil society, in which these rights are voluntarily relinquished, is accomplished. By virtue of this, the government ("Leviathan") comes into being as possessor of virtually absolute authority, necessary for maintaining the peace. The best *form* of government, in Hobbes's view, is a monarchy. Whatever the form, the authority acquires the duties of defending subjects from one another, propagating the state religion, and acting as a censor. The duty of the subjects is to obey the sovereign, but with one theoretical loophole (in anticipation of Locke's doctrine of the right of revolution): only so long as the sovereign continues to fulfill his necessary and legitimate functions.

The importance of Hobbes for our purposes lies in his conception of human nature and the relation in which it stands to society. The individual, in Hobbes's world, is defined as a self-sufficient atom, a calculating entity that attempts to realize its interests of self-preservation and self-expansion. The *relations* this atom enters into (the convenants of society and submission: see below) result from and are determined by the inherent *presocial* qualities attributed to abstractly conceived isolated individuals. The specific nature of society as an authority relation between ruler(s) and subjects is derived from this postulated original nature.

Despite its formal elegance and internal consistency, Hobbes's system was vigorously attacked from various standpoints. For one, there is the mixing of normative and empirical elements. Cutting more deeply is the question of how it is that humankind, given the total freedom of the state of nature, would create a virtually unfettered state authority. Close by this point is the criticism that Hobbes fails to show that we would be any better off under the sovereign than in the state of nature. Furthermore, how is it that human beings, existing in a state so brutal and irrational, could exercise the vision and reason necessary to bring the contract into being? Other formulations of the contract idea, like those of Hugo Grotius and John Locke, . . . suggested alternatives that, in different ways, circumvented this difficulty. There is a further problem involving the virtual identification by Hobbes of social relations and state authority, as Cassirer puts it, collapsing the "covenant of society" into the "covenant of submission," leaving the latter as the only remaining form of social bond by virtue of which any sort of social life may arise (Cassirer, 1951, 256).

Hobbes's assumptions about human nature as exclusively self-interested and calculative have been criticized repeatedly. In a penetrating analysis of Hobbes on this point, McPherson (1962), following many others, argues that this is an unsupportable universalization of normative conceptions of the individual in capitalist society. In this view, Hobbes was the seminal modern liberal, and liberalism since can be viewed as a series of attempts to circumvent his depressing conclusion concerning the relation of self-interested individuals in their relation to or production of society.

The difficulties of Hobbes's theory, however, are of only minor relevance for our purposes. For these, Hobbes's significance lies in his influence on later thought, through establishing and legitimizing the domain assumption that the nature of social life can be explained by or derived from imputed presocial attributes of a supposed universal human nature. This presumption survived in the thought of many later thinkers, but during the eighteenth century came under increasing pressure from two very different sources: (1) the growing appreciation of the diversity of human life, and (2) the problem of explaining worldly evil without recourse to the Christian account of original sin.

THE FIRST DILEMMA: THE UNIFORMITY OF HUMAN NATURE AND THE DIVERSITY OF HUMAN BEHAVIOR AND CUSTOM

In progressive intellectual circles, an abstract belief in the basic unity of the species was perhaps as firmly entrenched a principle as one will find during the Enlightenment. It is an example that attests to the staying power an idea may have in the hands of those whose interests seem to depend on it. In the intellectual armament of eighteenth century progressive thinkers, the idea of the unity of humanity was a weapon in the struggle against Christianity, and they clung to it tenaciously, even as the astonishing variety of human cultures was being revealed. Formulated in Western thought first by Greek Stoic philosophers, and taken to be the first principle of sociology by Comte, it is perhaps the grandest, most hopeful idea ever to have emanated from the human mind. It is also arguably the most naive, and sociologically speaking, most unpromising one. Our interest here in this grand vision, be it noted, is not in its intrinsic worth or lack thereof, but in assessing its significance in a specific development of thought.

By the early years of the eighteenth century, innovations in technologies such as shipbuilding and navigation, combined with the centralization of political power into a relatively few major powers in Western Europe, were making possible an expansion of the European presence and consciousness on a scale not previously achieved since the Roman conquests. Reports of explorers, military colonialists, civil administrators, and religious proselytizers, of travelers in search of the exotic, were becoming commonplace. Travel in general, undertaken throughout the middle ages only rarely and at great risk, by the seventeenth century was becoming a realistic possibility for many. To a much greater extent than before, social thought in the eighteenth century takes as objects of interest the detailed differences not only between humans and nonhuman species, but also among the varieties of humans. For secular intellectuals, the growing sense of human diversity came to constitute a challenge to their conceptions of human nature. Generally they responded by theorizing the problem in two ways, one of which was relevant to the eventual emergence of sociology, and one that was not.

The nonrelevant line of response was to hold to the conception of a uniform and constant human nature. The relativity of "manners" revealed in works such as Montesquieu's *Persian Letters* and Voltaire's satires, was taken by some of the philosophies as a *challenge*, even an *opportunity* to uncover or reveal the wellsprings of a *universal* human nature. In his historical work, Voltaire revels in dramatizing the staggering variability of human customs, but then argues that this was actually the form in which reason, everywhere the same, reveals itself.

The tendency to retain original nature conceptions as explanatory of the social may be seen even in the sociologically inclined Adam Ferguson. Ferguson placed great emphasis on human inventiveness and went to considerable lengths to reconcile the resulting cultural diversity with the constancy of presocial human nature. Even the most recent cultural innovations, he argued, are really "the latest devices which were practiced in the earliest ages of the world, and in the rude state of mankind" (1767, 9). Seeming diversity reflects a true homogeneity or uniformity of "certain devices" (i.e., cultural practices or institutions). And the important point: This homogeneity *results* from humanity's limited array of presocial qualities:

> Men are themselves in different climates and in different ages greatly diversified . . . it appears necessary . . . that we attend to the universal qualities of our nature before we regard its varieities . . ." (Ferguson, 1767, 16–17).

In his view, the catalogue of universal qualities included (1) the "mutual inclination of the sexes"; (2) the "suckling instinct," which for him is identical with that of "natural affection"; and (3) the "spirit of clanship" (1767, 85). Ferguson thus dealt with the problem by conceptually limiting the range of cultural phenomena to a relatively few original inventions, and by emphasizing the continuities in their historical development, thereby bringing them into conformity with original nature.

Such attempts to cling to human nature explanations stand in contrast to the tendency that has occasionally been referred to as "environmentalism." Environmentalism may be thought of as a transitional period occurring prior to the gradual emergence of sociology as an identifiable discipline. Its essential character is the shift to "external" factors in the explanation of human behavior, with particular emphasis on the natural environment. It was Montesquieu who probably provides the best sociologically inclined form of environmentalism in the eighteenth century. Indeed, Montesquieu's environmentalism is probably the most sociological of the time. Raymond Aron says that Montesquieu was "first and forever intensely aware of human social diversity" (Aron, 1965, 1, 59). In *Persian Letters* he had displayed a quite remarkable detachment in chronicling a fictional journey through Europe taken by two Persians—a brilliant and witty inversion of European ethnocentrism toward non-Europeans. In *The Spirit of the Laws* (Montesquieu, 1966), hereafter referred to as *SL*, he observes "the infinite diversity of laws and manners" on which the entire analysis is predicated.

It is the central idea of *SL* that the political institutions of a society, and its central cultural forms as well ("manners" and "customs") can be accounted for by analyzing their "spirit," which Montesquieu subdivides into two categories, environmental and social. The diversity of forms of rule he classifies into three general types: monarchy, republic, and despotism, the republic taking either aristocratic or democratic form. Each type is defined in terms of the principle that informs it; "honor" for monarchy, "virtue," meaning something akin to patriotism, for the republic, fear for despotism. But also, and very importantly, whereas despotism is rule beyond the law, Montesquieu defines both monarchy and republic as different forms of rule of law. Size also enters the picture:. Like the classical authors from whom this (modified) classification derives, Aristotle in particular, he finds democracy possible only in small societies, thereby ruling it out as a realistic possibility in the large societies of eighteenth century Europe, a view quite congenial to Montesquieu, himself an aristocrat (see Vol. 1, Books 2–8).

Montesquieu goes on in later sections of *SL* to analyze the *relations* between forms of rule, on the one hand, and environmental and social conditions, on the other (see Books 14, 26). Environmental factors are classified according to climate and qualities of the land; social factors according to commercial, demographic, and religious groups. Countries where the productivity of the soil is great, for example, are more likely to produce a monarchy than a republic, because "a country which overflows with wealth is afraid of pillage, afraid of an army" (1, 271). This accounts for Greek democracy. Moreover, cold climates are conducive to greater vigor, which in turn "must produce . . . a greater boldness, . . . sense of superiority, . . . a greater opinion of security, . . . more frankness, less suspicion, policy, and cunning" (221). There is a great deal of this sort of environmentalism in *The Spirit of the Laws*, most of it worthless. On the other hand, many of Montesquieu's analyses of social factors are trenchant sociological observations. Consider two examples of this. The first has to do with the relationships between economic life and social mobility based on merit. It is contrary to the spirit of a monarchy, Montesquieu holds, to allow aristocrats to enter into commerce, and this practice, he thinks, has weakened the English monarchy. French practice is "extremely wise" in excluding the nobility from commerce but not barring merchants from entry into the nobility. This encourages efficient management, for it is the successful merchants who will gain entry into the superior class (327)—even if through the widespread purchase of titles (a detail unmentioned by Montesquieu).

The second example has to do with the broader matter of Montesquieu's observations and analysis of the English polity and society. These led him to a theory of rule that is partly an overlay, partly an extension of the classically derived but modified types. A moderate, and therefore humane rule, which for Montesquieu meant one guaranteeing liberty, he argues, arises out of social divisions, most importantly those of rank. The English constitutional monarchy rests on a balance among classes (1, Bk. 11). In France, with its strong aristocracy, moderate rule must necessarily be aristocratic. Montesquieu wrote at a time, during the mid-eighteenth century, when the power of the monarchy was growing, thus threatening the rights and powers of the aristocracy (and therefore Baron Montesquieu himself). The basic idea is that the aristocracy checks the power of both the masses and the monarchy; all therefore exercise only limited power relative to the others. This is an important idea, influential for later French thinkers, in particular (and also for the American colonial elite seeking to define the proper constitution after the revolution). For formulating and applying ideas like this Montesquieu has been justly credited with being the first empirically-oriented "pluralist" political sociologist.

What is important in this is the way in which Montesquieu's environmentalism shades off into true sociological analysis. Indeed, once the "environment" is constituted as a category bearing explanatory power with regard to human behavior, the *principle* of a more general "external" explanatory paradigm is already implicitly in being. The door is then open to custom, law, economic factors, and much more. At some point the proliferation, and of course, actual use of such categories begins to look like something approximating a relatively systematic sociology.

It is worth noting that environmentalism, like its extensions into the political, cultural or economic aspects of social life, must virtually unavoidably attend to the given complexity and multidimensionality of the category. This encourages, at least in Montesquieu's case, a somewhat systematic, if uneven observational method. And indeed, the sociological merit of Montesquieu's work rests on the spirit of observation that pervades it. It is "multicausal," presuming that a variety of factors of varying weights must be invoked in order to provide adequate causal explanations.

The philosopher Helvetius, writing somewhat later than Montesquieu, provides a very different type of environmentalism, one centered on education. Helvetius was a prominent figure in the French philosophical materialist school of the late eighteenth century, and his basic concept of human nature was a materialistic and utilitarian behaviorism.

> Men have not changed their nature, and they will always perform nearly the same actions for the same rewards (Helvetius, 1810, 113),

and

> Corporeal sensibility is the sole cause of our actions, our thoughts, our passions, and our sociability (135).

At the root of all experience lies a balance of pain and pleasure. Helvetius tries to show that such common social relations as friendship and power are derived from experiences of pleasure. Now pain and pleasure are environmentally induced; all that original nature provides is the corporeal material. Particular types of social relations, for Helvetius, are not reflections of original nature, but result from different types of *education*. Helvetius's behaviorism is at the root of his extended treatment of education, which he saw as a *panacea* for everything wrong with the world.

> All men, commonly well-organized, have an equal appetite to understanding (82).

and

> The inequality in minds or understandings, is the effect of a common cause, and this cause is the difference of education (94).

For Helvetius, education becomes virtually coterminous with the totality of experience—it is lifelong, proceeding not only from schooling, but from "the manner (the) form of government gives to a nation," from "books, friends, mistresses" (25–26). His discomfort with the present system has to do only with the fact that most of it remains in the hands of chance. This he would set right. "To render it perfect," he proposes, "it must be directed by a public authority and founded on simple and invariable principle."

More generally, the importance of education to the philosophes as a world-transforming agency could hardly be overemphasized. As a liberal panacea, education has its modern origin in this period. Doctrines such as Locke's had to be invented to accommodate theoretically the interests of reformers in formulating the nature of the human mind as a receptacle open to new ideas of a progressive sort. Many of the would-be reformers constructed educational schemes. A vast faith in education is found in the reformism of Diderot and Condorcet. In *Emile* (1979), Rousseau struggles with the absolute imperative of some kind of education, against the backdrop of his theory of the "noble savage" of his earlier work. The theorists of the future were publicists, constantly bombarding the literate public with the books, essays, pamphlets, edicts, plays and poetry, and even musical works, that bore their message. All of it was, in their understanding, an educational undertaking. Their belief that even despots could be educated, which is to say "enlightened," reveals their great faith in education as a prime mover. The author of *Candide* could attach himself to Frederick II who, to his great disappointment, before long showed himself to be king first and philosopher second.

Even this brief review of a few selected texts suggests that the growing sense of the diversity of human collective life could not indefinitely live in peace with the doctrine of a presocial constant human nature as an explanation of social phenomena. Although even the greatest minds among them continued to at least genuflect in the direction of original nature, the attempt to ground explanations of the diversity of social phenomena in this domain was perhaps bound to undergo severe reformulation, if not outright rejection. Either the diversity had to be reduced, as Hume put it, to a "variety of maxims which still suppose a degree of uniformity and regularity," or the movers of human action would have to be relocated outside a constant and uniform human nature—the crucial step on the road to a genuinely sociological statement.

Environmentalism not only points in the direction of considering social life as an autonomous ontic realm, but also toward an observational, empiricist *style* of social science, as well, perhaps on the order of Montesquieu's beginning, or of the Scots'. This was not, however, to be the main line of presociological development in the late eighteenth and early nineteenth centuries. Rather than the growth of an empiricist sociology along these lines, what occurred was that social and cultural diversity came increasingly to be framed by the doctrine of progress, as this began to approximate a hegemonic intellectual ethos among progressive intellectuals and their off-shoots. We might say that the diversity problem came to be seen as the stuff with which thinkers like Turgot, Condorcet, and even Ferguson, and later more systematically and remorselessly Comte and Spencer, fleshed out the *stages* defining universal human progress.[5] In this fashion the "elective affinity," to borrow Max Weber's idea, between the idea of progress and the need to explain diversity was at the root of sociology's first systematically elaborated explanatory paradigm. The diversity gets explained, and in the process is massively, perhaps exponentially enhanced (for a discussion, see Bock, 1978).

In the course of these developments the incompatibility between the doctrines of original nature explanations of social phenomena, on the one hand, and of universal human progress, on the other, did not go unnoticed. This had the effect not of leading to an abandonment of the premise that original nature had to be implicated in explanation of human action in some fundamental way, but of contemplating a challenge to the premise of its immutability. Eighteenth century thinkers needed such a revision in order to explain the stretched-out diversity constituting human progress. But prior to the development of evolutionary biology, any and all attempts to formulate such a theory were necessarily entirely speculative, of no more scientific worth than the theological conceptions they wanted to displace. The strategy of linking a reformed plastic conception of human nature to the doctrine of human progress would become practically possible only with the displacement of the Linnean static taxonomy by the evolutionary biology beginning with Lamarck, and eventually in the sociological fruition of this in Spencer's sociology.

The eighteenth century thinkers were essentially unable to jettison the principle of explanation by original nature itself. This ingrained collective habit of the time remained the main obstacle to the kind of fully sociological scheme implied in Montesquieu's rather chaotic *oeuvre*. It would have been impossible for them to realize that in this environmentalist *cum* protosocio-

---

[5] Comte's claim to be a follower of Montesquieu must be judged as largely fraudulent; his evolutionism is certainly outside both the spirit and practice of Montesquieu's sociology.

logical scheme they had at hand the instrument that could make obsolete the very idea of original nature as relevant to social explanation.

THE SECOND DILEMMA: THE PROBLEM OF EVIL
AND THE DOCTRINE OF ORIGINAL NATURE

If one grants the doctrine of original sin, Christian theology proposes an internally consistent explanation of evil. Evil appears in the world because of our corrupted nature; the goodness in the world depends on Christian faith and its practice. The world as it is thus rests on the dual nature of human nature.[6] Serious reforms of social institutions, in *this* framework, are in general irrelevant, because the end transcending all others is individual salvation. (This fact makes those efforts at social reconstruction undertaken as Christian casuistry particularly interesting from a sociological standpoint.)

The problem of evil was perhaps the most vexing of all for the philosophes. If the evil of the world cannot be explained by the doctrine of original sin, why has the world been so full of it throughout history, and why does it continue unabated? Much reflection on this question was confined to conventional and theoretically unimaginative observations. Diderot, expressing a rather characteristic Enlightenment view, maintained that although human beings were born innocent, perhaps even good, they still had a *capacity* for evil. This dualism is expressed even in the title of his play, "Est-il bon? Est-il méchant?" Says Diderot, "The heart of man is by turns a sanctuary and a sewer." At various points, Voltaire, too, along with many others, frequently expressed the view that the species was composed of a mix of good and evil.[7]

Such views suggest the extent to which some aspects of Enlightenment thought remained tied to basic Christian doctrine, but obviously not entirely. The problem of evil was too pressing, much too critical in terms of the "modernism" and reformist interests of the philosophes, to indefinitely resist new intellectual departures. Its relevance for early sociology lies in these innovations.

The problem of evil was important to the development of sociology

---

[6] The nature of Christian dualism differs from other non-Christian forms, e.g., Manicheanism. In theologies or metaphysical systems such as the latter, two *distinct* principles govern the world, in Manicheanism, specifically, through struggle. In Christianity, on the other hand, the dualism is fused, or constituted *from* a monist principle to begin with. Augustine cries,

... I understand ... how the flesh lusteth against the spirit and the spirit against the flesh. Myself verily either way; yet none myself, in that which I approved in myself, than in that which is myself I disapproved." (Augustine, 1949, 153)

For Augustine,

". . . will is divided against itself. Our will, like Adam's after the fall, is not wholly bad . . . part of it yearns for the good it has lost, and would, if only it could, turn back to it." (Jones, 1952, 372).

[7] Pope reflects the eighteenth century sense of this ancient doctrine, shared by thinkers of every stripe:

"Two principles in human nature reign; self-love to urge, and reason to restrain . . .

and

"Self-love, the spring of motion, acts the soul; Reason's comparing balance rules the whole."

because it moved theorizing about the nature of moral conduct in the direction of social institutions. As the center of speculation moved from God to humankind, the problem of the source and justification of evil became increasingly acute. One way to tackle this problem was to reformulate the Christian doctrine of original sin in natural law terms, i.e., along Hobbesian lines. The difficulties of this approach—generally those mentioned in our discussion of Hobbes—led later thinkers like Bernard Mandeville to reconstruct the nature of the *relation* between a more or less Hobbesian original nature and human conduct in society in the form of the rhetorical device of irony. Somewhat paradoxically, it then becomes virtue, not evil that requires an explanation.

The Moral Wisdom of the System

Writing early in the eighteenth century, Mandeville in his *Fable of the Bees* presented an analysis that begins with essentially Hobbesian assumptions but that draws decidedly non-Hobbesian conclusions for society. Mandeville argues that the unhampered play of the individual's selfish interests produces not the absolute authority of Hobbes, but a social order resting on essentially utilitarian needs.

> Men are naturally selfish, unruly creatures, what makes them sociable is their necessity and consciousness of standing in need of others' help to make life comfortable . . . (Mandeville, 1729, 1, 10–11).

Mandeville observes the beehive, his model of human society, and concludes:

> Every part was full of vice . . . yet the whole mass a paradise (1, 24).

Universally selfish and egoistic, all cloak their actions as virtuous, in pride and notions of honor, and society itself can exist only through the free play of the appetites:

> . . . whilst luxury
> Employed a million of the poor,
> Were ministers of industry;
> Their daring folly, fickleness,
> In diet, furniture and dress,
> That strange, ridiculous vice, was made,
> The very wheel that turned the trade. (1, 25)

Society is truly held together through utilitarian interests, and virtue arises only through the masks by which we delude ourselves and others about our essential nature. Social life reflects the *representations* individuals advance regarding their natures; indeed it is these constructions, those of each individual, that literally constitute society.

> The first rudiments of morality, broached by skillful politicians, to render men useful to each other as well as tractable, were chiefly contrived that the ambitious might reap the more benefit from them . . ." (1, 47).

This seems not only irretrievably cynical, but very modern-sounding, as well. But Mandeville is very much an eighteenth century thinker, particularly in his understanding of society, indeed, of everything social, as "artificial." The manipulative and ego-satisfying arts of interpersonal relations derive from our truly basic nature. So, although he brilliantly describes the inner dynamic of social life, Mandeville still considers it artifice—not a domain with an inner structure of its own, but just a set of arrangements created by atomistically conceived individuals.

Adam Smith's study of the conditions of the "wealth of nations" in his great book of that title, although formally limited to economic life, also belongs in the category of irony-transformed Hobbesianism. Smith shows that the creation of wealth has two main causes: the developing division of labor and capitalist accumulation. These, in turn, are explained by the principle of self-interest, found in the breast of every man, "the propensity to truck, barter and trade."

Smith's analysis parallels formally (and is in part influenced by) that of Mandeville in its derivation of an essentially automatically functioning economic system. In following their "natural propensity," all people contribute unintentionally to the increase in wealth. My selfish interests naturally lead me in the direction of satisfying some need of yours. You, therefore, benefit from my self-interest. My purely self-interested action is thereby transformed into a socioeconomic function, transcending my private self-regarding action. Furthermore, to inhibit or attempt to suppress this naturally functioning system of self-interested wills is to inhibit the growth of wealth, which is self-evidently an inherently good thing.

In systems such as these, the Hobbesian formula of deriving the nature of the social order from the individual is retained, but the substance of the argument is modified. Hobbes had deduced the necessity of authority as the foundation of social order. Mandeville and Smith showed that it was possible to infer a completely different sort of order from essentially the same assumptions about human nature. Such systems thus illustrate the metamorphosis of Enlightenment thought in the direction of those conceptions of society we may call "systemic." The baser instincts of the race are surely there, but their unfettered expression produces beneficence on a *collective* plane. Evil, if not totaly eliminated, is at least ameliorated. Historically, the movement of society—seemingly away from the authoritarianism of theocratic and secular despots—seemed to promise a future that would wed individual freedom and collective order. This, of course, is the liberal formula: the freely acting individual, in serving him- or herself, produces social order with no authorities required. It was a formula that was to have a profound influence not merely on the nascent sociology of the time, but on the conventional wisdom of all the liberal societies of the West, and on sociology as well, of course, particularly although by no means exclusively, on the functionalist school.

Natural Sociability and Morality as a Law of Nature

A second line of thought addressing the problem of evil and bearing on the emergence of a conception of an autonomously constituted social level emerged in the eighteenth century. Here we find theories that retain the principle of an original nature, but reconstitute its substantive nature by introducing beneficent, sociable, or morally acceptable elements as explanatory of society, and then, by one expedient or another, theorize the persistence of evil as somehow inherent in or a consequence of this emergent social order.

Postulation of a social or gregarious instinct to explain human association is perhaps as ancient an exercise in thought as can be found. In antiquity Aristotle maintained that we are naturally "political" (meaning "social") animals (Aristotle, 1941), and St. Thomas Aquinas traced this predisposition to the original creation (1945). Jean Bodin argued that the social instinct, at first anchored in the family, but eventually expanding to wider circles, served the function of making life tolerable, despite the power and capacity for violence of the state (Bodin, 1962). Later, Hugo Grotius held that society was founded on a "social appetite," a position he maintained against contract theories emphasizing the instrumental foundation of human association (Grotius, 1964).

The English philosopher Anthony Shaftesbury stands in this tradition and is of importance partly because of his influence on the Scottish school (to be discussed in Chapter 5). His philosophy is a good example of a relatively modern attempt to resolve the problem of evil by rejecting both Hobbesian formulations resting on self-interest and Locke's doctrine of the external source of ideas, in favor of what he calls the "associating inclination." Shaftesbury holds that the associating inclination is "natural;" that is, it exists, as he puts it, in "original and pure nature" (Shaftesbury, 1, 1964, 110).

> If eating and drinking be natural, herding is so too. If any appetite of sense be natural, the sense of fellowship is the same (1, 110).

The inclination is further manifested in wider social groupings:

> And thus a clan or tribe is gradually formed a public is recognized [sic]: besides the pleasure found in social entertainment, language, and discourse, there is so apparent a necessity for continuing this good correspondency and union, that to have no sense or feeling of this kind, no love of country, community, or any thing in common, would be the same as to be insensible even of the plainest means of self-preservation . . . (1, 110–11).

Shaftesbury's estimation of theories that locate self-interest at the base of society is explicit—he does not reject outright the existence of self-interest (how, indeed, could anyone?), but plays down its significance in the context of motives resting on the supposed inclination to associate:

> . . . passion, humor, caprice, zeal, faction, and a thousand other springs, which are counter to self-interest, have as considerable a part in the movement of this machine. There are more wheels and counterpoises in the engine than are easily imagined. Tis of too complex a kind to fall under one simple view, to be explained thus briefly in a word or two. (1, 115)

The result is society as a complex clockwork. Shaftesbury employs the Deist argument for the existence of God to refute Hobbesian theories of society.

In this connection, possibly with Mandeville in mind,[8] he attacks those theories that

> ... would explain all the social passions, and natural affections, as to denominate them of the selfish kind. Thus civility, hospitality, humanity towards strangers or people in distress, is only a more deliberate selfishness. An honest heart is only a more cunning one. (1, 118)

With Hobbes in mind, spontaneous or nondeliberative acts are contrasted with calculative ones.

> For a common honest man, whilst left to himself, and undisturbed by philosophy and subtle reasonings about his interest, gives no other thought to the thought of villany than that he can't possibly find in his heart to set about it, or conquer the natural aversion he has to it. (1, 132)
> Speculative men find ... many ways of evasion; many remedies (1, 133)

Throughout, Shaftesbury identifies the associating inclination with a moral sense, referring to it as "this force of nature ... this moral magic" (1, 136). All the passions in which it is expressed are therefore, in part, moral in character, although Shaftesbury's understanding of morality connects it very closely with the aesthetic sense. The morality present in an amorous relationship, for example, residcs in "the curious search of sentiments," the "tender thoughts," the "*je-ne-scai-quoi* [*sic*] of wit," the "graces of the mind which these virtuoso-lovers delight to celebrate" (1, 137). Expressed naturally, i.e., without calculation, the associating inclination manifests itself in relations that are moral because of their *honesty*. Indeed, the test of morality for Shaftesbury is honesty: "with respect to morals, honesty is like to gain little by philosophy ..." (1, 132). Honesty, especially in the sense of noncalculative expressions that involve an aesthetic delight, is the common denominator of moral conduct.

The associating inclination manifested in much larger social units is no less moral.

> The relation of countryman, if it be allowed anything at all, must imply something moral and social. The notion itself presupposes a naturally *civil* and *political* state of mankind, and has reference to that particular part of society to which we owe our chief advantages as men, and rational creatures, such as we are, naturally and necessarily united for each other's happiness and support, and for the highest of all happinesses and enjoyments; the intercourse of minds, the free use of our reason, and the exercise of mutual love and friendship (3, 146).

[8] In an earlier footnote, Shaftesbury explicitly mentions Hobbes only. These quotes are from the 1723 edition, but the first printing was in 1708. Mandeville's *Fable of the Bees* was brought out in 1714, but a pirated edition of *The Grumbling Hive*, which expressed the essentials of his philosophy, and which was incorporated into the *Fable*, appeared in 1705. Shaftesbury was quite likely familiar with the essentials of Mandeville. That Mandeville was familiar with Shaftesbury's early work is not in question, since he is explicit in presenting his own *against* Shaftesbury's (1729, 1, 324). For a general discussion, see Horne (1978).

But what of evil? Shaftesbury's analysis of and celebration of the associating inclination makes it impossible for him to simply assert a *natural* source of evil. He argues instead that conflict results from the functioning or operation of the associating inclination, i.e., conflict is not inherent in human nature but occurs as a *consequence* of the actual social manifestation of the inclination, at an especially intense level. Warfare, party struggles, the conflicts of religious societies, are a few of the forms of conflict touched by Shaftesbury. In his view,

> the associating genius of Man is never better proved than in those very societies, which are formed in opposition to the general one of mankind . . .
> (1, 114).

The significance of this for us lies in Shaftesbury's tendency, in effect, to characterize conflict as a *social* phenomenon rather than as an emanation of original nature. Of course, he does not develop this *as* a sociological principle; this was not his purpose. And the logic of his argument is open to devastating critique. But in locating evil in the form of conflict outside of original nature, he takes a step on the route to an explicitly sociological formulation of an autonomously constituted social level.

These beginnings that are discernable in Shaftesbury were developed by later thinkers of the eighteenth and nineteenth centuries. If evil is exorcised from the soul, it must find a home elsewhere; some began to post its new address in the institutions of society. To his mistress, Sophie Valland, Diderot writes,

> No, dear friend, nature has not made us evil; it is bad education, bad morals, bad legislation, that corrupt us (Gay, 1969, 2, 170).

This theme, the corrupting effect of corrupt institutions on individuals came to be increasingly evident in the thought of many of the philosophes, and eventually received what was perhaps its most extreme formulation at the hands of the late eighteenth century thinker, William Godwin.[9]

Godwin and the Logic of Radical Individualism

In his *Enquiry Concerning Political Justice* (Godwin, 1946), Godwin attempts to show that all history has been no more than a "record of crimes," that all evil has its source in social institutions, and that the condition for the full realization of human reason is that the individual stand outside of

---

[9] Although long forgotten, Godwin for a time was regarded as one of the leading thinkers of the day. Barnes and Becker cite the contemporary evaluation of Hazlitt. "No work of our time . . . gave such a blow to the philosophical mind of the country as Godwin's celebrated *Enquiry Concerning Political Justice*. Tom Paine was considered for the time as a Tom Fool to him; Paley, an old woman; Edmund Burke, a flashy sophist. Truth, moral truth, it was supposed, had here taken up its abode, and these were the oracles of thought. 'Burn your books of chemistry', was Wordsworth's advice to a student, 'and read Godwin on Necessity'. 'Faulty as it is in many parts,' wrote Southey, 'there is a mass of truth in it that must make every man think.'" Godwin influenced Robert Owen and other utopian reformers (Becker and Barnes, 1, 473).

virtually all institutions, rejecting not only the state and other prima facie repressive forms of social organization, but even friendship and the reading of books, to achieve the end of a rational social order. The contradiction is patently obvious. Although the attribution of evil to social institutions has been one extremely important point of departure for the making of a true sociology, this end is short-circuited when subordinated theoretically to any form of human nature-grounded ethical idealism. Godwin remained tied to an ethical individualism grounding reason in the atomized individual, while simultaneously holding that all evil originates in social institutions. So he never got on to any analysis, which is to say sociology of the actual workings of these institutions to the end of *explaining* their evil nature.

Godwin saw his work as a kind of completion of Rousseau's idea that government was incapable of conferring any benefit on humankind. Ironically, despite his admiration for Rousseau and his feeling of intellectual kinship with him, he failed to perceive that the Genevan had already superceded him theoretically. Although he refers to *Emile* as "one of the principle reservoirs of philosophical faith, as yet existing in the world" (2, 129–130), in his own writings Godwin gives little evidence of grasping the profoundity of Rousseau's paradoxical conception of society, or of the complexity attending the growth and development of the individual in any society. He shared with Rousseau a rejection of the doctrine of progress and a belief in the evil nature of institutions. Rousseau, however, in his mature work, revealed both a sophisticated sense of the means or process whereby society socializes and oppresses the individual, and of the conditions necessary to facilitate the development of what we today would think of as an autonomous individual. Like Godwin, Rousseau salvages the individual theoretically; unlike Godwin, he does so while recognizing not only the devastating consequences of authority and hierarchy, but the inevitability of some form of social organization as well. Whereas Godwin merely asserts the ethical primacy of the individual—a reiteration of early natural rights doctrine now stripped of most of the old metaphysical underpinnings—Rousseau theorizes both about the possibilities of the actual *creation* of the individual in oppressive society (in *Emile*), and the possibilities of a society in which the principles of individual autonomy are built into its very social structure (in *The Social Contract*).

Godwin's work shows how the shift in the locus of evil from the individual to society could easily lead, though a moral rejection, to a profoundly nonsociological formulation. His weakness lies in failing to perceive that relocating evil in society requires that society be *theorized* not only to explain the evil, but to establish the ground for an emancipatory theorizing of the possibility of the good society as well. This was Rousseau's project.

ROUSSEAU

Among Western political philosophers, Rousseau has always seemed the most troubling and difficult to interpret. There is scarcely a political ideology with which his name has not been associated in one way or another, and he seems a morass of contradictions: a liberal individualist, but also a collectivist; a democrat, but, in the doctrine of the general will, by implication at least, a seeming totalitarian; a natural law philosopher, but perhaps more profoundly, a truly sociologically oriented thinker. These difficulties have been the despair of many Rousseau interpreters, and something of a tradition understanding him as near-hopelessly inconsistent has persisted.

Some have attempted to resolve this seeming inconsistency by distinguishing two Rousseaus: the first, he of the earlier works—the *discourses* and perhaps *La Nouvelle Heloise*; the second the author of *The Social Contract* and *Emile*.

Interestingly, Rousseau himself, in his *Confessions*, maintained that his work in its entirety was not inconsistent:

> all that is daring in the *Contract Social* had previously appeared in the *Discours sur l'inégalité*; all that is daring in *Emile* had previously appeared in *Julie* (Cassirer, 1963b, 3).

This is the position taken by Cassirer in his excellent *The Question of Jean-Jacques Rousseau*, as well as by a number of others, and it will be accepted as the foundation of the discussion to follow.

Rousseau has by and large been ignored by sociologists, and in any strict sense he was obviously not a social scientist in the sense of contemporaries like Montesquieu and Ferguson. Early nineteenth century sociologists like Comte, Le Play, and Spencer found in his work nothing of sociological value. He is dismissed by Comte as a "mere sophist" (1896, 2, 200). Marx, on the other hand, was impressed by his critique of eighteenth century bourgeois society. In this latter connection, although Rousseau was not the first to link the advancing division of labor with inescapable inequality, he was probably the first to develop the implications of this critique in the direction of modern conceptions of individual development and the nature of the community.[10] He was among the first to reflect on the nature of the individual as truly *problematic* from the standpoint of society. Rousseau's philosophical anthropology appears throughout his work, from the early two discourses through *Emile* and *The Social Contract*, which he worked on simultaneously. The theories of the ontogenetic development of the individ-

---

[10] The full range, direct and indirect, of Rousseau's influence is beyond the requirements of this project. He was, of course, of considerable political importance for the early egalitarians of the French revolutionary period, particularly Babeuf, and through him Buonaratti and Louis Blanc. More generally, perhaps, this influence appears in the socialist movement that was gaining power in the 1830s (see Talmon, 1952, 38 ff., and Lichtheim, 1969, Chapter 1). More important for our purposes was Rousseau's reception in Germany, not only by Kant, but more generally in the Romantic movement. Here the idea of the development of the faculties most evident in *Emile* appears in the more individualistic idea of *Bildung*. This concept and its significance will be discussed in Chapter 13. Rousseau was also of considerable importance for Durkheim, not only because of his ideas about the social formation of the individual (about which Durkheim remarks) but in other ways as well. In this regard it is worth mention that Durkheim's central concept of the collective consciousness, despite its evident differences, bears more than a passing similarity to the General Will, evidenced not only in the commalities, but in the criticisms brought against them as well, as being "mystical", "metaphysical", and so on. See Chapter 11.

ual and of the nature of community necessary for nonoppressive existence, worked out in *Emile* and *The Social Contract* respectively, are best treated in the context of what Cassirer has called Rousseau's "critique of modernity," which appears mainly in the two discourses.

Rousseau's Critique of Modernism

It was while on the way to visit Diderot, imprisoned at Vincennes but permitted visitors, that Rousseau, according to his account in the *Confessions* (1936, 540–541), found in the literary document *Mercure de France*, the announcement of a prize to be awarded by the Dijon Academy to the winner of an essay contest on the topic of whether the progress of the sciences and arts had contributed to the corruption or purity of morals. Rousseau says that he decided to defend the thesis that the arts and sciences had had a corrupting influence.[11] His essay *Discours sur les sciences et les arts* (Rousseau, 1964: *The First Discourse*) captured the prize and catapulted its author into the status of a reluctant celebrity. Three years later, in 1753, Rousseau submitted another essay to the same competition, this time on the topic of the origin of inequality. The *Discours sur l'origine et les fondements de l'inégalité parmi les hommes* failed to win the prize, but added to Rousseau's repute.

In the *First Discourse* Rousseau mounts what seems, at least on the surface, to be an unqualified attack on learning. What others idealized as progress, Rousseau perceives as progressive degeneration. The Renaissance, far from being an advance over the Middle Ages, was the beginning of a decline that has continued ever since. This condemnation of the cultivation of the arts and sciences is pressed on several grounds. For one thing, speculation is clearly more likely to lead to error than to truth. Furthermore, knowledge, or at least the form that learning has taken, provides little that is useful. Rousseau furthermore associates learning with luxury and the consequent dissolution of morals and military virtue.

If the cultivation of the sciences is harmful to warlike qualities, it is even more so to moral ones. The arts and sciences do no more than serve the ego needs of those who cultivate them, says Rousseau, and are essentially divorced from any significant communal utility. They are corrupt, therefore, because they arise with and serve the needs of men and women in corrupt society.

This critique of contemporary knowledge and learning remained a central theme in Rousseau's writing. Although it was formulated well before his disillusionment and break with Diderot and other Parisian intellectuals, and before he left Paris intending never to return, it was an attitude doubtless reinforced and sustained by his experience in *salon* circles. He remained uncompromising on this. For example, he later predicted that Peter the Great's empire would be destroyed because of the emperor's policy of attempting to disseminate the arts and sciences.

---

[11] Rousseau says that Diderot encouraged him to pursue the idea, and that "from that moment I was ruined," "all the misfortunes during my life were the inevitable effect of this moment of error" (1936, 541).

Rousseau's attack on knowledge in the *First Discourse* has often been taken as an unqualified condemnation, but this understanding has been challenged, particularly in recent interpretations. The critique is probably better comprehended as the first analysis of the function of knowledge as practiced by bourgeois intellectuals in a society undergoing extensive bourgeoisification. Perkins has shown, quite convincingly it seems to me, that numerous passages in the *First Discourse* reveal Rousseau's intention to limit his critique to the nature of current organization and practice (Perkins, 1974, Chaps. 2 and 3). This interpretation is also consistent with, and virtually required by Rousseau's larger vision of the potential inherent in the race.

In what sense, then, is society corrupt? "Man is born free, we see him everywhere in chains," proclaims Rousseau in the opening sentence of *The Social Contract*. But this is a theme already present in the *First Discourse*. The corruption of society results from the introduction into human affairs of the utilitarian principle of the division of labor; the cultivation of the arts and sciences have grown hand in hand with the expansion of the division of labor and the inequality it produces.

> What brings about all these abuses if not the disastrous inequality introduced among men by the distinction of talents and the debasement of virtues? (*First Discourse*, 58)

This theme is pursued further in the *Second Discourse*. Here the condition of humankind in a state of civil society is contrasted with the "state of nature." In the latter, human beings live in symbiotic relation to each other, but are not bonded by social relationships. Rousseau describes the state of nature as an idyllic one in which the relations among humans are essentially the same as those between animals: "the noble savage" fantasy. Rousseau's notion of the presocial state requires the assumption of plenitude, obviating the necessity of anything like a Hobbesian war of all against all. Everyone lives in a state of freedom, since no one is constrained by the exersize of anyone else's will. Everyone is dominated by *amour-de-soi*, the disposition of self-preservation, on the one hand, and the feeling of pity (*pitie*), on the other, but pity is a passive feeling akin to that of the animals, and not the basis for any sort of enduring association. Perkins has summed up nicely Rousseau's conception of the state of nature.

> All the aspects of the "natural" environment are dovetailed to provide (a) habit and feeling of liberty. The forest offers an abundance of foods, makes shared or sustained labor unnecessary, maintains in man sufficient vigor to assure fitness, the survival of only the strong. Submerged in the present, man is without sickness. Death goes unnoticed, the idea of duty and obligation to others is nonexistent. Since pity is not a positive force for altruism, it cannot turn man against himself. Whenever the individual is threatened, ego always asserts its right to the degree required for self-preservation. Man's passions are undeveloped and do not victimize him. He is free from the biologic drive of ego for power and more power described by Hobbes. Pity balances ego, restrains it to a sane *amour de soi* consistent with animal behavior. No pressure, it is clear, bears upon man. His only curb is the timeless, static order which cradles him, of which he is uncounscious, a curb only to his will's potential aspirations (Perkins, 1974, 87–88).

In his characterization of the state of nature, Rousseau departs significantly from much of the social thought of the seventeenth and eighteenth centuries. Against all those who posited a social instinct to explain the existence of society, he argues that the state of nature reveals no sympathetic or social bonds—only the essential independence of the individual who possesses the disposition of self-preservation and the capacity for feeling pity, or compassion. Far from attempting to *derive* society from either of these presocial dispositions, Rousseau suggests that their importance in society is greatly diminished, that pity is a feeling more intensely felt in the state of nature than in society, that civilization, in fact, weakens natural passion (130, 132). In this way he sets the stage, so to speak, for the philosophical anthropology later developed in *Emile*. His critique of Hobbes is precisely on this point—that Hobbes had illegitimately attributed to presocial humankind qualities that are, in fact, a product of society.

Rousseau's reformulation of Hobbes's instinct of self-preservation is related to his rejection of the Englishman's theory of contract. Hobbes, the reader will recall, failed to discriminate between the principles of association and of governance. Rousseau does not make this mistake. His account of the passage of the race out of the state of nature is of an exceedingly prolonged process that moves through several stages. For Rousseau, society has its origin in the initial exercise of the intellect, especially in the use of tools permitting a more efficient environmental adaptation. Reason is not present in the state of nature, that is, in *original* nature, but arises only with human association. This is a clear departure from what was generally "mainstream" Enlightenment doctrine. Language itself was not created until relatively late in the history of the species; early man required no language more refined than that of crows or monkeys. (Indeed, in the presocial state, the species was "without industry, without speech, without a dwelling place, without wars and without allies"). Rousseau explains the emergence of society on the ground of the *absence* of any socially predisposing traits. Having no instincts, the species was not only free, but in effect *forced*, to develop the intellect, or reason, and the power to act on it. But this was a long and protracted process that proceeded on a trial and error basis, as the species responded to the challenges of the environment, and in the process gradually developed the capacity for rational reflection. In hunting and gathering and in learning to utilize fire, human contact was intensified; individuals slowly came to understand that an isolated if free existence could be improved through utilitarian relations with other.

The appearance of the family and the beginnings of communal life emerged gradually from this earlier period. The division of labor had yet to appear. In this earliest form of group life, everyone remained independent of others and therefore "free." But the gradual growth of a materialism rooted in increasingly effective environmental adaptation and the seductive gratifications of group life began to undermine this primeval state. Somewhere along the line, the ideas of private property and the sharing of work came into being. This is the critical watershed in human history. The development of large-scale organized agriculture and of metallurgy, according to Rousseau, are the long-drawn-out revolutions that effect a transformation in the nature of the species. Procuring commodities jointly, he says, was "the first yoke they imposed upon themselves."

> . . . as long as (men) applied themselves only to tasks that a single person could do and to arts that did not require the cooperation of several hands, they lived free, healthy, good and happy. . . . But from the moment one man needed the help of another, as soon as they observed that it was useful for a single person to have provision for two, equality disappeared, property was introduced. Labor became necessary, and vast forests were changed into smiling fields which had to be watered with the sweat of men and in which slavery and misery were soon seen to generate (*Second Discourse*, 1964, 151–152).
>
> The first person who, having fenced off a plot of ground, took it into his head to say this is mine . . . was the true founder of civil society (141).

The millennia following are a descent into greater and greater corruption. With the advent of social organization and its inevitable accompaniment, inequality, we find the beginnings of morality and the accompanying introduction of draconic punishments. Rousseau writes ironically of "the progress of inequality" as the race passes through stages characterized by the law of and rights of property, the rise of the institution of the magistracy, and the transformation of legitimate into illegitimate power. His analysis of inequality, for its time, was quite sophisticated.

He also had a clear understanding of the meritocratic principle that ideologically, and to some extent in fact, was beginning to barge its way into the old society. He understood that the regnant forms of power and status of present and past—monarchy, aristocratic privilege and license, guild monopoly—were fated to be inundated and destroyed by scientific and commercial progress. Finally, he extended his critique of the division of labor and the inequality associated with it to all those spheres of contemporary life most celebrated by progressive thinkers as harbingers of the society of the future. He condemns the city ("the abyss of the human species"), the increasing scope and power of the state, the extension of commercial activity, along with, above all, the progress of knowledge.

In this connection it must be said that despite the seeming historical nature of his account, Rousseau's method is not truly historical. In fact, he says at the outset that a true historical method is impossible, and proposes to substitute an analysis of contemporary man essentially to discover the "natural man" within the civilized one. The fiction of the state of nature serves Rousseau as an ideal standard against which corrupt reality can be measured. The importance of the state of nature really lies in its theoretical *irrelevance* for Rousseau's characterization of society. No sociable instincts, no utilitarian cooperation, no Hobbesian struggle requiring a contract, but sheer historical drift as environmental adaptation, accounts for society.

Rousseau's early works pose the problem of the individual and society in a way more acute and problematic than does any other philosopher of the eighteenth century (excepting possibly Kant, who said Rousseau was the Newton of the century). His problem is that first raised by the Greeks, to explore the manner in which the individual can conduct himself or herself in the face of a society that, in its very nature, implicates people in corruption and evil. Rousseau is perhaps the modern thinker to formulate this problem most incisively as a paradox: One cannot become a moral being without entering into social relationships that affect one profoundly; yet those relationships, which are the stuff of society, are inherently corrupting.

In his later works Rousseau proceeds to grapple with this problem at two levels. In *Emile* he explores the condition under which a moral life becomes possible through education. And in *The Social Contract* he reflects on the form of association that would be necessary for all to realize themselves as moral beings. Especially in *Emile*, the distinctively sociological themes of the earlier work are developed, even though they remain in tension with natural law thinking.

Emile

The continuity between Rousseau's earlier works and *Emile* is evident in an early passage of the latter work.

> All our wisdom consists in servile practices. All our practices are only subjection, impediment, and constraint. Civil man is born, lives, and dies in slavery. At his birth he is sewed in swaddling clothes; at his death he is nailed in a coffin. So long as he keeps his human shape, he is enchained by our institutions (Rousseau, 1979, 42–43).

This passage crystallizes the essence of Rousseau's thought. The savage lives nobly but without reason. Society is the essential condition of reason, and reason the essential condition of progress. But the work of reason, called progress, "consists in servile practices." It follows that either reason is evil, or that our entire cultural association of progress with reason is a monumental confusion, a mistake of gargantuan proportions. The first implication must obviously be rejected, since it entails an absolute fatalism. The second invites, indeed demands, theoretical and practical exploration, an exploration that we might liken to an odyssey probing the unfolding dimensions of modernity. *Emile* may be understood as such an exploration. It is a work at once profoundly modern, yet one that, unlike the *Discourses*, reveals more explicitly the tension between natural law doctrine and the complexities and uncertainties that inevitably attend a sociological view-point.[12]

At one level *Emile* is a treatise on the principles of education that must inform the growth of a true (i.e., independent) individual by circum-venting social institutions. But beyond this it is a treatise setting forth what it must mean to be a whole individual *in relation to society*. Kant thought its publication was an event comparable to the French Revolution and placed it on a level with Plato's *Republic*, calling Rousseau the Newton of moral

---

[12] See, for example, Cassirer (1963b), Gay (1966), Winch (1972), and Perkins (1974).

philosophy, and Bloom finds it "a *Phenomenology of the Mind* posing as Dr. Spock."

The fundamental principle informing the education of the young Emile follows from and extends the critique of modernism of the earlier works. As a child Emile must be kept in dependence only on things, never on others, since dependence on things has nothing to do with morality and therefore cannot inhibit freedom or encourage vice (95).[13] This could be Godwin speaking. But for Rousseau it is only a temporary state. The principles of the *Social Contract* will be presented to Emile, but only at his full maturity. Before this they would be incomprehensible to him. This stoic emphasis on the necessity of living according to nature is perhaps the most profound link between Rousseau's early work and the early (but not the later) sections of *Emile*.

In all things the child must experience independence. Swaddling and other forms of physical constraint are condemned. As the child grows older, he is encouraged to learn everything for himself through direct experience. One must never attempt to reason with children, or worse, to inculcate in them any moral sense by stricture. The conventional pedant is banished from the scene. All education must come from the natural encounters of the child with the environment. Rousseau thinks of early education as "negative": it consists not at all in teaching virtue or truth but in securing the heart from vice and the mind from error (93).

As the child grows older, the same principle holds, but now comes the times at which he must become acquainted with the essential principles of the utilitarian foundations of society. According to Rousseau, "it is impossible to bring a child along to the age of twelve in the bosom of society without giving him some idea of the relations of man to man and of the morality of human actions" (97). The moral principles associated with utilitarian interdependence must be acquired by direct experience of their immediate utility.

Rousseau (or "Jean-Jacques," who is, ever present, the overseer of Emile's education) arranges an encounter with a gardener. Emile now learns that the principle of private property rests on the labor theory of value in its early Lockean form (cf. Locke, *The Second Treatise on Government*). The gardener instructs him:

> Pardon me, my young fellow, but little gentlemen as giddy as you do not often come our way. No one touches his neighbor's garden. Each respects the labor of others so that his own will be secure (99).

Since no moral doctrine is *imposed* on Emile, it follows that he will receive no punishments, except as "the natural consequence of their bad

[13] Rousseau immediately follows this by anticipating the analysis of the *Social Contract* (which he had been preparing simultaneously with *Emile*). If there is any means of remedying this ill in society, it is to substitute law for man and to arm the general wills with a real strength superior to the action of every particular will. If the laws of nations could, like those of nature, have an inflexibility that no human force could every conquer, dependence on men would then once again become dependence on things (Rousseau 1979, 85).

action" (101). A good deal of manipulation will probably be involved here, as elsewhere:

> you will not precisely punish them for having lied; but you will arrange it so that all the bad effects of lying—such as not being believed when one tells the truth, of being accused of the evil that one did not do although one denies it—come in league against them when the have lied (101).[14]

Emile is discovering the principle of the significance of private property as it connects with the division of labor through a specific concrete experience.

As the child reaches adolescence, new departures are necessary, but again they are to be informed by the same principles. Emile is still unprepared for conduct at a higher moral level although, as Rousseau puts it, "his strength develops far more rapidly than his needs" (165). Also during this period the main preoccupation is the acquisition of a trade. Rousseau's approach to this is consistent with his underlying principles. Occupations can be ranked in terms of their social utility, those most widespread and most indispensible being most highly valued. Agriculture, accordingly, ranks first, followed by metallurgy and woodworking. Robinson Crusoe's existence is idealized; this is the only book that will be allowed Emile for some time, and it is on the basis of the nature of Robinson Crusoe's existence that Emile should judge the others. He will observe the whole complex division of labor and the dependence it engenders, and observe the stupidity of such an arrangement.

Emile will learn a trade that he will select himself. His training up to this point ensures that he will select one on the basis of the independence it assures him. Rousseau's preference is that of carpenter: "it is clean, it is useful, it can be practiced at home" (201). Others among them as stonecutting, stocking making, and weaving, are summarily dismissed as creators of human automatons (1979, 201). Policemen, spies, and hangmen are useful, it must be admitted, but theirs is a utility owed entirely to the government, and one's trade must not demand from those who practice it "qualities of soul that are odious and incompatible with humanity" (197). Those trades that can be performed only in aristocratic or genteel circles, such as embroiderer, guilder, or varnisher, are also rejected. Neither does Rousseau want Emile to become a musician[15] or writer. Although agriculture is "man's first trade," and consequently, "the most decent, the most useful, and . . . most noble,"

---

[14] Rousseau's insight into lying is brilliant. He perceives that lying is not "natural" to children, but results from "the law of obedience which produces the necessity of lying." "In the natural and free education why would our child lie to you? What has he to hide from you?" Lies in the form of promises of future conduct are not natural, "since promises to do or forbear are conventional acts which depart form the state of nature and impair freedom." Furthermore such commitments are, in Rousseau's view, null, simply because the child, in his or her limited experience, cannot be held responsible for the uncomprehended situations and consequences of the future. "It follows from this," Rousseau insists, "that children's lies are all the work of masters, and that to want to teach them to tell the truth is nothing other than to teach them to lie" (1979, 102). Nested in this irony, of course, is a concept of lying as *social* behavior.

[15] Whether this has anything to do with the fact that Rousseau earned much of his living as a music copiest is difficulty to say.

one's inheritance in land can be lost. Emile, of course, will know that he should learn agriculture, but beyond this, that he should also acquire a trade.

All this, however, leaves Emile in a state of possessing "only natural and physical knowledge" (207). He cannot generalize or abstract. What he knows, he knows, "by the relations which are connected to his interest" (207). He remains essentially amoral, demanding nothing from others and thinking he owes them nothing; he is, in effect, an isolate in human society. Up to this point, the essential principal of the child's education has been to keep him as remote from social influence as is practically possible. He has been removed from the artificial environment of the city to the natural setting of the countryside. His nanny is enjoined to eschew most of the conventional training practices. He has no teachers. Even the master, Jean-Jacques, never actually directs him in anything. He has no significant personal attachments. Now, however, arrives the time for entry into true social relationships. It is a moment of great danger. Rousseau says that everything that has thus far transpired is unimportant, that childhood itself is essentially unimportant. Throughout childhood Emile's education has been restricted to the development and extension of *amour-de-soi*, the innate, primitive passion of self-love. *Amour-propre*, a sense of self that arises from participation in society, has yet to take root. *Amour-propre*, says Rousseau, "is still hardly aroused in him" (208). Indeed, forestalling its arousal has been the basic intent of the entire educational program.

Amour-propre comes into being only as one becomes involved in social relationships and is related to the form of those relationships. In a society based on an extensive division of labor and therefore institutionalized inequality, it assumes an alienating, or negative, form. It is a form of self-love dependent on the opinions of others. The dependency thus created brings into being a type of bond appropriate to the principle at the root of the division of labor, i.e., utility. Rousseau depicts an individual motivated by a form of self-interest that can be realized only by continuous manipulation and eventual domination of others. Cunning, deceit, flattery, ostentatious displays of learning and talent, are its mark. His characterizations evoke Mandeville earlier and a host of others later. "To be and to seem to be become two altogether different things" (*Second Discourse*, 155). No one, therefore, "dares to appear as he is." In consequence, ". . . one will never know well those with whom he deals" (*First Discourse*, 39). Especially in the leading centers of progress is *amour-propre* manifest. ". . . Under that much vaunted urbanity," he says, there exists "no more sincere friendships," but only "suspicions, offers, fears, coldness, reserve, hate, betrayal . . ." Furthermore, *amour-propre* is the essence of inequality itself: "The rich and the powerful would cease to be happy if the people ceased to be miserable." Inegalitarian relationships breed satisfactions that are inseparably linked to maintenance of the inequality itself. Works of art are enjoyed by the rich precisely because the poor cannot afford them.[16]

---

[16] In these and other passages, Rousseau adumbrates principles of stratification theory that had to be rediscovered by later generations. In the mainstream sociologies of the nineteenth century, most importantly those of Comte and Spencer, inequality is represented as serving essentially benign and socially constructive ends. Marx, of course, is the greatest but by no means the sole nineteenth century exception to this.

Rousseau's experiences of alienation in Paris led him, after twelve years, to abandon the great center of progress in total disillusionment. He came seeking a true community, but found only artificiality, vanity, and duplicity among the intellectuals of the salon culture. He was discovering, he says in the *Confessions*, that he was a "different sort of being." After leaving Paris, he sought a home at various places: Geneva, with the Duke of Luxembourg, with Hume in Scotland. Personal or political troubles drove him from these and other temporary domiciles.

In all of this Rousseau locates the nature and development of the self squarely in the social milieu. The individual does not, as in mainstream Enlightenment thought, bring to social experience presocial dispositions that are, in some sense, impressed on or injected into social life. But this insight creates for Rousseau a profound dilemma: How is he to make Emile into a social being and yet avoid the trap of *amour-propre*?

Essentially his answer is to build on the purely natural sexual drive, but to transcend it, by literallly *sublimating* it in love. Emile is provided with Sophie, who will eventually become his love-mate. But before this union can be consummated, Emile (and Sophie as well) must go through years of preparation. Emile must learn to truly know and understand Sophie. Friendship must precede sex. Other aspects of his education also commence at this point (e.g., selected readings in theology and travel literature). Above all, to avoid negative *amour-propre*, Emile must have available what we today call role models, through which the study of society proceeds. Society can be studied only "by means of men," and significantly, "men by means of society" (235). Emile's company must therefore be selected with extraordinary care.

> I would want a young man's society to be chosen so carefully that he thinks well of those who live with him; and I would want him to be taught to know the world so well that he thinks ill of all that takes place in it. Let him know that man is naturally good; let him feel it; let him judge his neighbor by himself. But let him see that society depraves and perverts men. Let him find in their prejudices the sources of all their vices; let him be inclined to esteem each individual but despise the multitude; let him see that all men wear pretty much the same mask, but let him also know that there are faces more beautiful than the mask covering them (236–237).

Rousseau's highest ideal of humankind was the citizen. The role of citizen, however, is in no way realizable in the present condition of society. Indeed, it is, in principle, possible only in the ideal commonwealth described in *The Social Contract*. There, the free and equal wills of all coalesce in the *volonté general*, the grand egalitarian consensus from which no one can, or would ever care, to remove oneself. In this the freedom of all is assured, obviating the need for deviance or dissent.[17]

Instruction in these matters comes only at the end of Emile's education, for their comprehension is possible only after the fullest *experience* in the right company and the fullest appreciation of the corruption of present

---

[17] This early formulation of the modern democratic idea, of course, has often been attacked for the seeming totalitarian implications.

society. Undoubtedly the extraordinary measures required to bring into being a moral person in corrupt bourgeois society would be unnecessary in the ideal commonwealth, for such a community would be founded on, and therefore continually propagate, virtue in the first place. The maturing individual would not have to be removed to the country, shielded from all manner of social and cultural experience, and carefully guided into the mid-twenties.

Of course, in telling the tale of Emile's education—including the necessity of a sophisticated, full-time "Jean-Jacques"—Rousseau is maintaining that moral education is virtually impossible in the corrupt milieu of urban commercial society; that in fact, it requires the existence of a community based on an intense value consensus—one like that described in *The Social Contract*. In removing Emile from every societal influence, and especially from educational institutions, Rousseau recognizes the extraordinary effectiveness of those institutions in forming the individual. But he is also asserting the potentially equal power of a completely different kind of social *milieu* as a seedbed for encouraging, even requiring, the development of the principled moral actor. Society is the source of evil, but paradoxically also the necessary condition of its transcendence. The theoretical difficulties of the theory of the *volonté general* should not be allowed to deflect us from recognizing it as an early attempt at a sociological theory of the community, and an explicit attempt to formulate the relationship between the structure of the community on the one hand, and the nature of human character on the other. Rousseau theorizes that the continuity of any society rests on the functioning of its agencies of socialization, or of indoctrination; that the formation of the individual is inevitably and necessarily a social process, even though the foundations of this process are in some sense "natural," and that the results depend on the specifics of that process, i.e. the nature of social practices and institutions. In the last analysis Rousseau endorses the classical Aristotelian standard: truly *human* i.e., moral or "virtuous" beings, can be nurtured only in the milieux of the oversized primary groups we call communities.[18]

Conclusion

In all this Rousseau advances a sociological perspective that may be framed in terms of the three problematics. Despite his conceptions of nature and continual references to natural law, he is the first modern to enunciate a clear and unequivocal conception of the fundamental social nature of the

---

[18] Interestingly, although Jean-Jacques arranges for Emile to acquire what are in effect elements of what we would today recognize as revolutionary consciousness, the end of the whole process for Emile and Sophie is a retreat into intimacy, a principled obliviousness to the social and political surround. Everything culminates not in efforts by Emile to revolutionize, or even modestly reform society, but in his ecstasy upon learning that he is about to become a father. In this utterly conventional event he finds his fulfillment, confiding to Jean-Jacques that "I need you more than ever now that my functions as a man begin" (1979, 480). Rousseau's thought is revolutionary but he himself is not. Like Voltaire in Candide, Rousseau *privatizes* and *personalizes* the manner of dealing with the devastations of society. The availability of such solutions has always been one of the more important sources of the relative stability of capitalist societies.

individual as an entity divorced from presocial determination. In this he was as far ahead of his time as Hume was in the theory of knowledge. (See chapter 4). And Rousseau's philosophical anthropology was inseparably linked to his rejection of the doctrine of progress. This was most emphatically not because he rejected the possibility of a better world; indeed, the very writing of *The Social Contract*—granted its contradictions—proved otherwise. Rousseau could not accept the doctrine of progress as the march of reason because he believed that the new scientific form of knowledge, despite the grand ideal, was inseparably linked to an emerging and corrupt bourgeois society. Neither did he, like the other *philosophes*, believe that abstract timeless moral principles that could be applied to a reordering of the future were discoverable by science. Rather, he held that all forms of knowledge must be subordinated to moral principles—specifically in the form of the general will, i.e., in the *human community*,—in order to be used in humane and effective ways.

The three problematics, in Rousseau's thought, exhibit a close interpenetration. The nature of the human activity is social and this means that moral principles are either codes hammered out by individuals in the face of oppressive social institutions, or the collective will of all acting in concert to bring into being a larger consensus. Since inequality corrupts everything, progress is not possible so long as society is inegalitarian; and since inequality is rooted in the division of labor, which itself expands with social scale, moral consensus is possible only in the small community.

The political and social difficulties inherent in this formulation are well-known and have been much commented on. But from a sociological standpoint, what is important is that Rousseau has dealt with the three problematics in such a way as to produce the rudiments of a theory of different *types* of society in terms of the nature of the relation of the individual to the whole, the significance of common values, the role of knowledge, and the stark facts of inequality and hierarchy. In this he anticipates such modern polar opposites as Tönnies' *Gemeinschaft* and *Gesellschaft* and Weber's societal and communal types.

Without the critical perspective that draws the distinction between moral and utilitarian relationships, Rousseau's prescription for Emile's education would make no sense; there would be no point to such an exercise. The very idea of an autonomous self derives from a conception of society as repressive. Rousseau's theory of the path of development of the autonomous individual is possible only in relation to a theory of how modern society represses individuality; his "analysis" of the division of labor and inequality is his account of this.

It is paradoxical that this sociological conception of the self and its formation appears in Rousseau, for it seems to be irreconcilable with his powerful emphasis on the natural. The education of Emile, in its entirety, is the charting of a course intending to preserve the natural self by *transforming* it into an *autonomous yet social* self. If one thinks of the character of Rousseau's natural state as a *standard* against which present actualities should be judged, and a future ideal measured, the essentially modern sociological quality of Rousseau's concept is evident. *Emile* is revealed as anything but just another natural law tract. Education was accorded great prominence in liberal eighteenth century thought, but Rousseau's conception is different from all others in that it advances a clear conception of the developmental nature of the self in relation to the specific character of social organization. In other treatments of education, for example, those Locke sometimes called the "disciplinary theory of eduction" (Locke, 1690), it was assumed that education was a matter of exercising the faculty of reason, which could discover truth if allowed unfettered scope. For Rousseau the entire relation between education as the development of the self in *society* is problematic.

CONCLUSION

From Shaftesbury to Rousseau and Godwin, then, we see how the problem of evil encouraged the beginnings of a specific conception of society, one originating in a *critical* perspective that has as its fount the rejection of the corrupted nature of human nature. The later influence of this tendency was exerted not only on practical matters like the French Revolutions and the early socialism of thinkers like Mably and Owen. It also placed its impress on some of the major sociologists of the nineteenth century, especially the line of socialist theorizing culminating in Marx and Engels.

This highly selective survey of some of the tendencies in the social thought of the eighteenth century relevant for the emergence of sociology proper is intended to show that two factors, the perception of human diversity and the moral dilemma in the problem of evil formulated in secular terms, were the source of certain important sociological tendencies. The first challenged the doctrine of a uniform and unchanging human nature, thereby tending to devalue its significance or relevance in explaining social phenomena. The second led to two very different conceptions of society: (1) the systemic idea, in which society functions more or less automatically but with at least some significant degree of autonomy from the impress of human nature; and (2) the idea that since social institutions are the source of evil, they invite analysis as independent of human nature, a sociological project. These projects were realized only later, in the nineteenth century sociologies proper, but these sociologies would not have assumed their particular forms had it not been for their roots in these questions raised during the Enlightenment.

4

KNOWLEDGE AND HUMAN SCIENCE

Knowledge has always been a factor in human social existence, but until recent times it has been essentially practical and *adaptive*. Practical ends have been achieved not so much by mastering nature as by existing in harmony with her. Machiavelli's advice to Lorenzo illustrates this. The prince receives a series of recommendations based on Machiavelli's ransacking of ancient and modern history. He is advised on various means of keeping his subjects loyal, whether or not to rely on mercenary armies, the merits of various administrative procedures. Framing these is the famous cynical realism about human nature, rendered in aphorisms such as, "men must be either caressed or annihilated"; or "A man striving in every way to be good will meet his ruin among the great number who are not good." But in all of this Machiavelli never imagines his knowledge as an instrument to be employed in *mastering* or *transforming* the world, even the north Italian city-state world of Lorenzo the Magnificent.

This adaptive function of practical knowledge, even systematized as scientific knowledge, was still very much alive during the Renaissance, as it is today. The seventeenth and eighteenth centuries, however, witnessed the growth of the Baconian ideology stressing the possibilities of mastery and transformation not only of the physical world, but of the human domain as well. In this sense, the Enlightenment, in its unerstanding of the proper role of knowledge in human affairs, departs dramatically from the past. A science of human nature is envisaged which is invested with revolutionary significance. The idea that knowledge has an end beyond the employment of the speculative faculties of the individual, as in Aristotle, beyond the glorification of God, its justification for the scholastics, beyond the solution of practical problems confronting men of affairs, is now embraced with near-chiliastic fervor.

Although there were continuities, the contrast between medieval and modern understanding of the proper status of *reason* and *knowledge* could hardly have been more stark. Aside from its employment in practical matters, reason in the Middle Ages was considered a gift of God enabling humans to understand their proper (i.e., God-ordained) niche in the scheme of things, and perhaps for some, at least, to enable them to grasp His greater glory. This last, however, is a delicate and dangerous matter, since it may be taken to imply that God stands in need of glorification by the creatures He created, and even that He created them for this purpose. In the historic context of received Christian doctrines this is, of course, an unthinkable contradiction, which is one reason why faith always took precedence over reason, as in the theology of Aquinas. Certainly the idea that reason could be turned *against* God was heresy, as the reaction of the church to the movements among the Waldensians, Franciscans, and others shows. Theologically, the social order was a static organic whole (a point to be elaborated on in Chapter 6); sociologically, it was a society whose stability rested on tradition, including the legitimation of authority mainly on traditional grounds (to use Max Weber's term). Things sanctified by tradition and justified doctrinally by sacerdotal authority leave little room for the unfettered play of reason, and none at all for a reason that would upset the existing order of things to make room for the new.

Beginning with the Renaissance, the meaning of reason and knowledge, and of the relation between them, at least in some of those circles relatively free from church authority, began to be radically transformed. Two interacting tendencies seem to have been centrally implicated in this. The first of these was the association of reason with science, originally a Greek, not Christian, idea. The medieval conception of nature as the *creation* of God was during the Renaissance gradually displaced by the idea that it was God's *expression*. This is a critical shift because it elevates natural law in its significance, thereby encouraging a greater respect for the power of reason as the instrument necessary for understanding nature, and of viewing nature as accessible to reason (Hawthorne, 1976, 8). Second, also during the Renaissance, the idea arose that the human world was comprised of activities and institutions that are expressions of human intelligence and creative faculties. Two centuries later, reason had come to be understood as a *natural* faculty that finds its clearest and highest expression in science, and in the view of some, like Hume and Vico, that a *human* science was not only a desirable end, but necessary to *ground* all the others. Hume's expression of this is perhaps the most elegant and exact of the time.

> All sciences have a relation, greater or less, to human nature . . . Even *Mathematics, Natural Philosophy*, and *Natural Religion* are in some measure dependent on a science of man; since they lie under the cognizance of men, and are judged of by their powers and faculties (Hume, 1949, 19).
> There is no question of importance, whose decision is not comprised in the science of man; and there is none, which can be decided with any certainty, before we become acquainted with that science (of human nature).

In pretending therefore to explain the principles of human nature, we in effect propose a complete system of the sciences built on a foundation almost entirely new (1949, 20).

Ernest Becker identifies this "placing man before nature" as nothing less than a "Copernican shift":

> How does one make science significant? Diderot had the answer upon which we cannot improve today. The sciences should be centered on man, and the various sciences would be considered in relation to him and his needs: lines would radiate out from man to all the sciences. Instead of being woven at random, like an afterthought design, into an alien fabric, man would be the central line on a switchboard (Becker, 1968, 12).

The sense of urgency regarding a science of human nature in the eighteenth century in itself implied nothing about its nature and characteristics. Prescientific forms of knowledge—practical adaptive knowledge, folk widsom, theological and metaphysical speculation, mystical transcendence—provided little in the way of a guide to a science of human nature. The eighteenth century reacted not only against Christian theology, but against systems in general: The great rationalist philosophies of Descartes, Spinoza, and Leibnitz were in varying ways suspect and in varying degrees rejected. This was a time of fabulous success for the natural sciences and mathematics; it is not surprising that to many of the progressive minds; particularly *late* in the century, an extension of the natural sciences seemed to hold out the promise of an understanding powerful enough for a material and moral remaking of the world.

The passage of the idea of the primacy of the human sciences from the early eighteenth century to the beginnings of sociology early in the nineteenth was a process critical to the form taken by these sociologies. Over this period the siren song of the success of the natural sciences subverted the principle to the point of virtually reversing the ideal relation as expressed by Hume, ironically all the while embracing ever more confidently the immanence of its realization through the working of natural law (by that time increasingly understood as evolution). We could say that positivism, in its basic sense of assimilating the socio-cultural world assembled by humans to the nature world as given, was constructed out of its opposite, the ideal of a human-centered science.[1] Comte's hierarchy of the sciences may stand as an exemplar of this process, making, as it does, the achievement of sociology conditional on the prior development of all the other sciences, mathematical, physical, biological (see Chap. 7). Although Comte's ideal of a knowledge-emancipated and knowledge-guided human future is of course derived from and identified with his eighteenth century precursors, his religion of humanity works only through bureaucratically administered knowledge, the foundation of which is mathematical truth, not "knowledge of human subjects."

The philosophy on which the positivistic nineteenth century sociol-

---

[1] This is one of the themes of Max Horkeimer and Theodore Adorno in their *Dialectic of Enlightenment* (1973).

ogies were grounded was the atomistic empiricism of Locke and his followers, including Hume, and its application in Hartley's associationist psychology. This constructs human social action as an object unequivocally *given* in experience, having the same status as the givens of the natural world, and the human mind as homologous with the structure of that natural reality. In this, the focus on human agency and constructivism present in thinkers like Vico (see Chapter 6) and (perhaps to a lesser extent) the Scots (Chapter 5) could find no place.

Embedded in the program to create a science of humankind were two dilemmas of knowledge important in shaping the contours of nineteenth century social science. The intellectual fulcrum of both was the principle of natural law, inherited from Greek thought, modified and adapted for the growth of the natural sciences, then injected powerfully into the service of the eighteenth century passion to create a human science. On the one side, the natural law conceptions faced the empiricism of science; on the other, the ethical ideal of freedom. Together, these questions constitute the problematic of social knowledge as it appears to the progressive philosophers of the eighteenth century.

NATURAL LAW METAPHYSICS AND SCIENTIFIC EMPIRICISM

Just as natural scientists were revealing a lawful universe designed by God, convinced that He would "not play dice with the universe," so the protoscience of human nature of the eighteenth century would reveal the parallel moral laws of the species. On the one hand stood the empiricism without which scientific discoveries would not be possible; on the other were the assumed-to-exist laws governing the nature of the species, the latter being the discoveries-to-be of the former. Scientific empiricism, resting philosophically on the epistemology beginning with Locke and running through Berkeley and Hume in England and Condillac and Helvetius in France, connected with the science of Galileo, Newton, and Boyle. This empiricism was practiced within the framework of the idea of a complex universe—a "clockwork" created by design.

Attempts to model a science of human nature on the natural sciences typically assumed that the physical and human domains possessed parallel structures. We have seen the way in which Hobbes approached this question— the structure of human nature was conceived as an analogue of the physical world essentially as portrayed by Newton. Isaiah Berlin expresses one form of this doctrine of parallelism.

> The mind (is) a container within which ideas like counters circulate and form patterns as they would in a complicated slot machine; three-dimensional space has its counterpart in the inner "space" of the mind over which the inner eye—the faculty of reflection—presides (Berlin, 1956, 19).

The idea that human nature has a structure parallel to that of the natural world was the *metaphysical justification* undergirding the belief that human behavior could be analyzed and understood in the same fashion as the natural world; indeed, in its most extreme form it is a conception that places the species squarely *in* the natural world. This is the root idea underlying the movement Comte would label positivism in the nineteenth century.

Now this conception of scientific empiricism is incompatible with rationalist metaphysics—despite the likelihood that science as we understand it would never have taken root in the West had not the rationalist, and even before this, the theological, conceptions of natural law constituted such widely held beliefs and intensely held domain assumptions (see Whitehead, 1955, 119). This contradiction was revealed over the course of the development of British empiricism. Beginning with Bacon, and running through Locke and Hume up to the nineteenth century utilitarians, this *epistemological* framework of analysis came into conflict with but did not displace the *metaphysically grounded* idea of science and of natural law. The beginnings of this are found in Bacon.

Bacon

Bacon was born in 1561, attended Trinity College at Cambridge, and by 1584 was a member of Parliament. He was an exceedingly ambitious man of affairs and has often been described as inordinately power hungry. During his life he held a number of government posts and loved the rituals and ceremonies through which power is exercised and maintained. Although probably no more corrupt than the average politician of the time, in 1621 he was convicted of bribery and forced from office. The remainder of his life he spent in private pursuits.

Bacon's philosophy, or at least his philosophy of science, seems fully consistent with the political side of his life. What distinguishes him from others is his conviction, not only that science as a career could be the foundation for the exercise of personal power, but that "a knowledge whose dignity is maintained by works of utility of power" was possible and should be pursued. Starting from this conception of the utilitarian possibilities of science as an instrument of power, Bacon moved on to the question of the practical kind of exercise that must be performed in order to *do* science. Bacon's strictures have to do with the way the scientist approaches his materials, and in an important sense, they reveal the fashion in which the natural law and empiricist aspects of science were held together in a fragile intellectual suspension. Bacon predates Locke in enunciating the doctrine of the mind as a *tabula rasa*. Originally, the mind was "like a fair sheet of paper with no writing on it" or "like a mirror with a true and even surface fit to reflect the genuine way of things" (Jones, 1952, 599). Although a blank slate originally, in practice all minds bring to the scientific quest the accumulations of experience and the volatile urgency of the passions. Bacon, we must recall, was a pre-Enlightenment figure, writing well before the philosophes began the rehabilitation of the passions. For him, as for Hobbes, basic human nature is composed of irrational and self-interested motives. The mind as receptive to impressions and capable of recording them accurately, is indeed hard to come by.

"The *idols* and false notions which have already preoccupied the human understanding and are deeply rooted in it, not only so beset men's minds, that they become difficult of access, but even when access is obtained, will again meet and trouble us in the instauration of the sciences, unless mankind, when forewarned, guard themselves with all possible care against them" (Bacon, 1889, Sect. 38)

Four species of *idols* must be overcome: (1) Idols of the Tribe, or those inherent in human nature; (2) Idols of the Den, or those peculiar to each individual, whether from nature or learning; (3) Idols of the Market, or the obfuscations of language arising from human association in general; and (4) Idols of the Theatre, misconceptions derived from belief systems of all sorts, of which the religious are the most important (1889, Sects. 39–44).

W. T. Jones has trenchantly characterized Bacon's approach to science as a kind of "epistemological Protestantism" (1952, 599). The baggage the mind brings to experience will distort that experience and make the knowledge based on it invalid or unreliable. The mind must be purged of the idols if the practice of science is to go forward. For Bacon, the *ideal* of a scientific recording instrument is the mind as *tabula rasa*. The scientist may then go forth in humility: Bacon speaks of "the true and legitimate humiliation of the human spirit." The mind is an acceptable instrument of scientific investigation only if "restored to its perfect and original condition."

In a sense, Bacon advances a characterization of the subjective attitude or orientation that supposedly provides the foundation for pursuing the practical methodology of science, including human science. Scientific objectivity rests on a cleansing of the apparatus of perception. The passions can be damped only by a procedure that Bacon transparently describes as an essentially religious exercise. But why, Spence (1978, 38) along with others has asked, should anyone submit to such humiliation? The answer is as old as Western thought: Knowledge is the road to power. For Bacon this meant power in the sense of mastery over nature and ultimately over human destiny. Thus the Baconian formula: One masters nature by obeying her. To search out and discover her laws is a quasi-religious act of humiliation—a humiliation before the grandness and magnificence of the laws of nature. But here the parallel with religious experience ends. Once in possession of such knowledge, the possessor becomes like a God, as mastery and control come within the scientist's grasp.

In Bacon many of the basic themes of institutionalized Western science can already be found, in particular, science as mastery of nature and; the presentation of the scientist as a quasi-religious figure possessing esoteric knowledge, not at all unlike a priest. Belief in natural laws and faith in an empiricist doctrine of scientific discovery unite here in the ideal of the scientist.

Locke

Bacon's program for science was mainly an attempt to state the conditions under which the human mind could adequately come to know the natural laws governing the world. With Locke and his successors, the very assumption of whether there are any natural laws that can be known comes to be challenged. Bacon had specified the state of mind necessary for the practice of science; Locke asked a more fundamental question: What is the nature of the mind as a knowing instrument, and what are the implications of this for what can be known? He then pursued this question by analyzing the very origin of ideas, i.e., the nature of experience itself (Locke, 1894).

Experience, Locke maintains, reveals that there are but two sources of ideas: (1) our sensations, and (2) the functioning of our minds. This duality underlies not only all of Locke's philosophy but also frames the increasingly skeptical approaches of his successors, Berkeley and Hume. Whether they originate in sensation or the mind, ideas may be of two types, simple or complex. Simple ideas are those such as solidity or motion, or, from within the mind, the idea of willing. Complex ideas are those that join simple ones together. It may be seen that, like others at the outset of modern human science, Locke's approach uses an atomistic one.

Alongside his analysis of experience, Locke places a doctrine of substance, the philosophical centerpiece of practically all previous philosophies. Although his characterization of this is unsatisfactory even to himself (it is "something, I know not what"), it figures importantly in his theory of knowledge. Locke distinguished so-called "primary" qualities from "secondary" ones, the former being expressions or manifestations of the "essence" of a thing. Thus, motion or duration express essential characteristics of, say, a kicked soccer ball. Its spheroid shape and its black and white colors, on the other hand, are mere secondary qualities having nothing to do with its essence, but dependent on our perception. Primary qualities, then, inhere in and are essential to the nature of real objects, while secondary ones come into existence only as we exercise our senses.

For Locke there still exists an unequivocal object world independent of the senses, and our knowledge of its aspects is unequivocally a reflection of the real nature of those aspects. In this Locke retains the essential metaphysical assumption that the science of the time had always taken for granted: an orderly knowable object world. However, in his doctrine of secondary qualities, he opened the door to a full-scale critique of the nature of our sensory experience as it relates to that presumably existent object world. It was Hume who carried the implications of Locke's epistemology to their radical conclusion.

Hume and Natural Law Doctrine

For our purposes the significance of Hume's philosophy lies in two closely related arguments. First, he demonstrated the fateful consequences of a rigorous analysis of experience for all natural law and related doctrines. Second, he showed that the human sciences can be grounded in an empiricist philosophy in precisely the same fashion as were the natural sciences.

Hume showed that belief in natural law as constitutive of reality could not be sustained by a rigorous analysis of the nature of experience. The doctrine of natural law, whether imposed by the deity or immanent in the nature of things, but constitutive of human as well as physical reality, was toppled by Hume's analysis. Hume does, of course, continue to speak of natural law, but the meaning is now radically changed, become subjectivized

as "observed persistence," or as statements of observed fact, thereby jettison-
ing all conceptions of scientific law as imposed by God or immanent in
nature.[2]

Following Locke, Hume distinguishes from the flow of consciousness
two kinds of perceptions—impressions and ideas (1949, 1–7; 1912, Sect. 2).
The latter are distinguished as "faint images" of the former, i.e., the criterion
of difference is one of degree, or intensity of perception. Hume also
characterized the difference as one of feeling and thinking. Both impressions
and ideas, furthermore, must be subdivided into simple and complex. The
most fundamental tenet of Hume's philosophy is that all ideas are derived
from impressions.

> ... our simple ideas in their first appearance are derived from simple
> impressions, which are correspondent to them, and which they exactly
> represent (1949, 4).

Hume goes on to demonstrate the validity of this assertion by an examination
of experience and concludes that "our impressions are the causes of our
ideas, not our ideas of our impressions" (5).

Now for Hume all knowledge may be divided into two categories:
matters of fact, and relations of ideas. The latter has to do *only* with logical
relations, the former with the flow and relations among impressions. Hume
distinguishes seven "philosophical relations," three of which, relations of
space and time, the idea of identity, and that of cause and effect, are derived
from experience.[3] The relation of cause and effect is a special one, of
particular importance because, as Hume says, "it is the only one that can be
traced beyond our senses, and informs us of the existence and objects which
we do not see or feel." (74). That is to say, the other six philosophical
relations are either indisputably relations of ideas, or simple relations between
impressions and ideas. Furthermore, the idea of causation is of particular
importance for science, since, as compared with other relations (resemblance,
contrariety, etc.) it is by far the "strongest."

Hume goes on to ask from what impressions the idea of cause and
effect is derived. Clearly, this idea cannot result from any particular quality
or qualities of objects, since there is nothing that could not be considered to
be a cause or effect; neither is there any one quality belonging to all of them
which could be designated as a cause. The idea of causation, Hume concludes,
"must be derived from some *relation* among objects" (75). He then proceeds
to argue that the relations of *contiguity* and temporality, or *succession*, are
clearly indispensible to that of causation. But beyond this, and in Hume's
view far more important,[4] is the idea of *necessary connection*. From whence
does this idea derive?

---

[2] For a good discussion of different conceptions of natural law, see Whitehead's *Adventures of
Ideas* (Whitehead, 1955, Part 2, Section 8). In addition to the older conceptions of being
imposed (by God) or immanent in nature, Whitehead identifies more recent *semantic* and
conventional variants, these latter two being, it seems to me, only marginally distinguishable.

[3] The others, resemblance, quantity, degrees of quality, and contrariety, derive from ideas (1949,
69ff.).

[4] "Contiguity and resemblance have an effect much inferior to causation" (1949, 110).

Now, all philosophy has assumed or supposedly demonstrated that, in some sense, "causation" is a constituent of reality, or "being." This is true of systems that differ radically in other respects, whether the teleology of Aristotle, the "prime movers" or "first causes" of scholastic philosophy, or the immanences supposedly present in more scientific conceptions of natural law. Even the *"esse est percipi"* of Berkeley (1901, 1, 3) rests ultimately on the necessity of God causing the things that we know only at the moments of perception. Hume's analysis reveals the idea of causation to be a complex relation of ideas, or, more precisely, an idea of reflection, not an association of impressions.

> There is no impression conveyed by our senses which can give rise to the ideas of necessity. It must therefore be derived from some internal impression, or impression of reflection (1949, 165; see also 1912, 64).

When the same object is always followed by the same event, Hume says, "we begin to *feel* a new sentiment or impression, to wit, a customary connection in the thought or imagination . . ." (1912, 81). The idea of causation, then, results from the liveliness of the imagination, not at all from a direct impression. Causation is nothing more than the constant conjunction of objects as they are related in the imagination. And if this is so, the idea of natural law as constituent of an object world must be abandoned.[5]

There are a number of important aspects of Hume's discussion which it is here necessary to ignore, but one is so important that it requires a brief discussion: the general nature of scientific knowledge. Hume clearly conceived virtually all of his work, and the *Treatise* in particular, as scientific in a specific sense. Early in the *Treatise* he distinguishes three branches of human reason: (1) reason from knowledge; (2) reason from proofs; and (3) reason from probabilities. By "knowledge" he means "assurance arising from the comparison of ideas;" by "proofs," "those arguments, which are derived from the relation of cause and effect, and which are entirely free from doubt and uncertainty," and, by probability, "that evidence still attended by uncertainty" (1949, 124). The entire discussion of the idea of necessary connection in the *Treatise* follows this tripartite distinction, and the examination of this idea is Hume's central purpose. It is in this conceptual frame that he expresses his famous skepticism,[6] arguing that "all knowledge degenerates into probability" (180), or "all knowledge resolves itself into probability" (181). And even more generally, with regard to cause and effect reasoning, Hume is convinced that it is ultimately rooted in *custom*, which underlies *belief*, and is "more properly an act of the sensitive, than of the cogitative part of our natures" (183). Hume clearly holds that all knowledge of cause

---

[5] That Hume was fully cognizant of the revolutionary implications of this approach is beyond doubt. "I am sensible," he writes, "that of all the paradoxes, which I have had, or shall hereafter have occasion to advance in the course of this treatise, the present one is the most violent, and that 'tis merely by dint of solid proof and reasoning, I can ever hope it can have admission, and overcome the inveterate prejudices of mankind" (1949, 166).

[6] Hume calls his position "mitigated skepticism," which is somewhere between the poles of total doubt, exemplified in "Pyrronism" and the various forms of faith in an object world. See the discussion in the *Enquiry*, Sect. 12.

and effect is probabilistic in nature.[7] Our cause and effect reasonings are essential to life in virtually all its aspects; we become inured to particular beliefs regarding cause and effect because of custom, i.e., their regular concurrence. This knowledge, however, is inherently imperfect: changes in the succession of impressions sometimes occur, or beliefs are shaken in various ways, not the least of these being pursuit of philosophic or scientific inquiries such as those of Hume himself. No cause and effect knowledge, then, can be regarded as certain.

The general thrust of British empiricism was to reformulate epistemologically certain questions that had until then been framed metaphysically. Locke, in his doctrine of primary and secondary impressions, had, so to speak, gone halfway with this program, and Berkeley had taken it in the direction of a reductio ad absurdum. Hume completed the job Locke had begun by demolishing the distinction between primary and secondary characteristics. In so doing, he undermined the received conceptions of natural law as imposed or immanent. His skepticism demolished Locke's distinction and, in the process of bringing all qualities within the phenomenal world, drove all succeeding attempts to defend empirical science on rational grounds to one or another form of pragmatism (Scheffler, 1957).

The founding fathers of the discipline, although rejecting metaphysical thought in principle, failed to follow Hume in expunging the natural law doctrine; rather, they converted it into a moving substratum of history. For Comte, it is the *evolution* of the mind that makes possible the massive changes in society, past, present, and future. It lies at the heart of Spencer's evolutionism and is the object of Marx's critique of "bourgeois" social science, i.e., economics, or political economy.

Actually, Montesquieu best articulated the spirit of Hume. Although he does hold that there is a natural law antecedent to positive law, this plays little if any part in Montesquieu's actual analysis (see Chapter 3). His study of the roles of environmental and social factors was carried foward in an empirical and probabilistic spirit. Montesquieu everywhere remains open to the atypical, the skewing of effects due to the play of factors not present elsewhere, in general, to the difficulties attending generalization. And above all, he held no brief for any law of progress that could inform social analysis. In the spirit of the classical authors, his heavy emphases, like Hume's, are on the political, particularly the internal structuring of social and political formations in their relevance for the political process. Such formations fall into no historical pattern, and judgments about their consequences in terms of forms of rule can be only relative and conditional. The progress doctrines, distinct from such classically derived moderation, are associated with thinkers who insist on seeing history as driven by ideas, like Comte, with those maintaining the primacy of economic or material factors, like Marx, or those

---

[7] This was anticipated by Locke, for whom there were three kinds of knowledge: *intuitive*, which is knowledge of ourselves, and beyond any doubt (the Cartesian starting point); *demonstrative*, which is knowledge of God revealed by reason; and *sensitive*, or knowledge of the sensible world. Locke says that the latter comes close to being nothing more than a matter of "faith or opinion," or is "probability, not knowledge" (1894, 4; 11, 9).

who discover the prime movers in biology, like Spencer and other nineteenth century evolutionists.

Hume and the Empiricist Foundations of the Human Sciences

The second and for us more important aspect of Hume's contribution to the foundations of nineteenth century social science relates to the *manner* in which he established the legitimacy of applying natural science principles to the human realm. Hume stripped the rationale for the scientific study of the soul of any need for metaphysical attributions or analogies with the physical world and laid the foundation for human studies on purely episte-mological grounds. He not only destroyed the metaphysical claims, but provided a grounding for a human science positivism that remains today, whether exploitly recognized or not, the epistemological foundation of all "objectivist" sociologies.

In the *Treatise* Hume asserts that "the common distinction betwixt *moral* and *physical* necessity is without foundation" (1949, 171). By this he means that the experiences we have of our inner states—ideas and emotions—have identical epistemological status as those originating externally: They are all impressions. The fact that there is a difference between impressions of sensation and impressions of ideas is of no consequence whatever for the pursuit of scientific knowledge of moral, i.e., human action. Why is this so? Very simply put, our experience of the human world is constituted to a great extent by recurring events, and these experiences are in no wise different from those of natural events. Indeed, Hume argues, our typical experience involves an interpenetration or close association of natural and human sequences:

> And when we consider how aptly *natural* and *moral* evidence link together, and form only one chain of argument, we make no scruple to allow that they are of the same nature, and derived from the same principles (1949, 93–94).

Hume goes on to reinforce his point by describing the inexorable nature of the events leading up to the execution of a prisoner. The prisoner will perceive the discipline of the guards and soldiers, the preparatory actions of the executioner, and other related events as being interlaced with the purely physical events, the prison itself, the executioner's ax, and so on. All are parts of a chain of causes and effects that stimulate no differences of *perception* on the part of the prisoner (1912, 93–94). The nature of events as impressions, then, Hume argues, is identical in the natural and moral or social realms. In so far as the possibility of a science of any sort rests on the perceptions of the constant conjunction of events, it cannot be held—on this ground—that a human science must be subject to special limitations or stipulations not applicable to the sciences of the natural world.

Hume then raises some possible objections, the most important being the alleged relative absence of uniformity in the moral sphere. This Hume disputes.

"Is it more certain that two flat pieces of metal will unite together, than that two young savages of different sexes will copulate?" (1949, 402)[8]

The unexpected behavior of anyone must be treated in the same fashion as inconstancies in nature. The problem? A lack of knowledge of all the elements in a given situation. "A person of an obliging disposition gives a peevish answer: but he has the toothache or has not dined" (1912, 90). To Hume, there is no difference between a seeming irregularity such as this and the observed irregularities of the weather, which are, nevertheless, "supposed to be governed by steady principles" (91).

The *observable* uniformities of human life, then, are on this line of argument established as no different than those of the natural world. But what of the subjective side? Hume might have ignored this reality, thereby perhaps limiting or weakening his case for the essential identity of natural and human events. But Hume clearly intends his theory of science to include, and to include unequivocally, the subjective content or side of human behavior. Far from expressing any Cartesian doubt regarding the possibility of knowledge of subjective states or events, Hume takes it to be self-evident that they are a reality. The problem is *how* knowledge of subjectivity is to be constituted, and Hume has no doubts that it can and must submit to the same epistemological canon as all other scientific knowledge.

Like so many Western thinkers Hume conceives of this reality in terms of motivation.[9] Motives, says Hume, are inferred on the basis of our observations of *action*, and these inferences, in turn, assist us in further observations.

> ". . . we mount up to the knowledge of men's inclinations and motives, from their actions, expressions, and even gestures; and again descend to the interpretation of their actions from our knowledge of their motives and inclinations. The general observations treasured up by a course of experience, give us the clue of human nature, and teach us to unravel all its intricacies" (1912, 87).

The paradigmatic methodology of the human sciences, then, requires a principled focus on *both* actions and motives, and Hume's way of describing

---

[8] As acknowledged in *custom*, Hume might have said. Hume's emphasis on the significance of custom not only in human life generally, but as the experiential foundation of regularities as well, cannot be overemphasized.

". . . like objects, placed in like circumstances, will always produce like effects; and as this principle was established by a sufficient custom, it bestows an evidence and firmness on any opinion" (1949, 105).

In this and related discussions, Hume can be read as locating the foundations of scientific methodology, or better, scientific thought itself, in common everyday experience. This was a decidedly "unenlightened" doctrine; Enlightenment philosophers, as we have seen, pre-ferred to locate the scientific mentality in the higher reaches of reason. But in this Hume foreshadows, we might say, *launches*, the *pragmatic* conception of science, as this ultimately came to be formulated by Dewey and others. The late nineteenth century philosopher Wilhelm Windelband considered him to be the father of pragmatism as well as radical empiricism. See Whitehead's remarks in *Adventures of Ideas*, Part 2, Section 8.

[9] This is one form of the teleological view of the world derived from Aristotle, and buttressed throughout Western history by the ethical individualism which has been so central to the history of the West since both Greek and Judeo-Christian antiquity.

scientific procedure clearly suggests not only that they have equal epistemological status, but that they can be studied *only* in their interconnections.

> When I see the *effects* of passion in the voice and gesture of any person, my
> mind immediately passes from these effects to their causes, and forms such
> a lively idea of the passion, as is presently converted into the passion itself.
> In like manner, when I perceive the *causes* of any emotion, my mind is
> conveyed to the effects, and is actuated with a like emotion (1949, 576).[10]

Hume is satisfied that any given acts are always produced by the same
motives and so allows himself the comforting belief that the difference
between actions and motives present no special problem of observation, even
though he also writes of "interpretation of their actions, from our knowledge
of their motives and inclinations."

Note that Hume writes that his mind "passes" from effects (actions)
to causes (inner states conceived of motivationally). This is obviously a gloss.
Does his claim to knowledge of inner states not in reality imply a form of
knowing standing outside a rigorous empiricism? If passions are not directly
observable, on what grounds can we claim knowledge of them? Hume dealt
with this critical issue mainly through elaboration of his theory of *sympathy*,
derived in part from Hutcheson, but very significantly modified.[11] Sympathy
is that capacity of human beings to come, in some sense, to know, or to feel,
the inner state of another, "a power of the imagination which communicates
to us the inclinations and sentiments of others even when they differ from
ours" (Bryson, 1945, 129). This proceeds at first through familiarity with
the outward signs or manifestations of these states, but, because of the great
resemblance among all human beings, i.e., their common human nature,
these observations may stimulate a "weak perception" by the process of
intuition,[12] and this perception may itself become a passion. Essentially, this
involves the "doubling" of the generic relation of coming to know: An idea
is converted into an impression, and this process accompanies the reverse,
but "parallel," process of the production of an idea from an impression. In
Hume's view, sympathy is fundamental to many of our most common
experiences, e.g., engendering and maintaining consensus, making education
possible, or motivating people to become successful or famous.

It is interesting and somewhat puzzling, however, that Hume never

---

[10] This passage occurs in the course of Hume's discussion of what he defines as natural virtues
and vices, i.e., those having no dependence on "the artifice and contrivance of man, those
most closely connected with the basic principles of pleasure and pain," e.g., joy, grief, hope,
fear, in which the force of sympathy is invoked" (1949, 576). In the following chapter we
shall have more to say about this.

[11] The substantive importance of both Hume's and his friend Adam Smith's theories of sympathy
will be discussed in Chapter 5.

[12] Intuition is one of the five types of knowledge distinguished by Hume. Intuition and
resemblance are forms of knowledge involving only immediate perceptions. A third general
type, imagining, comprises three subtypes: (1) "fancying," the wild play of the imagination;
(2) "understanding of demonstrable systems" by which Hume means comprehension of
logical truths such as algebra and geometry; and (3) "demonstration of natural systems,"
roughly speaking, knowledge of probabilities, or all knowledge derived from experience (see
Stewart, 1963, Chap. 2, for a discussion).

theorized the process of sympathy as a methodology. His analysis proceeds on the assumption that like everything else, it can be comprehended by cause and effect reasoning about impressions that present themselves in our experience. This may have been due to his distrust of introspection as a philosophic or scientific method, expressed clearly in several passages. In the introduction to the *Treatise*, for example, he describes the mental operations of "reflection" and "premeditation" as *obstacles* to a science of human nature. Indeed, in this regard Hume is a rather strict Baconian. Unlike natural science, moral philosophy is faced with a disadvantage in that the reflections of the "experimenter," when introduced into a social situation, may, indeed almost surely will, influence and so bias the perceptions of the events of interest (1949, 23). The moral scientist is then enjoined to exorcise these idols, to "clean up our experiments in this science . . ." (23).

It is somewhat ironic that the same thinker who thought through the decisive arguments against metaphysical elements in science also not only provided both the most powerful grounding for a positivist human science, but was also the first to deal with one of positivism's most troubling problems, the seeming unobservability of inner states, and to have done so in a surprisingly modern, if inevitably unsatisfactory fashion.[13] Comte and other positivists to follow ruled human subjectivity in is various forms out of legitimate human science; behaviorism, the employment of an extremely stringent protocol of observation ruling out as scientifically illegitimate all events not directly observable, is the extreme form of this. Modern sociology rejects this and claims, although not without challenge, that human subjectivity may legitimately be brought within the positivist model of science. In this, modern sociology, at least since Durkheim, has been heir more to Hume than Comte.

The implications of Hume's analysis of the scientific status of causality and law, and his assimilation of human subjectivity to a positivistic conception of science, went largely unrecognized not only by his peers[14] but by generations to follow. Empiricism was honored in word while various metaphysics of human nature and history became the staple of most late eighteenth and nineteenth century sociology, a condition which persisted, indeed persists, well into the present century.

NATURAL LAW METAPHYSICS AND THE IDEAL OF FREEDOM

The juxtaposition of the idea of freedom with that of natural law, understood as a *moral* law, was a volatile one that lay at the root of much creative thought in the eighteenth and nineteenth centuries. On the one hand, there was the

---

[13] In this regard, the reader might wish to examine Hume's theory of the self, which has some tangential relevance to the present discussion but which cannot be discussed in detail. Hume argues that the "self" is acquired from a whole series of quite diverse impressions, and is therefore a "fiction," in reality a whole array of fractionated "selves," depending on the relations of resemblance, contiguity, and causality, a "bundle" pulled together by "force of association," itself an irreducible aspect of human nature (Hume, 1912, 245–246, *et passim*). This clearly anticipates a variety of modern self theories.

[14] Even the itinerant Rousseau, whom the generous and congenial Hume put up (and up with) for a considerable time, evidently had little understanding of or interest in Hume's work.

tendency in writers like Hartley, LaMettrie, Holbach, and Maupertuis, closely following and emulating the structure of Newtonian theory, to formulate the moral law of human nature in highly mechanistic and deterministic fashion. Human nature in this view is a clockwork, a mechanism in which all parts mesh wonderfully with each other.

On the other hand there was the concept of freedom, an intensely held practical *ideal*, not only of a few progressive intellectuals but of classes or class fractions coming newly to power, particularly businessmen attempting to extricate themselves from the mercantile system and other social and political constraints of societies based on privilege associated with rank. Much philosophical thought of the time defended the principle of freedom by attempting to provide for it some solid philosophical ground. Now, there is a sense in which the ideal of freedom and the principle of natural law appear to stand as an irresolvable contradiction. Freedom seemes necessarily to imply the making of choices, implying the availability of *criteria* of choice, of whatever sort: moral, technical, political, and so on. A freely acting being is one who makes, or is thought to be capable of making, conscious and rational choices regarding his or her conduct. Behavior that is in some clearcut sense "determined" (e.g., the reflexes, conditioned or utterly habitual behavior, action that unavoidably proceeds in ignorance of something that would otherwise give it a different direction and consequence), regardless of its consequences, we place in a moral category other than that of the making of choices.

The nature of the contradiction seems transparent. A deterministic account of human action seems to exclude the possibility of choice, and therefore of what, in our human conceit, we like to think of as the distinctively human quality, the capacity for *moral and ethical conduct*. If our behavior is determined, then choice, by definition, is excluded. On the other hand, if one regards one's action as freely undertaken, i.e., involving a choice or choices of different paths of action, then behavior seems not to be determined. To speak of a "determination of choice" seems a contradiction in terms.

The implications of this for budding conceptions of social science in the eighteenth century were considerable. Knowledge of human nature was regarded as the key to progress, to the remaking of the human world. But this knowledge, on the model of the natural sciences, was conceived as deterministic in form. Would a scientific grasp of the principles of human nature, then, not show what was necessary? But if the principles of human nature are necessary, then how is it that their expression in the future will be different than at present, or in the past? History, on this view, would seem to be a record of broken laws of nature.

Furthermore, acquisition of knowledge is thought to be liberating. But in what sense can this be? Does not the liberated condition achieved through knowledge itself contradict our understanding of the system of explanation as deterministic? The idea of knowledge as a practical instrument of social reform or mastery necessarily implies a concept of knowledge bearers who actively seek to *create* and implement *new* values, to transform existing conditions. This presupposes the freedom to do so. But progressive thinkers, in their rush to apply science to human activity, and understanding science as modeled on physics or mechanics, held to a deterministic conception of science. Their idea of "law," in either the imposed or immanent sense, although generally rather loose and ambiguous, was a rendering of two constituent principles: generality and necessity. A principle was a law if, even in some unclearly specific sense, it was thought to undergird a range of particulars, and if the described connections among things were thought to permit of no other ones.

The philosophes and others were troubled by this problem of law as determination versus human freedom, and the literature of the eighteenth century includes many attempts to effect one or another sort of reconciliation. Kant's philosophy, for instance, was an attempt to establish ethical conditions as necessarily *outside* the framework of scientific explanation, a philosophical exercise that continues to have profound ramifications. Another was Condillac's *Treatise on Sensation*, a work in the French materialistic tradition. This is worthy of a short review.

Condillac

In his *Treatise* (Condillac, 1930) Condillac sets out to establish in a quasiexperimental fashion the Lockean doctrine that all ideas and feelings arise from experience. Employing something on the order of what we would today call a "mental experiment," Condillac asks us to imagine a marble statue, or, more precisely, a man with a marble exterior. Initially, the statue has no experiences; the marble is impervious to everything. Condillac then introduces the five senses, beginning with smell and followed by taste, hearing, sight and, finally, touch. At each stage, he analyzes what he imagines the statue's experiences must be, in consequence of the most recent addition. From the base point of his pleasure-pain formula, he deduces the full range of human experience from the senses, considered singly and in relation to each other. Finally, it is only with the acquisition of the sense of touch that the sense of external *objects* appears in the statue's experience.

Although, in the understanding of the time, this was a philosophical undertaking, the *form* of Condillac's procedure is more like a scientific experiment than a conventional philosophical inquiry. If only in the imagination, Condillac manipulates "variables" to establish a hypothesis. Furthermore, the issue of whether or not the statue experiences a real object world independent of our sense experience, after acquiring the sense of touch, is for Condillac merely metaphysical, "one of the questions God has left to the philosophers to dispute about" (216). Condillac confines himself to "positive investigations." In summing up, he concludes:

> "In giving it successively new modes of being, and new senses, we saw it form desires, learn from experiments, to regulate and satisfy them, and pass from needs to needs, from cognitions to cognitions, from pleasures to pleasures. The statue is nothing but the sum of all it has acquired. Why not this be the same with men?" (239).

Clearly, the environmental determinism of Condillac's experiment (and of his earlier work, *Traité des systèmes* as well) was a concern for him, for he was moved to append a "Dissertation on Freedom" to the *Treatise on*

Sensations. In this short tract he attempts to assimilate the question of freedom to his deterministic analysis of experience. The statue is confronted with diverse objects in its experience and, over time, makes selections in accordance with the desires it has acquired. If events follow their "natural course," the statue will sometimes meet obstacles to its desires and often fail to find the pleasure in the objects it seeks. "In such a situation," writes Condillac, "it will recall happier circumstance," and come to "judge that it was in its power to prefer them" (244). It now experiences regret, the pain of comparing experiences, or repentance. Repentance, in turn, "teaches it how important it is for it to deliberate before deciding" (245) In deliberation, the statue acquires the power to act or not to act, and this, for Condillac, is freedom.

> Freedom consists then in determinations, which, in supposing that we always depend in some way on the action of objects, are a series of deliberations we have made, or have had the power to make (250).

Condillac's analysis, like others in the eighteenth century, is an early form of a problem that remains with us today in the terms of *agency* versus *structure*.[15] Of course, thinkers like Condillac were employing the idea of natural law in its immanent sense, which makes the problem insoluble from the outset. If determinism and freedom are defined in ways contradictory or exclusive of one another, no possible exercise in logic or science can reconcile them.

Condillac's effort, in attempting to assimilate freedom to determination, or the other way around, was perhaps characteristic of eighteenth century treatments of the question. Hume, however, attacked the problem from the standpoint of his "mitigated skepticism," treating it as essentially a semantic one.

Hume: The Problem of Freedom

Hume, in his analysis of causality and related writings, moved epistemological thought away from a naive assumption of the existence of an object world and toward a phenomenalistic account of science. It was not, however, Hume's intention to destroy science, but to explore the sense in which claims regarding science, i.e., a body of laws of human nature, could be established. The *Treatise* is subtitled "An Attempt to introduce the experimental Method of Reasoning into MORAL SUBJECTS." What Hume actually does is to shift the locus of natural law from the object world, where its presence cannot be defended, in the direction of the realm of language, i.e., to *conventionalize* it. Hume does not say explicitly that scientific laws are propositions, but he comes close to it, so it is probably not much of an

---

[15] The most recent sustained and systematic effort to achieve a practically usable resolution is Giddens's concept of "structuration" (Giddens, 1983, 1985).

overstatement to think of Hume as the first true logical positivist or logical empiricist.[16]

Hume is everywhere sensitive to the misuses of language, to the fallacies, pseudoproblems, and absurdities to which an incautious employment of terms and arguments can lead. He understands that much of what has passed for argumentation about substantive philosophical matters has been no more than a series of futile exercises in semantics. In both the *Treatise* and the *Enquiry* he argues that, if we insist on opposing liberty to necessity, the only thing the former can possibly mean is the absence of being determined, i.e., chance, which "is universally allowed to have no existence" (1912, 100). Yet he agrees that liberty is essential to morality. Whenever freedom of action is absent, we cannot speak of morality. Action can be moral only by virtue of "indications of the internal character, passions, and affections" (103).

In the *Treatise* Hume analyzes three reasons accounting for "the prevalence of the doctrine of liberty" (1949, 407): (1) the difficulty we have of persuading ourselves, after the fact of any action, that we were governed by necessity; (2) a "false sensation or experience of the liberty of indifference, which is mistaken for its real existence" (403)—an intuitive feeling; and (3) religion. Hume dismisses all three: the first as an obvious rationalization; the second as clearly false, because although "we may feel a liberty within ourselves, . . . a spectator can commonly infer our actions from our motives and character (408); the third as an absurdity, since religion is in fact dependent on the doctrine of necessity, rather than liberty, in its doctrine of morally acting subjects.

Hume thus seems to treat freedom, from the standpoint of science, as error; our rationalizations, our intuition, foolish religious doctrines, all easily shown to be partial or mistaken forms of experience, provide the ground for this idea. Yet on the other hand, "liberty is essential to morality." How is it that the idea of liberty, so casually disposed of by Hume from a scientific standpoint, is yet fundamental to all moral action, the object of the human sciences? Is Hume a Kantian, radically separating the domains of science and human moral conduct? Consider his argument.

Hume asks us to consider the case of "mad-men," who, "it is commonly held, have no liberty, yet, whose behavior we observe, is anything but regular." Instances such as this reveal the muddled quality of our thought.

---

[16] The intent here is not to attribute to Hume a unique or special concern with or interest in the functioning of language. The eighteenth century was fascinated by language from different standpoints. Kames (1774) wrote six volumes on the origin of language. Adam Smith, in his "Considerations Concerning the First Formation of Languages" (1966, 507–538), speculated brilliantly on the subject. Language was central to Vico's analysis of the differences between "ages" (i.e., cultures) and was important for Herder. Neither is it suggested that such concern for analysis of language is that new; it runs through the entire history of philosophy. The medieval debate between nominalists and realists, for example, involving John Scotus, Odo, Anselm, William of Champeaux, Duns Scotus, and others, was partly over the ontological status of language. Ockham's "razor" is wielded from an essentially linguistic perspective. Later, Leibniz attempted to create a language for science that would be universal in scope, precisely because of the same problems with natural languages that later exercised Hume: vagueness, uncertainty of meaning, and therefore, scientific unreliability.

And this brings us to the root of the problem. This issue (of "mad-men") is but

> . . . a natural consequence of these confused ideas and undefined terms, which we so commonly make use of in our reasonings, especially on the present subject" (1949, 404)

The problem is one of clarity and consistency of usage. If we attend scrupulously to our *language*, pseudoproblems such as "the fantastic doctrine of liberty" would never exercise our intellectual energies.

A slight rephrasing of Hume's argument might go as follows. The idea of liberty makes no sense within the necessary cause-and-effect or deterministic language of science, since its meaning is necessarily reduced to the operation of choice, which, by definition, can be no part of scientific explanation. However, the idea surely does have *meaning* to us, but from the standpoint of practical action, and appears in the language of practical action. Hume's political essays and historical writing deal repeatedly with the importance of liberty as *practically* of great significance in life. In passages like those above, he seems to wish to *subjectivize* it, seeming on implicit Baconian grounds to place it outside the sphere of phenomena appropriate for scientific study. Liberty seems to be merely a feeling that accompanies human moral activity, but does not enter its constitution. Yet we saw earlier how, although Hume distrusted subjective states and wished on Baconian grounds to exclude them as objects of scientific investigation, he not only included "motives" in the framework of his moral science, but quite explicitly designated them as indispensible to scientific study of moral subjects. He thus appears to be on *both* sides of what was eventually to become perhaps the most fundamental schism in the grounding conception of sociology, that between an objectivist-positivist orientation and a subjectivist-constructionist one.

Although an inconsistent and intellectually troubled one, Hume is clearly a positivist. Since he was evidently the first to systematically theorize the epistemological ground of a positivistic *human* science, it may be worth our while to systematize the way we may legitimately inquire as to what the essential elements of this positivism were. They seem to be four.

> First, in his "mitigated scepticism," Hume established the basic foundations for a human science on epistemological grounds, specifically, our experience of recurrence or regularity in human affairs.
>
> Second, he construed the practical method of the human sciences as "experimental," i.e., as in some sense copying that of the natural sciences. Strictly speaking, of course, Hume did not perform experiments in the usual sense. Rather he engaged in two kinds of intellectual exercises: (1) more or less systematic observations; and (2) what we would today call "imaginary experiments." The important point is that Hume was attempting to introduce the *form* of the natural science experiment into the science of human nature.
>
> Third, he proposed applying the experimental method to the full range of human activity, including moral and cultural life. Hume divides the human sciences into four subdisciplines: (1) logic, (2) morals, (3) criticism, and (4) politics. These divisions do not correspond very well with present-

day academic disciplinary specialization—perhaps unfortunately! Logic explains, "the principles and operations of our reasoning faculty"; morals and criticism, "our tastes and sentiments"; politics, "men united in society, and dependent on each other" (1748, 19). Hume refers to all of these collectively as "moral subjects," meaning that all human conscious activity is in some sense moral.

Fourth, although he does not express it systematically as a doctrine, Hume wishes to distrust or avoid subjective elements in scientific knowing, and this is a tendency perhaps inconsistent with that described just above.[17]

CONCLUSION: KNOWLEDGE, HUMAN NATURE AND SOCIAL CHANGE

The general point of this chapter has been to establish the importance of natural law in the proto-social science of the eighteenth century and the attendant difficulties. Both the epistemological and ethical dilemmas of knowledge remained centrally implicated in the early sociologies, and interacted with conceptions of human nature and history as progress to give these sociologies their definitive shape.

I have said that the three problematics display a close interweaving at several points. One of these had to do with maintaining a doctrine of the constancy and immutability of human nature in the context of a powerful and intensifying commitment to massive social change. Eventually, the enlightenment theory of human nature had to give way, or, perhaps more accurately, undergo severe modification. Although early sociologists tended to cling to the Enlightenment formula of explaining social phenomena as effects of presocial human nature, they did convert the substantive conception of human nature into a historical variable. Comte does this, for example, as does Marx, who, working partly with materials from a different tradition, carries it through to its logical conclusion.

In Chapter 3 we saw how the contesting philosophical anthropologies of the eighteenth century moved toward an increasingly distinctive sociological conception, as they grappled with the problems of cultural diversity and mundane evil. Amelioration of evil, in particular, comes to depend on the new comprehension of true human nature; in this the outlines of a new, liberating human science is understood as indispensable—a science of human freedom. The human science of the Enlightenment, however, remains

---

[17] In all of this Hume was somewhat ahead of his time. For years, his philosophical works were scarcely read. In his autobiography he remarks that the *Treatise* "fell dead-borne from the press." Even the *Enquiry*, published ten years later as somewhat of a popularization of the first book of the more demanding *Treatise*, was ignored for some time. It was after this that a discouraged Hume turned his hand to the writing of history and essays, and it was in these fields that he finally made a reputation. Only in the 1760s did his more strictly philosophical works come into greater demand. Scientists of human activity honored empiricism more in the breach than in their practice. Indeed, the movement of sociology throughout the last half of the eighteenth century and throughout the entirety of the nineteenth generally ignored most of what Hume had to say. The incredibly grandiose program that Comte a century later labeled "positivistic" not only extends far beyond the limited positivism of Hume, but incorporates elements profoundly inconsistent with it, as we shall see.

atomistic, reductionist, and mechanistic. In these aspects it clashes with the master principle of change, for how can a human nature that functions on deterministic principles become the fulcrum of the creation of a new order?

Beyond this there is the *double* dilemma of knowledge as the new motor of history, i.e., as an *instrument*. If we are to organize the future on the principles revealed by science—a human science—it had better be as much a veritable embodiment of truth as Newton's physics. Just as problematic is the question of who is to wield this new instrument, and to precisely what ends; knowledge in the wrong hands serves evil as efficiently as it does socially beneficent ends in the hands of the morally incorruptible.

The Janus face of science is not a comprehension sprung just lately to the contemporary mind. Enlightenment optimism is powerfully tempered with attention to the themes of both error and evil as these related to a human science. *No* science, of course, is possible at all, until superstition is eradicated from the mind. Bacon's program for overcoming the idols already presents the essence of what being objective has come to mean. Superstition and the like are *error*, of course, in that they are a cognitive misrepresentation of what is true. But they are also an *evil* in that they continue to make impossible the realization of conditions that would assure a humane existence for all. In this sense they block realization of what may *become true* in the future.

The cognitive problem is understood to be solvable by way of making human science objective. From Bacon through Hume and Condillac to Mill and beyond, this faith underlies the progressive construction of empiricist epistemology and logic. Hume is a critical figure in this progression; well before the natural law conceptions derived from earlier centuries had begun to be disgarded, or at least significantly modified, he had erected the essentials of the epistemological bridge to the world of modern positivistic social science, even though this was not well understood.

An historic irony, however, attends this faith in and advance of scientific objectivity. The value of knowledge wielded as an instrument increases as its truth and potential efficiency are augmented. And within this one is nested another. The Enlightenment advances the ideology of scientific knowledge as the instrument for the discovery of the foundations of evil, and for the attack upon it; the other face of this science makes it potentially, at least, into an evil greater than that it is designed to overcome. The Enlightenment had some understanding of this. Most obviously, of course, there is Rousseau, with his attack on everything "civilized." Cynical realists like Mandeville had some grasp of it. Gibbon analyzed the power of Roman statesmen in terms of their ability to manipulate religious superstitions they did not share.

But what sort of a clockwork is this? The gods who made it must be chuckling at the supreme irony—and genius—of a machine that runs through history by constantly negating itself; even as it begins to dawn on the machine's creators that their magic, like that of the sorcerer's apprentice, forever threatens to turn on them with uncontrolled fury and malevolence. Euripides understood something of this:

> There be many shapes of mystery
> And many things God makes to be

Past hope or fear
And the end man looked for cometh not
And a path is there where no man thought
So hath it fallen here

Bacchai, 1388–1392

It is only a short step from Enlightenment idealization of knowledge to conversion of its creators into high priests of a universal religion, as Comte wanted to become. A somewhat longer stride through history is required to transform the critical-minded positivism of the Enlightenment into a technicist, "value-free" science at the disposal of any buyer who can find some use for it. These and other related consequences of Enlightenment thought have been at the center of the growth of sociology from the beginning. But they have not stood there alone. Conservative thought both before and after the French Revolution had a central role, which we shall review in Chapter 6. But before this we shall look at the group of thinkers that may, with some stretching of the idea, be thought of as loosely constituting the first sociological "school," the Scottish moralists, and examine how their thought took its shape in as addressing the axial questions raised in these chapters.

5

THE SCOTTISH MORALISTS

Rousseau's thought had only slight influence on the development of sociology in the nineteenth century. During his own life his rejection of the ideology of progress and the eighteenth century ideal of knowledge seemed unenlightened, and he alienated himself from the reigning intellects of salon circles. His influence, therefore, was transmitted less through the dominant Anglo-Franco sociologically inclined intellectual circles of the late eighteenth and early nineteenth centuries than through the egalitarian revolutionaries during and following the French revolution and in the romantic movement. The early nineteenth century radical egalitarianism that reflects Rousseau's thought was of little consequence for early sociology.

Unlike Rousseau, the Scottish moralists were men of position and in some instances—even in barren Scotland—substantial means. Many of them—Hutcheson, Smith, Ferguson, Millar, and Stewart—were academicians, and Kames and Monboddo were jurists. Hume was born to the lower gentry. Their political leanings or doctrines, which, reflecting their position in society, ranged from conservative to liberal, but which in no case embraced the radical egalitarianism of their Genevan contemporary,[1] were also quite unlike those of Rousseau. The Scottish enlightenment, however, certainly in comparison with contemporary English letters, has been commonly judged

---

[1] From the standpoint of contemporary conservatives, of course, the liberal doctrines of some of them, Smith and Ferguson in particular, seemed radical enough. Ruskin's judgment on Smith was that he was a "half-bred and half-witted Scotchman who taught the deliberate blasphemy 'Thou shalt hate the Lord thy God, damn his laws and covet thy neighbor's goods'" (Bryson, 1945, 212).

to have been enormously creative[2] and influential, especially the work of Hume and Smith. Although England was inhospitable to the Scots, many of the French *philosophes* held it in the highest regard. In Prussia, Kant understood fully the implications of Hume's *Treatise*, announcing that it had "awakened him from his slumbers." Both Ferguson and Smith were well received in Germany, and the seeming contradiction between Smith's moral philosophy, in his *The Theory of Moral Sentiments*, and his economic theory, in *The Wealth of Nations*, published seventeen years later, was first formulated in Germany as "das Adam Smith Problem." Scottish thought was also well known and appreciated in the United States; it was to Dugald Stewart that Jefferson turned for assistance when staffing his newly formed University of Virginia. But influence is always a matter of the backward vision of the contemporary and therefore a special or particular way of receiving or interpreting the thinker or thinkers in question. The nineteenth century thinkers drew on the Scots for their skepticism, their utilitarianism, their liberalism, and their progress-colored historical work. With considerable justification, Hawthorne maintains that in utilitarianism and evolutionism "the sociological insights of the eighteenth-century Scots were to be lost" (Hawthorne, 1976, 31).

It is at least this—the fate of their sociological insights—that the Scots have in common with Rousseau. The developing mainstream of nineteenth century sociology, while celebrating—and distorting—other aspects of their thought, for the most part ignored their sociological insights, and was the poorer for it. Part of the reason for this was that these insights were nested in the framework of their moral philosophy, and they of course did think of themselves as moral philosophers. But regarding moral philosophy, as Stewart remarks, "The Scots had in mind what we, for lack of better terms, probably would call 'humanities' and 'social sciences'" (Stewart, 1963, 10).

The Scots' sociological thought reveals a novel interplay of elements within the problematics of progress, the possibilities of social knowledge, and conceptions of human nature, which held substantial sociological potential but that remained essentially unexploited for many decades. Whereas most eighteenth century philosophers emphasized the powers of the mind in ultimately bringing into being a better world, the Scots, on the whole, downplayed the role of reason and relocated the motor of advance not in the old polar opposite of and obstacle to the exercise of reason, the passions, but in a somewhat resurrected and resituated form of the category of interest, and by extension, in the rather despised sphere of economic life. Some of their works were, for the time, sound historical analysis displaying a strong sociological cast. But they also produced the beginnings of a theory of types of social relationships sounder and potentially more fruitful than anything in previous social theory. We shall refer to these two sides of their sociology as (1) their theory of personal and societal relations (mainly in Hume and Smith), and (2) their theory of the institutional nature of liberal market society.

---

[2] Whitehead's judgment: "Throughout the greater part of the eighteenth century the intellectual life of England, so far as concerns any originative energy, is negligible" (1955, 36).

THE SCOTS' CONCEPT OF PERSONAL AND SOCIETAL RELATIONS

Hume: On Personal and Societal Relationships

Although obviously not the first to announce that human life was in some sense social, a good case can be made for the proposition that the Scots were the first to flesh out in analytical detail just what this might mean. Central to their thought is a distinction between two types of social relations: (1) the "natural" relations found within the family and other face-to-face groups, and (2) the "artificial" relations of the larger society. These are Hume's terms, but similar distinctions are to be found in the works of the others. In the discussion to follow, I shall render this distinction in the terms *personal* and *societal*.

Stewart says of the corpus of Hume's works that they, "constitute a system of thought which is not only highly unified, but quite valuable as a description of the rock and the sand on which our modern world is built" (Stewart, 1963, 19). It was this understanding of the modern world as it was coming into being that lies at the root of Hume's distinction between personal and societal relationships.[3] The reader will recall (from Chap. 4) that Hume made a fundamental distinction between "direct" and "indirect" passions, the former arising out of impressons experienced immediately as either painful or pleasurable (and thereby creating the basis for the moral distinctions of good and evil). The cause of why it is that anything in particular is experienced as pleasurable or painful lies in the recesses of human nature, beyond the powers of the mind. The "direct" passions are those arising directly from these aspects of human nature. The "indirect" passions, by contrast, are those that involve a perceiving subject and an impression, pleasurable or painful, as in the direct passions, but also the *idea* of the person who is the *perceiver* of the perceived pleasure or pain. This triadic relation is thus both natural and social. The indirect passions—most importantly love, hatred, pride, and humility—are possible only within society because they presuppose social experience mainly in the form of comparisons made in accordance with what we would today call normative standards.

Hume goes on to analyze the manner of the emergence of personal relationships in terms of his concept of sympathy.

Hume locates sympathy in the relationship between impressions and ideas. It will be recalled that the differences between these two forms of experience is one of degree: They "differ only in the degrees of force and vivacity with which they strike upon the soul" (1949, 319). Ideas, however, "are borrow'd from impressions"; i.e., an impression, particularly a very strong one, may give rise to a related idea. However, once an idea related to an impression has been formed, it may itself evoke the impression, as in the case of our imaginings of pain and sickness. This process, says Hume, is particularly important in the formation of "the opinions and affections."

---

[3] In the following discussion I lean heavily on Stewart's excellent *The Moral and Political Philosophy of David Hume* (1963), as well as on Hume's own works.

Our affections depend more upon ourselves, and the internal operations of the mind, than any other impressions; for which reason they arise more naturally from the imagination, and from every lively idea we form of them. This is the nature and cause of sympathy; and 'tis after this manner we enter so deep into the opinions and affections of others, whenever we discover them. . . . When we sympathize with the passions and sentiments of others, these movements appear at first in *our* mind as mere ideas, and are conceiv'd to belong to another person, as we conceive any other matter of fact. 'Tis also evident, that the ideas of the affections of others are converted into the very impressions they represent, and that the passions arise in conformity to the images we form of them (1949, 319).

Although Hume identifies sympathy as a capacity of human nature stemming from the "great resemblance among all human creatures (1949, 318), and dependent on the fact that "the minds of all men are similar in their feelings and operations (575–576), it is clearly a capacity realized only in and through social intercourse. "The minds of men are mirrors to one another," (365) he writes, in a modernity-tinged metaphor.

A man will be moritified, if you tell him he has a stinking breath; tho' 'tis evidently no annoyance to himself. Our fancy easily changes its situation; and either surveying ourselves as we appear to others, or considering others as they feel themselves, we enter, by that means, into sentiments, which no way belong to us, and in which nothing but sympathy is able to interest us. And this sympathy we sometimes carry so far, as even to be displeas'd with a quality commodious to us, merely because it displeases others, and makes us disagreeable in their eyes; tho' perhaps we never can have any interest in rendering ourselves agreeable to them (589).

In passages such as this, Hume seems to at least adumbrate the idea of personal relations as an autonomous plane of analysis. Might we say that his "actors" come close to taking the "standpoint of the other"? Perhaps Hume should be accorded some recognition for anticipating the later interactional theories of thinkers such as Baldwin, Cooley, and Mead. He seems to be suggesting that essential properties of social life arise directly through sympathetic interaction, that the sense of self (or, for Hume, more properly, our "selves") is known to us through acts of perception occurring within social intercourse, and that although these perceptions are possible at all, to be sure, because of the basic species similarity, they depend in their "strength" on (1) "similarity of manners, or character, or country, or language" and (2) the strength of the relation "betwixt ourselves and any object."

Hume's theory of sympathy anticipates the ideas of later interactionists in its larger constructionist implications as well as in its internal mechanics. Earlier moral sense philosophers, Hutcheson in particular, and Shaftesbury (although of course not a Scot), who influenced him strongly (see Chapter 3), had located the moral sense in original nature, defending this on theological grounds. Hume departs from this received doctrine, proposing that "sympathy is the chief source of moral distinctions" (1949, 618). Sympathy, he holds, is the source of the moral approbation attending our sense of justice (500), the chief source of the moral distinctions inherent in social life. As such, it becomes that essential bond between people which prevents their isolation; it is the relation at the very root of, or constitutive of, society itself.

The family, friendship, and humanitarian activities are the basic types of relationship that come to be constituted on the basis of sympathy. These relations constitute a sphere that fosters development of a sense of duty or obligation (that Hume still continues to think of as "natural"). It is a sphere that rests on the indirect passions manifest through sympathy.

Social bonds based on sympathy are in their nature limited to the immediate and the personal. They are unreflective, nondeliberate, nonrational. If sympathy were the sole principle relating human beings to each other, society as we know it would be impossible. Hume therefore coupled his analysis of sympathy with what he called the principle of comparison. Pain and pleasure in their primitive sense give rise to a purely self-interested moral sense. Genuine moral judgments (i.e., those rising above the former), on the other hand, are made from a neutral standpoint (471ff.), where one arrives not solely through sympathy, but by way of the process of comparison. Through sympathy we do no more than enter the feelings of others. By comparison we are enabled to judge their comparative worth: "*Objects appear greater or less by a comparison wtih others*" (375). Comparison, in Hume's formulation is "directly contrary to sympathy in its operation" (593). Sympathy remains irrevocably tied to the parochial *milieu*; freedom from this particularism proceeds through comparisons of various sorts, especially of one's own self with others. *Disinterested* judgments are those that transcend the immediacy of particular sympathetic ties, and whose worth is evaluated in the context of general rules. We might say that, for Hume, this is the meaning of objectivity.

> Tho' sympathy be much fainter than our concern for ourselves, and a sympathy with persons remote from us much fainter than that with persons near and contiguous; yet we neglect all these differences in our calm judgments concerning the characters of men" (1949, 603).

In such judgments, a variety of considerations may appear, all rooted in comparison: differences in immediate circumstances, actions considered appropriate to various social roles, and differences in ability, for example. The critical point is that the genesis of general rules is to be found in the process of comparison, that comparison is a rational process ("all kinds of reasoning consists in nothing but comparison" [1949, 73]), and that the presence of general rules is the decisive test of the presence of a "civil society."

Thus, societal relations are those that acquire a collective *utilitarian* nature through rules enforced by the state, but they may also both rest on and be mitigated by the presence of a common morality (or "custom"). It is in this sense that Hume, in the fashion of so many eighteenth century thinkers, characterized society as "artificial" (recall Mandeville): its self-interested (essentially economic) activity is regulated in the utilitarian interests of the collectivity, by a set of general rules that soften the destructive consequences of competition while yet retaining its individually and socially beneficial aspects. The critical principels of regulation, according to Hume, are those of private property, free markets, and the sanctity of contracts (501ff.).

Normative standards defining societal relationships and derived from the process of comparison, then, are "artificial," which may be understood to indicate that they constitute a plane remote from human nature. These standards define relationships that differ fundamentally in principle from personal relations. This difference is summed up succinctly by Steward.

> ... [Hume] distinguishes ... between family, friendship, and humanity, on the one hand, and the civil relationships, society and state, on the other. The former are the direct results of the feelings men have for others, and therefore they can be called 'natural.' The latter are artificial: when men are seeking scarce economic goods, when the natural relation among them is competition, and society and state are the framework within which this competition can go on with results most satisfactory to all (Stewart, 1963, 302).

At this point we shall leave the topic of Hume's theory of personal and societal relations, and turn to an examination of Adam Smith's theory of sympathy, which is both an extension and modification of Hume's.

Smith's Theory of Moral Sentiments

As with Hume, the essence of Smith's position is that the moral sense is not to be found implanted in original human nature, as is true of the "passions," but rather, acquired socially. Smith's central intent was to work out a moral philosophy, and took the critical problem to be *explaining* the making of moral judgments about our own and other's conduct. This differs somewhat from Hume's project, which was more on the order of working and the implications of his basic empiricist axioms and postulates for various spheres of experience. But it is precisely because his main interest was on working out a systematic moral philosophy that the *sociological* contours of Smith's thought, particularly in his theory of sympathy, are elaborated more fully. Like Hume, Smith resituated the genesis of the moral sense in the process of social interaction. "How is it," he asks, "that when our passive feelings are so sordid and selfish, that our active principle is often so noble" (1966, 193)? Any modification or control of such natural proclivities presumes the operation of a moral sense, which Smith says is acquired only by removing ourselves from our "natural station," by acquiring a "certain distance" from these propensities of our nature. This distancing from our impulses, he says, can occur only when we attempt to look at them *as others do* or as they are likely to do. A solitary human being, he thinks, would find it impossible to reflect on himself or herself as an object, or to conceive of the propriety or impropriety of any particular act. But "bring him into society and he is immediately provided with the mirror which he wanted before" (162).

The capacity for self-judgment leads Smith to what may be the first technical elaboration of the interior structure of the self in the social sciences.[4] "When I come to examine my conduct, Smith writes, I necessarily see myself as two persons," and

> That I, the examiner and judge represent a different character from that other I, the person whose conduct is examined into and judged over. The first is the spectator, whose sentiments with regard to my own conduct I endeavor to enter into, by placing myself in his situation, and by considering how it would appear to me, when seen from that particular point of view. The second is the agent, the person whom I properly call myself, and of whose conduct, under the character of a spectator, I was endeavoring to form some opinion. The first is the judge; the second the person judged of (164–165).

The presence of the "spectator" is possible not only because of a quality of our imagination that enables us to place ourselves in the position of another, but because of the objective existence of others and relations with them, as well. By virtue of the imagination, we put ourselvves in the position of the other and are thereby able to duplicate or share other's experiences, even "become in some measure the same person" (4). Smith gives as examples our tendency to emphathize with someone about to receive a blow, or with a dancer or acrobat hanging and twisting by a rope.

In this Smith takes an important step in extending Hume's theory of sympathy. Hume had formulated this as an *objective* social process. Smith does so as well, and although not as clear about the matter as we might prefer, he *extends* this idea by proposing that the mental deliberations constituting our moral judgments are derived from or perhaps are a homologous reflection of, our paradigmatic social relations. This does not sound very different from the internal conversation described by Charles Cooley and G. H. Mead a century and a half later (see Chapter 15).

Other aspects of Hume's theory of sympathy may be profitably compared to Smith's.

Hume had rooted the development of sympathy squarely in the experiences of pain and pleasure, a reflection of his strongly utilitarian side that we here prefer to recognize but not emphasize because of our particular interest in recovering the sociological elements in his thought. Smith, by contrast, explicitly rejects such integration of the utilitarian and moral sides of our activity. To be sure, moral activity may also be utilitarian, but it never has a utilitarian genesis; it merely acquires utility as it persists. Smith's insistence on this point—the nonutilitarian character of sympathy—seems to be related to his desire to characterize sympathy, in Dugald Stewart's words, as "always agreeble to both parties," and to thereby provide the foundations of the general propriety essential for the integration and continued functioning of society. Hume, who was not very favorably inclined toward *Theory of Moral Sentiments*, himself criticized Smith on this point, arguing that limiting the moral sentiments to positive, or agreeable senti-

---

[4] Western thought, of course, is replete with theological, literary, and other depictions of our inner life. One thinks immediately of Augustine, along with other religious conceptions.

ments, was unjustified (letter to Smith, in Stewart, 1963, 351). Hume himself, always more the cynical realist (despite his personable disposition) had, the reader will recall, explicitly included the sentiments arising from aversion or hate in his own analysis of sympathy.

Adam Ferguson, in his discussion of moral sentiments some eight years after publication of *Theory of Moral Sentiments*, reinforced and amplified this point. The imperative of "the care of subsistence," he writes, accounts for technical progress, the material forms of stratification, the distribution of power, and the experiences of joy and grief that accompany success and worldly disappointment. Yet, such purely utilitarian considerations fail to set humankind off from "mere brutes" (1971, 47–48). Far from utility, it is the "principle of affection to mankind" that is "the basis of our moral approbations and dislike" (65). This, the essence of Smith's thesis, Ferguson supports by further observation. If the utilitarians are right, how is it that our languages are replete with terms that designate aspects of experience in our relationships that are remote from, or have nothing to do with, our interests in the transactions themselves? Again, frivolous matters often assume significance beyond their seeming import and beyond the importance of the transactions themselves. And we engage each other on business, but "whether as friends or enemies, a fire is struck which the regards to interest or safety cannot confine" (49), and it is surely obvious that many things are simply not measured by the yardstick of calculation (50).

Smith extended Hume's theory of sympathy in another, more sociological, direction. After reviewing a series of cases to exemplify the nature of sympathy, he goes on to conclude that

> sympathy . . . does not arise so much from the view of the passions, as from that of the situation which excites it. We sometimes feel for another, a passion of which he himself seems to be altogether incapable" (7).

Smith here seems to assert that evocation of sympathy is situational; it is evoked by empathizing with someone in the context of a specific situation. It is to the situation that we respond, or, perhaps more accurately, to the individual-in-the-situation. We "sympathize" with a lunatic who sings and laughs seemingly without provocation or reason. Clearly, in such instances, our sympathy does not directly reflect the sentiments one may be momentarily experiencing.

In contrast with Hume, Smith advanced a somewhat broader and more convincing characterization of the relation of the self as an at least partially constructed entity to an interaction process that he described intersubjectively. Hume's depiction of the empirical self as no more than a series of momentary awarenesses fails to cohere well with either the problem of moral order or that of the persisting identity of the individual. In Smith's version we find for the first time the essence of the idea of the relationship of self to interaction—a momentous conception—as well as that of interaction itself as a process that can be described independently of the aspects of presocial human nature.

The Scots, it seems, had at least begun a breakthrough in the individual and society problematic. But their theories of moral sentiment, couched in the terms of moral philosophy, were not exploited by the sociology of the nineteenth century. Nineteenth century thought, in various of its forms, would incorporate both conservative and progressive conceptions of the self and the individual-society relation, and these would be passed on to the turn-of-the-century generation of truly seminal sociological theorists. Among the few fundamental weaknesses of even the great syntheses of Durkheim and Weber would be their failure to come to terms in a satisfactory way with the problem of the nature of the individual in society. The insights of the Scots would have only limited influence on the investigations of the self by either French Liberals or German romantics and would await rediscovery in the turn-of-the century sociology of thinkers such as Baldwin, Cooley, and Mead (see Chapter 15).[5]

THE SCOTS' THEORY OF PROGRESS AND THE LIBERAL MARKET SOCIETY

In his discussion of the historical writings of the philosophes, Gay remarks that their works reveal no system: Gibbon, Montesquieu, Voltaire, display "a cavalier evasion of analysis," seem to reflect an attitude of being "at play," and are preoccupied more with literary elegance than analysis (Gay, 1969, 2, 388–389). This is certainly true of many of them, but scarcely applies to the Scots, who went some distance toward establishment of a systematic theory of the liberal market society. They achieved this by working out an essentially sociological theory of progress centering on the division of labor.[6]

For both Hume and Smith, the liberal market society supercedes feudalism because it is, in the large, we might say, a vast utility. But it is also a far more cosmopolitan entity. General rules come into being through the impartiality of the spectator which transcends the old parochialism. Thus,

---

[5] Others who are sometimes mentioned in this regard are, mainly, Franklin Giddings and perhaps Albion Small. Giddings's reformulation of the theory of moral sentiments, however, is somewhat unSmithian. We learn that there are a variety of "modes of resemblance," such as the similarities deriving from kinship, and those of mental similarity, and of "potential" resemblance, which "makes society possible" (Giddings, 1898, Chap. 6). The logical problem here is obvious. The principle of consciousness of kind seems to drop out of Giddings's later work. In his *Studies in the Theory of Human Society*, published in 1922, there is only one mention of it (163). More important, Giddings attacks Baldwin's theory of the dialectic of personal growth, the central idea of which is the relation of the self to interaction (162). On this point see Chapter 15. Small discussed Smith in his *Adam Smith and Modern Sociology* (1907), but the sociological sense of his theory of moral sentiments seemed to elude him.

[6] I employ the term "liberal market society" in preference over several alternative possibilities. "Capitalist society" I find too broad, embracing as it does nonliberal as well as liberal capitalist societies, which would certainly not be an accurate reflection of the Scots' intent. Nor is their sense of the emerging society restricted to commercial practices, thus ruling out "commercial society." "Industrial society" neglects the market element (at least explicitly), but even "industrial market society" is flawed in its seeming economistic focus, a narrowness that does not accurately render the Scots' broader interest in the theorization of *society*. "Liberal market society" best captures the dual emphasis that I think correctly defines their interest: (1) on the functioning of the market including its economic consequences, conceived as (2) situated within the broader environing society, implying the need to theorize this society as one defined by liberal social relationships.

the emergence of modern commercial society is constituted of both an expansion of the economic division of labor and a culture in which universal standards come into being, a culture of civility, we might say. How does this transformation occur?

In some of his political writings (1963), Hume suggests a three-stage progression, from hunting and fishing through agricultural, to civil, or commercial society. This scheme was modified somewhat by his followers, who added a herding, or pastoral stage following that of hunting-fishing. The hunting-fishing and herding stages are referred to as "savage" and "barbarian," respectively, or designated as "rude" as over against "polished" societies (e.g., Ferguson, 1971, Part II). Recognition of the pastoral stage was important, for it was the point at which, in Smith's judgment, "the notion of property is ext(end)ed beyond possession" (Smith, 1978, 107). Difficulties in subsisting off the natural produce of land and sea, occasioned by population pressure, lead eventually to innovations in agriculture (15). Game taken or wild fruit plucked from a tree are "possessed" sheerly by virtue of being in hand; possession of herds of flocks, by contrast, requires recognition of a *right* of possession and guarantees of its enforcement. The first governments appear in the herding stage (206ff.) specifically to guarantee property. Herding societies are warlike in character and engage routinely in conquest (Smith, 1978, 202ff.; Millar, 1806, 59, and passim; Ferguson, 1971, Parts 2, 3, p. 186). "Every nation is a band of robbers, who prey without restraint, or remorse, on their neighbors" (Ferguson, 1971, 150). Herding societies also introduce new forms of inequality. Societies of hunters display only inequalities resting on age and differences in personal qualities, whereas herding societies come to be stratified on the basis of economic differences and birth (Smith, 1963, 2, 231). Millar's treatise, *The Origin of the Distinction of Ranks* (1806)[7] appears to have been the first systematic treatise ever published on the topic of social stratification and is well worth the attention of contemporary scholars, especially for its treatment of gender stratification and the position of women in different types of society.

Herding societies require institutions of property, but not much of an expansion of the division of labor. The latter requires a settled way of life made possible only by the systematic pursuit of agriculture. Agriculture began to develop in situations where bands of roving herdsmen found conditions propitious for permanent settlement. In some cases they united and formed relatively large settlements, originally somewhat democratic, but later developing into aristocracies. Such permanent communities make possible a substantial expansion of the division of labor, encouraging extensive proliferation of technical and occupational differentiation and a corresponding expansion of the system of internal exchange.

The shift to settled agricultural societies occurs as the delights of expanding consumption and leisure gradually undermine the war system. Expansion of the division of labor underlies this, but it is in no sense either

---

[7] For the most part it is an expansion of ideas evidently drawn from Smith's lectures at Glasgow, which Millar attended as a student of Smith and which were published much later as the *Lectures on Jurisprudence* (1896).

foreordained or planned, a point reiterated everywhere by Ferguson in particular.

> Every step and every movement of the multitude, even in what are termed enlightened ages, are made with equal blindness to the future; and nations stumble upon establishments, which are indeed the result of human action, but not the execution of any human design (Ferguson, 1971, 187).

Smith argues along the same lines, rejecting the notion that human intelligence or foresight had very much to do with the advance of the division of labor (Smith, 1963, 2, 570). Progress occurs by slow increments and the future is always difficult to foresee. Indeed, a more intelligent engagement in the future of commercial society was the driving interest behind the Scots' scientific approach to moral philosophy. History reveals no significant rational component and is largely an account of the unanticipated consequences of the "establishments"—we would say "institutions"—resulting from self-interested activity. At the same time, expansion of our knowledge of "moral subjects" may increase our rational understanding of and command over such institutions. In this sense, although they generally denied the presence of any plan or hidden agency in history, the Scots shared, if more cautiously, and in differing degrees, the general Enlightenment optimism about science (Hume, of course, being the most skeptical).[8]

In Europe profound changes occurred in the agricultural societies following the fall of Rome. Until around A.D. 900 property was "allodial," i.e., comprised of relatively small holdings with little political centralization. The tenth and eleventh centuries were a period of increasing consolidation and centralization of property and of political control, a process that eventually brought into being the powerful European feudal aristocracy. European feudalism existed for five centuries—perhaps longer—but was eventually undermined by the gradual expansion of "luxury and the arts." This development broke the back of the aristocracy, an essential condition for the emergence of a more democratic order. "The power of the nobles must always be brought to ruin before liberty is possible" (Smith, 1978, 264; cf. Moore, 1966). The stage is now set for the beginnings of liberal market society (Smith, 1978, 250ff.; Millar, 1806, 176ff.).

Liberal market societies are marked not only by an expanding division of labor and commerce beyond societal or national boundaries—thereby increasing productivity and encouraging development of the arts and sciences—but also by the movement of the people toward greater political participation. Although harbingers of democracy may appear in late agricultural societies, anything approaching a full democratic ideal—by the lights of liberal eighteenth century philosophers, who were generally rather distrustful of placing anything like absolute power in the hands of the people—

---

[8] Monboddo is the principal exception. In his *Of the Origin and Progress of Language*, 1792 he proposes that humankind was originally an intelligent being—below God, the angels, cherubims, and seraphims—but lost this facility through the sin of intellectual pride. "Wild Peter," a celebrated deaf and dumb youth supposedly reared in the wild, proved the existence of this earlier mute period. Civil society is the medium for the moral rehabilitation of the race, mainly through reacquisition of language.

is possible only in liberal market society.[9] In these terms the Republican period of Rome and the eighteenth century were comparable; both were periods of rising commercialism and democratization. There is a functional, if not causal, relationship between commercialism and democratization. A commercial society brings into being a new social type that becomes widespread—the citizen who acquires, indeed, must acquire, habits of independence that manifest themselves in both economic and political activity. But the continued presence of such a citizenry is, in turn, dependent on institutions of a certain type. In working out these relationships, the Scots, like so many of the philosophers and historians of the time, were profoundly influenced by antiquity, particularly Rome, and among individual thinkers, by Montesquieu. Comparison of the world of antiquity, with its commercial growth rooted in the expansion of the division of labor, with the modern world of the eighteenth century, was the methodological touchstone of much social analysis of the time[10] and was very important to the sociology of the Scots. Their theory of the liberal market society was formulated in many of its aspects by comparison—explicit and implicit—with antiquity. The expansion, internal transformations, and ultimate fate of Rome, in particular, constituted a model within which their analyses and judgment on societies of their own time were framed. An example of this has to do with the relationships between the division of labor, militarism, and democracy. Greek democracy and the Roman Republic, of course, were based on slavery, and, in the Scots' view, this accounted for their warlike nature. In a slave economy, freedmen are not essential for the functioning of the economy and can therefore be more or less continually prepared for or engaged in warfare. A slave state, therefore, tends to be militarily durable (Smith, 1978, 242). In a nonslave commercial society, where most of the populace is of necessity engaged continuously in essential economic pursuits, the tendency is in the direction of military weakness and enervation of the state. Often the army will become mercenary; mercenaries follow generals rather than the people and so are "dreaded in all republics" (Smith, 1978, 236; also Millar, 1806, 220–225).

The Scots' analysis of commercial society centers not only on the division of labor as engine of development, but also as generator of a variety of unintended consequences. Indeed, the real power of their analysis derives from this (along with their broad comparative and historical consciousness). We could say that, although property was valued and celebrated more or less unambiguously (despite its being the first cause of social inequality), their attitude toward the division of labor was one of considerable ambiva-

---

[9] It should perhaps be noted that the Scots were working out a sociological characterization of what they regarded as a necessary relation between a developing commercial life and democratic political institutions. This has long since, of course, become a central tenet of conventional liberal ideology, but in the middle of the eighteenth century it was decidedly innovative. Even in Britain the actual extent of democratic practice, by contemporary standards, was slight.

[10] The idea of the seeming sociological parallel between antiquity and the modern world, it should be emphasized, was rather widely held. After reviewing the factors involved in the fall of Rome, for instance, Gibbon admonishes us, "This awful revolution" may be usefully applied to the instruction of the present age" (1960, 530).

lence. They regarded it as the indispensible condition of economic expansion, and thereby, of increasing material well-being (*The Wealth of Nations* is based on this premise), but they also characterized it in surprisingly negative terms. Theirs was an acute sense of the play of irony in history, a sense, like that of so many of the most creative social thinkers—Marx, Weber, and Veblen spring to mind at once—was the intellectual leaven in terms of which they worked out their concept of liberal market society.

One of the most imporant of these ironies rests on their conception of the individual in liberalizing society. Here is an ideal figure, independent, rational, active, engaged in the full development and exercise of the faculties—a spirited and enterprising personality. Such idealized figures stand in stark contrast to those of the precommercial society with its aristocratic arrogance, its servile, ritualized inequality, its structure of dependency.[11] It is continuous expansion of the division of labor and the growth in commerce associated with it that gradually bring into being the conditions under which such independent and rational citizens become possible. This is, however, no unambiguous blessing, for the division of labor, not unlike those gods of antiquity who often took such delight in frustrating the aspirations of their followers, also has unanticipated but near-inevitable consequences of great ironic import, a tendency about which Smith and Ferguson, in particular, were unequivocally clear.

> In the progress of the division of labor, the employment of the far greater part of those who live by labour, that is, of the great body of the people, comes to be confined to a few very simple operations, frequently to one or two. But the understandings of the greater part of men are necessarily formed by their ordinary employments. The man whose whole life is spent in performing a few simple operations, of which the effects too are, perhaps always the same, or very nearly the same, has no occasion to exert his understanding, or to exercise his invention in finding out expedients for removing difficulties which never occur. He naturally loses, therefore, the habit of such exertion, and generally becomes as stupid and ignorant as it is possible for a human creature to become. The torpor of his mind renders him, not only incapable of relishing or bearing a part in any rational conversation, but of conceiving any generous, noble, or tender sentiment, and consequently of forming any just judgment concerning many even of the ordinary duties of private life. Of the great and extensive interests of his country he is altogether incapable of judging; and unless very particular pains have been taken to render him otherwise, he is equally incapable of defending his country in war. The uniformity of his stationary life naturally corrupts the courage of his mind, and makes him regard with abhorrence the irregular, uncertain, and adventurous life of a soldier. It corrupts even the activity of his body, and renders him incapable of exerting his strength with vigor and perseverance, in any other employment than that to which

[11] "Dependency," says Smith, "debases the mind." He employs the idea of dependency throughout his work. For example, contrasted with the (supposed) low incidence of crime in Glasgow, he attributed the social disorders in France to "the vast numbers of servants which it is fashionable for the great to maintain," in that land (1978, 333). Modernization would presumably go some substantial distance in remedying this: "Commerce is one great preventative of this custom" (333). Note the form of Smith's explanation: He advances a *structural* theory of crime, in the context of a theory of social change.

he has been bred. His dexterity at his own particular trade seems, in this manner, to be acquired at the expense of his intellectual, social and martial virtues. But in every improved and civilized society this is the state into which the labouring poor, that is, the great body of the people, must necessarily fall, unless government takes some pains to prevent it (Smith, 1963, 2, 284–285).

Nine years earlier in 1767, Ferguson had written:

> Many mechanical arts, indeed, require no capacity; they succeed best under a total suppression of sentiment and reason; and ignorance is the mother of industry as well as superstition. Reflection and fancy are subject to err; but a habit of moving the hand, or the foot, is independent of either. Manufacturers, accordingly, prosper most, where the mind is least consulted, and where the workshop may, without any great effort of imagination, be considered as an engine, the parts of which are men" (Ferguson, 1971, 280).

The idea that progress was inevitably accompanied by widespread misery and alienation was a pervasive Enlightenment understanding: D'Alembert called this the "law of compensation." But no one perceived with such clarity its locus in the *specific* human consequences of the division of labor applied to the factory as did the Scots. The dehumanization inherent in the treatment of human beings as means was itself, of course, a common enough theme: Critiques and denunciations of slavery and various forms of bondage, for instance, appear everywhere during the Enlightenment. But the perception that dehumanization was now being caused by the very institution central to progress—the workshop "considered as an engine, the parts of which are men," (here again the mechanical metaphor, that staple of the eighteenth century), and that it was *intrinsic* to this new form of work organization—was a striking theoretical innovation, and an important aspect of the sociological genius of the Scots.[12]

There is another irony in the social thought of the Scots that is also linked to the idea of the independent citizen. This has to do with the commonly expressed idea that the decline of Rome was due, at least in part, if not mainly, to internal factors. The growth of luxury, made possible by the division of labor and a money economy, tends to degenerate into "sordid pursuit of avarice" (Millar, 1806, 235). Revealing the interesting mixture of John Knox Presbyterianism and classical Stoicism that runs through the school, Millar holds that the love of pleasure engendered by increasing opulence, when carried to extreme, destroys the very passions it is intended to gratify—a principle that applies with special force to women: "great luxury and dissipation . . . diminish the rank and dignity of women" (102). In this connection he holds as well that although increasing material resources of the pastoral and agricultural stages encourage a "refinement of the passions"

---

[12] It is clear that Smith grasped not only the central principle relating the division of labor to productivity, but perhaps its alienating nature, as well, at least as early as 1761. The essentials of *The Wealth of Nations*, including the famous description of pin manufacturing, were clearly set forth in an early manuscript definitely prepared no later than 1761 (see Smith, 1978, 561ff. and editor's note under "Introduction," 560).

(57) and "heighten and improve sexual passion" (76), love of pleasure carried to extreme destroys the passions it was intended to gratify" (99). Differing sexual dispositions are thus depicted as *consequences* of different forms of social arrangements.[13] The Scots clearly had some understanding of what Weber later called the "Protestant ethic."

More importantly, perhaps, are the political implications of the growth of luxury, a point enlarged upon by Ferguson. "Many of the boasted improvements of civil society will be mere devices to lay the political spirit at rest," he writes (1971, 339). A society that seeks to "secure the person and property of the subject, without any regard to his political character . . . may immerse all orders of men in their separate pursuits of pleasure, which they may now enjoy with little disturbance; or of gain which they may preserve without any attention to the commonwealth" (340). He goes on to conclude:

> If this be the end of political struggles, the design, when executed, in securing to the individual his estate, and the means of subsistence, may put an end to the exersise of those very virtues that were required in conducting its execution. A man, who, in concert with his fellow-subjects, contends with usurpation in defence of his estate or his person, may find an exertion of great generosity, and of a vigorous spirit; but he who, under political establishments, supposed to be fully confirmed, betakes him, because he is safe, to mere enjoyment of fortune, has in fact turned to a source of corruption the very advantages which the virtues of the other procured (1971, 340).

And later, in discussing liberty, he opines that

> this blessing (is never) less secure than it is in the possession of men who think that they enjoy it in safety, and who therefore consider the public only as it presents to their avarice a number of lucrative employments (343).

Ferguson warns against mistaking "for an improvement of human nature, a mere accession or accommodation, or of riches" (344). Mere scientific and technical advances in themselves, far from guaranteeing progress, can engender a privatization of life centering on exploitation of one's self-interest that, ironically, undermines the very order that makes it possible. A viable society requires strong, public-spirited, and resolute citizens. The arts of policy and war cannot be subjected to the subdivisions that, in order to improve their practice, properly occur in the arts and professions, for this would be "to dismember the human character, and to destroy those very arts we mean to improve" (353).

The boasted refinements, then, of the polished age, are not divested of

---

[13] Sexual behavior was treated as a social phenomenon rather routinely by the Scots. In this connection the reader might look at Smith's interesting treatment of incest in the *Lectures on Jurisprudence* (159–171). He argues that incest results from the understanding that women thus "defiled" would be unacceptable mates, and, by implication, that this would undermine the marriage system. Smith captures the essentials of the (very probably incorrect: see Lévi-Strauss, 1949) modern functionalist treatment of incest by Kingsley Davis (1949, Chap. 7).

danger. They open a door, perhaps, to disaster, as wide and accessible as any of those they have shut (355).

In this fashion the Scots explicated the character of liberal market society in terms of the ironic consequences that may follow in the train of an expanding division of labor and the material bounty it increasingly brings into being. Dehumanization and privatization are profound consequences for the individual: the workmen whose minds have become emptied of the liberal outlook and whose sensibilities are limited to an interest in economic gain, are unfit for participation in political *society*.[14] But this redounds upon the very structure of society itself. An expanding division of labor cannot release many workers from their tasks for too long. The lesson of Rome suggests that this leads to the replacement of citizen armies with mercenary ones, with all that this implies,[15] particularly the likelihood of Caesarism. Centralization of power, in turn, will tend to damp, if not obliterate, that very spirit of invention and independence which lies at the core of all progress.

The great questions of war and conflict were never far from the minds of the Scots. They generally agreed that warfare and conquest were among the great movers in history, and that the expansion of the division of labor and the growth of commerce were intertwined with violence. In this they seemed to differ somewhat from what was perhaps the "mainstream" Enlightenment view, as expressed by Gibbon, that "the more useful . . . arts can be performed without superior talents or national subordination," and that there does occur "a kind of subterranean progress despite the warfare and destruction" (1960, 530). "It is vain," writes Ferguson, "to affirm that the genius of any nation is averse to conquest" (1971, 235). Warfare and conquest, like the division of labor and commerce, they thought, had played a double role in history. Conflict, despite its obvious destructive consequences, is not only natural, but historically has had social consequences of enormous import as well. This idea appears in its most developed form in Ferguson's *Essay*.

Those who have argued that the race was originally "either in a state of alliance, or of war," maintains Ferguson, advance one-sided explanations. "The history of our species indeed abundantly shows, that they are to one another mutual objects both of fear and of love" (24). In the constant conflicts that mark human history, it would be a mistake to conclude that conflict was

---

[14] The fateful implications of this view were very likely one reason, at least, that Smith included the lengthy section on education in *The Wealth of Nations* (1963, 2, 268–289). The state of affairs described in the passages reproduced above was one with which the people "must of necessity fall," he wrote, "unless government takes some pains to prevent it" (285). He goes on to advocate a national system of public education, the expense of which is "so moderate, that even a common laborer may afford it" (287). Such a system will achieve not only basic literacy and ability in geometry and "mechanics," but also help to indoctrinate children in the "martial spirit" on which "the security of every great society must always depend" (288).

[15] Use of mercenaries has been denounced by Western social and political theorists for centuries, especially since Machiavelli (1963). This attitude accompanies rising nationalist sentiment. Western political nationalism has always been fundamentally expansionist, and citizen armies, indoctrinated with nationalist ideology and identifying with war making, have been (generally rightly) regarded as more reliable than mercenaries.

uniformly evil: "War does not always proceed from an intention to injure," and "even the best qualities of men, their candour, as well as their resolution, may operate in the midst of their quarrels" (30). But even more important, although human beings "appear to have in their minds the seeds of animosity, and to embrace the occasions of mutual opposition, with alacrity and pleasure" (30), conflict can really be understood only in terms of the fact that human life is, and has everywhere been, incorrigibly social. "Mankind have always wandered or settled, agreed or quarreled, in troops or companies" (23), he writes. In all the varied and diverse situations in which we find human life,

> they affected a distinction of name and community. The titles of *fellow-citizen* and *countryman*, unopposed to those of *alien* and *foreigner*, to which they refer, would fall into disuse, and lose their meaning. . . . We love our country, as it is a party in the divisions of mankind; and our zeal for its interest, is a predilection in behalf of the side we maintain (31).

Aggression, far from being opposed to the more amiable qualities of our nature, must be understood as the other side of the coin. "Sentiments of generosity and self-denial . . . animate the warrior in defense of his country," (35) he says, and in an anticipation of Summer's theory of the in-group and out-group, allow that "it is vain to expect that we can give to the multitude of a people a sense of union among themselves without admitting hostility to those who oppose them" (37). In these and other passages, Ferguson insists that humans are social, and that conflict is incorrigibly enmeshed in that very social nature.

But even beyond this, conflict must be understood as a historically inevitable aspect of social life without which the progress of the race itself could not have occurred. This echoes Hume's view, in "Of the Original Contract" (Hume, 1962). There, Hume devastated once and for all the assumptions of contract theories, in part, by an empirical argument emphasizing the demonstrable importance of warfare and conquest in the creation of governments. "Almost all the governments which exist at present, or of which there exist any record in story," he writes, "have been founded originally, either on usurpation or conquest, or both . . ." (151), and observes that, in the dissolution of great empires, colonization, and "migrations of tribes," there is nothing to be discovered but "force and violence" (152).

In this understanding of the progressive function of conflict, the Scots were, by and large, at variance with the general atitude of the Enlightenment, and this is a measure of their strong sociological bent. Although engaged in moral philosophy, they were able to extricate themselves to a considerable degree from a framework defined simply in the moral terms of good and evil, and to take an objective and empirical stance toward their materials.[16]

The idea that inequality not only antedates government, but that it brings it into being because of the conflict it inevitably engenders is central

---

[16] Ferguson was most explicit in his criticism of such moral dualism: "The division of our appetites into benevolent and selfish has probably, in some degree, helped to mislead our appreciation on the subject of personal enjoyment and private good" (1971, 79).

to the Scots' theory of progress and the liberalizing society. Ferguson followed Hume in the very characterization of this idea, referring to the existence everywhere of a "casual subordination" not only independent of government, but which seems to arise from the distribution of property, and which "gives the state its tone, and fixes its character" (1971, 204). The government, he says, "takes its rise from casual subordination" (207). It is not surprising, in view of this, to find him maintaining elsewhere that "some mode of subordination is as necessary to men as society itself" (94–95). On this question Smith is just as unequivocal. Inequalities rooted in personal qualifications and in age differences, which appear in hunting societies, and those resting on the amassing of fortunes and rights of birth, appearing in societies of shepherds, he says, are all antecedent to civil institutions. "Property," he says, echoing Rousseau, "presupposes a certain subordination" (1963, 2, 230), and he goes on, in this vein, to maintain that the government owes its very existence to the necessity of protecting the rich from the poor.

Smith on Inequality in Liberal Market Society

Although the Scots understood that industrializing process would ultimately eliminate the hoary forms of inequality known to feudalism and earlier periods, then they did not believe that liberal market society would bring about anything like complete egalitarianism. On this point alone they did not differ from the great majority of other social thinkers. Smith, in particular, however, is important for sociology because he went beyond this generality and attempted to show how inequality is created and maintained in commercial society.

Smith was clearly cognizant of the fact that important forms of inequality were coming into being that had to be understood outside the traditional and legally guaranteed inequality of feudalism; that what would come to be thought of as "normal" functioning of capitalist society would generate and perpetuate new forms of inequality. His understanding of this was probably the main reason he introduced an extensive discussion of the legal problems thus created in the section on "justice" in Book 5 of *The Wealth of Nations*. Here we find him announcing that "wherever there is great property, there is great inequality" (2, 229), and "for one very rich man, there must be at least five hundred poor . . ." (2, 229). Smith has no doubt that this situation will cause great disorder, and that the near-sole object of the legal system is to protect property. "Civil government, so far as it is instituted for the security of property, is in reality instituted for the defense of the rich against the poor . . ." (2, 233), and it is "only under the shelter of the civil magistrate (that) . . . the propertied can sleep one night" (2, 229, 30).

It should be reiterated that, although Smith's social analysis is framed within natural law doctrine, much of what is innovative and of value in it transcends that framework. Even the famous "propensity to truck, barter and exchange one thing for another," it seems to him, is probably *not* "one of those original principles in human nature of which no further account can be given" (1963, 1, 2). This propensity is much more likely to be "the necessary consequence of the faculties of reason and speech . . ." (1, 2). Far from defending the notion of natural law liberalism that social inequality is a reflection of the distribution of natural presocial talents among individuals, Smith argues that differences of natural talent are not only "much less than we are aware," but also "not so much the cause as the effect of the division of labor," occurring "not so much from nature as from habit, custom, and education" (1, 7).

The philosophical anthropology implicit in such abstractions is embodied in much of Smith's more concrete and detailed analyses of inequality in industrial societies. The structure of economic inequality, he thinks, is quite complex and has a number of sources that can be located in their very functioning. These are worth mention: (1) "the agreeableness or disagreeableness of the employments themselves; (2) "the easiness or cheapness, or the difficulty and expense of learning them"; (3) "the constancy or inconstancy of employment in them"; (4) "the small or great trust which must be reposed in those who exercise them"; and (5) "the probability or improbability of success in them" (1, 79–80).[17] Smith goes into some detail about all of these, and, in effect, not only produces the first systematic classification of factors affecting occupational stratification, but also goes beyond this to elaborate the first modern form of what has come to be known as the functional theory of stratification (Davis and Moore, 1945; Davis, 1950, Chap. 14; Parsons, 1949). The important point is that he establishes the inevitability of economic inequality in liberal societies as a consequence of the process of occupational specialization and interrelatedness. This idea—that occupational differences inevitably produce inequality—remains the core proposition of the functional theory of stratification in liberal market societies.

It is not only in connection with the objective, or external, aspects of the emerging form of inequality that Smith develops a modern sociological analysis. Even as early as *The Theory of Moral Sentiments*, in 1759, he had developed a most perspicacious and trenchant analysis of its inner meaning. "From whence . . . arises that emulation which runs through all the different ranks of men and what are the advantages which we propose by that great purpose of human life which we call bettering our condition?" (1966, 70–71) he asks. "To what purpose is all the toil and bustle of this world? What is the end of avarice and ambition, of the pursuit of wealth, of power, and pre-eminence?" (1966, 70). All this, he says, has but little to do with our material interests, or satisfaction of our material needs. In a striking anticipation of Weber and Veblen, he observes:

> The rich man glories in his riches, because he feels that they naturally draw upon him the attention of the world, and that mankind are disposed to go along with him in all those agreeable emotions with which the advantages of his condition so readily inspire him. At the thought of this his heart seems to swell and dilate itself within him, and he is fonder of his wealth, upon this account, than for all the other advantages it procures him. The poor man, on the contrary, is ashamed of his poverty. He feels that it either places

---

[17] All five of these, Smith says, apply to wages. But only the first and last mentioned affect the profits of entrepreneurship (1, 88).

him out of the sight of mankind, or, that if they take any notice of him, they have, however, scarce any fellow-feeling with the misery and distress which he suffers (1966, 81).

The great and powerful, he says, inspire in others sympathy, awe, admiration, compassion. The disposition of mankind is, in effect, to regard their wealth and the actions producing and maintaining it as legitimate, and this is the foundation of social inequality. This he reiterates: "Our obsequiousness to our superiors more frequently arises from our admiration for the advantages of their situation, than from any private expectations of benefit from their good-will" (73). Against the critics of this view, he repeats, "rank, distinction, pre-eminence, no man despises,"[18] and "compared with the contempt of mankind, all other external evils are easily supported" (83).

The sentiments generated among men by the glories of those of high station and the miserable condition of the lowly are the meanings in terms of which people acquire a taste for bettering themselves. In these passages Smith adumbrates what Max Weber would later call status stratification (Weber, 1978b, Chapter IV: 6), an arena of struggle distinct from the objective system of class stratification rooted in the occupational division of labor, and Veblen's theory of emulation (Veblen, 1899).

Smith did not restrict his theory of inequality in liberalizing society to the material and honorific consequences of the division of labor as such. He also worked out the rudiments of the first theory of classes in capitalist society. Starting from the proposition that the entire produce of land and labor can be divided into three parts, land rent, wages, and profits, he then goes on to inquire into the *interests* and *knowledge* of these "three great, original, and constituent orders of every civilized society" (1963, 1, 199). The interests of rentiers, he says, is "inescapably connected with the general interests of society," because progress entails an increase in rent payments. The price of land rises when it is placed under development. The owners of land, however, characteristically fail to understand this truth, and as often as not are found resisting progress (199). Rentiers' profits "cost them neither labor nor care" (199), and "they love to reap where they never sowed" (1, 21). Smith, with his strong puritannical streak, clearly finds this displeasing. Their ignorance results from the "ease and security of their situation" (199); it is a condition under which any systematic application of the mind is rendered practically impossible.

Wage workers also have an objective interest in growth because it creates high labor demand, which in turn brings high employment and high wages. Furthermore, slowed growth exacts much higher costs from workers than from the other orders (evidently because of the absence of any other resources to fall back upon). In an analogue to the situation of rentiers, workers also are supposedly unable to understand this.

But though the interest of the laborer is strictly connected with that of the

---

[18] Excepting what must be supposed to be two rather rare exceptions: those raised well above, or placed well below, the general standard, and significantly, "anyone confirmed in wisdom and real philosophy" (81). In this latter we find the germ of the later nineteenth century alienation of intellectuals from capitalism (see Graña, 1967).

society, he is incapable either of comprehending that interest, or of under-standing its connexion with his own. His condition leaves him no time to receive the necessary information, and his education and habits are commonly such as to render him unfit to judge even though he was fully informed. In the public deliberations, therefore, his voice is little heard and less regarded, except upon some particular occasions, when his clamor is animated, set on, and supported by his employers, not for his, but their own particular purposes (1963, 1, 199–200).

Smith's long section on the need to educate the workers later in *The Wealth of Nations* should be understood in the context of this understanding of their subjective class situation. In contrast to both of these groups, the interests of employers do not lie in growth, because the rate of profit falls as prosperity increases and, in fact, "is always highest in the countries which are going fastest to ruin" (1, 200). Smith finds merchants and master manufacturers to be superior to rentiers and workers in the comprehension of their interests, and it is by virtue of this that they are able to maintain a strong position in society. Basically this understanding boils down to the principle of restricting competition. It is always in their interests, says Smith, for businessmen to both widen the market and to narrow the competition, but the latter can never be in the interest of the public. Accordingly, Smith points out, while the interests of rentiers and workers are consistent with the interests of the public, those of merchants and master manufacturers never are. He is therefore at pains to warn us that, since the success of the businessman depends on the systematic deception of the public, all proposals for new laws or regulations coming from that quarter should be viewed with great suspicion, and never adopted, "till after having been long and carefully examined, not only with the most scrupulous, but with the most suspicious attention" (210). This, after all, is an order of men

> whose interest is never exactly the same with that of the public, who have generally an interest to deceive and even to oppress the public; and who accordingly have upon many occasions, both deceived and oppressed it (201).

Harsh words for capitalists from the champion of capitalism!

The importance of this lies not only in the fact that Smith has moved in the direction of a theory of classes related to interests, for he was not the first to do this, but that he clearly separates objective interests from the subjective disposition and knowledge that come to be characteristic of the *culture* of classes, and that have powerful implications for their political orientations. This, in short, is a rudimentary theory of class consciousness, conceived at the very dawn of the industrial form of class society.

The hard-headed realism informing Smith's notions about classes and the basis of conflict in class interests is a theme running through his treatment of various groups in capitalist society. He has a sure eye for perceiving group interests and the conditions and means for advancing them. Common examples of this are the characterizations of mercantilism as a system and ideology "for the benefit of the rich" (1963, 2, 177–178), and attacks on the colonial system partly for the same reason. But he also notes and denounces combinations of master manufacturers: They are "always and everywhere in a sort of tacit but constant and uniform combination" (1, 54). Even professors are not spared:

> The discipline of colleges and universities is in general contrived, not for the benefit of the students, but for the interest, or . . . the ease of the masters (2, 272).

He understands the importance of ideological legitimation in the pursuit of interests. The sole motive of Castile in the New World, he opines, was the hope of finding treasure there, but "the pious purpose of connecting them to Christianity sanctified the injustice of the project" (2, 110).

In all this Smith advances at least the beginnings of an understanding of liberal market society as one in which structured but shifting occupational and class interests give rise to differing forms of consciousness—including false consciousness—and political potential. Always the tendency toward monopolistic formations threatens both political and economic freedom. It was necessary, and probably inevitable, therefore, that commercial societies would erect legal frameworks to curb the tendencies toward private power inherent in commercial society. The latter sections of *The Wealth of Nations* are devoted to this task. Even in Book 4, which attempts to establish the proposition that laissez-faire best promotes the public good, he discusses many exceptions. Book 5, which comprises about thirty percent of the entirety of *The Wealth of Nations*, deals with the legal and social institutional framework within which the principle of private self-interest must be made to function, in Blaug's words, within "a framework of social institutions that channel and harness pecuniary motives" (1963, ix). Ruskin's judgment on Smith, quoted earlier, although inexcusably scurrilous, was by no means entirely a misperception. Smith was, of course, a believer (although not a traditional one); what seems to have disturbed Ruskin was the remoteness of Smith's social science not only from the imprint of the hand of God, but from our "human nature." Despite his natural law framework, Smith lays out the beginnings of a sociology of liberal market society that transcends that framework and that comes alive on a relatively autonomous social plane.

CONCLUSION

I have attempted to show in these pages that the Scottish moralists developed a fairly sophisticated theory of both social relations and of the capitalist society that was coming into being, and that Hume at least tried to bridge the two. Central to this effort was their partly implicit, partly explicit, rejection of the Enlightenment conceptions of blind agencies in history and the principle of explaining social level activity through characteristics of a posited human nature.

The Scots shifted the analysis of moral conduct, and so in principle human action in general, away from the Christian doctrine of the soul and thus from original nature. In the process they effected the beginnings of a recasting of the nature of the individual as shaped by social experience. And in their theorization of the liberal market society they tended strongly to frame individual action and to explain its specific properties in terms of the theoretically formulated properties defining this new order.

The "Adam Smith Problem" can be viewed from this perspective. As Hirschman has shown (1977), they resolved the theoretically intractable polarity of the passions and the intellectual faculties by formulating the category of interests as distinct from both, and *dissociating* it from the blind and often uncontrolled and destructive character of the former (with which it had generally been viewed in early modern thought). But in the context of a moral philosophy that still formally attributes the moral sense to the divine touch, the powerful implication of this was to not only dissociate the individual's interest from the passions in general, but to theoretically detach it from the original nature bundle and reinstate it in the framework of the workings of society. Redefining self-interested action as a *social* force (mainly the market) goes a decisive step beyond merely distinguishing it from other original nature-based behavior.

The work of the Scots was thus both a departure from received conceptions and a major innovation in social theorizing. The fact that this was not understood at the time probably reveals only that the necessary conditions for its perception—concretely, the incredible social, political, and economic ferment following the French revolution—had not yet come into being.

6

CHRISTIAN SOCIAL PHILOSOPHY AND THE CONSERVATIVE IMPULSE

Enlightenment thinkers portrayed humankind as part of the natural order struggling to throw off the yoke of "artificial" institutions: Humans were thought to possess a capacity for reason that might manifest itself if oppressive social institutions, church and state in particular, could only be eliminated. But this liberal and radical thought of the Enlightenment was only one of the two main intellectual sources out of which sociology was born. The other was the hoary tradition of Christianity, rooted in the uprooting and captivity of the Israelites and their communal Yahweh religion, the Christianity of Paul, the Church Fathers, Saint Augustine, a thousand years of feudalism and the codification of this order in the *Summa Theologica* of Saint Thomas Aquinas. Despite its theological and nonempirical nature, Catholicism bore within its belief and practice a set of ideas very amenable to sociological interpretion, reformulation, and technical elaboration. At the core of this historically developing complex of ideas stood the conception of the human community with an internal order constituting a reality *sui generis,* and its source ultimately in God's providence. Whereas Enlightenment thinkers were wedded to an individualism that continued to obstruct the full emergence of an autonomous social level, this came ready-made in Catholicism. Christian thought, from Augustine to the great synthesis of Aquinas, insofar as it was preoccupied with social speculation or social issues, viewed society, if only indirectly, as the result of the workings of God's providence, and thus as anything but artificial.

   The forms of Christian social thought that were most important for early sociology in the eighteenth and early nineteenth centuries are found in the works of writers such as Vico, Herder, Burke, von Savigny, de Maistre, de Bonald, and Lammenais.[1] There is little doubt that these and other writers were of importance for Comte and other early sociologists. There were, however, important differences among them, the principle one being the gulf between the prerevolutionaries and those who wrote in reaction to that great historical watershed. Before getting into this, however, it will be useful to briefly sketch those aspects of early Christian thought that constituted the tradition within which these eighteenth and nineteenth century sociologically oriented thinkers were working. The historically dominating figure in this tradition was Saint Augustine.

AUGUSTINE

Saint Augustine was a convert from both neo-Platonism (which he continued to praise as a philosophy close to Christianity) and Manichaeanism (which he denounced and attacked critically, especially in his *Confessions*) who became the Catholic Bishop of Hippo (today Bône) in Africa. Augustine wrote at the tail end of the decline of the Empire, a decline that had been going on for several centuries due to the increasing difficulties of obtaining slaves (or reproducing them under the Roman barracks system) for the slave-based Roman economy after the Empire's boundaries ceased to expand. It was during this period of decline that Constantine established Christianity as the official religion of the empire at the Council of Nicea in A.D. 325. In the context of the growing identification of Christianity with the empire during Roman decline, the sack of the city by the Goths in A.D. 410 was a devastating experience for Christians. The early sect leaders of the religion had no reason to regard the fate of the empire as a problem (except that it might have meant less persecution). But despite intensified persecution,[2] Christianity had been disseminating upward from its lower-class urban origins, and had taken root among the Roman middle classes, a process that culminated in the conversion of Constantine himself in A.D. 312.

By the time of the sack of Rome by Alaric, Christianity had become closely associated with the empire, both ideologically and organizationally (to the point of having acquired a parallel bureaucratic structure). The end of the empire was thus as much a crisis for the church as for the empire, and it was widely believed that the end of the world was imminent. Many attributed the fall of the empire to the rise and prominence of Christianity, a theme upon which Gibbon would confer authoritative historical status fourteen centuries later. The rise of Christianity to official status and the resulting scapegoating of Christians were the conditions under which Augustine set himself to the task of writing *The City of God*.

Much of the early teaching of the church Fathers was an attempt to

---

[1] See Nisbet (1978) for a review of conservative thought of this period.

[2] Persecution of Christians, who for some time were regarded by the Romans as just another Jewish sect, was not conducted systematically before A.D. 250 and the reign of Decius. Prior to this it appears that Christians were not singled out for special treatment, but merely repressed along with others by Roman governors carrying out their general charge of maintaining law and order.

demonstrate that God, in the act of Creation, had created the fact or potential of human freedom. The elevation of the principle of freedom of choice recurs repeatedly in Christian history, especially in those variants interpreting the salvation doctrine as a volitional act by the individual conscience. From such a pure theological and ethical position, it is only a further step (although in many concrete historical situations a very long one) to extend the principle to political, intellectual, and other types of action. During early Christianity the Genesis tale was commonly interpreted in this fashion. To mention one such instance, sometime during the second century Justin argued that the freedom to rule oneself was conferred on Christians through baptism.

Positions such as this, however, were generally understood to be at odds with Christian sanctification of secular power, and some had initiated the development of a doctrinal form of Christianity mainly by interpreting and extending Paul of the Epistles, and by adapting these doctrines to Greek and Roman philosophy (especially Stoicism and Seneca's doctrine of a Golden Age in the past). This social philosophy was intent on reconciling what came to be understood as the Paulinian doctrine of the Fall ("All have sinned and fall short of the glory of god": Romans 3:23), in which all are *equal* not only in their sinful state but in their potential state of grace as well, with the justification of inequality and exercise of coercive power (mainly by the state) in temporal affairs. Church Fathers such as Irenaeus and Ambrose argued that the coercive nature of the social order was the *direct* work of God rather than the necessary consequence of the dark side of human nature.

> For since man, by departing from God, reached such a pitch of fury as even to look upon his brother as his enemy, and engaged without fear in every kind of restless conduct, and murder, and avarice, God imposed upon mankind the fear of man, as they did not acknowledge the fear of God, in order that, being subjected to the authority of man, and kept under restraint by their laws, they might attain to some degree of justice, and exercise mutual forbearance through dread of the sword suspended full in their view . . . Earthly rule, therefore, has been appointed by God for the benefit of nations and not by the devil. (From "Against Heresies," Bk. V, Chap. xxiv, Sect. 2, in *Anti-Nicene Fathers*, vol. 1; cited in Becker and Barnes, 1961, I, 239).

In this fashion worldly inequality and the coercive power of the state, even the Roman state, far from being evil, were justified as necessary instruments of God's will on earth.

This was a view shared by Augustine: "Human kingdoms are established by divine providence" (1950, 142–143), he writes. There is, of course, the problem of why God would impose earthly rule more or less evenhandedly on the pious and just as well as on the wicked. Augustine's answer is that "earthly kingdoms are given by Him both to the good and the bad; lest his worshippers, still under the conduct of a very weak mind, should covet those gifts from Him as some great things" (1950, 140), in other words, as a hedge against the sin of pride. The earthly ruler has not only a right, but a duty, to demand the obedience of his subjects, who are in turn, therefore, obligated to obey.

Augustine's great contribution to Christian thought was to provide a framework within which both the "egalitarianism" of the states of sin and of grace are reconciled with the inequality and injustice of earthly existence. His solution to the problem posed by the threatened destruction of Roman— and Christian—civilization was to separate the workings of providence in the world from the secular rise and fall of dynasties or states, indeed, from any of the mundane conditions of earthly life. In fact, one sees that even as Rome was in decline, the church was rising with the future standing revealed as a kind of progress, predestined by God, toward the final heavenly state. It is in this context that Christians are enjoined to accept worldly realities, however harsh they might be.

Throughout the last part of the *The City of God*, Augustine elaborates in detail the distinction between the two cities. The essence of his argument is:

> The two cities have been formed by two loves; the earthly by the love of self, even to the contempt of God; the heavenly by the love of God, even to the contempt of self. The former, in a word, glories in itself, the latter in the Lord (1950, 477).

These principles are manifest in the world.

> In the one, the princes and the nations it subdues are ruled by the love of ruling; in the other, the subjects serve one another in love, the latter obeying, while the former take thought for all. The one delights in its own strength, represented in the persons of its rulers; the other says to its God, "I will love Thee, O Lord, my strength." And therefore the wise men of the city, living according to man, have sought for profit to their own bodies or souls, or both, and those who have known God "glorified Him not as God, . . . (but) glorying in their own wisdom, and being possessed by pride" (1950, 477).

The "cities" are thus both conditions of the soul and objective social or political arrangements, communities of those professing and practicing Christian love, on the one hand, and on the other, the wicked who stand outside the pale. The "City of God" is an ideal commonwealth here on earth, but more importantly, manifest in all eternity. This is the foundation of the doctrine of predestination, in which believers are united in love and in an absolute faith in the unknowable but providential will of God.

If earthly history is moving in such a direction, mundane events such as the rise and fall of empires, even bloody wars and tyrannies, cannot be the measure of Christian aspiration. The true Christian, finding his or her place in the City of God, will accept his or her lot in life (indeed, the doctrine of predestination demands it). Augustine justifies slavery, for instance, as retribution for sin, holding that the master is as much a slave as his chattel— a "slave," that is, to his passions or lust. Since slavery is instituted by God, not only should slaves "serve (their masters) heartily and with good will . . . not in crafty fear, but in faithful love" (1950, 694), but even understand that "beyond question it is a happier thing to be the slave of a man than that of a lust" (694). Such sentiments led Nietzsche to call Christianity a slave religion.

In this fashion Augustine advances an idealistic conception of society in which all must accept their lot, because this must reflect God's will, with a philosophy of history which projects a spiritual form of progress leading up to a final state of grace. This combination of elements became the dominant theology and eschatology of the church for many centuries, and, despite many modifications, remained essentially intact right up to the modern era.

The view of the church Fathers and of others that God intervenes directly to establish mundane institutions as punishment or for purposes of social control may be seen as virtually inseparable from the argument that all must accept their lot in the hierarchically ordered, authority-based social order. To reject this would be to challenge the will of God, who is omniscient. Later church authorities, for the most part, adhered to Augustinian conservatism and even advanced arguments to strengthen it. In the thirteenth century, the schoolman Saint Thomas Aquinas, for example, agreed with Augustine that society was appropriately an ideally unified, hierarchical entity in which all had their proper place, but also, following Aristotle, held that social inequality emerged in primitive times, *before* the Fall, and was a reflection of *natural* inequalities that developed in noncoercive fashion. The Fall then made coercion necessary to maintain already present social inequalities. Aquinas developed in some detail the specifics of the proper functioning of society conceived of as an organic unity, arguing that both the finely graded hierarchy of medieval society and its related functional division of labor are willed by God and therefore not to be tampered with by human beings. This included a justification not only of slavery (justified on utilitarian rather than natural law grounds), but of the absolute subjugation of woman as well (as a social reflection of alleged natural inequalities), on Aristotelian as well as Augustinian grounds.

John of Salisbury, English churchman and secretary to Thomas à Becket, had a century earlier advanced a detailed conception of the organic nature of society. Like other scholastics, John maintained that society exists by divine will and that as the representative of God on earth, the Prince is the embodiment of reason, while the clergy is the soul of society. John expands the organic principle, claiming that the heart of society is the senate, that various public offices correspond to the internal organs and that the eyes, ears, and tongue are represented by provincial governors (John of Salisbury, 1979, Bk. VI) "Inferiors should cleave and cohere to their superiors, and all the limbs should be in subjection to the head" (258), he insists, although this holds only so long as "religion is kept inviolate."[3]

Although the Augustinian doctrine of God-willed inequality and suffering justified by a theodicy having its roots in the scriptures held sway in official churchly circles right up through the Enlightenment, and even to the present, it was repeatedly challenged in both thought and deed. Marsilius of Padua, for example, in his remarkable *Defensor Pacis*, was heretical in the extreme. And especially during the late Middle Ages, dissident and possibly heretical, although very different, movements within the Church, like the Pelagians, Lutherans, Franciscans, and Uniates, occurred with increasing

---

[3] It is on this basis that John justifies tyrannicide, which he calls "a lawful and glorious act" (1963, 367), even while he acknowledges that tyrants are "ministers of God" (350).

frequency and were either repressed, as in the instances of the first two, or eventually coopted and incorporated, as in those of the latter. Virtually all such movements were, at least in part, energized by one or another form of religious "individualism," and new challenges continue right up to the present.

Much the same can be said of the plethora of dissident and refractory challenges to Protestant orthodoxy, whether the authoritarian Lutheranism that took root in German-speaking lands, or the state churches of England, Holland, or elsewhere. Pietists, Colonists, Anabaptists, Quakers, Methodists, Swedish "free churches," Congregationalists, and others all opposed church authority in the name of one or another verison of the free exercise of conscience.

The heterodoxies of the Renaissance are a somewhat different matter. Galileo, Copernicus, and others undermined the natural philosophy doctrines of the Church, but for the most part Renaissance social and political thinkers posed no direct threat to Catholic orthodoxy. It was for the most part only during the Enlightenment, in part in the ways I have suggested earlier, that serious challenges began to appear.

But apart from the increasingly secularized thought of the philosophes, novel and essentially *sociological* versions of the social order began to appear *within* the framework of the hegemonic churches. During the eighteenth century prior to the French Revolution, the best representatives of this effort are perhaps Giambattista Vico and Johann Gottfried von Herder, whose systems of social thought, although religiously framed, were strongly conditioned by enlightenment. After the revolution, the Irish-born British Whig Edmund Burke, various French noblemen, and others, reacted with outrage against what they regarded as revolutionary excess, and in the process elaborated a somewhat sociological version of Christian doctrine as a reactionary challenge to the Enlightenment. As a matter of convenience, we may label these two forms of Christian organicism "progressive" and "reactionary."

VICO

The Italian philosopher Giambattista Vico, a Neapolitan professor of rhetoric who wrote early in the eighteenth century, has been credited by some with formulating the first true sociological system (Martindale, 1981, 75–76; Rossides, 1978, Chap. 5; Bierstedt, 1978, 22–25). Despite Karl Löwith's judgment that his thought is "more penetrating than Voltaire, far profounder than Comte and Condorcet, and more inspired by original intuition than Hegel" (1949, 135), of all the early forerunners of sociology, Vico has probably been the most neglected. Although the post-revolution conservative Joseph de Maistre was apparently familiar with Vico's main work, the *Nuova Scienza*, or *New Science*, he makes no mention of it, or of Vico, in his major works. Hardly known at all through much of the nineteenth century, Vico was not read by Comte until 1844, who, although referring to him as "eminent," dismisses his theory of history as a "radically misconceived social dynamics" (Comte, 1957, 3, 501). Marx, on the other hand, knew his work and appreciated it greatly. Bierstedt thinks that if Vico had coined the term *sociology*, he, and not Comte, would be celebrated as the founder of the discipline (1978, 24). The ("New Science"), was first published in 1725, but it was a book Vico worked on and revised continuously throughout his life. The title is taken from Bacon and reflects Vico's great admiration and respect for the English philosopher.

Vico's significance lies in the fact that, although he remained a believer, and although the *New Science* is replete with references to the workings of providence, he incorporated into this framework a conception of progress, a philosophical anthropology, and a theory of knowledge amounting to a creative syncretism that goes some distance in transcending the dilemmas of progressive eighteenth century thought.

It will be useful to begin with Vico's conception of history, because this frames his system as a whole. Vico accepts the essence of the Christian idea of divine progress, but with two significant alterations. First, although history, to be sure, is in some sense determined by providence, the form it takes is cyclical. Cyclical theories were advanced by pagan philosophers such as Plato, Aristotle and Polybius in antiquity, but throughout the Middle Ages received only subterranean recognition within the framework of Christian thought.[4] At root, the doctrine is clearly incompatible with the Augustinian synthesis, because the latter presumes a definite beginning and end to mundane human history. Second, although the form of history is indeed providential, its course is viewed by Vico as a human social construction, being, as he puts it, "made by men."

> The world of civil society has certainly been made by men, and that its principles are therefore to be found within the modifications of our own mind (Vico, 1948, 33).[5]

Taken together, these two ideas were a stunning departure from received Christian doctrine.

A review of the substance of the *New Science* will reveal just how creative an innovation it was. Vico believed that a prehistorical "age of giants" (a common belief of the time) gave way to the age of human history after the giants diminished in size due to the ablution rituals following sacrifices and the feminization of the gods and early patriarchs (1948, 371). Human history occurs in cycles, each of which is constituted of three ages: those of

---

[4] Particularly, in the twelfth century, by Abbott Joachim and also by Tommaso Campanella, a monk who lived in the sixteenth century. Joachim thought that history proceeded through three states, each of which contained seven periods. The theory, modeled on the doctrine of the Trinity, was presented in his *Concordance of the Old and New Testaments* (orig. publ. 1519). Joachim became controversial because of his doctrine that a spiritual state of grace would appear on earth. Influenced by Joachim, Campanella enunciated a similar doctrine, prophesying that a "City of Sun" would appear on earth. For his labors he was rewarded by the church with torture and long periods in prison. Manuel makes the interesting point that cyclical theories seem endemic among a whole string of south Italian writers and tentatively attributes this to their geographic location at the center of so much Mediterranean commerce and movement of peoples. (For a review and discussion of the reappearance of "pagan" cyclical theories within the Christian framework see Manuel, 1959, Chap. 2).

[5] Citations refer to paragraph numbers introduced by Nicolini, Vico's twentieth century editor.

gods, those of heroes, and those of men—a reiteration and adaptation of ideas first propounded by Herodotus.

The Age of Gods was patriarchal; fathers exercised total dominion over their families, the first institution, and instructed them in religion and were revered by their sons. This is a period totally enveloped in religion, and the religious experience is represented in the form of myth. Fables created by poets were the form in which comprehension of God's intent appeared. The Age of Heroes comes into being through the expansion of the family by inclusion of refugees and with the conquest by patriarchs of those still at a lower stage.[6] This is an aristocratic age, thus one of inequality and of constant struggles between rulers and their subjects. In the Age of Heroes the mythological meaning systems of the Age of Gods are displaced by metaphorical ones. The first cycle of human history may be seen in the movement through antiquity up through the fall of Rome, and within this cycle Homer is seen as the greatest poet of the Heroic Age. Homer represents a transition from a mythic to a metaphorical type of meaning system. Vico's analysis of the Homeric epics is a tour de force of cultural sociology; he interprets them not as just the work of creative individuals, but as the metaphorical representations of an entire age, in the process introducing and employing what would later come to be known as historicist principles of analysis. The Age of Heroes gives way to the Age of Men, a time of mutual recognition of equality on the basis of a common human nature, and the establishment of the original popular commonwealths, and later, monarchies. The Age of Men is an age of rationality, in which equality is extended and social relations become more civil and refined, in which the authority of the father wanes and equality and justice spread throughout the "nations" (Vico's term for society). With the creation of the systematic alphabet, language becomes more precise and the expression of culture as myth and fable disappears. Religious life takes on more the form of an expanding morality and eventually undergoes a partial displacement by philosophy and by a more skeptical outlook in general.

The Age of Men ends in dissolution and decay. Great inequalities of wealth come into being, bringing in consequence a train of evil—corruption, poverty, political unrest, and a reign of individual greed and isolation. There is something of the spirit of Machiavelli[7] in Vico's depiction of the dissolution of the Age of Man. Although optimistic about the rather distant future, he theorized that the world was nearing the end of a second great cycle, which had begun after the fall of Rome, and which recapitulated in form the first cycle of the classical world. The Age of Men ends in a condition of "misbegotten subtleties of malicious wits," a "barbarism of reflection" worse even than the barbarism of the first men.

Described in this fashion, the final dissolution is a condition containing the elements of a renewed historical cycle. With Rome as his model, Vico

---

[6] Vico thought that areas of the world other than Europe were generally at stages of development substantially earlier than was Europe, essentially because of Christianity.

[7] An influence of Machiavelli, along with other more secular writers of the Renaissance has been suggested by some. More generally, Vico interpreters have frequently approached him as a late Renaissance thinker (Manuel, 47, et passim; Berlin, 1976, 137ff.).

theorized that there were two possible consequences: either the rise of an authoritarian leader, i.e., a Caesar who restores order, or barbarian conquest from without. The failure of Caesarism and resulting barbarian conquest sow the seeds of a new cycle.

> Peoples who have reached this point of premeditated malice, when they receive this last remedy of providence and are thereby stunned and brutalized, are sensible no longer of comforts, delicacies, pleasures and pomp, but only of the sheer necessities of life. The few survivors in the midst of an abundance of the things necessary for life naturally become sociable and, returning to the primitive simplicity of the first world of peoples, are again religious, truthful and faithful. (1948, 1106)

Vico's syncretic philosophy of history fuses the pagan idea of historical recurrence with the Christian understanding of history as providential. The cycles are not mere eternal redundancies, but occur historically as spirals. The movement from the Dark Ages through the Middle Ages, the Renaissance (the beginning of the second Age of Men), and up to the present, although constituting a formally similar cyclical pattern, was culturally different in substance, and, Vico hoped, in its eventual historical destiny as well. Each new cycle, for Vico, is a renewal of humanity; this is the manner of the working of providence. One must speculate, then, that there is a kind of progress occurring in history, although this has little in common with the secular idea discussed in Chapter 2. Vico rejects equally all views of history as fate, or as no more than sequences of chance events.

The lawlike nature of history may thus be assured by providence, but this is a providence that neither intervenes directly in human affairs nor directly predetermines them in their particulars. Rather, providence works through the free will of men. In this fashion the nature of the cycles are tied closely to, in fact explained, by the practical, real ends men seek, and the consequences of such seeking. The institutions and cultures that define the three Ages are, in fact, great historic ironies resulting from human purposeful action.

> Men mean to gratify their beastial lust and abandon their offspring, and they inaugurate the chastity of marriage from which the families arise. The fathers mean to exercise without restraint their paternal power over their clients, and they subject them to the civil power from which the Cities arise. The reigning orders of nobles mean to abuse their laws which establish popular liberty. The free peoples mean to shake off the yoke of their laws, and they become subject to monarchs. The monarchs mean to strengthen their own positions by debasing their subjects with all the vices of dissoluteness, and then dispose them to endure slavery at the hands of stronger nations. The nations mean to dissolve themselves, and their remnants flee for safety to the wilderness, whence, like the phoenix, they rise again. That which did all this was mind, for man did it with intelligence; it was not fate, for they did it by choice; not chance, for the results of their always so acting are perpetually the same. (1108)

This is a fully sociological characterization of society as the work of men, a paean to human agency, yet the point of theorizing and understanding it is religious: It is through our understanding of human history as a parade of unintended consequences that the working of a supreme intelligence is perceived. It is a close parallel to the scientific-deist view of nature as a clockwork. Humans cannot know the mind of God directly,[8] but human knowledge of human creations achieved through scientific study allows at least a partial knowledge of God's works as he envisioned them flowing from the free creative capacities with which he endowed the race.

Not content with a statement limited to an analysis of *political* cycles, as were Aristotle and his later classical and Renaissance imitators and epigoni, Vico *relates* the forms of government to religious practice, to forms of the family, and ultimately to basically different forms of human nature. In fact, the *New Science* can be understood as a book about fundamental transformations in human nature and the cultural and political changes to which these are related. "He held that certain periods of history had a general character, coloring every detail," writes Collingwood (1946, 67). The nature of any age is to be understood in terms of the interrelatedness of its chief elements. Thus, the Heroic Age is agricultural, is dominated by an aristocracy that celebrates the virtues of individual heroic prowess, a meaning system in which language was metaphorical and manifest in a ballad literature. All the elements of a society, Vico is saying, fit together and acquire their unity through the meaning system of the society. Whether Vico was an absolute idealist, as Benedetto Croce claimed (Croce, 1963), may be debatable; that he advanced an idealistic and organic conception of society cannot be doubted.

If Vico's idea of history and society both drew on but departed profoundly from received Christian thought, the same may be said of his conception of the nature of the race. On the one hand, the human race is the creation of God. On the other, although he accepted the doctrine of the Fall (which explains our inability to know God directly), Vico's emphasis was at all times on humankind as active and creative, as a culture-building species. Vico's characterizations of "human nature" follow consistently from his postulate of a basic human creativity; the result is everywhere an emphasis on "man making himself," as it were, through creation of the variety of societies and cultures revealed throughout history. Far from deriving the nature of social life and institutions from any imputed qualities of human nature, in describing the general character of his new science, Vico asserts that

> our science comes to be at once a history of ideas, the customs and deeds of mankind. *From these derive the principles of human nature,* which we shall show to be the principles of universal history. (1948, 368; underlining mine)

This fundamentally modern principle of Vico's philosophical anthropology was summed up by M. H. Fisch as follows:

> Vico shared with the Marxists and the Existentialists the negative view that

[8] With one exception: Vico thought that God had revealed himself directly just once, to the "philosophical Jews" of the Old Testament.

there is no human essence to be found in individuals as such, and with the Marxists the positive view that the essence of humanity is the ensemble of social relations of the developing system of institutions. (cited in Berlin, 1976, 114)

Croce was so impressed with this aspect of Vico's thought that he went to some lengths to interpret it as "dialectical" in nature (Croce, 1963).[9]

Vico's theory of knowledge is tied closely to his conception of human nature. Contrary to the prevailing style of the eighteenth century, he does not propose to study human history by assuming that its evident diversity reflects a universal human nature discoverable by the objective methods of natural science. For Vico, history is rather an integral segment of the great chain of being constitutive of nature. Vico insists that historical knowledge is fundamentally different from knowledge of nature. His starting point is a critical discussion of the Cartesian position that mathematical knowledge is the only true form of knowledge and that the practice of science is the discovery of mathematical laws of nature. Vico argued that we do indeed have precise knowledge of mathematics, but only because it is a construction of mathematicians. Vico rejects the assumption that mathematical propositions reveals truths about nature, an epistemological centerpiece of rationalist and Enlightenment thought. He argues, very much like Hume, that the clarity of our ideas has nothing to do with their truth—this merely accounts for our belief that they are true. There is no reason to accept mathematical characterizations of the workings of nature as true.

What is needed, Vico goes on to argue, is some criterion whereby the true ideas can be distinguished from those that stand as items of mere belief. And it is here that we locate his great methodological discovery, a discovery derived from his philosophical anthropology. For anything to be known to the human mind, Vico argues, it must be a construction of human activity. This is the epistemological status not only of mathematical propositions and systems, but, far more important, of all history as well. We can know the truth about human history *not* because it is the handiwork of God, but because and *only* because it is in its entirety the work of human beings.

> In the night of thick darkness enveloping the earliest antiquity so remote from ourselves, there shines the eternal and never-failing light of a truth beyond all question; that the world of civil society has certainly been made by men, and that its principles are therefore to be found within the modifications of our own human mind. (1948, 311)

Vico is astonished that philosophers throughout the ages have misspent their energies attempting to fathom the mysteries of nature, which, having been made by God, are knowable only by Him.

> Whosoever reflects on this (that history is "made by men") cannot but marvel that the philosophers should have bent all their energies to the study of the world of nature, which, since God made it, He alone knows; and that they

---

[9] Recall that Marx was familiar with Vico and evidently thought highly of him. (M. Lifshitz, 1948, cited in Löwith, 1949, 240).

should have neglected the study of the world of nations or civil world, which since men had made it, men could hope to know. (311)

In passages such as these in which the possibilities of a true human science is envisioned, Vico stands as an exemplar of Enlightenment thought, remote from the Christian theology and dogma. This quality of the *New Science*, and its implications, were evidently clear enough to the Italian Churchmen of the times, for they attacked it as incompatible with the principle of God's transcendence. And its import must have been equally clear to the anticlerical Italian socialists who, toward the end of the nineteenth century, brought it back into print for use as weapon in the revolutionary cause (Löwith, 1949, 136).

Since for Vico the central feature of any society is the unity of its collectively created meaning system, the centerpiece of the method of understanding it scientifically is, broadly speaking, the analysis of language. Myths and fables, religious creeds and rituals, exist *as* language. Berlin holds that Vico's basic discovery was that "the development of the morphology of a symbolic system is one with the growth of the culture of which it is the central organ" (1976, 48). The method of studying culture is philological. Vico calls it "Fantasia" and it rests, to reiterate, on the postulate that human societies actively and collectively create meaning systems through which they come to know themselves, in effect, become what they are. The Age of Gods is a period in which societies are *defined linguistically* by their mythic nature, by communication occurring through sentiments appearing in inexpressed symbols such as the flight of birds or the patterns appearing in the entrails of an animal. The Age of Heroes is understood as one in which societies are what they are by virtue of the concrete metaphorical personifications that *define* the Hero. The Age of Men has as its central feature precisely the *rational* use and manipulation of language, whether in science, politics, economic life, or other spheres of experience. For Vico, the fundamental nature of societies appears in their forms of communication. Berlin expresses this as a conception in which the mind, society, and language are but three modes of one reality (1976, ix). It follows that these forms of communication can properly be taken as "data" for the *interpretive* understanding of all ages, even the most remote ones.

Vico thought of his interpretive method as standing in bold contrast with the methods of the natural sciences. In this he adumbrates the distinction between *Naturwissenschaften* and *Geisteswissenschaften* of a century later. The original technical formulation of the doctrine that the study of human history cannot be assimilated to natural science methods is Vico's. And it is worth emphasizing that, after two and a half centuries of growth and development of the social sciences, Vico's basic argument, that we can know our social milieux precisely because it is of our own making, and that this form of knowing is basically different from that appropriate to the natural sciences, remains the basic axiom of the interpretive sociologies.[10]

---

[10] Vico was quite aware of some of the difficulties attending an interpretive science such as he was proposing. Along Baconian lines, and in anticipation of such late nineteenth century sociologists as Herbert Spencer, in his *The Study of Sociology* he discussed various sources of bias or error.

Let us reiterate the connection in Vico's thought between his philo-sophical anthropology, his conception of society, and his interpretive method. Although the periods occurring with a cycle exhibit broad formal similarities, they are comprehensible only in their uniqueness and cultural specificity. As I have pointed out in Chapter 3, the great cultural diversity of the world was a central appreciation in the social thought of the foremost thinkers of the Enlightenment, but by and large they never got beyond trying to *explain* that diversity within the natural law framework of an imputed common and universal human nature. Vico, on the other hand, not only emphasized the specificity, and thus the diversity of cultures, but insisted that their uniqueness resulted from the fact that human nature is constantly *changing*, and doing so in relation to cultural changes. It is "constantly generating new character-istics, new needs, new categories of thought and action" (Vico, 1948, 128). Vico's philosophical anthropology is the intellectual root of both his innovative concept of culture and the method employed to study it.

Finally, it should be noted that there remains in Vico a conservatism, and even an anticipation of the romantic sensibility, that follows from all of this. If God's purpose is reflected in the institutions and cultures human beings create, and if the upwardly spiraling cycles are somehow reflective of this, then there seems to be something of inevitability in history after all. And if there is a plan, and especially one whose end is in the nature of the case beyond the powers of the human mind, then the tampering of social engineers or struggles of revolutionaries seem pointless at best. Although it cannot be said that Vico shared the estranged and pessimistic temper that later came to characterize the romantic reaction against everything modern, his *theory* nevertheless locates eighteenth century Europe at the downturn of the second cycle, i.e., undergoing dissolution. In fact, his expectations for the future, in this context, seem a bit implausible; they have a hopeful, and even at times a utopian tone, particularly his expectation that the future will see the establishment of an ideal monarchy. But then, the second cycle *is* an advance over the first. It is difficult to say whether these passages are anything more than a prudent adjustment to Christian doctrine in early eighteenth century Naples. As a Catholic professor of rhetoric (at the University of Naples from 1699 to 1741) living under rather depressing conditions,[11] Vico was, perhaps predictably, no reformer and might even have been prepared to trim his theory a bit to maintain the meager existence that was his.

Vico's scheme for the interpretive analysis of societies as cultural unities that pass through clearly definable stages and that experience periods of breakdown, was a powerful historical-sociological innovation in social thought. It was, in fact, in some repects so radical in its innovativeness that it went largely unrecognized in its genius until its partial and selective recovery in the nineteenth century. But today it appears so significant that Berlin identifies Vico as the true founder of the *German* historical school, of

---

[11] Vico helped to support himself by composing commissioned works such as wedding poems, funeral orations, commemorative remarks and elegies. Mooney calls him "a wordsmith of high society" (Mooney, 1985, 12).

decisive importance for sociology. We turn now to the first important representative of this school, Johann Gottfried von Herder.

HERDER

Johann Gottfried von Herder (1744–1803) in important ways bears a striking similarity to Vico, a similarity that has not gone unnoticed by later inter-preters.[12] Albeit in somewhat different ways, both formulated sociological conceptions of history that attempted to fuse elements of Christianity and the Enlightenment; both, in this connection, rejected or radically revised central tenets of the Enlightenment theory of progress, philosophical an-thropology, and theory of knowledge. Both adumbrated what is essentially the modern concept of culture, emphasizing its uniqueness, historical spec-ificity, and organic unity, and, in so doing, became major figures in the development of the discipline of history. Both were major precursors of the forms of romantic conservatism that more immediately influenced Comte and other early sociologists of the first half of the nineteenth century. Both were religious professionals and analysts of language, which was of great significance for their theories.

There are, of course, significant differences between them. Vico was a Catholic south Italian, Herder a Protestant German. Vico adopted the pagan idea of historical cycles as the theoretical underpinning of his "new science," but the idea of cycles is scarcely to be found in Herder. Vico's fusion of seemingly inconsistent elements is effected with an untroubled, even serene magnificence; Herder's works are excited and agitated, leap from the polemical to the sublime, and defy consistent interpretation. In this regard, Manuel says that Herder is "a primitivist worshipper of folk cultures: an "enlightenment exponent of the values of reason and Humanity," an "educator of German liberalism," a "propagator of irrationalism," a "militant exponent of Germandom who can be attached to that long line culminating in the Nazis," a "crucial figure in the modern historicist revolution," a "philosophical precursor of Darwin" (x), and, given all this, elsewhere concludes that he is "by far the most difficult thinker of the German Enlightenment to pigeonhole" (Manuel, 1965, 83). This is a recurring theme in Herder interpretations. His biographer Haym likened his masterwork, *Ideen zur Philosophie der Geschichte der Menscheit* (translated as *Reflections on the Philosophy of History of Mankind* by T. Churchill), published between 1784 and 1791, to, "a bush whose branches and twigs sprouting in wild profusion end up by breaking each other" (Herder, 1968, x).

The inconsistency of Herder's thought is nowhere more evident than in the way he deals with the concept of progress. Bock concludes that Herder's discussions of the concept are so confusing that it is a theme not even worth pursuing (Bock, 1978, 55), although he adds that Herder's "pluralism" was indeed destructive of the classical theory of progress. But there are passages in Herder that, rather analogous to Vico, reflect a view

---

[12] Isaiah Berlin's *Vico and Herder* is an important recent work that curiously leaves their commonalities and differences essentially undiscussed.

of the workings of providence in history. Herder wonders whether there will come a time in the future ("the fullness of time") when we will have knowledge sufficient to discern "the end of the chain which links peoples and continents, observe how it forged its links hesitantly at first, then with increasing vehemence and clamor, began to weld the nations together, more firmly though less perceptibly?" (Barnard, 1969, 223),[13] Despite the great diversity and uniqueness of cultures, there is nevertheless something we may think of as progress. Egyptian culture could not have been what it was without its Oriental predecessors, nor Greek without Egyptian and Roman without Greek. The Roman "carried on his back the whole world (188). Although our "shallow histories" can scarcely reveal any true purpose or final end, we can achieve "glimpses of a divine theatre" in the ruins of particular cultures. Like Vico, Herder thinks that God has placed the fate of humans in their own hands, that the destructive elements of nature must ultimately yield to the powers of human reason and sense of justice, since the extension of humanity is the "destiny" of the human race, and that, in Flint's words, a "wise goodness dispenses the fate of mankind," requiring that all cooperate in its designs (for a good summary of Herder's doctrine of progress, see Flint, 1894, 386).

The sociological significance of Herder's work, however, does not lie in these rhetorical flourishes paying homage to providence. The more significant side of Herder is to be seen in the prominence of his concept of a *Volk* and related ideas. By this concept Herder and other German thinkers understood a people united by virtue of having formed and lived within their unique cultural tradition. Traditions are rooted in religion and expressed in gradually changing forms of literature, music, art, and even science. Such traditions tend toward a unity, and toward a *uniqueness* of form or pattern. The idea that human communities are unique cultural configurations that may advance in their creativity is essential to Herder's work, and, indeed the central idea of German historicist thought. While it is true that Herder embellishes this *early* historicism by maintaining that the culture created by a people develops through the realization of a common humanity (*Humanität*)—nowhere adequately—the dominant thrust of his thought falls on the *opposed* principle that the standards in terms of which its concrete forms must be judged can never be the universal abstractions propounded by philosophers.

Every *Volk* forms a society at the core of which is its "Seele" or "Geist," its "inner spirit." The culture of a *Volk* represents its special genius and is an entity sui generis. Although they may be in some indeterminate sense comparable, cultures are incommensurable with one another, at least in terms of value judgments about their progress. Much of Herder's most important and ambitious work, the *Ideen*, is taken up with what one can only describe as ethnographies of peoples the world over; not only the Greeks, Romans, early Germans, and Persians found so commonly in eighteenth century social science and history, but Chinese, Indians, Hebrews, Arabs, Lapps, Frisians, and so on. Indeed, he thinks the true philosopher must be an anthropologist, and his work is both an early attempt at scientific

---

[13] In his useful *Herder on Political and Social Culture*, F. M. Barnard has edited and brought together sections of several of Herder's works.

ethnography and the study of national character.[14] In all this, Herder has in mind a unity supposedly manifest in the common understandings held to underlie the literature, music, art, and science of a people. He emphasizes, like Vico, the profound significance of religion and above all language as the foundation of all community life. In this respect one can perceive the close family resemblance to Vico resulting, in part, from the influence of the organicism of earlier Christian thought.

For the time, Herder's conception of the nature and significance of culture was profound. Although the human race is "the first of creation left free," all individuals are shaped by association with others at all times and places, and the uniqueness of human cultures means that "each form of human perfection is . . . national and time-bound and, considered most specifically, individual" (Barnard, 1969, 184). "Human nature," he says, "has to learn everything, develop through progress, keep on advancing through gradual struggle" (184). "Even the image of happiness," he says, "changes with each condition and climate" (185). The notion that "the image of happiness changes with each condition" is a recognition by Herder that the very standards in terms of which individuals experience "happiness" are culturally relative, and so incommensurable. It is a doctrine at fundamental variance with all versions of universal history. Collingwood believes that Herder was the first "to recognize in a systematic way that there are different kinds of men and that human nature is not uniform but diversified" (1946, 90–91). He might have added that this diversity results from the very nature of culture: there is no human nature as such, only the various "human natures" formed sui generis within diverse cultural milieux.

Nowhere is Herder more at variance with the *Philosophers* than in his treatment of the nature of reason, which he regards not as a property or potential of the individual mind, but as formed through experience; and because experience varies with one's cultural milieu, there can be no universal reason. "Reason (is) the creation of man," he declares (Barnard, 1969, 264), "nothing more than something formed by experience . . . , an aggregate of the experiences and observations of the mind" (20). And most importantly, he proposes in quite modern vein that the very presence of reason in human experience results from the emergence of language as a distinctive human creation.[15]

---

[14] Although his conception of cultures as unique gives rise to a methodological rule prohibiting the making of comparative judgments, Herder's work, not surprising for the times, is by no means free of various prevailing stereotypes or celebrations of certain cultures. He clearly admires and prefers ancient Greeks and Germans, for example; Orientals, on the other hand, are "deformed" (due to the rigidity of their ancient culture, a point that Herder may well have intended against his long-time protagonist Voltaire, who admired and eulogized Chinese culture); Hindus are "the gentlest" of people, Frisians . . . "honest," the ancient Persians were "ugly mountaineers," Tibetans "contemplative solitaries," like children "in a gentle slumber." One of the books written late in his life is entitled *German National Glory*, a tract that expands on the intrinsic values of Germanic culture (an effort that earned him the reward of being labeled as one of the intellectual precursors of German nationalism and Nazism). Indeed, as Barnard says, "one does not have to look hard for Herder's German, middle-class prejudices" (Barnard, 1969, xi).

[15] Although he also holds to the "enlightened" idea of there being just *one* reason expressed in language, a contradiction, since the categories of reason cannot both underlie and emerge from language.

Herder's analysis of human language is quite sophisticated. Animals may have languages of their own, he grants; unlike animals, however, human language does not develop out of instincts. Yet neither is language of divine origin (but see footnote 16), as later conservatives such as de Maistre and de Bonald insisted. Observing the incredible diversity of languages, he wonders why the deity found it necessary or desirable to invent seventy words for "stone" in one language. The idea that language resides at the very core of culture, that it is constitutive of it, grounds Herder's analysis of culture.[16]

Despite the predominance of these non-Enlightenment ideas, Herder did not escape a considerable influence of Enlightenment individualism. His reception of this, however, was framed by a rejection of the Cartesian mind-body dualism in all its variants and he insisted that human experience is a unity. He especially rejects the separation of the rational from the emotional or affective. "Words, rhythms, actions are aspects of a single experience," writes Berlin, in characterizing the central thrust of Herder's philosophical anthropology (Berlin, 1976, 174). God has implanted in everyone the potential for creativity and freedom of choice, and the realization of this is the highest of human ends. But such an individuality is possible only within and in terms of one's culture. In this sense, human creativity, by which Herder understands essentially aesthetic expression—in poetry, song, visual art—is the other side of the coin of cultural development. But for Herder this does not imply an out-and-out cultural determinism. Individuals realizing their potential for freedom through aesthetic expression simultaneously revitalize the culture in which they participate. Just as all cultures are incommensurable, so too, therefore, are the activities and experiences of those immersed in them. No one, not even the greatest genius, ever transcends his or her cultural traditions.

In this fashion Herder links together his ideas of *Volk* and the individual, and even progress. Just as all cultures are unique because of the configuration of meanings of which they are comprised, so also is the experience and activity of the individuals, for they are conceived of as the bearers and expressors of their cultures. Communities that experience cultural growth and retain their authenticity are the necessary milieux for continuing creative expression; if there is anything that can be identified as progress, it is this continuing gradual modification of cultural tradition that enhances the real possibility of the creative growth and expression of the individual.

It is this formulation of the individual-society relation that is so epochal in Herder's thought. Not Godwin nor the Rousseau of *Emile*, nor even the Scots, ever fully abandoned the "human nature causes society"

---

[16] Herder's emphasis on language and his historicism was derived mainly from his teacher Hamann. Herder inherits from Hamann, says Berlin, "the desire to seize the whole in its fullness, in all its peculiar, complex, historically changing manifestations" (1976, 164), and derives from him "his notion that words and ideas are one" (165). It should be noted that Herder's analysis of language involves yet another inconsistency, in fact a flat contradiction, stemming from his reception of both Christian and Enlightenment thought. Although the incommensurability of languages was central to his thought, he nevertheless maintains elsewhere (against Lord Monboddo and others) that language was the "gift of God." The mouth, he announces at one point, is "rendered divine" by the faculty of speech.

formula of enlightened philosophical anthropology. None of them were able to formulate, within the framework of their liberalism, an intellectual anchor adequate to effect this. Only with Herder's developed concepts of the *Volk* and *Seele des Volks*, essentially the idea of culture, is this achieved. It is this that Cassirer had in mind when he wrote of Herder's "conquest" of the Enlightenment.

The fusion of Enlightenment and anti-Enlightenment elements in Herder's conceptions of progress, culture, and the individual is, if anything, even more striking in his idea of the possibility of true social knowledge. The spirit and intent of his theory of knowledge is essentially no different from what we find in the leading exponents of a liberating human science. Herder wants to create a human science in order "to know all past ages and to use this knowledge rightly." Although a devastating critic of the programs of the philosophes, he was impressed by and celebrated the science on which their moral doctrines were supposedly based (see Nisbet, 1970). In his more optimistic passages, he allowed himself a vision of a world in which peace and freedom would reign as the fruit of growing knowledge of humanity. He admired the culture of ancient Greece in part because it nurtured and supported a progressive scientific outlook. And not the least of his reasons for denouncing despotism in any of its forms was the fact that despots suppressed the growth of the arts and sciences. "History shows," he remarks in his sociologically sophisticated *Dissertation on the Reciprocal Influence of Government and the Sciences*, that "as soon as freedom was lost . . . the spirit of the sciences likewise disappeared" (Barnard, 1969, 239). The celebration of knowledge as the means of the emancipation of the human spirit was as alive in Herder as in any of the philosophes.

It is when he turns to the *method* of social or historical inquiry that Herder departs from the dominant Enlightenment theory of knowledge and takes up company with Vico. His rejection of methodological ideas and practice of the leading Enlightenment intellectuals—Montesquieu, Voltaire, Ferguson, Hume, Millar, Diderot, Bayle—is unequivocal. In his critique of rigor, clarity, order, rationality, Berlin pronounces Herder to be "the profoundest critic of the Enlightenment, as formidable as Burke, or de Maistre," but, quickly he adds, "free from their reactionary prejudices and hatred of equality and fraternity" (Berlin, 1976, 165). Anything that smacks of generalization, of abstraction, becomes a target for his methodological polemic. It is for these sins that he excoriates Montesquieu.

> The history of all times and peoples . . . is reduced to ruins divided neatly into three heaps, to a mere collection even though it does not lack noble and worthy material. O, Montesquieu! (Barnard, 1969, 217)

For Herder, even Montesquieu's *Spirit of the Laws* ends up as superficial, as a kind of scientific artifice. It glosses over the profound realities of cultures and languages—the real stuff of human experience, to concentrate instead on a superficial taxonomy of forms of government—a taxonomy that itself has to be broken down into a dozen permutations in a vain attempt to capture the deep truths of the vast array of unique cultures—vain because governments themselves, in contrast to the "natural" form and evolution of human communities, are artificial, superficial constructions. Montesquieu fails because his science never gets beyond externals; this is so because *generalization* is, in principle, limited to externals. True understanding of human cultures must penetrate to their inner spirit, and to the extent that this is achieved the entire matter of generalization, in the nature of the case, is rendered vacuous. Herder's basic methodological dictum for understanding anything at all about human communities follows from his concepts of culture and the community. The student must enter the "spirit" of a people in order to understand *any* of its thoughts or deeds.

The idea of penetrating to the spirit is rendered by the German noun *Einfühlung*, which translates as "empathic understanding." One must "feel" one's way into the Geist of a culture; only then can one grasp the sense of anything in particular about it. Berlin describes the process as follows:

> To explain human experience or attitudes is to be able to transpose oneself by sympathetic imagination into the life situation of the human beings who are to be "explained," and this amounts to understanding and communicating the coherence of a particular way of life, feeling, action; and thereby the validity of the given act or action, the part it plays in the life and outlook which is "natural" in the situation. (Berlin, 1976, 154)

Herder is not very clear about the technical nature of this process (less so than Vico, perhaps, when compared with the latter's idea of *Fantasia*), but this, after all, is not surprising for it remains a question not fully explicated in the social sciences even to this day (see Chapters 13 and 15). However, it was clear enough to Herder, as it was to Vico, that the route to the inner life of any culture was through its language. Everything about a culture is expressed in its language; the language is itself the indubitable expression of the culture, and it follows that the indispensable procedure for a human science is the study of language. One must read Herder's own "ethnographies" to fully appreciate the seriousness with which he followed this path. Much of his later work follows this course, but even as early as his *Travel Diary* one finds him engaged in sophisticated national character analysis through study of the nuances and complex meanings of the living languages of Europe.

Herder's insistence on sympathetic imagination as a method moved him to criticize sharply much eighteenth century thought on the ground that it proceeded apart from an adequate canon of empirical verification. He regarded his own method as the truly empirical one.[17] He was especially critical of French thought, which he thought showed little concern for proof, but was preoccupied with "esprit." Of course, Herder's is an empiricism that

---

[17] In a strict sense this is correct. If we understand "empirical" to designate the truest and fullest report or description of an object possible, even while recognizing the impossibility of a completely exhaustive account of such an object, it follows that any generalizing procedure is unempirical to the extent that aspects of the object go unreported, glossed, or distorted. This seems self evident. Science, of course, is and must be empiricist, but also is and must be something more than empiricist. On this issue see Northrup, 1945. See also Chapter 13 of this work.

revels in the particulars and the informing spirit that connects them. It is an empiricism that halts at the gate of generalization and that insists that "all comparison is unprofitable." But it is an empiricism that, once injected into the nascent social science of the time, has, if in modified forms, refused to relinquish its claim to a legitimate status in the repertoire of social science right up to the present.

Finally, and very importantly, there is Herder's theory of social change. Whereas his wishful and mushy passages on universal progress can only be dismissed as the lingering dream of the true workings of providence, of a God still at work in human affairs, Herder's actual analysis of social change in the eighteenth century is a concrete and powerful indictment of modernism cast in unmistakable sociological terms. In formulating this critique his concept of the *Volk* served as an early ideal type against which European modernization could be set. In this regard, much of what the philosophers celebrated as progressive and liberating was attacked by Herder as a movement from the organic completeness of the older communal forms to a condition of "soulless" mechanistic functioning. "The strong vital ties of the old Republics and eras are long since loosened," he writes, and "everything tends to erode the more delicate ties of our time." He everywhere employs the metaphor of the machine, of mechanical functioning, especially in connection with the state and commercial life, and it is on this ground that he rejects so much of what is celebrated by the Enlightenment, particularly the burgeoning commercial economy and the expansiveness of the state. "A large part of this so-called new civilization is actually a piece of mechanism . . . , in fact the essential characteristic of the new spirit" (Barnard, 1969, 196).

Herder was not the first to express this theme. Kant, in particular, antedates Herder here, but the latter's critique of modernism entails the first, clear version of the modern concept of the culturally unified community so critical to the topologies of nineteenth century sociology, as opposed to the modernizing forces of economy and state which are indicted as *mechanisms* inherently opposed to and destructive of the organic unity of the culture of the Volk. This is the concrete form in which the "natural" and the "artificial" oppose each other: The community is the natural organic form of life upon which the mechanism of the state and money economy impose themselves. One sees this new spirit arisen in many places; in the military, for instance, where, with the invention of artillery, "the army has become a hired machine without thought, force, or will, which one man directs from above and which he employs as pawns, as a living wall to dispatch and to intercept bullets" (197). Herder interprets the inegalitarian and authoritarian systematization of relationships throughout society as a consequence of this new spirit that has invaded the militiary. Writing well before Hegel's famous elaboration of the master-slave relationship, Herder argues, "The master-servant relationship is . . . the most pervasive characteristic of our offices of state, or the trades and of all social orders from peasant to minister and from minister to priest" (197).

The sense of a world poised on a knife-edge of catastrophe caused by the expansive power of the state was perhaps felt more keenly by Herder than any contemporary. The expansion of state power is accompanied by "the resignation of the individual human being," he writes, and he insists that inequalities imposed by the state are unnatural. In a savagely ironic and sarcastic commentary, he decimates the idea of European "progress."

> It really is a great century, both in its means and its ends; without a doubt we stand at the very top of the tree in regard to the previous centuries! We have drawn from our roots, trunk and branches, as much sap as our slender topmost bough could contain. We look down on Orientals, Greeks, Romans, especially on the Gothic barbarians of the Middle Ages! From what a height we look down on the world! In a sense, all peoples and continents stand in our shadow, and if a storm in Europe shakes two tiny branches, how the whole world trembles and bleeds! (Barnard, 206)

The obliteration of local cultures by imperialist expansion may be seen in its most disastrous aspect in the replacement of indigenous languages by the *linguae francae* of the dominant powers.

> The princes speak French, and soon everybody will follow their example; and then, behold, perfect bliss: the golden age, when all the world will speak one tongue, one universal language, is dawning again! There will be one flock and one shepherd! National cultures, where are you? (209)

The idea that the administrative domination of the state and of the organization of economic life could produce a profound alienation was an idea that by the end of the eighteenth century was becoming commonplace. As we have seen, there was some understanding of this by Rousseau, Godwin, and the later Scottish moralists, and by others as well.[18] But no one in Europe, not even Rousseau, polemicized against inequality and political domination more eloquently than Herder; the difference is that his conceptions of culture and the community allowed him to go a step beyond this. Although there is not much in the way of rigorous conceptual clarity in Herder (he was, after all, more or less against it in principle!), it seems fair to understand him as suggesting that there is a form of human experience that results from a fractured or decimated culture, and that this is not identical with the effects of inequality and domination. The expanding power of the state may be the driving agency, but the disastrous consequences are experienced on a cultural plane. The authenticity of individuals depends on

---

[18] Adam Smith's indictment of colonialism should be understood, in the context of his celebration of free trade, as an unfortunate adjunct of mercantilism that concentrates wealth in the hands of a few through the subjugation of native peoples everywhere (see Chapter 6). Edmund Burke denounced colonialism in even stronger terms (see Burke, 1906, in speeches in House of Commons, 1–139, passim), regarding the operations of the East India Company, for instance, as "a system of oppression and tyranny, that goes to the utter ruin of thirty millions of my fellow-creatures and fellow-subjects" (1906, 128). Herder's attack on colonialism, if no more of a polemic than Burke's, is more thoroughgoing in the double sense of being an application of the conceptual polarity of the communal and the mechanical, and as the consequence of a master trend in history, namely the increasing scale of relationships that have inevitable destructive consequences. Herder sees what the others do not: that colonialism means the destruction of indigenous culture, and this, in turn, or actually simultaneously, the destruction of the individuals who are the individuals they are because of their culture.

the continuing unity of their cultural milieux; it follows that anything destructive of such milieux will have profound consequences for those who must endure their dissolution.

In this polemic, Herder gives a novel twist to the near-universal eighteenth century theme of the opposition of the "natural" and the "artificial." In some respects there are clear parallels between Herder and other Enlightenment thinkers adhering to this distinction, like the Scots. Herder thought of the primary relations of the family as primordial and therefore natural, as did the Scots. "Nature extends the bonds of society only to families" (Barnard, 1969, 322). And the idea of tradition is not absent from the Scots' work, especially that of Hume. But in Herder the nature-artifice polarity is rendered in different and novel form. The Scots elaborated their idea of the commercial society in terms of primary relations made possible by the capacity for sympathy, on the one hand, and the other, the institutions of society that are created more or less by rational design for utilitarian purposes. The latter, on the whole, were thought to serve human needs in adequate fashion despite the limitations of human reason that inevitably introduce into societal functioning a variety of unanticipated consequences. Herder's formulation of the folk culture with its organic unity manifest in language, religion, folk music, and indigenous aesthetic expressions, goes beyond this, locating the theoretical center of gravity in the *collective products* of association rather than the technical qualities of associational forms themselves, the *culture* rather than the *social structure*. The creation and historical perpetuation of meaning systems in their totality are for Herder the essence of what is natural in human social life.

The power of Herder's conception lies, in considerable degree, in the way he realizes the Enlightenment tendency toward rejection of the Christian doctrine of evil inherent in the race and its relocation in social institutions. What is a tendency and a puzzle for Diderot, Voltaire, and the utilitarians, what turns out to be a logical cul de sac in Godwin's anarchistic liberalism, and what in Rousseau finally ends up cast in rationalist and nascent totalitarian political form, in Herder finds its expression as the dissolution of culture when subordinated to the functioning of the utilitarian mechanisms of modern monarchical states and interest-based commerce. Evil is located not so much in the mechanism itself, but in the *consequences* for the unity of the folk community and its individual members. And this destructive modernism cannot escape Herder's Christian sense of just retribution. With a fine sense of outraged irony, he predicted that these imperialist chickens would ultimately come home to roost. The more that Europeans create the technologies or other means with which other peoples are brought into submission, the more complete, Herder thought, would be their ultimate victory. In connection with his discussion of the Persian Empire under Cyrus, he exclaims that "it is a rigorous yet beneficent law of fate, that all overgrown power should destroy itself" (326).

In all this, Herder's work is perhaps the most powerful of all eighteenth century formulations of the halting movement toward a sociological conception of a social level sui generis deriving from the problem of the need to relocate the source of evil. That this should appear in the work of a Lutheran parson is another of those ironies of which the history of social thought is so replete.

Herder is the principle source of the idea of the opposition of society, meaning economic and state and related spheres of instrumental action, and culture, designating shared meaning systems, including language, which is understood to be essential to the process of the formation of individuals. I shall refer to this opposition as the inner-outer polarity, and later, in Part III, propose that it is the central paradigm of the German historicist tradition as this unfolded during the nineteenth century. In this context, it is also the condition within which the interpretive, or *verstehende* method, which is the method of historicism, came into prominence. We will later see how this polarity undergirds Max Weber's historical sociology at the moment of the crisis of positivism around the turn of the twentieth century, in Chapter 13.

THE REACTIONARY CONSERVATIVES

There can be little doubt that not only Comte's sociology, but that of other nineteenth century social scientists as well, including Le Play and Tocqueville (as Nisbet points out: 1978, 108ff.), would not have been what they were had the postrevolutionary conservatives not created their *oeuvres*. Although their influence has sometimes been exaggerated (see Nisbet, 1978, 105–107) it is perhaps reasonable to assess this as roughly equal to that of the Enlightenment. This has the merit of being Comte's own judgment, insofar as this is possible to determine.

Many of the main elements of the reactionaries' thought are to be found in the writings of both Vico and Herder: the organic unity of cultures founded on religion, the emphasis on the centrality of language, the idea that the family constitutes the fundamental unit of society and the sense of decay and dissolution in Europe. But, as I have tried to show, Vico and Herder are important because they formulated their ideas of society, history, and the individual in an intellectual dialogue with the central tenets of the Enlightenment, to the *spirit* of which, in the last analysis, they must be judged as having remained philosophically true. The reactionaries, on the other hand, set out to develop the conservative Christian themes already formulated in their predecessors' thought as an intellectual staging-ground from which an unremitting attack on the Enlightenment in its every aspect could be mounted.

It will be useful to treat the reactionaries by pursuing the theme of differences between their work and that of the progressives, through a review of their rejection of the doctrine of progress, acceptance of Christian philosophical anthropology, and conception of the nature and possibilities of knowledge of society. Rather than take up a great deal of space, I will treat the three leading reactionaries together, a procedure I believe justified on the grounds of their striking similarity,[19] although I will place somewhat more emphasis on Maistre than the others.

---

[19] Becker and Barnes for instance, find "a resemblance between (Maistre and Bonald) so close as almost to constitute identity" (1960, 2, 494).

Although Berlin's assertion that the reactionary conservatives "virtually invented" the doctrine that the West was "rotting," cannot be accepted without qualification (What does he make of Rousseau, or of Herder, in particular?), it is certainly true that their relentless expression of this idea rises to a level of polemic that has perhaps rarely been matched. Maistre believed that the French Revolution was a divine punishment visited upon those who had strayed from the Catholic faith. "It is long since such an appalling punishment has been seen, visited on so many sinners" (Maistre, 1965, 50), he announces, but the revolution was, in one of his lines of argumentation, only the manifestation of the evil incarnate of the Enlightenment. He regarded all Enlightenment thought as destructive at its core: Enlightenment philosphers "detect without exception every distinction they do not enjoy; they find fault in every authority; they hate anything above them" (269). He regarded the freewheeling intellectual style of the Enlightenment as a disease of the soul, "an insurrection against God," deserving only of the harshest punishment. Burke's characterizations are less eschatological, but reflect the same theme. "The age of chivalry is gone—that of sophisters, oeconomists, and calculators has succeeded" (Burke, 1790, 89).

Far from believing that anything like progress was occurring, Maistre, in particular, believed, in good Christian tradition, in a Golden Age in the past, an age before the Fall in which everyone possessed divinely-inculcated wisdom. Man's slight capacity for reason or understanding of nature or history is a punishment imposed by God for Original Sin. In Vico this is a doctrine muted to the point of insignificance, and Herder dissociated it totally from his philosophical anthropology. But in the thought of the reactionary conservatives, it looms as a brooding centerpiece, affecting their social thought in manifold and potent ways. Thus, while the Enlightenment and revolution are a revolt against God, they (especially the revolution) are also punishment meted out by God. If this seems contradictory, it should be understood as just another expression of the inherent contradiction between the ethical Christian doctrine of free will, and the Christian philosophy of history in which God is thought either to have determined earthly history, or at least to "intervene" at crucial moments in order to set things on their proper course. The conservatives were what we might call "strong" interventionists, but not full determinists, for the latter implies either that humans have no freedom of will, or that their belief in free will is a kind of diabolical game God plays with his human puppets to some end no one could possibly comprehend.

The reactionaries' vision of the history of human society is thus both a religiously determined and ironic one. On the one hand stands their recognition of history as carnage, a conception within which the Revolution was only one, although admittedly the greatest of upheavals. Burke informs us that "history consists of miseries brought upon the world by pride, ambition, avarice, revenge, lust, sedition, hypocrisy, ungoverned zeal, and all the train of disorderly appetites," and that it is these vices that are the causes of the "miseries," not "kings, governments, priests, or magistrates" (Burke, undated, 156). For Maistre, "war . . . is the habitual condition of mankind" (1965, 61), and the hangman the "cornerstone of society." "Human blood must constantly flow somewhere or other on earth; and that for every nation peace is no more than a respite" (1965, 62). He writes with approval of Louis XIV's atrocities against French Protestants, echoing Machiavelli's dictum that men must be either "caressed or annihilated." He regards war as God's best, most effective means of punishment (superior, evidently, to His alternate means: pestilence, earthquakes, and other disasters). Lammenais remarked that Maistre's work read "as if written on a scaffold." And yet, from this "terrible purification" springs everything good in history. Sounding much like Ferguson or Kant, Maistre insists:

> The true fruits of human nature—the arts, sciences, great enterprises, noble ideas, manly virtues—spring above all from the state of war. It is well known that nations reach the apex of the greatness of which they are capable only after long and bloody wars (1965, 63).

"Blood is the manure of the plant we call *genius*," the mysterious working of God's will in the world (or, we might say, with Hegel, his "cunning of history").

It is thus an understanding of history as a remorseless charnel house that grounds their theory of society. Evil and recalcitrant human nature must be made subject to various "natural" forms of social control. In this they reflect not so much Vico or Herder, but the organicism of Catholic social thought. The conservatives' conception of society, like that of so much early theorizing, is at once empirical and normative, a classical and medieval identification of jus gentium with jus naturale. It is rooted in the twin pillars of authority and common belief as the sine qua non of such social stablity as is attainable in a carnage-ridden world. The facts of human conflict *demand* the imposition of authority and the maintenance of common belief in the form of a state religion. Burke is not without some feeling for the down-trodden and professes a desire to "rescue (workers) from their miserable industry" rather than disturb the "tranquil repose of monastic quietude" (undated, 176), but is prepared to accept their oppression for fear of worse: because "property and liberty require it" (178). The close interpenetration of authority and belief may be seen in Maistre's doctrine that patriotism and religion are identical, because "there is no patriotism without religion." Without religion one's actions are "misguided and degraded," a "mindless selfishness" (1965, 110). Bonald emphasizes the Latin root of the term religion, *religare*, "to bind together," and proclaims that without such binding together no society is possible. For Maistre, "men are made for authority," which emanates from God, a proclamation commanding obedience as proper and necessary on the grounds of our sinful and evil nature.

The image of society that pervades the work of the reactionary conservatives is obviously that of society as an organic whole, derived essentially from Christian teaching. Although all the reactionaries were singleminded in emphasizing society as an organic entity, the most developed form of this appears in Bonald, who formulated his version in a series of analogies likening society to the organic constitution of the individual body and to the family (Bonald, 1880, passim). The God-ordained link of the authority of the sovereign over his subjects is a replication of that of the father over the family. In Bonald's formulation, just as the mind is the "cause" of the functioning of the body and the consequences of this action are its *effects*, within the family the father/husband is held to be the *cause*, the *wife* the *means*, and the children the *effect*, a set of relations directly analogous to that in the state, where the monarch is held to be the *cause*, the ministers the *means*, and the subjects the *effect*. As cause, the father must have both moral authority and literally unlimited physical power. The proper functions of the wife are reproduction and obedience to her husband, while obedience is the sole responsibility of the children. A division of labor in terms of authority is similarly formulated for the larger society. The nobility is charged with all intellectual functions and the general guidance of society, along with its defense, while the "ordinary" classes serve exclusively repro-ductive and economic functions. Among the reactionary conservatives, Bon-ald is perhaps the most sociological, and his analysis of the proper functioning of the family includes an early distinction between the rural and industrial family types (which would later be of some importance for Le Play in his study of European families [1982]). Anticipating many later writers, he argued that the spread of urbanism and industrialism were destructive of the organic unity of the rural family, in undermining its economic inde-pendence and leading to the emergence of individualistic sentiments and actions.

An integral part of the organic metaphor is the idea of slow or gradual growth. Just as organic bodies only gradually assume the properties of their maturity, so also must societies and their subunits grow and change by virtually imperceptible degrees. A quite literal reverence for the "wisdom" of tradition is at the center of the reactionaries' theory of society. Becker and Barnes claim that "what they have accomplished, above all, is an excellent analysis of an ideal type of the traditionalist society in general . . ." (1961, 497). The traditionalism associated with their organicism is the ground of their diatribes against rationalistic theories of social innovation or reform. Particularly anathema are any and all social contract theories and the schemes and proposals for enacted constitutions based upon them. According to Burke, civil society is the offspring of convention, and it follows that "conventions must limit and modify all the descriptions of constitutions which are formed under it" (Burke, undated, 72). If there is anything at all like a contract, it is an understanding between the dead, the living, and the living-to-be, "a fixed compact which holds all physical and all moral each in their appointed place" (110). This is an idea Comte appropriated. And indispensable to the maintenance of tradition, of course, is an organized religion with great social authority. These ideas are echoed by Maistre: "Mankind cannot make a constitution and no legitimate constitution can be written" (Maistre, 1965, 162) for the simple reason that, "every constitution is of divine origin." Institutions should change only with history, custom, climate, and changing political situations, and then only very gradually (100). "Nothing great has great beginnings" (158).

It is of some importance to recognize that the reactionaries imagined the working of authority, however socially necessary, as a function always to be wielded within a tradition of communal religious belief. They display a healthy distrust of *uncontrolled* power. Despite the fact that the main thrust of his polemic remains always on the wisdom of tradition, the whiggish

Irishman Burke worries that constitutionalism would separate secular power from the constraints provided by law and religion. Such power would be "unbounded" (Burke, undated, 68). Bonald, in particular, argues that although sovereignty is acquired solely as a divine gift, its manifestation in our world is properly fragmented: The church, the secular state, the guilds and universities, all have a part in it, and this "pluralism" is a safeguard against tyranny . . . And perhaps most important, he insists that the family must remain independent of state authority in order to retain its idealistic organic unity. The fear of centralization appears in Maistre as well, albeit in softer form. Although "all men are born for monarchy," it becomes clear that the king really expresses the interests and ideals of the aristocracy, a not so surprising idea for one who was himself an aristocrat (see Maistre, 1965, 116, 119). The monarchy is a "centralized aristocracy," and religion, laws, customs, and opinion serve to restrain sovereign power. After observing the consequence of what he regarded as the treasonous actions of the Republicans and others who had appropriated so many high state positions, Maistre concluded that the interests of peace and stability, and of the people generally, were properly served only when aristocrats occupied all positions of importance in the state.

The importance attributed to language by Vico and Herder is present also in the conception of society of the reactionaries, but the *nature* of its importance is different. Whereas Vico and Herder understood language as the medium of human creativity and its manifestation in the imaginative forms of poetry, fable, song, and epic, and as basically constitutive of the culture of any society, the reactionary conservatives perceived in language proof of the divine origin of everything not only human but social as well. Bonald goes to great lengths to establish that language could not have been a human invention, since, for this to have been the case, the prior existence of ideas would have been necessitated. Language must therefore be the creation of God. This logic is then applied to social institutions generally to establish society as of divine origin. Beyond this, language is linked functionally to the principle of tradition. Language is the vehicle of tradition, and no human institution can last very long, Maistre argues, if it has no religious foundation, *and* if it does not have a *name* generated gradually from within the national language, but definitely not the result of rational deliberation (Maistre, 1965, 172). Since God has named everything through a crescive generative process, men have no right to name anything. The introduction of foreign words into a national language is an indicator of its degeneration (176–81). One sees that, despite some similarity of formulation, the reactionary conservatives held a relatively superficial conception of the social significance and functioning of language when contrasted with their Enlightenment-influenced predecessors.

In all of this a rejection of any sort of philosophical individualism is also clearly to be seen. Indeed, the "retrograde school," as Comte called them, is rightly considered to be the central inspiration for a century of social realism in French social thought and developing sociology. They formulate the relation of the individual to society in a twofold manner. On the one hand they attempt to derive the necessary nature of social institutions from the dual nature of the race; on the other, they theorize the individual as a product of society. Humans are, in Bonald's phrase, "naturally depraved"; yet, as Maistre writes, it is necessary to recognize unequivocally the "primacy of society over the individual." It is this dualism that is the main legacy the reactionary conservatives bequeathed to later thinkers. On these and closely related matters, the striking contrast of their philosophical anthropology with that of Vico and Herder is clear, for the latter insisted not only on the organic nature of culture and the importance of language, but also attempted to conjoin this to the principle of the individual and individual creativity as culture creators and agents of social change. In this regard the relation between their theories of progress and their philosophical anthroplogy is all-important. The reactionaries reject the principle of progress on the basis of their philosophical anthropology, whereas both Vico and Herder advance variants of that idea on the basis of their Enlightenment-influenced philo-sophical anthropology. For Vico and Herder the future is open to the working of human agency; for the reactionaries it is closed by virtue of the immutability of the soul under the doctrine of original sin, and the functional imperatives of authority and belief derived from this.

Nowhere is the opposition to the Enlightenment in the thought of the reactionary conservatives more evident than in their understanding of knowledge and its social function. On the one hand, it should be recognized that they shared with Herder, in particular, but Vico as well, a rejection of the positivistic empiricist epistemology so central to Enlightenment thought. However, unlike Vico and Herder, their outlook was basically antiscientific, at least insofar as a scientific approach to social life was concerned.

Vico's formulation of a historically oriented social science was based on his conviction that the sociocultural order, being entirely a product of human collective activity, was therefore necessarily meaningful to its creators and could therefore be *interpreted* in a manner which he thought of as essentially objective and scientific in character. The reactionary conservatives, on the other hand, believed that any knowledge of society that we might come by was, necessarily at best, severely limited in scope. Maistre maintains that our knowledge of society can only be intuitive, like that of primitive men during the Golden Age (Maistre, 1965, 16). Our ignorance is part of the eternal punishment visited upon man by God, and therefore inescapable. Berlin says that Maistre seeks "to establish the eternal frontier of our knowledge and power, to demarcate them from what cannot in principle even be known or adduced by men" (Berlin, 1957, 110). It is clear that this demarcation prohibits virtually any serious application of reason to human affairs. Burke, too, holds that whatever knowledge we have of human affairs must be intuitive. Ultimate causes, he says in a critique of Bacon, cannot be discerned by the mind of man. Whatever we know of society is not only intuitive, but a revelation of God (Burke, undated, 201–202).

What we may learn from history is that the application of reason is folly. Since, according to Burke, "the nature of man is intricate," it follows that "the objects of society are of the greatest complexity" (Burke, undated, 73) and must give us pause in contemplating any sort of intervention. Although history "is a great volume unrolled for our instruction, drawing the materials for future wisdom from the past errors and infirmities," we glean from this only the dictum that—in anticipation of Spencer three generations later—it is folly to attempt to apply reason to the remaking of human institutions. Vico constructed a patterned philosophy of history in the spirit of the Enlightenment, but the reactionaries rejected in principle any sort of historical pattern. Not only is it the case that "the splendid theory of invariable laws would lead us straight to fatalism and make an automaton of man: (Maistre, 1965, 217), but there can, in any case, be no laws to discover. History unfolds not, as Vico and Herder would have it, through the collective creation and modification of cultures by participants in a community, but by the actions of great men acting in the grip of divine inspiration. Vico—and to a lesser extent, Herder—formulated a theory of history and culture while also attempting to retain a theoretical status for the individual, and in so doing took a giant step in the direction of transcending the liberal Enlightenment formula of deducing and analyzing society from the standpoint of putative qualities of human nature. The problem of the reactionary conservatives was defined by their *interest* in undercutting and abolishing any theoretical status for the individual in social thought or theory of any sort (except the actions of great men). Although they grounded their *polemic* against the Enlightenment in the fundamental Christian doctrine of the dual nature of human nature, their technical "solution" of the problem took the form of developing the idea of the organic nature of human social life into a more elaborated, more *sociological* doctrine, in which society takes absolute priority over the individual, the "social realism" paradigm so important in the sociology of Comte and those who continued his tradition.

CONCLUSION

We have seen in earlier chapters that the philosophical and technical assumptions embedded in the thought of the Enlightenment philosophers made it difficult for them to formulate the idea of society and culture as independent planes of analysis, even though the idea of a human science was becoming strongly implanted during the course of the eighteenth century. It is fascinating and ironic that the idea of the primacy of the social emerged most clearly within the framework of the Christian tradition. And this is the reason why Comte, although inspired by Enlightenment ideals and epistemology, drew upon this tradition as it was formulated in the work of the reactionary conservatives following the French Revolution.

There was both triumph and tragedy in this. The triumph lay in the fact that, in the 1830s, Comte was finally able to synthesize these elements into the first sociological system and thus set the stage for the continuing development of a more or less scientific sociology; the tragedy lay in his ignorance of (or disregard for) the earlier synthesis of Enlightenment with Christian elements attempted by Vico and Herder. Vico and Herder had taken a large step in the direction of a scientific science of society by transcending the natural law framework of liberal social philosophy, by formulating a conception of culture as a collective meaning system, and by suggesting a method whereby it could be studied. But the "enlightened" elements in this early synthesis were lost in the "revision" of the reactionary conservatives.

By the turn of the nineteenth century, virtually all of the elements essential for the working out of the early "classical" theories of midcentury were present. The second chapter in the development of a systematized science of society would take the form of syntheses constructed out of elements drawn from the competing philosophical anthropologies, theories of social change, and conceptions of social knowledge, syntheses created by the great exemplars of the century—Comte, Spencer, Hegel, and Marx. To these we turn in Part II.

The Sociologies of the Nineteenth Century

7

AUGUSTE COMTE
Sociology and the Enlightenment Vision

In Part I, I have tried to show that the emerging sociological perspective of the eighteenth century can be accounted for, at the level of ideas, by the intellectual struggles of secularized social philosophers with the dilemmas inherent in the problematics of progress, human nature, and the possibilities of a human science. Both the growing appreciation of the diversity of human cultures and the banishing of evil from its Christian locus in the human soul, were changes that tended to undermine the old paradigm of explaining human behavior by invoking qualities imputed human nature, and to redirect theorizing in the direction of a conception of a distinct social domain amenable to scientific analysis. The contradiction between the secularized conceptions of natural law as imposed or immanent, and the empiricist epistemology, originating with Bacon, was exposed by Hume, who grounded the human science of the future in the same essentially phenomenological frame as the natural sciences, thereby providing philosophical ground for what would become an expanding inclination in social philosophy and social science. At the same time, the idea of progress, increasingly rooted in a utopian conception of human perfectibility, provided the ideological foundation for belief in the possibility, even the indispensibility, of a human science. But the doctrine of progress was ambiguous, two-sided in its meaning. On the one hand, it was understood as a possibility resting on the exercise of the human will, and thus located in the concrete realm of human action; on the other, there was the tendency, powerfully influenced by earlier Christian thought, to attribute progress to a secular equivalent of God's hand in history.

These dilemmas were interlaced with one another, and an understanding of their impact on an emerging sociological perspective, as I have argued, is greatly enhanced by attending to these relationships. Despite the skepticism of thinkers like Hume, Rousseau, and Montesquieu, the siren song of progress as suprahuman historical force and future necessity continued to be understood in terms of the idea of natural law—a seeming natural affinity—in no small degree because the idea of natural law provided the future-oriented progressive thinkers of the time with a ground for optisim regarding the shape of that future. The mechanical conception of human nature as environmentally formed that dominated eighteenth-century thought was also conditioned by the century's idea of knowledge as knowledge of laws. But such a conception of human nature seemed inconsistent with the ideal of human freedom, a principle seemingly indispensible to any conception of human beings as moral agents. And finally, there were the problems of theodicy and diversity: If history was and would continue to be a tale of progress, on the one hand, and if, on the other, human nature was both a fixed array of entities but no longer the repository of evil, how could the horrors of actual earthly existence be accounted for? And how could the doctrine of progress be reconciled with the belief in the fixity of human nature?

In Part II we shall see how these questions led into and channeled the emergence of the major sociologies of the nineteenth century, those of Comte, Spencer, Hegel, and Marx and Engels.

By Comte's time, roughly the third through the sixth decades of the century, the actual shape of the new society, necessarily beyond the vision of earlier thinkers (even, in important respects, Adam Smith) was coming into being in increasingly well-defined shape. A class of *organizers* of *industry* rather than just merchant capitalists, quantitative growth of the *industrial proletariat*, expansion of the state bureaucracies (especially in France and Prussia), along with a burgeoning gaggle of "free-floating" intellectuals and the early stirrings of mass culture, in short, the social structures most definitive of the modern world, were becoming prominent enough to demand theoretical recognition and explanation. There were, of course, a variety of responses to these and other aspects of modernism. The Romantic movement, in its essentials, was a rejection of everything mechanistic and thereby "soulless." There were socialists whose utopianism took the form of rural communal movements, along with others who tried to come to some kind of terms with the new industrialism. It was also the time during which the modern "alienated intellectual" made appearance (see Graña, 1967). Of immediate importance for Comte and his mentor Saint-Simon was the rapid expansion of the numbers of educated intellectuals, especially in Paris, the creators of a large bohemian community and the modern form of bohemian life (see Manuel, 1956, 1962).

Saint-Simon and Comte, living and working under the new conditions of the beginning of modern industrial organization and the growth of what Mannheim would later call "free-floating intellectuals," along with the French Revolution and the conservative reaction it inspired, did not reject Enlightenment ideas, but they did reformulate them. By way of introduction to Comte, we will briefly consider the work of his predecessor and mentor, Saint-Simon.

SAINT-SIMON

The comte de Saint-Simon,[1] born into the French aristocracy in 1760, was without doubt one of the most fascinating figures of modern history. He was a rebellious child who refused his first Communion at the age of thirteen, an act for which his father promptly had him thrown in prison. Always a romantic, he tried to enlist in the army at the age of sixteen, but failed; however, he received his commission the following year. By the age of eighteen he was a captain and within a year saw action in the Caribbean and was present at the British surrender at Yorktown. For a time imprisoned by the British, he later developed a proposal for a canal across Central America linking the oceans. His later life was as eventful as his youth: He once reportedly traveled to Geneva to propose to Madame de Stael, claiming that the world should not be denied children by the union of the greatest man and greatest woman of the time. In order to finance his grandiose schemes for the reorganization of society, he speculated in confiscated church lands and after initial failure, realized substantial success. He later fell into poverty and was fortuitously rescued by his former valet, with whom he lived and who supported him for several years. His intellectual productions began to appear in 1802 and continued to his death in 1825. During his later years, from 1818 to 1824, Comte was his personal secretary (having succeeded August Thierry), and some of the work published under the master's name was undoubtedly written by Comte. A disagreement over some of this led Comte to break off relations, and he not only failed to acknowledge Saint-Simon's clear influence on his own work, but had only the harshest of words for him, once referring to him as a "depraved juggler."

We may begin by recalling Condorcet's proclamations on progress, particularly in the course of his ninth stage, from DesCartes to the present (the last decade of the eighteenth century). For Condorcet changes in politics and society were consequences of advances in the intellectual realm, especially the sciences. The future would bring further advance, a prognosis rooted in Condorcet's conviction that the human domain, just as nature, was in its totality subject to universal law.

Saint-Simon's work is at once an extension of Condorcet's and a clear anticipation of Comte's, even though it is more materialistic than either. He agreed that there had been an evolution of the mind which he characterized in religious terms as a movement from idolatry through polytheism, invented by the Greeks, through the deism of the Romans, to the idea of a universe governed by multiple causes, and that the period in Europe from Charlemagne to the present had been a preparation for the final positive state in which the conception of a single universal law ruling the universe would emerge (see Taylor, 1975, 115). This final stage would culminate in the acceptance of the scientific worldview, in which all knowledge would be modeled after physics.

There are no phenomena which cannot be observed from the viewpoint of

---

[1] For a detailed treatment of Saint-Simon's life, see Dondo (1955); for a briefer one, Taylor (1975, Introduction). See also Iggers, 1958.

the physics of inorganic bodies or the physics of organic bodies, which is physiology. (Taylor, 1975, 113)

His ideal of unified science embracing the organic and inorganic, and his argument that the reorganization of society could proceed only on the foundation of such a science, were the bases of his attack on the French scientific establishment of the time. He accused the scientists of unconcern for the unity of social purpose and the knowledge necessary to achieve it and even went so far as to prepare a treatise expressly for them, entitled *Travail sur la gravitation universelle*, which was intended to provide a foundation from which all other scientific principles would be deduced! Here was the seed of Comte's hierarchy of the sciences.

Along more practical lines—again anticipating Comte—he devised a scheme for the political reorganization of Europe and bombarded kings, ministers, politicians, and others with this and other proposals. Late in life he founded a sect, the "New Christianity," which his disciples, especially Enfantin, were quite successful in spreading through parts of Europe.

Saint-Simon, however, was extraordinarily unsystematic in the expression of his thought, much of which was polemical, anecdotal, and epigrammatic. So that although a good deal of what Comte eventually introduced into his positivistic system was first expressed by Saint-Simon, it is only with Comte that it is rendered in systematic and more or less scholarly form.[2] His deathbed statement, "It would be wrong to conclude that religion tends to disappear, only that it should adjust itself to scientific progress," is an apt prolegomenon to the work of Comte.

AUGUSTE COMTE

Comte was born into a Catholic Royalist family in 1798. In 1814 the family moved to Paris, where Auguste was accepted at the prestigous École Poly-technic. Like Saint-Simon he was somewhat of a rebel; in 1816 he was one of the ringleaders of a student revolt. Later, he was employed part-time at a miserable salary at the école grading mathematics papers, an occupation for which his training had prepared him, but he never realized his wish to become a professor. One wonders what the shape of positivism—and sociology—might have been if he had. In 1818 he became secretary to Saint-Simon and remained with him for about six years, at which time he broke away and set himself up as an independent intellectual. Two years later, after delivering only a few of what was to have been a year-long series of lectures, he had a nervous breakdown and was institutionalized. After several months he was rescued by his wife, a former prostitute who remained devoted to him throughout their sixteen years together. But Comte was an incredibly difficult person to live with, and she finally left him in 1842.[3] In 1844 he

[2] For an argument downplaying Saint-Simon's importance for understanding Comte, see Simpson (1969, 3).

[3] A measure of Comte's high estimation of himself is reflected in the fact that he signed his marriage certificate "Brutus Bonaparte Comte."

fell in love with a woman named Clothilde de Vaux, with whom he had an apparently platonic relationship until her death a year later. After this he decided to practice what he called "cerebral hygiene," avoiding all works with which he disagreed, not only in order to secure the mental tranquility and harmony necessary to continue his work, but also apparently as an application of his "positive" theory of the relation between mind and body, which emphasized the dependence of physical health on mental harmony.[4]

Comte's intellectual life can be separated into three periods. During his Saint-Simonian period and its aftermath, he published several works, the most important being his 1922 essay "Prospectus des travaux scientifiques nécessaires pour réorganiser la société," in which he condemned the political struggles of the time and proposed that the society of the future would have to transcend politics and take the form of a new order in which scientists would replace priests and industrialists replace soldiers. This essay was reprinted and appended to his last work many years later to indicate the continuity of his life's work. During the second period, following his mental recovery, he published the massive *Cours de philsophie positive* (between 1830 and 1842) which was translated and edited by Harriet Martineau as *The Course of Positive Philosophy*, in which he laid out his system in detail. In 1844 he prepared a succinct essay summarizing this system as the introduction to his book on astronomy, "Discours sur l'esprit positive," and following this, a somewhat lengthier statement translated as *A General View of Positivism*. Between 1851 and 1854 he brought out his *Système de politique positive, ou traité de sociologie, instituant la réligion de l'humanité*, in four volumes, later translated as *A System of Positive Polity*, in which he reiterates everything set down in the *Cours*, but places considerably more emphasis on human feeling, as against the intellect, and in which he includes a long eulogy idealizing women, probably in consequence of the tragic episode with Clothilde de Vaux. (In the following discussion I will, in general, avoid the encumbrance of identifying the various ideas of Comte as "early," "middle," or "late," except where necessary, since his system is, as he himself said, an extraordinarily unified one.)

Comte is often called the "father" of sociology[5] for several reasons: (1) most obviously, for establishing the linguistic hybrid by which the discipline continues to be designated (in 1839, because he objected to Quetelet's use of the term "social physics," which had been in common usage during the early part of the nineteenth century [see Quetelet, 1835]); (2) more importantly, for his claim that social life has characteristics and therefore laws of its own, and so must be recognized as a domain of analysis independent of others; (3) for establishing social statics and social dynamics as the principle branches of sociology (although both Condorcet and Bichat had anticipated him in this; (see Comte's references in 1875–1877, 3, 528), and for carrying

---

[4] It is of some interest that Comte's physician, who was philosophically a disciple of Comte and a believer in his positivist system, interpreted Comte's final illness in terms of this conception of "positive medicine." Comte, he diagnosed, fell ill due to "agitation" following the death of a disciple, made a partial recovery, but experienced a relapse that proved fatal when another disciple, a certain Blignères, published an "exposé" of positivism.

[5] The "father-in-chief" by Hankins, and "a better founding father than Saint-Simon" by Gouldner, because of the latter's socialism!

through a form of sociological analysis in these terms; (4) for his discussion of the methods proper to sociology and the relation of these to those employed in other disciplines; (5) for his delineation of the so-called "law of the three stages" (or "states"); (6) for his doctrine of the hierarchy of the sciences; and (7) in his later years, for his prescriptions for a universal religion.

Sociologists and others of a later day have not, of course, received all of this with equal enthusiasm. The main stream of the discipline has generally accepted the first three, been equivocal about the fourth, but quite unequivocally rejected the latter three.[6] However, the law of the three stages and the hierarchy of the sciences are not only central to Comte's positivism, but were formulated, as I shall argue, as a solution to the unresolved dilemmas discussed in the first part of this book. We shall consider Comte's work within this framework.

THE THEORY OF SOCIAL STATICS: COMTE'S RESOLUTION OF THE DILEMMA OF THE DOCTRINES OF PROGRESS AND THE FIXITY OF HUMAN NATURE

Comte divided sociology into two main parts: social statics and social dynamics. Social statics corresponds more or less to what we today would refer to as social structure, social dynamics to the history-long process of social change that embraces all of humanity. In his theory of social statics Comte is concerned both with linking together theoretically what he thinks of as levels of social organization, and with grounding this conception of social structure on his theory of human nature.

Although he systematically excluded the individual from any theoretical status in his sociology, Comte nonetheless worked out a highly complex scheme of human nature, the "Tableau cérébrale." He holds that the individual must be thought of as having a dual *nonintellectual* nature, on the one hand selfish or egoistic, but on the other socially inclined and altruistic. "Within the individual are to be found both individual and social or altruistic propensities, or instincts, but the former are overwhelmingly dominant" (1896, 2, 277–278). These include the sexual, nutritive, maternal, military, and industrial impulses, as well as those of pride and vanity, all egoistic in nature, but also the altruistic ones of friendship, veneration, and kindness,

---

[6] Reactions to Comte's work among sociologists have always tended to the extreme. John S. Mill had high praise for the *Cours* (but not the *Système*), assigning Comte a rank equal to that of Leibniz and DesCartes (Mill, 1865, 199–200), despite various criticisms of Comte, and despite the fact that he also compared him to Calvin, for, "taking a leaf out of the book of the despised Protestantism" (1961, 144–145). Herbert Spencer, in his "Reasons for Dissenting from the Positive Philosophy of M. Comte," was mostly negative. Among recent and contemporary sociologists, the pattern continues to prevail. "To know Comte's writings is indispensable to an understanding of both sociology in general and of research and explanation in its subsidiary fields. . . ," writes George Simpson (1969, v), but Andreski calls Comte a practitioner of "pompous verbiage" and "a true begetter of the style dominant in the social sciences today" and contends that the "Communists have implemented Comte in the name of Marx" (1974, 13, 14).

to be ultimately realized with the advent and spread of the Religion of Humanity (for a discussion see Aron, 1965, 89–90; also de Coppens, 1976, Chap. 2). One sees here the clear secular reincarnation of the Augustinian dualism of orginal nature.

Throughout his writings Comte strives everywhere to disqualify the individual as a legitimate sociological category. He inveighs, for instance, against the individualism of the political economists following Adam Smith, judging their work to be "metaphysical throughout" and maintaining that it "systematizes anarchy" (1896, 2, 206). His attack on the status of the individual in economic theory has its parallel in his excoriation of the celebration of the individual in political theory. He denounces the doctrine of popular sovereignty on the grounds that it condemns the superior to "an arbitrary dependence on the multitude of the inferior" (155–156) and argues that public order is dependent on "the uniform assent of the individual wills to invariable and general rules, adapted to fix . . . the true idea of the public good" (169–170). "All true moral order is incompatible with the existing vagabond liberty of individual minds" (170), and individualism is assuredly "the disease of the western world." Positivism itself, in its totality, Comte intended as a systematic refutation of the doctrine of individualism and individual rights (see Becker, 1968, 355).

It is obvious that Comte's rejection of methodological individualism as the foundation of sociology follows from his rejection of economic, political, and ethical individualism. It then follows for him that the family constitutes the basic and indispensable unit connecting the individual to society. "The whole human race," Comte quite astonishingly suggests, "might be conceived as the gradual development of a single family" (1896, 1, 145). This is effected through an organic union (decidedly not, Comte made clear, a mere parallel presence) of the different natures of men and women. Women possess a greater "social feeling" but men are more rational. On the basis of this presumption, it is one of the tasks of sociology to show that "each sex has a natural function in the economy of the human family" and "prove that the equality of the sexes . . . is incompatible with all social existence" (1896, 2, 284).[7]

The family is not only an organic unity resting on an instinctive social feeling, but simultaneously performs the function of curbing the egoistic impulses so destructive to social order. In the individual, "the lowest and personal propensities have preponderance over the nobler" (277), and it is the office of the family to "subordinate" these to the social impulses. Here Comte stands under the influence of his conservative forerunners. Central to their thought as well was the doctrine of the repressive function of the family (see Comte's remarks on "the illustrious Bonald" regarding the family: 150). Like them, Comte wants no part of what he thinks are the implications of making the individual's real but exaggerated capacity for reason and consequent claims to rights of all sorts, a basic category of social analysis. Granting the individual theoretical status in his sociology, Comte

---

[7] Comte's views on women do not appear to have undergone any really *fundamental* change between publication of the *Cours* and the *Système*, despite the passages idealizing them in the latter.

evidently thought, would open the theoretical gates to everything the philosophers of the Enlightenment—especially Rousseau, who was something of a bête noire for Comte—had celebrated in the name of individual freedom. For Comte individual freedom was unprincipled moral license, and the play of individual sentiments, if left to itself, "would put a stop to social progression in all important respects" (293).

While the family serves the function of creating morality, it is not an institution that can or should attempt to foster development of the innate intellectual faculties. This is an office appropriate to more comprehensive forms of social organization, in particular, society itself. While society for Comte is to be thought of as comprised of families, it nevertheless assumes properties that differentiate it structurally and functionally from the family. With some oversimplification, his theory of society may be thought of as composed essentially of three elements: (1) the expansion of the division of labor and the consequences of this, (2) the function of government, and (3) the necessity of social inequality.

The division of labor may be contrasted with the family in that it is based on rationalistic or utilitarian considerations (on this point recall Hume and the other Scottish moralists). Its expansion is therefore a progressive tendency; it is "the principle by which alone general society could be developed and extended" (293). However, Comte also had some serious reservations about the "dysfunctional" consequences of the division of labor that both anticipate later and reiterate earlier thought. Anticipating Durkheim's theory of anomie, he says that the division of labor threatens "to decompose (society) into a multitude of unconnected corporations, which seem almost not to belong to the same society" (293). Like Smith and Ferguson, he also thought that the division of labor tended to engender a sense of dependency, which he deplored but did not dwell on (perhaps because of the seeming inconsistency between this and his rejection of individualism).

Comte's antidote for these and other difficulties presented by the expanding division of labor was more government, which would have to "intervene in all aspects of the functioning of the social economy" (214); the more extensive the former, the more necessary the latter becomes. So coercive power or authority is something society cannot do without. Despite this admission, Comte nevertheless wanted to think of government as exercising mainly a moral influence, based increasingly on the growth of science, and especially of course, sociology, as requiring a minimum of force. On this point he stands as a major precursor of Durkheim. Indeed, the prevision achieved through sociology, he evidently actually thought, would eventually make the exercise of force all but unnecessary.[8]

The division of labor not only requires expansion of government, but implies the inevitability of inequality manifest in several spheres of experience.

> An elementary subordination must always be growing out of the distribution

---

[8] For an extended discussion of Comte's conception of force as central to his system, see Marvin (1965), Chap. 8.

of human operations. (This is) not only material but intellectual and moral; that is, it requires, besides practical submission, a corresponding degree of real confidence in both the capacity and probity of the special organs to whom a function, hitherto universal, is confided (1896, 2, 295).

In this system of stratification, ranks are assigned by Comte in terms of the generality of the function performed. Intellectuals exercise the most generalized function, so they are assigned the top rung. Laborers, because of their specialized functions, are at the bottom. Every occupation, including those of artists, serves a function strengthening the unity of the whole. In this connection, we should take special note of Comte's awareness that the system of inequality in industrial society does not do away with the need for legitimation; industrial society also requires "intellectual and moral" justification.

It was therefore for good reason that Comte, in the *Système*, finally came to think of this system as a religion. Comte expounds a principle that is ever since to be found in the *mainstream* of the social sciences: that all social systems require inequality and that inequality must be established and made acceptable to those subordinated within it. For Comte legitimation in the positive society of the future would take the form of teaching the positive philosophy, and especially sociology, to the workers. Indeed, he believed that his system would find its most receptive ground among the working class, because (in an argument not too dissimilar to that of Veblen nearly a century later) of the practical circumstances in which they find themselves (Comte, 1844, 74–75), and that positivism would come to power through a coalition of positive philosophers and workers (*Système*, in Lenzer, 1975, 367ff.). Scientists, on the other hand (as mentioned earlier), could be expected to reject his system (as they were for the most part already doing) because the increasing specialization of the scientific pursuits tended to freeze their thought at the metaphysical stage of development.

We now see that, despite his insistence on the social as an independent domain requiring a special science, Comte's characterization of social structure rests on a philosophical anthropology that combines various elements of Enlightenment and pre-Enlightenment thought. From the latter are taken the Christian dualism of human nature and the distrust of the individual and defense of repressive forms of social control that follow from this; from the former comes the emphasis on the potential of the intellectual faculties and their linkage to different types of social structure. Comte brought these elements together in a fashion that reconciled the Enlightenment doctrine of progress with the philosophical anthropology that viewed human nature as uniform and constant. He accomplished this by formulating the principle of reason as a social function and maintaining that it had undergone and would continue to exhibit a historical growth as a movement making universal history.

COMTE'S THEORY OF SOCIAL DYNAMICS: SCIENCE AND THE LAW OF THE THREE STAGES

Comte regarded his theory of the three stages of societal development as his most innovative achievement. He proposed that the history-making advance of the mind had created successively three types of society, which he labeled "theological," "metaphysical," and "positive," the last just beginning to emerge. What is essential to each of these types is their mental or intellectual outlook; the organizational aspects of each, for him, apparently must be understood as consequences of the former (although he is not entirely clear about this, in some passages allowing for degrees of reciprocal influence). The mind in its functioning, Comte says, must be understood in its milieu, and in the stages of human prehistory that lie almost entirely beyond our powers of empirical reconstruction, the powers of the mind, relative to the personal or individual instincts, were undoubtedly exceptionally weak. To be sure, human social existence would at all times have been impossible apart from at least some rudimentary practical intelligence, a *bon sens* of a sort. Human history is a long struggle of the mind to extricate itself from this early and almost endlessly protracted state in which its powers were indeed "feeble," to the very recent past in which it begins to command and canalize the individual and social instincts, themselves constant, rather than merely serving as their practical instrument. In his *Tableau cérébrale*, intelligence has the function of "steering" or *progressively constituting* the active and affective components of human nature. "Feeling," the emotional side of human nature, becomes progressively constituted in communities of increasing scale: it takes "civic" form in antiquity, "collective" form in the Middle Ages, and will be universal in the future, coming to constitute the sentimental foundation of a universal order in which evil is banished.

The theological stage is defined by its fundamentally religious outlook, and so encompasses the vastly greater part of human history. It is perhaps for this reason that Comte subdivided it into three subperiods, which he called "fetishistic," "polytheistic," and "monotheistic." Fetishism refers to a form of explanation of the world in terms of the belief that external bodies have within themselves some principle of life of their own. Polytheism is distinguished from fetishism as a belief in invisible beings distinct from the empirically experienced diversity of the world. Monotheism condenses the explanatory principle into a supernatural unity. The change from fetishism to a polytheistic outlook is an advance because it necessarily involves a much freer and speculative exercise of the imagination. Monotheism is superior to polytheism in being "an imperfect way of philosophizing" and an essential phase in the "constant development of human speculation" (Comte, 1844, 6); it "joins the present state of the human spirit indissolubly to the totality of its antecedent states" (4).

Related to the collective outlook defining the reality of a stage (or subperiod) are a variety of organizational characteristics. Central among these in the case of theological societies is a movement in the direction of an established professional priesthood that has the historic role of advancing the speculative function. The metaphysical stage, identified with the period following the Middle Ages and especially the Enlightenment, is one during which "reason acquires a greater extension"; in fact, in Comte's judgment, it becomes "exaggerated." Nevertheless, it was an essential stage in that it assisted the basic direction of modern civilization by gradually decomposing the theological system and served the important transitional function of advancing familiarity with the idea of regularity. The metaphysical (or critical-metaphysical) was—and there are still-powerful vestiges—essentially transitional, however, for the sheer play of reason always "tends toward a futile restoration of the theological state of mind" (1844, 10).

The positivist, or empirical-scientific stage into which, according to Comte, the advanced European societies were entering, is defined by its empiricist doctrine of the basis of belief, its conception of knowledge as relative, and (derived from the critical-metaphysical stage) its search for laws. This type of society, Comte argued (as had Saint-Simon before him), would be organized with sociologists headed by Comte himself at the top, together with a panoply of scientists and industrialists to manage the necessary organization of industry, and workers performing specialized tasks at the bottom. This was not, however, just another utopian scheme along Platonic lines, where all positions were essentially fixed. Although he greatly admired the Indian caste system, Comte believed that talent was distributed more or less evenly among individuals, and so it was necessary to provide some degree of opportunity for their expression in industrial society. The Comtean hierarchically ordered society would be one to some extent open to those displaying merit, although private ownership and free competition—institutions uncomfortably close to "anarchical" individualism—would not be allowed. In this respect Comte's utopia sounds closer to state socialism than to free enterprise capitalism. Comte recognizes the inevitability of social mobility in the expansion of industrial society, but insists that it be accommodated to the principle of hierarchy itself, in the form of an incredibly doctrinally rigid system presided over by Comte's cadre of sociologist-priests. This is transparently authoritarian. It is a measure of Comte's faith in the power of his own analysis that, with a serene confidence, he is able to dismiss the need for force in maintaining order in this system. Rather, the positivist doctrine itself, when recognized as true by everyone, would find nothing but morally committed adherents. Given this analysis, it seems that government would become little more than a succession of moral exercises on the part of its officials.

The genius of Comte's conception of the three stages lies in the fact that, far from rejecting the past as having any relevance for the present or future—even as a lesson in what to avoid, in discerning Hegel's "cunning of history," as it were—the stage theory incorporates that past as providing social elements that become constitutive of present and future. Slavery, for example, common to societies in the polytheistic period, made its contribution by inculcating habits of discipline essential for later forms of society. The separation of sacred and secular authority achieved during the monotheistic period Comte regarded as its greatest contribution to the times that succeeded it. Even the essentially transitional critical-metaphysical stage established the principle of regularity, or law, without which positive science would be unimaginable. The radical left has made its contribution too. The Communists, "put forth the question of property, which evidently needs a moral solution" (*Système*, in Lenzer, 1973, 362).

Through this scheme Comte "solved" the problem of evil by reformulating the shaky Enlightenment faith in reason as the force, partly realized, partly potential, for future reconstruction, in conservative terms. Whereas Enlightenment thought had been caught between the tendency to theoretically reconstitute the Christian conception of human nature by assigning it a positive valence, on the one hand, and the necessity of accounting for the continuing presence of evil in the world, on the other, in one fell swoop Comte incorporated all the evils of history into his theory of the three stages and pronounced them essential to the historical process itself. In Christian theology evil was forever (until Judgment Day) a necessary worldly presence; without it there could be no understanding of the good (nicely put in Herder's pithy aphorism: "Folly must appear that wisdom might surmount it"). For Comte, evil has the status of a historical irony approaching a dialectic: It continuously creates the force that ultimately brings about its own extinction. Comte's law of the three stages is in this sense a metaphysical secular theodicy that resolves the incompatibility between the enlightened faith in progress and the problem of evil.

In adopting the conservative doctrine of the overwhelming importance of continuity and tradition, and thereby accommodating the existence of evil to the idea of progress, Comte was also able to contextualize, or relativize, the post-Revolutionary sense of cultural and social dissolution within the historical process. For Comte, feudal society was surely in process of dissolution, but this was a good and necessary thing, a preparation for the rise of positivity in which the essence of Catholicism would be preserved. Catholicism, says Comte, was an effort to organize humanity, "made under intellectual and social conditions which precluded the possibility of success," . . . and "Positivism will always acknowledge the close relation between (itself) and the memorable effort of medieval Catholicism" (1875–1877, 69). It was such statements that led Thomas Huxley to label the religion of humanity "Catholicism minus Christianity."

The essence of the theory of the three stages was a fusion of liberal and conservative thought that Comte summed up in his aphorism that progress was the growth of order, that progress and order were two sides of the same process irrevocably wedded together. He showed that conservatism, with its central principle of the organic nature of things, including society, need not be just a static conception of social order rebelling against any sort of change, but could be constituent of change itself, in fact, the inner principle of progress. The problem that Vico and Herder faced but failed to resolve—Vico because his thought remained within a fundamentally religious framework, Herder because he never reconciled his passion for everything individual with his organic conception of society—Comte resolved in his syncretic version of history.

If human history is in process of culminating in a new age marked by the ascendance of science, what precisely is the relation between the origin and growth of the sciences themselves and the three stages of societal growth? Comte's answer to this question is less than satisfactory.

First, with regard to the growth of the sciences, he claims to have discovered a "great fundamental law," in which societies themselves, like "each branch of our knowledge . . . pass successively through three different theoretical conditions: the Theological or fictitious, the Metaphysical, or abstract, and the Scientific, or positive" (1896, 1, 1–2). These stages, however, do not actually correspond very well with the stages of *societal* change. Astronomy, for instance, was a positive science since Alexandria, but physics became so only with Galileo, and chemistry even later. Sociology became metaphysical at the hands of Aristotle (during a phase of the theological stage), advanced somewhat with Montesquieu (over two millennia later!), whose contribution was to conceive of social phenomena as subject to "invariable laws" (a misrepresentation of Montesquieu), but remained basically metaphysical. Condorcet's sociology was "premature" because true social science can only be established "after the revolutionary spirit has begun to decline" (1896, 2, 302).

In this connection, Comte in various passages also points out how developments *within* a science follow on one another. This process is one in which the critical attitude is especially important, in order to "disengage real science from the influence of the old metaphysical philosophy" (1896, 1, 310). Comte himself frequently undertakes this task. He attacks Leibniz's mathematics (the calculus), for example, as "radically vicious," declaring "the notion of small quantities to be a false idea," . . . it being "impossible to conceive of them clearly, although we may sometimes fancy that we do" (728). The division of chemistry into organic and inorganic he declares "irrational" and "impossible to maintain" (330).

Second, the growth of the sciences has been sequential: the appearance of each has had as its necessary requisite the development—up to a point, at least—of those others thought to be more fundamental. Thus, the order in which they have become, or are still in process of becoming positive, is astronomy (itself dependent on mathematics), physics, chemistry, biology, and finally, social physics or sociology. Sociology, for Comte, is "rooted in biology," which in turn, was possible only after the development of chemistry into an authentic positive science. Montesquieu's sociology, like Condorcet's, was "premature" because "no social science was possible before the development of biology" (1896, 2, 201).[9] The reason for this lies in the alleged differences in the complexity of the different sciences, which will be discussed in the following section.

THE DOCTRINE OF THE HIERARCHY OF THE SCIENCES: COMTE'S RESOLUTION OF THE DILEMMA OF THE NATURE OF A HUMAN SCIENCE AND THE PROBLEM OF HUMAN NATURE

Although sentimental human nature is uniform and fixed, the forms of social organization that constitute its manifestations change historically through the growing capacity of the mind. But this implies that knowledge of human nature *as such* would qualify at best as inadequate and at worst as irrelevant, in discharging the function of guiding the future social reconstruction. Knowledge of a fixed human nature, Comte evidently realized, cannot constitute the basis for understanding social change. The seeming implication is that the process of change must be understood on its own

---

[9] Aside from its validity, this principle allows Comte to dismiss earlier developments in a science. This is especially true of sociology, for which Comte clearly wanted as few forerunners of himself as he could possibly justify, since he considered himself its founder. Everyone previous is conveniently dismissed as metaphysical. The list is scurrilously brief, including only the three mentioned above: Aristotle, Montesquieu, Condorcet.

terms, and it is but one step further to the notion that this demands a science of its own. The social must be conceived of as a domain requiring its own independent explanatory science, a domain sui generis. Yet, at the same time, the realm of knowledge for Comte had to be a unified one, if as so many of the Enlightenment philosophers always insisted, it were to be capable of accomplishing the enormous task with which it is charged: the remaking of human morality. And Comte embraced this basic axiom with a passion exceeding any of his eighteenth century predecessors. "The positive spirit will embrace all and systematize human morality" (1844, 52), he writes. Fragmented knowledge was at best inadequate knowledge, at worst—as with Hegel, perhaps the greatest metaphysician of theoretical unity—no knowledge at all. Comte has nothing but words of condemnation for the current array of what he regarded as disunited sciences and for the scientists who, immersed and interested only in their own bailiwicks, thereby continue to exacerbate the problem.

So Comte is seemingly faced with another form of the dilemma of knowledge and human nature. How can a science be both capable of comprehending and analyzing a domain of nature that has to be conceived of as independent of other domains, yet simultaneously constitute a region within a unified system of scientific knowledge, and this without being reductionist? Comte's answer was his theory of the hierarchy of the sciences. He was quite dissatisfied with all previous classifications because they proceeded on the assumption that each science showed the development of a new or different faculty (see Simpson, 1969, 6). Such schemes represented the sciences as fragmentary in nature and advanced no ground for their unity.

In his description of his hierarchy, Comte is so concerned to establish its unity that he sets out to convince us that there are two principles rather than just one on which it is grounded. There is, first, the doctrine of the relative complexity of the sciences, closely tied to the sequence of their historical emergence, and second, that of the various methodological similarities and differences properly attributable to them. We have touched briefly on the first of these earlier. Comte held that the relative complexity of the sciences reflected the relative complexity of the different realms of nature, from the simplest, astronomy, through physics, chemistry, and biology, to sociology.[10] This is not for Comte an a priori judgment. The fact that they have emerged historically in the sequence delineated by Comte is *evidence* of their differences in complexity, and he advances a number of

---

[10] Note certain omissions which, even for the times, seem surprising. Comte objected to political economy because of its overly abstract nature and his belief that it failed to deal with the realities of economic life. Psychology he regarded as a pseudo-science that advances in biology would do away with (mainly, it seems, because of Gall's phrenology, which he thought would eventually provide the developed biological science in which social life is rooted). "It is a science without an object," he says, and inveighs against its attempts to utilize concepts designating subjective phenomena (1896, 2, 119). This, of course, was a departure from the tendency of eighteenth century thought, in which psychology was assumed to be central to any authentic human science, but a strategy consistent with and supportive of Comte's interest in establishing a social plane sui generis and a science taking this as its object; the possibly "contaminating" psychological phenomena are banished from the scene.

arguments purporting to show how developments in one or another were essential for those in others. He argues, for instance, that scientific astronomy would have been impossible without prior developments in mathematics; the laws of physics proved indispensible for the development of scientific chemistry; scientific biology is inconceivable without knowledge of the chemical properties of the organic world. The laws of planetary motion formulated by Kepler would not have been possible had they not been preceded by Tycho Brahe's work. Descartes's doctrine of "mechanism" was essentially metaphysical, but without it Newton could not have discovered the laws of gravitation. These arguments all rest on a version of the science-as-cumulation theory, which, until fairly recently, remained essentially unchallenged by scientists and philosophers of science.

As important as their relative complexity, however, are the methodological commonalities and differences of the sciences. In fact, at one point Comte tells us that "the only necessary unity is that of method" (1875–1877, 1, 49). There are methods that are appropriate for each of the sciences, but no science possesses a method (or battery of methods) exclusively its own. It is Comte's view that accompanying the increasingly complex nature of the sciences as we ascend the hierarchy is not just the possibility, but the necessity, of employing a broad spectrum of methods. Methods overlap or are shared, at least by neighboring sciences, some having greater importance in a particular science than in others. The physical sciences utilize observation, experimentation, and mathematics, but physics more so than chemistry. Biology makes but limited use of the experiment and relies mainly on comparison. Both mathematics and experiment are virtually excluded from the armamentarium of sociology; mathematics because, in Comte's opinion, the application of probabilities to historical phenomena (as LaPlace, for instance, attempted) is "misguided,"[11] the experiment because of the complexity of social phenomena. Sociology does, however, make some use of observation, which is central to astronomy and employed also by others higher in the hierarchy.

The relations between sociology and biology are of particular importance for Comte. Biology constitutes an indispensable body of knowledge for the sociologist for reasons both substantive and methodological. In contrast to the sciences of the inorganic world, which proceed by *analysis*, those dealing with organic phenomena are of necessity *synthetic*, i.e., they are grounded in a conception of the whole, and a knowledge of the whole is theoretically necessary for understanding the parts. Scientific biology rests on the idea of "consensus" among the parts, the essence of any organic entity, and it is this domain assumption that sociology draws from it, and that constitutes the basic affinity of the two sciences. It follows from this that the comparative method, essential to biology, is also employed by sociology, in fact; it enjoys the status of being its principle method. To this Comte adds

---

[11] This does not constitute, it should be added, a justification for short-circuiting the education of sociologists by ignoring mathematics, which still must be studied to acquire the basic attitude of "positivity" (and perhaps to become convinced of its inapplicability to social life, as well!). The fact that Comte himself was well trained in mathematics and managed to eke out a miserable living by reading student math papers, is perhaps not irrelevant to his views on this point.

the historical method, which he conceives of as a form or extension of comparison, but which is available to sociology alone.

Comte connects the two unity of science doctrines through his universal history scheme. The process of the progressive unification of knowledge is *identified* with the march of social progress as the development of order: Order in the domain of knowledge will bring order in the realm of social life. Already, according to Comte, the sciences exhibit a methodological unity, and the entire history of human knowledge (as written by Comte) convinces us that this is a state of affairs inevitably *in transit* to a *substantive*, or *moral* unity of knowledge. The methodological unity of knowledge, for Comte, does *not* therefore have the status of being the *final* form of unification, but is only evidence of progress toward the final goal of a unified humanity.

In the course of these discussions, Comte elaborates aspects of theory and method that remain central to the positivistic orientation in the social sciences to this day. His emphasis on laws that take the form of a deductive system explicitly modeled on astronomy and physics (again following Saint-Simon) remains the idealized paradigm of theory in positivist social science generally. Comte rejects empiricism understood as mere accumulation of facts, on the one hand, just as he does "mysticism," or any belief in nonobservable entities, on the other. Somewhat in the vein of Hume's methodological protocol for his "modified scepticism," he stipulates that positivism must find a path between these two extremes, and he thinks that this path lies in the direction of formulating empirically derived laws within a deductive system. "Science consists in the systematizing of facts under general laws" (1896, 2nd para., Chap. 6 on electrology). It is a measure of Comte's influence that this fundamental idea has ever since remained the ideal of theory in what must be considered the "mainstream" of social science. And Comte's argument for the necessity of a deductive relation between laws and facts, namely, that explanation, and therefore prediction (prevision) is otherwise impossible, has also been generally accepted—by those who believe that prediction is in fact possible—at least as the framework for the debate over the similarities and differences between explanation and prediction (see, for instance, Keat and Urry, 1975, 71–75).

Interestingly, Comte inveighs against any search for "causes." "Causes," he says, can never be "penetrated"; we learn through astronomy "what is the real meaning of the *explanation* of a phenomenon, without any impractical inquiry about its *cause*, first or final, or its mode of production" (1896, 1, 237). He explicitly rejects the use of terms such as *attraction*, in connection with the movements of heavenly bodies, which he thinks designate nothing observable (1896, 2, 180), and following what he regards as the principle of Newton's discoveries of the laws of motion, would "cast aside all inquiry into origins and mode of production" (Chap, III, Book on Physics, 1896, last p.). In this rejection of the notion of cause, Comte is perhaps both rejecting its usage in earlier philosophies (e.g., Aristotle and the Schoolmen, in which it designates hidden entities or beings), and attempting to follow the spirit of Hume in the latter's analysis establishing the locus of "cause" in the impressions of reflection. We can see here the survival and influence of the eighteenth century problems with the concept of law as an explanatory principle. Comte needs laws to explain the movement of history and predict the future, but feels compelled to banish "cause" as metaphysical, which is to say, as the essential idea of the imposed or immanent conception of law. This seems to be a partial affirmation of Hume's argument, but there is no recognition of Hume's restatement of the idea of causality as conventional or as resituated in the linguistic apparatus (see Chapter 4). This is, of course, a confusion. John Stuart Mill took Comte to task on this point, noting that all laws are necessarily formulations inherently involving causation, and that at least by implication, science cannot get along without the idea of cause; all that is at issue is the meaning that can legitimately be attributed to it (Mill, 1865, 57ff).

All this is taken by Comte as a set of principles that can, in fact, must be transferred *in toto* to sociology. The rejection of causes has its direct application to sociological methodology in a parallel rejection of anything suggesting introspection or search for meanings understood as subjective or mental phenomena. Intellectual functions cannot themselves be observed; only their *results* are available to our legitimate scientific operations (see Comte, 1896, 3, 308, *et passim*). In this fashion Comte thought he had established a scientific unity based on a methodological canon common to all the sciences.

We can now see why Comte found it necessary to establish the unity of the sciences through two, rather than only one argument. He sought to establish a scientific unity founded on the human domain but that would simultaneously be grounded in history. The development of the sciences must therefore be the central driving agency of that history, and Comte thought that he had proved this to be a process conforming to the law of the three stages. At the same time, the sciences taken as a whole must reflect the nature of this reality, a reality that, from an experiential standpoint, is incredibly diverse. The theory of the hierarchy of the sciences, at present (i.e., Comte's time) only a methodological unity, brings this diversity which the various sciences seek to comprehend within the larger unity of the abstract law of the three stages.

Neither of these forms of unity, however, provided Comte with theoretical assurance of the sort of final, unchallengeable knowledge that would be up to the task of guiding the radical reorganization of human society. Scientific generalizations forever subject to falsification are mere conventions and can therefore never inspire more than the most tentative confidence. And the theory of the hierarchy of the sciences culminates in an elitism that fatally decenters any scientific unity grounded on a sense of moral subjects, thereby undermining the emancipatory purpose of the enterprise itself. In the last analysis Comte falls back on the God of universal history,[12] investing it with the power of the developing human mind itself. And in this invention, all the evils of history are, as in Hegel, swallowed up in the grand cunning of its expanding rationality.

In the last analysis these two forms of explanation are contradictory: The first, a fundamentally teleological and scientifically unacceptable con-

---

[12] For a discussion of the influence of Enlightenment universalism on Comte, see Goudsblom, 1977, 16ff.

ception of law, breaks the very rules on which the second is grounded. This contradiction evidently went unperceived by Comte. In this connection it is illuminating to recall Raymond Aron's contrast of the interests driving Comte and Montesquieu. Montesquieu, he says, was the observer of the French monarchy, and his sociology bears the mark of that time. Comte was the observer of the clash of two types of society, and he wanted to hasten the metamorphosis of this condition into the synthesis of a third (Aron, 1965, 1, 6). The Catholic and aristocratic Montesquieu saw no need to invoke a law of history (although the idea was very much alive at the time he wrote *The Spirit of the Laws*) as the framework for his sociology; indeed, his work suffers from too weak a historical method. Montesquieu essentially confines himself to the sort of Humian relationships for which observables can be designated. Comte, the ragged prophet living among fellow jobless intellectuals in the Bohemian community in Paris, needed a universal law to guarantee his vision of the future.

It is not too difficult to see why some first-rate nineteenth century intellectuals, like Mill and Littré, had such high praise for Comte's system, despite the fact that, as sociology proper, it was greatly inferior to much that had long since been achieved. Montesquieu's empirical sociology, for instance, as well as that of the Scots, or much of Herder, or even Bonald, or for that matter, the brilliant analysis of culture contact and acculturation of Ibn Khaldoun (1958), were all superior to anything empirical produced by Comte. But Comte constructed a system that transcended the Enlightenment dreams and efforts in the direction of a human science by inventing what seemed to be an authentic *social* science, and provided, for the first time, a powerful rationale for pursuing scientific analysis of social life *as such*, to the end of perfecting the human race *through* society, through what seemed a powerfully formulated theory of the unity of knowledge. Comte apparently had convincingly and successfully converted scientific rationalism into an ethical rationalism; he had, it seemed, unlocked the secret of the future through the discovery of the meaning of the past.

THEORY AND PRACTICE

The growth of scientific knowledge is the engine of progress for Comte, but science is the work of men and women, a form of social action. How does Comte conceive of the relation between theory and practice and the working of universal law in history? All teleological theories present a difficulty in this respect: If historical agencies, whatever they may be, are driving us to some final state, what of the willful, acting individual? Is the belief in the relevance or significance of one's action to be regarded as a pointless conceit irrelevant to the course of events? Not quite. Peel makes the point that, seemingly confounding all logic, deterministic progressive schemes of history are associated with great psychological confidence on the part of their creators, and this confidence may as often lead to deep commitment and involvement in social action as to passivity and a sense of historical fatefulness (Peel, 1971, Chap. 4). Comte was not one to endorse withdrawal from the world of events, whether into mysticism, cynicism, or other belief. He preserves a place for action but he is careful to circumscribe quite severely the conditions under which it is likely to be effective, and not surprisingly, he does so within the framework of the hierarchy of the sciences.

The possibilities of effective intervention in social affairs, says Comte, depend on the degree of complexity of the domain in question, for in those that are more complex, relationships are less determinate. Thus, intervention in matters astronomical is out of the question, but at the other extreme of the hierarchy, in the realm of the social, certain possibilities do present themselves, for the limits of variation here are less rigid than they are elsewhere. Comte specifically mentions race, climate, and politics as having some impact on social change, but these effects are only "modifications," themselves subject to "fundamental laws" (1896, 2, 236). This "looseness" is the basic condition permitting intervention and the possibility of exerting some degree of influence on the direction of events. In addition, the capacity for *intelligent* intervention comes into being only with the growth of sociology, since it is necessary to understand the basic direction of social change in order to act rationally. However, social action cannot be political in nature, for the central objective of the new society of the future is the elimination or transcendence of politics through universal morality.

In this fashion, Comte formulates the essence of what has become part of the liberal creed of social action: Effective intervention is rationally possible only if it is undertaken in accordance with the already progressive direction of society. The standard governing social action is derived from presumed knowledge of that direction, or more practically, in support of already existing and identified trends.[13]

The elitism of Comte's positivist society is a direct implication of this code of social action. Being the most complex, sociology is also the most difficult to master, and is therefore accessible intellectually to only a few. Others, like sailors in their faith in astronomy, must have confidence in the direction given human affairs by the elite.

> Can it be supposed that the most important and the most delicate conceptions, and those which by their complexity are accessible to only a small number of highly-prepared understandings, are to be abandoned to the arbitrary and variable decisions of the least competent minds . . . ? Anarchy would result. (1896, 2, 153)

From this follows the entire system of organization described by Comte in the *Système*, with its sociological priesthood, its calendar of positivist saints, its repression of all intellectual life not controlled by the elite (only one hundred books would survive), its minutely systematized industrial organization—all under the new secular pope, Comte himself.

Despite the necessity for allowing some space for social action, at least until the arrival of the full-blown positive society, Comte in the last analysis places his decisive emphasis on the *limits* rather than the *possibilities* of intervention. This position follows logically from his doctrine of law. The

---

[13] For a recent expression of this Comtian creed in social movement theory, see Kloss and Roberts, 1974.

possibility of achieving anything, he says, is very limited. Even the greatest statesmen are presented with near-insuperable difficulties since, in whatever they undertake, theirs is a "struggle against natural laws." In these stipulations, Comte is quite aware that he is caught in the dilemma of the two meanings of progress and the implications of these for our conception of a human science. If great changes could be brought about by intervention in social affairs, he says, *no social science would be possible* (1896, 2, 235). Sociology therefore can exist only because of the impotence of the objects of its analysis. In the last analysis, the determinism seemingly required by science rests on passivity in the face of events!

It may be instructive at this point to briefly recall the main achievements of the Scots, as I have attempted to define them earlier. First, as I argued, they had in the latter decades of the eighteenth century laid the foundations of a workable sociological paradigm in their theories of sympathy and the commercial society. This achievement was due in part to the fact that, under the powerful influence of Hume's skepticism, they had significantly deflated the role of reason in human affairs, and partially, replaced it with the category of interest. The historic role assigned the intellect—the channeling of the passions—came to be reassigned to the play of interest. It was on the basis of this shift away from domain assumptions elsewhere still potent that they developed their realistic approach to social life that included such a prominent place for conflict. Indeed, their social theory was in large part an attempt to understand and account for the nature, significance, and consequences of conflict, perceived as an incorrigible component of human social life. The noncynical realism that informed this was certainly one of their great strengths. Comte, by contrast, worked out a system of sociology that *celebrated* the alleged growth of the social significance of the mind and recognized conflict only as an evil to be banished from human affairs. And, finally, whereas Comte opted for a faith in the working of law in history, the Scots emphasized the active character of human life, a practical voluntarism from which Comte, with his distrust of the individual, could never incorporate into his positivism.

Even as Comte's idealistic form of sociology was becoming disseminated in the marketplace of ideas, the undercurrent of the greatest intellectual revolution of the nineteenth century (some would say of all time) was about to become a torrent that would descend upon and divide not only the intellectual world, but social and political life as well. The theory of evolution, which had had some precursors in the eighteenth century, became with Lamarck, Galton, Darwin, and others, the revolutionary movement of the nineteenth, and the form it took in Herbert Spencer's system (and even in Marx's) would ensue in a quite different resolution of the philosophical dilemmas raised by the philosophers of the eighteenth century.

8

HERBERT AND EVOLUTIONARY SOCIOLOGY

Herbert Spencer was born in 1820 in the Midlands in Derby, a provincial town that had been undergoing industrialization from an early date, and Spencer's later intellectual career was profoundly influenced by the Derby milieu. By the late eighteenth century, the local elite included a coterie of scientifically oriented intellectuals and industrialists, an offshoot of the Lunar Philosophical Society in nearby Birmingham, which had been organized in the 1780s and included such famous scientists and industrialists as Dr. Erasmus Darwin, grandfather of Charles; Joseph Priestley, one of three claimants to the discovery of oxygen; Josiah Wedgewood, who industrialized the manufacture of pottery; Samuel Galton, a physicist and grandfather of Francis; James Watt; Matthew Boulton; and others. When Darwin moved to Derby in 1782, he founded the Derby Philosophical Society on the model of the Birmingham group, intending to reproduce there the enlightened intellectual atmosphere of Birmingham. Some of the other members of this group also had close ties with those in Birmingham.

The prevailing atmosphere in these circles was a large sense of optimism regarding the possibilities of a rebirth of society through the marriage of science and industry. Many of the members of this local bourgeoisie were either early industrial entrepreneurs or innovating scientists and craftsmen, or both. They were also mostly adherents to dissenting religions, Unitarians or Quakers (Darwin was a Deist), and in resolute opposition to the High Church (along with the old landowners and Tory worldview generally) and indeed the very principle of a state church. A critically important segment of England's modernizing elite, they saw themselves as executors of that great spread of human ideals, to be achieved through social transformation, that was the vision of the Enlightenment, and understood their concrete actions as practical realizations of that vision in the here and now (see Peel, 1971, Chaps. 2 and 3).[1] It is fair to say these figures, the leading ones of the late English Enlightenment, were to a much greater extent practical men of industry and science than was true in France, Scotland or Germany.

Theirs was a worldview that exuded the optimistic and future-oriented radicalism of early nineteenth century science and industrial expansion within the framework of dissenting religious and philosophic radicalism. It coupled a commitment to an economic liberalism derived from Adam Smith, expressed with special force in the journal *The Economist*, with a view of the world and of society as organic entities compounded of elements exhibiting a natural, law-given coherence, and above all, *developing* in the direction of an integrated condition wherein all the parts collaborate freely as *constituents* of that unity. The ideas of a struggle for existence and the survival of the fittest, the "social Darwinism" of Spencer, were scarcely in evidence. Rather, this view of the world was an organic version of the eighteenth century's more mechanistic secularized theology, but without the "biologization" it was to receive at the hands of Spencer.

Spencer's parents were second-generation middle-class adherents of Wesleyan Methodism, a religion that, in its earlier years, had attracted mainly working-class members. The original emphasis on emotional states and *feeling* as against *intellectualizing* religious experience among its middle-class devotees such as the Spencers, had given way, as Peel puts it, to "a restrained Biblicism and a middle-class ethic of individual attainment" (Peel, 1971, 40).[2] Spencer's father Thomas was a member of and for a time during the 1830s secretary of the Derby Philosophical Society, the members of which were still known as "Darwinists." So as a youth Herbert, who was kept out of school and educated by his father and uncle, was fully exposed to these ideas. His life's work was to be a development and extension of them in systematic fashion.

The social and political conditions under which Spencer came to maturity and worked out his theories could hardly have been more different than those under which Comte labored. Especially in England, the six decades or so of the nineteenth century following the Napoleonic wars up to the intensification of imperialistic conflict during the later decades of the century, was a period of relative foreign and domestic peace. The Chartist rebellion of the 1830s had petered out in the 1840s, partly because of a split in the movement itself, partly because of the beginnings of reform. The

---

[1] Of the general works on Spencer's sociology, Peel's is in my opinion, not only the best, but also a valuable examination of a variety of related aspects of nineteenth century English thought and society. Also useful is Turner (1985), especially as a much-needed corrective to misleading conceptions of Spencer's work introduced into sociology early in the century and perpetuated by virtually everyone writing on the history of sociological theory since. Wiltshire (1977) and Andreski (1971) go over much the same ground as Peel, adding little. Rumney (1934) was excellent for the times but is now dated. Textbook treatments tend to be superficial, with the exception of Rossides (1975), and Coser (1971).

[2] On the effects of economic success on religious ethics, especially those of Methodism, see Niebuhr (1929). More generally, of course, there is Max Weber's *The Protestant Ethic and the Spirit of Capitalism (1905) (See Chapter 14).*

continental revolutions of 1848 scarcely touched English domestic politics—indeed, England was haven for many fleeing the repression that followed in their wake. From the standpoint of the industrial middle class, it was a period of political success marked most dramatically by the success of the Anti-Corn Law League, which established the principle and fact of free trade and symbolized the coming to power of the burgeoning industrial capitalist class.

Spencer's popularity was greatest during the decades of the 1850s, 1860s, and 1870s, but declined thereafter, especially in England, as events seemed to diverge more and more from the future anticipated by his theories. Spencer himself, like so many Victorian intellectuals, was throughout his life subject to periods of depression and sometimes became quite despairing, even to the point of wondering if his life's work had been a total loss.

THE PROBLEM OF HUMAN NATURE

Comte had resolved the Enlightenment dilemma centering on received conceptions of human nature and the problems of cultural diversity and evil by "stretching out" the social manifestation of these in culturally distinct forms, under the determining influence of the growth of Mind. This was not very satisfactory, as we saw, since it left the changes in the world of ideas unexplained. Comte toyed here and there with social explanations of these changes but never seriously attempted to formulate them systematically. To have done so would have cut the ground out from under his domain assumptions regarding the primacy of the ideational sphere and weakened his claims regarding the three stages and the changes yet to occur.

Spencer's way of dealing with this problem was, in a sense, the direct opposite of Comte's. His problem in his first major work, *Social Statics* (Spencer, 1896), was Enlightenment-derived—how to reconcile the diversity of the social world with the seeming need for a universal morality on the basis of which a new regime of peace and freedom would come into being. The problem of the relativity of human conduct and culture discussed in Chapter 3 remained central to philosophical and quasi-sociological speculation in the times that followed. Moral philosophers like Hutcheson had supposed that God in his wisdom had implanted a sense or instinct of morality in every human being, but as we saw earlier, Hume and Smith took this belief in the direction of a "naturalistic" but somewhat sociological interactionism. Generally, the "environmentalism" characteristic of Enlightenment thought presented a challenge to the notion of a God-given moral sense. This was important for the evolutionists who followed, since it provided already established ground for situating the moral sense problem in the framework of a *changing* and *evolving* relation between organism and environment.

The conception of evolution provided a new way to think about moral conduct in all its complexity. The old problem of how it was that a sensibility conferred by the deity could be manifest in so many different—and evil—forms now had a new solution. It could be held, for example, that although some moral attitudes were associated with *particular* external circumstances—an explanation of the variability—there were still others,

Darwin's belief in the universality of sociable and altruistic relations between neighbors being a case in point, that could only be rooted in a moral sense acquired through habituation of activities beneficial to the perpetuation of the race. Linking the moral sense up with the functionalist utilitarianism of evolution through the principle of adaptation became the centerpiece of Spencer's philosophical anthropology. What Comte had superficially adumbrated, Spencer rendered scientifically concrete by assimilating it to evolutionary biology.

The idea that organic species were mutable is actually an old one that can be traced to antiquity and had been broached by Locke a century earlier, but it began to receive serious and systematic attention only in the late eighteenth century. Darwin credits Lamarck with being the first to "excite much attention," initially in 1801 with his *Système des animaux sans vertebrates* (Darwin, 1936, 3). With other naturalists around the turn of the century, Lamarck was involved in a debate as to whether animal behavior was unlearned or whether (along with anatomical structure) it resulted from the inheritance of habitual practice. By 1809 he came to the conclusion that animal behavior was adaptive to the environment (climate, temperature, etc.), and that the resulting changes were heritable. The mechanism whereby this occurred was a flow or movement of bodily fluids ("subtle fluids") within the tissues, eventuating in the formation of new organs (by "spontaneous generation"). In this fashion the internal milieu of the body created species-specific needs along with the more general ones of self-preservation, the sexual instinct, and so on, that came to be satisfied by habitual behavior. Repetitive or habitual use of organs strengthened them and brought into being new felt needs. This doctrine, known as use-inheritance,[3] was the dominant theory of evolution for most of the nineteenth century, despite many theoretical and empirical difficulties. Hawthorne suggests that its very vagueness made it adaptable to a wide variety of *both* hereditarian and environmental positions (Hawthorne, 1976, 97). Although Darwin's great contribution to evolutionary science was the linking of the idea of adaptation to that of natural selection through the struggle for existence engendered by the expansive tendencies of all species populations, he by no means rejected use-inheritance categorically; rather, he accepted it as one among several other contributary, if perhaps secondary, evolutionary mechanisms.[4]

The idea that species were mutable seemed to challenge the received religious orthodoxy,[5] of course, but the early evolutionists (along with quite a few of the later ones) were able to reconcile religious faith with evolution.

---

[3] For a discussion see Richards, 1987, Chapter 1. In the following discussion *The Origin of Species* and *The Descent of Man*, initially published in 1859 and 1871 respectively, will be referred to as *Origin* and *Descent*, respectively.

[4] In *The Descent of Man* Darwin alloted more space to sexual selection than to natural selection. He seems always to have had reservations about the latter. Late in life in a letter to Huxley, he writes that he is troubled as to "what the devil produces each particular variation" if, as he says he thinks, "external conditions produce little direct effect" (Darwin, 1888, 232, quoted by Quadagno, 1979, 106).

[5] Well understood by representatives of the religious establishment, as attested to by the celebrated debate between Bishop Wilberforce and Thomas Huxley in 1860.

For one thing, there was doubt as to whether the evolutionary process applied to the human higher faculties. In *Origin* Darwin avoided the entire topic of human evolution, and his famous colleague and rival, Alfred Wallace, as late as eight years after its publication, held that both the origin of life and of the moral and higher intellectual nature of the species were "difficult to conceive as originating by any law of evolution," but must have evolved under the guidance of a higher power (Wallace, cited in Richards, 1987, 178).

In the longer run, of course, the implications of evolutionism were clear, and no struggle in the modern history of science has been as intense and protracted as that between scientific evolutionists and those holding to a Christian interpretation of nature and the origins of the human species. The current creationist movement is just one more episode in this history.

Although Darwin put off the question of the evolutionary origins of the human mental and moral faculties until *Descent*, the issue of moral evolution—inevitably perhaps, once the idea of evolution was around—had long occupied naturalists and moral sense philosophers. We have earlier discussed the treatment of the idea of the moral sense among the Scottish philosophers, but it was the utilitarian side of their work that was taken up— and in Smith's case overstated—by later thinkers as the industrialization of England began to spread apace. During this period the theological-philo-sophical problems of the moral sense came to be appropriated by evolutionary biology, a radical turn from the earlier more or less sheerly taxonomical interests.

Darwin held that altruistic behavior was rooted in instincts that became modified by natural selection. But the evolutionary reduction of moral behavior to biology carried with it a number of difficulties. Once established, would not altruism work to impede the evolutionary process by selecting the weak, thus preserving them? And can it not be strongly argued that, far from constituting an advantage, altruistic behavior works to *harm* those who practice it by placing them at a competitive disadvantage relative to those following the law of tooth and claw? Darwin in later editions of *Origin* advanced a variant of natural selection that operated at the group or community level, proposing that individuals could be altered by natural selection if the changes were to the benefit of the community as a whole in its relations with other communities (see Richards, 1987, 213ff.). He evidently thought of the group effects of natural selection as merely additive or aggregative. This had no lasting scientific value: Its twentieth century reincarnation (Wynne-Edwards, 1962) has failed to establish itself, precisely in the need to *theorize* the social level in order to salvage the very conception of evolution.

Spencer's formulation was innovative, in good part because it joined Darwinist to Lamarckian ideas, (even before publication of *Origin of Species*), linking the evolution of the moral sense to a differentiated and sophisticated conception of the group level. Spencer argued that instincts, including human instincts, are *complexes* emerging from a *lower level* of reflexive response. Instincts constitute an *integration* of behavior, resulting from environmental changes, particularly population pressures (Spencer, 1852).[6] Later, in *Principles of Biology*,[7] where he first coined the phrase "survival of the fittest" (only later adopted by Darwin), Spencer argued strongly that natural selection was deficient insofar as it formulated the evolutionary process as a series of specific or individual trait adaptations. The great rack of the Irish elk is adaptive, but requires the *simultaneous* emergence of a heavier chest, expanded vascular system, and other functionally related features. None of these changes alone is adaptive; rather, only the entire complex occurring in concert (Spencer, 1866, Chap. 12). This *functional* inheritance goes beyond simple use-inheritance not only in the complexity of its conception of instinct, but also in the manner in which it is integrated with the level of social organization. The differentiation of reflexes and their integration into instincts has its parallel in group organization in the unfolding of the division of labor. (Indeed, Spencer's characterization of biological evolution as differentiation and integration at higher levels was doubtless actually modeled on the social division of labor.) Acquired traits and associated behaviors are inherited organically and then engender social changes in the form of an increasing division of labor, which is to say social organization of greater complexity. In turn, adaptation to the expansion of the social division of labor demands higher levels of the exercise of the faculties. As this process unfolds, the mental and moral faculties become increasingly important and eventually replace physical adaptations. With the achievement of a high level of rationality and moral sense, fertility is reduced, ending population pressure and ushering in the era of the happiness and well-being of all—the final realization of the Derby Philosophical Society's conception of the "ethical society." The moral sense is understood as a developing human capacity rather than one fixed in human nature, with human progress the measure of its evolutionary growth. The Enlightenment belief and faith that evil could be collapsed into ignorance and error, is in Spencer's hands, now fortified by scientific authority. The two great problems implicated in the eighteenth century problematic of human nature—the diversity of human behavior and culture, and the persistence of worldly evil—are thus framed and explained historically. Spencer's answer to the many faces of and persistence of evil is new evolutionary wine in the old Comtean bottle: characteristics of earlier adaptations somehow live on as "survivals" (as they came to be designated in anthropological parlance). Evil is the nonadaptation of the organism to external conditions. Diversity is the evolutionary mani-

---

[6] Emphasis on population pressures was nothing novel on Spencer's part, since it was shared by the evolutionists in general. Evolutionary theory had to respond to Malthus's arguments regarding the implication of the alleged exponential increase in population when compared with linear increase in the food supply. If Malthus was right, evolutionary theory is obviously reduced to so much nonsense. The evolutionists, we might say—to borrow the famous epigramatic metaphor of a great contemporary—"stood Malthus on his head," building population pressure into evolution as a *progressive* factor. This line survives in sociology in later evolutionists like Durkheim in France and Sumner in the United States.

[7] In the remainder of the chapter, Spencer's work will be designated as follows: *Principles of Biology, PB; Social Statics, SS; Descriptive Sociology, DS; Principles of Sociology, PS; Principles of Ethics, PE; First Principles, FP;* "Progress: Its Law and Cause", *PLC; Principles of Psychology, PP;* "Reasons for dissenting from the Philosophy of M. Comte", *RD;* and *The Study of Sociology, StSoc.*

festation of functional inheritance. Evolution is inevitable in its course, although not particularly orderly or linear, exhibiting periods of stagnation and even retrogression.

So science now shows indubitably that progress is no mere dream but a necessity. With mind and its evolution firmly ensconced in biology, civilization ceases to be thought of as artificial and becomes part of nature, "all of a piece with the development of an embryo or the unfolding of a flower," as Spencer, with rather uncharacteristic felicitousness, put it. And the same iron necessity that guarantees the final achievement of human happiness through the growth and exercise of the faculties of the individual, justly interdicts any meddling in the process. Interference with the adaptations that constitute human history are necessarily ill-fated and anti-progressive, for they impede the "natural" advance of evolution. And here the received meaning of good and evil is transformed. In this newly revealed natural order of things, a society is constantly "excreting its unhealthy, imbecilic, slow, vacillating, faithless members," and "any interference slows down or halts the purifying process" (Spencer, 1896, 151). Of course, certain costs must, in the short run, be accepted.

> It seems hard that an unskillfulness which with all his efforts he cannot overcome, should entail hunger upon the artisan. It seems hard that a laborer incapacitated by sickness from competing with his stronger fellows, should have to bear the resulting privations. It seems hard that widows and orphans should be left to struggle for life or death. Nevertheless, when regarded not separately but in conjunction with the interests of universal humanity, these harsh fatalities are seen to be full of beneficence—the same beneficence which sends to early graves the children of diseased parents, and singles out the intemperate and the debilitated as the victims of an epidemic (Spencer, 1896, 151).

Passages like this certainly seem on their face to qualify Spencer as the greatest promulgator of "social Darwinism." In fact, he never unambiguously embraced the principle of natural selection as the fundamental law of evolution in favor of Lamarckian inheritance of functionally acquired characteristics (although he claimed to have anticipated Darwin), and in later years was even subject to criticism on precisely this score. From the beginning of his work in the 1840s through the "middle" period to which most of his sociology can be dated, to the end of the century, Spencer never wavered on the question of the heritability of acquired characteristics, despite its displacement by natural selection during this period. Two decades after the above passage was written, we find him in *StSoc*, at the point of embarking on his strictly sociological work, informing us that "human nature will adapt" to the evolutionary process (Spencer, 1873, 318), that "permanent bodily and mental differences will be produced" (308). In a letter to J. S. Mill in 1879 (reprinted in Part I of *PE*), he summarizes the doctrine and his commitment to it.

> To make my position fully understood, it seems needful to add that, corresponding to the fundamental oppositions of a developed Moral Science, there have been, and still are, developing in the race, certain fundamental

moral intuitions; and that, though these moral intuitions are the results of accumulated experiences of Utility, gradually organized and inherited, they have come to be quite independent of conscious experience. Just as in the same way that I believe the intuition of space, possessed by any living individual, to have arisen from organized and consolidated experiences of all antecedent individuals who bequeathed to him their slowly-developing nervous organizations—just as I believe that this intuition, requiring only to be made definite and complete by personal experiences, has practically become a form of thought, apparently quite independent of experience; so do I believe that the experiences of utility organized and consolidated through all past generations of the human race, have been producing corresponding nervous modifications, which, by continued transmission and accumulation, have become in us certain faculties of moral intuition—certain emotions responding to right and wrong conduct, which have no apparent basis in the individual experiences of utility. I also hold that just as the space-intuition responds to the exact demonstration of Geometry, and has as its rough conclusions interpreted and verified by them, so will moral intuitions respond to the demonstrations of Moral Science, and will have their rough conclusions interpreted and verified by them (Spencer, 1904, 1, 123).

Finally, in 1891, with Weissman's recovery of Mendel's research as well as Darwinism now on the scene, he reiterates this.

When the circumstances of a species make certain relations between conduct and consequence habitual, the appropriately-linked feelings may come to characterize the species. Either inheritance of modifications produced by habit, or more numerous survivals of individuals having nervous structures which have varied in fit ways, gradually form guiding tendencies, promoting appropriate behavior and deterring from inappropriate. The contrast between featherless birds found on islands never before visited by man, and the birds around us, which show fear of man immediately they are out of the nest, exemplifies such adaptations (1904, 4, 27).

Lamarckian inheritance was for Spencer the counterpart of Comte's theory relating the innate social sense to its various historical manifestations. Like Comte's effort, Spencer's was a way of resolving the dilemma posed by belief in the constancy of human nature and the problem of giving a rational account of the process of social change. But Spencer's formulation cut deeper than Comte's. Whereas Comte held only that the social *manifestations* of the social instinct underwent transformation, and basic human nature itself remained unchanged, Spencer proposed that original human nature itself was being progressively transformed.

The main implications of this were two. On the one hand, linking social change to organic transformation obviously roots social analysis more firmly than ever—more firmly than in Comte—in human nature, and strongly instantiates the human nature-society paradigm of social analysis. But at the same time, since the point of sociological analysis is to understand society as it changes, the need for a precise scientific conceptualization of the nature of those changes becomes evident, and this presupposes an elaborated conception of the particular nature of society. Such a theory ought to be historical in order to reveal the direction—and future—of human development by penetrating to its inner dynamic. But to claim the authority of science, this program would have to ground its findings on a convincing application of *scientific method*, now applied to the social realm. Spencer attacked the first of these over a period of two decades in his massive *Descriptive Sociology* and *Principles of Sociology*, mainly the latter. But preparatory to this he found it necessary to secure the second, the methodological foundations of sociology. He did this mainly in *The Study of Sociology*, a semipopular work, brought out in 1873, to which we now turn.

SPENCER'S THEORY OF SOCIOLOGICAL KNOWLEDGE

Spencer's methodological precepts are of a piece with both his philosophical anthropology and his evolutionary organicism, and, as we shall see, designed to produce the conclusions at which he had long since arrived. He begins *StSoc* with a defense of sociology. Sociology, he says, is needed to supplant the operation of a variety of "biases" (which he treats in detail in the middle section of the book) with reliable knowledge. Why should not the "rigor of inquiry," which in sciences like astronomy and meteorology have proven their utility, not be applied to society? Not to do so he finds "an immense incongruity," for the common form of social belief, "common sense," is demonstrably more often wrong than right. Spencer had little doubts about what such a "rigor of inquiry" would reveal. Societies are immensely complex and, in accord with the law of evolution, becoming ever more so. Sociology will demonstrate this complexity, and thereby "dissipate the current illusion that social evils admit of radical cures" (Spencer, 1873, 19). Sociological knowledge thus has for Spencer an end the opposite to that which it serves for Comte, and one that, as we shall see, leaves it in a fundamentally ambiguous status.

Having settled the question of the social function of sociology, Spencer goes on to dispose of a variety of objections to the possibility of its actualization: divine explanations, the role of great men, free will, the supposed uniqueness of historical epochs. Some of the issues he discusses are still matters of debate, and Spencer's treatments are sometimes surprisingly modern in content and tone.

The various doubters refuted, Spencer takes up the question of general sociological methodology, and like Comte, his strictures here follow directly from his theory of human nature. The characters of aggregates are determined by the characters of their constituent units. "The natures of units necessitate certain traits in the aggregate," he maintains (44); and *observation* shows that "cardinal traits in societies are determined by cardinal traits in men" (47). The theoretical foundations of this methodological individualism are developed throughout *StSoc*, especially in chapters on "preparation" (for doing sociology) in biology and psychology. Biology must be studied because the vital functions of the organism underlie social life and because society as a whole presents phenomena of growth, structure, and function like those of the individual body. Here is the celebrated organic parallel with which we shall deal in the following section. Psychology must be studied because "everything originates in the motive of an individual or some united individuals, and this always involves a feeling guided by the intellect" (349). One has no hope of even approaching explanation of social phenomena without recognizing sentiments as critical factors in the determination of societal-level phenomena.

The significance attached by Spencer to the relationship he perceives between his concept of human nature and evolution of the moral sense, on the one hand, and his methodology, on the other, is reflected in his argument that preparation in psychology is important—critically so—because through the study of it we come to understand that the objects of study of the various disciplines are linked together as related domains of nature. Through the study of psychology, Spencer says, we learn that the natural forces that comprise the individual's faculties must never be overlaid by social institutions. All should be free to struggle and thereby assure the survival of those who make the superior adaptation (336ff.). Spencer needs psychology for the opposite reason that Comte banishes it.

Spencer's methodological individualism is barely distinct from the ethical individualism of his moral sense doctrine (and the broader "Darwinism" of the Derby Philosophical Society), as the following example illustrates. Freely willed action, such as the marriages entered into by the constituent members of an aggregate will result in uniformities, such as the birth rate, at the level of the aggregate. Far from being incompatible with sociological inquiry, the free exercise of the faculties is for Spencer a *natural* phenomenon, as we saw earlier, indispensable for evolution itself. "Social phenomena can follow a general (evolutionary) course only as social units *act out their natures*" (47), thereby producing regularities at the aggregate level. So sociology must engage itself at both levels if it is to produce sociological explanations. Explanation of aggregate level phenomena requires that the sociologist recognize the ethical or moral nature of the free excercise of the will. To reject methodological individualist explanation is equivalent to denying the law of evolution.

Despite the importance attributed to sentiments, and the moral sense, in particular, in the evolutionary process by Spencer, this does not for him constitute grounds for apprehending the sentiment-rooted actions of individuals at the subjective level. Indeed, on this point Spencer is strongly Baconian, regarding human subjectivity as an *obstacle* to scientific explanation. He regards what he calls "automorgraphic interpretations" as presenting a "subjective difficulty that must somehow be transcended." We necessarily interpret the actions of others in terms of our own perspectives: "Our interpretations must be automorgraphic," he says, but this is a condition that must "perpetually mislead us" (106–107). He presents a catalogue of his own "idols" that constitute important obstacles to an objective sociology (the "biases" of education, patriotism, class, politics, and theology: Chaps. 8–12). The social phenomena that constitute the objects of study for sociology have objective reality: The problem for the sociologist is to rid the mind of the welter of biases that cloud the view of that reality. Thus, the "class bias," rather than being taken as part and parcel of the class structure and class relations, is a view of the world to be expunged from the mind. This makes it easy for Spencer to dismiss the legitimacy of the economic and political beliefs of English workers (Chartists and Trade Unionists, for instance) as obstacles to rational thought that "obscure truth" and that will eventually be corrected—not entirely unlike the way Comte had it—by the spread of sociology.

The program advanced in *StSoc* was the first modern positivist sociological statement of method, and in many respects it remained superior to anything appearing in the next half century, perhaps including even Durkheim's *Rules* (on this point see Turner, 1985, Chap. 2). It remained for Spencer to make good his claim that an objective methodological individualism would reveal an evolution in society parallel to and functionally related to organic evolution. This was the task he set himself in *Principles of Sociology*.

SOCIETAL EVOLUTION

In his early writings Spencer had formulated his view of human nature and specified the mechanism of evolutionary change. The question now became, What is the nature of the *social process* whereby the moral sense comes increasingly to infuse the life of society? Spencer approached this question from both inductive and deductive directions. The deductive approach can be seen in his 1857 essay "Progress: Its Law and Cause," where for the first time he formulated what would become the general law of evolution expounded in detail in *First Principles*. He maintains that all spheres of Being, "astronomic, geologic, organic, ethnologic, social," should be manifested in one "fundamental necessity." Five years later in *First Principles*, this vagueness would become:

> Evolution is definable as a change from an incoherent homogeneity to a coherent heterogeneity, accompanying the dissipation of motion and the integration of matter. (Spencer, 1862, 291)

and further,

> That there are not several kinds of Evolution having certain traits in common, but one Evolution going on everywhere after the same manner. (188)

This "one Evolution" Spencer identified as the "Persistence of Force," in and of itself unknowable, but the final explanatory principle of all things in the universe. Spencer thus began by establishing as a "world hypothesis" (Pepper, 1970) the existence of "One Law" of the cosmos working in all orders of being, a metaphysical conception that he set out to demonstrate through science.

Spencer's "law" asserts: (1) that adaptation occurs through differentiation, i.e., that differentiation is adaptive, because (2) a differentiated entity is more stable than is a homogeneous one. As in the earlier essay on population, he argues again that the basic condition for the emergence of increasingly superior forms of adaptation in human society was population increase and the resulting pressure on the environment. Increasing numbers force more efficient adaptation, and this takes the form of greater specialization of tasks. Formally then, the sociological theory of evolution stands in deductive relation to the theory of "one evolution," or the law of "persistence of force."

PS, however, assumes the form, or in the view of some, perhaps only the guise, of inductive science. Spencer amasses his armies of facts from history and the ethnography of the time. The quantitative magnitude of this effort is best seen in *DS*, running eventually to fifteen volumes, on which Spencer and his assistant (and later biographer) David Duncan began work in 1867, but which was abandoned by Spencer fourteen years later (although the work was carried on and eventually published over several decades by others). *DS* was intended as a kind of massive file wherein the culture traits gleaned from manifold sources could be rendered in tables, ordered within a classificatory scheme derived from the general theory of evolution, and used in preparing *PS*. Incredibly detailed, it was perhaps at once a fitting epitaph to nineteenth century evolutionary sociology and an anticipation of the creation of the Human Relations Area Files at Yale University three quarters of a century later (for a generally positive evaluation, see Turner, 1985, Chap. 6).

Spencer's theory of evolution, then, has both a deductive and an inductive side and Spencer claims that the latter, based on analysis of ethnographic materials drawn from his welter of sources, proves the validity of the "One Law" of evolution. The main *logical* form of demonstrating this is the use of extensive alleged parallels between structure and behavior in the organic and social domains, supposedly establishing the latter as part of the natural order. And this is perhaps its greatest flaw, for the method of analogy is the weakest of all truth-establishing forms of argument.

It will be useful for purposes of exposition to think of Spencer's theory of evolution as involving three terms: (1) original nature, particularly the Moral Sense; (2) the social manifestations of this in various forms of social organization; and (3) environmental factors. Changing environmental factors such as population growth or warfare (which for Spencer was extremely important in the evolutionary process, especially at relatively "primitive" levels) cause changes in the existing forms of social organization. For example, the internal class divisions of a society that constitute an adaptation to the state of warfare, vertical and hierarchical in nature, under conditions of peace give way to functional or horizontal divisions that Spencer held to be characteristic of "industrial" societies. Or, conquest of one people by another results in a "compound society, which increases its "mass" and results in greater internal differentiation. The new forms of social organization then constitute the "environment" for changes in the physical, intellectual, and emotional composition of individuals. In this framework, as one might expect, Spencer worked out an elaborate theory of the differences between "primitive" and "civilized" types, firmly rooted in Lamarckian theory (which from another standpoint can be understood as a codification of Victorian prejudices). The intellectual ability of primitives is confined to simple ideas: They lack the ability to generalize and to exercise prevision (see *PS*, 1, Chaps. 4–7). Emotionally they are in "awe of power," exhibit a love for the helpless, and being well down the evolutionary scale in the development of the moral sense, have "a poorly developed sense of justice" (Spencer, 1961, 346). As social evolution proceeds through expanding differentiation, these traits of individuals undergo transformation: Expansion of the capacity of the mental faculties means that adaptation achieves a higher level of reason and of morality.

As a major participant in the protracted and often intense debate over the mechanism (or mechanisms: virtually all the evolutionists after Lamarck, including Darwin, as mentioned earlier were to some degree eclectic in theorizing multiple evolutionary mechanisms) of evolution, which of course continues today, Spencer was quite aware of the difficulties attending the scientific establishment of the theory of the heritability of acquired characteristics. This was a problem throughout the range of organic forms, but particularly acute, obviously, in the instance of human evolution. It was enough of a problem to cause Spencer to puzzle particularly over the brand of alchemy that transforms "natural" human egoism into altruism. In *SS* he had drawn on the moral philosophers, and Smith in particular, in attempting a resolution. The moral sense, he says, is "a divinely implanted instinct, which along with sex and hunger, assure the continuation of social life." But the *expression* of this takes the form of *personal rights*. This is the fundamental axiom which, in natural law terms, undergirds the whole of Spencer's individualism. He goes on to argue that those having the strongest sense of their personal rights will also have the strongest perceptions of those of others (which he calls "Justice"). Quaker ethics, with which he was quite familiar, is invoked to support this: Quakers exhibit both a strong sense of individual rights and personal liberty, along with a highly sympathetic understanding of the rights of others (Spencer, 1896, Chap. 8).

Years later, in *PE*, he is still troubled by this version of the "Adam Smith problem," i.e., the difficulty of reconciling the doctrine of the individual as fundamentally egocentric with the seeming—and one must emphasize the "seeming," because this conceals a world of issues—moral nature of social behavior.

> While we may thus understand how the egoistic sentiment of justice is developed, it is much less easy to understand how there is developed the altruistic sentiment of justice. On the one hand, the implication is that the altrustic sentiment of justice can come into existence only in the course of adaptation to social life. On the other hand the implication is that social life is made possible only by maintenance of those equitable relations which imply the altruistic sentiment of justice. How can these reciprocal requirements be filled? (Spencer, 1904, 4, 29)

According to Spencer, they can be filled "by the aid of a sentiment which temporarily supplies its place, and restrains the actions prompted by pure egoism—a pro-altrustic sentiment of justice, as we may call it" (Spencer, 1904, 4, 29). We learn that the "pro-altruistic" sentiment of justice has to do with various sorts of external restraints that work through fear: vengeance of a political sort, divine retribution, social disapproval, legal action. "Containing none of the altruistic sentiment of justice, properly so-called, this pro-altruistic sentiment of justice serves temporarily to cause respect for one anothers' claims, and so to make social-co-operation possible" (30–31). The pro-altruistic sentiment of justice thus has its origin in the *repressive* aspect of social institutions, which are in process of being evolved out of existence by Spencer's Lamarckism.

The pro-altruistic sentiment of justice, it appears, has its source in the *repressive* aspect of social institutions, which is to say, a social rather than a natural source. This would seem to imply the primacy of the social order over the individual, and among other things, constitute a challenge to Spencer's methodological individualism. It is also inconsistent with the most fundamental evolutionary process, the movement in the direction of the ethical society, which Spencer (drawing on ideas long present in the "Darwinism" of the circles in which he grew up) rendered empirically as a drift from the military to the industrial type of society, since the repressiveness of the former type is being evolved out of existence by the Lamarckism process. Here, in his last major work, the capstone of his system, the fatal flaws of Lamarckism, of the virtual identification of ethical and methodological individualism, and in the last analysis, of fatih in evolution as progress, remain a puzzle to Spencer.

In all this we see the interpenetration of Spencer's philosophical anthropology and his theory of evolution, particularly his Enlightenment-rooted identification of the problems of evil and error, these categories now assimilated to the evolutionary scheme. Superior adaptation occurs as the power of the intellectual faculties waxes and stimulates the growth of the moral sense; evil is reduced as intelligence is progressively brought to bear within the process of adaptation; the chief form of adaptive intelligence is science (including sociology, although it of course has no Comtean role). Spencer's theory of social evolution is both less and more than science; less because of the Lamarckian deus ex machina supporting the One Law of Evolution; more because it serves, and was intended by Spencer to serve, as a secularized theodicy. This was the Enlightenment paradigm realized in grand style.

But all this is only the foundational aspect of Spencer's evolutionary theory. We turn now to its sociological aspect.

Societal Evolution and the Societal Types

In *DS* and *PS* Spencer applied his Law of Evolution to human society.[8] Evolution proceeds by two basic processes: compounding and the multiplication of internal units. In the case of the former, a larger society may be formed by the joining of two or more smaller ones, without the necessary obliteration of the constituent ones, or one society may conquer another. This process may be carried to another level, which Spencer designates as "double-compounding," for example, the massing of already compounded small French baronies into provinces, and even "treble-compounding," exemplified by large modern industrializing societies. Multiplication of internal units is an adaptation occurring through differentiation in response to changing conditions, external or internal. Although evolutionary growth through multiplication of internal units was Spencer's political ideal,

---

[8] The following discussion is based on Chapters 3–9 of *PS* unless othewise indicated. Where convenient I employ Carniero's abridgement (Carniero, 1967).

the evidence forces us to recognize, he says, that evolution has proceeded mainly through compounding, or, as he otherwise says, more realistically, by "subjection to despots."

Whatever the causes, however, the creation of such larger units— increase in "mass"—as Spencer puts it, is destabilizing, encouraging an increase of structure, or further differentiation, as an adaptation to the new situation. The basic nature of this process Spencer formulates as a relation between structure and functions. All social change, i.e., all of evolution, is a matter of the relation of structures to functions. "Changes of structure cannot occur without changes of functions" (Carniero, 1967, 24), he says, and in this dictum establishes the fundamental nature of sociological analysis as structural-functionalist.

There is, he argues, a general relationship between structural development and function: the more complex the forms, the greater the functional dependence of the differentiated parts on one another because of their specialized nature. For example, in his analysis of political organization, he argues that the principle of inheritance comes into existence to resolve the instability that exists due to the differentiation of warrior from medicine man in groups that evolved somewhat beyond the simple primitive horde (126). Or, in the area of kinship analysis, Spencer judges a supposed early state of "promiscuity" (accepted by some evolutionists) to have been unstable because of the amorphous and variable and irregular nature of child-raising arrangements. Promiscuity gives way to polyandrous structures that have a selective advantage over promiscuity because of their superior, i.e., more adaptive, child-raising arrangements. This change, of course, occurs as an increase of structure because it involves a differentiation of roles beyond the previous condition. But polyandrous systems themselves give way to polygynous ones, which have the further advantage of fostering a stronger organization of male leaders and permitting a more rapid replacement of warriors, because males with more than one wife, according to Spencer, will produce more male offspring. Polygyny is in turn displaced by monogamy, which has its adaptive advantages (Spencer, 1898, 1, 652).

Attention should be drawn to the fact that in all of this Spencer proceeds strictly at the social level, with the Lamarckian trappings absent (at least explicitly) from the scene. This is of the greatest importance because, although Spencer still claimed in the context of discussing the One Law that acquired characteristics were heritable and that they were implicated in social evolution, his actual sociology is a powerful demonstration—for the time, and despite its serious flaws—of their questionable relevance for sociological explanation. Spencer's analysis in *PS* is the sort we find in modern structural-functionalism. Social structures are explained by the functions imputed to them, a simple enough sounding rule, but one that opened up a veritable Pandora's box of ambiguities and interpretations still far from being satisfactorily resolved.[9]

[9] Despite the rather extravagant claims of adherents of the functionalist (or structural-functionalist) school, from Durkheim to Talcott Parsons and now beyond, a century of functionalist sociology has failed to yield much in the way of accumulated systematic knowledge, the professed goal of members of the school (see Turner, 1985, Chapter 3, for a strong recent

Spencer's functionalism has its roots in his modeling of sociological analysis on the nature of the organism. Societies are held to be analogous to organisms in that both experience growth, progressive differentiation of structure and function, integration of functions, destruction of the whole prior to the death of the parts, and the extension of the life of the whole beyond that of the parts. There are also some dissimilarities (which Spencer generally plays down):[10] animal parts are concrete whereas the parts of societies are discrete; in organisms consciousness is concentrated in a small part of the whole whereas in societies it is diffused throughout; the migration of social units from one society to another has no parallel in the organism.

The systems of "organs" in human society are not only structurally homologous with those in the organic world, but also stand in the same and functional developmental relationship to one another. According to Spencer, organic functioning is defined in terms of three main systems, the sustaining, the distributory, and the regulatory. The functioning of all societies, like all organisms that have evolved beyond the simplest of forms, is possible only by virtue of the functional interrelatedness of the three systems. The simplest organisms and societies are little more than sustaining systems that develop out of interaction with the physical environment, but as differentiation proceeds, the functional requirements for distribution between the increasingly specialized parts increase. Regulating systems begin to develop through contacts with environing societies in the form of warfare, which may be either temporary, in which case a temporary chief appears, or permanent, resulting in the establishment of leadership on a permanent footing, and the appearance of a clearer (more "definite") internal subordination. The latter is more adaptive, and such societies survive, while the former tend to disappear, victims, in effect, of an adaptive struggle occurring at the societal level.

At every point Spencer employs organic analogies, at times fantastic ones, to show the workings of evolutionary law in the two domains. Technical terms drawn from biology are used to strengthen or establish the descriptive similarity and functional identity of social and organic processes. Manual occupations, for instance, are parallels of the alimentary organs, business of the vascular system. Spencer, of course, was very unhappy with the actual *governmental* regulation of nineteenth century industrial societies, a sentiment reflected in his sociology. His theoretical discussion of the regulatory systems of advanced industrial societies provides a particularly illuminating example of this. He says that there are, in fact, two distinct types of regulating systems: external ones, as described above, but internal ones as well, which have their beginnings when former military heads begin to assume control of internal functions. But in advanced industrial societies, the regulatory function becomes more complex. So now an industrial regulating system emerges and

---

reiteration of this position). And not only have the empirical results turned out to be embarrassingly meager, but many of the basic methodological and logical criticisms have never been satisfactorily answered. The revival of functionalism in the 1980s is mainly an exercise in pure theory, with little associated empirical work.

[10] I emphasize *generally*. In *MS* at one point Spencer actually says that such comparisons are inadmissible: "The social organism is not comparable to any particular type of individual organism" (592).

carries on its regulating independently of the political. Spencer goes on from here to argue that this further differentiation has been occurring in the form of the credit system. Just as in the organism local vasomotor centers possess local control, local banks have *their* local spheres of influence! This is a system

> called into action upon increased demand upon an organ—dilation or contraction of arteries. Neither volition in the organism can alter these supplies of blood nor can legislation affect bank credit (Spencer, 1898, 545)

This ingenious parallel between the expansion of the banking system independent of centralized control and localized vasomotor functions establishes the *functionality* of the former. In evolutionary terms it proves that industrial society is moving beyond the need for much *internal governmental regulation* to a state where regulation would inhere in the sheer adaptive systemic functioning of its interrelated parts. This is the industrial society that we shall shortly discuss in more detail.

Apropos of all this, Turner has argued that Spencer's main sociological interest falls on the origin of structures, and that his analysis of their functions is restricted to periods following their establishment, or institutionalization. On this basis he claims that Spencer was more of a conflict theorist than a functionalist, and that functional analysis was not really central to Spencer's sociology (Turner, 1985, Chap. 6). But it does not appear to have been Spencer's *intent* to make such a separation. For him, all structures come into existence only to serve certain functions, and what he calls the "consensus of functions (i.e., their close interdependence) "becomes closer as evolution advances" (Carniero, 1967, 25). Spencer would have regarded any basic separation of the questions of the origin and maintenance or continuation of structures as artificial or contrived. All structures come into being, in principle, to discharge functions having some adaptive value or efficiency. This is so even in the case of the conflicts that Spencer regarded as being so critical in evolution. And the fact that structures come into existence through conflict does not render them unsuitable as objects of sociological analysis. Unification of small groups into larger entities, for instance, serves the function of defense or survival in the face of external threat; in such a circumstance this is more adaptive than for each society to cope singly. The more efficient adaptation of the larger unit gives it a greater opportunity of being "selected" for survival. In this vein, the conquest and subjugation processes, like all others, are framed by Spencer in terms of the functions performed.[11]

There are a number of problems with Spencer's use of the organic metaphor, and it is this aspect of his sociology that has been subject to

---

[11] The contemporary distinction between functionalist (or "order") and conflict "paradigms" as fundamentally different forms of sociology—a distinction given impetus by the turbulence of the 1960s, but clearly antedated by Martindale among others (see Martindale, 1960)—is confounded by Spencer. For Spencer both order based on structures properly fulfilling their functions, and conflict are central to sociological analysis. He is perhaps properly identified as a "conflict functionalist."

especially critical review.[12] Although there can be no objection in principle to employing organic or any other type of model to elucidate otherwise unclear or undiscovered aspects of social life, the sheer extent and remorselessly systematic character of Spencer's procedure eventually leaves the reader with an overall impression of systematized absurdity. Beyond this, there is a logical difficulty involving the units being compared. The unit of evolutionary biology is the species; but in Spencer's sociology it is the *individual units* collectively constituting the "species" human society that undergo evolution. *Each* society must (generally speaking, although with certain qualifications) proceed through each of the evolutionary steps (see *DS* for the detailed classificatory scheme). Societies are compared in terms of the level on the evolutionary scale they have reached. Another problem is that heterogeneity and differentiation by no means necessarily imply superior adaptation; many relatively complex organisms have become extinct despite having evolved over millennia; on the other hand, many species low on the evolutionary scale in Spencerian terms (e.g., the amoeba) must be credited with astonishing adaptiveness (for a discussion of some of these points see Hawthorne, 1976, 97–98).

A final point brought against organicist theories generally, Spencer's included, is that they ignore or downplay the realities of class and power. Despite the centrality of the role of conflict in evolution in his work, this is a problem in Spencer, but mainly only because he limits his concept of class to purely political/military domination, thereby excluding it from societies of the industrial type, of which England in the nineteenth century was the preeminent example. This is a major flaw in his understanding of the basic processes of capitalist industrial societies.

The various criticisms leveled at Spencer are not unjustified. However, it is also true that his sociology went far beyond any other of the time in its grounding in massive empirical detail and in its clear, if flawed, conceptualization of the basic societal types thrown up in the course of evolution.[13] This brings us to what is probably Spencer's most important contribution: the theory of military and industrial types of societies.

Spencer thought that the grand sweep of evolution was a process that could be characterized as proceeding from forms of society based on birth, through those based on wealth (the present),[14] to those of the future based on the ethical or moral qualities of their members, the "Ethical Society." By 1870 he had come to characterize this development in terms of two ideal types, the "military" and "industrial" forms of society. Although this was a distinction long current in dissenting circles, Spencer must be credited with rendering it in substantially more rigorous sociological form.

Military societies[15] develop under conditions of continuing militancy

---

[12] See for instance, Martindale, 1981, 81–85; Rossides, 1975, Chap. 13; Wiltshire, 1977, Chap. 9; Peel, 1971; Carniero, 1967, Intro.; Hawthorne, 1976, 100.

[13] Jonathan Turner must be credited with being virtually the sole sociologist concerned with rehabilitation of the truly sociological Spencer (see Turner, 1985).

[14] Sometimes, borrowing from Henry Maine, expressed as a movement from status to contract. See Maine, 1862.

[15] The following discussion is based on *PS*, Part 5, Chaps. 17 and 18.

or warfare and constitute adaptations characterized by what Spencer designates as "compulsory cooperation." As the militarization of society proceeds, the ratio of fighters to workers increases, and the very distinction between civil and military becomes unclear, even obliterated. ("The army is the nation, the nation is the army") A hierarchical structure of command that exercises increasing control over all social activity comes into being. Related to this is a growth of importance of status as an organizational principle, and on this foundation the institution of inheritance[16] comes to be established. Compulsory forms of work, restrictions on freedom of movement, and repression of independent associations become the norm. The social significance of a hierarchically organized state religion increases in importance (a recognition on Spencer's part of the importance of ideological legitimation for governments assuming extensive functions). The sustaining system becomes self-sufficient and subordinate to the regulatory system. Under conditions of continuous warfare, the institutions of the military society become exceedingly rigid and unreceptive to change, a state that, as in Rome[17]—Spencer's principal model for the military society—may be maintained for a long period of time; it represents a virtual suspension, or regression, of the evolutionary process. Military societies are communistic in nature and create what might be called a modal character type that emphasizes courage, takes pleasure in destruction, displays no respect for life or property, and lives by "faith and passivity."[18]

The industrial society is one in which contract supplants status, and in which a severely constricted public administration goes hand in hand with an abundance of voluntary associations of all types. Virtually all communistic or communal arrangements are excluded in favor of the principles of individual freedom and individual rights. The modal character type then tends to be an active individual with a highly developed sense of independence (recall the discussion of Smith and Ferguson in Chapter 5 on this point), and little faith in (or need for) governments or leaders. Such a society is relatively open to change because it does not have the rigid internal institutions resulting from adaptation to a condition of warfare. Most generally, industrial societies are defined as being based on voluntary cooperation, as against the compulsory cooperation of the military society.

The greater significance of the military/industrial typology lies in the fact that Spencer applied it throughout his section on political institutions in *Principles of Sociology*, and so it assumed the form of a general political sociology. In this analysis movements in the direction of political centralization and decentralization (somewhat on the order of Weber: see Chap. 14) constitute the critical adaptations to a variety of conditions and to which the functioning of all other institutions adapt.

Recall that for Spencer, societies grow in size by both internal

---

[16] Inheritance was anathema to Spencer, despite the fact that he himself lived partially on one during the later decades of his life.

[17] Spencer implicitly employs the Enlightenment belief about Rome providing instructive parallels with contemporary times.

[18] In forming these types, especially the military one, Spencer anticipates in some respects much later work on totalitarianism such as Lasswell's concept of the garrison state (Lasswell, 1968).

multiplication of units and by compounding and recompounding, which is to say through amalgamation of smaller units, usually in the face of military threat, by military conquest, and incorporation. But it is not the internal multiplication of units, but, as mentioned earlier, "subjection to despots," Spencer says in summing up the evidence, that "has been largely instrumental in advancing civilization" (Carniero, 1967, 124).

Compounding not only increases the size of the social unit, which itself tends to initiate further differentiation, but requires stronger, more centralized government because of the conflict resulting from the clash between the traditions of compounded societies, the extreme of which occurs when the conquerors enslave the conquered. Further, any external pressure, especially but not exclusively military threat, has the same centralizing effect. As compounding proceeds, as the ruler's staff expands, as administrative agencies multiply, as formerly autonomous local political governing agencies are brought under the central power, as kinship systems are deracinated, the power of the ruler is clearly enhanced. But the identical developments serve also to decrease his power because his actions become, as Spencer puts it, increasingly modified by them (121). Furthermore, centralizing tendencies also have the effect of creating resistance among the subordinated, and this sets in motion a movement in the direction of decentralization. Thus, within the *general* evolutionary process, fluctuations or oscillations occur and re-trogression is commonplace. Furthermore, each step in evolutionary advance creates ever-greater obstacles for the next. Any growth of instrumentalities "increases the impediment to future modifications" (70) because more specialized structures are limited to serving their own narrow function and cannot be adapted to serve others. Greater efficiency is purchased at the cost of greater rigidity.

The internal arrangements characteristic of the military society will be maintained and expanded under certain conditions, by far the most important of which is continuous warfare. Peace, conversely, encourages the spread of industrial pursuits and the decay of the status system Spencer associates with militarism. History is replete with instances of retrogression to military type societies; indeed, this appears to be so common that it seems close to being the rule. Continuing militarism tends to narrow the range or composition of the elite, peacefulness to widen it.

Although the theory of military and industrial socieites was inter-woven throughout Spencer's political sociology, it has an ambiguous rela-tionship to the general theory of evolution. If "subjection to despots" has been the main engine of evolutionary advance, on what grounds are we justified in looking to the spread of the freedom, democracy, and enlight-enment associated with industrial society? We see here Spencer's inductive, empirical political sociology at war with his One Law of evolutionary advance. We might even go so far as to say that the extent to which the military/industrial society theory is bad evolution it is good sociology.

Spencer's theory of the military and industrial societal types was certainly one of his most acute pieces of sociological anlaysis. Formally, it is an analysis of how the strucures of entire societies adapt to changing function. Empirically it is an explanation of how continued militancy tends to fuse civil and military functions, and of the effects of social structures on the characters of individuals. It was, for the time, perhaps for any time, first-rate sociology. And it was possible in good part because Spencer, in effect, suspended his individualistic methodological protocol.

Late nineteenth century events, however, were anything but kind to the theory. At least as early as the 1870s (and perhaps even the Crimean war), it was becoming apparent that the industrialism-democracy affinity was anything but an undissolvable evolutionary necessity. In England the rapid pace of industrialization continued, but increasingly in concert with an expanding colonialism and intensifying jingoistic militarism, which reached a shrill climax during the period of the Boer War. And in autocratic Germany under Bismarck, where democracy had never taken root, an industrial society was rapidly coming into being under the sponsorship of an aristocratic class and military elite. Spencer's societal types were under challenge both as evolution and as a partitioning of mutually exclusive sets of functioning structures. The notion that industrialism itself could provide the societal foundations of global conflict raised to previously unimagined levels was an idea that strongly resisted assimilation to the nineteenth century creed of liberal dissent. Spencer himself, however, although assailed by waves of doubt and pessimism in his later years, never flagged in the defense of his theory of evolution against the increasingly critical judgments brought against it.

CONCLUSION: SPENCER, THE PROBLEMATICS, AND THE ENLIGHTENMENT

In the conclusion of this chapter, we will place Spencer's sociology in the context of the three problematics of the Enlightenment and the problems stemming from this.

First, consider the import of evolution as the theory of social change. The problems encountered by Spencer's theory of societal types having to do with its inability to convincingly explain the thrust of social change in the later decades of the nineteenth century have already been discussed. But more generally, Spencer failed to see the complex of problems that the expanding division of labor in industrial societies was creating. Comte was really more acute about this, as were Marx and other socialists, and even Smith and Ferguson, among others. Spencer's sociology fell short where both the Comtean and Marxian perspectives on the division of labor did display some sociology-rooted prescience in defining the central social issues of twentieth century capitalist societies. Closely related to this is the problematic nature of morality in Spencer's sociology. Spencer was obviously not unaware of the imperative of some form of moral consensus in any society, and did not claim that a stable human society could be based solely on purely utilitarian functioning or self-interested activity, a position attributed to him by many, Durkheim prominent among them.

Quite the opposite is apparent in his insistence that the good society of the future would necessarily have to be one suffused with the sense of morality. The problem lies in the fact that he provided no convincing *sociological* account of the origin, nature, and manner of the functioning of such a morality. Hawthorne remarks that Spencer's failure to show the evolutionary necessity of altruism was "so total as to make it seem to most that he was commending competition and struggle instead" (Hawthorne, 1976, 109). It would be precisely the greatest achievement of Durkheim, working in the Comtean tradition rejected by Spencer, to give this its sociologically most powerful classical formulation. But this was a sociological direction not open to Spencer because of the way he initially chose to deal with the Enlightenment problematics. Spencer inherited a utopian conception of the good society from the Enlightenment, transmitted through the social milieu described earlier, and his sociology is an attempt to show the path to its realization. This is the basic source of its contradictions and unworkability.

The status and function of sociological knowledge in Spencer's system is essentially derived from the evolutionary process. Evolution works through adaptation, which involves a growing significance of intelligence in human behavior, especially with the rise of science. But should not the growth of knowledge understood in this functional sense not only permit but in its very nature *imply* increasingly effective intervention and greater control over social evolution? Spencer's strictures on the social role of knowledge replicate the persistent difficulty attending nineteenth century evolutionism insofar as it attempted to encompass the seeming appearance of the higher human faculties. Human intelligence (however defined, a matter of controversy then as now) and seeming capacity for altruistic behavior (the behavioral expression of the moral sense) are adaptations appearing high in the evolutionary scale, and so must have a function. But evolution is a natural process working through selection and would presumably be disrupted in its course by the consequences of the effective introduction of organized altruism. It is the role of intelligence, and in Spencer's view to some significant degree intelligence in the form of sociology, that informs us of this dire consequence of any organized form of altruism (in practical terms, of course, meaning state intervention).

But this does not mean that social knowledge has no social function. Our evolved intelligence shows the evils of humanitarianism, and this proscribes its expansion in the societal regulating function, but it receives Spencer's imprimatur for application in the *specialized* organs of society (i.e., the "private sphere": business, religion, the family, and so on). Spencer, like Marx and Engels, although from a very different vantage point, here has his finger on the pulse of the liberal dilemma of the state-society relation. Knowledge is properly turned to private ends, which stimulates and guides the development of private "organs"; but in the terms of Spencer's own theory, this creates a growing need for greater coordination, in turn implying the application of knowledge to the *totality* of functions, in its strongest form centralized planning. But this is the socialist solution, precisely what Spencer wanted at all cost to avoid; in this context the moral sense comes to serve the absolutely necessary role of state-surrogate.

In those "modernized" but still minimally welfare-statist capitalist societies, like the United States, Spencer's ideas have life, if only as ghosts haunting their interstices in the various forms of charity, giving, and private benevolence (much of it, one must add, mightily fueled by tax advantages), as the states continue to exercise a vastly expanded set of functions. So far at least, history seems to have proven Spencer wrong about the possibility of a capitalist society of the purely unregulated type coming to be governed by the moral sense.[19]

Finally, the very idea of a moral sense, in its older usage, must obviously be questioned. Nesting it within evolution seemed—and was—an intellectually revolutionary act at the time, but it is easy to see today that it really amounted to no more than replacing one theology with another. The idea that morality somehow originates in the individual, whether placed there by God or nature, is one that seemed to gasp its last breath in sociology sometime in the early twentieth century, discarded with much other detritus of nineteenth century sociology in favor of a sheerly cultural and mostly relativistic conception of morality.[20]

In all of this the Scottish beginnings might have better informed Spencer's sociology had he been able to assimilate them differently. The rudiments of a theory of interaction and of the interactional genesis of morality were present in their writings. But Spencer could hardly be expected to have taken this line in the evolutionary, utilitarian, and laissez-faire ethos of the nineteenth century; few others did so. Spencer was very much a child of his time, perhaps the nineteenth century's greatest embodiment of Peel's observation that periods of rapid social change are unreceptive to theories emphasizing the guiding potential and power of the intellect, for in such periods events themselves seem to be in control (Peel, 1971, 244–245).

The sense of irony in the sociology of the Scots became, in Spencer's hands, wedded to an organic model, and on this basis converted to a general argument against the application of the intellect in social and political change. Indeed, we might say that establishing the affinity of irony in the dress of sociological functionalism to the requirements of the radical liberalism of the time was at the core of Spencer's sociology. In its earlier appreciation, even among the Scots, irony never had such an import. There is a strong component of Humean skepticism in Ferguson and Smith, but they never reduced knowledge to a social irrelevancy. Spencer was the first to convert the historic appreciation of irony as unintended social consequence into an argument establishing the impotence of knowledge in human affairs (while simultaneously implicitly implicating it in evolutionary advance).[21] In doing so, and in assigning to blind drift the task of spreading enlightenment, he turned enlightenment principles not only against his Enlightenment predecessors but against his own theory as well.

---

[19] Somewhat ironically, capitalists themselves, or to be more sociologically precise, the normal functioning of capitalism, has itself been a major, if not the major, factor in bringing into being the expanding bureaucratic state.

[20] Attempts to breathe new life into it have appeared now recently under the auspices of the new sociobiology (which might better be called "biosociology").

[21] It is worth noting that the utilitarian wing of social theory deriving from the "practical" or utilitarian bent of the Scottish moralists—Bentham and the Mills—avoided this contradiction. Utilitarianism required plenty of state action to put the new theory to work: thus, it served as the theoretical foundation for a theory of public administration.

9

BACKGROUNDS OF MARX

Hegel and the Young Hegelians, materialism, Feuerbach, and Marx's critique

Just after the turn of the nineteenth century G. W. F. Hegel inaugurated a revolution in philosophy by reformulating the way Kant had theorized philosophically the problem of human subjectivity as it is confronted by the objective world. Then, drawing from the powerful romantic currents of the time, and incorporating rationalistic accounts of history, for example, Leibniz's monadology, Hegel undertook nothing less than a total reformulation of the course and meaning of world history as a *Logos* at the core of which stood the dialectical progress of the human spirit or Mind (*Geist*).

As a concession to Hume and empiricism generally, Kant had agreed that everything known through experience was experienced as a phenomenal reality only and that there could be no certain knowledge of "things-in-themselves," or the *noumena*. Hegel rejected this fundamental conception of Kant's as being overly restrictive of the exercize of reason, limiting it to the realm of the contingent. Hegel wanted to show, in general, that the world of "being" was *necessary*, not just an array of contingencies, and in particular that the seeming irrationalities of history were in fact not only necessary, but the very essence of history (for an excellent discussion see Hawthorne, 1976, Chap. 2).

Hegel had died in 1831 and at least two competing schools very soon emerged, a conservative one emphasizing Hegel's theory of the state as realization of the idea of freedom, a doctrine pleasing to the Prussian rulers Hegel seemed to celebrate in his later writings, and a critical one, worked out mainly by the "Young Hegelians"—Arnold Ruge, Moses Hess, Max Stirner, Bruno Bauer, and others—the group to which Marx was drawn.

We will here take up Hegel's philosophical anthropology as this is worked out in his phenomenology (Hegel, 1971) and his sociological account of social change, mainly as this is given in his *Philosophy of Right* (Hegel, 1978).

HEGEL

For Hegel all reality is bound up in the subjective nature of our existence, in psychic processes that have no fixed forms, but that are continually coming into and going out of existence. All reality is found in a dialectical process whereby ideas come into existence, bring into being their negations, and synthesize in a new reality. Although Hegel's history incorporates extensive discussions of social institutions, law, the family, the state, and so on, these are always ultimately conceived of in terms of their inner *Geist*, or "spirit," and history itself thus becomes a series of dialectically emerging transformations of the inner nature of the spirit. The essence of being human, says Hegel, is the freedom of the will, but this freedom exists only as the free will *wills* itself free in accordance with the *idea* of being free. The will "becomes objective to itself" through "the immediacy of existence as external reality." Its activity "consists in annulling the contradiction between subjectivity and objectivity and giving its aims an objective instead of a subjective character while at the same time remaining itself even in objectivity" (Hegel, 1978, 32–33). Hegel's account of this process in his *Philosophy of Mind* takes the nature and transformations in human consciousness, or mind, as the foundation of all human reality.[1]

Hegel's Phenomenology of Mind

The earlier, or first, stage of self-consciousness is the "appetite" stage, the condition of the "natural" individual in which impulse rules, and self-consciousness is an "exclusive" self-consciousness. This self-consciousness

> remains absolutely certain of itself because it knows that the immediate, external object has no true reality but is, on the contrary, a nullity over against the subject possessing only a seeming independence, and is, in fact, a being which neither merits nor is capable of an existence of its own, but must succumb to the real power of the subject (Hegel, 1971, 168)

Here, "immediate self-consciousness is caught up in the monotonous alternation *ad infinitum* of appetite and its satisfaction, in the perpetual relapse into subjectivity from its objectification" (170). In this all self-consciousness is collapsed into subjectivity.

Hegel says that in this first or primitive process, "self-consciousness

---

[1] Hegel's text is considered by many the most difficult in all of philosophy. I personally find many of the welter of interpretations with which I am familiar to be even more confusing than Hegel's text. In any case, particularly in such a scandalously brief treatment as this, obviously no claim whatever to any enhanced intelligibility is made. It is important to consider Hegel's work not only because of its genius, but because of its importance in the growth of sociology.

knows itself implicitly in the object. As the object is experienced, in Hegel's terms "rendered subjective", the subjectivity "divests itself of its one-sidedness and becomes objective to itself" (168). This results in a "fast conjunction of the ego with itself, its satisfaction realized, and itself made actual" (169). It is here that we find the germ of an expanded or transcending self-consciousness; indeed, "self-consciousness is the truth of consciousness" (165).

It is in this process in which ego is, or becomes, at once *aware of* itself as an ego, and *outside it* (i.e., itself), in which Hegel discovers the essence of the human condition, the anthropological universal of human nature.

> Here there is a self-consciousness for a self-consciousness, at first *immediately*, as one of two things for another. In that other as ego I behold myself, and yet also an immediately existing object, another ego absolutely independent of me and opposed to me (170)

At once, Hegel seems to be saying, to have self-consciousness of oneself is "a self-consciousness for a self-consciousness": ego is both prehender and prehended. But it is also a beholding of an immediately existing object independent of me and opposed to me. Note that Hegel says this is a self-consciousness *for*, not *of*, a self-consciousness. This denotes that the object of the self-consciousness (in the sense of the first term) is not one that is somehow given in ego's experience, but an emerging object that is in some sense the future construction, or better, an object whose construction is always in process of *becoming*, and in this is always merging with self-consciousness (in the sense of the first term).

Now this process is incorrigibly mediated by the other, is necessarily constrained by the other as an object of self-consciousness. No self-consciousness, no ego-action, no ego construction, thus no ego whatsoever, is possible or conceivable apart from such mediation. This axiom stands at the root of Hegel's philosophy and is an absolute rejection of Kant's thing-in-itself. Further, says Hegel, this process is necessarily a contradition, and thus an opposition, and gives self-consciousness "the impulse to *show* itself as a free self, and to exist as such for the other" (170). That is, the condition of self-consciousness *as such* is the necessary mediation of the other. Hegel calls this *recognition*; recognition thus becomes the incorrigible binding of the process of self-consciousness to the immediacy and particularity of the other. Its existence always appears in the mode of being constrained *in* this particularity. This immediacy of self-consciousness in the other is a contradiction. The ego in its natural essence always seeks, as Hegel puts it, "to show itself as a free self", to transcend the particularity and immediacy of the constitution of self-consciousness through the other.

Both constraint, or unfreedom, and freedom are constituent of the nature of self-consciousness; the necessary implication of this is that the very mode of unfreedom and freedom is to be bound together, and this bound nature constituted in struggle. Unfreedom and freedom are not things-in-themselves, but relational, ever-changing, consisting *in* opposition, and whose particular forms, therefore, are incorrigibly constituted in struggles. These are clashes which result in outcomes that are transcending *syntheses*. In the very long run this process evolves toward a final synthesis in which the human consciousness achieves ultimate transcendence of all particularity and immediacy in the mind of God. But this movement, indeed, any movement at all, is possible only through the "other" side of this dialectic, namely, the process of production of *objectifications* of mind that we call history (to which we will turn our attention momentarily).

The struggle of self-consciousness to free itself of its dependency on, or domination by the other, Hegel says, is "a battle".

> The fight of recognition is a life and death struggle; either self-consciousness imperils the other's life, and incurs a like peril for its own-but only peril, for either is no less bent on maintaining his life, as the existence of his freedom. (172)

The *social* conflict appearing as a dialectic in history, the form of which was adopted by Marx, has its root here, in Hegel's philosophical anthropology.

The dialectical contradiction and opposition in self-consciousness is also the context in which Hegel formulates his famous metaphor of master and slave.

The master-slave relation is Hegel's paradigm of human social relations, grounded in and derived from the phenomenology of mind. The fights alluded to above are resolved as "a one-sided negation with inequality". The one surrenders his claim for recognition while the other asserts his superiority which is recognized by the former *in* the surrender of the claim. The master-slave relation is not only the general form which real social relations assume but the universal dialectical paradigm of the totality of world history. This is so because Hegel discovers in the master-slave relation the germ of the idea of freedom and therefore of the growth of or expansion of freedom which is the essential mark of human history. This is Hegel's essential idea: history is the growth of freedom, and this growth is rooted in the dialectical process of self-consciousness, and therefore necessary.

It was Hegel's genius to show that the necessary condition of freedom, or more accurately, the universal process constituting human consciousness, i.e., *self-consciousness, necessarily* moves itself forward as an intrinsically and necessarily self-moving real actualization of freedom. In his interest in theorizing freedom as a growth in history Hegel identifies himself as a liberal or progressive philosopher, at one with the eighteenth century philosophes and dominant sociological theorists of the nineteenth century. But Hegel's argument, compared with Comte's or Spencer's, is brilliantly ingenious.

Although Hegel was certainly not the first to suggest that domination has played an important role in human evolution (recall the discussion of the Scots, as just one example), no thinker before or since has, with such remorseless and inexorable logic, made the case that the growth of freedom itself, the essential thread of evolution, derives in its inevitable universality from the inner nature of domination. This idea suffuses not only Hegel's phenomenological analysis but the entirety of the *History* as well. It is necessary here to limit the discussion to Hegel's seminal presentation in the Phenomenology section of *Philosophy of Mind*.

In his servitude, Hegel says, the slave surrenders his self-will to the master. The slave receives into the content of his self-consciousness the "purposes of the master" whereas the master receives from the slave not the *will* of the slave, but only the necessary consideration for his physical support, in order that he, the master, may continue to benefit from the slave's labor. This remains purely external; the slave becomes an other to the master only in the qualities of his natural existence, his potential for labor and for the necessities of survival. The critical point is this. The self-consciousness of the master is such that he

> beholds in the slave and his servitude the supremacy of his *single* self-hood resulting from the suppression of immediate self-hood . . . " (Hegel, 1971, 174–75)

The slave, however, in the service of the master,

> overcomes the inner immediacy of appetite, and in this divestment of self and in 'the fear of his lord' makes 'the beginning of wisdom'—the passage to universal self-consciousness" (175)

The slave labors for the master, and this labor is, in the nature of the situation, not entirely of his or her own interests (this being, of course, in the nature of slavery). The slave's actions embody the desires not only of him- or herself, but those of the master as well (again, of course, in the nature of slavery). It follows for Hegel that the slave rises above the "selfish individuality of his natural will, and his worth to that extent exceeds that of his master", who is "imprisoned in his egotism" (175). The egotism of the master is the negation not of the slave's objective egotism, but of the subjugation of the slave's egotism (175). Now the critical point: this subjugation is the essential condition of the emergence of freedom, as concept and reality.

> This subjugation of the slave's egoism forms the *beginning* of true human freedom. This quaking of the single, isolated will, the feeling of the worthlessness of egotism, the habit of obedience, is a necessary moment in the education of all men. Without having experienced the discipline which breaks self-will, no one becomes free, rational, and capable of command. To become free, to acquire the capacity for self-control, all nations must therefore undergo the severe discipline of subjection to a master (175)

Hegel goes on to briefly exemplify this idea by reference to Greek and Roman experience and in his *History* illuminates it in detail (Hegel, 1956).

Hegel's theory of knowledge, or science, derives from and is integral to this analysis of consciousness.

The Theory of Science

Hegel's theory of science is rooted in the logically demonstrable contradictory nature of the phenomenal, i.e., experienced world. The ancient Greek philosophers had thought of the working of contradiction as logical in nature, and so outside of history. In all of the subsequent history of philosophy in the West up through Kant, logical canons of thought had been held to be arbiters of the validity of scientific knowledge, the principles of identity and noncontradiction being the fundamental ones. Thus, a thing could not be both "A" and "not A". Hegel showed, or claimed to have shown, that contradiction was no mere principle of logic, but constituitive of the world itself (Hegel, 1929). The idea of motion, for instance, involves the idea of something simultaneously being in and not being in a specific place. What was thought to be an idea confined to the realm of logic is thus made available as an object of scientific interest.

From this beginning, Hegel infers that the essential reality of the totality of the phenomenal world necessarily lies outside of its "essence", or identity—in its negation. All understanding of the nature of anything requires grasping its "is" and its "is not." This is a momentous revolution in philosophical thought. Not only does it challenge the principle of noncontradiction, but it also unites scientific thought with speculative reason, i.e., metaphysics, a separation that many scientists and other intellectuals had been working toward for centuries. The unity-in-contradiction that is constitutitive of all reality requires a conception of "totality" that bridges the separation of thought and reality: All aspects of reality become aspects of the totality, but now for Hegel, as a *process* constituitive of the world, i.e., in history. History itself is the unfolding of contradictions as the societies and civilizations that have peopled it come to ever greater understanding of their nature. The processes of coming to such self-understanding are a series of revolutions in what Hegel thinks of as the absolute spirit that moves the world.

Kant, in his critiques of pure and practical reason, had claimed to have established an unbridgeable barrier between human knowledge-creating activity, especially science, on the one hand, and ethically guided behavior on the other. It was Hegel's intent to destroy this barrier. He proceeds by simultaneously attempting to unify the subjective (will, thought) and the objective (events in the world), and yet recognize their distinctiveness as they appear in the real world.

Phenomenological analyses holding that all reality is somehow incorporated in the willing and perceiving of the individual mind, such as that of Husserl, do not have this problem; there is no need to *maintain anything* as possessing objective status; everything objective is collapsed into the subjective. At the other extreme are those systems that collapse the mind into the objective reality; e.g., behaviorism in its extreme forms. Attempts to work out sociological systems exclusively on the foundations of either of these have undertheorized or only partially theorized social reality. Social science must recognize, and theorize, an "objective" order both because this is given in our experience and is constitutive of that experience, and because *relations* between individuals are not self-evidently reducible to individual attributes or actors. It must also reserve theoretical space for the subjective, because following the Descartes-Husserl line of analysis, this is indubitably given in our experience, but also because we understand it to be definitive, in some sense, of our very humanity. And social science must also theorize the relation *between* these because an objective order cannot exist in independence of the subjectivity of its perceivers, or apart from its necessary origins in human agency and the subjectivity this implies, as Vico, among eighteenth century thinkers, understood most clearly.

The subjective-objective unity-in-opposition presenting itself as a dialectic in history, is a variant—a late one—of the Enlightenment theory of progress. In a sense it is, philosophically at least, a culmination and synthesis of all the earlier ones, which unifies the human agency-driven and covert agency-in-history forms discussed in Chapter 2.

On this basis, Hegel works out his sociology, which, it is easy to see, must be an historical sociology. This appears mainly in *Philosophy of Right*.

Hegel's Theory of Society and Social Change

The synthesis of the subjective and objective that Hegel effects is a thoroughgoing organicism, but one that differs from earlier organic characterizations of the world in two ways: It constructs the world as ever-evolving and self-moving toward a unified whole, and it characterizes this process as one in which conflict plays the central role.

Hegel's sociology has some similarities to that of Comte. Like Comte, he formulated it substantively in terms of the categories of family, civil society, and state. The family is unified by "intuition"; civil society, the sphere of economic interest, by "understanding"; the state is the province of "reason." The family, says Hegel, is "the only social relationship" responsible for language and is a form of consciousness distinctive of human life, wherein the archetype of all human social relationships comes into being. In its very nature, however, the family bears within itself the conditions of its transcendence. Families are property-owning units and multiply intergenerationally as children grow up, reproduce, and inherit. As families proliferate, they tend to become competitive, and this process prepares the ground of civil society (Hegel, 1978, 114–120).

Hegel's category of civil society is a somewhat modified version of eighteenth and early nineteenth century economic thought, especially of liberals like Ferguson, Smith, and Ricardo. The economists, of course, not only recognized, but celebrated the relative de facto independence of the emerging market system from the rest of society. Hegel rejects this, arguing that market society creates the conditions that bring about its transcendence by the state, and in the course of this propounds a critique of capitalism that would not have been out of place in *The Communist Manifesto*. In civil society the individual finds his satisfactions in working in and through others; "his particularity is mediated," says Hegel. Civil society provides the conditions for much more reflection than is possible in the family; this reflection becomes objectified in the system of justice necessarily brought into being in civil society, a system in which

> the idea is lost in particularity and has fallen asunder with the separation of the inward and outward. In the administration of justice, however, civil society returns to its concept, to the unity of the implicit universal with the subjective particular, although here the latter is only that present in single cases and the universality in question is that of *abstract* right. (145)

Hegel goes on to maintain that the actualization of this unity is the specific responsibility of the police.

Civil society exhibits the working of the dialectic in being, first, a "system of needs" that finds a degree of satisfaction through the principle of freedom imposed by the system of justice, itself an ideal principle that must be understood historically. The "subjective particularity" of civil society, which in other forms can be found everywhere in history, differs in contemporary European society in that it becomes established in the "objective order", thereby becoming the "animating principle of the entire civil society." This amounts to a recognition of a "right" of a certain sort, by which Hegel means the legal framework establishing capitalist social relations as legitimate.[2]

However, the system of needs on the one hand, and the workings of the system of justice on the other, breed class divisions in society. In civil society

> the infinitely complex criss-cross movements of reciprocal production and exchange . . . (become) distinguished into general groups. As a result the entire complex is built up into particular systems of needs, means, and types of work relative to these needs, modes of satisfaction and of theoretical and practical education, i.e., into systems, to one or another of which individuals are assigned—in other words, into class-divisions" (130–131).

Hegel thinks the class system is such that

> natural capacity, birth, and other circumstances have their influence, though the essential and final determining factors are subjective opinion and the individual's arbitrary will, which win in this sphere their right, their merit and their dignity" (132)

However, the expansion of the division of labor that results from this has the effect of reinforcing "natural inequality".

> Men are made unequal by nature, where inequality is in its elements, and in civil society the right of particularity insofar from annulling this natural inequality that it produces it out of mind and raises it to an inequality of skill and resources, and even to one of moral and intellectual attainment. (130)

Furthermore, for Hegel it follows that

> to oppose this right a demand for equality is a folly of the understanding which takes as real and rational its abstract quality and its 'ought-to-be.' (130)

---

[2] A "Right" is an extent of any sort embodying "free will", says Hegel (Hegel, 1978, 33). One's character is built up throughout the course of one's life through acts of will, but the nature of that character at any particular time was implicit in childhood. A personality always struggles against the restrictions inherent in the world, and these struggles of will continuously transform both the individual personality and the world itself. This idea, which became central to the historicist movement in Germany during the nineteenth century, will be discussed in Chapter 13.

Class inequality inevitably creates conflict between classes; the interests of producers and consumers, for instance, may come into collision with each other (147). Hegel even seems to suggest that this conflict may be unresolvable in principle.

> It . . . becomes apparent that despite an excess of wealth, civil society is not rich enough . . . to check excessive poverty and the creation of a penurious rabble (150)

Attempts at reform that leave the basic workings of the system intact are, for Hegel, unworkable. To receive welfare for no work is, in his opinion, to violate the principle of civil society. But to *create* work, leading to an "excess of production", does so as well (151), since not enough consumers are also producers. In England and Scotland, the solution to this state of affairs has been to "leave the poor to their fate and instruct them to beg in the streets" (150). In these passages Hegel prefigures Marx's theory of class and class conflict.[3]

The contradictions of civil society, conceived of by Hegel as occurring in the sphere of the "spirit", eventually give rise to the state, gradually at first, through the creation of the police function, and "corporations", which Hegel thinks of as guildlike multiple-function organizations, in which the necessary functions of the family are unified with those of civil society. The state, however, is truly realized only through the actualization of the ethical idea. We must not, Hegel insists, mistake the true end of the state with its police function, for this would be tantamount to identifying it with the interests of individuals ("subjective particularity"). Specific historic issues that may attend the emergence of states have nothing to do with the *Idea* of the state (156). The state emerges dialectically in unifying the contradictions between family and civil society, and within civil society itself, transcending them in an idealized unity. This is a unity that must never be identified with the mere *organization* of the state (e.g., the division of powers between legislative and executive branches) but rather only as it realizes the *principle* of unity—in the case of turn-of-the-century Prussia, the monarchy.[4]

The difficulty with all this, and with Hegel's philosophy in general, Marx would later conclude, is that the world of the spirit, or thought, can never in itself have any effect on the real world of human practical activity. It is not that intellectual activity is of no account or of no significance, but that it is not *in and of itself*, as Hegel would have it, capable of transforming the world.[5] Hegel's thought exemplifies the general tendency of German

---

[3] He does so in his understanding of the global tendency of capitalism, as well. In a short but prescient paragraph, Hegel says that this "inner dialectic drives a specific civil society to push beyond its own limits and seek markets, and so its necessary means of subsistence, in other lands which are . . . deficient in the goods it has overproduced . . . (Hegel, 1978, 151).

[4] One sees the similarities to Comte: the idealistic conception of history and social life, the dialectical principle that proposes that everything prior historically (especially civil society) makes a necessary contribution to the emerging forms of political organization, and the claim that an absolute form of political domination (however idealistically characterized in the enlightenment language of freedom) represented the final highest and *immanent* form of human social organization.

[5] For Marx's critique of Hegel, see Marx (1843) and (1956).

idealism, including that of the Young Hegelians, to maintain, as Lichtheim puts it, "an unbridgeable barrier between criticism and action, theory and practice, philosophy and revolution" (Lichtheim, 1971b, 191), summed up in his famous aphorism "The real is rational and the rational is real."

In rejecting this, Marx broke not only with Hegel, but with the Young Hegelians as well because he concluded that their attempt to extract or derive an activism from a conception of human nature in which the mind dominates all else was programmatically fruitless. It was the intent of the Young Hegelians to strip away the master's conservatism but extend his idealism as a revolutionary force.[6] Marx and Engels, however, perceived in this a fundamental error.

> Since the Young Hegelians regard concepts, thoughts, ideas, and all products of consciousness, to which they give independent existence, as the real fetters of man—while the Old Hegelians pronounced them the true bonds of society—it is obvious that the Young Hegelians have to fight only against illusions of consciousness. In the Young Hegelians fantasies, the relationships of men, all their actions, their chains, and their limitations are products of their consciousness. Consequently they give men the moral postulate of exchanging their present consciousness for human, critical or egoistic consciousness to remove their limitations. This amounts to a demand to interpret what exists in a different way, that is, to recognize it by means of a different interpretation. The Young Hegelian ideologists are the staunchest conservatives, despite their alledgedly 'world-shaking' statements. The most recent among them have found the correct expression for their doings in saying they are fighting only against "*phrases*". They forget, however, that they fight them only with phrases of their own. (From *The German Ideology*, in Easton and Guddat, 1967, 407–408).

This critique of the Young Hegelians, which is simultaneously an attack on all idealism, also conveys the essence of what Marx meant when he spoke of the "end of philosophy" and its supercedence by science, and the sense in which he rejected the label "philosophy" for his own work.[7]

The importance to sociology of Hegel's depiction of self-consciousness and the self-moving course of history derived from it can hardly be overemphasized. Most obvious, of course, is Marx's and Engels' appropriation of the dialectic and turning it to the radical end of a materialist account of history. But Hegel's intellectually revolutionary account of the self as relational and oppositional rather than linear influenced powerfully a whole array of later schools and thinkers, including, of particular importance here, various German and other Romantics and the American pragmatist school, especially as represented by G. H. Mead.

---

[6] For a good treatment of the various Young Hegelians, see Hook (1950). For Marx's treatment, see especially *The German Ideology* (1845–1846).

[7] At least from 1846 onward he always understood his work as science. On this point one can easily see the stamp of the Enlightenment on Marx, Comte, and Spencer alike; all are Saint Simonians in pronouncing the superseding of philosophy by science (although Spencer still retained the term in designating his work "synthetic philosophy").

THE MATERIALISTS

The other side of the coin of Marx's critique of Hegel was his evaluation of the philosophy of materialism, especially French materialism. The materialism of eighteenth century French philosophers such as Holbach, Condillac, Lamettre, and Helvetius[8] was of importance for Marx's for two reasons.

First, these thinkers advanced a view of human nature quite different from that of idealists like Hegel and thereby provided a foundation for a *critique* of idealism. As Marx (and Engels) understood it, materialism developed "as an open outspoken struggle against the metaphysics of the seventeenth century and against all metaphysics" (from *The Holy Family*, in Easton and Guddat, 387), including the metaphysics of Descartes, Spinoza, and Leibniz. These reemerged as "a triumphant and substantial restoration in German philosophy, particularly in the speculative German philosophy of the nineteenth century" (387), the apotheosis of which is found in Hegel.

Second, materialism in its essential character, Marx and Engels thought, had displayed a consistent affinity for socialism and communism. On this point, after a review of the theories of the leading French materialists, they wrote:

> No great acumen is required to see the necessary connection of materialism with communism and socialism from the doctrines of materialism concerning the original goodness and equal intellectual endowment of man, the omnipotence of experience, habit and education, the influence of external circumstances on man, the extreme importance of industry, the justification of enjoyment, etc. If man forms all his knowledge, perception, etc., from the world of sense and experience in the world of sense, then it follows that the empirical world must be so arranged that he experiences and gets used to what is truly human in it, that he experiences himself as a man. . . . If man is by nature social, then he develops his true nature only in society and the power of his nature must be measured not by the power of the single individual but by the power of society (from *The Holy Family*, in Easton and Guddat, 1967, 394–395).

The influence of eighteenth century materialism on both the French and English communism of the nineteenth century was of enough significance to Marx and Engels (a topic needing "a detailed presentation": 397) that they may have entertained the ideal of preparing a major work on the subject.

But materialism, of course, was the philosophy of the bourgeoisie, and even though in its French form it, "endowed English materialism with *esprit*, with flesh and blood, with eloquence, (and) civilized it" (303), and even though this French variant represented a *"fighting bourgeoisie"* in contrast with its English counterpart—a "ruling bourgeoisie"—Marx and Engels rejected it. Although efforts like those of La Mettrie and Condillac were immensely valuable in displacing the idealistic metaphysics of earlier philosophy, both the French and English forms of materialism were at bottom deterministic philosophies. Whatever the intellectual prestidigitations of its

[8] See Chapter 3 for a discussion of certain aspects of the philosophies of these thinkers.

proponents (like Condillac's arguments regarding free will at the end of *L'homme machine* discussed in Chapter 3, to note one example), it allowed no space for human agency. And it was in good part to redress this defect of received materialism that Marx and Engels extracted and retained that kernel of truth from Hegel—the essential voluntary nature of mental activity. When Marx broke with idealism, Hook says:

> it was not in order to return to the simple materialism which made thinking appear to be either unnecessary or miraculous, but to provide a materialistic basis for the genuine discoveries the idealists made in their analysis of consciousness. . . . Not only the simplest thought but even the simplest perception cannot be plausibly explained as an effect of a mechanical impulse, for the very description of the mechanical impulse as an object of knowledge presupposes some active subject who approaches it with *this* category rather than *that*, with a whole set of values, assumptions, memories and anticipations which, whatever their origin, *now* contribute to what is seen and thought. (Hook, 1950, 275)

In his final thesis on Feuerbach, Marx asserts, "The Philosophers have only *interpreted* the world, in various ways; the point, however, is to *change* it." In this fashion Marx, as Worsley says, "slides between" idealism and materialism (Worsley, 1982, 30) and sets the stage for a science capable of energizing a revolutionary practice. Both determinism and agency were built into Marxism from the beginning.[9]

This science takes as its object both an understanding of the dynamics of capitalist societies (and to some extent, rather unfortunately, earlier ones as well). The theory is worked out around the concept "mode of production" and takes the processes of class formation and class action as the main motors of human action and historical change. The proletariat becomes the agency of the transformation of capitalism into socialism and then communism. The material condition of this class was described brilliantly and savagely by Engels in his *The Condition of the Working-Class in England* (1844). In comparison with other socialists during their lifetime, it can be seen that it was really only they who succeeded in formulating the situation of this class *theoretically* as it was coming into being and developing, and then, especially in Marx's later economic works, *explaining* this condition as a consequence of the inner functioning of the capitalist economy. The first of these tasks involved working out a structural and developmental theory of the industrial capitalist *working class*, the theory of "alienation". The second, broader and more ambitious in its scope, entailed the economic and sociological analysis of capitalist society. Only the first of these can be said to have approached completion by Marx. Taken together, they constitute Marx's theory of social

---

[9] At another level was the problem of the relationship between the intellectuals and the movement itself. Marx thought there was an affinity between the determinism of materialism and elitist political practice, wherein intellectuals' claims to knowledge were deductions from abstract theorizing. Somewhat ironically, later revolutionaries like Lenin and Mao, in greatly transformed historical circumstances, were forced to *dissociate* determinist theory from elitist practice. Lenin's elitism rests on a philosophical *voluntarism*. Mao's cultural revolution asserts the primacy of *ideal* over materialist factors.

structure and social change and will be discussed in the following chapter. But first it is necessary to introduce the concept of alienation, so important to Marx's sociology,[10] as it was developed by Hegel and Feuerbach.

THE THEORY OF ALIENATION: HEGEL, FEUERBACH, AND MARX

Marx's theory of alienation was rooted in a critique of both Hegel and the Young Hegelian, Ludwig Feuerbach. The general idea of alienation as an estrangement of the spirit is a religious idea and can be traced to the very origins of the Judeo-Christian tradition. It is the master theme of Augustine's *Confessions*, and of the Christian dualism of the soul, which struggles with itself seeking a unit that can be finally achieved only in the supreme act of faith and achievement of a state of grace in the world beyond. In Christianity a total abolition of alienation is perhaps impossible, even in sainthood, for the flesh and the objective conditions of life can never by totally transcended even through the most devout and powerful means of self-abnegation.

For Hegel all process, all history, proceeds through a dialectical process in which any thing, any moment, or "notion", by its very existence implies its opposite, or negation. In world historical terms this is understood by Hegel as a dialectic of subject and object, and Hegel's entire philosophy, as earlier depicted, is an attempt to resolve the subject-object dichotomy of Western philosophical thought, especially in the sharpened form in which Kant had left it.

The principle of alienation is constitutive of the dialectic: The social formations appearing in history are *objectifications* of contradictions resulting from the exercise of the will. They are in their nature separate from further willful action, forms of the *other* limiting the action of that will. It is this relation of separation, a ceding of power to another, that defines the alienated condition. As we have seen, the master-slave relation is the paradigm of this. As Hegel puts it,

> It is just in this concept of mind as that which is what it is only through its own free causality and through its endless return into itself out of the natural immediacy of its existence, that there lies the possibility of a clash: i.e., what it is potentially it may not be actually . . . , and vice versa what it is actually . . . may be other than what it is potentially. Herein lies the possibility of the alienation of personality and its substantive being, whether this occurs unconsciously or intentionally. Examples of the alienation of personality are slavery, selfdom, disqualification from holding property, encumbrances on property, and so forth. Alienation of intelligence and rationality, of morality, ethical life, and religion, is exemplified in superstition, in ceding to someone else full power and authority to fix and prescribe what actions are to be done . . . or what duties are binding on one's conscience or what religious truth is, etc. (Hegel, 1978, 53)

---

[10] A point with which many would disagree, especially Marxist "structuralists" and those who perceive a radical disjunction between Marx's early and later works. See especially Althusser, 1969.

We shall see later how Marx assimilated this idea in his early work.

In his earlier critique of Hegel, Marx had already exposed the problems in the *Philosophy of Right*, essentially from a liberal humanistic standpoint. A year or so later, after having moved to Paris and having enjoyed continuous contacts with French (and emigré German) working-class associations, he turned his hand to a critique of Hegel's philosophy in general. It was partly from this critique that he worked out his idea of alienation and of the proletariat as an alienated class.

Marx says that in Hegel "all the elements of a critical theory" are present, "but in alienated form" ("Economic and Philosophical Manuscripts"; hereafter designated "EPM," in Bottomore, 1964, 202). Hegel's error, he says, lies in the fact that he (Hegel) conceives of the alienation of objective entities (e.g., state, wealth) only in their "thought form," i.e., they are conceived of as being alienated only from abstract thought. "For Hegel, *objects* are appropriated only as thoughts and movements of thoughts." In characteristic ironic vein, he then goes on to turn Hegel's theory back on the latter's own thought, charging that the philosopher (i.e., Hegel himself, but also philosophers in general), is "an abstract form of alienated man . . . (who) sets himself up as the measure of the alienated world" (200).

However, Marx's critique is not a rejection of Hegel in toto. Indeed, he maintains that "the outstanding achievement of Hegel's *Phenomenology*— the dialectic of negativity as the moving and creating principle—is that Hegel grasps the self-creation of man as a process, objectification as loss of the object, as alienation and transcendence of this alienation, and that he, therefore, grasps the nature of *labour*, and conceives objective man . . . as the result of his *own labour* (202). It is this that is meant when it is said that although Marx rejected Hegel's idealism, he appropriated his method as a framework for his own work. And the most critical sense of this lay in its significance of Hegel for Marx's theory of alienation.

Marx actually attributes much of the foregoing to Feuerbach, who in 1841 had published his *The Essence of Christianity* (Feuerbach, 1893), something of a philosophical and theological bombshell and of momentous importance to the Young Hegelians. In an earlier work Feuerbach had reversed the Hegelian order of things, arguing that intellectual activity was the *result*, not the origin, of practical worldly activity and rejected the master's attempt to demote sense experience to an irrelevancy, arguing instead that it is indispensable to the development of any theoretical knowledge. And because of this, he had asserted against Hegel that philosophy ought to concern itself in the first instance with the seemingly unphilosophical problem of the concrete needs of humanity as these are found in the real world.

In *The Essence of Christianity* Feuerbach continued this line of thought but now taking up the problem of religion. This was a period in Germany during which the state religion, Lutheranism, was being subjected to various criticisms, especially by other Young Hegelians like David Strauss and Bruno Bauer. Strauss (1953) had shown that the accounts of the gospels were contradictory and so could not be accepted as legitimate history, and then gone on to argue that all such accounts should be treated as myths and analyzed *historically*, rather than naively being taken as revealed. For expounding these ideas, he was declared by the state to be unfit for an academic position. Bauer had gone even beyond these near-heretical pronouncements of Strauss, raising questions of the authenticity of events reported in the Bible, and denying the existence of Christ as a historic individual (Hook, 1950, Chap. 3, Pt. 1). Bauer thought that his work had not only undermined the historical foundations of Christianity, but that it delivered the critical coup de grace to all of religion.[11] Not surprisingly, although Bauer himself eschewed political action on the grounds that history itself would eventually do away with religion, he was forced from his position at the University of Bonn.[12]

Feuerbach went beyond both Strauss and Bauer. Religious ideas, he maintained, were no more than illusions resulting from humankind's self-alienation. God is imagined as the perfection that is at once the opposite of his own frailties and suffering and a projection of everything he wishes to be. The poorer, the more miserable, the more abjectly degraded, the greater the need for a transcendent belief. "The poor man has a rich God," he says, and in elaborating this provides the direct antecedent of Marx's theory of religion as "opium of the people."

Feuerbach then argued that religion arose out of humankind's unconscious deification of itself, thereby existing as a distorted reflection of the real life of human needs and drives (the antecedent of Marx's later characterization of religion as the "heart of a heartless world"). He maintained that the characteristics attributed to God are identical with those of human nature and that this required religion to be understood in terms of the natural concrete conditions of human existence. Theology, then, is no more than a systematic idealization of real human relationships. Thus for Feuerbach, all existing and historical religions are forms of alienation, which, being created unconsciously, rule people's lives on irrational grounds. This state of alienation, however, could be transformed if the material foundations of life were clearly recognized; he thought that a critical philosophy could be formulated on the basis of a humanistic ethics (indeed, that a kind of "humanistic religion," fully cognizant of its nature, would come into being in the future).[13]

Throughout his life, Feuerbach thought of himself and his humanism in the tradition of Spinoza, referring to his books as "letters to mankind." His humanism is an attempt to unify the "natural" with the social aspect of the species. There exists, he believed, a profound continuity between the

---

[11] Hook remarks that whereas "a Christian might make peace with Strauss, . . . from Bauer he was separated by an abyss" (Hook, 1950, 93).

[12] The suspicion with which the Prussian state viewed the Young Hegelians is reflected in the state edict prohibiting them from lecturing on any subject other than aesthetics.

[13] Along with Marx (and Engels), Feuerbach represents more than anyone else during the first half of the nineteenth century the continuation of the Enlightenment critique of religion. The German Enlightenment came later than the French, and the German attack on religion recapitulates much of what had transpired earlier in French thought. In France at the time, the issue of religion had lost some of its saliency. Many of the German socialists arriving in Paris in the 1840s were quite surprised at the rather unproblematic attitude toward religion found among French socialist workers. This was the beginning of the accommodation of Catholicism to a nonrevolutionary socialism that in Catholic Europe mainly took the form of Catholic workers parties.

natural world and the human socialized species. Transcendence of estrangement for him meant an organic union of the natural and human, a humanistic
religion of universal love, not unlike Comte's religion of humanity.

Marx thought that Feuerbach was "the only person who has a *serious*
and *critical* relation to Hegel's dialectic, who has made real discoveries in this
field, and above all, who has vanquished the "old philosophy" (*EPM*, in
Bottomore, 1964, 197). Feuerbach had shown the negation of the negation
to be a "contradiction *only* within philosophy itself," which—again, nicely
ironic—"affirms theology after having superseded it" (198). His treatment
of religion as alienation thus went beyond Hegel's, which existed only in the
realm of thought. Marx regarded Feuerbach's analysis as "materialist"
(although Feuerbach himself persistently denied that he was either a materialist *or* an idealist)[14] and his own theory of alienation is both an extension
of and critique of Feuerbach's.

Marx accepted Feuerbach's central idea of religious alienation as
estrangement[15] from the very products of one's activity. Feuerbach provided
an indispensable corrective to Hegel in demonstrating that civil society, not
the state, was the true sphere in which humanity's potential for freedom
must be realized. In his earlier critique of Hegel, Marx had followed
Feuerbach, arguing that the state, as the apparatus of oppression, would
disappear. But in the *EPM* he extended Feuerbach's critique to the principles
of capitalist economy (i.e., Hegel's "civil society"), arguing for the first time
that capital was, in fact, a form of human labor, "alienated labor," and that
it was the essential condition of the estrangement of labor. This was quite
daring, but critically foundational to Marx's later work. It was a reformulation
of Feuerbach's rather vague materialism in terms of practical activity, i.e.,
labor. It is also an intellectual watershed in the sense that here Marx
transcends the Enlightenment belief—of which Feuerbach may be the last
gasp—that the abolition of religion would be a more or less sufficient
condition for the realization of the good society through the growth and
application of scientific knowledge. For Marx the critique and essential
abolition of religion are necessary, of course, but only as a preliminary to
the more fundamental and demanding task of formulating a critique and
analysis of alienation as it actually was manifest in the *material* foundations
of social life and on this basis proceeding to the work of developing an
emancipatory science of human social life.

The *EPM* were the first writings in which Marx's materialism appears.
Although they doubtless remain the most humanistic of Marx's works, human
labor is even here characterized as the "essence" of private property, or
capital, which must be "abolished." "Communism is the *positive* abolition of
private property, of human *self-alienation* (Bottomore, 1964, 155). Recalling the

---

[14] He argues systematically against materialism understood in any "absolute" sense. For a
discussion see Hook (1950), 239–242. Later in life he adopted a radical physiological
determinism, this perhaps bearing out Marx's early judgment.

[15] Despite traditional usage, I shall henceforth follow Walliman in employing the term *estrangement*
(usually *Entfremdung*) to refer to the process of being ruled or dominated by the products of
one's own activity, and *alienation* (usually *Entäusserung*) to designate the sense of being
separated from something or someone. Walliman's analysis is a convincing textual exegesis
of Marx's usage of *Entfremdung* and *Entäusserung*. See Walliman, 1981.

spirit of Rousseau, Marx inveighs against the division of labor as the social process underlying private property and class divisions, and therefore (seemingly) scheduled for abolition in the communist society of the future; "although the division of labor increases the productive power of labor and refinement of society, it improverishes the worker and makes him into a machine" (75).[16] The *EPM* reflect Marx's attempt to approach analysis of capitalist society still essentially within Feuerbach's humanistic framework, but in identifying alienation and estrangement in the economic sphere as fundamental, he goes beyond Feuerbach as well as Hegel. He thought of criticism of religion not only as preparatory to criticism of the state, but also as preparatory for the more fundamental task of criticizing the material foundations of religion and the state. Both political and religious estrangement appear "only in consciousness," whereas economic estrangement is a phenomenon of "real life."

A year or so later, in the "Eleven Theses on Feuerbach,"[17] we find an expansion of these remarks and, in fact, a systematic if terse critique that many think of as Marx's decisive break with idealism.[18]

Although he still agreed with Feuerbach's "unmasking" of the material foundations of religion, in the "Theses" Marx not only attacks Feuerbach on a series of interrelated issues, but more importantly, adumbrates with admirable economy the essential domain assumptions of the general science that would frame his own work. These domain assumptions, I think, can be reduced to three:

1. The "essence" of humankind consists in practical activity in which objective relations with nature and with others are created and modified, and in the course of which the *meanings* of these relations are also constructed and changed.
2. Human activity must be grasped in its *concrete* reality and not in terms of alleged universals whether they be of the spirit or the flesh.
3. Scientific knowledge of these relations can be acquired only in close association or involvement in transformative action; tests of and establishment of knowledge must take the form of submitting it to the test of change-oriented action (praxis).

In what follows I will discuss these using material from the "Theses."

1. "Social life is essentially practical. All mysteries that mislead theory into mysticism find their rational solution in human practice and in the

---

[16] He expands on this theme in *The German Ideology*, where the expansion of the division of labor is explicitly identified as the process underlying estrangement in capitalist society.

[17] The "Theses" have been reprinted in many places. See Easton and Guddat, 1967, 400–402. They were evidently written in March of 1845 but published only by Engels as an appendix to his *Ludwig Feuerbach* in 1888, not too long after he had discovered them in one of Marx's notebooks. For a detailed analysis of the "Theses," see Hook (1950), Chapter 8.

[18] Whether it also constitutes a break with his early humanism, as some (principally Althusser) have maintained, or whether Fromm, (1941), Schaff (1970), Kolakowski (1978), Walliman (1981), and others are correct in asserting the essential humanism of all of his work, despite changes in terminology and theoretical emphases, remains a point of debate. It seems to me that the weight of the evidence lies with the latter.

understanding of this practice." So writes Marx in Thesis VIII. If materialism is to constitute the foundations of science capable of informing the transformation of society, it must be stripped of its deterministic character and somehow be brought into conjunction with the great insight of the idealists, the idea of the mind as active and potentially world-transforming. The materialistic philosophies of the past were ahistorical and deterministic. The French in particular understood human nature in mechanistic, static, typically physiological terms, heavily influenced by developments in French medicine. There is also a fundamental logical difficulty; even the claim that such a theory is true leads to a logical impasse, since the theory itself must then be determined, and this admission undermines its nature as an explanatory theory.

Marx's critique eventuates in a radically transformed materialism. The foundation of a scientific materialism must be constituted on the basis of an understanding that human activity is incorrigibly, necessarily practical, or at least that this is so for the massive majority of all human beings who have ever inhabited the real world. This understanding of materialism, Marx thought, circumvented the determinism problem, since human practical activity is clearly—to Marx—*transformative*, or else nothing in this world would ever have changed. It is inherent in man's practical engagement with the world, then, that it brings about change not only of the natural world, but of the human agents engaged in practical activity.

Marx's formulation reserves a theoretical place for the mind as indispensable in the transformative process, but—and this is crucial—leaves open as *contingent* the extent to which the *rational potential* of the mind can be brought to bear on that process, a potential contingent on the specifics of concrete historical conditions. Feuerbach, says Marx, "regards only the theoretical attitude as the truly human one" and "does not grasp the significance of 'revolutionary' . . . practical, critical, activity" (Thesis I).

2. Feuerbach's theory of religion takes religion to be a universal, a construction resulting from what he thinks of, in effect, as the existential condition of man, believing that a humanistic religion will some day transcend religious estrangement. Marx rejects this universalizing of the religious experience and proposes instead to locate the human powerlessness that underlies religion in the *concrete* powerlessness of specific social relations. Religious myths and theologies are not universal human wishes projected into consciousness in different forms, but reflect the human powerlessness built into real social relations, especially relations of production. Religion, like all other productions of the species, must be understood historically, in its concrete specificity. The fact that religion has appeared everywhere means only that exploitative and repressive social relations have been at the core of all human societies. But is also means that a humane society will, of necessity, be one in which religion is abolished (Theses I, IV, VI, VII).

These two tenets, taken together, imply a conception of human needs that is central to Marx's philosophical anthropology and that departs totally from the doctrine that human beings possess a constant human nature that could be invoked to explain events occurring on the plane of social life. For Marx, human needs are historical, always a fact of life of a particular society, and a creation of the social relations of production of that society.

As such they themselves become material for analysis and explanation rather than principles to be invoked as *explanans*.[19] Finally, the principle of human needs as social and as changing had important implications for Marx's diagnosis of capitalist society in his later works. In all this, Marx is sociological to the core.

      3. "The question of whether human thought can achieve objective truth is not a question of theory but a *practical* question. In practice man must prove the truth" (Thesis II). If the nature and functioning of the mind depends on the practical nature of the situation, then knowledge cannot be acquired in isolation from such situations. Knowledge thus always has a foundation in the life-situation, and to think otherwise, e.g., to proclaim the universality of one's truth or to regard ideas as somehow having a life of their own, is to mystify the incorrigible relation between theory and practice. We can only know whether or not a seeming truth is true by *acting* on it. "Philosophers have only interpreted the world differently; the point is, however, to change it" (Thesis XI).

---

[19] For an excellent and detailed explication of Marx's concept of needs, see Heller (1976).

10

MARX AND ENGELS
Historical materialism and the sociology
of capitalist society

INTRODUCTION

Comte and Spencer were self-consciously engaged in the task of creating
sociology. On the face of it, it might seem that sharing this common goal
would set them off in the sharpest possible manner from Marx, for Marxism
is obviously many things that sociology is not or at least claims not to be: a
political ideology, an economic theory, a philosophy of history (on some
interpretations, at least); and sociology is many things Marxism is not: an
academic discipline, a "profession" (if only self-styled), a conception of the
world generally congenial to capitalism and the capitalist state. Yet there are
clear commonalities as well: Both claim scientific status; both have centered
upon understanding the nature and direction of capitalist (and to a lesser
extent, unfortunately, socialist) societies, although it must be said that in the
case of sociology this interest has tended to become secondary to others,
especially in the United States, as various sorts of mostly ahistorical quantitative analysis in sociology have come to define the meaning of becoming
"professionalized"; both claim to be embodiments of the Enlightenment
vision of achieving a future humane and emancipated world through
knowledge, although in sociology this has to a large degree become an empty
formalism, and the practical embodiments of Marxism have increasingly
come to be revealed as humanly intolerable bureaucratic despotisms.

    In the light of even these ever so cursory remarks, it should not be
surprising that the relationship between Marxism and sociology has been
formulated in the most varied ways. There have always, of course, been
those on both sides of the fence who have maintained that the differences

are such that the two could, indeed, *must* never meet. In years past, sociologists of the mainstream typically rejected the ideological intent of Marxism, on this basis denying it any legitimate scientific status. Martindale, for example, in 1960 grouped Marxism with the economic and racist variants of Social Darwinism as just another "major nineteenth century ideology" (Martindale, 1960, Chap. 7). Marxists have—as often—dismissed sociology as ideology masquerading in the persona of science (e.g., Therborn, 1976). Today, the general trend has been for academic sociology to accept, rather grudgingly, a sanitized, non-action-oriented Marxism, but to compartmentalize it or subsume it under other supposedly broader principles, and to disconnect from its understanding of the theory-practice relation. In this view Marxism is alternatively a form of sociology, a special way of doing sociology, an emphasis within sociology, or a needed corrective to other sociological perspectives, or any or all of these simultaneously. These marginally discriminated variants have become crystallized in the view that sociology is a "multiparadigm science," incorporating "consensus," "conflict," and "interactionist" paradigms (the view advanced with special vigor by George Ritzer [1975]). Somewhat distinct from this domesticating, or "sociologizing" of Marx, is the position taken by Gouldner, which understands sociology and Marxism as parallel "sister disciplines" (Gouldner, 1980, 22) having "much to contribute to understanding the other" (23).

Marxism has indeed played a large role in the history of sociology. Of the three dominant nineteenth century sociological theories dealt with in this section, those of Comte and Spencer exerted immediate and profound influence on the development of sociology, on Ward and Sumner in the United States, Durkheim in France, and other lesser figures. Marxism was important in a different way: as a set of ideas and movements to which sociology was often quite self-consciously intended as an *alternative*, even where, as was sometimes the case, some of its elements came to be incorporated into those very sociologies. While it would be a mistake to maintain that this was the whole of the story, as Karl Korsch, for example, comes very close to doing (Korsch, 1963, Chap. 2), it is nevertheless true that Comte thought of his positivism as a true science that would wean the working class away from dangerous socialist ideas, and that Spencer intended his system to demonstrate the folly of any intervention in the "natural" workings of capitalism—precisely what the collectivist movements of the nineteenth century believed to be necessary if a humane order was ever to be brought into being.

This was as true in the United States as it was in Europe. All the important American sociologists of the late nineteenth century, including not only Sumner, but Ward and other liberals as well, for the most part shied away from anything socialistic. Ward's idea of telesis, for instance, was a theory of the *gradual* growth of intelligence in shaping the social order that drew from both Comte and Spencer. When Albion Small proposed to set up the first sociology department in the world at the University of Chicago, which was funded by Rockefeller money, he was explicit in characterizing sociology as an alternative to socialism (Mathews, 1977, 95–

96), in spite of the fact that parts of his own work have a rather Marxist tone.[1]

This short review suggests not only that Marxism and sociology have indeed been parallel intellectual—and perhaps political—tracks, as Gouldner says, and that Marx and Marxism have made a substantial contribution to social science and sociology, but also implies that there may well be a sociology of sorts in Marx. A somewhat "weak" form of this view is expressed by Lefebvre, who maintains, somewhat confusingly, that "although Marx is not a sociologist, . . . there is a sociology in Marx" (Lefebvre, 22) and that "it is possible to recognize in Marx's works a sociology of the family, of the city and the countryside, of subgroups, classes, and whole societies, of knowledge, of the state, etc." (24). Somewhat distinct from this is the view that Marx formulated an essentially sociological conception of society (at least, of capitalist society), but was unable (or unwilling) for various reasons to develop it in directions parallel to the ways in which Comte, Spencer, and their various followers worked out their sociologies. Bottomore maintains, for instance, that Marx's project was, "an attempt to construct a historical social science (Bottomore, 1956, 20). Lichtheim holds that standing "behind" a whole series of issues implicated in assimilating German, French, and British intellectual currents is the fact that Marx went "behind them to the central issue of his age: the genesis and functioning of modern society" (Lichtheim, 1971b, 187). Perhaps this is the nub of the question. Can one formulate a better definition of the central task of a sociologist? Could not one say the same of Comte and Spencer, and maintain that precisely this makes them sociologists?

What does seem fairly clear is that Marx and Engels together envisioned a general science of society that would be realized in revolutionary practice, and that this vision involved something of greater scope than just an analysis of capitalist economics. Already in the *Paris Manuscripts* of 1844, at the age of twenty-six, Marx stated his intention of publishing

> my critique of law, morals, politics, etc., in a number of independent brochures, and finally . . . in a separate work, to present the interconnected whole, to show the relationships between the parts, and to provide the critique of the speculative treatment of this material. That is why, in the present work, the relationships of political economy with the state, law, morals, civil life, etc., are touched upon only to the extent political economy itself expressly deals with these subjects" (Bottomore, 1964, 63).

Marx never got beyond the "first brochure," which was eventually published as *Capital* (in four volumes), and what we have in Marx's and Engels's other writings are some quite brilliant political analyses, most importantly Marx's analyses of class politics in France and Engels's *The Peasant War in Germany*, some cogent and insightful but sketchy and unsystematic remarks about the nature of social classes, along with a variety of provocative sketches dealing

[1] See Aho (1975) for an excellent analysis of how European conflict theories were modified in the American socioeconomic climate of Progressivism.

with religion, the family, and various other topics, much of it in popular or journalistic form, or in Marx's voluminous correspondence. But years later we find Engels reflecting on the early days of their association in the *"Anti-Dühring"*, or *Herr Eugen Dühring's Revolution in Science*, recalling that

> it was therefore a question of bringing the science of society, that is, the sum total of the so-called historical and philosophical sciences, into harmony with the materialist foundation, and of reconstructing it thereupon (Engels, 1939, 20).

The key idea here is the "reconstruction" of the "science of society" clearly something larger than just economics.

If Marx and Engels were aiming for a comprehensive human science, of which the economic analysis of *Capital* was to be only a part, their project can be thought of as *programatically* akin to those of Comte and Spencer, a fulfillment of the Enlightenment vision of a body of knowledge capable of being "midwife" (as Marx referred to himself in connection with the problem of material versus ideal causality) in bringing into being the socialist society of the future. Indeed, the not uncommon idea that Marx was the nineteenth century's "true heir" of the Enlightenment (e.g., Zeitlin, 1981, vii), while perhaps an extreme interpretation, has a good deal to recommend it.

The incomplete (and in some respects ambiguous) nature of Marx's and Engels's work has brought into being a host of Marx-Engels interpreters, critics, literary epigone, and those who aspire to complete his system: an army of Marxologists far too vast to enumerate here. (In any case many extensive Marx bibliographies are available.) Every conceivable aspect of Marx's thought has been examined, expanded, rejected, canonized. In this situation, any claim to have identified the "true" Marx must be at least mildly suspect. At the same time, one must stake out one's position. Accordingly, although in the account to follow the sociologically important aspects of Marx's Marxism will be discussed in terms of the framing ideas of this book, I shall attempt to do justice to those many aspects of Marx's and Engels's work that remain controversial.

MARX AND ENGELS

Marx was born in Trier, in the Rhineland, and spent his early years there. Germany during those years was a relatively backward land both politically and in terms of its economic development, at least when compared with England and France. This was a fact of some importance for Marx's early intellectual development. The Rhineland, however, more so than other parts of Germany, had come under the influence of the French Enlightenment after having been annexed by France during the Napoleonic period. During Marx's youth, the Saint-Simonian religion had taken root there and Marx's father—originally Jewish, but later a convert to the Lutheran State Church—had been attracted to it. So Marx was exposed early to what at the time were the most avant-garde socialist ideas in Europe. In this respect, it might also be noted that two of the three main sociological developmental streams of the nineteenth century have at least this very important common root.

In 1836 Marx left Trier and enrolled in the university at nearby Bonn, but soon became dissatisfied, and the following year transferred to Berlin, where Hegel's philosophy, the greatest intellectual influence on Marx's life, was regnant. After his dissertation was accepted at Jena in 1841, Marx seemed to be set for an academic career, but the dissertation itself, an examination of the philosophies of Democritus and Epicurus, heavily influenced by Bauer's critical analysis of Christianity, proved too radical for this in conservative Germany. So after a short period at Bonn—with Bauer, just before his dismissal because of his radical ideas—Marx soon became associated with the journal *Rhenische Zeitung*, published in Cologne, eventually becoming its editor. This journal, to which other young Hegelians contributed, was suppressed in 1843, however, and Marx was again cut adrift.

In the fall of 1843 he moved to Paris, and there, along with others founded the *Deutsche-Französische Jahrbuch*, in which some of his early articles appeared. It was here also that the *Economic and Philosophical Manuscripts* were written, although they were not to become available until well into the next century. But once again Marx fell afoul of the authorities and left Paris for Brussels, where he (again) encountered Friedrich Engels and began a lifelong collaboration that stands as one of the greatest and most creative partnerships in intellectual history. During these years, Marx and Engels published many works, including *The Holy Family, The German Ideology*, and *The Communist Manifesto*. Once again, Marx found himself in difficulties with the authorities, this time being accused of treason. He was tried, and after conducting his own defense, acquitted but exiled. Marx finally settled in England, where he lived until his death in 1883.

In London Marx was at times—mostly later in life—active in the international Communist movement and became one of its best-known figures. But most of his time was spent in the library preparing and eventually writing the great works of his maturity, especially *Das Kapital*. Much of his life there—mainly the earlier years—was lived on the brink of, if not in abject poverty. He and his family subsisted on stipends from Engels and by writing articles for various publications, particularly the New York *Daily Tribune*, at that time a radical paper. Much of his later work, including volumes two and three of *Capital* and the *Outline of a Critique of Political Economy*, were not published until after his death.[2]

What about Engels, and the Marx-Engels relationship? He and Marx met early on, but even before this, and before Marx had "discovered" economics, Engels had published his superb *The Condition of the Working Class in England* and "Critique of Political Economy" in 1844, the latter in Marx's journal. Throughout his life, Engels was very self-effacing relative to Marx, always praising his contributions and playing down his own, but as Collins has recently argued, Engels was not only a powerful intellect in his own right, and original fount of many "Marxist" ideas, but the more sociologically inclined of the two (Collins, 1985, 56–62).

Despite the fact that he came from a business family, Engels was a

---

[2] For Marx's life, see McClellan (1973).

revolutionary and had actually led the 1848 revolution in his hometown of Barmen. After his and Marx's exile from Belgium in 1850, Engels also settled in England, and became first a clerk, then manager of his family's factory in Manchester. For over twenty years he remained for the most part uninvolved in day-to-day radical politics, but contributed fairly regularly to supporting the ever-impoverished Marx and his family in London. Only in the 1870s did he return to active involvement in the socialist movement, and then to the editing of many of Marx's works posthumously, and the writing of his own.

While a separation can be made between Marx's and Engels' works, and in some respects between their basic intellectual orientations, the approach here will be to emphasize their commonalities, with regard to their writings both jointly and singly authored, unless there is reason to proceed otherwise.

MARX'S PHILOSOPHICAL ANTHROPOLOGY

As I have tried to show earlier, the Enlightenment was a time during which the tension between the notion that knowledge of an invariant human nature that would constitute the key to the understanding of both past and future on the one hand, and the doctrine of progress, on the other, was a critical factor impelling the social thought of the times in the direction of a genuinely sociological conception. The systems of Comte and Spencer, as we have seen, acquired their sociological character in good part *because* they were worked out as partial resolutions of those incompatible doctrines. Yet, as we have seen, even Comte and Spencer only modified, but did not abandon, notions of original human nature derived from their eighteenth century forerunners.[3] Comte held closer to the eighteenth century, maintaining that original nature was, indeed, unchanging, but that its *social* manifestations, under the directing influence of the mind, constituted the subject matter of sociology. Spencer accommodated the received idea of human nature to the principle of progress by abandoning the idea that it is constant throughout history, and in this formulation made a significant break with eighteenth century social science.

Marx's philosophical anthropology, when compared with that of Comte or of Spencer, is distinctive precisely in this respect: Although Marx shares, in a general way, the Enlightenment ideal of progress—indeed, more than any other thinker of the century, he points up or reveals the tension

---

[3] Various forms of biological or psychological reductionism continue to be promoted as indispensable to sociological explanation. Sociobiology is only the most obvious of these, but they appear in "mainstream" sociology as well; particularly in some rational choice and exchange theories. See also Lenski's *Power and Privilege* (1966), a historical theory of social stratification cast in evolutionary form, in which the author finds it necessary to advance a series of postulates defining *individual* qualities—derived from the liberal tradition of Hobbes and Smith, to underpin the entire sociological analysis (see Chap. 1); or Collins's *Conflict Sociology* (1975), in which a similar, but more sophisticated construction of basic human nature of an ethological character is presented, again as the foundation of a general sociology of social stratification (see especially chap. 3).

between the two versions of it—he formulated his conception of human nature *independently* of this theory of social change. By this I mean that it is not causally implicated in the nature, direction, or ultimate destiny of that process of change. Neither Marx's theory of "historical materialism" (which was not Marx's term) nor his conception of capitalist social structure and dynamics theoretically require a formulation of human nature *as an explanatory principle*. In this sense it is with Marx that the decisive transcendance of the Enlightenment dilemma of human nature and progress occurs.

The essence of being human, says Marx in the *First Manuscript*, the quality that sets human beings apart from animals, is what he terms, borrowing from Feuerbach, "species-life." Although human life, like that of animals, is unequivocally part of nature, human beings must be distinguished from animals: "Conscious life activity distinguishes man from the life-activity of animals" and "Only for this reason is he a species-being" (*EPM*, in Bottomore, 1964, 127). The significance of this for Marx is that "man makes life-activity itself an object of his will and consciousness" (127). It is in this sense that *production* through the manipulation of the inorganic world acquires its significance.

> It is just in his work upon the objective world that man really proves himself as a *species-being*. This production is his active species-life. By means of it nature appears as *his* work and his reality. The object of labor is, therefore, the *objectification of man's species-life*; for he no longer produces himself merely intellectually, as in consciousness, but actively and in a real sense, and he sees his own reflection in a world which he has constructed (128).

Now this work of self-production is an incorrigibly social process. "In *species-consciousness*," Marx writes, "man confirms his real *social life* and reproduces his real existence in thought." Specifically referring to Communism, he says that "individual human life and species-life are not different things, even though the mode of existence of individual life is necessarily either a more *specific* or a more *general* mode of species-life . . . " (158). "Activity and mind are social in their content as well as in their *origin*" (157). And in the sixth thesis on Feuerbach, he says that "the essence of man is not an abstraction residing in each single individual. In its reality it is the whole of social relationships." The human essence is "the ensemble of social relations."

For Marx the social character of all human existence arises from the natural conditions under which production is instituted: All forms of human production are social. Given the physiological commonalities of humans, which they share in general with the animals, human nature is historically variable because the forms of production are variable. Production and reproduction of the means of subsistence implies, for Marx, the simultaneous production and reproduction of the social relationships that constitute human society itself.

All this has been discussed and summarized admirably by Planenatz. Existing as a "species being" means that *acting* as members of the species, men and women necessarily recognize themselves as belonging to it. Being and acting as a human being presupposes that one knows one is human; the knowing presupposes the being. But this in turn presupposes membership in a community and awareness of one's relationships with others (even if they are mistaken about their nature). In relation to the environment, we are producers of things that satisfy our wants and in the process acquire the need for self-expression and *understand* our actions as forms of self-expression. So we come to know ourselves as creators through our labor, through this acquiring the understanding that we can change our nature. Because we are social and our labor is social, this understanding may come to encompass a full grasp of how our natures are formed through collective or communal involvement in the labor process (Plamenatz, 1975, 69–77).

In general, it may be said that most contemporary sociological interpretations of Marx follow this line. Giddens, for example, has argued that Marx's idea of alienation should be understood as an alienation from historically variable social conditions (Giddens, 1971, 15–16) rather than from some postulated essential nature. On the other hand, interpretation of Marx's conception of human nature as historical has at times been challenged by those who have understood Marx as advancing an "essentialist" theory of human nature. In this vein, for instance, Joachim Israel maintains that Marx's concept of human nature incorporates "metaphysical" elements and emphasizes their alleged untestable nature (Israel, 1971, 24).

In the course of his recent work clarifying Marx's theory of alienation, Isador Walliman has argued that Marx in fact had a double theory of human nature (Walliman, 1981). There is first a biological one, in which he (Marx) distinguishes humans from animals in terms of the human capacity for willful and self-conscious creative activity and the capacity to relate to the needs of others specifically as *human* needs. But there is also a historical human nature that encompasses everything not included in the biological conception—everything, in short, that is historically variable (15–16). Walliman goes on to argue that Marx thought of alienation in the context of original nature, not historical nature, a controversial position. At one level this dispute is semantic. The very idea of "human nature" has ordinarily been intended to designate an "original nature," an *anthropology* that, by definition, is transhistorical. Substantively, however, Walliman's point is well taken; while Marx clearly advances a social conception of the species, there are also points at which he seems to revert to an original nature idea (even though he used the term *"Gattungswesen,"* translated as "species being," and generally avoided terms such as "original nature" and "human nature".)

In any case, Marx certainly carries forward his analyses of capitalism and class conflict, and of precapitalist historical transformations, quite independently of any considerations centering on original human nature. He understood fully that historical change cannot be accounted for by human nature constructs of any sort, and indeed, that the very notion of human nature has no *technical status* in such an analysis. In this sense Marx's philosophical anthropology was a clear break with the remnants of the received original nature theorizing and a sociological fruition of the Enlightenment "environmental" tendencies. This is evident throughout Marx's work. He attacks economists like Smith and Ricardo for reading as human nature the acquisitiveness he regarded as specific to capitalism. In *The German Ideology* he and Engels dissect utilitarianism in a brilliant and scathing critique in which the idea of the self-interested individual as the foundation of society is rejected as a universal and shown to be the particular manifestation in consciousness of capitalist social relations. They label a "nursery tale" the idea that societal inequality resulted from individual differences.

Logically the social order must be considered to be prior to the individual, and the idea of the individual must thereby be constructed as fundamentally social and *historical*.[4]

DYNAMICS OF CHANGE: HISTORICAL MATERIALISM AND THEORY OF CAPITALIST SOCIETY

Marx's and Engels's Historical Materialism and the Theory of Alienation and Estrangement

Marx's critique of Feuerbach in the "Theses" was already anticipated in the *EPM*, as I have said, and this is particularly true of the most important part of the manuscripts, the theory of alienation. Although the "Theses" were written a year later than the manuscripts, they can be thought of as establishing the ground not only for other aspects of Marx's social theory, but for the theory of alienation as well.

Recall that Feuerbach had located human alienation in the religious experience. Religion was the form of experience through which human wretchedness expressed itself, a fantasy life or displaced meaning construction that veiled the realities of the human condition. At one level, this is still Hegelian, because the decisive factor remains in the sphere of the ideal. The "Theses on Feuerbach" are a critique precisely of Feuerbach's idealism. The critique of religion, Marx realizes at this point, is indispensable, but only as a preliminary. In and of itself, it will change nothing, being just so much more idealist philosophizing, still another indictment and "correction" of the "error" of religious thought. Feuerbach's position is thus basically that of the Enlightenment critics of religion like Voltaire, who regarded it as an obstacle to progress because it was an erroneous form of thought. But alienation rooted in the material foundations of life is not susceptible to philosophical correction as error; it cannot be touched by ideas as such.

Marx's and Engels's theory of alienation/estrangement was *materialist*, and *historical*, in the sense that the property relations defining different historical societies were at once conditions incorporating different forms and degrees of alienation. It is to Marx's and Engels's construction of this history that we turn next.

Before we begin this, however, recall the point made in footnote No. 15 of the preceding chapter regarding Walliman's clarification of Marx's general, although not fully consistent use of *Entäusserung* and *Entfremdung*.

---

[4] In these discussions Marx perhaps laid the groundwork for a theory of a social conception of the self, as some have claimed. His and Engel's interests, of course, lay in a quite different direction. In *The German Ideology* they were interested in establishing the ground for a materialist analysis of society by showing the unworkability of idealistic philosophy for this task. In this sense, *The German Ideology* can be read as a methodological treatise grounding the social sciences in a very general way.

These are translated as "alienation" and "estrangement" respectively, and designate, respectively, the forcible removing of some sort of power, mainly power over the disposal of one's labor, from one's possession, in the case of alienation; and the condition in which one's creations become instruments of others' wills employed to satisfy *their* needs, and in the process perpetuate the exploitation inherent in the relation, in the case of estrangement. "The producer is estranged (*entfremdet*) from his product because he was forced to alienate (*entäussern*) his labor power in return for a wage and the abandonment of control over his product of labor" (Walliman, 1981, 42). We shall employ this distinction as we proceed.

In *The German Ideology* Marx and Engels distinguished a series of stages of societal development, defined in terms of the nature of their *mode of production*, or property relations: tribal societies, where property was communal (and which years later seemed—at least partly erroneously—to be confirmed by the anthropological research of Lewis Henry Morgan (Morgan, 1877); ancient society, based on slavery or other types of bondage; feudal society, where much property is private (thus preparing the way for capitalism) but subordinated in its use and transfer to strong traditional and legal prescriptions, and in which church and state property are also very significant; capitalist society, which comes into being with the freeing of private property relations from feudal constraints; and communist society, in which capitalism and the class society it produces are abolished; and communal property in the Communist societies of the future, in which some not very clearly specified form of communal organization is reintroduced.[5] In the *Communist Manifesto* they maintain, in a famous phrase, that "the history of all hitherto existing societies is the history of class struggles (Marx and Engels, *Communist Manifesto*, hereafter designated *CM*, in Feuer, 1959, 7). With the dissolution of tribal societies, "society begins to be differentiated into separate and finally antagonistic classes" (Engels's note to the English edition of 1888). This view of history as one of varying degrees of development and intensity of class conflict accounting for the great societal transformations of human history was often reiterated by both Marx and Engels in later works. Indeed, Engels, who later (in 1892, in *Socialism: Utopian and Scientific*) labeled the theory "historical materialism," says it was one of the two great discoveries made by Marx (the other being the law of capitalist accumulation). Classes, then, defined in terms of their relation to the means of production, and thereby constituting the *modes of production* have existed since the dissolution of communal property.

Throughout all of this, the central theme is that the really fundamental struggles are over control of the means of production and that this is true of all societies that have progressed beyond the tribal level. All societies

[5] There is also the controversial "Asiatic" mode of production, bureaucratic and centered on water control. For an excellent discussion of this, and quite devastating critique of Marx, see Anderson, 1974, Appendix B. For a systematization of Marxian concepts into *three* types, "transhistorical" (e.g., relation of production or mode of production), "particular" (i.e., applied within a mode of production—Asiatic, feudal, capitalist, etc.—such as exchange value, constant and variable capital), and "regional" (i.e., those applied to different levels or sectors within a mode of production, e.g., "commodity" within the capitalist mode of production), see Althusser, 1969, Intro.

with a division of labor, in effect, tend to form into classes that are antagonistic because some have control over the means of production while others do not. It follows by definition that any groups or individuals in such a situation are *alienated*, and indeed regarding both feudalism and slavery, Marx is explicit: "Already, in feudal landlordship the ownership of the soil appears as an alien power ruling over men" (*EPM*, in Bottomore, 1964, 114). And his remarks on the brutality of slavery and the manner and consequences of appropriating surplus value through slave labor leave no doubt that he regarded it as an alienated condition. There is therefore a sense in which the idea of alienation is employed in a way that transcends capitalism.

But there is another theme in the *Manifesto*. It is clear that Marx and Engels there and elsewhere intend to establish a *fundamental distinction* between capitalist society and all earlier forms of precapitalist society. And here the concept of alienation is employed as specific to the capitalist mode of production.

Although the historical scheme described above was fleshed out in detail only in 1846 in *The German Ideology*, Marx had already begun his analysis of the decisive differences between capitalist and precapitalist (especially feudal) societies. His characterization of feudal property in *EPM* emphasizes the *limits* of alienation. Even though "the rule of private property begins with the ownership of land," Marx writes, "landed property assumes an individual character with its lord, . . . (and) appears as the inorganic body of its lord" and not "as the direct rule of capital" (*EPM*, in Bottomore, 1964, 114). Estate workers are not day laborers but in part the lord's property. Relations of respect and personal obligation are present and may even be "agreeable." Custom to some degree constrains the impulse to exploit labor (114–115).

Marx much later depicts feudal relations in a similar vein. They are *personal* and involve dependence, he writes in the *Grundrisse* (McLellan, 1971, 72 ff.); even when, during late feudalism, they begin to recede before the advance of market relations, the *appearance* of (and one supposes, the *belief in*) relations as personal remains. Under these conditions of precapitalist societies in general—even in slavery—exchange appears only in the form of exchange of *use-value*; *exchange value* is virtually nonexistent (106 ff.). Later in *Capital* he remarks along the same line that

> in any given formation of society, where not the exchange value but the use-value of the product predominates, surplus-labour will be limited by a given set of wants which may be greater or less, and that here no boundless thirst for surplus-labour arises from the nature of production itself. Hence in antiquity overwork becomes horrible only when the object is to obtain exchange value in its specific independent money-form. . . . Compulsory working to death is here the reconized form of overwork. . . . Still there are exceptions in antiquity. (Marx, 1906, 260).

While there are exceptions to this in precapitalist societies (e.g., Marx describes in some detail the corvée system of the Danubian Principalities), in general he wishes to make the point that regardless of how terrible conditions may be—and often have been—in precapitalist societies, there have always been, on the positive side, various natural limits to the demands made by those in control of the means of production, and negatively, an absence of the remorseless, machinelike, and impersonal quality of production and expanding demand for labor inherent in capitalism. Work in earlier societies has indeed often enough been barbaric, but the internationally expanding mode of production grafts the "civilized horrors of overwork," onto "the barbaric horrors of slavery, serfdom, etc." (1906, 260). In the slave system of the American South, for instance, when export of cotton came to be vital for the southern states, "it was no longer a question of obtaining from (the slave) a certain quantity of useful products," but of "production of surplus labor itself" (1906, 260).

The empirical prototype of this condition of labor, of course, is the factory, especially with the continuous introduction and elaboration of machinery, but it is a condition that can be and sometimes has been met elsewhere, for instance, in the course of the commercialization of agriculture. Thus, Marx gives evidence that the condition of English agricultural workers deteriorated during the nineteenth century to the point where it compared unfavorably not only with the condition of urban workers, but, in terms of diet, with that of inhabitants of English jails and prisons and that of transported prisoners (Marx, 1906, 739ff.), and that this deterioration occurred because of the fact that, during this period, English freeholders were undergoing extensive expropriation, which is to say, were being relieved of their control over land, the primary means of production. This is contrasted with the worker's at least partial control over the use of land earlier during the feudal period, when "the laborer . . . could live in plenty, and accumulate wealth" (74).[6]

Marx extends the comparison with feudal property relations to an organically related aspect of alienation, the worker's connection with the *product* of his or her labor. "The alienation of the object of labour," he says, "merely summarizes the alienation in the work activity itself" (*EPM* in Bottomore, 1964, 124). This condition stands in stark contrast with the ability of the feudal producer, whether peasant, yeoman, or craftsman, to appropriate the items produced and to dispose of them more or less in accordance with his or her own judgment.[7] He then goes on to argue that these two dimensions of alienation imply a third, alienation from the *species*, by which he means the transformation of productivity, the essential practical condition of all life, from an end into a means. "Labor, life activity, productive life, now appear to man only as a *means* for the satisfaction of a need, the need to maintain his physical existence." This negates the potential for "free, conscious activity," which is the "species-character" of human life itself (127).

Alienation from species-life, in turn, implies a final aspect of alienation, namely, alienation from others. "A direct consequence of the alienation of man from the product of his labor, from his life-activity (i.e., free engagement in production)[8] and from his species-life, is that man is alienated

---

[6] See Marx's account in *Capital*, "The So-Called Law of Primary Accumulation" (Marx, 1906, 784–848), and his extensive treatment of capitalist agriculture in *Capital*, 3, Section 4.

[7] In various places Marx emphasizes the independence of the peasant when compared to the industrial worker.

[8] Parenthetical clarification mine.

from other men" (129). Here Marx doubtless has in mind Engels's description of the misery and demoralization of the English working class in his *The Condition of the Working Class in England* (which he often cites). In later works he would reiterate this theme: the destruction of the working class family through the forced prostitution of wives and daughters, the "sale" of children to mines and mills, the general reduction of family relations to a purely materialist basis, all specifically in consequence of everyone being nothing more than the bearer of a commodity—labor power—and thus necessarily in competition with everyone else.[9] And this stands in contrast to the feudal family, in which the organic relation with land and lord remains more or less intact.

As Marx says, up to this point he had merely analyzed "an economic fact." His analysis of alienation is thus far only descriptive and is not absolutely incompatible with the appearance of alienation in conjunction with industrialization in any system of property relations (in fact, it does appear in industrialized socialist societies). The real theoretical significance of alienated work under capitalist property relations lies in the fact that it produces and continues to *reproduce* the conditions of exploitation and domination. Just as all men and women realize themselves, i.e., their humanity, only through the continuity of their social relationships, so the social relationship of alienated production *reproduces* that alienation through *estrangement*, the *objectification* of labor in the form of capitalist property relations. It is in this sense, as Marx says, that "private property is thus derived from the analysis of the concept of *alienated labor*" (131), although "at a later stage . . . there is a reciprocal influence" (131). In the drawing of this implication of *estrangement* from his analysis of alienation, the influence of Hegel in particular, on Marx is evident.

Now Marx's historical theory of alienation and estrangement was linked to his philosophical anthropology through his theory of needs.

For Marx, of course, the material foundations of life are the fundamental and inescapable conditions under which all life activities are carried forward, and within which they are at least powerfully constrained, if not determined. "Men make their own history, but they do not make it just as they please; they do not make it under circumstances chosen by themselves, but under circumstances directly encountered, given, and transmitted from the past," he would later write in 1852 in *The Eighteenth Brumaire of Louis Bonaparte*. The primary relationship of everyone is to nature, and this relationship exists in the form of the satisfaction of human *needs*. Needs, however, are not be to thought of as constant and unchanging, but as changing with historical circumstance, as continually undergoing modification, in short, as *products* of specific material conditions and the specific relations of production characteristic of a particular historical period. They are, we may say, the creations of objective relations. Under capitalism, human needs become, so to speak, a rational consideration built into capitalist

[9] The bourgeoisie has "torn from the family its sentimental veil, and has reduced the family relation to a mere money relation" (*CM*, in Feuer, 1959, 10). "Previously the workman sold his own labour-power, which he disposed of nominally as a free agent. Now he sells wife and child. He has become a slave-dealer" (Marx, 1906, 432).

exchange relationships in a volatile and dynamic fashion evidently not present in precapitalist societies. The degradation imposed on human beings laboring for wages under capitalism takes the form of *extinguishing* all human needs; "even animal needs disappear" (170), and "all passions and activities must be submerged in *avarice*" (172).

But if human needs can be virtually obliterated under capitalism, the other side of the dialectical coin is that under socialism they can experience "a new manifestation of *human* powers and a new embodiment of the human being" (168), a coming into being of a *wealth* of human needs going far beyond the sheerly material ones, into moral, spiritual, intellectual, and aesthetic realms (See Heller, 1976).

It has sometimes been claimed that this theme of alienated and estranged labor was confined to Marx's early writings of 1840.[10] But, as many critics of this view have maintained, the same theme is central to much of the *Grundrisse* (Marx, 1973), written fifteen years later, although not published in Marx's lifetime. Here he says that production on the basis of exchange values "creates an alienation of the individual from himself and others," and that "while living labor is executing the process that reproduces its objective conditions, it has at the same time established raw materials and instruments in such proportions that—as surplus labor, i.e., labor beyond what is necessary—it can realize itself in them and thus make them into material to create new values" (97).

Although continuing the alienation/estrangement theme, Marx's analysis in the *Grundrisse*, in fact, goes somewhat beyond the *EPM* in more definitely placing the theory in the theoretical context of political economy. In 1844 Marx was poorly read in technical economics, but during the years following his removal from the continent to England he undertook extensive study of the subject, leading up to the publication of the first volume of his greatest work, *Das Kapital*, in 1867.

The *Grundrisse* is probably best understood, as McLellan (1971, intro.) argues, as a transitional work bridging the early more Hegelian and Feuerbachian with the later more economistic Marx, but simultaneously demonstrating that the early themes are continuous with rather than disjunctive from the later ones. In the *Grundrisse* we find the elaboration of the distinction between use-value and exchange-value that would become the theoretical foundation of *Capital*. There, as Mandel and Novak put it, the concept of alienated labor was broken down into its elements and "integrated into a comprehensive exposition of laws of motion of capitalism" (Mandel and Novak, 1970, 65), laws of motion that Marx would soon be dissecting in detail in *Capital*.

If the *Grundrisse* incorporates Marx's early theory of alienation and

---

[10] As mentioned in Chapter 9 (footnote 20), the relation of Marx's early to his later work is a controversial matter and has tended to polarize into two positions. One holds that the "romantic" early works are of little importance for understanding the later "scientific" ones. Louis Althusser is perhaps the leading exponent of this view. Those holding the opposed position argue that Marx's works represent a developmental unity, one, to be sure, in which a growing maturity can be seen (as Marx himself says), but in which the early writings constitute an essential grounding for the later, mainly economic ones (for a discussion defending the latter position, see Walliman, 1981, chapter 1).

estrangement into the framework of political economy, in *Capital* we witness its extension beyond the sphere of production and its elaboration in terms of the concept of "commodity fetishism." Indeed, in the first sentence of *Capital* Marx establishes the centrality of the concept of "commodity."

> The wealth of those societies in which the capitalist mode of production prevails, presents itself as "an immense accumulation of commodities," its unit being a single commodity. Our investigation must therefore begin with the analysis of a commodity. (Marx, 1906, 41)

Commodification of everything, consumables as well as land, labor, and resources, is the most generalized feature of the alienation of capitalist society.

The last element in Marx's historical theory of alienation was the formulation of the concept of the proletariat. Throughout the early writings there is, of course, considerable discussion of the alienated condition of the proletariat under capitalism, along with allusions to, if no real analysis of, classes generally and their role in history. And there were the criticisms of "utopian" socialism in the *Poverty of Philosophy*, directed mainly against Proudhon, in which, among other things, Marx charged utopians with failure to perceive or attribute to the emerging working class a progressive historical role.

These elements are brought together in the *Communist Manifesto*, where the nature and historic role of the proletariat is succinctly formulated. Marx's theory of the proletariat may be said to incorporate four themes: (1) its historical emergence as a structural necessity as capitalism develops, (2) the process of its organization into a class, (3) its function within the capitalist society and economy, and (4) its historic future role.

The proletariat, Marx says, has been "called into existence" by the bourgeoisie (*CM*, in Feuer, 1959, 13). With the progressive development of the forces of production, labor increasingly becomes "socialized," i.e., production is carried out collectively, as the *detail* division of labor expands, breaking the production process down into increasingly minute segments. This process, in conjunction with the continuous rationalization of the mechanical foundations of production through the introduction of machinery, cheapens the value of the product by cheapening the price of labor. Factories become larger and greater numbers of workers are agglomerated, creating great collective productive mechanisms. The growth of the proletariat is one side—the progressive one—of the same coin on which the death throes of various feudal classes are inscribed: craftsmen, small farmers, *petits bourgeoisies*, and so on. As these older feudal forms of production and the societies based on them are ground out of existence by triumphant capitalism, members of the old classes are thrown into the expanding capitalist labor market, there to sell that last commodity possessed by everyone of minimally sound mind and limb—their brute labor, or, as Marx would later carefully clarify, their *labor power*.

As this new working class grows larger, it begins to assume increasingly organized proportions, a process linked by Marx at every point with its emerging and intensifying struggle with its master, the bourgeoisie. First carried on by individual laborers, this struggle, says Marx, becomes factorywide, then begins to mobilize members of entire trades within particular localities. Much of the struggle in these early stages, however, is directed not against the bourgeoisie, with whom workers are, in fact, allied, but against the remnants of feudalism—monarchy, landowners, nonindustrial bourgeoisie, *petit bourgeoisie* (15–16). But as industry advances, the introduction of machinery "obliterates all distinctions of labor and nearly everywhere reduces wages to the same low level" (16). As capitalism displaces the older forms of production, insecurity spreads throughout the system, and workers begin to form organizations independent of their capitalist masters. Larger unions of workers appear, assisted by modern communications, and increasingly take political form. As contact and organization proceed, the "consciousness" of workers expands and they begin to understand something of the nature of their common plight, i.e., they begin to acquire a view of the world appropriate to their class situation. Despite many setbacks rooted mainly in the enforced and unavoidable competition among themselves, the organization grows and eventually some successes appear—most notably, at the time of the publication of the Manifesto (1848), the 10 Hours Bill (of 1844).

The process of organization and expanding class consciousness seemed for Marx and Engels at the time of the writing of the *Manifesto* inevitable, because capitalist appropriation of the labor power of human beings by means of the wage has the inevitable consequence of grinding down the life conditions of the workers and their families to the level of brute survival, the "immiseration" that turned out to be perhaps the most momentous of Marx's and Engels's errors regarding the future of capitalist societies. They expressly designate the proletariat as the first class in history to exist under conditions that fail to assure its very existence, however oppressed or impoverished these might be.

> In order to oppress a class, certain conditions must be assured to it under which it can, at least, continue its slavish existence. The serf, in the period of serfdom, raised himself to membership in the commune, just as the petit bourgeois, under the yoke of feudal absolutism, managed to develop into a bourgeois. The modern laborer, on the contrary, instead of rising with the progress of industry, sinks deeper and deeper below the conditions of existence of his own class . . . He becomes a pauper and pauperism develops more rapidly than population or wealth. (19)[11]

The proletariat is here described as a class without a culture. This once again stands in sharp contrast with the worker under feudalism.

---

[11] It is worth noting at this point that in certain passages in their later writings, after observing the substantial staying power of capitalism along with the beginning of increasing affluence of at least certain small sectors of the working class, Marx and Engels can be interpreted as suggesting that the economic deterioration of the situation of the proletariat was a relative, not an absolute matter. This, of course, accommodates the facts of increasing worker affluence, even into and throughout the twentieth century. See the discussion later in this chapter.

> The proletarian is without property; his relation to his wife and children has no longer anything in common with the bourgeois family relations; modern industrial labor, modern subjection to capital, the same in England as in France, in America as in Germany, has stripped him of every trace of national character. Law, morality, religion are to him so many bourgeois prejudices, behind which lurk in ambush just as many bourgeois interests. (18)

Finally, because of this condition, the proletariat is said to be not only a revolutionary class, but the *only* revolutionary class. All others are not only conservative, but reactionary. Therefore, the proletariat alone "holds the future in its hands." This is guaranteed, for unlike all previous classes, the proletariat is at least in process of becoming, if it is not already, the majority, possessing nothing, and therefore having nothing to lose. "The proletarians have nothing to lose but their chains. They have a world to win" (41). But however propitious for its internal organization the expanding infrastructure of capitalism might be, the proletariat can never act in a revolutionary manner without theory, and this is to be supplied by intellectuals like Marx. As Gouldner puts it, the proletariat is the "heart" of a revolution whose ignorance must be "pierced by the lightning bolt of theory" (Gouldner, 1980, 29).[12]

The proletariat is Marx's surrogate agency for a Reason Engels thought had become "the idealized kingdom of the bourgeoisie", a Reason that seemed to be realizing the worst of Rousseau's visions. What was obviously in order was to bring into being a reason in new dress, tailored for modern times, something like Vico's *New Science* carried forward by an agency new to history. The proletariat was Marx's theoretical response to a reason gone awry, *not* because of the sorcerer within, but, as he and Engels insist in the *Manifesto*, iron historical necessity without. The bourgeoisie could never have "burst the fetters" of feudal society and brought into being the modern forces of production without incorporating, developing, and employing science in a myriad of ways. The irony of the very existence of the modern bourgeoisie, which "cuts from under its (own) feet the very foundation on which (it) produces and appropriates products" (19–20), rests on the fact that in being the "*involuntary* promoter" (italics mine) of industry, it becomes increasingly dependent on continuous *scientific* development and application. It is inherent in the control of science by the bourgeoisie that it be deployed against the worker (Marx, 1867, 397).

Rejection of science in the hands of the bourgeoisie, coupled with the absolute need for some *assurance* of what the future would bring, were the linked conditions for both Marx's theory of capitalist economics and his

---

[12] There is more than a little of the Prometheus myth in this. The proletariat, like Prometheus, struggles through defeat after defeat, persistently renewing itself following the depredations of its vitality. Like Prometheus bringing the fire, the proletariat, through the fire of its waxing revolutionary outrage enlightened by scientific socialism, brings liberation to humankind. Fascination with Prometheus was lifelong for Marx. Already as a student, he wrote that among all the gods "there is nothing equal to him." The fact that he lived most of his life in fear of cancer of the liver, which had killed his father, is perhaps not unrelated to this, and to his own seeming identification with the god. See the discussion in Levine (1975), 8; Gouldner (1980), 235; and most importantly, Wessell (1984).

theory of knowledge. One could hardly ask men to assume the risks involved in enlisting in the struggle for a future ideal in the absence of pretty sure knowledge that the direction of history was on their side.[13] At the same time, the continued expansion of scientific knowledge as a bourgeois activity would achieve no more than a perpetuation of, indeed, an exacerbation, of the existing state of affairs. And Marx had already laid the groundwork for a theory of practical action that would simultaneously both incorporate and generate a new science rooted in his philosophical anthropology. These imperatives constituted the main aspects of the situation under which Marx worked out his theory of capitalist development in *Capital*.

THE LABOR THEORY OF VALUE: USE VALUE AND EXCHANGE VALUE

Marx and Engels had thus arrived at a clear conception of the nature and direction of the emerging working classes of Europe by the late 1840s, and despite the setbacks of 1848 remained convinced that the workings of the capitalist economy would continue to bring into being conditions favorable to their continued agglomeration and eventual politicization. But there was no particular *theoretical* reason to believe that this process was necessarily a linear one or that it would assume any particular form other than being punctured by periodic crises. So the last thirty years or so of Marx's life were devoted mostly to working out the inner "laws" of capitalist economics, a theory that would *explain* what seemed to be the momentous transformations—past, present, and future—occurring in the sphere of labor.

I mentioned earlier that Marx begins *Capital* by stating that the basic concept for analysis of capitalism is the commodity. Now a commodity is an item produced for exchange on a market, and while it is possible for such exchanges to occur as item-for-item transactions, as the commodity *system* expands, this very quickly becomes impractical, and a universal medium to which all commodities can be assimilated—money—appears. Money, of course, appears even in antiquity, but money exchange had been institutionalized only in very limited sectors of precapitalist societies, for an entire set of reasons, of which the absence of a continuous supply of scarce metals is only one. Now the existence of a system of economic exchange based on money is for Marx a sine qua non of capitalism, for it is in this form alone that a society in which everything is up for sale can exist. This, of course, includes resources utilized in production—the least of the problems involved in the transition to industrialism—but land as well, a major obstacle under feudal forms of tenure, and most importantly—and historically momentous—

---

[13] It is an interesting sociological fact that, while logically, deterministic theories obviate the need for action, they may often be powerful, even indispensable, ideological and thus motivational elements in rebellion or revolution, or even reform: thus, the determinism of *The Communist Manifesto*, a political pamphlet written following the convention of the International Workingman's Association in Belgium in 1848. In this same connection, see the discussions of the same problem in connection with Spencer, by Peel (1971), in Chapter 8, by Hobsbawm in *Primitive Rebels* (Hobsbaum, 1965), and by Zaret in his *The Heavenly Contract*, (1985) Chapter 4.

human labor. Here we have the elements of capitalist production, what Marx called the "trinity formula" (Marx, 1967, 3, Chap. 48), all of which must be converted from their "natural," or purely useful form, to their *alienated* form: capital mobilized for *profit*, land freed from traditional forms of tenure to yield *ground rent*, and human labor from its form as useful work to the commodity of *labor power* sold for a *wage*. The principle of alienation is here generalized within the framework of political economy to ramify through every structural feature of the capitalist economy.

Central to Marx's analysis is the labor theory of value and the way this is construed in his distinction between use-value and exchange-value. The utility of a thing makes it a "use-value", says Marx, and use-values "constitute the substance of all wealth" (Marx, 1867, 42–43). The concept of use-value must be clearly distinguished from that of exchange-value, which *appears* as "a quantitative relation, in which values in use of one sort are exchanged for those of another sort . . . " It is this *seeming* to be constituted of a double property, its *intrinsic* value (i.e., its utility), on the one hand, but a *relational* character (i.e., equivalence in exchange), on the other, that occasions our interest and calls for analysis.

The idea of exchange-value was not Marx's, but goes back to the commercial and early manufacturing predecessors of industrial capitalism. Locke had formulated the first systematic account of the nascent medieval theory of value as constituted of labor, not only as a justification of private property per se, but of private property as the foundational institution of capitalist society, (Locke, *Second treatise*), but this was a justification of wealth and its accumulation in the form of agricultural enterprise and handcrafting, *not* as a standard of value in exchange. As the progressive European societies became increasingly commercialized, and as manufacturing enterprises grew in size and significance, in short, as the movement away from feudal agricultural society progressed, it became increasingly apparent that substantial profit could be taken in consequence of economic activity remote from agricultural or rural handicraft production. This was an idea, as Lichtheim points out (1971b, 127),[14] lacking in respectability in the late medieval view of things economic.[15] To bring diverging practice within received theological boundaries, William Petty proposed late in the seventeenth century that values appearing in exchange could be traced to the labor invested in the exchanged commodities.[16] Although intended to provide a legitimation for capitalist trading and profit taking, and in one version or another to be found in the work of economists of the "classical" school up through Ricardo, the proposal contained the germ of a profoundly anticapitalist critique, namely, that capital is constituted at least partly from labor (*albeit*, in their view the labor of property *owners*, not propertyless *workers*) and thus ought to be thought of as "stored-up" labor.

Well before Marx, earlier socialist theoreticians had attempted to

---

[14] This account follows Lichtheim, 1971b, Chap. 8.

[15] Although "merchant capital," as Marx emphasizes, has a long history during the late Middle Ages; in fact, it was the first form of "liberated capital" (Marx, 1967, 3, Chap. 20).

[16] Marx identifies the beginnings of true, as against vulgar political economy, with Petty (Marx, 1906, 93fn).

employ the labor theory of value as a critique of capitalism by arguing that labor was not just one, but the original factor in production, and to dissociate this from property-associated labor. It thus became, for Marx, an idea whose time had come. Essentially, what Marx did with the concept of exchange value was to argue that it was entirely determined by the investment of labor, but, further, to *oppose* it to use-value. He begins by asserting that a use-value, which by definition is constituted of some sort of utility, "has value (i.e., exchange-value)[17] only because human labor in the abstract has been embodied or materialized in it" (1867, 45). Use-values, however, are inherently *qualitative* in nature: if I am a potter and I produce a pot for my own use, the pot has utility for me and a value based on my labor, but this cannot be quantified, since the utility of things is relative. My neighbor, for instance, may have no use at all for pottery. At the same time, some things, like air and virgin soil, may have use-values independent of labor. There is thus a principled relativism, a sense of the great diversity of needs and wants, of their fundamental subjectivity, implicit in the concept of use-value.

Now, items that are produced for sale (i.e., commodities), one might think, acquire their market value by virtue of being exchanged for others of equivalent use-value. If this were so, everyone's needs would presumably be satisfied. However, since the use-values served by the utilities of exchanged commodities are variable and have different sources, it cannot be so. Exchange-value, therefore, must be something independent of use-value, and this something, Marx argues, is nothing other than the labor invested in production. In short, exchange-values *appear* in exchange, but the magnitude of the values exchanged is determined entirely by labor. What is being exchanged is the labor-power "in the abstract," as Marx puts it, and it is this having in common *nothing other than* being an embodiment of abstract labor-power, that defines the nature of commodities. With this, Marx begins the working out of his theory of the capitalist economy, seemingly showing the manner in which it *necessarily* exploits the labor of all who must sell their labor-power for a wage.

Marx goes on to argue that the appropriate way of measuring exchange-value is by the *duration* of the labor involved in its production. By this Marx means "homogenous" labor, or the *average* of all the not-so-homogenous units of labor-power, as an average degree of skill and intensity prevalent at the time" (46), and that, further, "each individual commodity . . . is to be considered as an average sample of its class" (46).[18]

Now nothing could be exchanged, of course, if it had no use-value, and if it were exchanged (sold) for its use-value, i.e., the value of the labor

---

[17] Parenthetical clarification mine.

[18] At the very outset Marx struggles with the problem that, from a theoretical standpoint, would more than any other bedevil his economics. The labor theory of value was a late medieval idea, appropriate perhaps for an agricultural/handicrafting society where the work of one individual was more or less apparent in what was produced. In modern technical-scientific societies it has become increasingly unworkable precisely because the total mass of what is produced *cannot* be regarded as the product of "units . . . the same as any other" (46). Even the Soviets jettisoned the labor theory of value. For a recent penetrating critique of the theory, see Macy, 1988. In particular, Macy shows that the labor theory of value can't explain class exploitation (37).

invested in it measured by the duration of that labor, there would be no problem. This is, however, not the case. Indeed, it cannot be, since it is self-evident that capitalists must, and do, in fact retain at least some of their income for purposes of further investment. If a worker were paid precisely the value of the labor invested in producing a commodity and if this commodity were sold for this value, there would be nothing to invest. Distinct from such *logic*, there were also, as I have noted, the seeming facts regarding the impoverishment of the English working class during the first half of the nineteenth century, i.e., the apparent increase in the number of paupers accompanied by growth of the mass of accumulated wealth. This, it seemed, could not occur if workers were paid wages equal to the fair value of their labor. In fact, classical economy had always assumed that the price of labor and commodity prices were in a general equilibrium, and, on another, but decisively related plane, that the *classes* that formed around basic market relations were essentially complementary, rather than antagonistic (although some of Adam Smith's comments, cited in Chapter 5, suggest that he was, at best, of two minds on this point; capitalists needed workers and workers needed work, landlords needed rent returns from their land, and agricultural workers, of whatever type, needed land to produce agricultural products). The play of interest at the individual or subunit level somehow produced complementary functioning of classes at the societal level.

From a theoretical standpoint, Marx and Engels's observations thus took the form of an *anomaly* relative to classical economics, and it was but a short step to the conclusion that workers were not in fact being remunerated in full for their labor. The actual (average) wage of the worker, Marx argued, was in fact that wage required to keep him or her maintained at a minimum level, i.e., continuously available for work and able to prepare the next generation for more of the same, the functions of production and reproduction. This is achieved only under conditions of formally free labor, i.e., where workers are *not* legally or traditionally tied to feudal institutions and thereby become totally dependent on employment for a wage. The labor required for this purpose Marx called "necessary" labor.

But beyond this, Marx argued, the capitalist extracted additional labor as "labor power" for which the worker was unremunerated, and this he called "surplus labor". Surplus labor is the necessary condition for the production of "surplus value", the portion of capital available for further investment.

Now, because all historical societies since primitive communism have been class societies of one sort of another, they have all, by definition, been based on the extraction of surplus value from the propertyless by those owning or controlling the means of production. The creation of surplus value under capitalism is therefore *something* like the feudal arrangements whereby the peasant would work a certain number of days (or weeks, or even hours) to fulfill his obligations to the lord, with the remainder of the time available to work for himself and his family.

Two aspects of the extraction of surplus-value under capitalism, however, make this a very different process. First, feudal society was essentially an economically stagnant one. The feudal nobility did not extract a surplus primarily to invest or to expand the operation. They were landowners interested mainly in maintaining their life-style, not businessmen producing for a market that made continuous demands for commodities and thus continuous demands for more production.

Second, as mentioned earlier, the social relations between agricultural workers and their masters (including the church and its parasitic hierocrats) were, as Marx had put it earlier, "personal," rather than "materialistic," and both the nobility and the church had obligations as well as rights vis-à-vis the peasantry. The peasants therefore lived for the most part within a system of substantial economic security, which not only possessed no inherent internal tendency to reduce them to material ruin, but even offered opportunity for some—not many—to rise above their lowly position (peasants could become free; commoners were occasionally knighted or entered religious orders).

At the same time, the actual distribution of the fruits of labor was fairly clear to everyone—the lord (and church) getting so much, the peasant so much. The amount of surplus value extracted and its manifestation among his masters were, so Marx thought, not only plainly obvious to the peasant, but generally accepted as just[19] as well, apparently (it is not entirely clear in Marx) both because of "services" rendered by the lord (security, adjudication, representation, military protection), and the religious legitimations provided by the church. The great difference in capitalism is that the ratio of necessary to surplus labor, or even the fact of the latter's existence, is obscured by the very nature of the way the system works. The transformation of the value and the price of labor into the form of wages, says Marx, is important, in fact decisive, because it *appears*—all of it—as being paid for by the capitalist. It makes the actual relation invisible, a "phenomenal form," a "mystification" (Marx, 1906, 591). Moreover, the form mystifies not only the worker, but the capitalist himself, for whom the profit (based on surplus value) *appears* as a wage paid, both necessary for his exertions in exploiting labor and for mastering the complexities of management (Marx, 1967, 3, 380). For Marx, the capitalists' "wage" is just so much unpaid labor. It is not so much that workers accept capitalist ideology (the theme of "cultural hegemony" emphasized by a later generation of Marxists), which to some extent is doubtless true, but that the very objective conditions of capitalist economic organization cloud and obscure the realities of exploitation. In this situation, as distinct from feudalism, the most obvious need is for a *critique* and a clarification of how that system functions—precisely what Marx set out to provide.

The labor theory of value and the analysis of use-value and exchange-value leads directly to Marx's theory of exploitation.

THE THEORY OF EXPLOITATION

Marx's appropriation of the labor theory of value and his analysis of use-value and exchange-value is the foundation of his analysis of exploitation in capitalist society. This is a theory of production that *explains* the worsening

---

[19] But note the many peasant rebellions throughout the Middle Ages, about which Marx says nothing in *Capital*. See his remarks on the French peasantry in *The Eighteenth Brumaire of Louis Napoleon*, and Engels' *The Peasant War in Germany* (Engels, 1966).

condition of the working class and (in Marx's view) the political future of that class as well.

Exploitation occurs when capitalists appropriate some portion of the product workers produce for the purpose of accumulation, thereby withholding from the workers full value for the labor power expended, measured in terms of its duration. Although all value comes into being in consequence of labor power expended in production, it appears in any immediate situation in differentiated form. Marx distinguishes between "constant capital" and "variable capital". Constant capital, by definition, refers to stock and materials employed in production and thereby added to the value of whatever is produced (referred to variously as "congealed labor", "materialized labor", "stored up" labor, etc.). This is to be distinguished from immediately or presently available labor, from which labor-power must be extracted in order to produce anything. Variable capital, in Marx's formulation, in addition to reproducing the equivalent of its own value in the productive process, possesses as well the critical property of creating a "surplus value", which Marx claims to be indispensible to ongoing capitalist production.

Surplus value refers to that value created by the worker and appropriated by the capitalist, but for which the former remains unremunerated. The *rate* at which this occurs is defined as the rate of exploitation of labor. The profit realized by the capitalist is not identical with surplus value, but is based on the rate of the latter.[20] Without the constant extraction of surplus value, it is obvious that no capitalist enterprise could long survive. Now, political economists in general had worked with the assumption that the price paid for labor (its wage) was identical to the value received by the capitalist. Under this assumption, the capitalist could also be conceived of as a worker, albeit one possessing higher skills and knowledge (thus justifying his higher wage). This might not occasion much of a problem if restricted to managerial functions, but greater difficulties arise in spheres such as profits in the form of interest, or various forms of commercial capital.[21] Marx, naturally enough, was unwilling to exclude managerial "wages" from the category of surplus value, and thus from the capitalist's profit, although essentially in response to what he regarded as utopian claims made by

---

[20] $C = cv$, where C = Capital, c = constant capital, and v = variable capital. Since surplus value is extracted only from v, the ratio of extraction or of exploitation, if s = the *magnitude* of surplus value and s = the *rate* of surplus value, $s' = s/v$. The rate of profit (p) is then $p' = s/c+v$. See Marx (1906), Chap. 9. For the technical arguments far too extensive to reproduce here, the reader must consult *Capital*. It should be noted that since Marx, alternative proposals for measuring surplus value have been advanced (Sweezy, 1974; Mandel, 1968). The more or less standard method has been to subtract the total wage package plus production and materials costs from commodity prices. For a review of the seemingly insuperable difficulties involved in this, see Murphy (1985).

[21] See Marx's discussions in *Capital*, Vol. 3 (1967), Parts 4 and 5. The problem of "unproductive labor" goes back to Adam Smith and was a chronic problem for economists that followed. The fact that Marx embraced the principle had the consequence of converting it to socialist doctrine, bringing with it all sorts of difficulties when socialist regimes in power attempted to apply it. A strict Marxian interpretation would seem to rule out what is today the bulk of the labor force: clerical workers, technicians, intellectuals, scientists, not merely those exercising managerial functions or that are engaged in nonproductive financial or monetary manipulations.

anarchists, he did recognize a legitimate coordinating function required wherever a division of labor in production appears, but distinguished this from the supervision required by the class antagonisms arising from the exploitative nature of capitalist production (Marx, 1967, 3, 383–384).[22] More of this later.

During feudalism, production was localized, carried out within small units, typically by individual peasants and their families or by individual craftsmen with a few apprentices and helpers. The transition to capitalist production occurred when the handicraft system was modified in the form of the "putting-out," or "cottage" system, in which the various steps involved in the production of a *number* of articles were "subcontracted," so to speak, to a number of individuals typically working in their own homes. Here we find the beginning of what Marx and Engels called "socialized" production, meaning production organized on a collaborative basis, in which it is no longer possible to attribute the finished product to this or that worker, because it is, in fact, produced by a whole ensemble of workers.

The purpose and consequence of this form of the division of labor and of its heir, the "detail" division of labor celebrated by Adam Smith in *The Wealth of Nations*, is increased productivity and economic growth. It is specifically to conditions where production is socialized that Marx's analysis of constant and variable capital, and the relation of his concept of surplus value to this, applies. The key lies in the fact that cooperation

> produces a greater quantity of use-values and, of course, diminishes the labour-time necessary for the production of a given useful effect" (Marx, 1867, 361).

A "greater quantity of use-values," of course, is nothing other than growth or accumulation, so that as productivity increases "the labour-time necessary for the production of a given effect" is shortened. The necessary consequence is an increase in the proportion of constant capital to variable capital and the growth of the total mass of capital.

Extraction of surplus-value under feudal conditions of production, mostly nonsocialized and employing a relatively primitive and slowly changing technology, has little accumulative potential. Under capitalism it is very different. Because of the massive structural changes brought about during the transition from feudalism, particularly the presence of workers "freed" from bondage to the land and the elimination of the old "fetters" on production and markets, the capitalist producer faces a competitive market, which forces him, on the one hand, to engage in commodity price competition, and on the other, to drive down the cost of production. He effects the latter in various ways, but central to the process is the cheapening of the cost of labor (variable capital), by expanding constant capital. Now it is at this point that Marx's assumption regarding the measure of the value of labor-power is crucial. Price competition in the commodity market forces the capitalist (at least in the long run, although there may be fluctuations in the short

---

[22] Much later Engels took over and embellished the same theme, again in opposition to the anarchists (Engels, "On Authority," in Feuer, 1959, 481–85).

run) to pay for labor power that price which is the lowest he can possibly manage to pay. This is the price equivalent to the cost of subsistence of a worker for one day. But the cheapening of labor-power means that the ratio of variable to constant capital declines, with the necessary consequence that the part of total capital (C), i.e., variable capital (v), from which the capitalist must extract his surplus continuously, declines relative to constant capital (C). Constant capital thus increases the productivity of variable capital, resulting in continuous (though fluctuating) accumulation. The capitalist manages his enterprise, in short, only by compensating for the shrinking of the portion of capital from which surplus value is extracted by continuously expanding production, thereby cheapening his products. This is the central contradiction of capitalist production, and Marx calls it the Law of the Changing Organic Composition of Capital (Marx, 1967, 3, Chap. 8).

If the ratio of variable to constant capital decreases, it follows as an *abstract* necessity that the rate of profit, based on the rate of extraction of surplus value, must fall, because surplus value can be extracted only from variable capital (Marx, 1967, 3, Part 3). This must be understood, Marx repeatedly emphasizes, to be a *relative* matter, not an absolute one. In fact it is possible—indeed, in the long run from the standpoint of any given capitalist, a *necessity*—that accumulation continue and that the level of employment grow; expansion *compensates* for the contraction of the relative base from which surplus value is extracted by enlarging that base quantitatively. Thus, although the rate of profit must fall, the total mass of profit may actually increase, since the magnitude of the accumulated enterprise grows. This, however, is dependent on continuously expanding markets and constitutes the inner dynamic of capitalism's drive to convert the entire world into a vast market, this latter being one of only three "cardinal facts of capitalist production" (Marx, 1967, 3, 266). The world, however, is finite, and in the long run the Law of Falling Profit will bring about capitalism's final dénouement, in the form of not just one more crisis and recovery, but of a final collapse.

This central contradiction of capitalism brings about a number of economic, social, and eventually, political consequences that Marx in *Capital* generally characterized as ultimately inescapable. Among the essentially economic ones, three are of particular importance. First, competition among capitalists inevitably results in increasing concentration of capital ("one capitalist always kills many").[23] Indeed, the argument that competition is an essentially unstable, rather than a naturally equilibrating type of organization, is one of Marx's great insights and opposes (correctly) an idea that was always central to classical and now neoclassical economics, namely, that a consistently accumulating system organized in terms of "natural" competition (i.e., without having some sort of order imposed from without) could also be a stable one (i.e., that Adam Smith's "hidden hand" in itself is adequate to stabilize the economy, and thus society). Marx was basically right about this. Today's massive concentrations of capital can be explained essentially on the basis of Marx's critique.

[23] This is a second "cardinal fact of capitalist production," the third being the capitalist organization of labor.

Second, the decrease in the ratio of variable to constant capital, of course, when translated into human terms, means growing numbers of unemployed workers. Periods of rapid accumulation, of course, create increased labor demand, and during these times women and children are drawn into the labor force, for their labor can be exploited more intensively. But the long-run tendency for the changing organic composition of capital, or the cheapening of the price of labor, to swell the ranks of the unemployed, and the increasing concentration of capital itself, barring intervention, continues to produce unemployment. The "reserve army" has the critical function of keeping wages at or near the level of subsistence.

Third, inherent in the macroeconomic process of accumulation is a tendency toward violent periodic (more or less decennial) fluctuations in employment, as a consequence of the changing organic composition of capital. Periodic crisis is also inherent in the limited capacity for consumption under capitalist production. This is so because the commodities produced embody greater value (and thus must command higher market prices) than the value of the labor power actually remunerated. There is then a necessary discrepancy in the supply of commodities and the capacity of consumers to purchase them. The result of this is periodic overproduction, causing further unemployment and augmentation of the reserve army.

The policies pursued by capitalists in order to counteract the remorseless Law of the Falling Rate of Profit are several. First, it may be possible to lengthen the working day itself and thus increase the number of hours beyond which the worker labors for his subsistence. This form of "intensification" Marx calls "absolute surplus value" (Marx, 1906, 345). The descriptions and accounts of conditions in factories and mines in his chapter on the working day in the first volume of *Capital* show the extensiveness of this policy: young children forced to perform for incredibly long stretches, 14 or 16 hours, or even longer, in some cases not even allowed to leave the factory, and even found chained to the machines, where they would eat and sleep. This and many other accounts reveal the incredible brutality inherent in the lengthening of the working day in Victorian England.

Alternatively, the capitalist may—indeed, since there are inherent limits to lengthening of the working day—*must* attempt to shorten the labor-time required for the production of any given set of commodities, and this Marx calls relative surplus value (352). This entails, more than anything else, the increasing employment of machinery, the significance of which for Marx can scarcely be overstated.[24]

Competitive commodity markets in conjunction with the consequences of the Law of the Falling Rate of Profit in the workplace, then, constitute the two poles that define the essential realities of capitalist society for Marx and that led him to characterize it as "anarchy in society, despotism in the workplace" (more of this later). Production, much of which even in feudal society served real human needs, in the capitalist scheme becomes a *means* to the end of making profit (demonstrated by, among other things,

---

[24] The chapter on machinery in Vol. I of *Capital* runs to nearly 150 pages. This alone, contrary to the view of some (see, for instance, Aveneri, 1968, 153), would seem sufficient to confirm its central significance for Marx.

the fact that capitalists so often attempt to bypass it by various expediencies, such as getting the state to print more money).

The changing organic composition of capital thus constitutes an explanation of the nature and direction of the proletariat. Capitalists and workers alike do what they must to survive, thereby continually fueling the inexorable movement toward monopoly capitalism. Hegel's dialectic is rendered as the law of capitalist accumulation, but now in materialist form as the contradiction at the core of capitalist production imposing on all a necessity that the philosopher's dialectic of ideas never possessed.

But in all this there remains a problem of interpretation. Did Marx mean that the impoverishment of the working class was a "tendency" but not a prediction of the actual course of capitalist development, one that could, perhaps would, be countered by other forces? Or did he mean that increasing misery was an absolute inexorable movement of capitalism? Consider these in turn.

The first interpretation is based on the presumption by some that Marx could not have been so wrong about anything as fundamental as the future of the working class. Generally Marxists favorably inclined toward Marx, they interpret the immiseration doctrine as one at "a high level of abstraction," to be understood as a "tendency" but not considered by Marx to be an actual prediction. Zeitlin, for instance, has examined this question and concluded that this understanding is the correct one (Zeitlin, 1967, 97–99). He takes Marx's statement asserting that the number of paupers increases with every crisis, and diminishes with every recovery, as implying that the numbers do *not* increase in the long run, an obvious error (98). And he interprets Marx's reference to "many circumstances" under which "all laws" work as an injunction to eschew the making of predictions (99). Furthermore, and a critical step, he converts Marx's remarks about the fluctuations in the absolute numbers of paupers into a test of whether or not Marx held that misery would continue to increase (98–99). But Marx does not appear to have restricted the immiseration thesis to pauperization. Although paupers form "the lowest sediment of the relative surplus-population" (Marx, 1906, 706), this is only one of *four* categories of which the latter category is comprised, and it seems evident that Marx regarded those included in the other three also as victims of progressive impoverishment.

The first of these, those ejected from the "centres of modern industry," the productivity of their youth have been largely used up, become part of the "floating surplus-population," "growing with the extension of these branches of industry" (704). Such individuals "fall into the ranks of supernumeraries" (704).

Second, there is the rural-urban migration resulting from the declining demand for labor associated with the industrialization of agriculture, reducing agricultural laborers to "the minimum of wages," and "always standing with one foot in the swamp of pauperism" (705). This source of the augmentation of the surplus population, Marx says, is "constantly flowing." (705).

Third, there are those who are part of the "active labour army," but whose employment is "extremely irregular." This component of the surplus-population "furnishes an inexhaustible reservoir of disposable labour-power," just as "its conditions of life sink below the average normal level of the working class." Significantly, Marx says of this category, that as "its extent grows, as with the extent and energy of accumulation, the creation of a surplus population advances" (706).

It seems, then, that Marx did not restrict the thesis of growing misery to the unemployed and unemployable, but on the contrary, included within it vast sections of the employed. And of course, this is precisely what one would expect on the basis of Marx's own theory, which claims to establish the necessity of the capitalist to drive *wages* down to a subsistence level, and therefore obviously includes the *working* population as well as paupers, as victims of increasing misery.

A more general problem with this interpretation is that it explicitly ignores the unquestionably deterministic character of *Capital*. Marx says that "the natural laws of capitalist production (work) with iron necessity towards an inevitable result" (Marx, 1906, 13). In his preface to the second edition of the first volume six years later, Marx took account of some of the reviews it had received, and in one instance went to some pains to quote at length from and endorse as "generous" the judgment of an unidentified Russian reviewer who had described Marx's conception of social evolution as "governed by laws not only independent of human will, consciousness, and intelligence, but rather, on the contrary, determining that will, consciousness, and intelligence" (23).

Now consider the second interpretation. Is it really believable that, as scarcity gradually recedes before the advance of accumulation, the great mass of the population must sink into ever-greater poverty? Marx's explanation, of course, centers on the conditions of capitalist production, the changing organic composition of capital, and the falling rate of profit, and the consequence of this, periodic overproduction.

However, if the mass of capital is constantly increasing but cannot be consumed by its producers—the workers who constitute the great majority of the population and who are growing in numbers—it seems to be implied that either (1) the population must be increasing at a rate faster than the growth of the mass of capital, or (2) consumption by the capitalist class increases at a rate equal to the rate of increase of the mass of capital, or (3) both.[25]

Marx treats the question of population increase as production of "relative overpopulation" resulting from the presence of an excess of surplus capital over the existing working population. On the one hand, this leads to greater labor demand and higher wages, thus in consequence making marriage easier, which in turn leads to a *gradual* increase in the population. But on the other hand, employment of such capital to produce greater relative surplus value "would be a breeding ground for a really swift propagation of the population, since under capitalist production misery produces population" (Marx, 1967, 3, 218). Here we are offered two *theoretical* alternatives, but Marx himself is quick to draw the implication that "the increased mass of means of production that is to be converted into capital

---

[25] I exclude a third, systematic waste, since it is really a structural phenomenon of developed monopoly capital. See Baran and Sweezy (1966).

always finds a correspondingly increased, even excessive, exploitable worker population" (219). It does seem that Marx is here maintaining that the necessary misery accompanying capitalist accumulation in fact results in rapid population increase, and this lends some support for the first implication stated above.

What about the second, the rate of consumption of the capitalist class? Marx is quite clear on this issue. In the earlier period of accumulation still dominated by scarcity (later to be called "primary accumulation"), the capitalist perceives his own personal consumption as "a robbery perpetrated on accumulation" (Marx, 1906, 649), but "as capitalist production, accumulation, and wealth, become developed . . . , he becomes richer, not like the miser, in proportion to his personal labor and restricted consumption, but at the same rate as he squeezes out the labour-power of others, and enforces on the labourer abstinence from all of life's enjoyments" (651). He is "able to smile at the rage for ascetics, as a mere prejudice of the old-fashioned miser" (650). Furthermore, a normative or institutionalized requirement that wealth be displayed now appears as "a conventional degree of prodigality" appearing as a "business necessity," as Marx puts it, and "luxury enters into capital's expenses of representation" (650).[26]

These passages seem to suggest that Marx thought not only that the changing organic composition of capital and falling rate of profit would perpetuate the misery of the quantitatively expanding proletariat, but that the growing surplus would be channeled into an increasing level of consumption by the capitalist class, thereby transforming their "work ethic" into a "consumption ethic" that would never be possible for the working class. This lends support to the doctrine of the increasing misery as an inevitable accompaniment of capitalist growth. If this is so, it could be concluded that Marx failed to appreciate the incredible power and creativity—Promethean powers—that he himself attributed to the bourgeoisie (especially in the *Communist Manifesto*). Despite his empiricism, Marx's conclusion about the fate of the working class was, in the last analysis, a deduction based on the "law" of the falling rate of profit. But he was mostly wrong about this. All the old capitalist societies have experienced a "trickle-down" of wealth in the form of income that has *raised* the absolute level (and standard) of consumption for the great majority in all of them, even though significant differences among them remain, and even though in some of them the tendency toward the concentration of wealth has continued.

Despite this seemingly rather heavy "tilt" toward the deterministic side, the fact that this and other aspects of Marx's economics and sociology have been the object of such diverse interpretations may itself be most significant. And this may be the consequence of Marx and Engels having *two* theories, a *scientific* one and a *critical* one, the former deterministic, the latter voluntaristic, and that these in a myriad of ways intertwine throughout Marx's and Engels' works, and in so doing, have lent themselves to chronic

---

[26] Despite this, in the 1860s Marx could still imagine that the capitalists of the time experienced a "Faustian conflict" between the "passion for accumulation and the desire for enjoyment" (651). After the passing of three decades of massive accumulation, we find in Veblen's expanded examination of the same theme no mention of it (Veblen, 1899).

polemic over the "true Marx." This is Gouldner's position, and it will be discussed in the final section of the chapter.

MARX'S SOCIOLOGY OF CAPITALIST SOCIETY

Marx's sociology is rooted empirically in a series of contrasts between capitalist and (mainly) feudal society, in which the nature of exchange and production are contrasted. In feudal society, exchange is contained within an array of social frameworks (manor, guild, even church), is generally based on need, and is carried on within a framework of social relations that are personal rather than materialistic and that are generally conducive to an understanding by all, including those exploited, that the values of the commodities exchanged are materializations of social labor time. Capitalist exchange is structurally isolated from any form of social control, based on profit (production being merely the *means* for making profit), and generates *illusions* or *appearances* regarding exchange that obscures the roots of exchange-value in social labor-time.

Relations of production in feudal society are characterized by a substantial *social*, but no-*detail* division of labor, direct personal relations in or at the workplace (whether rural or town), and again, *transparent* relations in the workplace, since production is carried out mostly in primary or face-to-face situations. Relations of production under capitalism are based on a constantly expanding detail division of labor, the sale of labor-power for a subsistence wage, and a *mystification* of the basis of the relations of production in social labor-time.

The underlying contradiction in the capitalist mode of production ramifies first of all in the economics of the workplace and the commodity market. The capitalist is driven to expand production, thereby increasing the size of the workplace and agglomerating ever more workers, and to reduce production costs through the extension of the working day and intensification of work itself. In the commodity markets the manifestation of labor-power in exchange-value determines or powerfully conditions the changing forms and level of needs as capitalist development unfolds.

These economic consequences of the basic contradiction of the capitalist mode of production are manifested in parallel form in the social relations of workplace and market, characterized in the pithy phrase of Marx and Engels, "despotism in the workplace, anarchy in society." The length of the working day and the way in which production is organized are the battlegrounds of class struggle in the workplace. The lengthening of the former and intensification of the latter increase the need for authority in the workplace, a growing quantum of "despotism" beyond that necessary for the sheer coordination of tasks. In the market, the "anarchy" of unregulated competitiveness governed by exchange-value has as its consequence the coming into being of a new, estranged form of experience, the "fetishizing" of consumption, a layering-over of consumption by a "cash nexus" in which money and the power it brings becomes the arbiter of all human need. Workplace and society, in this sense, are the loci of Marx's sociology of capitalism.

WORKPLACE AND SOCIETY

Marx's depictions of the various actors in capitalist society, especially in the workplace, are commonly stated in terms of direct or immediate material constraints that they cannot escape. "Men make their own history," he had written earlier in *The Eighteenth Brumaire of Louis Bonaparte*, "but not of their own free will, not under circumstances they themselves have chosen but under the given and inherited circumstances with which they are directly confronted" (*Eighteenth Brumaire*, in Fernbach, 1974, 2, 146). And it is this past, which Marx calls "the tradition of dead generations (which) weighs like a nightmare on the minds of the living" (146), embodied in human institutions particular to their times, that sets the boundaries of action, that closes off the actualities of choice. Years later, this working guideline for the 1848–1851 research becomes a cardinal theoretical axiom. In the preface to the first edition of Volume I of *Capital*, Marx makes clear that "individuals are dealt with only insofar as they are the personifications of economic categories, embodiments of particular class-relations and class-interests" and goes on to maintain that this view of the workplace "can less than any other make the individual responsible for relations whose creature he socially remains" (Marx, 1906, 15).

Industrial workers are constrained by the necessity of selling their labor power, and the dependence on the capitalist that this creates. And in the process, of course, they reproduce those very conditions of constraint. The dialectic of alienation and estrangement constitute the constraining nature of production.

But the capitalist is no less constrained, for he must accumulate to survive and must therefore seek to grow through expanded markets, and increasing intensification. Marx illustrates the position of the capitalist in this respect in the instance of the outcry over child labor. In 1863, twenty-six pottery firms, including that of Josiah Wedgewood and Sons, petitioned Parliament for legislation that would limit the working time of children, since, as the companies stated, "much as we deplore the evils . . . mentioned, it would not be possible to prevent them . . . (without) some legislative enactment" (Marx, 1906, 297n.). The good or ill will of the capitalist is simply irrelevant: "Free competition brings out the inherent laws of capitalist production, in the shape of external coercive laws having power of every individual capitalist" (297).[27]

Parallel to the constraints arising directly from the inner workings of capitalist economics are those that are brought into being as the class struggle intensifies, a "despotism" of the workplace. "As cooperation extends its scale," writes Marx in *Capital*, "this despotism (of authority in the workplace)[28] takes a form peculiar to itself" (364), which he then compares to *military* discipline, likening managers to officers, foremen to sergeants, and so on. As mentioned earlier, he insisted on a conceptual distinction

---

[27] See Gouldner's interesting discussion of Marx's principle of constraint understood as "structure" and then compared to the conventional sociological rendering of the latter as normatively stabilized role relationships.

[28] Parenthetical clarification mine.

between the supervision necessary for the coordination of tasks, which would later be called "functionally necessary," and that arising from class antagonisms, which is therefore repressive (Marx, 1967, 3, 383–384). The "general laws" of capitalist accumulation clearly imply the necessity for an increase in the latter. Marx here clearly anticipates Weber's hierachical conception of bureaucracy as an instrument of domination, a topic to which we will return later in this section.

The *representation* of these social relations in the workplace, however, *appears* as something very different. Capital, writes Marx,

> becomes a very mystic being since all of labour's social productive forces appear to be due to capital, rather than labour as such, and seem to issue from the womb of capital itself. Then the process of circulation intervenes, with its changes of substance and form, on which all parts of capital . . . devolve to the same degree that the specifically capitalist mode of production develops (Marx, 1967, 3, 827).

And later he says that the various determined forms of capital in circulation conform to an inner law, "invisible and unintelligible to the individual agent in production" (828). He specifically designated capital as a fetish "which reaches its height in interest-bearing capital" because "it attributes to the accumulated power of labor . . . the inherent secret power, as an automation, of creating surplus-value in geometrical progression . . ." (399).

Finally, even though classical economy has to some extent penetrated the realities of surplus-value formation (i.e., in this context by reducing interest to a portion of the profit, and rent to the surplus above average profit), even their best spokesmen "remain more or less in the grip of the world of illusion which their criticism had dissolved" (830). In an implicit parallel to religious illusion, he says that here

> is an enchanted, perverted, topsy-turvy world, in which Monsieur le Capital and Madame la Terre do their ghost-walking as social characters and at the same time directly as mere things. (830)

And, more broadly, of course, the liberal ideology celebrating the freedom of the individual to enter into and disengage from contracts is the form in which these basic property relations *appear* in the workplace, acquire their meaning, and mask the necessity of the "wage-slavery" imposed on all who must survive by selling their labor-power.

Comparing the modern "wage slave" to his Roman counterpart, he writes, that "the Roman slave is bound by fetters; the wage-laborer is bound to his owner by invisible threads" (Marx, 1906, 628), and that "the appearance of independence is kept up by means of a constant change of employers and by the *fictio juris* of a contract" (628). Freedom merely *appears* to be greater under capitalism, he says in the *Grundrisse* (Marx, 1973, 72) and in *Capital* calls it a mystification, a "phenomenal form" (Marx, 1906, 591), but one essential to the system, since the truth about the actualities of capitalist social relations would be intolerable.

The other pole of his sociology of capitalism—society—Marx likewise characterizes in terms of both structure and process versus appearance: structurally and processually as increasingly leveled and atomized; in appearance, or culturally, as afflicted by "commodity fetishism" and its consequences.

The structural-processional account follows directly from his characterization of the transition from feudalism, in which "ties of personal dependence are in fact broken, torn asunder, as also differences of blood, educational differences, etc.," (Marx, 1973, 72). The class and stratum distinctions of feudal social organization are obliterated, creating a *leveled* society; simultaneously, the personal social bonds through which the dense network of feudal obligations were maintained are fast being destroyed, resulting in a *atomized* society.

There is nothing original about this in and of itself; such expressions of what would later come to be called mass society were becoming common.[29] But for Marx it acquires a heightened theoretical significance when taken in conjunction with his claim regarding the increasing misery of the working class and the implications for the growing repressive function of the state apparatus.

The growing immiseration of working-class life was the other side of the coin of Marx's description of the destruction of feudal communal and occupational structures. Influenced perhaps by Engels' description of working class life as anomic, Marx evidently thought that the only organizations of any significance likely to arise—or survive—in capitalist society were unions and political parties. His portrayal of the working class is one of disorganization and mutual exploitation—breakdown of family life, prostitution rampant—a total absence of moral order. This understanding of capitalist society as atomized and leveled is not unrelated to the idea of constraint, for individuals by themselves are powerless. Just as the "emancipation" of the workers from the feudal condition of economic security determines their labor power, so the atomization of civil society determines the powerlessness of the individual citizen confronting the organized power of the state.

Parallel to his conception of capitalist society as leveled and atomized is Marx's theory of capitalist or *bourgeois* culture, in which all spheres of experience are increasingly penetrated by what Carlyle called the "cash nexus," i.e., the "fetishizing of commodities." Beliefs and morality in capitalist society have to do almost entirely with *appearances*. Marx says that commodity exchange fosters the illusion that the value of the commodities exchanged somehow lies in the exchange itself, because the commodities are produced in different places, often remote from one another, and people come together only for the purpose of buying and selling. This belief is an illusion because the actual value of all commodities, Marx regards as proved, results from the labor time socially necessary for their production. Commodity fetishism is a type of alienation, akin to religious alienation and estrangement, wherein what appears to be a natural thing, permanent and unalterable, is in reality social in its basic nature, and historically transitory. Fetishism is that "which attaches itself to the products of labor," but "is a secret, under the apparent

[29] E.g.; Tocqueville, in *Democracy in America*. (1835).

fluctuations in the relative values of commodities." Since commodities are exchanged habitually, they attain a stability in their value relative to other commodities, and this Marx calls the "general form of value," the essential condition for bringing into being one value to which all commodities can be compared, the universal commodity of money. "The simple commodity form is the germ of the money form" (Marx, 1906, 81).

Money is a kind of alchemy whereby the money form of commodities under capitalism transforms the entire view of the world. To perceive the objective world in terms of money means that the values intrinsic to the things of the world are lost. Money transforms the particularity, the richness, of the world into a unidimensional object grasped through the prism of one abstract and universal value. To perceive objects or others in this fetishized form is to be dazzled and therefore confounded by one aspect of reality, a *societal* alienation in the form of a perverse reality construction that veils the realities of actual capitalist social relations.

This formulation of the culture of capitalist society makes it virtually coextensive with bourgeois ideology, an ideology not only interwoven with actions of the class whose interests are served—the bourgeoisie—but with actions of the proletariat, as well. In this formulation there is only one ideology in capitalist society, the fetishism of commodities, a set of illusions shared by capitalists and proletarians alike.

There are problems with this. Just how, for one, does this total domination of ideas created by the dominant class maintain itself throughout the process of capitalist growth and development? And related to this, how do counterideologies, and especially the revolutionary ideology of the proletariat, come into being? The conception of ideology employed here is quite different than that advanced by Marx and Engels earlier, especially in *The German Ideology*. There, ideologies were depicted as direct productions of classes, as the latter came into being with the expansion of the division of labor. In this view a capitalist society at different stages of development would contain ideologies of differing patterns and strengths at different stages of capitalist development. And it is this conception of ideology that still informs Marx and Engels's theory of the proletariat in the *Manifesto*. Compare, for instance, the passages describing the fetishism of commodities with the earlier depiction of the proletariat as a class to which (bourgeois) "law, morality, religion are . . . just so many bourgeois prejudices" (Marx and Engels, *The Communist Manifesto*, in Feuer, 1959, 30). The proletariat of *Capital* remains the victim of the false consciousness of bourgeois ideology; the proletariat of the *Manifesto* is a class-conscious entity that sees through the culture of capitalism as so many "bourgeois prejudices," and is thus prepared to adopt its own revolutionary conception, and this will not, of course, be an ideology in the sense of bourgeois ideology as false belief.

The strength of this earlier formulation of Marx and Engels lies in its greater capacity to explain and deal with class conflict and the changes in such conflicts over the course of capitalist development. It was, for instance, this conception that was employed by Marx in his political analysis of the 1848–1851 revolution in France (to be discussed later), both as a product of class formation and a weapon in the class struggle, and so a causal agency of revolutionary change.[30]

The parallel analyses of workplace and society reveal the basic structuralism of Marxism. More or less hidden structures produced by hidden processes sometimes referred to as "laws of motion" determine the "surface" world of "appearances", that world which "bourgeois" positivist science takes as the entirety of social reality. This is the essence of Marxist realism.

THE STATE

Marx's analysis of capitalist economics and the workplace seems to imply an increasing need for repression in the workplace, and perhaps in society, as well, as the contradictions attending the changing organic composition of capital increasingly bring into being conditions facilitating the heightening of class consciousness within the working class. And indeed, Marx's and Engels's' view of the state follows from their analyses of workplace and society. However, this analysis goes well beyond the rather simple view of the state as the "executive committee of the bourgeoisie."

It is true that in the *Communist Manifesto* Marx and Engels took the position stated above, and that in later works they sometimes reiterated this. In *The Origin of the Family, Private Property and the State*, for instance, Engels calls the state "an instrument of exploitation of wage labor by capital" (in Feuer, 1959, 392). Indeed, they always held that the state had originated as an instrument for managing class conflict.

> At a certain state of economic development, which was necessarily bound up with the cleavage of society into classes, the state became a necessity, owing to this cleavage (Engels, in Feuer, 1959, 394)[31]

If the state is the creation of private property, it follows that, with the expropriation of the latter, it will cease to exist ("wither away"); communist society is stateless society.[32]

[30] For a good discussion of the ideology problem, see Benton, 161–165.

[31] For a recent analysis generally supporting this position, see Fried (1967), especially Chaps. Five and Six.

[32] The fact that the expropriation of private property would require not only capturing the state, but might well lead to its massive expansion, perhaps on a permanent basis, was from the beginning a troubling possibility recognized not only by those to the left (the anarchists) and the right (liberals and others) of the Communists, but in the very doctrine of the latter, in the transitional stage of "the dictatorship of the proletariat." This is a form of "nightmare Marxism," to employ Gouldner's insightful idea, nascent in every theory, comprising hidden or unemphasized elements that imply a reality quite different, even the opposite, of what the theory "officially" claims. Socialist experience has obviously brought into social existence this particular "nightmare" to a degree that it now constitutes the central anomaly relative to the theory. Whether the state socialist societies have been classless in the technical sense of having generally expropriated private property (although there are some important exceptions to this), or whether social inequalities are appropriately designated as "nonantagonistic classes," seem minor issues in the face of the existence of the powerful party and state bureaucratic elites, and the recent popular rebellions against them in these societies. This situation also helps account for the virtual neglect of the development of the Marxist theory of the state by socialist scholars, especially in the three decades or so between the publication of Lenin's *State and Revolution* and Milovan Djilas's *The New Class* (for which he was labeled a heretic and jailed).

While the deterministic scheme advanced in the *Communist Manifesto* became socialist doctrine, it should be noted that as the working classes of the advanced European societies began to acquire some influence and to exact some concessions, Marx and Engels were often given to less than deterministic formulations about economy-state relations. Marx's famous statement that he was no "Marxist" goes to just this point, and more importantly, we find in the substantive work of both quite nondeterministic formulations. Even in the passage quoted above, Engels qualifies—rather severely—the idea of the state as agency of the dominant class. "By way of exception," he writes, "periods occur in which the warring classes balance each other so nearly that the state power, as ostensible mediator, acquires, for the moment, a certain degree of independence" (Feuer, 1959, 392); he then continues by citing a whole array of instances in which this is true, including the Germany of the 1880s. Marx's studies of French politics relating to this question can be interpreted as reflecting a less than deterministic, theoretically relatively flexible view of class-state relations, just as easily as it can be interpreted as simply anomolous to the theory itself (see Gouldner, 1980, Chap. 11, for an argument supporting this latter view). In his *Eighteenth Brumaire*, he characterizes the state of Louis Bonaparte as standing above the specific interests of *all* classes, of necessity requiring a relatively high degree of autonomy, if only to advance or protect the *long-term* interests of the bourgeoisie, who were given to potentially destructive, short-sighted action. In such a situation, which Draper calls a "frozen class struggle," the state is not the instrument of any particular class, "*but still the resultant of class society taken as a whole* in its current constellation of countervailing powers" (Draper, 1977, 499).

There is yet another way in which the state acquires some autonomy from direct control by the bourgeoisie. This appears in Marx's early writings when he was occupied with Hegel's political theory and the repressive nature of the state.

Despite his critique, Marx thought that there was a sense in which Hegel had been right in emphasizing the ideal nature of the state, although he was wrong in regarding this as its "true" nature, as well as in his account of the reason for its development. As theorists long before Marx or Hegel well understood, coercion must be accompanied by a belief in its "rightness." Marx extends this idea, again in partially Hegelian fashion, by arguing in his "A Critique of Hegel's Philosophy of Right" (Marx, 1964) that the state is "transmuted" into a kind of civil society in and of itself; that is to say, it becomes a social entity unto itself. This is so because the very function it discharges *requires* this separation from society, requires that the state stand *above* society. And this is a contradiction, for it implies that, distinct from the *functional* requirement the bureaucracy serves, it cannot tolerate the natural forms of social life that constitute any civil society and is therefore inherently *destructive* of society. This makes it necessary that the bureaucracy *appear* as the creature *of* the society rather than the apparatus of its domination, which is to say that it must *represent* its true raison d'etre as *universal*, as rule in the interests of all and must, in short, render bourgeois *ideology* in universal form.

The bureaucracy is the form in which the state gives itself a content, Marx wrote, in "A Critique of Hegel's Philosophy of Right." It becomes thereby the *justication* for the existence of the state, and in so doing must foster the illusion that the state is both indispensible and rational in its functioning. Bureaucrats are likened to theologians who must provide for the bureaucracy a set of illusions. The very existence of hierarchy is transmuted into a social necessity as the embodiment of rationality based on the claims to knowledge by those occupying the upper echelons of that hierarchy. At the same time, it makes secret—and thereby sacrosanct—that very knowledge.

In these analyses, it appears that Marx reserved an important role for the state bureaucracy as both somewhat autonomous and yet simultaneously representing bourgeois interests (and in this foreshadowed the "instrumentalist-structuralist" debate of the present). In the growth of bureaucracy, Marx perceived not only the instrument necessary for the control of class antagonisms, but also an apparatus tending to require (and acquire) a good deal of autonomy of both action and the exercise of hegemonic function in which naked justification of class rule becomes transmuted into a quasi-religious veneration of the state and bureaucracy itself. And here Marx stands somewhat closer to Weber than most Marxists (and others) have commonly cared to recognize.

CLASSES AND CLASS CONSCIOUSNESS

All this is obviously central to Marx's and Engels's theory of class consciousness and false consciousness. If the ruling ideas are the ideas of the ruling class, their manifestation among workers is a *false* consciousness precisely because the ideas themselves are false, in the sense of being illusions about or mystifications of the actual nature of social relations in capitalist society. Political economy perpetuates this false consciousness by representing inherently antagonistic social relations as complementary, which is to say, by representing *social classes* as complementary. The ability to *assert* the existence of false consciousness then depends on knowledge of the realities claimed to underlie the appearance; i.e., it is a *truth* claim opposing the truth claims of the ruling ideology and of "vulgar" political economy.[33]

We see in all this that Marx thought that capitalism necessarily fostered a belief system that was mostly appearance, and that this was a necessary complement to the structural constraints of economic role and state power. In this sense ideas are critical in Marx's sociology of capitalist society.[34]

The question of whether and how workers become class conscious, however, is an empirical one requiring discussion in the context of Marx's theory of capitalist society. Marx himself, of course, never got around to making a full statement of his class theory. Aside from a few short passages in the *Manifesto* and *The German Ideology*, there is not a great deal to be found.

---

[33] This issue clearly raises further issues that belong in the following section on Marx's theory of social knowledge and will accordingly be taken up there.

[34] For a good analysis of Marx's concept of ideology, too extensive to detail here, see Lefebvre, Chap. 3.

Volume III of *Capital* concludes with one page of what was intended as a chapter on classes, but the remarks here are only prefatory. The subject has been and remains a tantalizing one, and quite a few have tried their hand at "completing" the theory of class.[35]

The conceptual ambiguities attending Marx's theory of classes can be related to what has been said above. Marx says that capitalist development creates classes, and that a class, by definition, must be *conscious* of itself. To be sure, there is plenty of semantic confusion in Marx's comments on classes, but when he comes down to the actual application of the concept—surely the acid test—it is clear that a class, to be a class, must exhibit characteristics well beyond mere structural position (*für sich* in addition to *an sich*). This is clear in his analysis of the situation of the French peasantry in *The Eighteenth Brumaire of Louis Bonaparte*. French peasants are only a *mass* (like so many potatoes in a sack), says Marx, not a *class*, because of the isolated conditions of their existence. Insofar as "the identity of their interests begets no unity, no national bond, and no political organization . . . , they do not form a class" (*Eighteenth Brumaire*, in Fernbach, 2, 1974, 239). In a letter to his friend Kugelman he reiterates this (Marx, 1941, 19). It seemed clear also to Max Weber, one of whose criticisms of Marx's class theory was that it conflated structural or economic position with the meanings and life styles that might or might not be associated with it (Weber, "Class, Status, and Party", in Weber, 1978b, Chap. 9, Part B, 926–938).

The distinction between a class *an sich* and one *für sich* is thus a critical one reflecting the status of structure and process, on the one hand, and of agency, on the other, in the theory. A class *an sich* is an abstraction designating a structural aspect of the capitalist mode of production, and thus has explanatory status. A class *für sich* designates the *social relations* that may appear as a consequence of this aspect of the mode of production.

Marx's actual political analyses reveal more about his concept of class than do his general theoretical pronouncements. Again, this is well illustrated in his analysis of the role of the peasantry in nineteenth century France in the *Eighteenth Brumaire*. Discussions of the significance of this work, in focusing on and criticizing his *concept* of class as he applies it to the peasantry, often lose sight of the central theme of Marx's analysis, announced at the very outset. Immediately following the famous lines about people making their own history, but not doing so under conditions they themselves have chosen, Marx goes on to say that

> The tradition of the dead generations weighs like a nightmare on the minds of the living. And, just when they appear to be engaged in the revolutionary transformation of themselves and their material surroundings, in the creation of something which does yet exist, precisely in such epochs of revolutionary crisis they timidly conjure up the spirits of the past to help them; they borrow the names, slogans and costumes so as to stage the new world-

---

[35] Perhaps the most extended and detailed of these in sociology is that of Ralf Dahrendorf in his *Class and Class Conflict in Industrial Society*, esp. Chapter Two. It should be noted that the concept of class was in use long before Marx, especially in the work of some of the earlier British economists (see Dahrendorf, above, p. 8).

historical scene in this venerable disguise and borrowed language (Marx, *Eighteenth Brumaire*, in Fernbach, 1974, 146).

It is not only the material conditions of life, the "dead labor" materialized in present objective institutions, but the *ideas* of the past as well, that constrain action in the present. In the case of the French peasantry during the revolutionary period of 1848–1851, the ideas that had accompanied its successful emancipation from feudal constraints—ideas fully appropriate to the time—now constituted an ideological albatross shackling their potential to perceive their "true" interests (i.e., alliance with the urban proletariat). This ideology, which Marx calls "Napoleonic" because practical policies based on them were instituted during the Napoleonic period, was comprised of the following elements: (1) the ideal of the privately held smallholding, (2) strong central government, (3) the "rule of priests as an instrument of the government," and (4) the predominant importance of the army as manifestation of the glory of the state. During the Napoleonic period these were appropriate to the situation of a class still in bondage to feudal lords, unorganized but requiring action on a national scale, "naturally religious in its accord with society, its dependence on natural forces, and its subjection to the authority protecting it from on high" (243), and requiring the army not only to enforce the transition, but to serve as a focal point for the nationalistic attachment of the peasant to the state. In the 1840s the peasants still cling to this ideology, despite the fact that nearly two generations have passed, and their objective situation has been greatly transformed. Now the size of the holding has become smaller, incapable of supporting the peasant and his family, leading to multiple mortages, economic destitution, and ruin. As independent property holders, and being by far the largest "class" (*an sich*), the peasantry has become increasingly weighted down by taxes imposed from Paris (because not being organized and aware of its interests—*für sich*—it has no representation). Under these conditions of economic deterioration, the hold of religion weakens, "heaven becomes an *insult* . . . ," and priests the "annointed bloodhounds of the terrestial police" (244). The army, once filled with the sons of proud peasants during the glory days of conquest, is now turned *against* the peasants and becomes a hated force (238–245).

In this analysis, Marx builds objective conditions, ideology, and changes in both, into a concrete political analysis. Unlike the peasants, other classes or class fractions obviously have a much more highly developed sense of their interests, access to the power of the state (at least to some degree), some degree of internal organization, and will to act, which is to say, they are morely highly developed *as classes* have more the quality of classes *für sich.*

Return now to the problem of definition. Making these distinctions may be seen to be important for Marx's depiction of capitalist society as leveled and atomized. The full comprehension of its exploited condition, the full realization of its potential as a material force, after all, marks the *end* of capitalist society, according to Marx. This is essentially Bertell Ollman's conclusion after an analysis of Marx's use of the concept "class." He shows that Marx regularly employed four defining components of class: (1) the presence of economic interests, (2) a consciousness of opposed interests, (3) cultural affinity, and (4) overt hostility occurring in actual struggle, and that *all* of them appear only in *advanced* capitalism, although admittedly Marx does sometimes use "class" in situations when not all are present[36] (Ollman, 1979, 41). The burgeoning incubus of the proletariat in capitalist society is the beginning of the growth of a *new society*, the beginning of the creation of a *new* type of human social relationship. A class becoming class conscious may be said to be *in*, but not *of*, capitalist society.

The fact that the working class has failed to fulfill its historic mission has commonly been taken as the single most telling blow to the credibility of Marxism.[37] Attempts to salvage it have taken the form of distinguishing Marxism as a general *model* of society, or as *methodological*, which makes possible the rejection of any particular empirical claim from historical or deterministic Marxism, and argues that the former can, even *ought*, to be assimilated to sociology (or more broadly, social science), but that the latter is to be rejected. This distinction has been employed—in somewhat differing forms—by C. Wright Mills, Ralf Dahrendorf, and Anthony Giddens, to mention only a few from among sociologists. It is a distinction that doubtless has certain advantages, among them the possibility of a certain type of assimilation of Marxism to academic sociological models and practice, or as put rather more bitingly by Gouldner, a program "of clubby academicians who want to 'normalize' Marxism into something familiar" (Gouldner, 1980, 20). Apropos of this is Applebaum's opposition to methodological Marxism on *substantive* grounds, namely, that C, v, and s (see f.n. #20) designate not only analytical categories for understanding structural relationships and tendencies, but also are "political indicators of the degree of the class struggle" designating different forms of that struggle (Applebaum, 1978, 76).

Ollman, in one of the better "completions" of Marx (in this case "textual exegesis" might be more appropriate), has approached this anomaly of Marxism in a very different way. Ollman argues that concealed behind the generalities attending most discussions of class consciousness is a *very*

---

[36] Thereby seeming to challenge the usage in the *Manifesto*. If "class" appears only in late capitalist society, how can history be the history of class struggle? Ollman seems to think that these usages are not entirely imcompatible because there is almost always some degree of manifestation of one or more of the several factors.

[37] Along with its historic corollary, the theoretical conundrum of the revolution appearing in preindustrial agrarian societies rather than capitalist ones, and now the spectre of the working classes of many of the socialist societies rising up against the very instruments that are officially representing their revolutionary will. At the level of theory, nested within the deterministic utopianism of Marx and Engels was a several-faceted dilemma inherent in the theorizing of the transition. One facet had to do with the relationship between theory and action. Dogmatic insistence that violent overthrow was necessary seemed reasonable in the face of the real human depredations of capitalism, but smacked of the very determinism Marx had sought to avoid in "sliding between" Hegel and the French materialists. In fact, there is substantial ground for the claim of Lichtheim and others that Marx, in effect, became a social democrat after the failed revolutions of 1848 (Lichtheim, 1971b, 87). In his 1852 piece on the Chartists for the New York *Daily-Tribune*, for example, he opines that universal suffrage would be an "equivalent of political power for the working class of England, . . . where it has gained a clear consciousness of its position as a class. . . . Its inevitable result, here, is the political supremacy of the working class" (quoted from Bottomore, 1956, 200).

complex, laborious, and difficult social process involving at least nine steps that constitute something approaching a Guttman scale and that proceed in face of a variety of obstacles, any of which one might expect to effectively deter class-conscious action.

These are worth mention, in part because they relate to the above discussion of the general features of capitalist society. Ollman interprets Marx as saying that we can speak of class consciousness only if the following are present: (1) recognition by workers that they have economic interests; (2) an understanding of their interests as individuals *in* their interests as members of a class; (3) the capacity to distinguish their *main* interests from others; (4) believing that class interests must be prior to other interests, such as national or religious ones; (5) hatred of capitalists exploiters; (6) the belief that their situation can be quantitatively improved; and (7) the belief that they themselves can bring this about; but also (8) the belief that Marx's strategy is the best means to achieve it; and finally (9) courage to act. All this must come to pass in a situation in which workers are being treated like beasts; in which job competition inhibits such long-range considerations in favor of short-term necessity; in which a whole array of other types of attachments, trivial perhaps, take precedence simply by being present in peoples' lives; in which ruling class ideology encourages workers to admire, not hate, capitalists; in which most are illiterate; and more. (Ollman, 1979, 10ff.)[38]

One further point relating to this should be made here. I said earlier that Marx's critique of capitalist society is at root a critique of the consequences of the division of labor, and thus even more fundamentally of the division of labor itself. But there is a contradiction here. On the one hand, everything progressive in industrial society is owed to the expansion of the division of labor; a part of Marx's Enlightenment spirit is allied with Adam Smith on the desirability of increasing productivity and therefore of the division of labor on which it is based. On the other hand, a detail division of labor underlies capitalist property relations, and on this ground the latter would seem to be necessarily scheduled for abolition in the communism of the future. In fact, in certain passages, Marx follows this line.

> In communist society, where nobody has one exclusive sphere of activity but each one can become accomplished in any branch he wishes, production as a whole is regulated by society, thus making it possible for me to do one thing today and another tomorrow, to hunt in the evening, criticize after

---

[38] Ollman's analysis brings into focus what have been two related difficulties attending the theory of class and class consciousness. The first has to do with the fact that the goals of the proletariat (or other historical agents) are determined externally by "objective interests", which undercuts the principle of agency. The definition of "interest" derives from the theory, presupposing a superior knowledge arrived at independently of the particulars of the situation on the part of the theorist. But this contradicts the basic theory of knowledge (to be discussed) of Marx, in which knowledge is always situation-linked, and in which it stands in a dialectical relation with the objective nature of the situation. This line of analysis leads to the problem of the difficulties attending the observation of workers (and others) who act in ways divergent from those predicted by the theory, even, as often as not, in ways supportive of capitalism. This necessitates the introduction of the category of "false consciousness" as an explanatory device, which brings in its train a set of difficulties too extensive to detail here.

dinner, in accordance with my inclination, without ever becoming hunter, fisherman, shepherd or critic (from *The German Ideology, in Bottomore*, 1956, 97).

This passage really fails to address the point, if taken literally. The question is not whether one can hunt, fish, criticize, and so on in communist society, but whether an industrial society without a *detail* division of labor—*not* a social one—is possible. Marx obviously would like to believe this, but his own understanding and analysis make it near impossible. So what is left unsaid is of greater significance than what is expressed. In a system of socialized production there will, of course, be no surplus value, and no profits, and therefore no "law" of whether or how the latter fall. But it will be machine operators, miners, and others necessarily incorporated in the detail division of labor, not hunters, fishermen, and social critics, who will have to continue to produce. Marx fails to deal with the master issue of capitalism and socialism as rival systems, of whether or not a detail division of labor will not always bring into being a hierarchy of authority, privilege, and exploitation even in the absence of private property. This is perhaps the central "nightmare" of Marxism.

One final point, the theory of class and class consciousness can be taken as a measure of Marx's debt to Hegel. The growth of class consciousness is Marx's sociological rendering of the slave rising against the master out of the condition of bondage necessary for the realization of freedom. Prometheus brought the fire, but the Promethean proletariat rises from the pages of Hegel's *History* and *Phenomenology*.

To sum up, it may be said that Marx's sociology of capitalism focuses on the poles of workplace and society. Production is maintained by the structural constraints arising from the laws of capitalist development and manifested in the basic property relations of capitalism and through coercion exercised by bureaucracies in both workplace and society. Ultimately, this structure will collapse as the contradictions become increasingly acute, but for an indeterminate period capitalist society takes the form of an increasingly atomized and leveled structure with a culture centered on money and what money can bring—an instrumentalized, consumer culture of a sort appropriate to a time of scarcity—now evolved into forms of consumership of which Marx could never have dreamed.

Marx never worked out the social science that he envisioned early in life; indeed, it would obviously have been impossible for him to have done so. But he did create the essentials of a theory that grasped the world in a way radically different than either Comte or Spencer. It was a theory that *political* men and women, if not academics, would before long employ to transform the world, and in that process, in their view at least, bring much of its truth to realization. This brings us to the matter of the conception of knowledge in the Marxism of Marx and Engels.

MARX'S THEORY OF SOCIAL KNOWLEDGE

The premise of the thought of the philosophers of the eighteenth century was that knowledge and action could be fused and set to the task of guiding or directing the restructuring of human society. In earlier chapters, I tried to show some of the dilemmas inherent in this and the directions taken in response to them by social thinkers insofar as they had some bearing on the emergence of sociology. These difficulties, however, become really clear, and acute, in the work of the early sociologists proper—to some extent the Scots, but more importantly Comte and Spencer.

Comte and Spencer both, although in different ways, formulated their sociologies in highly deterministic form. Both wanted to guarantee the future and this meant the elimination of conflict, particularly political conflict. But there is a fundamental and unavoidable theoretical dilemma involved in this.

If the transcendence of politics requires willful human action, i.e., engagement in politics, the means is self-defeating, and subverts the very legitimacy of the end. On the other hand, to remove the future from the province of the human will and to submit it to the play of providence or of covert agents in history abandons the conception of human individuals as possessing rights, and as rational and potent agents capable of taking the direction of things into their own hands. Comte's and Spencer's philosophies of science attempt to *guarantee* a humane future; to do so they *objectify* abstractly the purposeful exertion of the human will as the *immanent* law of change.

In Hegel we find a system similar to Comte's, although more complex, and one that makes a *virtue* of contradiction itself. The irony of Hegel's system resides in its being grounded in the irreducible and unchallengeable fact of human subjectivity and the assertion of freedom inhering there, but the wisdom and power of the individual is realized only insofar as it achieves unity on a collective plane, as it is "objectified" and therefore held to be the highest truth. Furthermore, since knowledge is identified with the dialectical unfolding of history, true knowledge is identified only with final knowledge. Prior to this, knowledge is incomplete, thus inadequate; once true knowledge comes into being, its very meaning is that history will have realized itself in the highest form of knowledge possible, thus making practical exertions based on it superflous. The Owl of Minerva ends up taking its flight under conditions that guarantee its impotence.

Hegel's manner of working out the implications of the Enlightenment idea thus subverts that ideal because it makes knowledge the consequence of action, rather than action itself the rational application of knowledge. Although Hegel's philosophy is intended to demonstrate the progress of freedom in the form of an increasingly enlightened subjectivity, it does so in a way that ends up by identifying that subjectivity in externalized, i.e., in estranged form. In recognizing the contingency of all human action upon the social world—that action being simultaneously a remaking of that world— Hegel's philosophy takes the form of identifying the process whereby humankind's naturally free subjectivity "realizes" itself, becomes congealed in the objectifications that constitute that world, a doctrine implying that rationality amounts to submitting to the fate—whatever that might be—that history has ordained for us all. For Hegel this turned out to mean canonizing the Prussian state of the early nineteenth century as the highest form of freedom, a "freedom" that would ultimately be spread to the rest of the world.

But Hegel had developed only the conservative side of his philosophy, and it was mainly—at that time—the Young Hegelians, whose program was rediscovery and extension of the *radical* roots of Hegel's philosophy. Marx, in turn, had rejected the Young Hegelians' idealism, but also retrieved the Hegelian theoretical centrality of the incorrigibly social and processual nature of the subjective and the nestedness of the knowing subject in the social process, and tried to bring it into synthesis with the developments in English and French materialist philosophy of the eighteenth and early nineteenth centuries.

Beyond his relation to German idealism and to materialism, at least three other intellectual sources were critical in Marx's formulation of his conception of social knowledge. These were the various socialist theories and movements of the early nineteenth century, the historical development of political economy, and Darwinian evolutionalism. It will be useful to briefly review them here, since Marx's conception of social science both criticizes and incorporates them all in an attempt at synthesis unique to nineteenth century thought.

Marx and Engels critiqued the socialists of the time—Proudhon, Owen, and others—in Marx's *The Poverty of Philosophy*, a critique of their doctrines later summed up by Engels in *Socialism: Utopian and Scientific* as being "the expression of absolute truth, independent of history" (Engels, 1977, 117), rather than addressing "the necessary outcome of the struggle between two historically developed classes" (124). The task of a scientific social science was "not to manufacture a system of society as perfect as possible, but to examine the historic-economic succession of events" (124–125). Earlier forms of socialism could not *explain* the nature of the capitalist appropriation. Like Marx in *Capital*, Engels here reiterates how the forces driving human history are like those of nature (140) and are thereby amenable to scientific analysis. One aspect of historical materialism, then, is its status as a critique of utopian socialism.

Marx also appropriated the essential corpus of political economy, a bit of which we have seen earlier, for his analysis in *Capital*. Although even the best of the political economists "remain in the grasp of illusion," and more than this, even though political economy is "the ideology of bourgeois society reflective of bourgeois property relations," and even though he and Engels in *The German Ideology* assert that the ideas of the ruling class are the ideas of the time and that the control of the "means of mental production" by the ruling class follows from its control of the means of material production, Marx nevertheless based his economic analysis squarely on classical economics. "The opponents of political economy—socialism and communism—find their theoretical basis in the work of political economy, especially Ricardo's," he writes in the *Grundrisse* (McLellan, 1971, 48). Without the tools of the labor theory of value and many other principles central to the economics of the time, including the idea of the falling rate of profit, Marx's analysis in *Capital* is inconceivable, for within this science he found the components of a theory that seemed to have the inexorable quality of natural law, the power of determination, thus allowing him to claim for his own radicalized version the prestige of science.

Finally, after 1860 Marx found in Darwin's *Origin of Species* (which he called "epoch-making" [1906, 375]) "the basis in natural history for our own view (of) the class struggle in history" (Gouldner, 1980, 72). If Gouldner is right, this served to further confirm and buttress the already firm determinism of his analysis in *Capital* (72), a kind of "scientizing" of Hegel. Later, in the first volume of *Capital*, he remarks, citing Vico, that such a history of the "productive organs of man ought to be easier to complete."[39]

The manner in which Marx criticized and appropriated these intellectual schools and traditions exhibits a struggle to transcend the various limitations of them all and to retrieve from them the elements of human science that might realize the Enlightenment vision. Marx took from Hegel the centrality of the subjective in history, but stripped of both its objective idealism and its universalim and reformulated by what Karl Korsch would much later call the principle of "historical specification" (Korsch, 1963, Chap. 2); from the Young Hegelians the critique of religion, but shorn of the idealism derived from Hegel; from Feuerbach the idea of religion as an alienated reflection of our real world, but without his universalism; from the materialists the fundamental principle that everything about human life must rest on a material foundation, and that this profoundly *limits* the will and the intellect, but not the manner in which this school understood the *scope* of the realm of the material, mainly as biological mechanism, or the doctrine of the full *determination* of ideas generally associated with the school; from the socialists elements of a *critique* of capitalism and of a vision of the communal restructuring of the future, but again, at once rejecting the various universalizing, romantic, religious, generally "nonscientific" emphases found in these in the past; from the economists the technical apparatus with which this critique could be carried out (but not, of course, what Marx regarded as the ideological baggage built into the conceptual structure of the theory); and from evolution, the confirmation of the *historical* lawlike character of this analysis, but without surrendering to the extinguishing of subjectivity implied by its vulgar application to human history (as in the case of Spencer).

The doctrine of praxis emerges as an attempt to bring together elements from all of these. It attempts to incorporate both the determinism associated with the concept of law, in order to ground the claim to scientific *explanation*, and simultaneously, tries to *theoretically intertwine* this with the principle of freedom, the incorrigibility of our complicity in the construction of our world, and at once, the possibility of modifying this as a necessary condition for the action that would ultimately change the world.

The dialectical relation between structural constraint and voluntaristic action can be briefly illustrated in the following interpretation of Marx's assimilation of political economy to his revolutionary end.

All societies employ knowledge to ends generally consistent with their functioning. This is obviously true of technologies: technical developments in shipbuilding and related arts put to the service of the commercial interests of early maritime peoples around the shores of the Mediterranean, for instance, converted that body of water into an international sea. But

---

[39] Citing Vico in the context of defending a deterministic theory of history is, in itself, of interest, for it suggests that even in such moments Marx does not jettison his sense of the need for the principle of agency in social analysis.

knowledge is also always embedded in the broader culture of any society, and this culture is powerfully influenced, if not determined by those who control the means of material and mental production. While theoretically distinct from the latter, the rational aspects or elements of knowledge are empirically difficult to separate out from the larger mosaic of illusion and appearance.

The appropriation of science by the bourgeoisie to ground and hasten the growth of capitalism is one historical instance of this. To a large extent eighteenth and nineteenth century science (like earlier forms of rational knowledge) became what it was not only because of some immanent stream of purely intellectual developments but partly because it was *fashioned* by those commanding the resources to channel its development. The findings of science have been put to specific technical uses, shaping the world in practical ways, and these practices in turn constitute the foundations for the further growth and development of science and technology which grows out of the obsolescence or perceived inadequacy of that technology at any particular point in capitalist evolution.[40]

The science of the nineteenth century, then, like the intellectual productions of any age, is to be understood in the framework of the class interests that dominate that period. Political economy, although framed fundamentally by concepts reflecting what the bourgeoisie wishes to believe about itself and its historic role, is nevertheless more than this, because the modern bourgeoisie have need not only of ideology, but also of real science, for practical reasons—understanding and managing a complex and expanding economy—in order to accurately describe and interpret it. In this sense much of the technical apparatus of political economy, like the proletariat itself, is a product of a dialectical process of development, from which Marx extracted the "scientific" elements and then rendered them as the *negation* of the larger ideological totality. Marx's own theory emerges as a Hegelian negation of bourgeois instrumental reason, Engels's "idealized kingdom of the bourgeoisie."

But is there a unity here? Following in the footsteps of Karl Korsch, Lucio Colletti, and others, Gouldner has argued the thesis that there are, in fact, *two* Marxisms that have always been not a unity, but in tension with and contradicting each (Gouldner, 1980). *Scientific Marxism*, deterministic, its emphasis on structure as constraining, its conception of change more evolutionary, gradualistic, politically social democratic, intertwines throughout Marx's work with *Critical Marxism*, voluntaristic and relationistic, emphasizing the openings history offers to the bold and creative, its conception of change catastrophic, its politics revolutionary. Recognition of this, of course, is part of the ground of the Young Marx-Old Marx argument, but as Gouldner shows, it is far more than this, and the constant tension between the two accounts for much of the confusing and ambiguous phraseology and locution—and repressed arguments—as well as the blatant contradictions, that run through the corpus of Marx and Engels's writings.

If Gouldner's argument is correct—and in my view it is strongly

---

[40] See various passages and comments in Marx's chapter on machinery in *Capital*, vol. 1 on this point.

argued—we have in the Marxism of Marx the first major attempt to both bring to the intellectual surface the contradictions inherent in the Enlightenment vision of a human science, and then to fuse them in a synthesis that neither celebrates the power of the mind as such, on the one hand, nor on the other, falls victim to materialist reductionism (since the material causation of ideas necessarily vitiates their nationality). And even though Marx's Marxism is in certain ways a technical failure, in part because it was limited by the state of development of the materials at hand, it was at the same time fantastically successful in forging a paradigm of a human science that continues to inspire a diverse array of continuing sociological work.

The theory of praxis irrevocably implicates the scientist as an actor in his own scientific activity. In Giddens's rendering of this, the social sciences differ from the natural in that their boundary conditions involve actors' knowledge, including knowledge of themselves produced by social scientists. This implies an inherent and incorrigible mutability of all such action. Therefore

> every generalization or form of study that is concerned with existing society constitutes a potential intervention within that society and this leads through to the tasks and aims of sociology as a critical theory (Giddens, 1981, 244–245).

Such action is linked logically to Marx's basic realist paradigm of hidden structures and processes as determinants of the more or less immediately observable facts of appearance. Knowledge of the laws of such processes and the forms taken by the structures they bring into being is at once knowledge that is a *revelation* of how our own actions are determined, and this knowledge then *negates* its own determined character, bringing our action within the realm of control and rational manipulation. Marx's theory of knowledge in this fashion thus establishes theory (even if not necessarily historical materialism) as necessarily constituitive of all emancipatory action. And it stands in fundamental opposition to the positivist tradition, whether of Comte or his various heirs, which means, of course, that the Baconian sense of objectivity is sacrificed, but in the name of a humane order possible only with the democratization of knowledge.

CONCLUSION

All this constitutes a quite unified realization of Enlightenment and early nineteenth century tendencies. The unfolding of history is still construed as progressive, and this is so *because* it takes the form of a movement from being determined by hidden forces to *rational* action based on acquisition of an understanding of these forces. This effects a resolution, in historical terms, of the two Enlightenment views of progress. As with Comte and Spencer, and Hegel as well, this knowledge is understood to be scientific, if in a sense claiming to depart in significant ways from the naive positivism of earlier thinkers.

Marxism also rejects entirely any explanatory theoretical status for original nature, thereby powerfully displacing the old paradigm that had held sway for so long in its various, if increasingly suspect forms. The causes of evil are not only located exclusively within the plane of the social, but theorized in their particulars, and then linked causally with the emergence of an order in which evil is banished. Human agency is *theorized* in the theory of class and class consciousness, the essential outlines of which, despite the attending difficulties, constituted the single most powerful framework for the analysis of social change for a century or more. If the particulars of this seem today to be hopelessly utopian, the paradigm of analysis on which they rest, one can surely claim, remains the condition of any knowledge-grounded and change-oriented action.

11

EMILE DURKHEIM I
Philosophical anthropology and the rules
for sociology

PREFACE TO PART III

By comparison with the "stuffy" decade of the 1880s (Hughes, 1958, 40–41), the last decade of the nineteenth century was one of incredible ferment and creativity. It was the time during which the strains and contradictions of European liberalism, building for a century, reached crisis proportions economically, politically, culturally, and intellectually.

In every major European society and the United States, the movements of the left—international socialism, anarchism, populism (especially in the United States) were growing in size and potential political power. In Germany, the Social Democrats, who had pursued the state-oriented politics introduced by Ferdinand LaSalle at Gotha[1] in 1873, in 1891 at their Erfurt meeting turned their doctrinal—if not actual—backs on moderation and endorsed a Marxist program. In France, a strong non-Marxist socialist movement was coming into being, but was split into parliamentary and anarchist wings, the latter stimulating the anarchist sociology of Georges Sorel (Sorel, 1961).[2] In England nonrevolutionary Fabianism had long been

---

[1] Mainly in the form of advocating state-run workshops somewhat along the lines of those set up by Louis Blanc during the 1848–1851 revolutionary period in France. Marx's reaction to LaSalle's doctrine appears in his "Critique of the Gotha Program."

[2] The strength of anarcho-syndicalism in France is partly accounted for by the moderation of the socialists who failed even to speak out in support of Dreyfus, thereby earning Sorel's contempt. It also perhaps helps explain why Durkheim could be as accommodating as he was toward socialism (see Durkheim, 1953b).

taking shape under the leadership of George Bernard Shaw, the Hammonds, the Webbs, Graham Wallas, and other middle-class intellectuals. In the United States socialist thought and action was considerably less genteel but still essentially nonrevolutionary, especially in the form given it by Eugene Debs; but the anarchist-inspired Wobblies were for a time a significant force in some parts of the land, and during the early 1890s the populist movement mostly of small independent midwestern and southern farmers posed a potentially serious threat to the rapid growth of monopoly capitalism until its cooptation by and absorption into the Bryan fusion ticket of 1896.

The international order, based for three quarters of a century on British industrial production, the British fleet, and the British pound sterling (and one might add, British social anthropology, which was everywhere deployed as an adjunct to British colonial administration) was coming under challenge, most importantly by the meteoric industrialization and militarization of Germany under Bismarck and Wilhelm I; but also—despite the old cultural ties—by the United States, and of course, by France as well. A century of peace in Europe lasting from the final defeat of Napoleon to the outbreak of World War II was, by the 1890s, degenerating into something very different from the progress celebrated by Spencer and other Victorians, a growing unsettling of the European balance of power.

Perhaps the most acute and prescient diagnoses of the time were the works of Rudolf Hilferding, a German Marxist (Hilferding, 1968), and the British liberal J. A. Hobson (Hobson, 1971). Hobson, in particular, argued powerfully that behind the rhetoric of the "white man's burden" and the nationalist jingoism, imperialism was a violent and destructive exploitation of native peoples which benefited mainly the economically dominant groups: industrialists, bankers, and their satellites. Fourteen years later at the height of the war, some of his and Hilferding's ideas were incorporated by Lenin into his analysis of imperialism (Lenin, *Imperialism*).

Today we also understand that internal unrest and violent external expansion were not unrelated; both Hobson and Lenin attended to this relationship, although in a less than satisfactory manner. Both thought that the basic interests of the working classes were opposed to imperialism, but they also recognized that at least some of the benefits of imperialist expansion accrued to nonbourgeois sectors of society. Lenin, in particular, in his theory of labor aristocracy, saw how at least certain sectors of the working class could be brought ideologically in line with imperialist ideology.[3]

Although the major industrializing nations experienced some central commonalities (e.g., the term "The social problem" came into use in all of them to designate first the misery of the working classes and second the threat they came to pose: see Merz, 1965, Vol. 4, 446ff.), national differences were of great importance for turn-of-the-century sociology. In each of the three major national contexts—France, Germany, and the United States—sociology in part defined itself in relation to socialism, but, more proximally or directly, the growth and direction of these sociologies was also powerfully

[3] Some recent scholarship has attempted to show empirically that internal unrest was an important factor in continuing and accelerating imperialist expansion. See Wolfe, 1975, Chap. 3.

influenced by already existing intellectual traditions, the *Weltanschauung* of the groups that were their bearers. These differences of national intellectual culture were the critical contexts of the sociologies worked out by the first generation of *academic* sociologists.

French national experience for a century had been one of recurring upheaval revolution: the great revolution of 1789 and the years following, the Napoleonic usurpation, the restoration of 1815 and Orleanist takeover in 1830, the struggles of 1848–1851, the revolutionary commune of 1871, the attempted coup d'état of General Boulanger following the left-wing electoral victories of 1885, the struggles over the conviction of Captain Dreyfus in the last years of the century. In conjunction with the progress of industrialization, this political history had since the early days of the century been preoccupied with the problem of social order, which had fostered a chronic sense of social dissolution, generally attributed to the growth of an uncontrolled and destructive individualism. This was a theme common to intellectuals of all persuasions, and although the concrete meanings they attached to it differed they all perceived it as a threat to social order (see Lukes, 1973a, 195–97).[4] Even Sorel's theory of the socially integrating function of violence, for instance, is interpreted by Edward Shils as the work of "a moralist distressed with the dissolution of traditional morals into rationalist individualism and hedonism" (Shils, in Sorel, 1961, 20). It is just this problem of order that became central to Durkheim's sociology (and which through Talcott Parsons's work was ultimately introduced into American sociology as the foundational question of social thought and sociology ever since Hobbes).

The intellectual traditions of the other big European societies, along with the United States, evolved quite different understandings of their histories and future fates. In Germany a sense of separation between "inner" and "outer", often expressed as a polarity of "meaning" and "mechanism," in conjunction with the historicism that suffused the understanding of the cultural sciences there, framed the tradition within which so much German intellectual and aesthetic work was carried forward. These ideas virtually define the romanticism of German social and historical thought.

Romanticism in its German sense acquires its very meaning in the opposition of inner "spirit" and external "lifeless mechanism." German historical experience has sometimes been understood as alternatively exploding outward to achieve a unity bringing alive the external lifeless shell through suffusion by the inner spirit (as for example in Naziism); or a near-total, often mystical escape *from* the latter into the inner recesses of the former, as in the idea of the "Volksgeist" and the romanticism of the great German poets. In one form or another, "spontaneity" is opposed to mechan-

---

[4] It should be said that there is perhaps an element of exaggeration in such accounts, especially regarding the last two decades of the nineteenth century, years during which Durkheim came to his intellectual maturity and produced most of his enduring work. (On the possible importance of this qualification, see Fenton, 1984, Chap. 1.)

ical routinization, whether it be in intellectual life, in art, or in politics.[5] We have already discussed the earlier elaboration by Herder (Chap. 6).

Sociologically, this polarity reflects the disjunction between the sense of cultural unity accompanied by still-surviving political fragmentation prior to unification begun under Bismarck in the 1860s, a unity undoubtedly magnified well beyond its real manifestations among the German-speaking peoples. It was in this context that Max Weber worked out his sociology.

In the United States, where in the absence of feudal institutions the business class came early to political dominance, an instrumental culture of enormous energy and practical inventiveness was quite early in evidence. Although regional differences were enormous, the dominant ideological outlook was unequivocally favorable to business and associated with an ascetic Protestantism described by Weber in his *The Protestant Ethic and the Spirit of Capitalism*. The American character has been persistently portrayed as one seeking to establish identity in a new land where status distinctions remain insecure or ambiguous, but where the passion for democracy eventuates in, among other things, continuing struggles over cultural—as distinct from economic—questions. The burgeoning of a polyglot array of immigrant cultures, especially in the decades around the turn of the century, tended to elevate cultural issues—generally in the form of assimilation and conformity—to a central place in the American consciousness, and to relegate the economic questions of class to secondary importance. Not the political consciousness of the expanding working class, but the ethnic conflicts, and then the mass culture emerging in part from the clashes among them, along with rising levels of consumption after the turn of the century, have been the critical foci of American experience.

This environment produced intellectual movements and viewpoints very different from those of the Old World. For our purposes, the most important of these is the uniquely American philosophy of pragmatism. This is a philosophy, as so many of its critics, such as Bertrand Russell—and even some of its friends—have maintained, that resonates with the coarsest values of the relatively unchecked form of capitalism in the United States. Like its European counterparts of the time, however, it is at base an attempt to come to terms with the individual-society relationship on a theoretical or philosophical plane, and then to apply this to the polyglot social *milieu*. So, although American sociology roughly up to World War I was simultaneously evolutionist in the Spencerian sense, and reformist in the tradition of the Social Gospel, it was not the sociologies of Ward, Sumner, Giddings, and Ross, but the *interactionist* pragmatism of Cooley, Mead, and W.I. Thomas—itself evolutionary—that came to exercise the dominant influence on later generations of sociologists.

In the chapters following, we shall concentrate on the work of only

---

[5] In the latter connection, to cite just one instance of a sociological expression of this, see Wilhelm Reich's interpretation of the government's repression of the Viennese workers' movement of July 15, 1927 (the event that evidently politicized him and set him on the mission of his life, to bring together Marx and Freud). The people, says Reich, behaved *spontaneously*, the police *mechanically* (Reich, 1953, 40–45).

a few of the sociologists of the period roughly between 1890 and 1920, those who, by general consensus, have exerted and continue to exert the strongest influence. There were, of course, many others. France produced Tarde, le Bon, and Bouglé as well as Durkheim, but almost everything of relatively lasting worth has its beginnings in Durkheim. In Germany, Simmel, Tönnies, Michels, Sombart, and von Wiese, along with Franz Oppenheimer and the Austrians Gumplowicz and Ratzenhofer, worked out sociologies of importance for their time, and all of them exerted some influence, especially in the United States, through Alion Small, W.I. Thomas, and Robert Park, along with others who studied and traveled in Germany during the late nineteenth century. We shall, in fact, take some note of the first three mentioned above, but our focus must rest mainly on the work of Max Weber, the sociological titan of the time, and perhaps of all time. In the United States we shall largely ignore the various reformist evolutionists, chiefly Ward and Ross, as well as their conservative counterparts, most importantly Sumner and Giddings, and focus first on the contribution of Charles H. Cooley, and the philosopher G.H. Mead, and then on work of the latter's student and then friend W.I. Thomas (along with Thomas's collaborator, Florian Znaniecki), and try to show the way in which their *The Polish Peasant in Europe and America* can be assimiliated to Mead's theory of interaction and the self.[6]

DURKHEIM'S LIFE AND CAREER

Durkheim was born into the family of a rabbi in 1858 in a village in a part of Lorraine not annexed by Germany following the war of 1870. Accounts reveal him as a studious and brilliant child, and at the age of 18 he was accepted in the prestigious Ecole Normal Superieur in Paris, the training ground of the French cultural and political elite during the Third Republic. There he became acquainted with such future luminaries as Henri Bergson, Léon Blum, Lucien Lévy-Bruhl, and Jean Jaurès. Among his more influential teachers were Fustel de Coulanges, from whose *The Ancient City* Durkheim probably first came to his appreciation of the significance of religion in communal life, and Emile Boutroux, who introduced him to Comte. He was also powerfully influenced by reading Charles Renouvier, the leading French neo-Kantian, whose work was an attempt to establish the compatibility of determinism in the sphere of science with the autonomy of the individual required by moral conduct (for more detail see Lukes, 1973a, Part 1).

After completing his studies at the école, Durkheim taught at several secondary schools (lycées) and during the year 1885–1886 traveled in

---

[6] The absence of significant sociological development in England—with the possible exception of Hobson—during this period is perhaps worthy of brief comment. The former has been explained by the sheer fact that in Victorian England little if anything seemed problematic, whereas the English social order being more or less taken for granted. English industrialism led the world, and the transition from the feudal world, although lengthy, had taken place *relatively* peacefully through reform, giving rise to a complacency regarding the "social problem." This fostered the attitude that only "common sense", not sociology, was needed to cope with time (Hawthorne, 1976, Chap. 8).

Germany under a state travel grant,[7] visiting several universities, including Berlin, where he became familiar with the work of Wundt. Upon his return he was appointed lecturer at Bordeaux. Although Durkheim had been trained mainly in philosophy, his appointment at Bordeaux was in education and social science.

While at Bordeaux Durkheim offered a variety of courses in sociology, including the sociology of the family and of education, as well as socialism, criminology, legal and political sociology, and religion. The struggle over Captain Dreyfus's conviction also occurred while Durkheim was at Bordeaux and he became a committed Dreyfusard. Durkheim was and evidently remained a republican of fairly *radical* stripe, fundamentally committed to the French understanding of this term, i.e., a separation of church and state along with opposition to all royalist movements, which recurred continually. It is arguable that Durkheim's Bordeaux period was the most creative of his life, for while there he published in rather rapid succession *The Division of Labor in Society* in 1893 (his doctoral dissertation), *The Rules of Sociological Method* in 1895, and *Suicide* in 1897. Excepting *The Elementary Forms of the Religious Life*, published in 1915,[8] none of his later work, although important in illuminating certain aspects of his sociology, approaches the originality of his work of the 1890s.

In 1902 Durkheim was called to the Sorbonne to accept a professorship of education. There he became one of the better-known figures in French academic life, and his sociology converged with the official ideology of the Third Republic, to the point that it came to be referred to as "State Durkheimianism."[9] His other important works, especially *Professional Ethics and Civic Morals, Socialism and Saint-Simon*, "The Dualism of Human Nature and Its Social Conditions," and *Moral Education*[10] were published during his tenure at the Sorbonne. His ideas regarding education were by and large adopted during the Third Republic, and indeed, in some circles came to be known as "State Durkheimianism." With the outbreak of the war, Durkheim became an avid publicist in its support but was psychologically broken by the death of his only son—a promising sociologist—in that conflict. Durkheim himself died soon after in 1917.

After the war Durkheimian sociology entered a period of decline; by the late 1930s there were only three chairs in sociology in the French academic system. It was not until after the war that the discipline became firmly established (for the details on this period, as well as a good description of the structure and functioning of French higher education, see Clark, 1973, esp. Chap. 6 and Besnard, 1983).

Like his Enlightenment predecessors, Durkheim believed that a

---

[7] From a fund designated specially for this purpose. German universities during this period were generally acknowledged as the world's finest and attracted scholars and students from around the world, including many early American sociologists. France was still recovering from the ignominious defeat inflicted by Germany in 1870–1871 and the travel fund was a recognition that much could be learned from the rapid development of the old enemy (see Tiryakian, 1978).

[8] Hereafter referred to as "*DL*," "*Rules*," "*Suicide*," and "*EF*."

[9] On these and related points, see Tiryakian's excellent essay (Tiryakian, 1978).

[10] Hereafter referred to as "*PECM*," "*SS*," "Dualism," and "*ME*."

reconstructed human future was possible only if a bona fide human science could be brought into being, and it seemed to him that not much approaching this existed at the time. He was critical of all those who claimed to have achieved such a science, including Comte and Spencer as well as the Marxists and other socialists. He thought that a science of society must show the conditions under which a stable and harmonious social life was compatible or consistent with an essentially liberal, Enlightenment-rooted conception of the self as both free and responsible. For this task, he thought—in the spirit of both the Enlightenment and the revolution—a science of ethics, or morality, was required. The idea that laws of morality can be discovered by science and that they can serve as guidelines for actors seeking to realize moral ends, is fundamental to Durkheim's sociology (see Durkheim, 1964, Intro. and Appendix). It becomes, Durkheim sternly announces, "man's duty to make a moral code for ourselves" (409). However, he stops short, or so it seems at least, of the Comtean claim that science could or would *constitute* the new morality, even though in its "pure sense" (i.e., science) it may be thought of as "conscience carried to its highest point of clarity."

For Durkheim sociology must be, on the one hand, a science of society conceived in moral terms but without Comte's totalist consensus—accommodated, in other words, to a more pluralist world—and on the other, must avoid reductionist explanation and establish the scientific legitimacy of explaining "social facts," as Durkheim came to call social phenomena in *Rules*, at their own level. As we shall see, both the genius and the main difficulties of Durkheim's sociology stem from this combination of interests.

DURKHEIM'S PHILOSOPHICAL ANTHROPOLOGY

Durkheim's philosophical anthropology is rendered in two related formulations, one in which he states a *social* concept of the individual, and a second wherein he asserts the dual nature of human nature. Both are critical for an understanding of his work. We will consider these in turn.

Although Durkheim criticized others for having allowed themselves to be too strongly influenced by various types of philosophy, he formulated his own conception of the nature of the individual, and of the relation of the individual to society, on the basis of a critique of Kant's ethical theory. He found Kant's conception of morality, in which the principle of obligation or duty is central, basically compatible with his own views. He agreed with Kant that since moral behavior presupposed freedom to choose, it also implied the necessary exercise of reason (Durkheim, 1887b, 139 *et passim*). And especially important for our purposes here, he sided with Kant against the "moral sense" school in rejecting the idea that ethical behavior resulted from an innate "moral sense" (see Chapter 3).

Durkheim departs from Kant, however, in rejecting his conception of the individual as acting essentially in isolation from social anchorages of any sort, and even goes so far in this respect as to place the Königsberg philosopher in the company of Hobbes and the economic liberals. Rather, although agreeing that reason was necessarily implicated in morality, he maintained that the actual source of moral conduct was to be found on the *social* rather than the individual plane of reality. This was so, he thought, because in essence morality has to do with the creation and imposition of *rules* (along with the imposition of sanctions for breaking them) and necessarily transcends the individual (Durkheim, 1887a). The significance of such rules for human conduct, in all their fantastic variability, implies that morality cannot be regarded as individual in nature.

Durkheim also, of course, rejects the utilitarian understanding of the social order in which morality is thought to arise in the form of a "calculus" through exercise of the rational faculty in discerning and evaluating all experience in terms of pain and pleasure. Utilitarianism, in both its Benthamite and Millian forms (Bentham, Mill, 1961) is a late Enlightenment philosophy in which the correct ethical properties of the social order are derived on the basis of characteristics of human nature ("Nature has placed mankind under the governance of two sovereign masters, *pain* and *pleasure*": Bentham, 17), and it bears with it the problems accompanying that formula discussed in Chapter 3. At various points in his work, Durkheim inveighs at length against this view, maintaining, for example, that the expansion of the division of labor has not fostered greater happiness and should not be expected to do so in the future (Durkheim, 1964, Book 2, Chap. 1); or criticizing what he understands to be Spencer's theory of the social order founded on contract (200–206).

Against all such lines of theorizing, which attempt to derive human moral action from individualized conceptions of human nature (whether those of Kant, "moral sense" philosophers, utilitarians, or liberal economists), Durkheim locates the source of morality outside the rational or self-interested exercise of the individual's intellectual faculties.[11]

As long as the remnants of the old individual human nature-centered philosophical anthropology retained a significant status in social theorizing, a fully *sociological* approach to social analysis remained blocked. The systems of Comte and Spencer, and those of Hobbes and Rousseau as well, were in this respect halfway houses on the road to sociology and were criticized by Durkheim on that ground.[12] So Durkheim's explication of morality, not only its functioning but in its origin or source as well, implies an analysis that must be carried out on a social plane sui generis. Durkheim's great intellectual innovation was to establish a way—a method—of doing this.

Of course, many writers during—and before—the Enlightenment had understood something about the power of social influences in inculcating morality; indeed, it was integral to the emphasis on education during the Enlightenment. It was not coincidental that Durkheim manifested a lifelong commitment to reform of the French educational system—among practical activities, this being the one to which he committed by far the most time and energy, and for which he became best known beyond purely sociological circles—and that in his lectures on educational theory he placed great stress

[11] For a collection of Durkheim's writings on morality, see Bellah (1973). For an excellent analysis of Durkheim's approach to morality, see Wallwork (1972).

[12] On Comte: for him, "the most complex forms of civilization are only a development of the psychological life of the individual" (Durkheim, 1958, 99). On Spencer: "It is . . . always in human nature, whether original or acquired, that everything is based" (100).

on that side of Rousseau discussed earlier in this book, namely, the immense power of society to form the moral individual (Durkheim, 1979d). In his article on childhood, which appeared in a French educational dictionary in 1911 (Durkheim, 1979a), he describes a regimen for the education of the child that, without mentioning Rousseau, seems to incorporate some aspects of Jean-Jacques's program for Emile.[13]

The essential point here is that in a way different from Marx, Durkheim took a giant step toward transcending the dilemma arising from the inconsistency of two of the beliefs central to the efforts of the eighteenth century progressive philosophies to create a new human science: the faith in progress, on the one hand, and the received belief in human nature as constant and uniform, and as causal of society, on the other. In discussing the transformations of consciousness that have accompanied the increase of the division of labor in his work of that title, Durkheim argues that it can only be that the latter has caused the former.

> Man depends only upon three sorts of *milieux*: the organism, the external world, society. If one leaves aside the accidental variations due to combinations of heredity—and their role in human progress is certainly not very considerable—the organism is not automatically modified; it is necessary that it be impelled by some external cause. As for the physical world, since the beginning of history it has remained sensibly the same. . . . Consequently, there is only society which has changed enough to be able to explain the parallel changes in individual nature (Durkheim, 1964, 348).

On this basis, Durkheim draws the distinction that would ground his sociology as he worked it out over the course of his career: that between the *conscience collective* (or "collective consciousness")[14] and that of the individual, and the dependence of the latter on the former. In 1885, in a review of the first volume of Albert Schäffle's *Bau und Leben des sozialen Körpers* (his first publication), he put it as follows:

> There exists a social consciousness of which individual consciousnesses are, at least, in part, only an emanation. How many ideas or sentiments are there which we obtain completely on our own? Very few. Each of us speaks a language which he has not himself created: we find it ready-made. Language is, no doubt, like the clothing in which thought is dressed up. It is not, however, everyday clothing, not flattering to everyone's figure, and not the sort that anyone can wear to advantage. It can adapt itself only to certain minds. Every articulated language presupposes and represents a certain

---

[13] Without, however, seeming to grasp the idea, so central to Rousseau, that a *small scale* moral unity very different from the *societal* morality might emerge under certain conditions, and that this could, in the fullest sense, ground the life-orientations of individuals (see also Durkheim's other works on education, particularly *Education and Sociology* [Durkheim, 1956]).

[14] The French *conscience* carries the double meaning of the English "conscience" and "consciousness." In his translation of *DL*, Simpson preferred the former, arguing that for Durkheim the concept did not mainly designate rational phenomena, but "the organ of sentiments and reputations" (Simpson, in Durkheim, 1964, ix). Many later translators, however (e.g., Traugott, Swain, Solnay, Mueller), have rendered this as "consciousness," reflecting a cognizance of Durkheim's apparent expanded usage in his later work, particularly in *EF*. This practice will be followed here (see footnote 10 in Chapter 3).

articulation of thought. By the very fact that a given people speaks in its own way, it thinks in its own way. We take in and learn at the same time. Similarly, where do we get both the rules of reasoning and the methods of applied logic? We have borrowed all these riches from the common capital. Finally, are not our resolutions, the judgments which we make about men about things, ceaselessly determined by public mores and tastes? That is how it happens that each people has its own physiognomy, temperament, and character. That is how it happens that at certain moments a sort of oral epidemic spreads through the society, one which, in an instant warps and perverts everyone's will. All these phenomena would be inexplicable if individual consciousnesses were such independent monads (Traugott, 1978, 102).

The basic idea in the review, the determination of the individual consciousness by the collective consciousness, appears and reappears in his early writings, first in his "German" essays, then in *DL, Rules*, and the essay "Individual and Collective Representations," published in 1898. But elsewhere Durkheim expresses the individual/society relation quite differently, as one involving "spontaneity." He describes the French Revolution, of 1789, for instance, in these terms (1956, 214) and at various places in *DL* writes of the "spontaneity" of the collective consciousness emerging with expansion of the division of labor. In connection with what he calls the "forced" division of labor, he argues that the collective consciousness of modern industrial societies can be consensual only if there is a "spontaneous" fit between the "natural" talents of individuals and external occupational requirements (Durkheim, 1964, Book 3, Chap. 2, esp. pp. 376–377). He credits the classical economists with having demonstrated that constraint could only make the spontaneity of social life deviate from its natural course (386), and discusses the spontaneous creation of occupational groups as the division of labor advances (3–4; 56; also 1897, 378). There are, then, two sides to Durkheim's formulation of the individual-society polarity: Durkheim both derives the concept of the individual from society's moral order and establishes spontaneous action as essential to the continuing existence of that order.

Although Durkheim injects the term "spontaneity" into his work at various points, and although he clearly intends to assign it important theoretical status, he nowhere provides a systematic account of its meaning. One is therefore left with an array of quite diverse usages, as even the few indications in the preceding paragraph suggest: the term encompasses such disparate phenomena as revolutionary crowd behavior and the acquisition of occupational skills and attitudes. What appears to unify these various usages, however, is not really so difficult to see. Durkheim everywhere opposes situations in which spontaneous action appears to those in which it is *constrained* by *external* social factors, the most important among these being societal rules or norms. It might be noted that this understanding was shared by Marx and Mead, and many present writers, as well (see, for a discussion, Lyng, 1990). Spontaneity appears and reappears in Durkheim's works without ever, until in his last important study, *EF*, published in 1915, he brought it into central focus in his analysis of ritual among Australian aboriginal peoples. This, in effect, was Durkheim's way of keeping the principle of agency alive, if undertheorized, throughout the theoretical evolution of his sociology. We shall be taking note of this throughout this and the following chapter.

If this first formulation is a modification and amendation of Kant, the second, the dual nature of human nature, is Cartesian with roots in Augustine. Durkheim expressed this systematically mainly in some of his later publications, most notably *EF* in 1915 and in "Dualism" in 1914, although he pretty clearly had the idea much earlier (He mentions it, for example, in *Suicide*: Durkheim, 1951, 213). In "Dualism" he begins—rather surprisingly, in the light of the foregoing—by announcing that sociology "draws on psychology and could not do without it" (Durkheim, 1973a, 150), and on this basis it must be asserted that human nature is dual, that there are "two poles of our being" (151), one sensory and egoistic, the other conceptual or intellectual, and moral. The first of these is "body-based," the second, "supra-individual." He quotes Pascal to the effect that man is both "angel and beast."

But Durkheim then gives the idea a new twist by linking it up to the distinction between the social and individual consciousness. The individual side is identified with what he calls the "organicopsychological" foundations of life; here is the egoistic, self-preserving, impulse-driven individual of Hobbes. This is distinguished from the *social* side of the individual, comprised of *rational* and *moral* elements that are social in origin and that include everything that makes us truly human. Social human nature is "the highest reality in the intellectual and moral orders that we can know by observation" (Durkheim, 1957a, 16). The consciousness of the individual is caught in the middle: It may be controlled from "below" by the instincts and urges, in which case states of mind have no rational content, or it may be formed from "above," the "heaven" of the collective consciousness, a "superimposition" of "social man" upon "physical man" (1951, 23).

Durkheim is nowhere explicit about the distinction between these two formulations, giving us reason to think that he himself probably was not clear about it. The manner in which he employs aspects of the collective consciousness/individual consciousness distinction in elaborating the *homo duplex* doctrine, as well as the fact that he expanded the latter only later in his career, suggest that he implicitly understood the *homo duplex* conception to be a reiteration, perhaps modified, of the former.

The presence of *two* dualisms in Durkheim's philosophical anthropology is of particular interest because a sheer interest in establishing a social level sui generis as the ground for sociology not only does *not* require the *homo duplex* doctrine, but ought logically have led Durkheim to downplay or exclude as irrelevant *any* original nature doctrine. The reason for the presence of *two* doctrines seems to be that it reflects two distinct components of Durkheim's theoretical interest. In the instance of the first, if the individual consciousness can be understood only in relation to *collectively* held sentiments, it follows that we must formulate a conception of the nature of that collectivity to facilitate its analysis. This addresses the theoretical interest of establishing an object conceptually distinct from the individual as the proper object of sociology. Elaborating the nature of this object—society—was a task Durkheim undertook in the *Rules*.

The *homo duplex* doctrine answers to a different (although related) theoretical interest: to establish the theoretical foundation, and perhaps even *justification*, for the exercise of social control. "Human passions stop only before a moral power they respect," writes Durkheim, in his preface to the second edition of *DL* (1964, 3). An egocentric and fractious original nature is one thing, always potentially capable of overwhelming fragile moral authority. But industrial society, with its inherent continuous expansion of wealth, its loosening of family ties, along with other similar tendencies, creates a condition in which the antisocial impulses are uncontained by the instrumentalities of social control. As dissolution and affluence spread, the "natural" constraints of poverty and isolation, and the moral code of the local community and organizational forms like the old guilds, are no longer capable of exercising constraint over the individual in the manner of the past. And to this may be added the ideological elevation of individual self-interest to a principle of social organization in the form of philosophies like utilitarianism, economic liberalism, and social Darwinism, that actually *celebrate* this state of affairs and so exacerbate its already destructive consequences. As the French put it, "*l'indiviualism odieux*" runs wild.

Defining society primarily in moral terms made it possible for Durkheim to attribute both the social function of repression and the power of commanding respect—a voluntaristic act—to society. Integration and repression are represented as two aspects of the same process, with both normally simultaneously present to some degree. In *Suicide* he maintains that "society is not only something attracting the sentiments and activities of individuals . . . (but) also has a power controlling them" (1951, 241). This assigning of *both* functions—repression and voluntaristic integration—to society defined as a moral order is perhaps the single most critical formulation in Durkheim's sociology, for it ramifies through its every aspect, as we shall see.

In building both the Kantian and Hobbesian variants of individualism into his philosophical anthropology, Durkheim draws on both the progressive and conservative traditions to ground his sociology, progressive particularly in its rendering of progress as the growth of individualism, conservative in its claims for the indispensability of the exercise of social control on the over individual.[15] Sociologically, these distinctions established both causal determination and human agency at the core of Durkheim's philosophical anthropology, and this had ramifications of great import throughout his sociology. We shall see this first in his analysis of the growth of the division of labor.

In his early work on the division of labor, Durkheim needed this conceptual ordering to deal with the problems seemingly attending its advance. The expanding division of labor releases and even encourages

---

[15] There has been a rather long and irregularly pursued controversy over whether Durkheim's work is in some fundamental sense conservative or liberal, and even over the sense in which it may be considered socialist. The former position has been most persistently maintained by Nisbet (Nisbet, 1966, 86; 1974, 26, 27; 1965, 25–28), the second by Giddens, Coser, and others, including most recently Fenton (1984, 32–37). Without at this point going into the various arguments on both sides of the issue, I would merely point out that from the standpoint of looking at Durkheim's work as I have formulated it here, we would expect it to be neither conservative *nor* liberal, but *both*, simultaneously but in different ways.

expression of both organicopsychological constants of human nature and socially molded dispositions. Durkheim set his task in *DL* as the discovery of the new emerging forms of the collective consensus that would, in effect, restore order to the Western world.

THE DIVISION OF LABOR

If the theme of societal dissolution during the nineteenth century was a central one among French intellectuals of Durkheim's time (see the preface to this section), it was part of Durkheim's genius to convert this diffuse ethos into a scientific problem, and in the doing, to create the first modern form of evolutionary and functionalist positivist sociology, or as Martindale has characterized it, positivistic organicism (Martindale, 1960, Part 2).

Comte, we should recall, had already done something like this. He had suggested that a form of solidarity would emerge from increasing occupational specialization and that it would be fully compatible with it, an emerging consensus centering on science and its progressive social functions. Of course, he had also argued that the division of labor was a source of social fragmentation and conflict, and in his time, political chaos. And in the *Système*, despite the idealizing of altruism, love, and moral consensus, he ended up by formulating what was, at least by implication, a highly statist solution to this dilemma. For Durkheim, this was unacceptable in principle, as his treatment of the state (to be discussed in Chapter 12) clearly shows. Durkheim also, of course, rejected the liberalism of Spencer, Mill, and the Manchesterites. His views were perhaps closest to the idea of the German "Kathedersozialisten" (Schmoller, Knies, Schäffle, and others to be discussed in Chapter 13), who advocated an expanded role for the state both as a principal economic actor and provider of the variety of functions now grouped under the rubic "welfare state." Durkheim was favorably inclined toward this type of theory partly because of its underlying organicism (see the quote from the review of Schaffle's book on pp. 244–45), even though he nowhere had much to say about the administrative organization of the state apparatus or the practical and political problems associated with bureaucracy. (Lukes, 1973a, 89; see also Therborn, 1976, 244–247.)

It was in *DL* then, that Durkheim first formulated the dissolution of moral consensus as a scientific problem, one that would provide a sociological diagnosis of the time and a guide to the future. Stated generally, the problem of *DL* is an investigation of the relation between the advance of the division of labor and the individualism it creates, on the one hand, and the nature and possibility of a collective morality that somehow must relate to that individualism, on the other.

> Why does the individual, while becoming more autonomous, depend more upon society? How can he be at once more individual and more solidary? Certainly, these two movements, contradictory as they appear, develop in parallel fashion. This is the problem we are raising. It appeared to us that what resolves this apparent antinomy is a transformation of social solidarity due to the steadily growing development of the division of labor. That is how we have been led to make this the object of our study (1964, 37–38).

The belief that the increase in the division of labor, described with varying emphases—the growth of industry, the expansion of trade, the development of technology—would bring with it a more harmonious world was a basic supposition of eighteenth and nineteenth century social thought. The late nineteenth century intellectual malaise of liberalism was in large measure constituted of a growing skepticism precisely about this, particularly among truly creative avant-garde thinkers like Nietzsche and Weber, and even Durkheim. Durkheim was an admirer of Rousseau, and one side of his approach to the division of labor was distinctly Rousseauean. Early in *DL* he asserts that the services rendered by the division of labor are "very near to being foreign to the moral life" (50). In a second preface to an edition nine years later, this view, if anything, was strengthened. Industrial activity is characterized as essentially anarchic, creating "an unruly state," bringing "the most profound disasters," and being a "source of general demoralization" (4). Industrial activities obviously have good reason for existing, he says; it is just that the needs they respond to are not moral ones, the civilization created by the division of labor being "morally indifferent." He defends this judgment in several ways, pointing out, for instance, that wherever the division of labor is most advanced, as in industrial cities, crimes and suicides are most common. Indeed, he opines that the "moral conscience of nations" is "correct" in preferring "a little justice to all the industrial perfection in the world" (51).

He goes on to contrast the division of labor with the domains of art and science. The realm of art cannot be one of morality since art, by definition, is "the domain of liberty," and all morality involves obligation, its antithesis. Science, on the other hand, is increasingly coming to be viewed as a duty, more or less obliging each individual "to develop this intelligence by learning the scientific truths that have become established." Science, in fact, is "conscience carried to its highest point of clarity" and the "enlightened conscience prepares itself in advance for adaptation" (52). In contrast, it is no one's *moral duty* to engage in labor of any *particular* sort; yet the necessary condition of engagement is abandoning that ideal of individual freedom necessary to the pursuit of artistic activity.

The fact that Durkheim judges the civilization created by the division of labor to be "morally indifferent" would seem to justify placing him at least as close to Marx as to evolutionists like Spencer, utilitarians like Bentham, or economic liberals like Ricardo or J. S. Mill. Indeed, passages like these have encouraged an interpretation of Durkheim that tilts him toward the socialists.[16] An example of this is to be found in the work of Alvin Gouldner, who in his introduction to *Socialism and Saint-Simon* assimilates Durkheim to Saint-Simon rather than to the more conservative Comte (Gouldner, "Introduction," in Durkheim, 1959), despite Durkheim's various rejections of socialism, (which he understood in a rather narrow economic sense).[17]

---

[16] While a professor at the Sorbonne he came to be thought of as a socialist (see Chap. 12, *fn* 6).

[17] For instance, in *PECM*, he writes: Let us suppose that by a miracle the whole system of property is entirely transformed overnight and that on the collectivist formula the means of production are taken out of the hands of the individual and made over absolutely to collective ownership. All the problems around us that we are debating today will still persist in their entirety. (Durkheim, *PECM*, 30) It may be noted in passing that Weber put the issue in virtually identical terms (see Chapter 12, pp. 286–88).

It is with this stark negation that *DL* begins. The division of labor is not a moral phenomenon, yet all societies *must* in their very essence be moral entities. Since the division of labor is not moral in origin, but at the same time is a permement feature of developing societies, it must itself in some sense be the generator of a societal morality.

Durkheim nowhere clearly defines or delimits precisely what he means by the division of labor. He fails even to distinguish between its social and detail forms which correspond to craft and industrial production. This was a startling omission, and one which greatly vitiated his argument resurrecting the medieval guild as the model for the type of organization that would best serve the function of maintaining social integration in the industrial societies of the future, as we shall see. However, it is evident that his usage is an expanded one encompassing *social* as well as economic differences. Indeed, this is precisely why it becomes problematic. A purely economic conception of the division of labor, at least in so far as it is framed by liberal political economy, is unproblematic, because by definition and in fact (as the evidence obviously shows) it expands the wealth of nations, *theoretically*, at least materially enhancing the lives of their people. Marx turned this formula inside out by claiming to have proved that the *real* logic of the division of labor (in its capitalist form, which is to say its *only* form at the time) perversely and paradoxically, not only failed to enhance the material condition of the producers, i.e., the laborers whose labor he held to be the sole source of value, but actually necessarily created a worsening of their condition. This left Marx's followers with the theoretical problem of the shape of the division of labor in postcapitalist socialist societies (see Chapter 10).

Durkheim's tack is different. It is only by broadening the definition of the division of labor to include its *social* forms of differentiation as well as its economic manifestations that he is able to make the argument that it produces an integrating moral code as well as enhancing the material conditions of life (an essential point on which he is in agreement with the liberal political economists). It is precisely the social aspects of the division of labor appearing in Durkheim's time as "abnormal," or pathological, that become the focus of his analysis in Part 3 of *DL*. This, it ought to be noted, is also a service for sociology as a discipline: At least implicitly, a merely economic perspective necessarily becomes inadequate as the basis of understanding modern society, in fact, any society. Sociology is born precisely of the separation of economic from social life, and therefore, of course, of the need to understand the nature of this separation along with its diverse implications for present and future.

Indeed, it can be argued that Durkheim's primary focus on the social aspects of the division of labor was purchased at the expense of downplaying its arguably more fundamental economic side. There is, for example, no mention of money and its immense role in modern economic life, despite his familiarity, obviously, not only with Marx but with Simmel's *Philosophie des geldes*, for example, which he reviewed in *L'année* (on this point see Luhmann, 1982, 15–16).

Before continuing on to a discussion of the thematic content of *DL*, we should note, and emphasize, that Durkheim's preoccupation with morality did not imply anything like a universally applicable moral code. In fact, his perspective on morality was grounded on a high appreciation of cultural diversity, an appreciation without which his sociological conception of the relation between the division of labor and moral codes probably would not have been possible. He was very early clear on this point; we find him in 1887 emphasizing the *differences* rather than the similarities between moral systems (1887a). And in *DL* he states bluntly, "What was moral for one people was immoral for another" (423). Like his Enlightenment predecessors, he took diversity to be the problem, and the search for *general laws* to be the route to discovery of the uniformities underlying it. And his rejection of rationalist and "moral" sense theories of morality (culminating in the tendencies described in Chapter 3) suggested that the variability of moral systems must somehow be rooted in differing types of *social organization*, and that a morality appropriate to one type of society would be inappropriate for another type. The existence of such variations then invites, even requires, the scientific study of moral codes in terms of their relation to the *different* forms of social organization, and further, although this does not follow logically, that they could be analyzed in terms of a *natural science* model, or as he says, "in relation to certain experimental conditions . . ." (423). This makes *DL* a work in comparative evolutionary sociology.[18] It appeared at a watershed in intellectual history, reflecting the evolutionism of the century on the one hand, and the just-emerging, more empirical-grounded emphasis on the other. Its immediate precursors were works like Henry Maine's *Ancient Law* and Tönnies's *Gemeinschaft und Gesellschaft* (reviewed by Durkheim in *L'année*).

There are two analytical themes in *DL*. The first deals with the causes of the division of labor. The proximate cause of the increase of the division of labor lies in what Durkheim calls "dynamic density," or "moral density," by which he means an increase in the scale or amount of interaction among the members of a society. This, in turn, is caused by the increasing concentration of population, particularly in the cities, and the expansion of the means of transportation and communication (259–260). But underlying the whole process is a "struggle for existence," albeit a significantly softened one. Population concentrations and improved communications and transport place occupational groups, in particular, in more intense competition with one another, thus inevitably leading to ever greater specialization. However, for Durkheim a struggle for existence implies *not* the survival of the fittest, but rather, a *coexistence* of differentiated units that results from the very nature of the division of labor itself. Sheer interdependence means that the competing units *must* survive, their very existence being necessary for the maintenance of the whole. This argument relates the very nature of the most fundamental changes in society, as Durkheim puts it, to "mechanical" factors, which seem to constitute a nonsocial substrate operating outside the sphere of the exercise of human mind and will. There is something of Spencer in this. Like Spencer, Durkheim advances an organic conception of society,

---

[18] But a qualified evolutionism. He was explicitly critical of both the Comtean and Spencerian variants, even though his own version was based on the same principles as Spencer's was (see Durkheim, 1958, 81ff.).

including comparisons to the nervous systems of living organisms (e.g., p. 121) and along with this a functional explanation of the expansion of the division of labor as adaptive. (However, the Spencerian *centrality* of conflict in evolution is deemphasized by Durkheim).

This analysis sets the stage for Durkheim to formulate the second, closely related, and for him more important problem of *DL*, to reveal the basis of societal integration in modern industrial societies, and to do so by demonstrating that the very conditions causing the fragmenting and conflictful tendencies of such societies were at once those of their integration and stability. Durkheim's analysis of this is prefigured in a short but significant discussion of the sexual division of labor, where he rather laboriously attempts to establish this as a *model* on which study of the societal division of labor might be based. It is precisely the *differences* between the sexes, he says, that constitute the foundation for the moral character of the conjugal relation. The purely sexual function that causes unions of males and females then "gives birth" to relations that are cooperative, but that go beyond sheer exchange (60ff.) Society, then, will be thought of as an analogue of the family.

Recall now Durkheim's discussion of individual and collective forms of consciousness, described earlier. This distinction Durkheim now relates to the theoretically substantive one between the two types of social solidarity, "mechanical" and "organic." The former, he argues, is characteristic of preindustrial societies generally. It is based on the *similarity* of the consciousnesses of the members of such societies and constitutes a direct link to their *collective* consciousness. Indeed, the consciousness of individuals in this instance is no more than a direct reflection of the collective consciousness. Mechanical solidarity achieves its "maximum" at that point where the *collective conscience* "completely envelops our whole conscience and coincides in all points with it." At this point, "individuality is nil" (Durkheim, 1964, 130). Mechanical solidarity is seen in its purest form in "segmental" societies, or those organized around clanship. In such societies each structural unit is a virtual duplication of all the others. Such societies are to be distinguished from those comprised of different kinds of structural units, particularly modern industrial ones with an advanced division of labor. In segmental societies the individual is completely encapsulated within the highly stereotyped social life of the clan, and apart from age and sex differences, everyone's individual consciousness is to be thought of as virtually identical ("individuality is nil"), because each is an "appendage" of the collective consciousness.

The introduction of this morphological or structural category intervening between the processes of population growth, dynamic density, and competition, on the one hand, and the moral facts of society, on the other, is of central theoretical significance for Durkheim, for it establishes a *social*, or better, *social structural* category (although in *DL* its status, i.e., being social or nonsocial, is somewhat ambiguous: see Therborn, 1976, 256) as the proximate causal domain of moral (i.e., "social") facts. This is important because it provides Durkheim with a theoretical elaboration facilitating the actual making of sociological explanations of social phenomena without reductions to any other nonsocial domains. This structuralism appears and reappears in different forms throughout Durkheim's work, initially in *DL*, where it is employed to explain differences in the nature of the collective consciousness in different societies, and thereby to provide a basis for comparative sociology.

It is thus on the basis of a society's morphology that a causal account of the collective consciousness may be given.

> We believe it to be a fruitful idea that social life should be explained, not in terms of the conception which its participants hold of it, but by reference to underlying causes which escape consciousness; and we also think that these causes have to be sought principally in the way in which associated individuals are grouped. (Durkheim, quoted in Giddens, 1972, 159)

This makes Durkheim, like Marx, a realist. It also establishes the essential ground on which Durkheim elaborated his methodology, with which we will deal in the last half of this chapter.

Durkheim sees the relation of dependence of the individual consciousness on societal consciousness as a kind of authority. Indeed, it is significant that, like Comte, he often speaks of moral authority, as distinct from political or state authority. This "authority" was rooted in the religions that in Durkheim's view, as in Weber's, were the source of morality up to the period of Western industrialism. Preindustrial societies were everywhere religious entities; what was and what remains central to them is their religious nature. "Religion pervades everything," says Durkheim; and moral systems are "nested in the bosom of the religion of the society . . ." (Pickering, 1979, 116). The unity of all previous societies rests on a sharing of such religion-rooted moral codes.

The sociological problem for Durkheim now becomes the form in which morality, with its evident religious foundation, can be maintained in increasingly differentiated societies. What *sort* of a moral system, we may ask, emerges in industrial society, with its proliferation of exchange relations and extensive division of labor accompanied by secularization and the waning of the significance of religion? At one extreme stand the Spencerians, utilitarians, economic liberals, *and* socialists, all in Durkheim's view asserting the impossible thesis that a stable social life can rest on economic, or, more generally, contractual relationships pure and simple; at the other extreme lies Comte's vision of a totalistic value consensus centering on science cum religion established as a benevolent bureaucracy of secular priest-enforcers. Durkheim wants to slide between these extremes. Industrial society, he maintains, brings into being a *cooperative* moral code, and it is here that the conjugal model of the division of labor has its relevance. The dissimilarities present in industrial society, Durkheim says, create "a system of rights and duties which link (people) together in a durable way" (Durkheim, 1964, 406), involving a recognition of both the rights of others, that is, of individuals and the rights of the collectivity. These might include, as part of the rights of individuals the availability of jobs or occupational opportunities fitted to the capabilities and talents of individuals; as part of the latter, the obligation of military service (last example mine: DLW). Such a moral code, Durkheim says, creates a form of social solidarity proper to industrial society, i.e., "organic solidarity." As the spreading division of labor weakens the hold of the old collective consciousness and makes increasing space for the play of

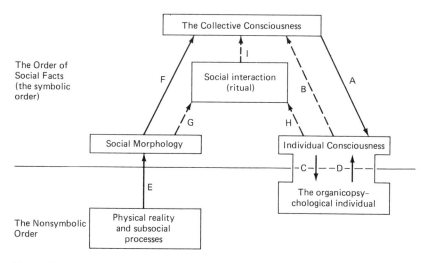

Figure 11-1 Durkheim's conceptual framework.

that of the individual, it also builds a new moral code rooted in differences rather than similarities.

But while differences may engender interdependence, economic differences as such are inherently unstable, as Durkheim repeatedly emphasizes, and therefore would seem to be more apt to breed breakdown and conflict than integration. Durkheim's response to this is given in a crucial passage in *DL*.

> As societies become more vast and, particularly, more condensed, a psychic life of a new sort appears. Individual diversities, at first lost and confused amidst the mass of social likenesses, become conspicuous, and multiply. A multitude of things which used to remain outside consciences because they did not affect the collective being become objects of representations. Whereas individuals used to act only by involving one another, except in cases where their conduct was determined by physical needs, each of them becomes a source of spontaneous activity. Particular personalities become constituted, take conscience of themselves. Moreover, this growth of psychic life in the individual does not obliterate the psychic life of society, but only transforms it. It becomes freer, more extensive, and as it has, after all, no other bases than individual consciences, these extend, become complex, and thus become flexible (Durkheim, 1964, 347–348).

Note the two themes in this passage. "As societies become more vast, and particularly more condensed, a psychic life of a new sort appears." But also, the "growth of psychic life in the individual . . . (transforms) . . . the psychic life of society." (This relationship is depicted in Figure 11-1 (p. 254) by lines A and B, line A indicating the primacy of the social determination of the individual, and dotted line B the less emphasized obverse relation). Here again is the first of Durkheim's dualisms, the moral ascendency of society on the one side, the spontaneity of the expanding self on the other (with primacy assigned to the first), used to describe the master trend of evolution.

We must now ask just what Durkheim means by the psychic life of society and of the individual.

Durkheim analyzes the collective consciousness into three components or dimensions, which may vary in: (1) their *volume*, meaning the degree to which moral rules and beliefs are held in common; (2) their *intensity*, meaning the extent of the emotional hold of the collectivity over the individual; and (3) the extent to which its components are *clearly defined*, or to which they constitute "uniform moulds" for ideas, allowing all consciousnesses to "vibrate in unison" (Durkheim, 1964, 152).[19]

Durkheim thought he could define the critical difference between the types of solidarities in terms of the decrease in volume, intensity, and clarity of collective representations, and its reciprocal in the consciousness of the individual, the enlargement of the sphere of psychic life. The existence of a massive range of sentiments, movements, and programs of all kinds, political, occupational, religious, educational, etc., has as its necessary consequence a condition in which individuals share only small bits of the sentiments, rules, and beliefs of the collective consciousness, while coming at once to share the common morality of those who are members of particular associations, particularly occupational associations: "where restituitive law is highly developed, there is an occupational morality for each profession" (227). In his later writings Durkheim elaborated on this point in a manner highly significant for his general sociology, as we shall see. Furthermore, the emotional commitments of individuals to the rules, and to the cognitive collective representations, may be greatly effaced. Many members of the traditional churches are minimally religious, remain as members for external or instrumental reasons, and may even be unbelievers. Even nationalistic sentiments—and nationalism is often understood as a kind of secular religion—are as often as not skin-deep, even though governments spend millions propagandizing their subjects or citizens to the end of bolstering them. Finally, the very meaning of collective representations may exhibit massive variation. For example, military service is held to be patriotic; yet others claim that conscientious objection is a higher service to the nation. In this and other ways, the "collective consciousness" becomes an arena of conflict from which selected aspects and interpretations are drawn to be used as weapons in ideological struggle.

The "psychic life of the individual" under the condition of organic

---

[19] To these Giddens adds the "content" of the collective consciousness, meaning the extent to which it is comprised of religious as over against nonreligious beliefs and sentiments, maintaining that, viewed from the standpoint of the movement from mechanical to organic solidarity, it is the devolution of its religious character that is of the greater importance, since changes in the other dimensions, by and large, all follow from this (Giddens, 1971, 5–6).

It should also be noted here that the precise nature of the consensus associated with the collective morality is left quite poorly theorized by Durkheim. Distinct from the three dimensions of the collective consciousness distinguished by Durkheim, there is the *prior* matter of their *content*. In this regard, Hawthorne points out that it is difficult (impossible might be more accurate: DLW) to determine whether Durkheim had in mind agreement on how moral arguments are to be conducted, agreement on the premises of moral arguments, or agreement on the substantive ends of action (Hawthorne, 1976, 120).

solidarity is not theorized very well, or very systematically by Durkheim, but we may interpret him as suggesting that this broad category encompasses at least three dimensions: (1) the relative freedom of choice and action of the individual; (2) the expansion of the individual conscience; and (3) the growth of the intellectual or deliberative powers of the individual, which is to say, the rational capacity, best reflected in the growth of science. Consider these in turn.

In terms of freedom of choice, the life possibilities of, say, the son of a shoemaker during the early Middle Ages in Europe were circumscribed by the religious rules and rituals of the Catholic church, the guild rules regulating entry to the occupation, and, quite likely, the rules of the commune or town imposing various kinds of sumptuary practices and communal obligations. Such a person would have relatively little freedom of choice in any of these matters, because of the very nature of the society; his life would be essentially bounded by membership in and the rules of these institutions. The idea that he might lead a different kind of life would probably never occur to him, except under extraordinary conditions. His "psychic life" would thus be severely restricted. In contrast, the differentiated economic life of the twentieth century in its nature presents opportunities of a greatly expanded nature, possibilities of occupational futures that are open (within certain limits, of course) to the choice-making of individuals.

This example can be used to illustrate the second aspect of our interpretation of Durkheim's "psychic life of the individual." Our medieval worker not only is faced with little in the way of choices to be made, but is therefore, in the nature of the case, unlikely to feel any sense of obligation to engage in making them. The twentieth century worker, on the other hand, not only finds it possible to make such choices, but is morally obliged, to some degree at least, to do so, and to do so in certain ways that best express his interests, and that conform to expectations arising out of his circumstances, i.e., class situation, available resources, personal identity (as intelligent, achievement-oriented, and so on), or whatever. The significance of individualism, for Durkheim, is not merely that it results from the condition of greater openness and thus de facto freedom of choice in societies with more highly developed divisions of labor, but that each individual becomes morally obliged to exploit this openness.

This example can in turn be extended to illuminate the third aspect of the psychic life of the individual. The growth of science as a major societal transformation is an objective fact. But this means that *individuals* acquire scientific knowledge and that this acquisition becomes to some degree constituent of their practical activities. Durkheim, already around the turn of the century, thought that the acquisition of scientific knowledge and keeping abreast of scientific developments, was becoming for the individual an obligation, a duty. Knowledge expands the intellectual horizons of individuals. Even apart from the intrinsic satisfactions it may bring, it becomes a critical component in the mastery of nature and the management of social situations, and an instrumentally important factor in the exploitation of the life chances of the individual.

Despite the difficulties mentioned earlier, in these descriptions we can glean some idea of what Durkheim had in mind in asserting that "as societies become more vast . . . a psychic life of a new sort appears." But how is it that, simultaneously, the individual somehow transforms the psychic life of society?

Of this side of the equation Durkheim has less to say. In general, what he has in mind is the growing possibility of spontaneous action that generates new collective representations. Individuals become "a source of spontaneous activity," "particular personalities become constituted, take conscience of themselves," writes Durkheim, and their actions bring about a "freer, more extensive" psychic life of society. But his particular descriptions of and references to such events (e.g., the French Revolution of 1889, the Crusades) are of *collective* actions in which individuals may, in fact, it ought to be noted, be acting in concert under the most intense social control. Durkheim frequently describes such processes with the metaphor "currents." Here individuals can indeed become receptive to ideas of all sorts, can make choices as to their value, combine voluntarily with others in movements of one sort or another, and possibly in this fashion effect changes in the societal collective consciousness. The problem with Durkheim's account at this early point in the development of his ideas is that he provides no *technical elaboration* of the ways in which individuals might effect social change—nothing, for instance, of Weber's theory of charismatic domination (however flawed that idea might be). This is a weakness of Durkheim's sociology attributable to the inflexible individual-society polarity that framed his sociology, and with which he struggled throughout his work.

In all this Durkheim can be understood in *DL* to be applying his first dualism historically. Societies exhibiting mechanical solidarity are defined in terms of the *total* "authority" of the moral order. Societies held together in organic solidarity are, again by definition, those in which the "spontaneous" action of the individual (or perhaps individuals organized in groups; glossing this distinction reflects a conceptual difficulty) becomes increasingly widespread and thus decisive in their continuing functioning. In this Durkheim seems to invite us to understand societal evolution as exhibiting a shifting *balance* between the two factors.

If this is correct, however, it conceals a problem. For if commercialism, industrialism, urbanism, and the rest of the modernist syndrome amounts to a devolution of authority and a growth of a spontaneous individualism that occurs within the framework of the moral order, where *is* the problem? Where is the crisis? In reality, the first dualism contains nothing in terms of which an answer to this question might be advanced. Individuals "internalize" the content of the moral order and act "spontaneously" to reproduce it. But the turn of the century crisis of the European industrial societies could not, as Durkheim well knew, be described in this naive evolutionist fashion. Despite his assertion midway through *DL*, in summing up the long section on the progress of organic solidarity, that society does not in the course of this progress "become a jumble of juxtaposed atoms, between which it can establish only external, transient contacts," but rather, that "the members are united by ties which extend deeper and far beyond the short moments during which . . . exchange is made," and that "each of the functions that they exercise is, in a fixed way, dependent on the others and with them forms a solidary system" (227), Durkheim concluded *DL* by reformulating his *sociological problem* in terms of three *pathological* forms of the division of labor which we shall discuss following the completion of our discussion of his general theory of the nature of societal solidarity.

Philosophizing about the moral codes of society without specifying empirical procedures for identifying their various states would have left Durkheim subject to his own criticisms of moral philosophy. It was necessary for him to provide criteria whereby such a diffuse phenomenon as social solidarity, which, he says, "does not lend itself to exact observation nor indeed to measurement" (64), could be made accessible to empirical procedures satisfying the rigorous canons of science. Accordingly, he proposes *law* as an appropriate indicator of the states of the collective conscience, arguing that social life always assumes *particular* forms, and that law always accompanies their coming with being and therefore stands in a direct relation to them. Simply put, custom is the basis of laws (65).

Durkheim then goes on to classify law into two basic types: repressive, or penal law, which inflicts some damage or loss on the individual, and restitutive law, which requires "the return of things as they were" (69). The law of preindustrial societies, Durkheim argues, is almost entirely repressive; as organic solidarity replaces the mechanical types, it is manifest in a growth of restitutive functions reflecting the necessity for a regulation of exchange relations between increasingly autonomous units. Durkheim specifically lists a number of types of differentiated restituitive law: the law of property, which is negative and therefore does not have an interacting function, but also domestic, contract, procedural, administrative, and constitutional forms of law, all of which are "positive" and so play an integrating role (119–122).

So along with his theory of the transformation of the collective consciousness goes a theory of a parallel transformation of law.[20] Although in this analysis law has the formal status of an indicator, i.e., methodological status, its usefulness obviously depends on its empirical or substantive validity, and to this there have been a number of objections. The very idea that simply by virtue of being codified law is necessarily something precise (and thereby scientifically serviceable), rather than a set of rules that continuously require interpretations and applications and that exhibit enormous variation, is something that Durkheim never entertains. The close relation between law and custom has also been disputed. In particular, Durkheim's formulation seems to rule out the possibility of conflict between them, a critical omission (Hunt, 1978, 70). About the *direction* of legal evolution he himself was evidently of two minds, contending in *DL* that repressiveness declined in the face of the expanding civil law, but later that the opposite was true (Durkheim, 1964). And the notion that "primitive" law was predominantly repressive, at least where the state is not present or is weakly developed, is evidently incorrect (see Hunt, 1978, 71). Growing repressiveness of law seems to be associated with class formation and conflict and the state-forms they bring into being, an observation more congenial to Marxist or Weberian views.

Although as abstract theorizing Durkheim's theory of the collective

---

[20] Durkheim's theory of law and crime before long became elaborated as the general functional theory of deviance, a topic that lies beyond the scope of this work (but see Merton, 1957a, Chap. 5).

conscience was a major advance in establishing a clearly defined focus for sociology, as a description of the actual state of affairs in France or other industrialized countries around the turn of the century it was somewhat less than convincing, even to Durkheim. Significantly, he concluded *DL* with three assays describing the actual state of affairs in industrial societies. These essays deal with (1) the weakness or absence of moral regulation in economic life (the "anomic" division of labor), (2) "overregulation" (the "forced" division of labor), and (3) inefficient coordination of functions because of ineffective management (Durkheim, 1964, Book 3).

The anomic division of labor results from the increasing scale and complexity of industrial organization as modern societies undergo the transition from mechanical to organic solidarity. In the small-scale forms of industrial organization of the past, especially the guild, production was adapted to consumption needs on a local basis. The productive enterprises were family or quasi-kinship-based workplaces in which the relations among workers were, to use Tönnies's term, essentially *gemeinschaftlich*, or communal. The workshop itself, and the associations of workers, along with the political authority of the towns, constituted a structure of moral authority that effectively regulated the entire process of production and guaranteed, more or less, that it was adapted to the needs of the local residents.

The emergence of modern industrial organization has transformed this world in such a fashion that production is carried forward sheerly in terms of the interests of the producers and is unregulated by any greater power, creating massive dislocations in virtually every sector of the production-consumption nexus. Like Marx, Durkheim identified the phenomenon of overproduction as central to the economic crisis in nineteenth century capitalism. Parallel to this, the destruction of the traditional workshop has meant the appearance of an increasing opposition between owners and workers, and therefore class conflicts of increasing intensity. Again, the reason for this is the destruction of the old forms of moral regulation, and the failure—as yet—of the emerging social organization of the societies of the future to create any new ones.

Durkheim specifically mentions economic crises, particularly sudden failures or successes that undermine one's moral world, along with major changes of role relations in marriage and family as major forms of anomie. And very interestingly, the bulk of his discussion focuses on anomie in the sphere of science, in which Durkheim takes a position very similar to Comte's (see Chap. 7). Elsewhere, he asserts that this development is accompanied by an *ideological* individualism that demands that satisfaction of the claims of individuals become the first principle of society itself. To somehow meet this unprecedented claim then becomes the indispensible condition of reinstituting order. But the very recognition of the legitimacy of the claim carries with it the danger that the demands themselves may become insatiable. Thus, although the fundamental roots of anomie lie in the organicopsychological, it is the fact that the absence of moral controls creates a "second-order," culturally induced individualism, that in its nature is self-sustaining.

The "forced" division of labor designates a phenomenon closely related to and interpenetrating the anomic division of labor. With the expansion of the division of labor and the creation of a welter of new occupations, the problem of the proper placement of individuals within this order becomes increasingly critical. Individual talents and abilities are greatly variable, and they must be fitted into the appropriate occupations.[21] However, this process is seriously hampered by the existence of accumulated resources and forms of social control, such as laws favorable to the interests of some but unfavorable to those of others. Here evil is caused by the rules themselves. Rigid forms of inequality, classes and castes are overly strict forms of regulation of the division of labor (374). In consequence, the proper, or "natural" relation between individual talents and interests cannot be instantiated. Durkheim repeatedly describes the normal form of this relationship as one in which "spontaneous" individual action finds its proper niche in the differentiated social structure. Although not particularly explicit about it, Durkheim may have understood this relation somewhat dialectically: On the one hand the evolving and differentiating social structure is, in fact, the *consequence* or creation of spontaneous action; on the other, given Durkheim's basic stipulation regarding the causal primacy of the collective consciousness, the social order itself facilitates the emergence of new differentiated forms of individual consciousness, and so new kinds of human experience. In this regard, there is the clear implication that an industrial society must be a meritocratic one in which channels of social mobility are open. The abolition of the inheritance laws, feudal survivals in Durkheim's view, would go a long way toward the elimination of the forced division of labor.

The third abnormality occurs when interrelated functions are not well adjusted, resulting in "very imperfect integration" due to the absence or ineffectiveness of management (389). Since social solidarity depends on functions being well integrated, ineffective or nonscientific management, as Durkheim preferred to think of it, may weaken it. Most importantly, the close relations among functions must *flow continuously*. The maldistribution of tasks, where too much is loaded onto one part of the system and too little on another, results in sporadic and interrupted work, and this discourages the sense of mutual dependence at the core of moral unity. In the past, work has been characteristically intermittent and unregulated, constantly interrupted by holidays, days of rest, the weather, its seasonal nature, and so on, but now it becomes more permanent, habitual, and inwardly motivated (Durkheim, 1893, 394). The condition of continuous involvement in work increases social solidarity not only by creating interdependency, but by increasing the activity and involvement of each worker. Evolutionary movement is in this direction. Durkheim's sense of social integration here seems to have some affinity with Weber's ideal of the spirit of capitalism, that lifelong devotion to work that in his (Weber's) view had its roots in Calvinist ethics.

The anomic and forced forms of the division of labor seem to have been constituted on the basis of Durkheim's two dualisms: the anomic form in terms of the doctrine, wherein the absence of moral rules allows the

---

[21] An idea evidently deriving, in its modern form, at least, from the zoologist Henri Milne-Edwards, who held that the extent of the development of the division of labor provided the criterion for the perfection of each species (see Merz, 1965, 4, 559, n.1).

organicopsychological side of the individual, manifest in *individual* forms of consciousness, an uncontrolled freedom of expression; the forced form in terms of the relations between the individual and collective forms of consciousness.

The great bulk of sociological interest in Durkheim's notions of pathological social states has fallen on his theory of anomie, probably because he continued to use the idea in *Suicide*, the work most commonly regarded by Durkheim's more positivistically oriented devotees as his greatest, but also perhaps because it locates the pathological form of society in the moral order. But on a broader, and certainly a Marxist view, and indeed, Durkheim's own scheme of analysis in *DL*, the forced form of the division of labor ought to be regarded at least as significant, because it addresses the problems of hierarchy and domination in both capitalist and precapitalist societies. The forced division of labor refers to the frustration of "spontaneous" society-creating and society-maintaining actions by various forms of socially structured hierarchy and domination. This condition demands the *removal* of such forms, in Durkheim's own terms, because the moral rules necessary to maintain social solidarity, and therefore social integration, can be realized only spontaneously, which is to say through the authentic and free expression of *individuals*.

The two abnormal forms seem to have been constituted on the basis of Durkheim's two dualisms: the anomic form in terms of the dualism of human nature, the forced form in terms of the relations between the individual and collective forms of consciousness. This is one of the crucial points at which Durkheim's philosophical anthropology exerts a clear and significant influence on his sociology. Both forms, he claims, are transitional, pathological states of industrial society, which is to say that they are not to be identified as necessary accompaniments of capitalism. In *DL*, however, both formulations are inadequately theorized and carry with them unclarified difficulties. In the instance of the anomic division of labor, this has to do mainly with the problems attending Durkheim's seeming inability or unwillingness even to speculate that the anomic condition itself might actually become the moral order of an ever-evolving capitalism, not pathological at all but appearing as successive forms of the capitalist—and perhaps socialist, as well—moral order, forms that have been documented for the several generations of evolution since Durkheim's time.[22] The case of the forced division of labor presents the difficulty of an undertheorization of the relation between the spontaneous action of the individual and the socializing process of society's moral order.

---

[22] This issue cannot be pursued here, except to note that ever since Tocqueville documented the inner contradictions of American political and social individualism, capitalist development in the United States has been accompanied by changing interpretations of the forms of its accompanying moral individualism. Representative of what has become something of a literary genre are James Bryce, whose *The American Commonwealth* dissected American political individualism just before the turn of the century; various of Walter Lippman's writings of a generation later; the shift to "other-directedness" and the organization-centered life analyzed by David Riesman and his colleagues and by William H. Whyte; and most recently, *Habits of the Heart*, by Robert Bellah and his colleagues, in which an emerging "therapeutic" individualism is described.

Whatever the merits and difficulties of *DL*, one of its most important aspects lay in the fact that in it Durkheim established the agenda that would frame virtually all of his subsequent work. This agenda may be stated as follows:

1. To render in a more formalized way an outline of what sociology ought to be as a generalizing science, in terms of criteria that would establish it on a footing parallel with that of the natural sciences. This task he would undertake in his *Rules of Sociological Method*, published in 1895.
2. To deal with the unresolved question of the appropriate form of social organization for an industrial society. There are three aspects to Durkheim's treatment of this, which broadly speaking constitute his political sociology: (1) the theory of individualism, (2) his discussions of occupation groups, and (3) his analysis of the state.
3. To demonstrate that his general conception of sociology was productive of specific research problems and that these could be *workably* formulated in terms of the theory of the collective (and individual) consciousness. His principle work in achieving this was *Suicide*, published in 1897.
4. The *general* theoretical task of exploring and locating the social process of the generation of the collective representations that comprise any particular collective consciousness. This would be the central task of *EF*, published in 1915.

In the remainder of this chapter and in the one following, we will take these up in turn.

THE RULES

Durkheim in the *Rules* has two closely intertwined objectives. The first and broader one is to establish the general outlines of sociology as a science parallel to the natural *sciences*, and to do this by demonstrating that the social plane could, in fact *had to be* unequivocally conceptualized sui generis, as independent of that of the individual. This frames a second objective integral to achieving the first: the unfinished substantive business of *DL*, theorizing the problems of regulation and inequality, and to do so by working out a coherent theory of just how organic solidarity is coming to function in industrial societies. Durkheim had labeled these abnormal in *DL* but even though he had there asserted that one of the three principal objects of that work was, as a theoretical necessity, a theorization of the distinction (1964, 45) and had done so in a preliminary way, proposing that it could be made on the same basis as in biology, i.e., by seeking the "average" type for any society at any given stage of its development, he had provided no well-argued rationale for this claim. It was now necessary to advance theoretical grounds to support this distinction, for without it the analysis in *DL*, and the claims that the industrial societies of the future—unlike those of the present—would be relatively harmonious ones by virtue of their integration through the medium of a spontaneously generated collective consciousness, could be dismissed out of hand (see Parsons, 1949, 4). As Durkheim himself says, the question of whether or not science has the ability to establish this distinction is, in effect, the most fundamental one of the social sciences, for the answer to it will determine the role they will play in any scheme of social reconstruction (Durkheim, 1958, 47). This is to say that it grounds his conception of sociology as a science of ethics (see this chapter, pp. 4–5).

Durkheim's Construction of the Social Level

Durkheim thinks what ought to be the fundamental subject matter of sociology are what he calls "social facts" (*faits sociaux*). These he defines along three dimensions: (1) their "generality" throughout a society, (2) their "exteriority" to the individual consciousness, and (3) the "constraint" exercised over the individual by virtue of this exteriority. These criteria, it is clear, are adopted by Durkheim because to his mind, they serve to distinguish specifically *social* phenomena from those that represent manifestations of *universal* aspects of human nature (Durkheim, 1958, 13), or as he sometimes put it, a phenomenon sui generis (lvi).[23]

The "externality" of social facts is self-evident to Durkheim: Every aspect of culture, language, custom, and knowledge is already objectively present and has to be assimilated by everyone, children in particular. The "unremitting pressure" exerted on the child exhibits "in a nutshell" the macrocosm of the larger historical process of the creation and maintenance of social order. Whether or not this exteriority is experienced *as* an exterior force is of little or no significance, since even fully internalized sentiments or feelings *originated* externally (1).

Durkheim goes on to further buttress this putative externality, and thus *objectivity*, of social facts by arguing that they are also "endowed with coercive power" (2), which is to say, are constraining. One *must* acquire the language in use to function at all. One can do nothing other than use the currency of the land. And there are the deeper foundations of life in society that require a continuous and repetitive process of socialization. Children, in particular, obviously can acquire their cognitive, emotional, and behavioral patterns only through continuous external pressure (6).

The criteria of externality and constraint are advanced by Durkheim in the face of our intuitive sense of by no means always, or even very commonly, experiencing social facts as external and constraining. Against this dictum of common sense Durkheim proposes a test. Note what occurs upon any attempt to resist or alter such profoundly internalized ways of acting: a reaction in the form of some sort of punishment, prevention of the act itself, or a restoration of the damage (2). In time, indeed, constraint may well cease to be felt *as* constraint as it engenders "habits" and "internal tendencies," that "render constraint unnecessary," although Durkheim is quick to add that this does not mean that it is abolished, for it remains the origin of these habits. This condition is in fact for Durkheim the "normal" state; the constraint imposed from without by violence or economic superiority is "pathological" (123).

---

[23] Nine years later in a preface to the second edition of *Rules* Durkheim used the term "institutions" to designate the totality of "all the beliefs and all the modes of conduct instituted by the collectivity" (lvi), in so far as they satisfy these criteria. Sociology then becomes the science of social institutions.

Durkheim goes on to further defend the protocol of constraint (and by implication, exteriority) as indispensable in formulating a social plane of analysis sui generis, by linking it logically with the third criterion, that of *generality*, meaning the extent to which a social fact is distributed generally throughout society. Generality and constraint are not independent modes of social fact: The generality of a social fact can be brought about only through imposition (10).[24]

In *Rules* Durkheim did not theorize the differences between the exterior and constraining qualities of the normative and non-normative orders, saying merely that the constraint inherent in such phenomena as businessmen employing methods from past centuries and suffering the consequences, for example, is "indirect." And he still insists on referring to such facts as matters of application of "rules," thereby seemingly conflating the two modes of control (3). Elsewhere, however, he does expand on this difference and its significance. He distinguishes the "mechanical" consequences of violating "rules" wherein the consequences of their "violation" are intrinsically connected to the violations themselves, as in the breaking of the "rules" of hygiene that "command" one to avoid sources of infection. Such "rules" are held distinct from those in which the connection between the obligations imposed on individuals to enact or avoid enacting certain acts, and the consequences of their violation, is "synthetic," i.e., constructed independently of the substance of the acts themselves (from *Sociologie et philosophie*, in Giddens, 1972, 96–97). This, however, is inadequate. On the one hand, Durkheim's insistence on the generic or class term "rules" for both types implies that both fall within the legitimate purview of sociology, yet, on the other, his strictures about sociology being a "science of ethics," and his persistent emphasis on morality or moral action as the *defining* aspect of the object of the discipline, confound this understanding.[25]

---

[24] The logical connection between generality and constraint has the further advantage of making constraint easier to identify empirically in the various milieux where this problem arises (in economic organizations, for instance, to cite one of Durkheim's own examples).

[25] In this connection it is of some interest that in the *Rules* Durkheim eschews almost entirely any direct discussion of sanctions, even though only two years earlier in *DL* the concept had assumed major proportions in connection with the problem of *identifying rules* (most obviously in his lengthy discussion of crime), and in fact, had been put forward as a central justification for sociology as a science of moral facts (Durkheim, 1964, 428). (But see the mention of sanctions on p. 41 of *Rules*.) More broadly, Parsons in his *The Structure of Social Action* made the changing character of Durkheim's category of constraint his central focus. Arguing that Durkheim progressively shifted the meaning of constraint from external environmental and genetic factors, to the application of sanctions, in *Rules*, to the introjection of norms into the constitution of the subjective perspective of the individual toward the close of *Suicide*, thence to a complete subjectivism and thus *voluntarism*, in his definition of religion as the *attitude* of respect in *EF* (Parsons, 1949, Chaps. 8–9).

Without doubt Parsons put his critical finger on the central problem of Durkheim's sociology, the theorization of the relation between the individual (whether as a social actor or psychological entity) and the nature of society sui generis. This polarity informs all the various problems theorized by Durkheim. It is open to question, however, first, whether Durkheim arrived at a "voluntarism" (which Parsons leaves undefined) only in his later works, and in *EF* in particular, and second, whether the "voluntarism" of that work is correctly located in Durkheim's definition of the sacred as the attitude of respect, as Parsons has it (see *EF*, pp. 413ff.). Regarding the first of these, we have already discussed the

If social facts are properly conceived of as external and constraining, it follows for Durkheim that they may be treated as "things" (*choses*), a principle he carried over into *Suicide*, there designating "tendencies" and "passions" as things (1951, 307). This much-debated and criticized protocol was formulated by Durkheim as an alternative to approaching social phenomena as if they were *ideas*, the fundamental error, according to Durkheim, of so many social philosophers in the past. It was by this expedient that Durkheim intended to assimilate conceptually the order of social facts to the domain of nature. Moral rules, he says, should be thought of as having a status directly comparable to those held by "things" in the natural sciences, and our *ideas* of moral rules (i.e., the ideas comprising sociology) regarded as being parallel to the *ideas* comprising the natural sciences. In both instances, Durkheim says, the latter are "derived" from the former (23). More than this, rules are like physical objects not only in being virtually intractable to efforts of the human will to modify them (28), but in their determination of the will "from without" (29); they are "like moulds in which our actions are inevitably shaped" (29). This deterministic formulation is Durkheim's way of establishing sociology as a naturalistic discipline on *ontological*, as distinct from epistemological, grounds (as in Hume's argument), by asserting that social objects really do have objective qualities *that are the same as those of the objects of the natural world*, not just that they designate phenomena that must be observed from without (on this point see Aron, 1970, 2, 71–73).

So much for social facts as things. Let us go on now to Durkheim's discussion of the concrete procedures appropriate for apprehending a subject matter defined in this fashion. There are three of these, and they constitute the basic framework of Durkheim's positivism. The first—for Durkheim the foundation of the others—is that the social scientist must, "eradicate all preconceptions," an exercise that will hopefully enable him to "emancipate himself from the fallacious ideas that dominate the mind of the layman," or at least make him aware of "their trifling value" (32). Second, the objects of sociological interest must be classified in terms of their "external characteristics" (which Durkheim confusingly also refers to as their "inherent properties") rather than in terms of "ideas" (35), the point being the necessity of freeing oneself from the errors inherent in "lay or practical knowledge" (44), even though, "in practice one always starts with the lay concept" (37n). And third, there is the requirement to at all times consider social facts from an

---

importance of spontaneous action in *DL*, and even in *Rules*, where despite the unquestionable emphasis on the external locus of constraint, Durkheim keeps the voluntarism alive, if sometimes only in footnotes, and often in the form of caveats qualifying his strongly deterministic pronouncements about "social facts" (see pp. 64–65 of this chapter; also *Rules* (lvi–lvii, n.7; 112, n.21; 111–112). Regarding the voluntarism of *EF* and Parson's location of it in Durkheim's definition of the religious attitude, it can be argued that Durkheim actually comes to situate it in the *social* process of *ritual* that is so central to *EF*. Parsons recognized the importance of ritual specifically to Durkheim's sociology of religion and analyzed it both from this empirical standpoint and from a broader epistemological perspective, but *not* from the standpoint of its *general* theoretical significance, as I suggest here and will argue later, of providing a nonindividualist category for the theorization of spontaneity and, seemingly therefore, of "voluntarism." Durkheim's theory of ritual can be understood as an alternative to, or as an *escape* from, the limitations and problems of scientific explanation attending the individual/society polarity. More of this in Chapter 12.

aspect "independent of their individual manifestations" (45), in both causal and functional types of analysis. This means that explanations of facts must be sought among other facts at the same level.

Durkheim's injunction to "eradicate all preconceptions" is obviously Baconian (indeed, Bacon's discussion of the *idola* is his model for the entire treatment [34]). We might call it the "tabula rasa" rule. Recall that his arguments defending the externality of social facts include the observations that much behavior is rule-bound, or in accord with morality or law, and so its source cannot be the individual, and that such rules are usually present prior to the existence of the individuals who end up following them, necessitating extensive socialization. One line of argumentation that could be drawn out from such observations is that the (putative) resulting standardization and orderliness of a society implies knowledge of the rules and moral principles on the part of the conforming individuals. Indeed, it would in one sense be an absurdity to suggest otherwise, if only because norms and values have to be learned. One implication of the axiom that social actors act on the basis of knowledge of this sort, however, might be that the tasks confronting the social scientist would have to include as a fundamental scientific operation some procedure for grasping or understanding the orientation of individuals to the rules and moral principles in all their specificity. This is the position taken by the interactionist and phenomenological schools, and, among others, by Max Weber and some types of later Weberian sociology, as well. In all sociologies of this sort, there is a clear desideratum regarding the condition essential for concept formation: It requires some grasp of the meaning of the actions of the subjects studied as the basis for the formation of the concepts. Indeed, this issue is the central one in the problematics of these sociologies, and we will be discussing some of them in chapters to follow.

Although Durkheim acknowledged that individuals sometimes do (must?) indeed have knowledge of the rules they conform to, the thrust of his discussion leads away from this issue and in the direction of seriously indicting the rationality of conforming to rules. For various reasons, he claims, social facts to which we conform are often not understood well or even known at all. The sentiments of individuals are a "refraction" of the forms of the collective consciousness and so—very surprisingly, one must think—irrelevant to sociological analysis. These "empirical categories of the layman" are, in fact, "ideologized," *notiones vulgares* or *praenotiones*, nothing more than Bacon's *idola*, "illusions that distort the real aspects of things," (17), that have become "tyrannical", and that must be "thrown off once and for all" (32). Only then can the facts of society be submitted to "cold, dry, analysis" (33).

Durkheim's characterization of the manifestation of social facts in the consciousness of individuals as ideological and illusory is clearly intended as a further argument establishing the domain of the collective consciousness on an *epistemological* footing parallel with those of the natural sciences (as he understands the latter). The sociologist must assume a mental set identical to that he attributes to natural scientists (xlv). And what is this state of mind? It is "to assume a certain mental attitude towards (the facts) on the principle that when approaching their study we are absolutely ignorant of their nature" (xliii).[26] This is true epistemological Protestantism. But is it possible to have *any* sensory experience apart from some given structure of perception? Today the stipulation that all observation is theory-laden, or theory-impregnated is broadly if not universally recognized, and even in Durkheim there are passages that could perhaps be interpreted as anticipating it. But these are not the central thrust of his account.

Another objection takes its point of departure from a critical Marxist standpoint. The whole program, it is argued, with its claims to methodological neutrality and objectivity, renders sociology devoid of any ground for assuming a critical stance, thereby affirming, at least implicitly, existing social arrangements. This itself constitutes an abandonment of neutrality, revealing the contradiction at the core of the doctrine, which then stands unmasked, leaving the entire enterprise undermined. This line of argument, however, can be countered by arguing that it creates difficulties as great as those it exposes, particularly the problem of where the scientific standards employed will come from in the first place. The critical theorist demands a standard that transcends any particular society; on what epistemological grounds, one may legitimately ask, can such a standard be defended (see Benton, 1977, 45)?

Durkheim discusses his second rule at much greater length than the others. Here he is concerned with definitions of objects of sociological study, especially *initial* definitions, and says that particularly in this early stage only their "externals" can be apprehended; "essences of reality" are to be avoided even though they may be "attained subsequently" (Durkheim, 1958, 42). In this exercise like things must be classified with like, and the criterion of this is whether or not they meet some test of having a common *external* quality. In order to determine whether some precept does or does not belong to the moral order, for example, it must be ascertained "whether or not it presents the external mark of morality, . . . a widespread sanction," . . . "a condemnation by public opinion that punishes all violations of the precept" (41). The crucial point follows as an implication of the first rule, namely, that the social scientist must "escape the realm of lay ideas." Scientific concepts must "adequately express things as they are, and not as everyday life finds it useful to conceive of them" (43). Even though Durkheim rather grudgingly grants that there is some kind of ultimate foundation of *all* knowledge ("the point of departure of science cannot be different from that of lay, or practical, knowledge"), social science must nevertheless "dismiss all lay terms . . . and return to sense perception" (44). This might be called the rule of the *objective* status of social facts.

Durkheim's second rule amounts, then, to a naive inductionism. To "dismiss all lay notions" in order to "return to sense perception" is to assert that an external reality of social facts can be apprehended apart from a grasp of their meaning, that is to say, *outside* their status in the life-worlds

---

[26] A principle he reiterated throughout his career. *EF* begins with the injunction that, in defining religion, "it is necessary to begin by freeing the mind of every preconceived idea" (1957, 23). Even in *EF*, it is interesting to note, Durkheim tends to avoid direct analysis of the emotional effervescence at the core of ritual, concentrating more on the cognitive "forms" emergent from or maintained by them.

of social actors. It is difficult to understand this as a "return to sense perception"; it sounds more like a radical *nonempirical* prejudgment of the nature of the object of study.

Durkheim's third rule is grounded in his formulation of the collective and individual forms of consciousness, in which society imposes and determines the actions of the individual. The more distinct from their individual manifestations social fact are, the more amenable to "objective" representation they become. This is so because objectivity requires that everything "variable and hence subjective" be eliminated (44). For Durkheim, it then follows that the "crystallized" forms of social life—laws, moral principles, "proverbs," and so on (45)—exhibit that substantial or solid objectivity that Durkheim seeks for sociology to qualify as a science. Thus the third rule: the sociologist must endeavor to consider (social facts) from an aspect that is independent of their individual manifestations (45). This rule is the core of Durkheim's attempt to transcend reductionist accounts of social facts. It might be termed the rule of the nonreductionist reality of social facts. We will encounter it again in the discussion of causality.

Durkheim has now defined the nature of social facts and laid down his rules for studying them. But the undifferentiated category of social facts demands an explication. Unfortunately, Durkheim nowhere undertook this task in any very systematic way. Therefore we shall have to interpret him.

What emerges in *Rules* regarding the order of social facts seems to be a classification into three categories: (1) morphological facts; (2) "crystallized" forms of the collective consciousness; and (3) "social currents," "currents of opinion," or "uncrystallized" forms of the collective consciousness. (For a slightly different interpretation, see Thompson, 1985, 16). There is also the further assertion that the facts of category (1) are the causes of those of (2) and (3), along with a very sketchily stated intimation of social "currents" being prior to and perhaps causal of the "crystallized" forms. Durkheim is—characteristically—anything but unambiguous about the content of these categories, or the relations between them, but we shall try to follow the main line of his thought.

Durkheim's characterization of the morphological facts of society derives essentially from *DL*, and although at one point in *Rules* he does give what he evidently regards as a representative listing—political structure, types of habitation, methods of communication, regular currents of commerce and migration, and law (12–13). These are later brought under the generalization "forms of association" (112), or alternatively, "the internal constitution of the group" or "human milieu" (113). The two abstract aspects of this human milieu so far discovered to have some influence on social life are those discovered by Durkheim himself in *DL*: the size and dynamic density of a society (113). This clarifies the status of the ambiguously a fixed morphological facts by unequivocally situating them in the category of social facts. This, we must presume, is an operation calculated to satisfy his rule (to be discussed shortly) that the explanation of social facts must be sought at their own level.

The distinction between crystallized and uncrystallized forms of the collective consciousness was already present in *DL*, then reasserted in *Rules*. Durkheim distinguishes between established, or "organized" beliefs and practices, such as "legal and moral regulation, religious faiths, financial systems, and so on, on the one hand, and the "social currents," to which he assigns a variety of more or less noninstitutionalized phenomena. The former constitute the main contents of the collective consciousness at any particular time and so are among—if not totally constituitive of—the central objects of interest of sociology. The latter include the "great movements" of enthusiasm, indignation, and pity in a crowd" (4), that is to say, collective behavior, along with the many minor currents that never achieve any significant degree of crystallization. There are also other beliefs and practices running more deeply within the interstices of the established institutions, but often lying somewhere below the threshold of social visibility. The great societally *general*, *external*, and *constraining* crystallized forms seemingly have their origins in the currents, or better, perhaps, in a variety of *complexes* of currents that may in rather rare instances achieve a general culmination (i.e., become general within a society, or become a general social fact), such as the French Revolution of 1789 and the years following. There is, however, no *fundamental* distinction to be made between uncrystallized "free currents" and crystallized social facts, the difference being merely those of "the degree of consolidation they present" (12).

Thus, we may interpret Durkheim in *Rules* to be theorizing two quite different lines of causation. One, the dominant one, runs from the what in *DL* is called morphological "substratum," which in *Rules* becomes the "facts of association," to the crystallized forms of the collective consciousness and probably uncrystallized ones as well. Durkheim gives his own analysis in *DL* as an example: Here the moral facts of society assume and change their nature as the advance of the division of labor erodes the segmental societies. This is the main, or "official" line of Durkheim's thought. Such explanations are structural, and Durkheim himself in a few places uses this term. The second, subordinate or secondary causal relation is found in Durkheim's few terse passages contrasting crystallized with uncrystallized social facts. Here, the former emerge from the latter. Interpreting this relation as causal rests on shakier ground than the first, even though in a few places Durkheim employs seemingly causal language of a sort, particularly in referring to the "genetic" development of social facts. (The problem with this is that, as we shall see, Durkheim elsewhere disassociates himself from historical accounts of causality as inappropriate for sociology, embracing instead John Stuart Mill's method of concomitant variation).

Now structural explanation, at least in its extreme form, moves toward the pole of excluding human agency, human purpose, and meaning, as having a necessary or significant place in scientific explanation. And although the main line of argument in *Rules* is clearly structuralist, Durkheim was never comfortable with the thought of unequivocally excluding purposive or subjective action from the legitimate purview of sociology. He says, for example, that he does *not* mean to say that sentimental factors have *no* impact on evaluation and even asserts that these can "hasten or retard its development" (92), even though, he qualifies, only on the condition that they themselves be subjected to causal analysis (93).

Durkheim never disregarded the principle of the importance of human agency in social life, and expressed this often, as discussed earlier, through the category of spontaneity. His unfortunately unembellished and scattered remarks regarding of the relation between the uncrystallized and crystallized social facts can be thought of as an early, if crude formulation of this. This idea would be developed further in *Suicide* and finally, in *EF*, achieve its highest theoretical systematization in the theory of ritual.

Having established the general categories of social life, Durkheim turned to what was for him the critical problem of defending the distinction between the normal and the pathological, critical because of the need to label the anomic and forced forms of the division of labor as instances of the latter, and therefore transitory.

The Normal, the Pathological, and Societal Evolution

Durkheim begins by reviewing various ways of formulating the concept of normality and rejecting them all as "aprioristic" (54). By applying the second of the rules discussed earlier, he says, we immediately come upon the critical "external" factor distinguishing the normal from the pathological, the generality of the social facts in question. Those most generally distributed are normal, those not so distributed, pathological (55). Such generally distributed social facts can be represented statistically, Durkheim seems to think, and this is the "standard of health" on the basis of which the "morbidity" of a phenomenon is to be determined (58).

Second, it is self-evident to Durkheim that normality can be defined only relative to a given species. This he claims to derive from the sheer variability of species in the organic world (56). Further, it will vary within the life of a species, if the species changes in relation to a given phase of its development. One sees the necessity of this rule, given Durkheim's prior stipulation regarding the relativity *and inherent validity* of moral codes. In taking this position, Durkheim again commits himself to and invokes an evolutionary conception of social change, despite his sometimes critical view of the evolutionism of earlier thinkers. If normality must be defined in terms of the variability appearing in the distribution of the representatives of a given species, and if the species itself exhibits variation, an evolutionary theory becomes indispensible for identifying pathologies. We must therefore ask how Durkheim formulated his theory of evolution.

He begins by asking how it is that the most common types of organization could have persisted in the aggregate had they not facilitated the resistance of destructive elements. Is it not evident that the reason for the rarity of other characteristics is "that the average organism possessing them has greater difficulty in surviving?" (58). Generality provdes adaptive superiority.[27] Indeed, it appears that Durkheim needed the evolutionary principle in order to classify societies into species, this being necessary, in his view, for determining their normality or abnormality.

---

[27] Some of the difficulties of evolutionary theories were discussed in Chapter 8 on Spencer. For the most part, those apply to Durkheim's half-hearted and abbreviated version of Spencer's scheme. In addition, there is the difficulty, raised by Parsons, of why any society conceived of in the evolutionary terms of the time, at least, should *not* fail to adapt, and give way to a higher form? (Parsons, 1949, 323).

Durkheim's discussion of his actual classificatory scheme is surprisingly brief, although a lengthier treatment was given in *DL*. By what principle, he asks, can societies be classified into different species? Clearly we wish to identify the "most essential properties," but by which principle? (79). After a short discussion of the possibilities that seem open to us, Durkheim quickly settles, as we would perhaps have expected him to do, on the *morphological* differences that societies exhibit, and specifically "on the nature and a number of the component elements and their mode of combination" (81), which is to say, with Spencer, their relative complexity (81–82).

Durkheim introduces what was—and remained—a cardinal presupposition of his sociology, namely, that since the basic principle of *social organization* (not morality) is the same for any society, we have only to study the *simplest* of societies in order to grasp at least the essentials of more complex ones. Since the parts of any society are necessarily simpler than the society in toto, we can formulate our sociological taxonomy by studying the manner in which simple societies combine to create more complex ones. This principle, of course, is a codification of his procedure in *DL*, and Durkheim never abandoned it. In his last major work, *EF*, he defended restricting his empirical focus to Australian peoples,[28] in part, on the grounds that Australian totemism was "the most primitive and simple religion which it is possible to find" (1912, 95).

Defending his procedure by citing Spencer (1958, 81), Durkheim then goes on to classify societies, beginning with the simplest society, the horde, which exhibits no evidence of earlier segmentation (83). Following this, Durkheim lists "simple polysegmental societies," essentially hordes that have developed internal clan structures (some Iroquois and Australian tribes; also the Kabyle); "polysegmental societies simply compounded," which are unions of the former (for example, the Iroquois federation); and "polysegmental societies double compounded" (city-states, Germanic tribes). This Spencerian classification is an incomplete and inadequately described one, Durkheim says, and there presumably are additional "higher" forms, including industrial societies, which Durkheim would obviously have to distinguish from city-states. In this context, however, he mentions only one additional type, the "empire" (Rome being the only example given), a species formed as a unification of societies from all levels of the societal geneological tree.

The extreme brevity of Durkheim's theorizing of the various "species" of society, squeezed into only five pages of *Rules* (81–86), perhaps reflects on the one hand his generally critical view of evolutionary theories (see, in particular, Chapter 5 of *Rules*), yet on the other, his evident need for a theory in the framework of which he could make a case for distinguishing

[28] This was a restriction he did not adhere to very rigorously, but which still left him open to criticisms from students of religion that he might otherwise have avoided. For instance, he equated the early tribal religions of the North American aborigines with those in Australia, suggesting that they were totemistic as well (see Lowie, Chap. 8). It ought to be noted, however, that in bringing in evidence from other culture areas Durkheim was following his own rules, in this instance comparing (in his eyes) societies of the same social type. What the critiques of Durkheim on this point ultimately come down to is that either there are forms of religion as "primitive" as totemism in some "primitive" societies, or that his principal of classification is unusable.

normal from pathological social facts. In fact, at one point he even tries, rather feebly, to exempt his theorizing of social species from evolutionism by arguing that it somehow is a middle ground between the evolutionary theories of progress advanced by philosophers, including Comte, and the historicism of most historians (76–77). But once having formulated the problem of distinguishing the normal from the pathological in the manner described above, and having taken relative complexity from Spencer as his basic classificatory principal, he remains, even if somewhat reluctantly, an evolutionist.

We have in this section done no more than shown that Durkheim's distinction between normal and pathological social facts is grounded in an adumbration of Spencer's evolutionary theory. But this does not, of course constitute an *explanation* of either type, and certainly not by Durkheim's own rules. So it is to the problem of explanation that we now turn. In the course of this exposition we will return to the normal-pathological distinction, and reveal its problematic nature from the standpoint of Durkheim's own explanatory logic.

Cause and Function in Sociological Explanation

Durkheim's conception of sociological explanation is somewhat complicated, mainly because he insists that there must be not just one, but two types, causal and functional. Why this is so very important for his sociology can be illuminated by his philosophical anthropology. This is the central point of this section, and we shall pursue it after clarifying just what Durkheim means by causality and function in sociological explanation.

Durkheim begins, as he usually does upon initiating a topic, by eliminating possible alternatives.[29] In this instance, he rejects any sociological explanatory scheme that gets its leverage in purposive rationality. If social facts were really the result of the pursuit of ends by individuals, a fantastic diversity of human action would be displayed. This is clearly not the case; in reality, social action reveals great regularity, commonly in the smallest detail (93–94). Furthermore, reflecting his first rule, Durkheim argues that such a procedure would have too much subjectivity to be scientific (95).

Although Durkheim rejects purposive rationality as a legitimate explanatory strategy, he is not prepared to exclude the *principle* of utility from sociology. Indeed, it is obvious that some social facts, at least, must be useful, since it is "generally necessary that (the social fact) be useful in order that it may maintain itself" (97). We may therefore speak of the *function* a social fact fulfills independently of the subjective ends or intentions of individuals. Functional analysis, although usually a necessary part of any sociological analysis, is logically posterior to causal analysis because it is "natural," but also because the discovery of the cause of a social fact may assist in the functional analysis. For example, drawing once again on *DL*, the *cause* of punishment is to be found in the intensity of the collective sentiments

---

[29] Which Lukes has called the method of elimination, likening it to a "cat and mouse game" (Lukes, 1973a, 38ff.).

offended by the crime, but it also has the *function* of maintaining those sentiments (96).

Durkheim goes on in familiar vein, excoriating individualistic explanations, as these are to be found, for instance, in Comte and Spencer. Much of this is reiteration of points already made regarding the external and coercive nature of social facts, the absence of any historical evidence that individuals ever deliberately planned their societies, of individual natures being only "indeterminate material" to be molded and transformed by society (106), and so on. In so far as psychological dispositions or biological phenomena have an effect on society, it must be presumed to be a general, or essentially constant one. At the end of this quite powerful exposition (97–110), Durkheim concludes, again employing the method of elimination, with a corollary of his third rule: Since social facts cannot be explained causally by the actions of individuals, "the determining cause of a social fact should be sought among the social facts preceding it and not among the states of the individual consciousnesses" (110).[30] And this applies to functional explanation as well (110–111).

After discussing the nature of morphological facts, which I dealt with earlier, Durkheim proceeds next to eliminate another possible category of causality: history. If we reject the internal milieu as the fount of causality, Durkheim argues (having already disposed of the individual level), the only remaining possible causal agency must be external. Durkheim associates external causality with historical causality, as if the working of history was for some reason excluded from the internal milieu. And indeed, this is just what he has in mind. On the one hand, "it is impossible to conceive how the stage that a civilization has reached at a given moment could be the determining cause of the subsequent stage" (117). On the other, rejection of the internal milieu as causal would imply that "there are no concomitant conditions on which social phenomena can depend" (117). In other words, as Durkheim very shortly argues, it is the "method" of concomitant variation (as described by J. S. Mill) that provides the proper causal model for sociology, and this, he seems to think, in some sense applies outside of history.

On what ground does Durkheim defend these assertions? One line he takes is to beg the question by identifying historical causality with evolution. By this artifice he permits himself the easy indulgence of inveighing against vital forces or other historical agents that have supposedly pressed civilization forward and that will continue to do so in the future. Of course Durkheim is correct in rejecting such formulations and broadly correct in identifying Comte and Spencer as exemplars (118–119), although, as we saw in Chapter 8, there is much more to Spencer's theory of evolution than this. But it is

---

[30] Yet even here Durkheim feels compelled to follow this long structuralist argument with the usual disclaimers: that he should not be understood to be saying that psychological facts are not indispensible to the sociologist, that individual life is "closely related" to collective life; and that even though "the latter cannot explain the forms, it can at least facilitate its explanation" (111), even though (elsewhere) "psychological phenomena can have only social consequences when they are so intimately united to social phenomena that the action of the psychological and of the social phenomena is necessarily fused" (172, n21) [The term *only* is, I think, misplaced, properly belonging between *consequences* and *when*: DLW].

Durkheim's reason for this rejection that is of the greatest interest and importance. He does not merely dismiss such constructions as unscientific because they are metaphysical or unconfirmable or too limited to explain the diversity of societies. All this he asserts. But in addition, he argues along two related lines that relate to the core of his sociology.

In the first line of argument, Durkheim asserts that history (qua evolution) is such a seamless developmental web that we are unable to make the sharp distinctions between societies or evolutionary stages required by the stipulation of the independence of cause and effect. Any society becomes merely the extension of its predecessor, a moment in a continuous evolutionary flow. It is not clear why this must be so. Surely there can be no good reason why historical causality necessarily precludes the conceptual operations of distinguishing types of societies occurring in temporal sequence. In fact, Durkheim's elaboration of his comparative sociology tends to undermine his own critique.

Durkheim's second reason for rejecting evolutionary causality as impossible is that it necessarily fails to fulfill just that purpose deemed essential by the philosophers of the Enlightenment, to allow us prevision of the future (118). Rather confusingly, Durkheim argues that

> All that can in any species be "experimentally" determined are *changes*, but not evidence of causality; there is only a "chronological" link between successive changes (118).

Because of this Durkheim holds that any possibility of "prevision" is abrogated. This confused reasoning is intended by Durkheim to deny the scientific claims of evolution as the agency of the realization of Enlightenment ideals. Although it is a valid critique of the evolutionary theories of the time, it certainly does not invalidate all historical conceptions of causality.

Durkheim's larger objective in these arguments rejecting any form of historical causality is, by means of the method of elimination, to clear the ground for the establishment of his own notion of what constitutes a truly scientific method for sociology, which he believes must be some form of the experimental method. He approaches this through a review of J. S. Mill's methods, and rejects those of residues, agreement, and difference, on the ground that they all suppose that the "causes compared agree or differ by a single point" (129). Durkheim selects the method of concomitant variation, which he identifies with (the statistical procedure of) "correlation," for the rather cloudy reason that this method displays the causal relationship "intrinsically" and not merely by "coincidence" (130) and reveals causes as "mutually reinforcing each other in a continuous manner" (130).

There are further reasons for employing concomitant variation as sociology's sole method. For one, unlike the methods of agreement and difference, which require extensive accumulation of data, concomitant variation can proceed with a relative parsimony of empirical material: "A few facts suffice." This permits the sociologist to limit "more intelligently the extent of his comparisons" and fosters a more "critical spirit" in their execution (134). Especially, most of the work of historians can now be more or less dispensed with, while at the same time their productions relevant to sociological analysis need no longer be welcomed "passively and naively" (134).

Although it employs only a single method, sociology should not be considered inferior to other disciplines. In fact, the method of concomitant variation is ideally fitted for application in the form of comparative analysis, given the welter of variations of social facts displayed over the great range of human societies. These variations result partly from the fecundity of evolution itself, which is constantly bringing into being new forms of social life, but also and perhaps even more importantly, from the variations on central themes produced by the diversity of human milieux, "new series of variations, outside those which historic evolution produces" (135).

The comparative analysis facilitated by the method of concomitant variation must be subject to theoretical discipline if it is to transcend the crude empiricism of just comparing any scattered cases that exhibit what may often be illusory external characteristics.[31] Comparisons must be made on the basis of theoretically systematized materials. Since sociology cannot perform actual experiments, the logic of the experiment must be applied to social facts as they are. But such bare bones are only a beginning.

Durkheim goes on to argue that, because social facts come into being gradually, becoming more complex in the process, it is necessary to analyze them "genetically," and to do so by "following (their) complete development through all social species." Because of this, comparative sociology is not just a branch of the discipline, but is identical with it. Further, because societies evolve from youth through stages of growth and development, the comparisons are properly made only of societies at the same stage of development (139–140). Durkheim specifically mentions "the curve which expresses the trend of suicide during a sufficiently long time" (136), and the "evolution of the patriarchal family through the history of Rome, Athens, and Sparta" (137), as examples of genetically conceived social facts. Such processes must be identified in their earliest manifestations and the mounting complexities described up to the point of their highest development. It would be insufficient, for example, to analyze the patriarchal family by merely tracing its development through the present modern European societies.

It appears that Durkheim has two kinds of comparison in mind, both anchored in evolution. The first is comparison of social processes across various societies at similar stages of development. Obviously, this presupposes the stipulation of the nature of the evolutionary sequence either for a given process or for the environing society, or, most likely, both, somewhat on the order of some types of modern comparative cross-sectional analysis. Second, developmental processes are to be correlated with other concurrent social processes, as, for instance, in Durkheim's own example mentioned earlier, of the correlation of suicide and educational level.

Thus, it is clear that Durkheim's strictures against reading causation into history do not to his mind imply that the evolutionary framework should

---

[31] Human societies, Durkheim believes, have the rather perverse power to assume "false" identities and in so doing throw sociologists off the correct investigatory track. The best examples of this are the survivals from earlier evolutionary stages, such as, presumably, the forced division of labor or inheritance laws.

be dismissed from scientific sociology. Indeed, he finds it essential to frame the comparative method, and thus sociology itself. And given all this, it is hard to see just what it is about "historical" explanations that Durkheim believes he is excluding. What is clear is that very much like Comte he rejects historical causation because it seems to him unscientific, different in kind from those formulated in the abstract, rigorous terms of logic. And above all, Durheim needs a method that appears indisputably scientific, both to separate sociology from history and to legitimize its very existence as a discipline capable of producing causal explanations.

Durkheim's framing of an evolutionary comparative sociology in these terms would seem, on the face of it, to be complete. Yet, although at one point he says that "sociological explanation consists exclusively in establishing relations of causality" (125), he nevertheless goes on to maintain that the pursuit of causal explanations on a social plane is not in itself a fully adequate methodological agenda for sociology. Despte his critical view of the employment of functional explanations by others (94–95), and his critique of evolutionary teleology, he holds that beyond the pursuit of causes there is still a need for *functional* explanations, which treat the question of "correspondence between the fact and the general needs of the organism" (95), or the *usefulness* of social facts for "established" society. Functional explanations, of course, stood at the core of the evolutionary schemes of Spencer and other evolutionists, and so it is perhaps not surprising that since Durkheim accepts the fundamentals of Spencer's evolutionism, he should also embrace functional explanation and even regard it as indispensible, even though this seems inconsistent with his own critique of evolutionary teleology, for the logic of these is one and the same (see Nagel, 1953). It is precisely the functionality of social forms, and therefore the need for functional explanations, that drive teleological evolutionary schemes. Durkheim evidently thought that rejecting *individual-grounded* theories, in which social facts are understood as consequences of individuals striving for particular *ends*, in the form of a variety of utilitarian needs, or for "happiness," left the door open to a strictly social or societal functionalism. This was a critically important theoretical step for the revival and extension of functionalist sociologies following World War II (see especially Merton, 1957a, and Parsons, 1951).[32]

---

[32] Early "individualistic" forms of functionalism (to stretch the term) got their power from showing the weakness of human reason: The higher ends and ideals were always subverted, either by *other* forces operating at the individual level (e.g., the passions) or by mysterious incomprehensible forces. The shift from reason to interest by Smith and other late eighteenth century thinkers (see Chap. 5) showed that a "higher" reason seemed to exist at a supra-individual level, based on nothing more than interest and blatant egoistic calculation. Sociological functionalism has one of its historical roots here; the other, of course, is in evolution. Fully developed sociological functionalism, as in Merton or Parsons or especially in systems theory, is able to dispense with the individual entirely. But perversely, the very rejection of rationality on which it is based, is undermined by the higher order, or emancipatory interests that the analysis serves. Logically, the rationality achieved by functional analysis (i.e., explaining the ways in which society works independently of individual motivation) would ultimately, if successful, put functionalism (of this variety, at least) out of business, because, in Merton's term, social functioning would become a manifest rather than a latent function operating behind our backs, as it were, as knowledge of these processes accumulated.

But why does Durkheim find it necessary to supplement causal with functional analysis? One clue is to be found in connection with one of his arguments for the necessity for causal analysis: Some social facts seem to have no function, i.e., no social usefulness, and for these a causal explanation is necessary. However, no society could exist for long if most of the social facts constituting it had no social functions: Too many such "parasitic" phenomena would add up to a situation wherein "the budget of the organism would have a deficit and social life would be impossible" (97). In a cryptic but critical passage, Durkheim asserts what Merton would years later term the fallacy of universal functionality (Merton, 1957a), namely that even though the usefulness of a fact is not the cause of its existence, "it is generally necessary that it be useful in order that it may maintain itself" (Durkheim, 1958, 97). The critical inference follows:

> . . . the fact that it is not useful suffices to make it harmful, since in that case it costs effort without bringing in any returns (97)

Functional analysis is necessary, then, because it is the basis on which the abnormal or pathological may be identified: Causal analysis cannot determine whether or not a contribution to the ongoing maintenance of society is or is not being made. In so far as it is deemed necessary to make such a determination, functional analysis cannot be dispensed with.

But the reader will recall that Durkheim has already given a definition of the pathological: those social facts not distributed generally. Why is another definition required? Although Durkheim provides no direct answer to this question, he does *link* the extent of generality of social facts to the protocol of harmfulness or nonutility. Pathological facts become, in effect, the not-so-general ones; if they were general they would necessarily—by definition—be "normal." Social facts of great generality must be making a contribution or they would not have survived the lengthy evolutionary process necessary to acquire that generality.[33]

As is typically the case with schemes that seemingly unknowingly confuse the normative and factual, as some forms of functionalism do, an otherwise unnecessary tangle of definitions, explanations, caveats, and denials is brought along in train. This may be seen in Durkheim's understanding of crime. In *DL* he had discussed crime at length in connection with the two types of law. There, crime was defined as violation of strong and defined states of the collective consciousness, exacting punishment graded in severity by the intensity of the moral rule violated. Punishment is vengeance. Now in *Rules* he takes the opportunity afforded by the theory of the normal and the pathological to designate crime as an example of the former. And indeed,

---

[33] It is somewhat ironic that after all his arguments against economic liberalism, methodological individualism, the impossibility of contract as the foundation of social order, and the like, Durkheim outlines a functional analysis at the core of which is a utilitarian argument. Social facts, in the last analysis, are characterized in terms of their usefulness to society. In the absence of this they will, for the most part, be unable to perpetuate themselves, although it is necessary to recognize the existence of "survivals," if only to provide a basis for identifying the pathological. Durkheim's functional analysis mirrors precisely that pervasive utilitarianism of industrial society that he rejected as providing an adequate account of its nature.

his arguments are convincing. Crime is universal, appearing in all societies, and appears to *increase* with movement up the evolutionary scale. There is indeed, says Durkheim, "no phenomenon that presents more indisputably all the symptoms of normality, since it appears closely connected with the conditions of all collective life" (66). Durkheim waxes eloquent in displaying the evolutionary role of crime: it firms up the social structure, bolsters the common morality, yet may also presage reform: Socrates and the heretics of the Middle Ages were necessary precursors of the liberal philosophers of the present (70–71).

All this might seem to suggest that crime is to be applauded, and the more of it the better. And indeed, Durkheim worries that the crime rate might fall too low (72). But having reiterated his point for the better part of a chapter, Durkheim then—in a footnote in a later edition—seems to want to banish the entire argument:

> From the theory developed in this chapter, the conclusion has at times been reached that, according to us, the increase in criminality in the course of the nineteenth century was a normal phenomenon. *Nothing is further from our thought* (75, n.15).

So much for the normality of crime.[34]

Functional analysis, then, is necessary for the normal/pathological distinction. But why should it be necessary to establish two different varieties of facts in the first place? As Hirst points out, this certainly does not follow from the demands of scientific explanation in sociology (see Hirst, 1975, 116ff. for a discussion of this and related matters bearing on the following discussion). Although many sciences do without the distinction, Durkheim says that it is one common to the vital sciences, indeed that defining and explaining the normal states and distinguishing them from pathological ones are the inescapable tasks of all the human sciences (Durkheim, 1958, 74). However, his account of the nature of *social* pathology is very different from its status in biology. The identification of pathologies in biology presupposes a scientific biology. Pathology is a branch of physiology that exists only as a consequence of knowledge of the general conditions of organismic functioning. Pathological states of the organism are not considered to be of a fundamentally different order. But this would have been impossible in Durkheim's time—and even at present—because a scientific sociology did not exist, as Durkheim himself emphasizes (xlvi).

But even the existence of a developed sociology would not have led Durkheim to a conception parallel to biology. The doctrine of a distinct order of pathological social facts is necessary for Durkheim because the very nature of his conception of collective consciousness as "sui generis" necessitated his conceiving of it as "normal." Since the commonly held beliefs and sentiments comprising the collective consciousness are what society *is* and so are necessarily normal, they cannot be the source of the pathological. Rather, Durkheim has a strong tendency, without ever being very clear about it, to

---

[34] Later scholars have fortunately ignored Durkheim's disclaimer. One of the most creative traditions in the study of deviance has built on Durkheim's original insight.

locate the *cause* of pathological facts in the eruption of the incorrigible organicopsychological nature of the *individual* into the social order, thereby creating the (pathological) unregulated states of the division of labor, and as we shall see in the next chapter, at least some types of suicide. As Hirst puts it, "by individualizing the *source* of pathology it de-socializes the pathological in society" (Hirst, 1975, 120). But if social pathologies are not caused by social facts, they cannot be explained sociologically in causal terms. In making social pathologies sociologically unexplainable in principle, Durkheim contradicts his own most basic methodological canon. Rather than being transcended, original nature Christian dualism survives in a post-Hobbesian secularized form to fulfill a necessary function in Durkheim's sociology.

CONCLUSION: CAUSALITY AND THE DOMAIN OF SOCIAL FACTS

The main theoretical emphasis of *DL* and *Rules* fell on the power of the collective consciousness and its autonomy as a domain awaiting its science. And especially in *DL*, there is a general morphological, or structural, account formulated within the even more general evolutionary framework. The bulk of our discussion has focused on this. But alongside it runs a complementary or reciprocal account emphasizing the importance of "spontaneity." Despite its lesser status at this point in Durkheim's work, the long-term significance of this second seemingly individual-centered conception should be made clear.

To this end we will profit by returning to an idea closely connected with his double account of social facts, indeed, one that I believe was nested within the problem inherent in the dual account. This is the distinction between "crystallized" and "uncrystallized" forms of the collective consciousness.

In *Rules* this distinction is little more than a way of classifying social facts and serves no end other than to reinforce his argument establishing the external and coercive nature of social facts: Just try and resist the crowd, he says, and you will quickly discover its irresistible coercive power (4–5). In later works, however, Durkheim brings the idea into greater theoretical prominence. In *Suicide*, in the course of defending his characterization of suicide as an "objective" phenomenon (i.e., existing as a social fact in the form of societal suicide rates), he *theorizes* the "currents" in a way that confers on them a heightened theoretical status. Below the "crystallized" forms lie the "currents," that "come, go, circulate, cross and mingle in a thousand different ways, and just because they are constantly mobile are never crystallized in an objective form" (Durkheim, 1951, 315). An example of this is the tendency of the group in the direction of individualism, then its redirection toward "social and philanthropic aims." Another is a shift from cosmopolitanism toward patriotism. Some currents may become crystallized— for a time—in rules or collective representations: legal rules, for example, or a whole variety of symbolic manifestations that "reflect," "sum up," or condense the currents themselves, such as the general acceptance of the appropriateness of the death penalty for murder. Durkheim employs the term *maxims*, evidently wishing to convey with this the idea of a social fact somewhat less crystallized than a rule. Maxims "merely express" currents: "they spring from . . . but do not supplant (them)." The living sentiments of the currents are "summed up by these formulae but only as in a superficial envelop" and would be meaningless if they did not correspond to the basic sentiments. There is here an anticipation of both the interpretation of "milieu" in *Suicide* and the analysis of ritual that would assume great prominence in *EF*. Durkheim's early theorizing of the social currents, we suggest, was a step in the direction of converting them from a subcategory of social facts to a causal agency *explaining* the crystallized forms of social facts, thus solving his human agency problem. There was no logical barrier to this since the stipulation of locating the causes of social facts in the domain of social facts is satisfied by the prior inclusion of the "currents" in that category. The shift in this direction in *Suicide* was not decisive, but it was a step on the way to what turned out to be his final formulation in *EF*.

Durkheim needed a conceptual innovation that would permit him to explain the collective consciousness without violating his basic causal axiom, as his scattered reductionist pronouncements seemed to do. This theoretical interest led him, willy-nilly, in the direction of seeking some *general principle* of interaction, which, with the limited conceptual kit of the time, he was able to formulate only metaphorically. What is important is that this was an early step in the direction of escaping the rigid individual/society polarity and establishing an explanatory conceptual ground apart from the "individual." In *EF* the interacting *ritual group* comes to be understood as the social vehicle within which sentiments and emotions are synthesized into emergent "collective representations" (i.e., symbols) of society in the process of becoming the constituent components of its religion.

Of course Durkheim never adequately theorized the nature of social interaction, an achievement that would have augmented considerably the power of his sociology. But it would have been virtually impossible for him to do so, if only because of his seeming unawareness of the beginnings of interactionist theorizing in the United States (despite his familiarity with the pragmatist movement (particularly the work of William James). And in any case it is an open question whether his basic theoretical and methodological axioms could have accommodated the human agency-infused type of inter-actionism necessary to provide causal grounding for his positivistic construction of the nature society.

But this is anticipation going well beyond *Rules*. Let us sum up. *Rules* was a project with the goals of establishing a formal paradigm for a *scientific* sociology and of accommodating the turn of the century social facts of anomie and class conflict to an evolutionary theory that would illuminate their transitional nature. Durkheim achieved the first of these in his arguments establishing human society as an object with properties parallel to those of the natural order, and therefore, as an object properly approached through the medium of a methodological conceptual armamentarium theoretically assimilated to those of the natural sciences. He achieved the second on the theoretical basis of his evolutionism and the functionalist account of social facts constituitive of functionalism, in conjunction with the dark side of the homo duplex doctrine.

In all this there was no mention of anomie or the forced division of labor. Was this deliberate on Durkheim's part, knowing that his sociology would be accepted only in the doing, only in the demonstration that it could be both diagnostic and illuminative of the future, on the one hand, and demonstrably capable of producing research grounded in rigorous scientific method, on the other? If this is so, it seems that the one consideration may have led him to his theory of occupational groups and the state, the other to the empirical studies of suicide and religion as social facts. It is to these that we turn in the next chapter.

12

EMILE DURKHEIM II
THE SUBSTANTIVE SOCIOLOGIES
a) Individualism, occupational groups,
and the state: Durkheim's political sociology
b) The sociology of religion and the
foundations of knowledge

Durkheim concluded *DL* with his diagnosis of turn-of-the-century industrial society as anomic and conflict-ridden. Anomie and the forced division of labor have their prime manifestations in the economic order, but also beyond economic crisis and heightened class struggle, there were other manifestations: family problems, for one, and high suicide rates, for another, the analysis of which Durkheim was already at work even as *Rules* was being prepared for publication. Durkheim had claimed in *DL* that increasing social heterogeneity would somehow create an ethic of cooperation embodying a moral authority adequate for eliminating or mitigating these pathologies, but his account of this remained abstract, relatively nonempirical, and was modeled on the domestic division of labor. If anything, the most convincing thrust of *DL* had been to suggest that anomie and the forced division of labor were conditions *endemic* to the expansion of the division of labor, that is, *normal* social facts. Durkheim was thus faced with a two-sided problem.

There was first the matter of the *content* of the collective consciousness. The old form of this, as Durkheim had formulated it, had been religious in nature, stressing consensus and conceiving of the community and the group (e.g., the guild) as associations that subordinated the interests of the individual to those of the collectivity. The growth of amoral or possessive individualism (McPherson, 1962), however, seemed, at least since the revolution, to be overwhelming the religious foundations of society. So one critical problem for Durkheim was to identify and analyze the nature of the emerging collective consciousness of industrial society.

Second, there was the question, following logically from the manner in which Durkheim had initially formulated the problem in *DL* and developed it theoretically in *Rules*, of the *relation* of the collective consciousness to differing forms of social organization—the morphology of society. This required that the forms of the collective consciousness were to be understood in terms of their relation to the morphological character of a society at all stages of evolutionary development. What form or forms of social organization, then, were appropriate for industrial society in the sense of constituting the proper foundations for the emerging (in Durkheim's view) collective consciousness of such societies? This was the master problem of Durkheim's sociology of social change, an exercise in divining the shape of the future in the chaos of the present, a legacy of the Enlightenment. In this regard, like Comte, Marx, and Spencer, Durkheim thought that he was engaged in displacing *philosophy* of history with a *science* that would master history through knowledge of society.

Durkheim's answer to the first of these two questions, given already of course in *DL*, but left unelaborated there, was something of a tour de force. Individualism itself, he proposed, would be the moral code of industrial societies of the future. And second, perhaps even more surprising, occupational associations modeled to some degree after the medieval guild would constitute the organizational matrix within which such a moral code would flourish.

INDIVIDUALISM AND THE CULT OF THE INDIVIDUAL

Although Durkheim addressed the "individualism" problem in *DL* and elsewhere, his most systematic theorization appeared in an essay, "Individualism and the Intellectuals" (*II*), published in 1898 in connection with "*l'affaire Dreyfus*." *II* was written in response to a defense of the actions of the French generals supporting the legal railroading and conviction of Captain Dreyfus by a well-known conservative publicist, Fredrick Brunetière. Brunetière had expressed the establishment position, maintaining that the issue had encouraged an anarchical *individualism* that had been exacerbated by the intellectuals supporting Dreyfus (Bellah, 1973, xxxvi; also, Clark, 1973, Chap. 6). Because of this, he argued, a moral consensus condemning Dreyfus was urgently required in the French national interest. Durkheim's *interest* in the matter was mainly to throw such weight as he had on the side of the *Dreyfusards*. To effect this, he advanced an argument that proceeded at a level ("the level of principles") quite remote from the actual issues. He attempted to show that the denunciations of individualism by the generals and their spokespeople failed to distinguish the utilitarian, self-interested form of individualism from the ethical type (See Chap. 11). The latter, he argued, could actually constitute, was in fact fact coming to constitute, the very foundations of the consensus the conservatives demanded.

Here again, is the *altruistic* individualism of Rousseau and Kant, springing "from *sympathy* for all that is human" (Durkheim, 1973b, 48) and is above all *disinterested* in the sense of being divorced from the pursuit of specifically personal interests. There is coming into being, he says, a "cult of the individual" that is a "glorification not of the self but of the individual in general" (48). Durkheim even invokes not only the general idea of humanity, which in other contexts he criticizes as obscuring the differences between societies and moral codes, but even a "religion of humanity," a term it is difficult to imagine him using for reasons other than to invite at least some degree of identification with Comte's program. The cult of the individual is the religion of humanity realized. "Man becomes a god for man" (52), he philosophizes and maintains that

> we make our way, little by little, toward a state, nearly achieved as of now, where the members of a single group will have nothing in common among themselves except their humanity (51)

Durkheim actually claims that this individualism "has become a fact" having "penetrated our institutions and mores . . ." (46)

The problem with *II* is that, aside from invoking Kant and labeling individualism a "cult," and implying that it might be an expression of the altruistic content of Comte's religion of humanity, Durkheim presents no *argument* capable of convincing us that the cult of the individual will to any significant degree transcend or displace *possessive* individualism.[1]

It might be argued that Durkheim's polarity of possessive and altruistic individualism fails to fully capture the richness and many-sidedness of this historic movement. In this regard it is perhaps worth taking note of an analysis of the rise of individualism from the perspective of a representative of a different European culture, Germany. Georg Simmel was an exact contemporary of Durkheim, and Durkheim was familiar with at least some of his works (including at least one version of Simmel's theory of individualism, in *Philosophie des geldes*).[2]

Simmel discerned a critical difference between the ideas associated with the individualism of the eighteenth century and those of the nineteenth century. During the earlier period the individual was understood as an agent exemplifying abstractions like natural rights ("the rights of man"), as manifesting a freedom grounded in natural law.[3] Throughout the nineteenth century, however, this conception was gradually displaced and superseded by one that construed individualism as *individuality*, uniqueness, or distinctiveness, an understanding quite at variance with the earlier categorical form. We may think of these as rationalist and romantic forms of individualism.

---

[1] *II* is of course more political than scholarly discourse, and at this level should be read as a defense of the liberal, socialist-leaning republicanism that had come to dominate social and humanistic thought during the 1880s and 1890s, a republicanism of which Durkheim was one of the acknowledged leaders (Clark, 1973, Chap. 6).

[2] Simmel contributed an article defining his conception of sociology in an early issue of *L'année sociologique*, the journal of reviews Durkheim founded and edited (along with others), and to which he contributed regularly. Durkheim reviewed *Philosophie des geldes* (*The Philosophy of Money*) in these pages in 1900 (see Nandan, 1980, 28, 88–89) and was familiar with some of Simmel's other writings. His initial enthusiasm for Simmel's work, especially its seeming affinity to his theory of the division of labor, evidently died out quickly as he came to see that Simmel's insistence on the restriction of sociology to the study of the *forms* of social interaction was incompatible with his own conception of the discipline (See Levine, 1985, 89–94).

[3] See the discussion in Chapter 4, where the difficulties of associating the idea of freedom with that of law are discussed.

The former is characteristic of Christianity and "ethical socialism," as well as Enlightenment rationalism, and is the moral or ideological basis for claims to dignity and human rights of all sorts (Simmel, 1979, 362). Its main thrust is leveling or democratic. This is Durkheim's moral individualism. The romantic conception, by contrast, has its roots in antiquity and conceives of the individual as a *bundle of qualities* that define his or her uniqueness. This lends itself to various types of rank orders of moral worth, in its extreme form even the justification of slavery (362).[4]

Now to think of individual freedom in terms of the *uniqueness* of every individual rather than in terms of the *formal* freedom common to all had profound implications for Simmel. Uniqueness implies separateness, a condition tending to produce seemingly contradictory consequences: a sense of isolation, but also an expanded sense of self. As Simmel put it,

> The individual seeks his self as if he did not yet have it, yet at the same time is certain that his only fixed point is this self (Simmel, 1950, 79)

He goes on to note that, far from resulting in a growth of reason, putting individual freedom into *practice* during the nineteenth century resulted in great inequality (thereby working a perverse irony on eighteenth century thought, which had generally assumed them to be harmonious).

In a manner parallel to Durkheim, Simmel points out that individualism as uniqueness has to be understood against the massive changes in social organization occurring during the nineteenth century. There is a paradox here, for while individualism was pervading every facet of social life, the *rationalization* of the workplace and the state's administrative system, along with the *urbanization* of community life, were simultaneously reducing the individual to a negligible quantity. And this is how things stood at the time of Simmel's writing. Without strong anchorages, he writes, "everyone must summon the utmost to preserve his personal core" (Simmel, 1950). Simmel reveals a different, darker, side of the unanchored, fragile, and

---

[4] Perhaps one extreme of what Simmel has in mind is that nineteenth century social type the "dandy," defined by Carlyle as "a man whose trade, office and existence consists in the wearing of clothes" (Moers, 1960, 31). Beau Brummel, the first dandy, spent at least two hours on his morning toilet alone, shaving, cleaning, brushing, washing, and then dressing, the end result a sartorial perfection—even, in Max Beerbohm's judgment, a work of art. All this for Brummel to convey, with a studied nonchalance, his superiority to the aristocrats, especially the Prince of Wales (in Georgian England) in whose circles he moved. The poet Baudelaire, another famous dandy, dressed all in black for audiences at the other social extreme, the bohemians of Paris. Both are systematic constructions of the self as presented in its uniqueness (see Moers's excellent *The Dandy*, [1960]; also Graña's depiction of Baudelaire [Graña, 1964, Chap. 5]). Another quite distinct nineteenth century type (still with us today), is the heroic genius. Here are protean archetypes of anarchistic individualism, personalities such as Victor Hugo, Richard Wagner, and Walt Whitman. Such larger-than-life figures share with the dandies their passion for uniqueness. Both, in their different ways, are manifestations of this prime romantic value. Both are off-centered refractions of the meritocratic work ethic central to modernization and a rejection of everything utilitarian, dandyism as a construction of a cultural reality in which appearance and performance are valued entirely for their own sakes, the genius in being a celebration of unique inner qualities appearing as a gift. Obviously, other forms of the individualistic uniqueness Simmel has in mind could be identified and described.

unique self: the inner reality perceived so acutely by Nietzsche and rendered so trechantly by him in his writings (and perhaps exemplified so tragically in his madness), a side reflected likewise in various forms of malaise (depression, hypochondria, etc.) evidently experienced by so many nineteenth century middle-class intellectuals (e.g., Spencer, Darwin, Max Weber; see Jameson, 1974, for a discussion) and revealed in such depth by Freud in his diagnoses of so many middle-class Viennese.

The weakness of Durkheim's theory of individualism, in the light of Simmel's analysis, is that it is polarized in terms of the two abstractions of the organicopsychological animal side and the socialized moral side. Durkheim reifies his ideal of altruistic individualism as the morality of the future. Simmel's treatment, by contrast, explores the inner or subjective meaning of modern individualism and displays a richer mosaic of the complexities of individualized existence not easily assimilated to Durkheim's polarity, an understanding more akin to Max Weber's view that "The expression of individualism includes the most heterogeneous things imaginable (Weber, 1948, 222, n.22). Simmel's main themes—increasing isolation, alienation, monomaniacal personalities forever seeking an elusive self—reveal a deeper and more complex dimension of individualism that calls into question Durkheim's rather rosy prognosis regarding the growth and expansion of individualism in the future.[5]

OCCUPATIONAL GROUPS

Theorizing the nature of the emerging collective consciousness of industrial society was only part of the task that emerged from the conclusion of *DL*. Religions, ideologies, moral codes—the ideal elements in human social life—do not exist in and of themselves or undergo change in purely immanent fashion. It is of the essence of Durkheim's sociology that the sphere of the ideal and that of social organization stand in close relation to each other. The segmental societies discussed in *DL* were integrated through a moral system that—Durkheim thought—imposed moral regulations essentially on everyone alike. But it was by no means established at the conclusion of *DL* that the anomic and forced forms of the division of labor were abnormal and transitional. To argue that they were transitional implied possessing some grasp of what the future would bring, and more specifically, just why it was that that future would see an end of, or at least a significant amelioration, of these maladies. On what organizational basis, then, might the industrial societies coming into being ground the "cult of the individual" that Durkheim thought was becoming the collective consciousness of the future?

It should be said at the outset that Durkheim exhibited a lifelong

---

[5] Any more extended review of works focusing on individualism is entirely beyond the scope of this work. Tocqueville's *Democracy in America* remains the seminal and still single most influential analysis. I have noted in Chapter 11 (see footnote no. 17) that the vicissitudes of individualism in the United States were a persistent preoccupation of European writers as long as this country was still perceived as the ripest ground for the realization of Enlightenment ideals.

concern with socialism, having early in his career begun a course dealing with its history (which he never finished due to the press of other duties, particularly the editorship of *L'année*). In these lectures, published years later (Durkheim, 1928), he undertook a sociological examination of socialism and found it unfit for the task of guiding the reorganization of an industrial society. It seems that like so many sociologists he saw it as a *competitor* of sociology, but an *unscientific* one. He thought socialist prognostications about the future of industrial capitalism were poorly grounded, and that socialism was therefore incapable of making the accurate predictions necessary for the functioning of the increasingly complex societies of the future (Durkheim, 1959, 5). His main objection to the substance of socialist *doctrine*, which he held to be its principal difference with sociology, was that it elevated the economic to a status of social primacy, and for him, of course, this reflected a fundamental misunderstanding of the basic nature of society. Actions or policies that followed from this erring conception, then, would inevitably be ineffective and inadequate. His remarks on economic inequality and poverty illustrate the kind of difference between economic and moral regulation Durkheim had in mind.

In industrial society poverty is partially ameliorated, but the breaking up of the older forms of communal life, coupled with a perception of the possibility of a better material life, tend to stimulate uncontrollable aspirations, an expression of *l'individualisme odieux*.

> What is necessary for (people) to be content is not that they have more or less, but that they do not have the right to have more. And for this it is absolutely necessary that there be an authority whose superiority they acknowledge, and which lays down the law. For never will the individual, left to the pressure of his needs acknowledge that he has reached the extreme limit of his right (Giddens, 1971, from Durkheim, *Le socialisme*, 177).

Under conditions of lessened *moral* regulation, imposition of rules limited to governing only economic functions, Durkheim argues, will do little to reinstitute the kinds of restraint necessary for the orderly functioning of the economy.

Durkheim objected also to the idea of a stateless society—the Marxian or anarchist utopias—which seemed to suggest that a stable and integrated economic life was possible without regulation. Neither did he believe that amelioration of the awful economic conditions of the time required intensification of class conflict; indeed, he rejected the doctrine of the necessity of class conflict in the transition to the Communist society of the future as a doctrine *unessential* to socialism.

Some of these views, especially the latter ones, reflect a somewhat peculiar definition of socialism, but one clearly suited to Durkheim's purposes. At least some elements of the socialist program (one should say "programs") were indispensable to future industrial society, he thought, and he therefore, in effect, incorporated them into his own sociology of that future society. We have earlier discussed Durkheim's indictment of the industrial capitalism of the time, a diagnosis on which the analysis in DL was predicated. And he did set down concrete proposals for the reform of certain aspects of capitalist social organization, such as the inheritance of private property, and for the regulation of class conflict. So while concurring in important respects with both the socialists' diagnosis of the problem and their solution, Durkheim (in his own view) went beyond them, contending that amelioration of the problems attending the abnormal forms of the division of labor had to be approached on the premise that what was required was the institution of some form of *moral* regulation.[6] This moral regulation, it is clear throughout Durkheim's analysis, had to be accommodated to a fundamental stipulation: Consistent with basic liberal principles, the role of the state had to be held to some necessary minimum. In principle, Durkheim rejected the *Machtstaat* with as much vigor as he did the stateless utopia of the socialists or the minimal state of Spencer and the economic liberals. There were, he believed, legitimate and necessary functions for the state; the problem was linking these with the drift of industrialism and protecting the expanding "cult of the individual" from the repression that is always a potential in the exercise of state power.

If the extensive regulating functions required by the expanding industrialism of the future were not to be exercised mainly by the state, they would obviously have to be discharged by other organs. What sorts of organizational forms, then, were consistent with both the continued existence of the state and the continuing expansion of the division of labor, but would not hamper the growth of the cult of the individual?

Durkheim proposes that it is to the medieval guild that social scientists (and the planners of the future) should look for their model of the emerging structure compatible with and capable of adapting to the continuing expansion of the division of labor. He defends this proposition by arguing along several lines. Since members of occupational groups, unlike the functionaries of the state, are intimately familiar with the problems in their particular branch of industry, it follows that such groups should *be* the organs of regulation, although the discharge of these regulatory functions would have to be consistent with the general national legal framework. And although Durkheim recognized that the future would doubtless bring into being regulatory functions for occupational groups that could not at the moment be foreseen, he nevertheless indicated an extensive array of functions that were at the time proper objects of group regulation. These included the general principles of the labor contract, salaries and wages, questions of industrial health and of the employment of women and children, the regulation of labor disputes, and judicial functions (Durkheim, 1957b, 40). Durkheim clearly believed that the exercise of these functions by the occupation group would effectively ameliorate the consequences of anomie.[7]

---

[6] For these reasons as well as his republicanism, Durkheim, along with many others of the academic elite of the time, was commonly thought of as a socialist. Indeed, he and his colleagues could be thought of as counterparts of the German "socialists of the chair" (see Chap. 13).

[7] The genesis of this idea appears in a lecture course during the 1890s and was first rendered in print as the conclusion to *Suicide*, in 1897. The theme was further developed in the preface to the second edition of *DL* in 1902. The relevant lectures appeared much later in *PECM*.

Durkheim characterizes the occupational groups not only in terms of their regulatory character, but of their spontaneity as well. The guilds of antiquity and the Middle Ages regulated not only economic activity, but much more broadly, community life in general. They were religious associations. But this regulation was possible only because they had fulfilled "profound needs" (Durkheim, 1964, p. 9). The guilds formed in part on the bases of common interests, "not only to defend those interests . . . (but) to associate, that is, not to feel lost among adversaries, to have the pleasure of communing, . . . to lead the same moral life together" (15). Here in the occupational group modeled on the guild Durkheim finds a form of social organization that meets the stipulations of his first dualism.

But what of the problem of the private appropriation and accumulation of productive capital? Durkheim clearly recognized that allowing the system of private property to remain in force carried with it both injustice in the system of social classes and chronic conflict in the industrial sphere. He does not, of course, propose a frontal attack on private property, in the form, say, of nationalizing the major industries. Rather, he proposes a number of reforms, two of which are especially worthy of mention.

Specifically apropos of the occupational groups, he maintained that the "supreme obstacle" to justice in the industrial sphere was the institution of inheritance of private property.

> Creating inequalities amongst men from birth, that are unrelated to merit or services, invalidates the whole contractual system at its very roots (213).

Inheritance must accordingly be abolished. This will go a long way toward bringing into being a society in which merit rules. And second, class conflict can be decisively reduced, he believes, with the proper matching of talent to position, a rationally managed type of social mobility that later became known as "sponsored mobility." Durkheim brings the problem of continuity and utilization of productive property within the purview of the occupational group, imagining a future in which the groups themselves will hold contractual property rights and discharge basic economic functions.[8]

Durkheim defends the occupational group modeled on the guild as the proper organizational form of the future on historical as well as functional grounds. The medieval guilds were independent, unlike the Roman *collegia* during the late Empire, and grew out of and appropriated many of the characteristics of domestic organization (a very significant point for Durkheim), thereby acquiring a range of social security functions, and developed

---

[8] In the light of later events, this appears to be a quite prescient prognosis on Durkheim's part. In recent years all capitalist societies have gone about creating various forms of worker's ownership of capitalist enterprise. In the United States this occurs mainly in the form of ESOPs and is as yet a movement of negligible scope. Probably the most extensive and even potentially quite radical such plan is the Swedish wage earner funds law, whereby labor unions acquire ownership of enterprises through a special tax pegged to the rate of profit and used to acquire owner shares in the business.

internal moral codes that were, in Durkheim's view, various forms of professional ethics. The new guilds of industrial society would replicate the older ones in all of these respects, each such group having its own quasi-domestic division of labor, security functions, and so on, bound together through the morality of the professional code.[9]

In all this Durkheim seems to have missed a quite fundamental point regarding the affinity between the guilds and the mode of production in the Middle Ages. The medieval guild was an organization that grew out of a handicraft system of production. It has been found in remarkably similar form in all of the agrarian societies of the past, and continues to survive in many of the present ones. Craft production was predominantly a system of household production, and craft guilds were associations of households. The collective interests of households engaged in the production of a particular product reflected the social division of labor characteristic of all agrarian societies. But the detail division of labor is based on the organization of production in factories which agglomerate workers whose jobs (i.e; roles in production) constitute a functional organization of many, not uncommonly hundreds, of occupations. The associations that grow out of factory production, even in socialist industrial societies, are labor unions, not occupational groups. Durkheim seemed to miss this difference, and its clear implication regarding the potential for the reemergence of craft guilds in an economy based on the detail division of labor, perhaps because his anti-economistic outlook led him to pay little attention to the actual organization of production as a critical sociological factor.

The moral code of the professional, discussed by Durkheim at some length in a series of lectures in the late 1890s and later incorporated into *PECM*, is of critical importance in Durkheim's scheme for the industrial society of the future. Because a professional ethic is a more or less *democratic* creation of the members of a group engaged in some *common* occupational activity, and because he thought that an earlier form of it had proved functional to both Roman and late medieval societies for long periods, Durkheim in effect took it as a model of *moral* regulation for industrial society. But he was evidently not entirely unaware of the possible dangers of this, particularly the potentially great monopoly power of organized group interests, although he probably underestimated them. He did realize that such groups, if given economic *carte blanche*, would likely, as he put it, "swallow up its members" (62). There must, therefore, be some structural arrangement to avoid such a tyranny. It was in large part on the basis of this consideration that Durkheim grounded his theory of the state.

---

[9] Durkheim's theorization of occupational groups stands in a long line of mostly counterrevolutionary writers who also had located the critical feature of the French crisis in the direct confrontation of the state and individuals, the early form of sociological mass society theory. Writers like Maistre and Bonald differed from Durkheim, of course, in their solution, the restoration of regional intermediate aristocrat-dominated *Parlements* (on this point see Aron, 1970, 97). The enlightened conservative Tocqueville theorized this problem in a progressive way, producing the first systematic mass-pluralist sociological theory in his *Democracy in America* and *The Old Regime and the French Revolution*. Durkheim could have profited from a more careful reading and reception of Tocqueville.

THE STATE IN INDUSTRIAL SOCIETY

Durkheim's conception of the state may fairly be termed pluralist. It derives from the tradition of French pluralism, of Montesquieu, Lamennais, and Tocqueville[10] and was reflected in such contemporaries of Durkheim as Leon Bourgeois and Clemeneau, and in the Radical Socialist Party. This view perceives the state as serving limited but important functions. For Durkheim these functions have to do mainly with protecting the rights of the individual from the tyranny of the group, and promoting moral individualism. Durkheim rejects the *natural rights* conception of individual rights, adopting the "positive" position that rights are created and guaranteed by the state. If the individual really had natural rights, he asks, why is it that their actual exercise appears and expands only with the rise of the modern state? His answer to this is that the state has evolved precisely to serve the function of providing "countervailing" powers against the group, such as the individual's rights of physical mobility and recourse to law. The state conceived in this way *checks* the actions of the group, just as it itself is checked by the very existence of occupational groups and the exercise by such groups of their indispensable regulatory function. Consistent with this, Durkheim assigned an important political function to the occupational groups of future industrial society, arguing that in the future they would displace the basic territorial structure of representation, and themselves become the units of representation at the state level.[11]

In essence Durkheim's pluralist conception of the state consists of inserting a conception of *society* between the individual and the state, much as Tocqueville had done in his analysis of the new society of the United States in *Democracy in America*. And just as Tocqueville emphasized the importance of private associations of various types—including religious groups—Durkheim saw a diverse array of occupational groups serving the same social function. Central to all such formulations is the principle of *balance*, of a balanced social order, that slides between absolutism or statism on the one side, and an anarchic, essentially stateless conception of the bases of social order on the other.

These structural features of the emerging state, however, are only part of Durkheim's account. Along with the role of *protecting* individual rights comes the *duty* to perpetuate and expand them. Durkheim's political discussions return constantly to the ideal or normative level. The state is the indispensible bearer and *propagator* of the ideas of individualism. The most important implication of this is that education becomes the central state function (perhaps excluding war-making). The expansion of public education centralized in a state bureaucracy was coterminous with Durkheim's academic

---

[10] For a discussion of the various forms of pluralist thought beginning with Aristotle, see Nisbet (1973), Chap. 6. We could as easily speak of a republican rather than a pluralist conception and better reflect the political rhetoric and sense of the time.

[11] This idea was by no means original with Durkheim. It was one of the tenets of the syndicalism prominent in France at the time, and also of British guild socialism. Durkheim rejected syndicalism as a program or movement *in toto* on the grounds that syndicates were autonomous of one another, limitless in their growth, and that they separated, rather than united, employers from employees (Durkheim, 1960, 6).

career, and at the core of his political agenda was the seizure of the educational function from the clerics by the state. This was effectively accomplished during the course of Durkheim's academic career, (the result being the main aspect of the spectre of "state Durkheimianism" raised by the enemies of republicanism). As educator, the state takes on something of a Comtean or Hegelian dimension. Durkheim viewed the state, as his former student George Davy put it (during the Great Depression), as a "Brains-Trust" (Davy, Introduction, in Durkheim, 1957b, xxxviii). The state, says Durkheim, is "the center of a particular kind of consciousness, one that is limited, but higher, clearer, and with a more vivid sense of itself" (50). It is charged with the responsibility "to work out certain representations which hold good for the collectivity" (50), is "the organ of social thought" (51), but very importantly, and astonishingly, "does not execute anything" (50).

Having emerged historically as the organizational bearer of ethical individualism, the state will continue to exercise this function in the future, since the rights of the individual are still evolving. The function of the state in this respect is to "call the individual to a moral way of life" (69), to bring into being an ethical individualism in which the state itself "merges with the human ideal" (74). The state will expand not administratively, but in the "clarity" of its consciousness. Through its connections with society it progressively synthesizes the inchoate elements of the collective consciousness in ever clearer forms, and in the process reflexively acquires a progressively clearer understanding of itself. The state as ideal "reflects" the passions that find their way into the political arena, but reconstitutes them in more rational fashion within the compass of a broader understanding of the collectivity as a totality. It becomes the organ of reason, qualified for *moral sovereignty* because the force of its morality is based on the extent to which it is *rational* (see Pickering, 1979, 66ff).

Durkheim's concept of democracy follows from this. It consists *not* in a theory of representation, but in the right and *duty* of the state to propagate its superior, clearer consciousness throughout society.

> The role of the state, in fact, is not to express and sum up the unreflective thought of the mass of the people but to superimpose on this unreflective thought a more reflective thought, which therefore cannot be other than different. It is and must be a center of new and origial representations which ought to put the society in a position to conduct itself with greater intelligence than when it is swayed merely be vague sentiments working on it. (92)

This is a formulation that would not be out of place in Comte or Hegel.

Finally, in addition to theorizing the ideological hegemony of the state, Durkheim in certain passages also seems to undermine his own strictures regarding the necessary independence of the secondary groups. He speaks, for example, of the "sovereignty" of the state over the secondary groups, and Davy describes his conception of this relation as one of the state "comprising within itself secondary groups of various kinds, which are of service to it rather than disservice . . ." (Durkheim, 1957b, xxxvii).

In all this Durkheim thought of the teacher as a conduit between the state and the individual, responsible for conveying the higher and clearer enlightenment of the state's evolving collective consciousness. He appears never to have seriously entertained the idea—despite familiarity with the *ideologues*, and with Marx and other socialist writers—that ideas might well serve dominant interests, or even classes, and that democracy implied, indeed *required*, continuous *struggle* rather than just a systematic propagation of the right ideas by a state-sponsored cadre of educators.

Perhaps the greatest theoretical deficiency that followed from Durkheim's tendency to elevate the collective consciousness above society was, as Giddens puts it, that "political power is implicitly assumed to be an outcome of a pre-established moral ascendency of the state" (Giddens, 1971, 509), or even more to the point, Hunt's judgment that his organicist view of the state and of law as "reflecting" passions of the collectivity, but then transcending them, in effect, abolishes the problem of power (Hunt, 1978, 75ff.). Such is the tendency of all absolute idealisms. Durkheim was no absolute idealist, but the "idealist" side of his theory of the state is not so remote from such philosophies as his republicanism might otherwise suggest.

Durkheim's "dual" theory of the state rather clearly reflects the basic features of both his philosophical anthropology and his conception of the drift of Western societies. The state clearly functions to keep the individual consciousnesses "vibrating in unison" by virtue of its reception of the ideals and rules of moral individualism. It is at least implied that, as the division of labor advances, the world increasingly comes to be ruled by humane reason, which obviates the necessity for much state repression. The manner of attachment of individual to collective consciousness seems therefore to be grounded in Durkheim's first dualism, that of the collective and individual consciousnesses.

As a corollary of this, Durkheim places the bulk of the burden of socially necessary repression on the occupational group rather than the state, an interpretation consistent with his tendency to associate egoism and hedonism mainly with economic life (along with the family). The regulatory function of the group thus appears to derive from the second dualism, *homo duplex*.

One could perhaps read Durkheim in such a way as to extract from his theory of the occupational groups and the state a form of conflict pluralism. The occupational groups might be interpreted as the main mobilizers of interests and therefore the major players in the pluralist political game. This would make the theory a (conventionally) liberal-democratic, although an elitist one. But Durkheim does not develop this line. For example, although from a present-day perspective it seems at least surprising if not incredible that Durkheim would have excluded political parties from the industrial societies of the future, he makes no mention of them in this exposition. Yet in Europe *circa* 1900 it should have been reasonably clear that political parties had become the main organizational forms of political action in all Western capitalist democratic states.

Finally, it does not seem as though Durkheim was a very good prognosticator of the contours of the shape of capitalism as it emerged in the middle and later decades of the century. The major actors that have emerged include, first and foremost, the great corporations that have concentrated their power through vertical integration, internationalization, and conglomeratization. The corporations have—admittedly in significantly varying degrees—in general become by far the single most potent shapers of the policies of the formally democratic states. Obviously neither the corporations nor their various trade associations are what Durkheim had in mind when writing about occupational associations, but neither are trade unions (although at one point he did suggest that unions could provide at least a partial model of the occupational association). And the power-concentrating and alienating nature of organizations generally, whether corporative, union, or other, seemed not to have found a place in Durkheim's imagination. On this point not only Marx, but a healthy dose of the Weberian understanding of bureaucratization and its effects, would have served Durkheim well.

SUICIDE

Suicide, published in 1897, was the culmination of at least seven or eight years of work. Durkheim had addressed the topic in a lecture course offered in 1889–1890, and assisted by Mauss, over the ensuring years he had collected, collated, and analyzed the statistical series on the distribution of suicide in Europe. *Suicide* is a statistical study, and although in certain respects—especially in the way in which Durkheim related theory and data—it was innovative and enormously influential in its long-term influence, the approach Durkheim took up was not in itself original. Europeans had been studying suicide for some time, and doing it in the way adopted by Durkheim, the so-called "moral statistics" approach (Douglas, 1967, Chaps. 1 and 2). The European concern with suicide was rooted in a *seeming* increase in suicide in all the modernizing European societies, and perhaps in France, in particular, it had for some time been thought to be related to just that growth of individualism and dissolution of social bonds discussed earlier. The genius—and failure—of Durkheim's analysis of suicide lay in the way he framed it within the general theory worked out in *Rules*.[12]

The selection of the suicide problem as the vehicle to demonstrate the scientific power of the new sociology, aside from the reasons given above, had to do with the nature of the act of self-destruction itself. If sociology was to carve out a recognized *niche* in the disciplinary firmament as a true science, it would have to show that the positivism of *Rules* really worked in analyzing the social level sui generis. This meant demonstrating that the social was a sphere of reality in which actual empirically grounded *explanations* were possible. From this standpoint selecting suicide as his research topic seems, on the face of it, a strange choice. What could be more private, more individual, more distant from the collectivity? All sorts of phenomena obviously social—the family, occupational groups, political activity, the state—would have qualified as bona fide sociological topics. Of course Durkheim did deal with all of these in his sociology but suicide was his major

---

[12] Undoubtedly due largely or even entirely to the fact that during the late eighteenth or early nineteenth century the states began to generate a variety of statistics, including statistics on suicide (see Douglas, 1967, Chap. 12).

monographic research effort. And yet, given his intent, what could have been more daring? The decision to study suicide seems in retrospect to have been somewhat of a calculated risk. If Durkheim had been unable to produce any significant results, this could and probably would have been attributed to the defects of his *theory*, and the weakened theory could thereby have been more easily dismissed by his competitors, academic and otherwise.[13] If, on the other hand, he was able to carry off a successful piece of research, the implications for the future of his brand of sociology would be substantially enhanced. To show that even such a seemingly private act as suicide was amenable to sociological analysis would be a powerful demonstration of the explanatory power of Durkheim's sociology (Hilbert, 1986, 5).

Durkheim proceeds, as usual, by the method of elimination, taking up and eliminating other general explanatory approaches—psychological, racial, the working of heredity, or pathologies such as alcoholism or mental disease. Factors such as these latter may be implicated in suicidal acts, but cannot be regarded as their causes. Durkheim sets out to establish the etiology of suicide in the central facts of society, the collective representations. It is on the *milieu*, to use the term he came to employ toward the end of *Rules*, that the sociological search for the causes of suicide must focus.

Durkheim disaggregates the concept of suicide into four types: (1) egoistic, (2) altruistic, (3) anomic, and (4) fatalistic. These Durkheim defines by so-called *causal definition* rather than independently of their causes, partly on the grounds that understanding the intrinsic aspects of the act of self-destruction is virtually impossible due to the unavailability of such information, but also because of his belief that the meaning of the act to the actor—the *intention*—had to be excluded from consideration on theoretical grounds already set down in *Rules* (Durkheim, 1951, 146–147).[14] But defining suicide in terms of its causes confounds the causal analysis itself and precludes the possibility of discovering additional types of suicide (for a discussion see Lukes, 1973a, 201ff.). In a strict sense this vitiates the analysis that follows in its entirety, since it *presupposes* the causal connections rather than establishing them by empirical procedures. But even granting some degree of plausibility to Durkheim's analysis and conclusions—which we definitely wish to do, both because of the real merits of the study and the fact that he seemed to have no alternative, given the sheer unavailability of proper data—we will see in the course of the following discussion that this basic conceptual strategy exerted a quite pernicious influence on important aspects of his analysis.

---

[13] Who were several, but especially Gabriel Tarde. Durkheim discusses and critiques Tarde's social psychology at various places in his work, especially the latter's theory of imitation, to which he devoted an entire chapter of *Suicide* (Book 1, Chap. 4).

[14] The idea of "causal definition," despite the confusing juxtaposition of terms, was evidently a common property of eighteenth and nineteenth century intellectuals, intended, in Cassirer's words, to "permit us to understand the structure of a complex whole; it does not, however, stop with this structure as such, but goes back to its foundations" (Cassirer, 1955, 254, and cited in Douglas, 1967, 31). The intent of illuminating larger "wholes" within which particulars are situated seems to stretch the idea of definition as it is presently understood, and to be more akin to describing a procedure for *investigating* complex phenomena. In any case, although Durkheim may have appropriated the term from the intellectual ethos of the time, he assuredly did not use it in the manner described by Cassirer.

Durkheim is intent on establishing suicide as a "social fact," and then, in rendering this social fact amenable to analysis. He does this by conceptualizing the study of suicide in terms of "suicide rates" and then claiming that these statistics are an adequate empirical rendering of "social fact." This excludes the meanings or psychological states of those who destroy themselves as sociologically irrelevant, in accord with his rules, a procedure that occasioned much criticism from later Durkheim critics and students of suicide. It should be recognized, however, that it was a direct and consistent attempt to apply the objectivism laid down in his own *Rules*.

Now Durkheim's disaggregated types are linked to his basic sociological interpretation of the drift of Western history, as a growth of individualism and dissolution of the social bonds.

Egoistic suicide occurs when the consciousness of a collectivity isolates the individual, weakens the bonds of dependence of the individual on the group, throws the individual back on himself or herself. Altruistic suicide, conversely, results from an overintegration of the individual into the group. Durkheim argued that the higher incidence of (egoistic) suicides among Protestants, as against Catholics and Jews, resulted from the greater emphasis placed on the self-determination of the individual in Protestantism. More specifically—and of considerable importance—he characterized this difference as one of a differing evaluation of the importance of *free inquiry*. The Protestant insistence on the individual's shaping of his or her own religious life, he argues, requires free inquiry, and this implies fewer beliefs held in common and so a weaker collective consciousness (1951, Book 2, Chap. 2).

Durkheim goes on to replicate this finding among other groups. Members of the liberal professions, because of their high levels of education, would be expected to kill themselves with greater frequency and the data suggest that this is so, as it is of other groups comprised of those more highly educated. Jews are well educated, of course, but they are an exception proving the rule because their learning actually forms the content of a highly integrating group consciousness that, significantly, stands opposed to that of the environing societies.[15] Durkheim then investigates this relationship in domestic and political milieux and his findings here evidently confirm the earlier ones. Suicide is rarer under conditions presumed to be highly integrating, in completed families as against married pairs, but also among the latter as against single individuals, and during movements of national political crises as against normal routine (Book 2, Chap. 3).

Durkheim's emphasis on knowledge and education points up one important connection with both his Enlightenment consciousness and his evolutionism. Committed anticlerical liberal that he was, he tended to equate progress with emancipation from traditional religion. Knowledge—and in the spirit of the Enlightenment Durkheim of course equated knowledge with scientific knowledge—was possible only as this process of emancipation continued. Egoistic suicide then, was essentially a phenomenon of recent evolutionary development and resulted from a central and necessary tendency of that development, the growth of ethical individualism. It occurs "in

---

[15] This is significant because it suggests that a group might have a low suicide rate precisely because of its opposition to the norms of the larger society.

societies where the dignity of the individual is the supreme end of conduct," where "the man himself is a God" (363).

Altruistic suicide is the other side of the coin of the egoistic type, resulting from "insufficient individuation" (217). This type is characteristic of traditional societies not yet differentiated by the expansion of the division of labor. One thinks of Japanese ritual suicide or even the suicides occurring in elite units of modern European armies, where an antiquated moral code survives (238).

Just as egoism and altruism constitute a polarized pair, so do the anomic and fatalistic types.[16] Anomic suicide results from a withdrawal or breakdown of moral regulation, mainly in two contexts, economic life and domestic relationships. Any abrupt change in one's economic circumstances, whether for better or worse, disrupts the existing balances between the expression of basic desires and wants, on the one hand, and the moral constraints imposed on them, on the other. Prosperity, if anything, creates a more anomic condition, for

> The social forces then free have not replaced equilibrium, their respective values are unknown and so all regulation is lacking for a time. The limits are unknown between the possible and the impossible, what is just and what is unjust, legitimate claims and hopes and those which are immoderate. Consequently, there is no restraint upon aspirations (253).

Breaking the domestic bond of marriage, Durkheim argues, results in a similar normlessness, for the moral bond of marriage has the function of restraining the expression of sexuality. And, indeed, he finds a significantly lower incidence of suicide in intact marriages.

Conditions under which lack of moral regulation is likely to occur make anomic suicide, like the egoistic type, a phenomenon of modernism, to be expected in societies "where progress is rapid" (364). In fact, he maintained that *chronic* anomie was "a regular and specific factor in suicide in our modern societies" (258).

Such characterizations, along with others describing egoistic as well as anomic suicide, suggest that, like crime, they might be thought of as "normal" phenomena of advanced societies. But Durkheim was ambiguous about the relation of suicide to his protocols of normality. At some points in his exposition, he does seem to perhaps at least imply that suicide might be considered normal. Certain levels of both types, and perhaps even the altruistic variety, are inevitable in rapidly changing societies. He writes of certain societal "currents" that tend in the direction of encouraging the autonomy of personalities, of others that lead to imposing restraints on them, and still others that demand sacrifice in the name of the group, as being present in varying degrees in *all* societies (309–310; 365). It is thus a matter

---

[16] Durkheim says little abut fatalistic suicide, except that it occurs in a condition of overregulation, where, for instance, people find themselves "with futures pitilessly blocked and passions violently checked by oppressive discipline," which seems to suggest that he might have thought of it as linked to the forced division of labor. His examples, however, "the suicide of very young husbands or of the married woman who is childless" (279n.), do little to clarify this.

of circumstance—or evolutionary stage?—which of them will at any particular moment be preponderant in its influence. This seems to provide a ground for regarding certain levels of the suicide rate as normal. Beyond this, one could even invoke the formal criterion of normality advanced in *Rules*, the generality of the social facts in question. Certainly the long-lasting high and increasing rates of suicide in the advanced European societies (the empirical validity of which presupposed a rather dubious act of faith in accepting the accuracy of the statistics, requiring suspension of the critical faculty) could have supported an interpretation qualifying them as normal under the rule of generality. And the "currents" that create the conditions for suicide, if not the suicides themselves, Durkheim evidently regarded as functional for society, as his judgments regarding education, rationality, and the growth of knowledge suggest. But Durkheim does not take up this line of argument.

It is reasonably clear, however, that Durkheim did not really wish to place the imprimatur of normality on suicide, did not want to say that the high suicide rates of the European societies around the turn of the century were normal. And, in fact, he eventually did assert that they were abnormal, "a pathological problem becoming daily a greater menace," a judgment he claimed to have made on the grounds of the evidence of "all proofs" that he himself had assembled (370).

Durkheim's inconsistency on this question reflects one of the central problems of constructing sociological analysis in terms of the organic metaphor, the implication that a society's normal and abnormal states can be stipulated, and even the necessity of doing so, as in Durkheim's case. But for how long, asked Durkheim's former student Maurice Halbwachs, can an entire grouping of societies be considered to be in a pathological state?

If egoistic and anomic suicide, whether normal or not, are both characteristic of societies at a certain state of development, it would seem that they might be related. And so they are, having "kindred ties": egoistic suicide, "recruits from the intellectual field, anomic from the economic."

> Both spring from society's insufficient presence in individuals. But the sphere of its absence is not the same. . . . In egoistic suicide it is deficient in truly collective activity, thus depriving the latter of object and meaning. In anomic suicide society's influence is lacking in the basically individual passions, thus leaving them without a check-rein. (258)

Anomic suicide here implicates the organicopsychological individual, occurring when the rules or norms fail to exercise their external constraining regulatory function. Egoistic suicide occurs where the norms themselves decree a condition "deficient in truly collective activity," throwing the individual back on himself or herself in arranging and carrying out life's activities; suicide may come to be seen as the only way out from being overwhelmed by it all.

Suicide is replete with questionable comparisons, inconsistencies, and obfuscations, doubtless to be expected in a work that in important respects was the first of its kind. To a considerable extent, these difficulties stem from the initial procedure of causal definition, as mentioned earlier. Durkheim's claim to have identified the cause of egoistic suicide is an important case in point. In the comparisons of the suicide rates of the different religious groups, Durkheim isolates the "spirit of free inquiry" as the decisive factor in the individuating process. This is clearly a rule or norm with specific substantive content. But in the comparisons of the suicide rates among married couples, the widowed, the single, and in expanded families, there is, of course, no spirit of inquiry, but only, as Durkheim puts it, "egoism" as against the condition of integration (209). There seems to be no parallel to the causal power of the *rule* of free inquiry, indeed, no rule or form of obligation at all. Here the processes of individuation in the domestic institution come to resemble more a *lack* of regulation as such, in other words a condition of *anomie*. This sort of sloppiness and confusion is made possible, perhaps near-inevitable, by the procedure of causal definition and its dubious supporting arguments. Definitions of the types of suicide in their own terms would constitute standards to which empirical realities would be held, and hopefully function as self-correcting processes in their very nature.

A somewhat similar problem arises in connection with Durkheim's analysis of altruistic suicide. Durkheim seems to consider the archetype or exemplar of altruistic suicide to be the instance where the act of self-destruction is performed as an obligatory act, as in the case of hara-kiri. But there are numerous other cases where no *rule* seems to be involved, particularly in various sorts of self-sacrificial acts. Durkheim recognizes that there is a problem here. While the former type, which Durkheim calls "obligatory altruistic suicide" (240), seems to define the category, others, where death is not itself the end of the action, are, he says, "only derivative forms" (240). The root cause then becomes "the state of altruism." Durkheim rejects any radical separation in these types, on the ground that it can only be made in terms of the motives or meanings of the acts to the individuals, precisely the procedure he has declared inadmissible from *Rules* on through the definitional sections of *Suicide*.

Partly because of these and other difficulties, *Suicide* has invited a welter of interpretations. Earlier ones tended to focus on various combinations of the strength and content of the collective consciousness. Parsons's is perhaps representative. Altruistic suicide is found where the collective consciousness is strong and collectivist in orientation; egoistic suicide where it is strong but substantively individualistic, forcing the individual to be free; the anomic form where it is weak or where the norms are weak and so fail to perform the regulatory function (Parsons, 1949, 324–338; see also Giddens, 1971, 82–85, and 1965). More recent interpretations (Hymes, 1975; Pope, 1975; Hawthorne, 1976, 129–132) have cut more deeply. Hymes has argued strongly that Durkheim's Cartesian mind-body dualism provides the basis for a more comprehensive interpretation. He claims that the dimensions of repression (regulation) and integration (direction toward society) are derived from the mind/body polarity. The functional requirement of some minimal fit between individual and society makes necessary some degree of both repression of the passions and positive orientation toward society. Hymes proposes that the four types of suicide result from the extreme states of each dimension, as given in Table 12-1. He remarks particularly on the difficulty of interpreting the integration dimension (Hymes, 89). In fact, this is not interpretable strictly within the framework of *homo duplex*, for, as we have

Table 12-1 Derivation of Durkheim's Suicide Typology*

SOCIALIZATION OF HOMO DUPLEX	QUANTITY INVOLVED	TYPE OF ASSOCIATED SUICIDE
Regression of drives (regulation)	(a) much	fatalistic
	(b) little	anomic
Direction toward social ends	(a) much	altruistic
(integration)	(b) little	egoistic

* From Eugene Hymes, "Suicide and Homo Duplex," *Sociological Quarterly* 16 (Winter 1975), 877–104.

seen, this dualism answers specifically to Durkheim's interest in regulation, not integration. It is Durkheim's other dualism, the distinction between the collective consciousness and the social consciousness of individuals, that is required to theorize the integration relation. In this formulation the altruistic and egoistic forms of suicide become functions specifically of the relationship between collective and individual forms of consciousness, while the fatalistic and anomic forms remain functions of *homo duplex*.

Suicide, to reiterate, was intended as a demonstration that the theory formalized by Durkheim in *Rules* could produce a work of true science which would unequivocally establish sociology as a science modeled on the natural sciences. And it has indeed repeatedly been acclaimed as the first truly theoretically grounded scientific monograph in sociology and continues to exercise great influence on sociological studies of suicide. It is ironic, then, that it is precisely in some of its most positivistic respects that it is found wanting.

One of these has to do, once again, with the employment of causal definitions. Durkheim's basic explanatory model includes (1) the types of suicide, (2) what he refers to as "suicidogenetic currents" that produce them, and (3) the associational life within which these currents are to be found. Currents with the potential of producing all four types of suicide are to be found in all types of associations, he says, and it is a matter of balance, or predominance of one or another, that accounts for the suicide rates of this or that group. Thus, there are currents of egoism, altruism, and anomy, which in differing balance account for the suicide rates of different groups. At one point Durkheim expresses this by saying that "at any given moment the moral constitution of society establishes the contingent of voluntary deaths," that there is "for each people a collective force of a definite amount of energy, impelling men to self-destruction" (Durkheim, 1897, 299). Very interestingly, he goes on to specify the "individual forms assumed" by each: "apathy" in the instance of egoistic suicide, "energy of passion or will" in altruistic suicide, and "irritation" and "disgust" in anomic suicide. Each of these, in addition, has an array of "secondary varieties": "indolent melancholy" or "the sceptic's sangfroid" as forms of apathy; feelings of "duty", "mystic enthusiasm", or "peaceful courage" as types of passion; and various sorts of "violent recrimination" as manifestations of irritation or disgust (Book 2, Chapter 6, esp. 293; also 299–300).[17]

Here the causal definition has a perverse effect. Remember that *as it is employed by Durkheim* it collapses effect into cause, thereby failing to identify the causal factors independently. In this instance, it amounts to a complete failure to identify the suicidogenetic currents empirically. Durkheim merely assumes, by virtue of his *attributions* of individualism, anomie, or altruism to Protestant, Catholic, or Jewish milieux, to the milieux of married as against single people, to that of officers as against enlisted men, to economically disrupted versus undisrupted conditions, and so on, that these milieux must contain or exhibit the specific preponderance of the type of suicidogenetic current he claims to be the appropriate one. But this is an entirely theoretical or speculative exercise. There is no independent verification that the suicides of Protestants really do result from *individualistic* suicidogenetic currents, that those experiencing disrupted economic or marital conditions kill themselves by virtue of the effects of *anomic* suicidogenetic currents, and so on. There is no empirical reason to accept those currents, as against others, as the true causes. Durkheim uses the causal definition not to explore and illuminate a larger whole, but as a surrogate for either an inability (because of the absence of proper data) or unwillingness, or both, to institute actual empirical specification of operations necessary to identify the different types of currents. In a strict sense, therefore, Durkheim can make no legitimate claim whatever to have discovered the causes of suicide.

A closely related point has to do with the consideration of *Suicide* as an application of the totality of the conceptual scheme laid out in *Rules*. Perhaps in part because of his inability to empirically identify the suicidogenetic currents of the groups he analyzed, Durkheim totally ignores the morphological facts that he says (in *Rules*) constitute the indispensible facts of the social milieux necessary for sociological analysis (despite his use of the term in Table 1 on page 293). According to the basic stipulation in *Rules*, discovery of such morphological facts, however conceived (see Chapter 11), is indispensible for sociological explanation in general. Recall that explanation on the basis of morphological facts is essentially structural explanation and is precisely what Durkheim claims sociology must do, in view of the fact that it ought not, indeed, *cannot* adduce sociological explanations by taking into account subjective meaning.[18] But in fact, if we understand Durkheim's account of the suicidogenetic currents as a causal one, it is apparent that it is based on subjective meanings; in the last analysis, how else can phenomena such as "the spirit of free inquiry" be construed? And this, if anything, is even more true of the "individual forms assumed," which Durkheim labels "Secondary Varieties."[19] The result is ironic. Durkheim claims that *Suicide*

[17] These attributions were drawn from various romantic writers (see Douglas, Chap. 2).
[18] Again, for ease and consistency of expression I employ Weber's term, which will be explained in Chapter 13.
[19] Table 1's headings and subheadings (293) are ambiguous and misleading on this point, a consequence, perhaps, of Durkheim's own partial confusion and sense of the difficulty he had gotten himself into.

will demonstrate the workability of his claims in *Rules,* but if he demonstrates anything, it is by virtue of breaking the most fundamental rule, that of treating social facts as things. In this sense, *Suicide* stands not only as the empirical work revealing the power of positivist sociology, but as one that in its most fundamental operations demonstrates, if not the necessity (which could be argued), at least the practical sociological fruitfulness of grounding sociological explanation on a recognition and theorization of subjective meaning.

In fact, Durkheim's analysis of the "individual forms" of the different types of suicide (Book 2, Chap. 6), despite the fact that they are based on virtually no data whatever, and relying as they do mainly on literary sources, is a veritable exemplar of the type of analysis, in form at least, that is implied in the first dualism. This is so despite its brevity and limited conceptual elaboration.The individual forms—apathy and melancholic reflection; energetic, duty-rooted, or mystic passion; and irritated disgust and recrimination—are shown (or so, at least, Durkheim claims) to reflect the egoistic, altruistic, and anomic suicidogenetic currents of the collective consciousness. They differ from the collective forms in their substance and in their variation among individuals, it appears, more or less as Durkheim had characterized this relationship in *DL* and *Rules.* The theorization of the individual as social, firmly establishing the theoretical status of the socialized individual in sociology, was perhaps Durkheim's most significant achievement. His theorization of the collective-individual consciousness link in *Suicide* was a demonstration, up to the publication of *Suicide* Durkheim's *only* empirical, if weak, demonstration that conceptualizing the social domain in terms of (at least) two internal levels was a fruitful, possibly even necessary, theoretical elaboration if sociology was to develop as a truly explanatory discipline taking as its object a fully comprehensive formulation of the social domain.

There remains an important general theoretic point that follows on and generalizes that made just above. I have earlier in this and the preceding chapter argued that one critical aspect of the conceptual development of Durkheim's sociology was a movement in the direction of escaping the constraints of the individual/society polarity and that in this regard one of the threads running through Durkheim's work is a persistent if unsystematic theorizing of the association process. His theorization of the suicido-genetic currents in *Suicide* was an important step in this direction.

Suicide reveals an enhanced or broadened perspective on the salience of association as such. Specifically regarding the individual/society polarity and reiterating many earlier statements, Durkheim writes that

> of course the elementary qualities of which the social fact consists are present in turn in individual minds

but goes on to declare that the social fact emerges from them only when they have been transformed by association, since it appears only then.

> Association itself is also an active factor productive of special effects. In itself it is therefore something new. When the consciousness of individuals, instead

of remaining isolated, becomes grouped and combined, something in the work has been altered (Durkheim, 1951, 310).

In *Rules* Durkheim's specification of the "milieu" was purely abstract and undifferentiated from morphological facts. In *Suicide*, although Durkheim's terminology is confused, an elevated degree of autonomy for interaction as such, distinct from morphology, makes a distinct if still undertheorized appearance.

Finally, it is worth remarking on *Suicide's* double irony, specifically with respect to the fate of Enlightenment ideals. The very success of the movement celebrating the individual, finally "crystallized" in institutional form, brings with it, in its egoistic form a *seeming* massive increase in the impulse of self-destruction. And the anomic form, appears as an unwelcome handmaiden of progress on the material side, as the advance of the division of labor demolishes the old moral order of regulation and replaces it with the new patchwork of special groups and interests unable to sustain any general collective consciousness.

THE SOCIOLOGY OF RELIGION AND THE FOUNDATIONS OF KNOWLEDGE

The roots of *EF* lie years earlier not only in Durkheim's concern with religion, on which he gave a lecture course in 1894–1895, but more broadly in his conception of science and its relation to evolutionary development and to culture in general.

In *DL* he had made passing reference to religion as a sharing of sentiments, writing that it "corresponds to a region . . . very central to the collective conscience," but had placed his emphasis on the progressive *withdrawal* of religion from the various areas of social life—the intellectual stance of the Enlightenment-rooted liberal (Durkheim, 1964, 169). Some of these earlier views appeared a few years later in his essay "Primitive Classification" (*PC*), written in 1901–1902 in collaboration with Mauss (Durkheim and Mauss, 1963).

In some respects *PC*, published ten years earlier, is an adumbration of *EF*, as well as being a reflection of Durkheim's general methodological canons. In part, it was directed against the vein dominant in psychology, as Durkheim understood it, holding that the development and functioning of the cognitive faculties was a problem having to do strictly with the individual mind (3ff.). It was also an investigation that Durkheim (and Mauss) thought of as having relevance for an understanding of modern rationality, and by implication, science (it "throws light on the genesis, and consequently the functioning, of logical operations" [88]). Like *EF*, *PC* relied heavily on available—and not too reliable—evidence about preliterate Australian tribal organization, supplemented by material on some North American tribes.

Like all of Durkheim's work, it was framed in evolutionary terms. Influenced to some extent by Levy-Bruhl (although Durkheim rejected Levy-Bruhl's theory of the qualitatively different and inferior nature of "primitive" mentality), Durkheim and Mauss begin by arguing that the cognitive categories of any society are reflections of its complexity. Thus, among certain "simple" Australian tribes that are divided into (two) moieties, each comprised of two "marriage classes," "everything in nature . . . is divided between the two classes," e.g., "the wind belongs to one, and the rain to the other" (12). Among tribes where the moieties themselves are divided into *four* marriage classes, the cognitive organization of the world is more complex. Or in a tribe organized into clans and subclans, the cognitive structure of knowledge is hierarchical, but if this structure breaks up and the clans or other units evolve into more or less equal and autonomous segments, the classificatory system reflects this change in conceiving of them all as being on the same level. Among the Zuni, for example, the division of the world into seven regions reflects the seven-clan structure of Zuni society, in which all objects and beings are associated or identified with a particular clan (44ff.).[20] Durkheim and Mauss then sum up what they consider to be the implication of evidence such as this:

> The first logical categories were social categories; the first classes of things were classes of men, into which these things were integrated (82)

And by extension, and of particular relevance in anticipating the two central theoretical propositions of *EF*, they proposed that "if the totality of things is conceived as a single system, it is because society itself is seen in the same way" (83), and that their collective representations are created from "motives of a quite different order" (85), namely, sentiments or affective states of mind. It is the "sentimental affinities" between individuals that are projected in such relations among things (85). In *EF* these "sentimental affinities" would be anchored sociologically in the ritual group.

Like *PC* Durkheim intended *EF* to be something more than a study of religion in some conventional sociological or anthropological sense. He thought of it as an investigation into the "origins of all categories of thought," as Thompson puts it (Thompson, 1985, 122), an intent clearly prefigured in *PC*, indeed, even in *Suicide* and before. This is discussed at some length in the introduction, where Durkheim tells us that "our study is not of interest *merely* (italics mine) for the science of religion," because every religion is also a cosmology and "philosophy and the sciences were born of religion" (9). The fundamental categories of knowledge—space, time, number, and so on—Durkheim seems to say, are *universal*, but receive different expression, or concrete manifestation, in different societies. It is this fact that, in Durkheim's view, makes religion and science related forms of the same underlying reality, and that makes the study of the religions of such "simple" peoples as the Australians relevant for understanding modern complex cosmologies, religious and scientific alike.

Durkheim justified studying the religions of the remote past or "primitive" present on evolutionary grounds. The essential qualities of modern belief systems, he believed, were more clearly evident in earlier, simpler forms of society. And so particularly in the early stages of the

---

[20] Based on Cushing's account (Cushing, 1883).

development of a science it seemed to him that studying the simplest manifestations of its objects would be scientifically most fruitful.

> A science in its infancy must pose problems in their simplest form, and only later make them gradually more complicated. When we have understood very elementary religions, we will be able to move on to others" (Lukes, 1973a, 458; from a work of Durkheim's published posthumously in 1919).

The Australian tribes practiced totemic religion; therefore Durkheim, following many earlier and contemporary anthropologists assumed that totemism was religion's most "primitive" form[21] and interpreted societies wherein its traits[22] were only occasionally or not fully in evidence as being at a point higher on the evolutionary scale.

I said at the conclusion of the section on the division of labor in the preceding chapter that *EF* represented the working out of one important strand of the unfinished business with which that work concludes. This was the matter of establishing the *process* of how the collective consciousness of a society or a group comes into being and is maintained, in short how it is caused.

For Durkheim, religious phenomena are defined *not* in terms of the *content* of the belief system (conceptions of gods, spirits, human origins, nature, etc.),[23] but in terms of an *attitude* that distinguishes all things by virtue of whether they are approached as *sacred* or as *profane*.

> All known religious beliefs, whether simple or complex, present one common characteristic; they presuppose a classification of all the things, real and ideal, of which men think, into two classes or opposed groups, generally designated by two distinct terms, . . . *profane* and *sacred* (Durkheim, 1957a, 37)

Sacred things are distinguished from profane by virtue of their being "considered superior in dignity and power to profane things," especially to

---

[21] Lukes points out a fundamental ambiguity in Durkheim's idea of the "primitive." It could (and did) mean, variously, either the *earliest* or the *simplest* type of society or social organization. Durkheim assumed an identity between these, but as Lukes says, the latter bears within it a basic evolutionary view, whereas the former understanding is divested of this and is associated with nonevolutionary theoretical frameworks. (Lukes, 1972, 456).

[22] Totemic emblems or symbols as sacred; myths regarding the origins of the group associated with the main totems, usually plants or animals; various rites practiced in connection with the sacred emblems; organization by clans (clan structure and totemism "mutually imply each other" [*EF*, 167]); and a cosmology in which all things in the world are organized in terms of their association with the totems and subtotems. Durkheim never questions the assumption, derived from his predecessors, particularly Smith, Tylor, and Frazer, that totemism was, in fact, an actual unified set of social beliefs and practices, and not just a collection of traits assembled by the ethnologist.

[23] Alternative ways of defining religion and theories of "elementary" religion are given extensive discussion by Durkheim (Book 1, Chaps. 1–3) and eliminated from consideration. There is no need to go into detail on all this, except to note that Durkheim, as usual, proceeds by the method of elimination, assuming that by eliminating *a*, *b*, and *c* as fallacious, that *d* and only *d* must be true. (For a critique specifically of Durkheim's use of this procedure in *EF*, see Lukes 1973a, Chap. 23).

humans in their base sense. Furthermore, "in the history of human thought there exists no other example of two categories of things so profoundly differentiated or so radically opposed to one another" (38). These are like two separate and mutually impenetrable worlds, and a movement of an individual from one to the other is, as in the initiation rites of the young among many peoples, a "metamorphosis, a "transformation *totius substanti-ate*—of the whole being" (39). The opposition is so great that it often becomes an antagonism, which may occasion total withdrawal from the profane into the sacred, as in monasticism, or "mystic asceticism" (40).[24]

Religious *beliefs*, then, are "the representations which express the nature of sacred things and the relations which they sustain, either with each other or with profane things" (41). And religious rituals, or *rites*, are "the rules of conduct which prescribe how a man should comport himself in the presence of these sacred objects" (41). These are the two fundamental categories of religion, representing thought and action (36). The beliefs and rites are always to be thought of as common to a group and constitute "the unity" of the group by virtue of the fact that the individuals comprising it "feel themselves united to each other" through this common "faith." The translation of beliefs into rites practiced in common creates a *church*, and there are no religions not embodied in churches.[25]

After distinguishing totemism (as in *PC* considered to be the most elementary religion) from "animism" and "naturalism," which he argues (on rather weak grounds) were derivative from totemism, Durkheim goes on to analyze its nature as a kind of archetype of all religion. The most sacred things are the *emblems*, such as the engraved *churinga* of the Arunta which represent the totem, in its *natural state* typically an animal. Their sacredness cannot be attributable to the totemic objects themselves, since these are "frequently insignificant" and ordinarily play little or no role in the actual religious life of the group (205). It is, Durkheim argues, *society* that "arouses the sensation of the divine" (206). It is the ritual group in which the central *collective representations* (Gods, divine entities, totems, icons, etc.) are brought into being as symbols of the group or society itself. Worship of the sacred totemic emblem is actually worship of the group. The feeling of dependence that all religions supposedly inculcate in their adherents Durkheim interprets as derivative of the sense of dependency inherent in social life itself, with its exteriority and constraint, i.e., the de facto dependence of the individual on the group. The sense of generalized power that Durkheim thinks is found in all religions ("mana," "wakan," "pokunt") symbolizes the power of the group. This construction of the sacred world "gives men a more active

---

[24] Durkheim here juxtaposes ideas which, in Weber's sociology of religion, are *opposed* as elements of mutually exclusive typologies. See Chapter 14.

[25] There is an ambiguity here. Durkheim *expresses* this relationship as an empirical one ("we do not find a single religion without a church") in order to differentiate religion from magic, in which the central relationship is then defined as one between the magician and his *clientele*, but which incorporates no "lasting bonds," unlike the church, which binds people together. The practice of magic, unlike religion, does not give rise to a *community*. This is an example of Durkheim's common practice of argument by *petitio principii*. The possibility of there being religions without rites and churches is eliminated at the outset, despite the seeming empirical foundation of Durkheim's definition.

sentiment of the double existence they lead and of the double nature in which they participate" (219). Individuals make themselves into sacred beings—although there is variation in the intensity of this—and in the hierarchy of sacred things, because they acquire their sacredness from participation in the totemic ritual, come to embody a lesser or inferior quantum of sacredness (221).

With the sacred-profane dichotomy as the conceptual base, Durkheim went on to the series of further issues. First and foremost among these is the question of explaining the very existence and nature of the sacred, i.e., of religion. Durkheim's theorization of this is a continuation of ideas appearing in his earlier works. In *DL* he had virtually identified the collective consciousness with religion in making his case for the causal status of morphological social facts. In doing so, he actually had identified two orders of social fact: a structural one, on the basis of which he distinguished segmental societies from those with an advanced division of labor; and another that was associational, stated mainly in his concept of dynamic density, but Durkheim had made no principled distinction between them. In *Rules* his treatment of the issue was ambiguous: On the one hand, he continued to use the term *morphology*, while seeming to shift its referent to the institutional orders of society; on the other hand, he introduced the term *milieu*, but never really gave it a definitive meaning. In *Suicide*, he quite clearly interprets the milieu as an interactional network, and then—against his own rules—empirically describes the various kinds of milieux, the suicidogenetic currents, in meaningful terms. But in *PC* we are treated to a thoroughgoing structuralist interpretation of the cosmologies of "primitive" societies.

In all this Durkheim kept alive both his primary structuralist and secondary but now somewhat more prominent human agency/interactionist lines of explanatory reasoning. Both appear in *EF*, but in different contexts: the former as "categories"of thought, the latter in the theory of ritual, which we will consider first.

Durkheim develops a fairly elaborate classification of rituals, distinguishing "negative," "positive," and "piacular" types. The first establishes taboos or interdicts and has to be clearly distinguished from magic, which does not involve the principle of sacredness (Book 3, Chapter 1). Positive rituals include the various types of sacrifice, "imitative" or homeopathic rituals, and "representative" rites (Book 3, Chaps. 2–5). The latter category is of particular importance because it is through representative rites that "the social group reaffirms itself periodically" (387). Indeed, Durkheim believes that the rituals of the first two categories are "probably only variations on this essential rite" (387). Piacular rituals (from the Latin *piaculum*) are those addressed to misfortune or calamity, to commemorate or deplore these realities.

These particulars, on which Durkheim elaborates in detail, are less important for our purpose than the overall or general significance of ritual. The very idea of society, of the group as a collective concept and as a unity, is *emergent* in the ritual process.

For a society to become conscious of itself and maintain at the necessary

> degree of intensity the sentiments which it thus attains, it must assemble and concentrate itself" (422)

"Assembling" and "concentrating" mean, for Durkheim, achieving "a state of effervescence which changes the conditions of psychic activity." The participants undergo a transmutation: They are "transformed," and do not recognize themselves; "there is an exhalation of the mental life" that "corresponds to this new set of forces" (422); a "super-excitation" echoes and reechoes through the minds of everyone, in which "every sentiment is expressed without resistence" (215).

It is this setting of concentrated and intense interaction that generates the power of creation. Rites transform the profane into the sacred. Youth undergoing initiation rites, for example, undergo a social death and rebirth (39). The totemic rites of the Australians not only "show one another that they are all members of the same moral community," but that the rite "makes it or remakes it" (358). The ritualization of beliefs serves to "sustain the vitality of these beliefs and keep them from being effaced from memory . . . (to) revivify the most essential elements of the collective consciousness," and to renew the group's sense of unity (375). Times of great creativity, of revolutionary zeal, like the Crusades and the French Revolution, are due to such intensification of interaction (210–211). "The religious idea is born of this effervescence" (218). To be sure, the stark polar contrast between the mundane and sacred is at its greatest in the early stages of evolution; in modern civilization this clear line becomes a blurred gradient (219).[26] But in principle, Durkheim seems to say quite clearly, in all human societies, religion frees the individual from the mundane world of necessity, the world dominated by individual drives and desires, the world of *individual* representations. The "sacred canopy," to employ a term coined by the contemporary Durkheimian sociologist of religion, Peter Berger, is "superimposed on the world of things" (299), thereby creating another very different world.

Now Durkheim acknowledges that this sharp dichotemization of sacred and profane is difficult to maintain; other nonreligious spheres can be ritualized in varying degrees, for example, in the approving or appreciative sentiments of others that result from having performed our duties well, or again, in the deference inspired by "men invested with high social functions," such as chiefs or nobles (213). This is important, for it provides a foundation, in Durkheim's own work, for expansion of the theory of ritual into a general interactionist and constructionist[27] theory of society.

This constructionist theorization of ritual interaction as producing and reproducing the collective representations is a theme that became central to Durkheim's sociology of religion. It represents the end point of his expression of an idea present in his sociology from the beginning, of

---

[26] Durkheim would have said that this is a good example of how the method of seeking the earliest or simplest form of a social phenomenon makes the discovery of its essential nature easier or more likely.

[27] I deliberately use both terms here. The idea of interaction as such does not necessarily imply a constructionist theory, for it is sometimes employed in the narrow sense of being the technology of human association, as, for example, in some exchange theories. *Constructionist* interactionism, on the other hand, designates interaction as the seedbed or generator of shared meaning. It is this sense at which Durkheim arrived in *EF*.

interaction as a level of social life distinct from those of individual and society. Theorization of ritual interaction dissolves the rigid and theoretically constraining polar opposition of society and individual. Theorization of ritual as interaction dissolves the rigid and theoretically constraining polar opposition of society and individual. This advance, incomplete though it was at Durkheim's death in 1917, has been taken by some as his most important and enduring achievement (e.g., Collins, 1975, Chap. 2; and 1981; also, more generally the work of Erving Goffman).

We find Durkheim repeatedly affirming the creative nature of ritual. Now recall that religion, by definition, is comprised of rites and beliefs, its two fundamental categories manifesting the spheres of thought and action, and that to describe rituals we must have knowledge of their objects, these objects being beliefs. We can define the rite only after having defined the belief. And Durkheim does in fact proceed to distinguish the different types of ritual on the basis of the nature of the beliefs that are their objects: negative, positive, and piacular rituals.

This, however presents us with a problem. While it may seem on the face of it perfectly reasonable to say that beliefs are the objects of rituals, Durkheim seems to take this to mean that we can in some sense have knowledge of the belief independent of the ritual: The rite can be defined only after the belief (36). But if this is the case, in just what sense are we to understand the effervescent creativity of ritual that Durkheim describes in such vivid detail? Evidently not in the literal sense of creating the beliefs. From whence, then, come the beliefs, and what is their status in Durkheim's theory of religion?

Durkheim tries to show that religious beliefs are "objective," in the sense of being grounded in the "realities" of the group. Beliefs are symbolic condensations, "collective representations" of *objective* aspects of group life. Drawing on the argument of *PC* Durkheim refers to these as "categories," and he regards them as a special type of "concept," special because of their universality. The rhythm of social life in the group underlies the concept of time; the human group itself finds its symbolic representation in the category of class; the territory it occupies grounds the idea of space; the elemental experience of the exercise of force by (but not, evidently, within) the group gives rise to the category of efficient force (440). The objective universality of the categories gives Durkheim licence to assert that there is

> something eternal in religion which is destined to survive all the particular symbols in which religious thought has successfully enveloped itself (427)

And this is so even though the intensity of religious commitment waxes and wanes (at the moment of Durkheim's writing it was, in his view, clearly at a low point.[28])

---

[28] In a moment of philosophical reflection he remarks, in Nietzschean vein, that (in contemporary Europe) "the gods are growing old or are already dead," but then adds, portentously, "but others are not yet born" (427). In a poetic passage, he presages a future secular rebirth of the revolution of 1789. "A day will come when our societies will know again those hours of creative effervescence, in the course of which new ideas and new formulae are found which serve for a while as a guide to humanity," . . . "and when those hours shall have been passed through once, men will spontaneously feel the need of reliving them from time to time in thought" like the holidays created by the revolutionary calendar (427–428).

These assertions at the very end of *EF* add little or nothing to the claims already advanced in *PC*. In the context of the concluding chapter of *EF*, Durkheim discusses them in only a cursory way, in order to establish the ground for his argument assimilating science to religion, a topic which we will treat shortly. But Durkheim's analysis of specific fundamental religious beliefs is actually grounded in the same objectivist claim. It should therefore be examined in this context.

We have already discussed the nature of the totem and Durkheim's argument that its source is society, and that it is the collective representation of society. In the chapters following this, he analyzes two fundamental types of religious belief, the concept of the soul and the concepts of spirits and dieties.

Durkheim asserts that the idea of the soul is possible only because of the nature of the collective representations themselves, and these are, of course, impersonal and universal. As in the philosophies of Leibniz and Kant, the individual personality is to be thought of as expressing universal, and therefore impersonal, ideals. Kant's categorical imperative is rendered rational because it is divorced from the uniqueness of the individual, universalized and depersonalized, thus becoming an expression of the collective will, rather than—as for Kant—the moral dictum of the individual.

Durkheim's sociological account of the soul is directly parallel to these philosophical understandings, which he believes are in advance of sociology (270). The differences between individuals arising from bodily sensory experiences do not discriminate personalities. Personalization, as distinct from individuation, involves the will, says Durkheim (following Kant) and implies a self-moving being to which considerable autonomy is attributed (171). This grounds Durkheim's idea of the soul as "mana individualized." (Note that individuals, as Durkheim puts it in unmistakable constructionist terms, are "attributed" a relative autonomy; they do not just have it.) Individuals as such, as distinct from personalities, are the slaves of environments, both inner and outer; they acquire autonomy only through the attribution and/or self-attribution (Durkheim is not clear about the significance of the distinction) of being willful and potent creatures; or more accurately, the willfulness and potency arise only as these very attributions are constructed.[29]

The soul is thus essentially the parceling out of the totemic principle, mana, into each individual clan member. It is the individualized form of the sense of moral authority deriving ultimately from the realities of social power or authority. This implies that the parceled out souls should have the essential property of their origin in the collective consciousness, i.e., impersonality. Why, then, is the soul so often represented as a "concrete, definite being, wholly contained within itself . . . the basis of our personality?" (264)

---

[29] Norbert Wiley has interpreted Durkheim's discussion of the sacredness of the individual in *EF* as containing a partially concealed theory of the origin of the self. The self, in this interpretation, is a historical creation originating in the intensely ritualized *milieu* of many early preliterate tribal, and perhaps other types of societies. This interpretation, Wiley argues, is at least as probable an account of the origin of the self as has been proposed in any other theory, including those of Cooley and Mead (Wiley, 1986b). For an earlier statement on Durkheim's tendencies toward interactionism, see Stone and Farberman, 1967.

Durkheim explains this seeming contradiction as a product of later historical development (264), and specifically as accompanying the rise of individualism. Among the primitive Australians it does not have this character. There, the soul is "a very vague thing" (264), "undecided and wavering in form," present here and there, perhaps everywhere; in other words exhibiting a diffused presence much like mana. Furthermore, the doctrine of reincarnation of souls, which Durkheim claims to have established as virtually universal, implies that each incarnate identity be "external" to its "true nature" (265). Again, the way in which we conceive of our own saints, specifically their ability to diffuse their power, understood as a survival of the primitive manifestation of mana, also supports this interpretation. All this suggests that the soul is "contemporaneous with humanity itself" and "not without a foundation in reality" (262), a foundation that is constituted of "the moral conscience" (263).

Now the close association of the soul with the body seems to imply that it could not survive the physical death of its host. Why, then, is this conception of the soul so common? Rejecting other received explanations, including the common interpretation that it provides a way of transcending death (268), Durkheim proposes that the soul's immortality is the only way whereby the fact of the perpetuity of the group could be explained: The forces that account for the perpetuation of the group must also themselves be perpetuated (268). By becoming a collective representation of the group, the idea of the soul (always, of course, some particular idea of the soul) in fact becomes (an important aspect of) the mode of group perpetuation. The collective belief then becomes the condition of its perpetuation in the consciousnesses of individuals.

Durkheim's discussion of the ideas of spirits, heroes, and gods is an extension of his analysis of the soul. Whereas the soul has virtually no power over the body it inhabits, spirits do have powers of specific sorts and the ability to move about. The fact that they are often connected to mythical personages with great powers explains the powers attributed to them. Spirits conceived of as returning souls of ancestors may have powers linked to specific locales where they reside, or to specific events. Belief in ancestral spirits explains the presence of *individual* totems—common in Australia— conceived of as the *externalized* souls of the individuals that possess powers exceeding those of the inner soul. Hence the "double" nature of the soul. In all this the conceptual paradigm of the individual versus collective consciousness quite transparently frames Durkheim's analysis.

The idea of a god is also rooted in totemism. Pantheons of gods of greater or lesser power derive from the idea of mythical ancestors. One or another may come to be attributed especially extraordinary powers; he is depicted as a great hunter, a powerful magician, a founder of the tribe, or the first man. Such a god transcends the clan boundaries and symbolizes the unity of the entire tribe. This is the highest evolutionary point of totemic relition (283ff.).

Many criticisms have been brought against *EF*. Some of these have to do with the errors and misconceptions attending both the data and the interpretations current and available at the time. We have now long known that totemism is not the primeval religion, that its elements probably do not constitute the sort of unity that Durkheim (and others) attributed to it, and that the sacred-profane distinction is probably sociologically near useless in analyzing religion. These difficulties are of no particular interest to us; they are of the sort that occur regularly and necessarily in the practice and advance of science.

There are other problems with Durkheim's analysis, however, that have to do with the very nature and form of his sociology. The most important of these in *EF* has to do with Durkheim's claims that religions, and specially religious beliefs, in some sense have an objective reality, and that this objective reality is akin to if not identical to that of the objects of natural science. Religions, he says, are "natural," "part of nature," in fact, nature's "highest representation." Even in *EF* Durkheim remains a fully commited positivist, and attempts to establish religion, like other social phenomena, in an ontological niche that opens it unequivocally to an approach parallel to that used in the natural sciences. He advances two arguments in defense of this.

The first is grounded in his evolutionary conception of society. Here again he employs the method of elimination. Society "must," he argues, be part of nature because it differs from nature's other realms simply in its greater complexity, and types cannot be discriminated on this basis. The main weakness of this argument is that it simply begs the question. One obviously cannot infer on this basis that *no* other significant differences exist, differences that would discriminate society as a special type. Furthermore, this stipulation could be interpreted as contradicting Durkheim's most important tenet, that human society is a domain sui generis. Something more than relative complexity must be involved, because the latter presupposes an already existing independent entity.

The second argument we are already familiar with: Religious beliefs are objective because they are grounded in the reality of the group. On the face of it, this seems to assume just what it claims to explain, i.e., *some* sort of cognition of the various aspects of group organization. If these realities exist as *prior* concepts, then it is not necessary to invoke the group's ritual experience to explain them. But if they do *not* have such prior existence, they must be pure *constructions*. (On this point see Lukes, 1973a, Chap. 23.) In a strict logical sense, the point must be granted. However, if our account of Durkheim's theorization of beliefs and rituals is correct, the criticism could be logically valid, but vacuous. Central to all societies are processes involving the construction of their own reality; and whether or not structural features of society which may be firmly or clearly articulated by its members are implicated in the construction of their belief systems, and how or to what degree this might be true, are both clearly empirical, not logical questions. Durkheim did not formulate this matter with the precision available in our now more finely articulated sociological language and our expanded understanding of the nature of such processes. But much credit must go to him for the initial insight.

How is Durkheim's analysis of religion in *EF* related to his philosophical anthropology and rules?

Durkheim introduces *EF* with a discussion of *homo duplex* that reiterates his discussion of "dualism." But given the main thread of *EF*, this seems off-centered. In *EF* the collective consciousness acquires a decidedly, even primary, cognitive dimension, as against the earlier emphasis on morality. The bulk of the discussion proceeds in terms of the way individualizing cognitions like the idea of the soul come into being as extensions or manifestations of the collective representations constituting the collective consciousness. The main theme of *EF* is not the repression of the organi-copsychological drives of the individual, but the process whereby the collectivity produces the *social* individual through the "effervescence" of ritual. Religion is a collective amalgam of ritual and belief. Ritual exerts a causal force by collectively emotionalizing, and in the process, transforming, unformulated marginally conscious understandings shared by all about their collective life.

Durkheim thus provides a causal account of the collective consciousness. "Objective" structures are reincarnated in cognitive beliefs through the *causal mediation* of ritual. The ritualizing group is inserted between the collective representations "above" and the morphology or structure "below." Durkheim perhaps sensed that he needed an intermediate interactionist category to break down the rigid polarity of individual and society. The theory of ritual was the last form this took in his writings, and although it was strongly developed in anthropological circles (e.g., by Mauss: see Mauss, 1967), at least four decades would pass before sociology would find itself able to assimilate his fundamental insight, mainly in the work of Erving Goffmann in the 1950s.

SCIENCE, RELIGION, AND SOCIETY

There remains one final aspect of Durkheim's sociology of religion to be discussed. As I noted earlier, Durkheim intended *EF* to be more than just an analysis of religion from a sociological standpoint. In fact, he believed that in *EF* he had established not only the origins of religion, but "that the fundamental categories of thought, and consequently of science are of religious origin" (418). The "categories" must be held distinct from all other aspects of cognition, i.e., from other collective representations (and of course, individual representation as well). They "are the permanent moulds for the mental life," and their role is basic to the development of all other concepts (440). This idea is a direct parallel of Kant's analysis of the transcendental analytic, in which the fixed forms that synthesize and unify all experience are elaborated. Thus, Kant's forms of quantity, quality, relations, and modality, with their trinitarian elaborations into twelve fundamental categories, are reincarnated by Durkheim not as a priori pure categories of the understanding, but as a constructed "social a priori" that frames all experience.[30]

In their religious manifestations, these categories are in varying degrees unsystematically elaborated, contaminated with other ideas not

---

[30] Durkheim more or less in passing claims to have solved the age-old rationalist-empiricist polarity, a quite audacious assertion.

possessing the same ontological status, buried within the welter of particular ideas of every sort. Science elaborates on these categories, which are already more or less objectified in religion, by introducing the critical spirit ignored by religion (420). Scientific thought is thus a "more perfect form of religious thought" (which is also to say a superior form of adaptation in evolutionary advance, therewith justifying its historic role of replacing religion). Science and religion are members of the same species both by virtue of being belief systems that incorporate general ideas founded in the "objective properties of the group" and in the functions they serve for the group.

It is in the elaboration of meaning in terms of the categories, then, that Durkheim finds the objective basis of *both* religion and science. Early in *EF* he argued strenuously that all religions were "true" in this sense (10), and now this argument is extended to science. "A collective representation presents guarantees of objectivity by the fact that it is collective, for it is not without reason that it has been able to generalize and maintain itself with persistence . . ." (436), and it could not have done so were it not in accord with the natural order (437).[31]

Being born of religion, science shares not only the latter's "objective" foundation, but its constructed nature as well. The concepts of science, Durkheim says, do not get their authority from their objective value; being true is not enough to make them believed. The inner power of science resides in the fact that its "force" is drawn from "opinion." Science, in fact, is "dependent on opinion" (436) and must be "in accord" with popular beliefs and opinion generally. The manner in which this occurs is rather mysterious.

> A higher life disengages itself which, by reacting upon the elements of which it is the product, raises them to a higher plane of existence and transforms them" (446)

Religion thus defines the unviersal nature of humankind. *EF* crowns Durkheim's lifework and endows it with its final irony. The Enlightenment philosophers thought that future emancipation required that religion be abolished so that a universal human nature might assert itself. Durkheim's work is a theorization of that human nature which ends up proving—for Durkheim—that future emancipation will, in the nature of things, come to be only with the continued evolution of science as religion.

However, Durkheim's assimilation of science to religion may be challenged. This assertion regarding their unity, or at least their similarity, may be decomposed into three claims: (1) Religion and science are in some common sense "objective" and therefore "true"; (2) they are alike in that their beliefs are in some sense grounded in the "objective properties of the

---

[31] In this and other passages dealing with this issue, Durkheim waffles between two senses of truth; one in which propositions acquire truth value to the extent that they correspond to the putative objective qualities of events in the world; the other, in which truth is understood as a consensus within a group. Durkheim interlards and conflates the vocabularies appropriate to each, for instance, applying the appelation "objective" to the consensus type, leaping from a (hypothetical) observation of a de facto consensus to a declaration that such a truth is thereby "objective".

group"; and (3) they serve a common function of constituting the most important collective representation.

In the case of the first of these, Durkheim seems to say that both religion and science are constituted of beliefs and that these beliefs do not differ in any fundamental way except that science possesses a "critical spirit" not found in religion. But this claim fails to recognize that the beliefs of science are always, at least in the long run, in principle validated by being subjected to criteria of empirical adequacy. Science is in this way a self-correcting enterprise (this is true at least of the practice of "normal science" within a given paradigm). Religion not only does not insist on such criteria for the validation of its beliefs, but typically assigns beliefs validated by faith or other subjective states, on the one hand, and beliefs validated by authority or sacred texts, on the other hand, a higher, frequently even infinitely higher, value than it assigns merely mundane beliefs. Durkheim's own distinction between sacred and profane provides the foundation for rejecting this alleged similarity between religion and science.

The claim that both religion and science have beliefs systems that are grounded in—and so explained by—the structural, morphological, or organization milieux of the group, as Durkheim puts it, the "objective properties of the group," fares no better when subjected to critical examination. Even if we grant Durkheim's claim that religious beliefs are collective representations of certain properties of the group or society, there is no reason to think that this is also true of science. It is easy to see why Durkheim provides no support whatsoever for this claim. For one thing, "science" is not some one simple thing, either today or during Durkheim's time. It is impossible to imagine how the constantly changing conceptions of say, microbiology, astrophysics, chemistry, and yes, even psychology and sociology, are in some sense "categories" reflecting the facts of social organization of a society. And even if Durkheim has in mind the most general characteristics of science, such as the norm of empirical validation, then he is simply wrong.

The main claim here would seem to center on the idea that scientific ideas increasingly constitute the content of the collective representations, displacing religious ones. This is a complex issue for several reasons. For one thing, and most obviously, religions still survive and prosper, and for many of their adherents it is the collective representations of the religion and not of science that command their respect and around which their activities are organized. The Enlightenment belief that religion would be displaced by science is at best a partial and complex truth. Second, there is the problem of definition, by no means an easy one. There are religions without any supernatural conceptions (which qualify as religions under Durkheim's definition), religions without much in the way of social organization (which might not qualify, since there is no "church"), religions that have adapted to most if not all of emerging scientific truth, but that still retain much of traditional belief, even when it conflicts with their scientific beliefs. There are "civil" religions with nothing whatever in the way of traditional or conventional religious content, but which celebrate and ritualize the "people," the "nation," the "state," and other such entities. Such religions may have little if any supraempirical content, and in this sense are not religious, but at the same time have little if anything to do with science. If traditional religions are being superseded by other belief systems, it appears that the most important forms of the latter are nationalism, communism, fascism, and various other "isms," but not science. The "functional substitutes" for religion are various, and science is perhaps one of them. However, it seems to serve this function mainly for its practitioners, less so for the average person. Durkheim's claim that science had to somehow be grounded in or respond to public opinion is a complex question with no clear resolution.[32]

CONCLUSION

In all this we can see how, as in earlier thinkers, the ways in which received conceptions of human nature, social change understood as progress, and ideas regarding the proper and possible forms of what is now clearly understood as a science of society, undergird and permeate the intellectual structure of Durkheim's sociology. The significance of Durkheim's two dualisms can be seen in their implication for his evolutionary scheme. On the progressive side, evolutionary advance will eliminate or at least ameliorate the "transitional" pathologies of anomie, class conflict, and the overburdening of the opportunity structure by seemingly insatiable aspirations. This will occur as industrial societies undergo major morphological transformations in the direction of a limited form of pluralism and a state that intellectualizes but administers little. The social order of the future will not have to be so repressive as the old ones were.

Yet Durkheim never was able to entertain the idea that social pathologies were actually the products of, part and parcel of, the social order itself. In elaborating the need for functional analysis beyond causal explanation, Durkheim tied the functional necessity of the regulation to the intractable egocentricity of human nature. But this is a betrayal of what is perhaps Durkheim's central achievement, the conceptualization—however flawed—of the social order sui generis. And as I have emphasized, the idea of the functional necessity to regulate antisocial behavior that springs from human nature is incompatible with the idea of change as evolutionary progress.[33]

[32] The assertion that science constitutes a new emerging form of religion sets up a clear-cut confrontation between Durkheim and Max Weber. Weber held that the growth of science, far from constituting a new religion, in fact was in the process of destroying received religions but placing nothing in their stead. The theoretical status of religion in Weber's sociology was at least as important as in Durkheim's, but unlike Durkheim, Weber clearly conceived of future societies without religion and without any functional substitutes for religion. Furthermore, he theorized powerfully the processes bringing it into being, the market and bureaucratic organization. Of course, there are problems with Weber's view, as there are with Durkheim's. More of this in Chapter 14.

[33] It may be that Durkheim's later view was more fatalist than progressive. He concluded his "dualism" essay, for example, with the though that "all evidence compels us to expect our effort in the struggle between the two beings within us to increase with the growth of civilization" (1973a, 164). Perhaps Durkheim discerned the portents of war in 1914, just before its outbreak.

Finally, it now seems fair to say that neither science nor the new individualism envisioned by Durkheim are very convincing as remedies for the ills of capitalism, even when conceived in Durkheim's terms. Science, at least insofar as it is assimilated to religion is as arbitrary a code as any other, even though Durkheim was never quite prepared to admit this. And the theory of the new individualism as the integrating moral code of industrial societies has presented little reason to accept it as capable of significantly ameliorating even the social maladies identified by Durkheim.

These deficiencies result in good part from Durkheim's persistent attempts to always see societies as wholes and to relegate to secondary status the forms of inequality and structures of power found everywhere. He insisted that the worst of the inequalities were survivals, that only a socially necessary amount would be manifest in the future, and that this would reflect emerging strong sentiments of justice that would take the form of the cult of the individual. It is easy to see today how pollyanish these ideas are, and in fact, it was not much less difficult to do so even in Durkheim's time. Theorists of the state and of power had for centuries been emphasizing just these themes Durkheim left undertheorized.

In these two chapters I have tried to show the ways in which Durkheim's project is connected to the intellectual movements emerging from the three problematics. As a final word, it may be said in this regard that the fundamental tension running through Durkheim's sociology results from the initial pretheoretical interest in creating a "science of ethics," and the conceptual and technical elaboration of the apparatus constituting its realization. A science of ethics requires that its object be a choice-making individual; an explanatory science (as Durkheim understood it) requires that the sociologically relevant aspects of this individual's action be explained causally. The rendering of the scientific interest in the form of society sui generis makes the individual theoretically derivative, a logical consequence against which Durkheim consistently rebelled. As he himself says in commenting in *Rules* on Hobbes and Rousseau, it is "contradictory to admit that the individual is himself the author of a machine which has for its essential role his domination and constraint" (1958b, 122). This is at bottom a struggle to find a niche for the reason that will show the way to an emancipated social life in the future. In the last analysis Durkheim fails to show just where, in the framework of his sociology, that reason is to be found, and how it will fulfill its historic charge laid down by his Enlightenment forebears.

13

MAX WEBER I

Philosophical anthropology and the
methodology of the historical and social
sciences

THE LIFE, THE WORK, AND THE TIMES

Max Weber (1864–1920) was born in Erfurt, Germany, but soon thereafter
his family moved to Berlin, where his father was a fairly important official
in the Prussian-dominated state bureaucracy of the Bismarck period (1862–
1890). Both the political environment and that of his home were critical for
Weber's later intellectual development and sociological orientation.

Weber attended the universities of Heidelberg, Berlin, and Göttingen
between the years 1882 and 1886, except for one year taken off for military
service. In his early years he seriously contemplated a life of full-time
engagement in politics and only rather reluctantly began an academic career
during the years 1894–1897, accepting professorships in economics, first at
Freiburg, then Heidelberg, which was to become his permanent home.
However, during the years 1897–1902 he fell into depressions so severe that
he was unable to teach, although he attempted to return to the classroom in
1899. Eventually he offered to resign his professorship and was tendered an
indefinite leave of absence by the Baden authorities. He resumed active
participation in academic life for a short time, but once again was unable to
continue, and between the years 1903–1918 he had no academic responsi-
bilities. During the last two years of his life, he accepted appointments at
Vienna and Munich.[1] He died in 1920 with the words "the only real thing
is the truth" on his lips.

[1] For Weber's life see Marianne Weber (1975), Zohn (1975), and Honigsheim (1968). For a neo-
Freudian analysis of Weber's life in relation to his work, see Mitzman (1969). For an account

Between 1903 and 1907 he published a number of essays on methodological issues[2] which became the center of one of the most intense, many-sided, and protracted methodological debates in modern sociology, centering on the issues of "value-relevance" and "value freedom." During this period Weber also began work on the series of works that would comprise his sociology of religion, beginning with his famous analysis of the historical relations between the rise of Protestantism and modern capitalism, later to be followed by his extended studies of ancient Judaism and of the religions of China and India. His works in economic and political sociology were mostly completed during the decade 1910–1920 and were capped by the massive *Wirtschaft und Gesellschaft,* never completed, brought into print only following Weber's death, and fully translated into English only in 1968. Other of Weber's important works have been translated and appear in various places. Important among these are the essays "Politics as a Vocation" and "Science as a Vocation," delivered at Munich before bewildered and disillusioned students following the military collapse of Germany, espousing a principled stoical attitude in the face of shattered ideals and expectations. Weber had also planned a comprehensive sociology of the arts, of which only one part, on the development of Western music, was completed.[3] Much of his other work also appeared posthumously.[4]

Weber was a complex man who lived and labored under great inner tensions that he faced with exemplary stoicism. Many who knew him were impressed by his struggle to lead an ethically principled life, both personally and politically. His was a turbulent and tempestuous personality; once when he was delivering a long and polemical speech during the course of the revolutionary uprisings of 1918–1919 in Bavaria and Berlin, someone suggested that he be stopped, whereupon one of Weber's friends responded, "Would you try to stop a volcano?" His rock-firm belief was that the good

---

of Weber's political thought and activity, see above all Mommsen (1984), but also Dronberger (1971), Honigsheim (1968), and Loewenstein (1965), although the last-named suffers from a somewhat uncritical outlook, perhaps because during his period of association with Weber the author was a young and impressionable marginal figure of Weber's Heidelberg circle. Interpretations of Weber's philosophical side are given in Löwith (1971), Merquior (1980), Brubaker (1984), Jaspers (1963), and Henrich (1953). Other shorter treatments appear in many places.

[2] Three of these were translated and published by Shils and Finch as *The Methodology of the Social Sciences* (Weber, 1949). Weber's general approach was developed at length in the 1903–1904 essays on Roscher and Knies (Weber, 1975) along with the "Logos" Essay (Weber, 1981). Additional untranslated essays are included in the collection prepared by Johannes Winckelman (Weber, 1968).

[3] For the sociology of religion, see Weber, 1948, 1951, 1952, 1958, and 1978b. For the economic and political sociology, see Weber, 1978a, and various short pieces appearing elsewhere. The essays on science and politics, along with various other selections, appear in Gerth and Mills's 1946 translations of various of Weber's works, under the title *From Max Weber: Essays in Sociology* (hereafter referred to as *GM*). The sociology of music appears in Weber, 1969. For a short general discussion of Weber's major contributions to sociology, see Westby, 1977. Even now only around 50 percent of Weber's texts have been translated into English, a fact that has led to a variety of distortions in his reception (see Sica, 1984).

[4] A recent fairly comprehensive bibliography of Weber's works and of the secondary literature appears in Murvar, 1983.

life was one guided by respect for and search for the truth, but also by a personal and passionate commitment to the highest ideals in both private and public life. This dual, and partly contradictory, commitment to both thought and action can be found embedded in Weber's works, particularly those on methodology and politics.

Weber was a liberal with ardent nationalist and strong imperialist sentiments, although late in life he evidently moderated these significantly. In his inaugural lecture at Freiburg in 1895 on the topic of the state's role in national economic policy, at the age of thirty, he could hold that "the *power* interests of the nation are, wherever they are in question, the ultimate decisive interests that must be served by the nation's economic policy" (Marianne Weber, 1975, 217). But during the war he stood with the moderates on the question of war aims—the extent of annexations following Germany's "victory" (see Ringer, 1969). Moreover, his nationalism not only failed to deter him from criticizing the government; it was the basis for persistent and vitriolic attacks not only on government policy, but personal denunciations of the Kaiser (Weber recommended in 1918 that he commit suicide in no-man's-land) and others, including Bismarck who he blamed for what he perceived to be a situation in which literally all German parties lacked both the political sophistication and will necessary for the tasks of the time (Weber, 1978b, 2, Appendix 2, 1381–1469).

Although Weber was never formally involved in politics (he was defeated in his only try for a Reichstag seat in 1918, perhaps because he deigned to "descend" to the level of grubby politicking), he became a well-known, and in certain limited circles, a highly respected figure. He was appointed a delegate to the treaty talks at Versailles in 1918 and was a member of the committee charged with drafting a new constitution. It is worth noting in this connection that although Weber's position reflected somewhat of a shift from his former views in support of a constitutional monarchy incorporating the *"Führerprinzip"* to one of greater support for parliamentary democracy, he never abandoned his nationalism and always regarded democracy less as an end worthwhile in itself than as a necessary expedient for mobilizing support for state policies, including expansionist ones (see, for example, Dronberger, 1971, Chap. 7).

Politically, the Prussian-dominated German policy was more or less polarized between the powerful Junker-based government allied with the Rhein and Ruhr industrialists as junior partners. Weber rejected the legitimacy and competence to rule of the Junkers on the grounds that they had turned themselves into capitalists with only a self-interested class ideology. But he also had a very pessimistic view of the capacity of any of the existing parties—whether liberal or socialist—to govern, especially in the absence of any strong, independent representation of the middle classes, elsewhere the leading modernizing force and bearer of liberal ideals and policies. The Weimar experience seems to have confirmed this view strongly (see Anderson, 1940). Much of Weber's disgust with the political situation, along with his (today) rather unpalatable political views, can be attributed to the fact that the rapid industrialization of Germany after 1870 was not accompanied by the political ascendence of the business-industrial class, as in Great Britain and the United States, and to a more limited extent in France. The German bourgeoisie remained politically—and socially—subordinate to the Junkers, who dominated the state, leaving little political space for an independent and influential politics of the middle.[5] Weber's pessimism about the future of the West runs both deeper and broader than this, but the absence of a viable political vehicle for his liberalism was the plague of his political life.

THE INTELLECTUAL SETTING: THE HISTORICIST MOVEMENT

Of decisive importance for understanding every aspect of Weber's sociology was the German nineteenth century historicist movement. With its roots in eighteenth century Enlightenment romantics like Herder, historicism flowered in the wake of the French Revolution and the devastation wrought by the Napoleonic invasions. It came to be a celebration of German history and culture invidiously contrasted with other modernizing societies, France in particular, but England, Russia, the United States, and others, as well.

Representative figures in the early period were the historians Wilhelm von Humboldt and Leopold von Ranke. Later in the century the historians Johann Droysen, Heinrich Sybel, Friederich Meinecke and Heinrich Treitschke, and the philosopher Wilhelm Dilthey were some of the leading bearers of historicist ideas. Historicism was a broad movement encompassing not just history but other disciplines as well, particularly political science and philosophy. Weber knew many of the leading representatives of the generation preceding his own and was variously critical of and receptive to their work. More of this later.

Since the movement grew up in response to the Enlightenment doctrines of universal history and universal reason and assumed its stance in opposition to them, I shall state its main identifying characteristics specifically in terms of this opposition. In what follows I rely mainly on the work of George Iggers (1968) and Jurgen Herbst (1965).

First, against Enlightenment universal history, the German historians advanced the idea of the uniqueness and specificity of historically emergent cultural entities. The units in question could be everything from an entire civilization to an individual. Often the specifically German uniqueness was compared with the unique emergence of Greek culture after about 600 B.C. Since the uniqueness of a culture was thought to consist of the particularity of its ideas, sentiments, emotional expressions, and the like, historicist doctrine was incorrigibly idealist and militantly antimaterialist.

Second, against the *mechanical* conceptions of social and individual functioning of the French Enlightenment, as in La Mettrie's *Man the Machine,* historicism states the idea of the essential nature of sociocultural entities as *organic.* As mechanism tends to be associated with materialism, the organic metaphor has an affinity with idealism when applied to human entities.

Third, and closely related to its organicism, historicism adopted the Romantic idea that the authenticity or *value* of organic entities springs from their *inner* nature, whereas the positivism of the Enlightenment, as we have

---

[5] Based in part on some of Weber's correspondence, Lawrence Scaff claims that Weber's persistent harsh criticism of Germany has a psychological substratum in Weber's puritanical belief that the nation had never gone through "the school of hard asceticism" associated with the struggles of *independent* bourgeoisies elsewhere (Scaff, 1981, 133).

seen repeatedly, tends strongly to reject inner domains, particularly inner meanings, emotional states, spiritual experiences, and the like, and generally anything "subjective", as having any legitimate scientific status in conceptualizing the proper objects of the historical or cultural disciplines. Closely connected with this is the rather uniquely German idea of freedom, as distinct from its French or English understanding. In this regard Hawthorne remarks that, whereas in England the individual had to *defend* himself against society, in Germany he had to *create* society. This meant that freedom in its English understanding was an *asocial* individualism, while in Germany it took the form of an "anti-individual holism" (Hawthorne, 1976, 112). We will return to this matter later.

Fourth, since the authenticity of things historical and organic is revealed only in their inner nature, the *method* appropriate for studying them must be one designed to penetrate their inner reality and grasp their unique particularity. Broadly speaking, this is the method of *Verstehen,* or understanding (developed mainly by Dilthey [1976, 1961]).

Finally, of quite singular importance, historicism came to focus on the state, in particular, as an expression of these ideas, as expressing a uniqueness in its historical development, and as resting on or reflecting the organic unity of the "people" (*Volk*). This opposes the understanding of the state and its legitimate functions in the liberal theories of the eighteenth and nineteenth centuries. Two rather different versions of this doctrine appear in nineteenth century German thought. The idea of the *Rechtsstaat,* in which, on the one hand, the state *reflects natural law* (a nonhistoricist idea), but on the other, is *ruled by law* in the interest of the freedom of the subjects, appeared during the early historicist period and was strongly influenced by Hegel. Later, with the unification of the many German-speaking principalities under Bismarck and then Kaiser Wilhelm, this idea was displaced by the concept of the *Machtstaat,* which glorified the necessity of a powerful state to defend the autonomy and freedom of the people in the broader political context of competing "Great Powers."[6]

Throughout all of this there is a persistent emphasis on the inevitable flux of things against the permanences of Enlightenment thought—reason, orderly evolution by stages, and related ideas. The world is a multiplicity, not a unity. There are patterns, but no laws. And conflict, not its abolition, tends to be thought of as an incorrigible part of the nature of things.[7]

I wish to emphasize in particular the emphasis on the inner/outer polarity, because of its thematic significance in Weber's sociology. For Weber, this serves as a framing model at all levels of his oeuvre: philosophical anthropology, methodology, theoretical elaboration, substantive analyses. Because of this centrality, some brief prefatory comments are in order.

Perhaps in good part due to the powerful influence of Lutheranism,

---

[6] Iggers points out that historicist ideas were more strongly represented in the smaller states of Germany where more communal institutions continued to maintain themselves against the (mainly Prussian) tendencies in the direction of absolutism (Iggers, 1968, 51).

[7] The term *historicism* has been employed in several not necessarily consistent senses, for example, Karl Popper's broadside against all conceptions of law in history, from Plato to Toynbee (Popper, 1954). For a discussion see Merquior, 1980, 140–142.

a sense of inner emotional experience as the source of whatever is valuable took root in German culture and came to be celebrated and elaborated by intellectuals (like Kant, Hegel, and Herder) in various ways. It has had a strong affinity for notions of organic development; in one fashion or another, historical development is understood as a growing expression of that value. German philosophy, beginning with Leibniz and running up through Hegel and his nineteenth century heirs, consistently expresses this notion in one fashion or another. Always the inner value is seen in terms of its potential for objectification. Objectifications of the inner spirit possess value only to the extent that, or in terms of the way in which they express that spirit authentically.

It is from this standpoint that the peculiarly German understanding of modernism takes its departure. We saw this earlier in Herder, where the commercial spirit, with its origin in the sheer egoism of the individual, expands in the form of a mechanism; society itself increasingly takes the form of a mechanism that not only is not an authentic objectification of the inner spirit, but that stands opposed to and is destructive of it.

This sense of experience polarized between its given "inner" form, authentic and possessing ethical value or validity, and the external mechanical functioning of society or its institutions on a purely rational and calculative basis, frames much of German historical and social science of the period. Furthermore, its significance goes beyond the social and historical sciences; it constitutes one of the major, if not the dominant, critical conception of modernity, a worldview manifested in a variety of ways, perhaps most dramatically in art. One of its most powerful forms, for example, is found in the German expressionist school of the early twentieth century, in the work of painters like Max Beckmann and Oskar Kokoschka. In much of German sociology the essential difference between communal and societal relationships lies in the organic nature of the former as contrasted with the mechanistic nature of the latter. For Tönnies (Tönnies, 1887), for example, *gemeinschaftliche* or communal forms of social life have an organic unity rooted in emotion and feeling, as against abstract reason and the rational calculating mentality of external *gesellschaftliche,* or societal relationships. Such organic conceptions were the principal way in which the conception of the social was formulated in nineteenth century German social thought.

Tönnies's theory of the movement from *gemeinschaftliche* to *gesellschaftliche* relationships, although an epitomization of this *Weltausehauung,* is only a particular case of a very general way of thinking among German social scientists and historians during this period of rapid industrialization, state formation, and bureaucratization. Theories like Tönnies's were, as Bendix aptly puts it, a fusion of romanticism and cynical realism (Bendix, 1960, 21). It is a fusion that lies at the core of Weber's sociology.

WEBER'S PHILOSOPHICAL ANTHROPOLOGY

For Weber, what is distinctive about human action is the capacity of every individual to construct the distinctively human world as meaningful, or more precisely, to *constitute* that world by investing it with meaning.[8] Outside of this human capacity there is nothing but the *meaningless* play of the forces of nature, including the materialistic foundations of human existence. The course of events is nothing more than blind drift. It was for this reason that Leo Strauss, among others, called Weber a "nihilist" and that Bendix understood his definitions of action and social action as formulations that "intended to break with the long Western tradition of a belief in objectively valid meanings" (Bendix, 1984, 40).

Positing meaning-construction as the defining human quality on the basis of which any scientific grasp of the human world would have to come to grips had at least two critical implications for Weber's sociology. The first is that, since ultimately only individuals are the creators of meanings, some conception of the individual must be a critical element in any construction of the social or cultural sciences. Weber's conception of the individual follows from this. Second, it implied a world of irreducible cultural diversity, the history of which could not be presumed to reveal any necessary "universal history," but only an "infinite multiplicity" of sociocultural phenomena. And further, since this diversity necessarily includes values and value systems, it can elicit ultimate commitments from their adherents, and this implies that conflict among and between them, at both individual and collective levels, is endemic to the human condition.

We will take up these topics in the following sections.

The Conception of the Individual in Weber's Philosophical Anthropology[9]

It should be emphasized at the outset that the primacy of the individual for Weber did not imply acceptance of natural law conceptions of human nature like those of the French Enlightenment. The essays in which Weber analyzes the methodological foundations of the economic historians Wilhelm Roscher and his former teacher Karl Knies, whom he succeeded at Heidlberg, contain a series of polemics against several variants of this position (Weber, 1975). He attacks Knies's conception of "basic instincts" of self-preservation and perfection, for instance, knowledge of which, according to Knies, is a requisite for historical study and explanation (199–207). Against this view, Weber maintains that any such "attempt to 'analyze' man into discrete 'instincts' is the fundamental error of the earlier (classical) methodology" (201). Similar points are brought against the psychologist Munsterberg, Roscher, the historian Benedetto Croce, and others. Elsewhere, he scores economic theory for its presumption of an unambiguous relationship between alleged psychological principles or axioms and the explanatory power of economic theory, maintaining that "on the contrary, insight into the psychological

---

[8] For discussions of Weber's philosophical anthropology, and its import for his sociology, see the following: Barker, 1980; Bendix, 1984; Brubaker, 1984; Brunn, 1972; Burger, 1976; Eisen, 1978; Henrich, 1953; Kronman, 1983; Levine, 1981; Löwith, 1982; Nelson, 1974; Oakes, in Simmel, Introduction, 1977; Portis, 1978; Schutz, 1967; and Swidler, 1973.

[9] Especially useful recent discussions of Weber's concept of the individual appear in Brubaker (1983), Oakes (1977), and Portis (1978).

preconditions and consequences of institutions presupposes a precise knowledge of the latter and the scientific analysis of their structure" (Weber, 1949, 88). Far from claiming that human economic (or any other) orientations can be adequately described by attributions of or generalizations about "fundamental" psychological motives held to be constants of human nature, Weber insists that what interests us about the attitude of an individual in any situation is "specifically particularized," depending on the significance of the situation (89).

The same sorts of strictures may also be found in the context of Weber's empirical work. Much of his long prospectus for the study of industrial workers prepared in 1909, for example, is an argument attempting to establish the inadequacy of an explanatory model that attempts to deduce worker's motivations from psychological (or biological) models, and establishing the necessity for analysis of the complex *meanings* that are collective in nature and that require *historical* explanation (Weber, "A Research Strategy for the Study of Occupational Careers and Mobility Patterns," in Eldridge, 1971b, 103–155).

For Weber, individuals have "personality" to the extent that their actions come to be self-reflective and more or less consistent attempts to realize ethnically significant values. This idea antedates Weber and runs deep in German culture, especially intellectual culture, epitomized in the concept of *Bildung,* meaning the process of education or cultivation of the individual, as distinct from instruction or training (*Unterricht*). Karl Jaspers, Weber's close friend and colleague at Heidelberg, distinguished between technical or practical education and "the forming of *personality*[10] in accordance with an ideal of *Bildung,* with ethical norms. . . . Education is the inclusive, the whole," and "related to the whole empirical existence of the individual" (quoted in Ringer, 1969, 87).

Weber's concept of "personality" is a close variant of this ideal, but with an emphasis on the existentialist idea of values being realized only through *struggle.* "Personality" emerges, grows, and is modified through struggles in which there is a constant *forming* of the individual. Although Weber nowhere elaborates this idea systematically, it is fair to say that for Weber, as for Simmel, the struggle to realize values implies both freedom and rationality: *freedom*[11] to make choices, and the exercise of *reason* in the process. Conflict is both *creative* and ultimately *tragic*: creative because the highest ideals are formed only in struggle with other ideals (Weber, 1949, 57), tragic because the objectifications brought into being through that freedom inevitably undermine the unity of self and culture. In this Weber shared in the tragic romantic outlook that became so central to Schopenhauer and Nietzsche. Early romanticism had understood the flowering of human culture as an expression of the freely acting creative spirit of the individual, culture of infinite variety and so not comprehendable through the dry

---

[10] *Underlining* mine.

[11] In its broadest concrete sense Weber understood freedom as the inner growth of the conscience, seen most clearly in his analysis of the Protestant ethic. This is essentially unconnected with the Anglo-American identification of freedom with political and economic liberalism. On this and related points, see Turner and Factor (1984), Chapter 3.

calculations of science. The pessimistic turn in the romanticism of the late nineteenth century sees such objectifications as a Frankenstein monster now out of control blindly subduing the very human creativity whence it sprung. The roots of this can be found in Hegel and Feuerbach, and its shoots and branches appear in Marx's theory of alienation. Elements of it appear in the work of other German sociologists contemporary with Weber, such as Simmel (see particularly his *Philosophy of Money*: Simmel, 1979) and Tönnies (Tönnies, 1963), but in Weber it is a *Kulturpessimissmus* that comes to be central to his entire sociology.[12] In much of what follows we shall see how this outlook shaped Weber's sociology virtually in its entirety.

Weber's philosophical anthropology is a form of *ontological* individualism, as distinguished from *methodological* individualism. In the former the individual reality is taken to be ontologically prior to all other domains. This carries with it problems to be discussed later. In Weber's case the most important of these probably has to do with his presupposition that the social order rests on the rational choice making of individuals qua individuals, sometimes referred to as his "decisionism" (Henrich, 1953; Habermas, 1975, Part 3, Chap. 1) and the relation of this to the formation of the nature of the social order although he held, that "one could as well claim . . . that 'irrational' emotions and feelings played the fundamental role in human action" (Weber, 1981, 152), and although he seemed to recognize that such a rationalistic foundation would have the consequence of distorting the entire science in a rationalistic direction, Weber, as we shall see, clearly did place rationality at the core of his formulation of social action. Despite this, however, nowhere in his mature writings does Weber provide an unambiguous account of what is involved in such choice making (thereby leaving him open to the charge that his conception of action is at root "decisionist" (e.g., Henrich, 1953).[13] The overwhelming emphasis throughout Weber's actual sociological analysis falls on the *constraints* within which human action occurs.

---

[12] On the significance and social origin of German *Kulturpessimissmus*, or the profoundly tragic outlook regarding the possibilities of the survival of Western culture, see Kalberg, 1987. For an argument assimilating Weber to the outlook as it appears in Jakob Burckhardt, as well as Nietzsche and Schopenhauer, see Bendix, 1965.

[13] In his speech "Politics as a Vocation," Weber does present a discussion that, if only indirectly, has some bearing on this issue. Here Weber distinguished between two types of ethics, that of "absolute ends," and rather ambiguously, of "responsibility." In the former, one acts without regard to the consequences of one's actions. Values are pursued as ethical absolutes, and this may permit the justification of any and all means (as in the instances of Bolsheviks, on the one hand, and the Sermon on the Mount, on the other [Weber, 1946, 118ff]). In the ethic of responsibility, consideration of the consequences of action is critical. Such conduct "takes account precisely of the average deficiencies of people" (121). It is thus a calculating practice involving a principled weighing of means against one another *and* with regard to ends, to the end of being able to assess as far as possible their unintended or unforeseen consequences.

Both ethics in their extreme forms tend to break down in paradox. Without the capacity to assign primacy to one goal as over against others, the ethic of responsibility becomes no more than "principled opportunism" (120), affording the politician justification to indulge his personal vanity. Politicians degenerate into "political philistines and banausic technicians" (125). The ethic of absolute ends inherently flirts with the "diabolical forces lurking in all violence" (125–126), and "goes to pieces" when confronted with a world

Weber's philosophical anthropology was mainly a product of a long development of German idealistic philosophy. After Kant, this became a series of attempts to reunite the moral and cognitive sides of human experience that had been so radically sundered by the Königsberg philosopher. Hegel had attempted this and in the process discovered that the self was not a static entity or some sort of essence, as in Greek and Christian thought, but rather a process in which thought was "self-moving" and the self as the subjective element in experience could be grasped only in terms of its relation to external or "objective" processes (see Chap. 9 of this book). This was a truly momentous *tour de force* in its implications for sociology, although flawed in its insistence that the dialectical process is a historical necessity.

Among Hegel's contemporaries, Fichte in particular came closest to identifying the manner in which the essential quality of the self, its reflexivity, was implicated in the social process. Fichte formulated a conception of the self, as Joas puts it, "dependent on objectifications of praxis and a dialectical relation between the delimitation of the self and its embeddedness" (Joas, 1985, 44). For Fichte, the individual realizes him or herself in action through identification with whatever it is that must be done. At any particular moment the world presents itself as a task to be achieved, and the individual, rather than being conceived of as an already realized or unchanging entity, realizes him or herself through this achievement. Fichte's self is thus an active entity standing in a continuous relation with the "non-self," i.e., the world. The transformations of the world that occur through human action are the objectifications of that action and constitute new conditions for a continuing but *changing* and *reflexive* self.

German philosophy and social science after Fichte, however, never carried these ideas forward in a manner that might have rendered them serviceable for a more explicitly sociological account.[14] What did emerge from this conception of the individual was a variant that found its "modern" formulation at the turn of the century in Weber and others like Karl Jaspers. In this doctrine the individual was the creator and bearer of all "value," and the "objectifications" of society were expressions of this. The German

---

"governed by demons." The great contradiction attending the practice of any ethic of ultimate ends has to do with its inherent unconcern with means ("the ends justify the means"), thus inviting employment of the ultimate means—violence. The textual evidence seems to suggest that Weber conceived of responsible political—and by extension, perhaps, social behavior in general—as a kind of balance of the two ethics. "An ethic of ultimate ends and an ethic of responsibility," he writes, "are not absolute contrasts but rather supplements, which only in unison constitute a genuine man—a man who *can* have the 'calling for politics'" (127). Politics requires "both passion and perspective," and "all historical experience confirms the truth—that man would not have attained the possible unless time and again he had reached out for the impossible" (128).

This seems to suggest that Weber's "personality" ideal is one that implies an ethic *transcending* the two ethics, one focusing on the *value* of *balancing* one against the other. The creative politician—or anyone else—must somehow find this point in the real demonic worlds of struggle and power. (See Brubaker, 1981, for a discussion.)

[14] An account that G. H. Mead was ultimately to formulate. Both Hegel and Fichte were appropriated by Mead in a powerfully creative way, such that much of what was valuable in their work still lives on in interactionist grounded sociology. See Chapter 15 of this book.

nineteenth century idealist tradition is thus an attempt to salvage theoretically the Romantic conception of the individual from submergence within or being overwhelmed by mechanistically conceived forms of social life. And historically, as commercialization of relations and industrialization of production proceeded apace and as the power of the reformed Prussian state expanded, this conception of the individual experienced an increasingly acute crisis. The Kantian duty-immersed moral individual metamorphosed through Hegel and Fichte into the free value-creating individual of late nineteenth century German idealism. This was the main source of Weber's philosophical anthropology, and the inner-outer polarity that frames his sociology. "What appears to underlie all of Weber's major statements," as Jones puts it, "is the neo-Kantian opposition between the world of the spirit and that of a mechanical rationality" (Jones, 1975, 751). The import of this can be seen in both Weber's methodology and substantive work.

History and Conflict: The Implications of Weber's Conception of the Individual

The sociocultural reality implied by Weber's understanding of the individual as a freely choosing and freely acting meaning-constructor is one of great diversity and constant flux. History appears as both a relativity and an "infinite multiplicity" of values constantly undergoing change and in conflict with one another.

Now, like his concept of the individual, Weber's view of sociocultural reality was no novelty entirely of his own making, but one with deep roots in German historical scholarship since Hegel. In Hegel's "magnificent conceptual apparatus," as Weber referred to it (Weber, 1975, 206), history was an immanent dialectical and *universal* unfolding in which higher and higher degrees of freedom were being realized (see Chapter 9 of the book). Even before Hegel's death in 1831, German historians such as Wilhelm von Humboldt (older brother of Alexander von Humboldt, the reformer of the University of Berlin) and Leopold Ranke both assimilated and reacted against Hegel's theory of history, retaining the organicist idealism but rejecting the speculative, universalizing side. For these and others like Alfred Droysen, Jacob Burckhardt ("one of the giants of the earth" [Weber to Honigsheim, in Honigsheim, 1968, 54]), Theodor Mommsen (so impressed by Weber's second doctoral dissertation, the *Habilitationschrift*, that he practically nominated "the esteemed Max Weber" to succeed him—at the age of 27!), and Treitschke (one among those against whom Weber directed his polemics regarding using their lecture halls for political purposes but whom he otherwise respected [see "Politics as a Vocation," in Gerth and Mills, 1946]), historical thought and scholarship was understood to constitute a special category, distinct from the science of nature, but also from that of speculative philosophy.

These scholars of history conceived of their task, in the famous historiographic epigram of Ranke, to reconstruct history "*wie es eigentlich gewesen.*" Ranke wanted to free history from philosophical speculation (of which Hegel represented the epitome) to "investigate the bare truth without embellishment ... through investigation of concrete, individual cases"

(Herbst, 1965, 103). Historical methodology was to reveal the *facts* of history, but more than this: to do so in the context of the understanding that those facts were the objectifications created by human actors in forms that reflected their valuational or ethical ideals. Here was the element of freedom. For Ranke, history was the discipline in which the facts are imaginatively reconstructed in their relation to the ideas that brought them into being through practical action. This necessarily becomes something very different from the kind of science practiced by natural scientists; it has more of an affinity with what the poet does, because it requires the exercise of the synthesizing imagination as an indispensable component of the method.

To reiterate insistence on the uniqueness or individuality of socio-cultural phenomena and the role of the imagination in investigating them are central principles of German historicism. As I said earlier, much of the work of these historians came to focus around the conception of *Volk*, understood as possessing a common language and culture on which their unity rests, and especially after Fichte, constituting a *national* unity, or nation, and ultimately a state that supposedly grows out of and reflects that unity. The concept of a *Volk* derived from the enlightened romanticism of the eighteenth century, and perhaps especially from Herder (see Chapter 6 of this book), expressed the ideal of a *cultural* unity under the condition of extreme political fragmentation prior to unification by Bismarck under Prussian hegemony. It was a concept employed not only by culture historians, but those in other disciplines as well, psychologists like Wilhelm Wundt, for instance, and members of the *Volkswirtschaft* school of economics like Knies, and even, in considerably modified form, by Tönnies in his concept of *Gemeinschaft*. The concept of *Volk* came close to constituting something like the "ethos" of German social science during the latter half of the nineteenth century.

Weber assimilated this conception of history, but by no means uncritically. Particularly critical of the organicism of the school, he takes Roscher and Knies to task for their Hegelian conception of society. To Knies's claim that "there is something eternal and invariable in all human life and activity . . . for no single man could *belong to a species* unless he, along with all individuals, were *bound to the common totality,*" Weber responds by saying that such formulations are conflations of actual collectivities and the "abstract concepts" that represent them, and that this sort of thinking is one example of the "rationalist consequences" to which "the epigones of Hegelian panlogism continue to cling . . ." (Weber, 1975, 206). Roscher is similarly charged with committing himself to "an organic mode of thought that borders on a Hegelian form of emanatism" (90), despite the fact that he self-consciously intended to distance himself from Hegel. In this critical respect Weber strenuously disassociated himself from *some aspects* of the romantic organicist "mainstream"[15] in German historiography.

Weber was equally critical of the practice of harnessing a psychobi-

---

[15] Meaning that there were important exceptions. Treitschke, for instance, rejected attributions of organic unity to state forms as totally misleading, on the grounds that the essence of the state was "will" and that this is not a property of organisms. "The state is power, precisely in order to assert itself against other equally independent powers" (Treitschke, 1963, 12).

ological conception of the individual to an evolutionist conception of history in order to ground the lawlike unfolding of the latter, on the one hand, and proclaiming the freedom of the individual (in the sense discussed earlier), on the other. He expresses astonishment that the same author (Knies) who in one section of his book celebrates the Enlightenment doctrine of the freedom of the individual, in another insists on characterizing history as the domain of "nomological regularity." And like others before him, he (Knies) is taken to task for grounding this claim in a notion of a "uniform 'instinctual force' which lies behind it" (207). Weber dismisses this as just one more unfortunate example resulting from the influence of "the atrophied remains of the great Hegelian idea" (207).[16] This is not unfamiliar terrain: A similar clash between the problematics of human nature and social change was a volatile incubator of the sociological outlook throughout the nineteenth century.

The human social order, as Weber thought of it, presents itself first, under material conditions of scarcity that constitute natural adversities for all human collectivities. The existential condition of all human life, individual or collective, involves struggle not only with the environment, but within the human world as well. There is more than a touch of Hobbes in this, and perhaps more yet of Marx and Darwin, but with a difference. There is and always will be a plenitude of conflict rooted in the scarcity inherent in the material conditions of life. But for Weber this was only part of the matter. Against Marx, he held that values are more than just reflections of, or "superstructures" rationalizing, material interests. The fact that they neces-

---

[16] Despite Weber's critical attacks on these various representatives of evolutionism, he himself has not infrequently been interpreted as an evolutionist. Parsons advanced this interpretation in his *The Structure of Social Action* in 1937 (Parsons, 1949, 621) and reiterated it in later work (e.g., his "Discussion," in Stammer, 1971, 27–50). Gerth and Mills write that "we . . . feel justified in holding that a unilinear construction is clearly implied in Weber's idea of the bureaucratic trend" (1946, 51). Badie and Birnbaum maintain that Weber is an evolutionist in his theory of the state (1983, 17–24), and Tenbruck argues that Weber's sociology of religion is evolutionary (Tenbruck, 1980).

On the other hand, this interpretation seems to be challenged by much that is central in Weber's work, a good deal of it along the lines of the passage just cited, along with some of his political writings (Roth, in Roth and Schluchter, 1979, 195–206) and has been rejected, at least in part, by many leading Weber interpreters. His close friend and colleague Ernst Troeltsch, for instance, wrote that Weber, in following Rickert, "renounced every kind of *dialectic* or *organicist* notion of development (and) consciously abandoned universal history and replaced it by comparative sociology" (Roth, in Bendix and Roth, 1971, 230; also Bendix, 286, and Roth, 1975). Schluchter thinks "Weber's work can be viewed as the gigantic effort to refute the basic assumptions of every kind of evolutionism" (Schluchter, 1981, 4). Honigsheim juxtaposes Weber to Hegel, whom he says Weber thought of as the man "having a position at odds with his own" (Honigsheim, 1968, 14, n.5). And Weber's critique of the idea of progress rested on his conception of the role of values in social science; specifically, that goals cannot be derived from "even the most unequivocal tendencies of development," is a clearly antievolutionist position. Certainly his attacks on universal history are a polemic applying not only to the German historians but to evolutionists like Comte and Spencer, and historical materialists alike. And he explicitly maintained that the history of Europe was comprehensible in terms of neither linear nor cyclical development (Runciman, 1978, 314), arguing specifically against the use of parallels for *the purpose of discovering laws*, by which he meant laws of universal history. (It is not that the discovery of parallels is itself scientifically objectionable; indeed, in a specific sense, as we shall see later in our discussions of ideal types and causality, their discovery is the very essence of historical science.)

sarily arise in the context of material interests of some sort—for such interests are fundamental to the human condition—does not mean that they are determined, or even in many instances very powerfully conditioned, by those interests. Weber held that individuals everywhere act on the basis of their life *meanings,* and these may or may not involve concrete material interests. This axiom led Weber to posit not only the partial, or better, the *variable* autonomy of the sphere of values, but also its incorrigible conflictful nature. Not only the material side of life, but the realm of meaning systems as well, he thought of as being suffused with conflict or the potential for conflict, and the entirety of his sociology reflects this. In his Munich lecture "Science as a Vocation," he pronounces as "the one fundamental fact, that so long as life remains immanent and is interpreted in its own terms, it knows only of an unceasing struggle of the gods with one another" (Weber, 1946, 152). Raymond Aron refers to Weber's metaphysics as "partly Darwinist,[17] partly Nietzschean" and avers that they define "the struggle for life" (Aron, discussion in Stammer, 1971, 93). For Weber, "a world without conflict is effectively inconceivable," "values . . . are in irreconcilable conflict" (94), and he was "obsessed by the vision of struggle everywhere and at all times" (95).

The clash of interests thus occurs in the domain of the ideal as well as the material. But this is not Hegelian or Comtean idealism, in which ideas *as such* are in control. Rather, "not ideas, but material and ideal interests, directly govern men's conduct" (Gerth and Mills, 1946, 280), Weber writes in 1915 (in his introduction to his series of studies in the sociology of religion). Ideas *as such* have no significance whatsoever from the standpoint of our sociological interest in them, but only in so far as they become constituent of interests, as in, variously, rationalizations of shared emotional states (e.g., in Nietzsche's theory of resentment), systematized articulations of a group's economic interest (e.g., in Marx's concept of ideology), or in defining an ideal of worldly service (e.g., in various branches of Protestantism).

In these and a variety of other forms, ideas become the stuff of struggle and in complex ways enter into relations with *material* interests. The interplay of material and ideal interests can be understood as having the theoretical status of a "world hypothesis" (Pepper, 1970) in Weber's sociology.

It appears that in this formulation, Weber was at once detaching himself from historical materialism while retaining what he regarded as indispensable in that theory. (In this regard it should be noted that at the time historical materialism was understood to be thoroughly and unequivocally economistic). The emphasis on ideal *interests* is in one sense a *broadening* of the Marxian restriction of the term to essentially economic matters, itself a product of the eighteenth century narrowing of the idea from the larger, essentially political, meaning it had acquired during the Renaissance (see Hirschman, 1977, 10, *et passim*). And in rejecting the Marxian determinacy (or near-determinacy, depending on one's interpretation; see Chapter 10 of this book) of ideas by the conditions under which they arise, Weber avoids

---

[17] Perhaps an unfortunate emphasis. Weber goes to some length in *Economy and Society* to downplay the sociological significance of selection, coming close to ruling it beyond social science analysis in defining it as struggle, "without a meaningful orientation in terms of conflict" (Weber, 1978b, 38).

the Marxian difficulty of having one's basic proposition come back to undermine the validity of the very theory to which the proposition is central. From *this* standpoint, Weber's "causal agnosticism," as Kronman has called it (Kronman, 1983, 119), is a strong point of his sociology.

Weber's concept of the individual and of history clearly situates Weber close to those who responded to Enlightenment thought by uncovering and giving primacy to the seemingly *irrational* side of human action. Philosophers like Schopenhauer and Nietzsche, the sociologist Vilfredo Pareto, and of course Freud, were among the more prominent figures of this anti-rationalist critique of the Enlightenment, carried forward later by twentieth century manifestations such as the Frankfurt School, which attempted to blend Marx and Freud during the late Weimar period and decades to follow. This movement goes well beyond, say, the reasoned skepticism of Hume, in not only downplaying the potency of reason as a social force, but in countering that emphasis with portrayals of human nature as incorrigibly irrational, and in predicting the decline and demise of Western culture on this basis (the "death of God," as Nietzsche expressed it), as the barbarian within overwhelms the sluice gates of religion and culture.

Weber's philosophical anthropology stands in a critical, but complex and ambiguous relationship to both his methodology and his theoretical and empirical work. Its significance for various aspects of the latter will be examined in the following chapter. We turn here to an examination of the methodology.

THE METHODOLOGICAL FOUNDATIONS

Apart from Marxism, an ambiguous case, the major sociologies of the nineteenth and early twentieth centuries, although often defining their subject matter idealistically, were generally positivistic in their basic methodological orientation. The most important exception to this generalization occurred in Germany during the latter decades of the century. There, the somewhat different understanding of sociocultural phenomena led to the debate known as the *Methodenstreit* ("controversy over method") in the discipline of economics. This amounted to a sustained inquiry into the foundations of the historical disciplines and involved an elaboration of a conception of social science quite different than that dominant in the Anglo-Franco tradition. The roots of the controversy can be traced to the late eighteenth and early nineteenth century thinkers, especially Kant, Herder, Hegel, and Goethe, but, more immediately and importantly, historians like Otto Ranke. The debate reached its high point in the 1880s with the rise of the marginalist school of the Austrian economist Carl Menger (see Menger, 1950), and the reaction to this by members of the "national economics" school, known as the *Kathedersozialisten*,[18] the most prominent of whom was Gustav Schmoller.

---

[18] A term of derision originating among nonacademic socialists, meaning "socialists of the chair," or "socialists of the lectern." They were mostly economic historians or economists who

Weber's essays on the theories of the economic historians Roscher and Knies were an attempt to resolve the question of whether, and in just what ways, the historical disciplines required a grounding fundamentally different from that of the disciplines dealing with nature. The essays are therefore more than just an inquiry into and critique of the theories of Roscher and Knies, ranging as they do over contributions not only of economists, but of historians, philosophers, psychologists, and aestheticians as well. It is characteristic of Weber in his generally polemical methodological essays to treat problems of general import in the historical disciplines in the context of a critique of specific authors or treatises. He clearly regarded his arguments in his essays on Roscher and Knies (Weber, 1975) as applying across the range of the historical disciplines.[19]

It is important to note at the outset that the *Methodenstreit* was a controversy carried on under the assumption that, whatever the differences between the natural and historical disciplines, there was a range of human activity that could be legitimately subject to *scientific* analysis. It therefore rejected the more extreme *historicist* position that the human sociocultural domain was amenable *only* to a historical, i.e., a nonscientific approach. More on this point shortly. The *Methodenstreit* was thus a controversy, first, over what aspects of social life this designation might legitimately include, and second (and more important), just what it must *mean*, in any case, to be an object of *scientific* knowledge.

Menger had argued that, although employment of historical materials and conceptions of historical phenomena were admissible, even necessary, in economic analysis, the search for and discovery of transhistorical "general" *laws* of economic activity was the sine qua non without which economics could never establish its claim to be a *scientific* discipline. The historians, or

---

opposed the marginalist variant of classical laissez-faire economics as a basis for state policies, advocating instead state intervention in economic matters. Many of Bismarck's social welfare innovations, such as pension funds and medical benefits, originated with this group. Menger was a marginalist. To some extent this pejorative identification was unmerited, since the group advocated a wide range of social policies (some never enacted) in Wilhelmenian Germany, including schemes to socialize the railroads, progressive taxation, factory inspection laws, social insurance, and collective bargaining arrangements (Ringer, 1969, 147). On the other hand, they had no connection with the real socialists of the time, most importantly the Social Democratic Party (SDP), and came to be increasingly identified with the conservative and authoritarian ideology and practice of the regime.

The principle organizational vehicle of the group was the *Verein für Sozialopolitik* (Social Policy Association), founded in 1872 by Schmoller and others, including Adolf Wagner, Roscher, and Knies, to counter the growing free trade ideology and practice centered mainly in the north. The central theoretical position of the group was an idealistic conception of history—naturally—wedded to a natural science methodology, including an acceptance of statistics (which for some of them seemed to be a way of reconciling their ethical voluntarism with their methodological determinism, of making history scientific without denying free choice). By the 1890s, with the infusion of new younger members, especially sociologically inclined ones like Weber, Tönnies, and Werner Sombart, a generation-based schism along both theoretical and political lines began to develop. Weber's critiques of Roscher and Knies reflect the former; his political liberalism (and even momentary dalliance with socialism) the latter. (For a short treatment see Ringer, 1969; a slightly more detailed one is given in Herbst, 1965, esp. Chap. 6.)

[19] See Oakes's discussion of this point in the introduction to *Roscher/Knies*.

some of them at least, argued that such abstract general "ahistorical" laws could never properly apply to the domain of human activity, even to economic activity, for various related reasons, which included the argument that such laws were inconsistent with their conception of human freedom. Human institutions, including economic ones such as markets and trade associations, should be conceived of as objectifications of the human spirit and will, and as such were infused with ethical significance. Such phenomena were necessarily beyond reduction to the type of laws that constituted the knowledge ideal of classical economics, modeled as this discipline was on mechanics. However, this did not preclude pursuing an understanding of economic life through discovery of so-called historical laws, which in more or less Hegelian fashion were thought to be expanding the sphere of human freedom.

The broader framing conception of knowledge within which the Methodenstreit was argued out was the distinction, essentially Dilthey's, between the *Naturwissenschaften* and *Geisteswissenschaften*. This distinction was not identical with the Anglo-Franco division between the natural and social or cultural sciences. The idea of a *Wissenschaft* corresponds more or less to that of a "discipline," understood in the sense of a systematic pursuit of knowledge of some domain of reality, and formulated in a systematic and unified way. Whether such a practice and body of knowledge was "scientific" or not was another question: some disciplines, like physics, were unequivocally so; others, for example, hermeneutically grounded biblical studies, were quite clearly not. Further, the idea comprehended by *Geisteswissenschaften* has no easy English equivalent. It designates something on the order of those disciplines taking as their objects the inner experiences of the human spirit, mind, and will, and the *objectifications* of these as they appear in history as unique and valuational manifestations. This again reveals the historicist inner/outer polarity. Objectifications of mind, spirit, and will have value insofar as they are *authentic* manifestations. To the extent that they are not, they are lifeless or mechanical, thus inauthentic. Idealist historiography had seemed to establish the domain of the *Geisteswissenschaften* as one that could *not* yield knowledge in scientific form, i.e., one not amenable to natural science methodology and principles of explanation (see Parsons, 1949, 473–487; Hughes, 1958, 186ff.; Herbst, 1965, 55–58). Such historical knowledge cannot take the form of explanation (*Erklären*), as in the natural sciences, but rather understanding (*Verstehen*). This requires a very different method, one involving use, but *systematic* use, of the imagination. The basic task, then, in the words of Dallmayr and McCarthy, becomes an examination of the "manifestations of human creativity and intentionality with the goal of recapturing in past documents and cultural records the original spirit that animated their authors" (Dallmayr and McCarthy, 1978, 4). This procedure can be expected to yield a form of knowledge superior to that of *Erklären*, since, with Vico, "only what mind has produced, mind can fully understand" (4). This case for such study was formulated in its most sophisticated form by Wilhelm Dilthey.

In Vician vein, Dilthey rejects all "objectivist" conceptions of history, insisting that history is a human creation, and that this is "the first condition that makes scientific history possible" (Dilthey, 1961, 67). However, *Verstehen* depends on access to what is inaccessible to the senses and can be experienced only "inwardly" (69). The source of the objectifications of history is the will: "The will strives to achieve development and form" (69). Such forms reflect only differences of degree rather than of kind and can be grasped as complex unities of mental qualities. However, they defy subsumption under laws. Nomological knowledge is appropriate to the spheres of nature, but cultural forms require a version of *Verstehen*.

> The various units (cultural systems, nations, states) have structures of their own and are complexly interrelated with each other. Hence they provide the historian with intelligible patterns which his research can recapture (Rickman, in Dilthey, 1961, 136).

Verstehen, then, Dilthey claims, can grasp the full range of human culture if developed by the historian in a systematic fashion.

But is not knowledge created in this fashion intrinsically relativistic? Dilthey's response is that there is something, some common "stuff," an original psychic type, something in ultimate human nature that makes it possible—if only for those possessing the requisite poetic imagination—to employ *Verstehen* in grasping the meaningful totalities of other times and cultures (Goodman, 1978). For Dilthey, far from implying a relativism of perspective which undermines the universalism of science, *Verstehen* equips a person with the means to grasp the organic totalities of history. This is not, it ought to be said, still another version of the eighteenth century epistemology in which the mind is assumed to possess a structure symmetrical to that of nature, thus making possible knowledge of natural laws. For Dilthey the ultimate grounding of our knowledge of history or culture rests on the assertion that what we create we can understand, and our ability to understand derives from no other source. The *possibility* of *Verstehen* inheres in human culture, but transcends it because the basic elements of culture and of the poetic imagination are expressions of an original unitary psychic type. (See Goodman, 1978; also Brown, 1978).

One can see in this the several commonalities between Weber and Dilthey in regard to their approach to the question of the appropriate methodology for the historical disciplines: the stipulation that the human reality is to be regarded as constructed by humans, the definition of meaning as the primitive form of this human reality on which all inquiry must ultimately be grounded, the emphasis on the concrete in history as the object of study, and the conception of history as a constantly emerging novelty.

On at least three points, however, Weber departs from Dilthey. The first is the critical question of the grounds on which the distinctions between the disciplines are properly to be made, and the resulting conception of the incorrigible foundations of the human sciences. The second is Dilthey's anthropological grounding of *Verstehen*. The third involves Dilthey's version of the Hegelian "emanatism" in which social institutions are regarded as objectifications of "spirit" or some essential quality of human subjectivity. Each of these leads to central aspects of Weber's philosophy of science and sociology. The distinctions on the basis of which the differences between the disciplines are drawn lead to the fundamental theory of value-relevance (*Wertbeziehung*) taken essentially from Rickert. The problematic aspects of

Dilthey's human nature-grounded formulation of *Verstehen* led Weber (and a host of others following) to ground-breaking and seminal discussions of the place of interpretation in the social sciences. The idea that social institutions are "objectifications" of "spirit" or some quality of subjectivity, when understood as science, eventuates in a form of methodological individualism. In the following sections we will see the centrality of all of these questions to Weber's philosophy of science.

The task that Weber set himself in the Roscher and Knies essays was to establish a form of *historical* inquiry—with its incorrigible subjectivist grounding—alongside and integrated with the generalizing nomological form, as legitimately scientific. He attempts to achieve this (in these essays *and* those that followed) by (1) establishing that it is on the basis of the *interest* of the historian or the social scientist, grounded in value-relevance, that the objects of scientific analysis are constructed and explained, and by demonstrating that this implies the employment of *two* types of concepts; (2) showing that the problem of formulating the basic methodology to be employed in scientific study of the historical domain requires a formulation of the *functions* of these two types of concepts in inquiry, and the relationships between these, an analysis establishing the *ideal type* as the principle methodological tool of the historical sciences; (3) arguing that this requires a formulation of a theory of causality specifically adapted to sociocultural inquiry; and (4) formulating the object of the historical disciplines as "social action" (*Handeln*), and establishing "interpretive understanding" as the unconditional presupposition of such knowledge.

Valve-Relevance and Concept Formation in the Historical Disciplines

For Dilthey, the type of knowledge appropriate to apprehending the domain of the sociocultural world is historical knowledge. Knowledge appropriate to nature is nomological in nature. Dilthey understands the distinction between types of knowledge as arising from the nature of the objects of study, an ontological adjudication. On this point Weber has little to say specifically about Dilthey, although in one rather terse passage he does point out that the dichotomy of inner and outer as formulated by Gottl, a well-known philosopher of language and science, and accepted by Dilthey "is not a purely 'logical' distinction," but rather "an 'ontological' dichotomy" and that this was accepted by Dilthey (Weber, 1975, 216, n.22). He then goes on to identify his own position as being "close" to that of Rickert (whose influence on Weber will be discussed briefly in the following section). This is the thesis that

> the manner in which mental entities are 'given' to us is *not* essential to any difference of concept formation between the natural and historical sciences (216, n.22).

Elsewhere in discussing Roscher's work, he notes that, for him, the differences between history and the exact natural sciences are consequences of the objects of study, or as he puts it, "the material with which they work" (68).

The problem with this for Weber is that it identifies the *scientific* disciplines as those seeking to establish nomological knowledge and establishes the *historical* ones as *nonscientific* (although by no means of lesser importance or significance) because of their necessary concern with concrete historical phenomena. Weber does *not* counter this position by merely asserting that the human domain, or even its historical aspect, is inherently amenable to scientific analysis. Rather, he attempts to establish the precise sense in which the historical disciplines may be considered to be scientific, on the basis of an analysis of the epistemological foundations of scientific concept formation. Critical to this inquiry is the concept of *Wertbeziehung,* or value-relevance.[20]

Value-relevance refers to our interest in identifying or constructing objects of scientific interest. Just as the objects of our social world come to be what they are through their value-relevance, so objects of social scientific interest are brought into being by a *selective process* of value-relevance. This idea was taken over by Weber from his Heidelberg colleague, the neo-Kantian philosopher Heinrich Rickert.[21]

Our basic cognitive experiences, Rickert argued, are given in our consciousness as undifferentiated impressions, beyond which (following Kant) nothing synthetic can be known. These impressions are the stuff from which we make sense of experience, in the form of *ideas*. Ideas are for Rickert the *content* of knowledge, as opposed to its *form,* and what we understand as knowledge is always some content wedded to a form, or a category such as "existence," "causality," or "possibility." All knowledge takes propositional form; thus, "This is a man" combines the form of existence with the content of "man." Instances such as this are "concrete facts," and their production regarded by Rickert as volitional acts.

Now, the fundamental process of constituting objects of knowledge, is, for Rickert, one of valuing. There are other dimensions of valuing, but we constitute all our *knowledge* of the world as concrete fact (in the above sense) because we *value* it as truth. This Rickert insists on, because the necessity or need to know, i.e., in Rickert's terms, to reproduce the world beyond our sense impressions, cannot be the ground on which we constitute our knowledge, because this "beyond" (in Kantian terms the *noumena*) is unknowable.

Now we bring the reality of our world into being not through valuing all, or just any facts; their infinitude makes this impossible. We therefore make a *selection* of this or that aspect, through some criterion of *value,* which is shared by at least some others. But how is this accomplished? According

[20] It is interesting to note that in this respect Weber's inquiry is Humian in its assertion that, in establishing the principles of concept formation in the sciences, there exists no basis for asserting any absolutely categorical differences associated with knowledge of the human and natural domains respectively.

[21] It has become generally recognized that in working out his methodology Weber was heavily influenced by Rickert. He regarded the latter's *Die Grenzen der naturwissenschaftlichen Begriffs-bildung* as "the fundamental work" dealing with the differences between the nomological and ideographic sciences. A translation of much that is relevant in Rickert appears in Rickert (1962). For a careful analysis of Weber's reception of Rickert, see Burger (1976). For a short qualified dissent, see Merquior (1980), 148. This brief account draws on both and also on Hekman (1983).

to Rickert, through the formation of *concepts*. Concepts "reduce the mass of facts representing the empirical world to proportions which the mind is equipped to handle" (Burger, 1976, 121). Without such concept formation, "any knowledge of the world, any grasp of physical reality, would be impossible" (Rickert, in Burger, 21). Concepts may be general, meaning they are formulated through abstraction of a limited number of properties from a range of ideas, or they may be "individual," designating a specific, or concrete "individual" as a phenomenon constituted by a set of concrete properties. In everyday life we have an interest in both, and we construct our cognitive world through both. We might say that we have an interest in knowledge of both sorts and accordingly *value* both the abstractness and generality of the former type of knowing, and the individuality and specificity of the latter, but in their respective relevances to our life situations. The former are relevant as instances of classes, the latter because of their uniqueness.

Rickert's interest in this line of argument was the fundamental neo-Kantian one of reformulating the realm of moral action in such a fashion as to establish it as a legitimate *scientific* object, i.e., as a domain to which *universal* concepts could be properly applied. In his own terms, he wished to replace the intrinsically individualizing or particularizing *Geisteswissenschaften* with the concept of *Kulturwissenschaften*, or cultural sciences (or a discussion see Makkreel, 1969). This universalization was to be achieved through the *valuing* process, since this is the universal form of constituting our reality. In this fashion the basis for a *scientific* approach to historical reality becomes possible. The category of the cultural sciences defines a sphere of interests distinct from that of those individualizing ones (*Geisteswissenschaften*) constituted by virtue of their taking as their object expressions of the human mind or spirit. Rickert's mistake in this effort appeared to be his conflation of the universal process of valuing with the pluralism of values constituting the substance of social action, or, at least, subsuming or deriving the second from the first. He thereby took valuation as such as an adequate conceptualization of a human universal adequate to ground a major category of scientific enterprise.

Weber accepted Rickert's formulation of the nature and significance of value-relevance and incorporated it into the foundations of his methodology. The central idea, that the nature and limits of scientific truth must be formulated in the context of valuation, underpins Weber's sociology in its entirety. Social scientific objects of interest are selected, or formed (there is a difference here, amounting to an important ambiguity never adequately recognized and treated by Weber, to which we shall return), on the basis of their "significance," which arises from the fact that it "reveals relationships that are important for us due to their connection with our values" (Weber, 1949, 76). It is from this standpoint that the conceptual schemes employed by the social sciences must be formulated.

The guiding "point of view" is of great importance for the *construction* of the conceptual scheme that will be used (76). Indeed,

> All knowledge of cultural reality ... is always knowledge from *particular points of view*. When we require from the historian and social research worker

as an elementary presupposition that they distinguish the important from the trivial and that he should have the necessary point of view for this distinction, we mean that they must understand how to relate the events of the real world consciously or unconsciously to universal "cultural values," and to select out those relationships which are significant for us (81–82).

All social-scientific problems are "selections" from among the "infinitude of possibilities" potentially definable from the meaningless flux. Weber gives as an example our interest in the money economy of contemporary capitalist societies. The *cultural* significance of this lies in the fact that "it exists on a mass scale as a fundamental component of modern culture" (Weber, 1949, 77), by which he means the scope of its actual ramifications in every aspect of the lives of people, in its real import as a pervasive condition of life. The capitalist money economy has come into being over a long historical period, and its significance for us rests on the ineluctable fact of our participation in this system. As historians we formulate the elements of the modern money economy as a complex object of scientific interest on the bases of its value-relevance.

Because it is in the nature of the interest of the historical disciplines to fall always on the particular, such as the money economy of a capitalist society, it follows that

> The type of social science in which we are interested is an *empirical science* of concrete *reality* (*Wirklichkeitswissenchaft*). Our aim is the understanding of the characteristic uniqueness of the reality in which we move. We wish to understand on the one hand the relationships and the cultural significance of individual events in their contemporary manifestations and on the other the causes of their being historically *so* and not *otherwise*. (72).

This follows from the valuational foundations of scientific interest.

> it is 'uniqueness' which establishes a relation to *value*. The specific *interest* in 'understanding' that which is significant because of its 'uniqueness' is based on this axiological relation (Weber, 1975, 259).

Here is the kernel of Weber's historicism. In this passage he means to convey that it is *not* the various and infinite abstract qualities of sociocultural phenomena, either in and of themselves, or as variables appearing in a law or empirical generalization (e.g., Gresham's Law), that constitute the scientific sociocultural significance or value-relevance of a phenomenon; rather, it is the constellation of elements of which it is constituted. The money economy of a given capitalist society, in all its empirical complexity, including the actual productive enterprises, the actual processes of exchange, and the actual meanings of all this to the actors involved, is the object, however complex, of scientific interest. Or, to take another example, it is the complex and interrelated and shifting actualities of Puritanism in the sixteenth, seventeenth, and eighteenth centuries which draws our scientific interest, not generalizations or "laws" that might purport to explain various abstract properties connected with religious behavior, e.g., "asceticism," "otherworldliness," or the process of "rationalization" (to mention just three ideal types created by Weber).

Within the framework of value-relevance, however, there remains the problem of defining actual concrete historical or social scientific problems. Weber's discussion of the possible scientific uses of Goethe's love letters to Fraülein von Stein may be used to illustrate this. They may be used to investigate Goethe's personality, for example, or to reveal his uniqueness, or as materials to analyze the nature of the Weimar culture of the time, or they may be employed in the development of a generalizing science (more of this shortly) like social psychology, or from the standpoint of studying mental pathology (138–142). Any and all of these problems, as Weber defines them, make sense only in terms of *particular* discipline-based perspectives. This is a critical point about which there has been considerable confusion. There is first of all the process of formulating objects of scientific interest, an operation distinct from construction of concrete objects for empirical study. Although he clearly recognized the distinction, Weber seemed to include both under the rubric of value-relevance.

> "Relevance to values" refers simply to the philosophical interpretation of that specifically scientific "interest" which determines the selection of a given subject matter *and the problems of an empirical analysis* (Weber, 1949, 22. Italics mine).

The importance of being clear about this distinction is, as Zaret has properly emphasized, that very *different* objects may be, and typically are, constituted as problems for empirical study. Today, for example, within the value-relevant field of social stratification we find, on the one hand, status attainment researchers defining research problems in terms of "variables implicitly specified by the value-laden notion of meritocracy in functionalist theory, and its economic analog, human capital," and on the other, "Marxist approaches, with their value-laden notion of class conflict" embedded in a quite different array of variables (Zaret, 1980, 1183–1184).

On the basis of his formulation of historical individuals as the objects of scientific interest, Weber argues that concepts of a certain special type are required to apprehend them. Such historical individuals are ordinarily quite complex configurations. His descriptive accounts of the "Protestant Ethic" or "rational bourgeois capitalism" exemplify this. The social scientist must formulate concepts capable of somehow grasping this complexity, concepts that are at once adequately representative of this historical complexity; and this is no easy task when one is faced with an "infinite multiplicity." Such concepts are historical ideal types.

This contrasts with the nature of the interest on the basis of which *generalizing* or *abstracting* concepts are formulated, a procedure more prominent in, but not exclusively characteristic of, the natural sciences. Such concept formation is a necessary condition for producing knowledge in the form of laws, the now conventional procedure whereby we attempt to specify relationships between *certain* aspects of various phenomena conceptualized in *class* terms. The *scientific* interest in apples falling from trees focuses not on their size, shape, sweetness, coloration, and so on, but on their rate of fall. And our interest in this derives from the fact that this rate of fall is in a particular instance subsumable under a "general law" (Weber has in mind what we today call an "empirical generalization"), which we consider to be the necessary form in which our knowledge of nature is rendered because there is no other scientifically-recognized basis of such knowledge, i.e., no other existing possibility of interpreting its *meaning*. In formulating such laws, we abstract not only from observations of falling apples, but of "falling objects" in general, i.e., the *class* of falling objects, and then proceed to create the abstract category "rate of acceleration," a *constructed theoretical property* of all falling objects. In elaborating this distinction, Weber built on and extended the ideas of Rickert.

Now, there is no reason why propositions of this sort cannot be formulated for sociocultural phenomena, or that they could not be cast in quantitative form; indeed, there are actually a good many such propositions, a few of which, at least, attain an even greater precision than do some of those in the natural sciences. And such propositions, Weber says, can perform a very important—even "indispensable," he says at one point (Weber, 1949, 77)—*heuristic* function in the historical disciplines. Thus, although individualizing concepts have as their objective the interpretation and explanation of concrete historical individuals, they may, indeed most surely will, find it necessary to employ generalizing propositions to achieve this end.

And just as the historical disciplines may make use of generalizing concepts, the natural sciences, in somewhat parallel fashion, may be found to exhibit an interest in "historical individuals" appearing in nature. In fact, Weber suggests in passing that entire disciplines, such as meteorology and geology, may be so characterized. And in *Knies* he seems to say that such employment may be mainly a matter of the presence of situations where a *historical* mode of explanation is the only procedure that presents itself, i.e., where explanation by subsumption under a general law or laws is not possible (Weber, 1975, 122ff.). Although he does not say so in so many words, Weber may be understood to be asserting that such occurrences would typically appear or be more prominent during the natural history stage of the growth and development of a science (104).

The importance of the fact that both types of concepts are employed in *both* domains is emphasized by Weber.

> With the exception of pure mechanics, on the one hand, and certain of the historical disciplines, on the other, it is certain that none of the "sciences" which in fact exist can develop their concepts exclusively from only one of these two metatheoretical points of view (58).

Weber has here broken the seemingly ontologically based association of the type of discipline with exclusive types of methodology, while at once recognizing that there remains an important difference. It is because of this that he has always seemed to have had one foot in the positivist camp and the other in that of the idealist historians, and thereby been an object of criticism of both.

Some of Weber's discussions of the differences and relationships between the two types of concepts might seem to suggest that these differences are categorical, i.e., a matter of differences of *kind*. His position that historical individuals can never be reduced to or rendered in the form of abstract concepts, for instance, might be interpreted as supporting this position. However, this is not the case. Wherever Weber systematically discusses the critical differences between the two types of concept, they turn out to be matters of *degree*. He describes "general" concepts as "becoming increasingly empty of content and increasingly alienated from empirically intelligible reality," and the logic of investigation in the natural science disciplines as requiring "the progressive elimination of individual entities and the deduction of established 'laws' . . . from other laws still more general" (1975, 64). This distinction underlies his discussion in "Objectivity in Social Science and Social Policy," (written in 1904) regarding the employment of the two types of concepts in varying research situations.

> . . . the greater the extent to which we conceptualize complicated historical patterns with respect to those components in which their specific *cultural significance* is contained, the greater will be the extent to which the concept—or system of concepts—will be ideal-typical in character (Weber, 1949, 101).

These characterizations of the "abstractness" of the concepts as a matter of *degree,* involving a procedure in which concrete bits of empirical description are, in Weber's terms, "abstracted," from concrete reality (see Burger, 1976, 72ff. for a discussion), are clearly of considerable importance for Weber's later purpose, to "make peace," as Brunn puts it (Brunn, 5), between the seemingly irreconcilable positions of the historicists and scientists. But he does this, in Habermas's words, by placing "the causal-analytical knowledge of empirical stereotypes at the service of a more extensive interest in knowledge" (Habermas, quoted by Dallmayr and McCarthy, 1977, 68). In this fashion Weber appears to have established a basis for asserting an essential unity of the social scientific and historical disciplines on an *epistemological*, rather than ontological or merely methodological ground, but one that has evidently never been systematically developed (but see Nagel, 1953).

The point of all this for Weber was to provide the presuppositions he regarded as necessary for the formulation of a method of concept formation that would incorporate essential elements from both camps. This is the theory of the ideal types, to which we now turn.

The Ideal Type[22]

It follows from the foregoing account of Weber's analysis that the concepts formed to grasp historical individuals would differ greatly from the generalizing types. And this is indeed the case. *Historical* ideal types are formed as syntheses of various manifestations of subjective meaning constituting a "configuration," or pattern. Generalizing concepts are formed by extraction of a single or limited number of qualities common to a range of phenomena

---

[22] There has accumulated a very substantial literature on the ideal type, beginning with von Schelting (1934). The most extensive and useful recent treatments are found in Burger (1976) and Hekman (1983).

and systematically exclude all other qualities of the empirical range of the phenomena in question: They "summarize the common features of certain empirical phenomena . . . (but) are not typifications" (100–101).

As an example of the former, we may take "bourgeois capitalism" (or, variously, "modern capitalism," or "rational bourgeoisie capitalism"), defined by Weber as "the provision of needs of a human group . . . carried out by enterprise," in which the enterprise "determines its income yielding power by calculation according to the methods of modern bookkeeping and the striking of a balance" (Weber, 1950, 275). He then goes on to list a series of "presuppositions," all of which are incorporated into the type because he considers them more or less indispensable to the actual functioning of modern capitalism, i.e., elements of the "concrete individual," modern bourgeois capitalism. These include a complex of social actions including free markets in commodities and labor, rational technology, a legal system allowing for high degrees of calculability in adjudication and administration of every form, and the general commercialization of life, and finally, of course, that complex of beliefs and ethical orientations he referred to as the "spirit of capitalism" (276–279, *et passim*).

This ideal type of modern capitalism, however, is not to be understood as a *description*. If this were the case, the methodology of the ideal type would, in principle, differ not at all from the procedure of the historical school that restricted the cultural disciplines to ideographic knowledge, and for which "the function of concepts was assumed to be *reproduction* of 'objective' reality in the imagination" (406). Rather, it is a way of analyzing a "historically unique configuration" (Weber, 1949, 90) through

> [a] one-sided *accentuation* of one or more points of view and by the synthesis of a great many diffuse, discrete, more or less present and occasionally absent *concrete individual* phenomena, which are arranged according to those one-sidedly emphasized viewpoints into a unified *analytical* construct. (90)

This one-sidedness results in the type having the quality of a "utopia," a term that Weber employs to emphasize the nondescriptive and constructed character of the type. In the same vein, he also sometimes refers to it as a "mental construct" (99).

Note the phrase at the end of the passage quoted above: "a unified *analytical* construct." This is a rule of type construction in general. The type complex "*conceived* as an internally consistent system" (90) is an essential aspect of historical type construction. The reason for this lies in the self-evident fact that just any congeries or concatenation of various features drawn from the infinitude of history and brought together as a "type" would have no more validity than would any other. As Weber says, the points of view from which they can be "significant" for us "are very diverse" (91). Such constructs must be stated in terms of relations "which our imagination accepts as plausibly oriented and hence as 'objectively possible,' and which appear as *adequate* from the nomological standpoint" (92). This last addendum is a critical one, for here Weber seems to say that while a sense of motivational adequacy in the eye of the researcher's imagination may legitimately serve as a preliminary criterion of type unity, all such types must be submitted to a second desideratum, namely, being situated in the framework of *causal explanation*. Positivistically inclined interpreters of Weber have usually preferred to understand this first moment of type construction as hypothesis formation, the second as verification. But Weber is explicit in rejecting types as hypotheses (even though they do have some of the characteristics of hypotheses, such as modifiability, and can even be *used* as hypothesis: 101–102). Rather, Weber's description of the desiderata employed in type construction reflects the influence of Dilthey and the historical school in general, whereas the second imposes a conventional *scientific* test involving the logical canons of explanation, which we shall take up later.

Such types will ordinarily be amalgams of two kinds of type-forming processes: an application of class or generic concepts (e.g., "exchange"), that have themselves no ideal-typical character, and "quasi-generic" concepts, which are always ideal-typical (100–101). "Exchange," for instance, is a "simple class concept," but may be brought conceptually into association with, for example, "marginal utility." It thereby becomes to that degree a construct, acquiring in some measure a "typical" character. The further this process is elaborated, the greater the ideal-typical character assumed by the concept. Thus, "every individual ideal-type comprises both *generic* and ideal-typically constructed conceptual elements" (100). Depending on one's project, the ratio of these is variable.

Weber gives as an example the concept of "handicraft," found in the industrial enterprises of many times and places, but everywhere in conjunction with diverse economic and cultural phenomena. From these diverse associations and connections (e.g., handicrafting in the medieval city carried out within the guild structure; craft work performed as wage labor, or in terms of a specific division of labor based on gender, or performed by communal groups formed for a specific purpose such as house building, or organized in connection with magical requirements, and so on), the historian or social scientist can extract what appear to be the essentials and in so doing formulate the type. Thus, by "handicraft" Weber understands "skilled labor carried on . . . in specialized form, either through differentiation of occupations or technical specialization, and whether by free or unfree workers, and whether for a lord, or for a community, or on the worker's own accounts" (Weber, 1950, 116). We are able to formulate the concept "handicraft production" only by associating it with some, and disassociating it with other, specific elements of production appearing in a number of situations. Or, to mention a familiar example, the "quasi-generic" ideal type, "inner-worldly asceticism," is employed, along with others, in construction of the *individual historical* ideal type, "Protestant Ethic." It is in this connection that Weber speaks of generalizing ideal types as "heuristic" in character, i.e., not being objects of interest in and of themselves, but employed for another purpose. Indeed, the goal of causal knowledge *requires* the consideration of generalizing concepts, because without them nomological knowledge (i.e., "knowledge of recurrent causal sequences" [79]) would be impossible.

Such quasi-generic, or generalizing ideal types, can be, and very often are, developmental or "genetic" in character. For example, they capture aspects of the shift from handicrafting to capitalistic economic organization (Weber, 1949, 101). Or in the case, say, of generalizing ideal types like "church" and "sect," in so far as the objective is something beyond a purely classificatory scheme, they have to treat "sectarianism," or the "sectarian spirit" genetically, as a process of growth. The broadest of all of Weber's ideal types, the concept of "rationalization" (to be discussed later) is formulated as a generalizing genetic ideal type.[23]

At a lower level of generality, generalizing ideal types of many sorts are constructed by Weber for the purpose of identifying "generalized uniformities of empirical process" (1978b, 19) to be employed in the analysis of concrete historical individuals. Weber's works abound with such empirical generalizations, sometimes cast in the form of "affinities" between ideal systems (ideologies, religions, etc.) on the one hand, and various politically, economically, ethnically, or militarily grounded social formations (e.g., classes, status groups, religious elites, etc.), on the other. To mention just two examples, there is the "affinity" between "otherwordly" salvation religions and depressed classes or strata, and between the professional interests of priests and anthropomorphically conceived of Gods (427–428). (The concept of elective affinity is discussed later in this chapter and in the one following.)

Although such empirical generalizations linking ideal types have the formal theoretical status of being "only heuristically" valuable, their formulation is "the distinctive objective of sociology," whereas that of history is "the causal analysis and explanation of individual actions, structures, and personalities possessing cultural significance" (19). Formally, then, the distinction between types of concepts translates into a more or less *practical* division of labor between history and sociology (and presumably the other social sciences as well).[24]

These features of the type, it may be well to reiterate, are not to be thought of as objective properties of the type, but as the products of the researcher's imagination exercised in a principled or systematic fashion, aspects "essential from the point of view of specific theoretical goals" (Weber, 1975, 168),[25] "logical constructs" (Weber, 1949, 42) exhibiting a "logical consistency" resting on the interrelations of the subjective meanings involved, and because of this, "not to be understood as averages" (Weber, 1978b, 1, 21–22).

History does not present itself in objective unitary forms independent of the observer's perceptions, waiting to be discovered in their pristine objectivity. The existence of "objective meanings" was, for Weber, a matter of faith alone. This was the sense of Bendix's quote asserting that Weber's sociology was intended "as a break with the long Western tradition of a belief in 'objectively valid meanings'" (Bendix, 1984, 40). And it was this, as we noted earlier, that was Weber's second point of difference with Dilthey. For Weber, ideal types acquire their meaning through the theoretically grounded problem orientation of the researcher exercised in the framework of value-

---

[23] Recall the discussion of Durkheim's treatment of genetic processes in Chapter 11.

[24] But one tempered by Weber's conviction regarding the basic unity of the disciplines, in a statement immediately following the last quotation, to the effect that the basic materials of the historian and sociologist were "to a very large extent, though by no means exclusively, of the same concrete processes of action . . ." (Weber, 1978b, 19).

[25] And so presupposing a given state of knowledge of a discipline.

relevance. And this observation has two faces: Subjectively, it points to the problem of the origins and nature of the researcher's criteria of unity, necessary for the construction of types, along with the specification of the nature of the *object* of knowledge—the *Verstehen* problem; externally, it leads to the issue of causality in history, because for Weber the historical disciplines as well as those dealing with the natural world were necessarily committed to the production of causal explanations of the phenomena that are the objects of their interest. We turn next to the latter.

Causal Explanation

The problem of causal explanation in history is broached in the "Objectivity. . . ." essay, but then taken up systematically in Weber's essay of the following year (1905), "Critical Studies in the Logic of the Cultural Sciences: A Critique of Edward Meyer's Methodological Views" (Weber, 1949). In the first part of this essay, Weber spends a good deal of time criticizing Meyer's historiographic views and reiterates much of what he had established in "Roscher and Knies . . ." and "Objectivity." He then goes on to formulate the issue of causality in the historical disciplines as the establishment of relationships between concrete historical individuals. In order to do this, we attempt to obtain a "judgment of objective possibility" (Weber, 1949, 181). By this Weber means a mental process in which the patterns or configuration of events thought to be the possible cause of the object of historical interest to be explained is modified or broken down in the "imagination." Included in the events defining the German revolution of 1848, for example, were the (two) shots fired in Berlin that were, as we would say today, the "precipitating factor" that touched off a series of significant events that, in their totality, could be called the Revolution of 1848." Of course, we also recognize an array of other factors of potential causal significance, perhaps including such specific concrete factors as aspects of class opposition, the repressiveness of the regime, conditions facilitating mobilization of struggle groups, the decisions of certain politicians, and so on,[26] any or all of which might well be included on various grounds: their partial confirmation in other research or their status in some theory, or because of the specific knowledge we have of the situation in question, or even (perhaps very importantly, in Weber's view), their sheer intuitive attractiveness. A judgment of objective possibility would involve an argument or inquiry focusing on whether or not any "significant" changes in the ensuing course of action (the Revolution of 1848) would be objectively possible if the shots had never been fired. In this instance the judgment (of Meyer) is that no changes would have occurred, thus, in Weber's terms, rendering the shots "causally insignificant" (181).

The degree of confidence one can have in such judgments, of course, varies enormously. Some events, if modified mentally, may involve elements enabling us to make very strong arguments that the modification or modifications would indeed have resulted in significantly different resultants. If

---

[26] These are my own examples. Weber himself does not in this instance go into such particulars because his interest is methodological, not substantive. Elsewhere he does.

the Greeks had lost the Battle of Marathon, for instance, it can be argued very strongly that a "Persianization" of the Greek world would have followed. The ground for this is found in a series of causal statements. If the Greeks had lost, they would never have been able to develop their fleet, which was indispensable for carrying on the war. Cultural developments central to the long-term development of the Western world would have been stifled had the Persians won. On the basis of such a line of argumentation, we may with great confidence attribute causal significance to the Battle of Marathon.

In general, Weber conceives of this process as one in which

> we can observe causal "factors" and can conceptually isolate them, and [that] expected rules must be *thought* of as standing in a relationship of adequacy to those factors, while relatively few combinations are *conceivable* of those conceptually isolated "factors" with other causal "factors" from which another result could be "expected" in accordance with *general empirical rules* (187).

Weber's italicization of "general empirical rules" here may be understood in the context of his assertion that "every *individual* ideal type comprises both *generic* and ideal-typically constructed conceptual *elements*" (100). Generalizing concepts formulated into "general empirical rules," or empirical generalizations,[27] provide the conditions under which judgments of objective possibility may be rendered in one degree or another. *In one degree or another* because, as Weber assures us, this is a matter of "gradations of degree" (181) and so dependent on the state of our knowledge. Weber refers to this as a dual process, one of "isolations and generalizations." Each of the "givens," he says is "decomposed" into "components," such that each is "fitted into an empirical rule," thus making it possible to assess the effects of each such component (depending, of course, on the actual state of our knowledge). The totality of judgments regarding all such empirical generalizations that have been "isolated" then constitutes a "generalization" about the objective possibility of the historical individual in question. In this conception of the elements of analysis, causal analysis virtually always involves *multiple* causal relations, each having a place in the larger *analytically* decomposed historical individual. And it also virtually always means that causality has to be understood as a *process* that is genetic in nature.

"Critical Studies in the Logic of the Cultural Sciences . . ." (hereafter referred to as "Logic") was published in 1905 and Weber wrote little about the theory of causality in the years following. Largely on this basis, Turner has concluded that Weber's optimism about the possibility of causal explanation in the social sciences at this point in his career later disappeared, and that Weber, in effect, came to limit the possible achievements of the social sciences to merely *understanding* sociocultural phenomena (Turner, 1983).

[27] For a discussion maintaining that the modern sense of "empirical generalization" is what Weber intends by all such formulations, including his references to "laws" and "nomological knowledge," see Berger, 1976, Chap. 4. In this usage, to truncate and simplify a rather complex topic, an empirical generalization designates a statement of universal form supported by empirical evidence, i.e., an induction. A "law," or "law-like statement" designates an empirical generalization that itself is incorporated within and subsumed under universal statements of a higher level of generality.

The main evidence for this is the absence in *Economy and Society* (hereafter referred to as *ES*) of terms used earlier: "generalization," "isolation," and "objective possibility." Interestingly, this is just the opposite of what has often been claimed for *ES*, namely that it was Weber's main attempt to *instantiate* the *generalizing*, i.e., the sociological, as against the sheerly historical, component of the cultural sciences.

Indeed, Turner's claim must be questioned. The conceptual exposition at the beginning of *ES*, written late in life, it is true, does not engage the causation problem, although Weber does briefly iterate earlier statements, clearly maintaining that sociology is concerned with "the interpretive understanding of social action and thereby with a causal explanation of its course and consequences" (Weber, 1978b, 4), a position also taken earlier (in 1914) in a letter to Georg von Below, where Weber states emphatically that "the . . . task of history is to find a causal explanation for . . . specific traits" (of social phenomena), and to do so through employment of the comparative method (quoted by Roth in intro. to Weber, 1978b, LXIV).

Furthermore, the entire section of *ES* labeled "Conceptual Exposition" was greatly "simplified," as Weber says (3), in response to collegial criticism of its complexity and difficulty, and Weber may have decided to restrict himself to the substantive level of concept formation and avoid the thorny metatheoretical problems of causality (perhaps because he regarded the earlier account as more or less adequate for his purposes). Such an interpretation would be consistent as well with Weber's well-known and publicly stated distaste for methodological issues, and his wish to put them behind him and get on with the research (see Oakes's introduction to Weber, 1977). Finally, there is the fact that *ES*, much of it in print earlier, to be sure, is nevertheless replete with causal statements of the generalizing sort; indeed, much of it stands as a virtual compendium of empirical generalizations.

Causal analysis in Weber's sense implies comparison, and indeed, this is central to Weber's usage. The manner in which he frames the empirical problem of the relation between Protestantism and capitalist development in Europe illustrates this in highly contracted but highlighted form, but it may be used to illustrate the point.

Weber frames the Protestant ethic-spirit of capitalism problem in world historical terms, even if retrospectively (Weber, 1905, Intro.). It is a causal problem, namely, the effect of a certain kind of "spiritual" disposition on the formation of a certain attitude toward economic activity. Weber begins by noting very generally some similarities and differences between the West and East. Many times and places in the world have known trade, even very extensive trade, have developed techniques of comparing income with expenses and even systematic calculation in decimals (in India), have experienced money and money lending and speculations of every conceivable sort, have created different types of economic organizations (guilds, companies, etc.), and have been familiar with economic class struggles. However, only in the West have the following developed to a significant degree: a rational form of labor organization (formally free labor brought together under the aegis of the capitalist enterprise), the strict separation of the business from the household, and rational bookkeeping as an *accounting* instrument (rather than as a mere budgetary expedient). The *significance* of the latter two, Weber says, rests on their connection with the first, for at least in their developed form they are inconceivable apart from the capitalist organization of labor. In addition to these essentially economic factors, Weber also says that the strictly Western principle of citizenship, the development of rational science, a rational law and administrative principles, and a legally autonomous form of the city separated from any traditional status or power formations, have also been critical. And finally there is the religious factor. Generally, Eastern religions threw up ethical or theological obstacles to capitalist activity, whereas the long and complex development of Christianity, by the sixteenth and seventeenth centuries, ended up creating a religious ethic and corresponding personality type with an "affinity" for systematic profit-oriented economic activity.

All this, of course, only epitomizes analysis either already performed to one degree or another, or envisaged as future projects (e.g., Weber's own studies of law, the city, or forms of political domination). In fact, it summarizes the broad outline of his life's work. But it also illustrates the way in which his methodological principles informed his own work. All of the factors mentioned are causal factors influencing in one degree or another the growth of capitalism in the West. Others, such as the role of the Jews as middlemen throughout the Middle Ages and beyond (Sombart's thesis) are rejected by Weber as causally inadequate. The real problems of analysis appear first in the need to clarify factors in a comparative way (as above), and second— and more difficult—to assess the *relative* causal adequacy of such an array of developments, as, for instance, in the statement above relating the three principal economic factors, in which the significance of the secondary ones increases when in association with the first, a kind of "synergism of meaning."

It perhaps ought to be noted that in all this Weber nowhere equates the causal relation with purposiveness, i.e., the explanation of *behavior* as *consequence* of subjective intentions, a position that has sometimes been attributed to him. Subjective inentions are, for Weber, constitutive of social action, make it identifiable as being what it is, which is to say, *meaningful,* but it is the actions themselves as so constituted—usually in collectivities— that have or that may have causal force. Merquior points out that restricting sociological explanation to sheer subjective intentions would make the explanation of unintended consequences logically impossible (Merquior, 1980, 164–168). This would have left the great bulk of Weber's sociology unpublished, since it deals mostly with precisely this category of social phenomena.[28]

Social Action, Subjective Meaning, and the Problems of *Verstehen*

The construction of ideal types and theory of causality presuppose a definition of subject matter appropriate to the historical/social sciences. For Weber this was framed by the doctrines of *Wertbeziehung* and *Verstehen*. The former

---

[28] Indeed, a fair although hardly conclusive case can be made for *defining* sociology as a science designed to explain unanticipated events. See Merquior, loc. cit.

establishes the incorrigibility of the *value-orientations* of the researcher in the framing of any and all research interests. The latter establishes the ineluctable *meaningfulness* of cultural phenomena, requiring that they in some sense be "understood" in terms of their nature. Given the first understanding, the second is necessarily "interpretive." The two taken together comprise the doctrine of "interpretive understanding." But this very phrase reveals the tension between the subjective and objective elements of social science inquiry. Historians and social scientists necessarily form concepts and formulate problems on the basis of their value-relevance, but sociocultural reality presents itself—or for scientific purposes must be assumed to present itself— as external, or as "objective." Dilthey had rendered the "inner-outer" conception by positing a universal *Verstehen* rooted in a common "psychic stuff" of the species. But this and other such universals were rejected by Weber. Somewhat ironically, the very doctrine advanced by Dilthey to establish the accessibility and comprehensibility of all cultural phenomena was given a particularistic interpretation by Weber, in this transmutation revealing its nested relativist implications.

Weber defines sociology as "a science concerning itself with the interpretive understanding of social action and thereby with a causal explanation of its course and consequences." He then goes on to define "action" as being present when "the acting individual attaches a subjective meaning to his behavior" and further clarifies this by stating that "action is 'social' insofar as its subjective meaning takes account of the behavior of others and is thereby oriented in its course" (Weber, 1978b, 4).

Meaningful social action has its boundaries or limits: At one extreme stands purely "reactive behavior" in which subjective meaning is not involved—much traditional action borders on this; at the other, highly emotional behavior may approach the point of noncomprehensibility, for both actor and researcher. In such instances, the degree of direct personal familiarity of the researcher with the emotional states in question is probably the crucial factor in facilitating his or her ability to clearly comprehend the state in question.

The forms of social action most comprehensible to a researcher are those that proceed on a rational basis, i.e., differentiated in terms of means and ends in the consciousness of the actor. At one extreme, says Weber, the proposition $2 \times 2 = 4$ is "unambiguously intelligible"; we have a "perfect understanding." Such logical or mathematical understanding is not, of course, very relevant to sociology. But much human social action is rational in other ways. Economic activity particularly can generally be understood in means-ends terms, and often quite unambiguously. On the other hand, behavior oriented to absolute values, although rational, presents greater difficulties. The important point here is that Weber attempts to formally delimit the sphere of sociological analysis in a way consistent with his philosophical presuppositions. In order to be an "interpretive" discipline, sociology must take as its subject matter that behavior which is meaningful to the actor; behavior nonmeaningful to an actor would therefore, for Weber, presumably preclude its construction or description *as* meaningful by an *observer*.[29]

---

[29] There are instances where this would not hold, Weber admits, e.g., psychoanalysis. But the psychoanalytic process is a fundamentally different one from what Weber has in mind as the methodological protocol of the social sciences.

Social action defined in terms of meaning is thus the "central subject matter" (24) of sociology. Weber moves from this definition in two directions: epistemologically, in distinguishing two types of understanding that may be employed by the social scientist; and conceptually, in delineating his four pure types of action.

Weber distinguishes between "direct" or "observational" understanding and "explanatory" (*erklärendes*) understanding. The former designates an understanding of the meaning of acts in and of themselves, as encapsulated wholes, so to speak. The proposition $2 + 2 = 4$, an emotional outburst, the act of reaching for a door knob or chopping wood, are examples (8). The meaning here is, one might say, internal to, or internally constitutive of, the act. Explanatory understanding, by contrast, situates the act in a wider context and grasps its meaning in "motivational" terms, i.e., the man chops wood to build a fire or to earn a wage. This amounts to a distinction, as Munch puts it, between the "what" that is occurring and the "why" that requires external or relational references to the intentions of the actor. Note that although Weber here uses the term *erklären,* meaning to explain or to account for, this does not refer to explanation of the analytical causal type discussed earlier, but rather, to a description of elements of meaning that are necessary to *understand* the nature of a given event, or complex or sequence of events, depending on just how we construct the differences between phenomena of scientific interest. To engage in such exercises is to constitute social realities in terms of value relevance.

It is central to Weber's methodology that the social and historical sciences have to employ this second form of understanding. While this presupposes the ability to grasp the meaning of the countless "atomized" actions that are constitutive of a large meaning complex—the objects of "direct" understanding—the *scientific* process of understanding must seek to grasp the relational complexities. The ideal type procedure is instituted in order to specify in a formal manner the way in which this is to be done.

The exact procedure involved in interpretive understanding has been the object of much discussion, and the difficulties in this will be taken up in the section following. Here it is only necessary to note first that Weber says next to nothing about the process itself. He does little more than to indicate that such understanding may be on either an emotional or a rational basis. For the social sciences the latter is by far the most important, although the former may have a significant supplementary role in some instances.

Weber rendered his presuppositions regarding meaning and the nature of *Verstehen* in his classification of four "pure" types of action. Action may be (1) instrumentally rational (*zweckrational*), (2) value-rational (*wertrational*), (3) emotional (*affektuel*), or (4) traditional (*traditional*). Traditional action constitutes the great bulk of all social action, or more precisely, suffuses most concrete human social action to one degree on another (for these are ideal types and are not to be found in their pure form in social reality). It is generally unreflective, and often, as Weber says, "almost automatic." But attachment to the habitual "can be upheld with varying degrees of self-consciousness," and so to the extent that this is true traditional social action is a critically important type in explaining social order.

The case of emotionality is similar, in that it too "stands on the borderline of what can be considered 'meaningfully' oriented" (25). But such experiences may often be "sublimated," i.e., given an interpretation that is meaningful, and as such they come within the purview of sociology.

Value-rational action is characterized by the pursuit of ultimate values in a self-conscious way. In common with the emotional type, it includes an emotional element, but finds its *differentia specifica* in the consistent and systematic manner in which actors pursue their values. The unqualified pursuit of honor or salvation, or of any "cause," or unswerving loyalty to a leader, are general empirical types of value-rationality. In its "pure" form, it takes no note of consequences and is in this sense "irrational" (26).

Instrumentally rational action is more complex. In this type "the end, the means, and the secondary results are all rationally taken into account and weighed" (26). This involves the weighing of alternative means, of the relations of ends to consequences, and of making judgments between ends. Thus, instrumentally rational action may, indeed, *ordinarily* does interpenetrate with value-rationality in particular concrete situations. This is so, for instance, in the sense of the latter being the ground for making decisions that are themselves reached through instrumentally rational action.

These *pure* types of action are ideal types designating "universal capacities of Homo sapiens," standing outside history (Kalberg, 1980, 1148). As such, they constitute the conceptual "bridge" between Weber's philosophical anthropology proper and the conceptual apparatus elaborated in *ES*. They are not categories to be applied *directly* to human sociocultural reality, but rather, conceptions that become constitutive of the structural or developmental ideal types employed. This is a central but controversial aspect of Weber's methodology, as we shall see.

INTERPRETATION AND CRITIQUE OF WEBER'S THEORY OF SOCIAL ACTION

Because he defines social action in terms of "subjective meaning," Weber has sometimes been interpreted as "psychologizing" social behavior. This is not entirely without justification, if only because his discussions of meaning are not always very clear. In certain passages he seems to identify it with purposeful or motivated action. For example:

> A motive is a complex of subjective meaning which seems to the actor himself or to the observer an adequate ground for the conduct in question (1978b, 11)

Processes or conditions, whether of the human world or not, are

> devoid of meaning in so far as they cannot be related to an intended purpose (7)

and

> that which is intelligible or understandable about (human activity and

artifacts) is . . . its relation to human action in the role either of a means or an end (7)

It is understandable that a "motivational sociology" has often been attributed to Weber, and that in this connection it is held that the essential "operation" of understanding is the attribution or imputation of a motive (Abel, 1948; Warriner, 1969; Parkin, 1982). Indeed, understanding *goal-orientations* to constitute the entirety of sociology's proper object seems to imply a subjectivizing of that object, because goals can be defined only in their *meaning to the actor*. In such interpretations action and meaning are often rendered as separate and independent "dimensions" of sociocultural reality, and *Verstehen* becomes a technique for penetrating to the meanings behind the action. One difficulty attending this understanding is that in his actual sociological work Weber does not seem to practice a psychologizing method. Accordingly, some have read Weber differently, downplaying or rejecting at least this type of motivational interpretation. Peter Winch, for example, prefers to interpret Weber's concept of meaning in terms of his analysis of rule-governed action in the earlier (1907) Stammler essay (Weber, 1977). There, as Winch understands him, Weber proposes that human interaction carries with it a commitment to acting in a certain way in the future. Such commitment is possible, according to Winch, only if the present action is an application of a rule. The existence of the rule is a necessary condition, we might say, of continuity in human affairs. It is Winch's contention that the nature of meaning is to be understood in this context: Human behavior is meaningful insofar as it is rule governed, and this makes it necessarily public in nature. Lest there be a misunderstanding regarding the implications of this, it applies as well to deviance and to outright rejection or deliberate rule breaking. None of these are even conceivable apart from the existence of the rule, and very importantly, of the specifications of the *correct* concrete ways of following it, as well (Winch, 49–51).[30]

Along this line, Peter Munch has argued that the "motive" interpretation of Weber has resulted from a misleading translation of key German terms, especially *gemeinter Sinn*. While such issues are inherently interpretive, and so debatable, in this instance Munch may well have a point. He points out that in his methodological essay "Some Categories of "Interpretive Sociology" (Weber, 1981; originally published in 1922) Weber devotes considerable space to clarifying this issue. At the very outset of the relevant section, he begins by announcing that "interpretive sociology (*verstehende Soziologie*) is not a part of psychology" (408) and then goes on to defend this in detail. The thrust of this argument does seek to establish a level of social experience that is public and accessible to interpretive understanding. Motives for action are distinct from the "sense" of an action, and Munch argues that this is indeed Weber's position.

> The "sense" of an action is inherent in the structure of the action itself, regardless of the mental state of the actor, and is directly comprehensible to

---

[30] For a critique of Winch's position, see Benton, 1977, 118–119.

the recipient as well as to the observer in terms of established expectations based on verified experience" (Munch, 1975, 62).

Human activity is meaningful or "makes sense" because there are norms for conduct, and this makes it publicly accessible. Weber's use of *"Zweck,"* or purpose, designates action in which, to go back to his basic definition, the actor "attaches a subjective meaning to his behavior," or, elsewhere, action in which "a motive is a complex of subjective meaning *which seems to the actor himself* an adequate ground for the conduct in question" (Weber, 1978b, 11). This formulation includes motives but is not confined to them. Weber gives as an example a person aiming a gun, as a member of a firing squad, or in battle against the enemy, or perpetrating an act of revenge (9). In each instance the aimer of the gun is motivated in the sense that this action (aiming, listening for the command to shoot, firing) is comprehensible in the larger context (in the first instance, for example, in understanding the nature and purpose of firing squads in wartime, including the valuational and legal context of the act, the nature and significance of the military echelon system and chain of command which, by its commands, sets actions in motion, etc.). This is quite clearly the sort of thing Weber has in mind as a "complex of meaning," the totality of which, or more correctly, certain selected aspects of which, seem to the actor an "adequate ground" for his conduct. In this sense, "motivations" are to be understood as designating the "sense" in which the intentions of actors are publicly accessible as selected elements of social situations, not actions bursting forth from within. The comprehension of such intentions necessitates formulation in terms of their relational aspects, and these relational aspects are intrinsically public. In this understanding *Verstehen* is a procedure for interpreting and relating the various meaning components of a situation as these are present in the more-or-less common understandings of the actors.[31]

The category of subjective meaning, then, cannot be reduced to rule-governed action, at least in the usual sense of that term. Weber, in fact, is clear in rejecting this equation. In "Categories" he is explicit, asserting that "consensus on content can . . . be quite concretely related to purpose without having the character of abstract 'rules'" (Weber, 1981, 170). Weber mentions the condition of "submission" to a despot, based only on "expectations" that, although perhaps a limiting case, nevertheless qualifies as action that is oriented to others on the basis of subjective meaning (169). One could as easily point to conflictual relations of many types, which may involve rules only minimally, yet clearly be carried forward in terms that satisfy Weber's definition of social action. Weber uses the terms *consensus* and *validity* repeatedly. Consensus refers to nothing other than "submission to the customary *because* it is customary" (177), a consensual validity resting on nothing more than its sheer facticity. Learning to use the multiplication

---

[31] Indeed, although virtually all of Western philosophical and legal thought makes a fundamental distinction between intent and action (a variation of thought and action), there are persuasive arguments, increasingly adopted by some schools of sociology, to the effect that it is impossible, in principle, to distinguish actions from the intentions imputed as their causes, because no adequate description of the action is possible apart from introducing the intent (Hamlyn, 1968, 57). Perhaps Weber had some understanding of this.

table, taking street cars, or riding elevators, we learn the "correct" way. It is in the sense, then, of learning the byways of culture that Weber understands social action. Today we would say that such "rules" are constitutive of reality, rather than regulative of behavior (i.e., norms), and that knowing them is the basic condition of participating in the life of any collectivity.

All this relates *Verstehen* directly to the nature of ideal types. Types are selected aspects of complex configurations of meaning. The public meanings of which they are comprised are shared understandings of the actors involved regarding the nature of their and others' actions. The sociologist must apprehend these meanings if he/she is to have any chance at *explaining* them (i.e., giving a causal account). In this sense *Verstehen* is a method of piecing together the meaningful elements of a configuration, of constructing its *unity*, as it were. The entire process is one of interpretive understanding, depending—obviously—on the knowledge available to the researcher, but also on his or her imagination, and "secondary" factors such as the ability to emphathize with an actor (or many actors) on the basis of personal experience. This stipulation holds even though some actions are virtually inaccessible, e.g., the irrational behavior of the psychotic, which is certainly *motivated*, but which does *not* make sense in the terms in which Weber constructs his category of "motivation/sense," i.e., in terms of shared public meanings. In such instances it is perhaps only the skilled psychologist who can "understand" what is occurring.[32]

It must be said, however, that even though the fundamental tenets of his methodology evidently do require it, Weber fails to provide any systematic rules or criteria for the procedures involved either in discovering unities in the world or building them into the ideal types. One can perhaps see why Weber skirts this issue, glosses it semantically, but never confronts it. To impose the unifying elements of the type would seem to violate the basic tenets of *Wertbeziehung* and *Verstehen*. But to claim a pre-existing unity in the world presupposes a prior (*a priori?*) knowledge claim on the basis of which the validity of this is established.

A look at two aspects of Weber's practice as well as theory might help illuminate to some extent what he may have had in mind.

First, we note that Weber employed the concept of "elective affinity" to designate the "attractions" that various social phenomena, perhaps especially ideal and material factors, may have for one another. Thus, he speaks of the elective affinity between the Protestant ethic and the capitalist form of enterprise,[33] or more generally that between a religious ethic and the material interests of its bearers. The existence of elective affinities might explain, in part, the historical occurrence of at least some phenomena appearing conjunctively and therefore formulable as ideal types with a unity based on the elective affinity.

A second aspect of ideal type construction bearing on the internal

---

[32] Interestingly, Weber suggests that this kind of behavior is probably only interpretable nomologically, i.e., by subsumption under law.

[33] See Chapter 14 for a more expanded discussion of the place of the concept of elective affinity, in Weber's Protestant ethic-spirit of capitalism analysis, discussion of which is taken up in the chapter following.

unity problem is the supposed provisional and self-correcting nature of types. At any particular moment, types are both the product of comparative study and subject to revisions occasioned by further study. Thus, it might be inferred that those elements of a type continually reappearing together over a range of cases, as against those not doing so, constitute a unity on the grounds of their persistent association. The several elements Weber identifies in his ideal types "bureaucratic domination" or "status group" are illustrations of this. Edwards has interpreted this as a kind of "shuttlecock" movement which never produces a final synthesis, but which is designed to yield progressively improved interpretations (Edwards, 1979; see also Outhwaite, 1975).

Observations such as these, however, cannot in themselves salvage ideal type construction as a basic sociological method *in principle*, whatever its evident or seeming practical utility. So despite its power in Weber's hands, type construction remains a promising but as yet inadequately theorized method.

This understanding of *Verstehen* would also seem to imply a rejection of methodological individualism[34] as an explanatory strategy, since public shared meanings are not reducible to the action of individuals. And as we have seen earlier, Weber consistently rejected the explanation of social behavior by reduction to the *psychological* level. And his research is not reductionist. However, there remains the indubitable fact that Weber's philosophical anthropology centered on the individual as meaning constructor. And some of his methodological pronouncements seem fully consistent with this, leading some of his interpreters to identify him as advancing a form of methodological individualism. His assertion, for instance, that collectivities such as the state or social classes have to be treated "as solely the resultants and modes of organization of the particular acts of individual persons, since these alone can be treated as agents in a course of subjectively understandable action" (Weber, 1978b, 13), is a case in point, as is his stipulation that the individual is "the only agent of meaningful behavior," and that the "single individual" and the action of the individual is the "basic unit," the "atom" of social action (Weber, 1981, 158).

In the light of both his actual research practice and theorization of causality in "Edward Meyer," however, the question of what he really intended

---

[34] It has been strongly argued that methodological individualism in the social sciences is (at least in most if not all of its forms) philosophically indefensible. Lukes, for instance, has shown that, as a general program, in the absence of clear specification of the particular aspects of the "individuals" in question—physiological, psychological, dispositional—methodological individualism is quite vacuous. More holistic descriptions such as role designations ("student," "worker," etc.) are meaningful only in the context of larger complexes of social interaction (Lukes, 1968). Further, as Benton shows, the methodological individualist finds him or herself in a regress ad infinitum, for there can never be any reason to suppose that units at any particular level are the ultimate ones (Benton, 1977, 115). And as has been argued earlier, recourse to generally distributed characteristics of the species is a strategy in principle *logically* incapable of *explaining* social and cultural differences. For an excellent discussion of the logical problems involved in any consideration of methodological individualism, see Danto, 1965, 258ff. While none of these arguments are absolutely conclusive, they do constitute a strong case against methodological individualism as sociology's sole or primary *explanatory* principle.

by this and a few other passages of like vein must be interpreted carefully. Weber's empirical work is not consciously or systematically metodologically individualist, being organized as it is around complex cultural configurations, the interests and actions of groups, social structures characterized in relational terms, and so on. And in "Edward Meyer" the individual-collectivity problem is nowhere in evidence. It therefore seems unlikely in the extreme that Weber intended such statements to be understood as a general *logic of explanation*.

But if Weber did not intend to frame his sociology in such terms, what was his intention?

It seems first of all that he was reiterating and emphasizing his basic *philosophical* or *ontological* individualism, and doing so in the dual context of (1) clarifying and emphasizing his concept of subjective meaning as the fundamental and irreducible object of sociological analysis, and (2) grounding his rejection of specifically organic or functionalist conceptions or other reifications of social life, as possible alternatives. The first passage quoted above from *ES* appears in just this context. Weber downplays functional analysis on the grounds that while such a frame of reference may be useful for purposes of "practical illustration and for provisional orientation," and in some instances may even be "the only available way of determining just what processes of social action it is important to understand . . ." (Weber, 1978a, 15), it ought to be clear that such a conception cannot *ground* the discipline: "Subjective understanding is the specific characteristic of socio-logical knowledge" (15). Weber says that collectivities are *constituted* of individuals' social actions, that the latter are the sole locus of subjective meaning, and that no existence can legitimately be attributed to the former apart from individual actions. But this is *ontological* as over against *methodological* individualism. It is not an *explanatory* pronouncement, but an account of the constitutive nature of sociocultural reality. Further, where Weber insists that because categories such as the "state," or "feudalism," do "indicate for sociology categories of certain kinds of joint human action" and that "it is therefore the task of sociology to reduce these concepts to 'understandable' action, meaning, without exception, the actions of the participating individuals" (Weber, 1981, 158), he may be understood to be providing a rule intended to guard against reification of collective concepts, the very common practice of investing collectivities with "higher" meanings, meanings derived from the interests of theologians or philosophers, like Hegel's glorification of the Prussian state, or the attribution of a higher unity to a collectivity by employing the organic metaphor, or for that matter, common everyday usage in its myriad forms.

All collective action for Weber is thus *constituted* through human meaning constructors engaged in social action. As Poggi puts it:

> Weber never lets us forget that any social system, no matter how solid and compelling in its apparent facticity, ultimately rests on, indeed consists of, flows of minded activity; and that such flows necessarily originate from individual human beings . . ." (Poggi, 1983, 34).

But to repeat, this is a presuppositional or metasociological statement, an ontology, not the formulation of a logic of explanation. It does not follow that the characteristics of collectivities or collective actions are explainable (i.e., in causal terms) by the properties of individuals (whether formulated in terms of meaning or not). The propositions of a philosophical anthropology must, in principle, be distinguished from those constituting a logic of explanation.[35]

Closely related to this issue is another thorny one: the relation between subjective meaning and ideal type construction. Sewart, for one, has maintained that Weber failed to make any sort of adequate connection between his concept of social action and collective entities like bureaucracy and class, which are characterized in structural terms, contending that such structural entities are formulated by Weber as independent or external to the subjective meanings of the actors involved (Sewart, 1978). Weber's own claim of course, is that the ideal types are constructed on the grounds of an understanding of actor's subjective meanings:

> The theoretical concepts of sociology are ideal types not only from the objective point of view, but also in their application to subjective processes (Weber, 1978b, 21).

It is another question, however, as to whether or not his operations were an adequate rendering of this intent. One approach to resolving this question lies in an interpretation of the early section of *ES*.

Weber's "conceptual exposition," appearing as the first section of *ES*, can be understood as a bridge establishing a theoretical continuity between elementary subjective meaning and ideal types. He proceeds by discussing in sequence the "methodological foundations" of sociology, "social action" and its four pure types, and the concept of "social relationship," and then he expands the discussion to an array of particular structural ideal types of differing levels of generality (4–55). This is a tightly and carefully organized discussion, in which the definition of each concept serves as the necessary basis for the introduction and definition of the one following. There appear here to be four stages in this process (although Weber does not so label them). First, subjective meaning is discussed at length. Then "social action" is differentiated from action in general and derived from subjective meaning: "Subjective attitudes constitute social action only so far as they are oriented to the behavior of others" (22). Then social action is differentiated into its four pure types, instrumentally-rational, value-rational, affectual, and traditional. Following this, Weber moves to the concept of "social relationship," which denotes "the behavior of a plurality of actors insofar as, in its meaningful content, the action of each takes account of that of the others and is oriented in these terms" (26). The significant additional element here is the stipulation that the "meaningful content" that "takes account of that of others" is now extended to a plurality. It is worth taking note of Weber's observation that the meanings in question may be quite complex ("not

---

[35] We might add that this assessment is consistent with Weber's definition of *social action*, not the individual as theorized in his philosophical anthropology, as the fundamental unit of sociological analysis.

necessarily the same for all parties" [27]). Throughout the discussion it is clear that social relationships have no other existence than that constituted from the subjective meanings among actors. The concept of social relationship is a critical one in that it functions as a sort of "bridge" between the foundational ideas of subjective meaning and social action, on the one hand, and the concepts of structure on the other.

Weber then goes on to differentiate the broadest or most general of action orientations insofar as they are associated with a collectivity. These are "usage," "custom," and "self-interest" (29–31). These concepts stand in a relationship of subsumption to both the pure types of action and "the social relationship." Instrumental rationality, for instance, is the essential quality of the orientation of self-interest, whereas tradition is the *differentia specifica* of custom (29). At this point Weber introduces the concept of "legitimate order," which in turn can be differentiated into types on the basis of the pure types of action (36ff.). Following this, an array of concepts designating the full range of empirical phenomena studied by sociology is worked out (38–54).

The important thing about this is that it has a sequential and developmental internal coherence. Each concept is defined and explicated in terms of the one introduced just prior to it: "Social action" is defined in terms of "subjective meaning," "social relationship" in terms of "social action," and the collective action orientations and the principle of legitimacy in terms of his definition of "social relationship." Throughout the entire sequence, Weber self-consciously strives to preserve the original principle of subjective meaning. The entire exposition should be thought of as an expansion, in the form of a logical progression,[36] of the basic concept of subjective meaning. Insofar as this exercise can be considered successful, the charge that Weber formulates his ideal types outside the basic theoretical framework of the concept of subjective meaning cannot be maintained. And at least in the sense of the logic of how he worked it out, Weber ought to be judged to have been, at least for the time, partly successful. The logical rigor of the entire operation is one basis for this claim. The fact that the content of the ideal types actually used in his research are formulated in terms of subjective meanings, is another.

Of course, what Weber did not achieve, and what still remains to be achieved in sociology, is an *empirical* demonstration of just how connections between the interactional and large-scale levels of collectivities are created and maintained, known today as the "micro-macro" problem. Taking "meaning" at the level of the individual makes the sort of transition to "social relationship" logically impossible. This is the problem faced by the early phenomenologists (especially Husserl) and their followers who attempted to ground social science phenomenologically. A relational term or concept— e.g., "social relationship"—is not derivable from one defined *essentially*, in this instance the subjective meaning of the individual. Logically, an array of such atomized conceptions yields only an *aggregate*, and terms or propositions

---

[36] Not of a "continuum," as Hekman puts it (Hekman, 1983, 54–55), although she is correct in emphasizing the internal consistency in Weber's concept of subjective meaning and principles of ideal type construction. See also Martindale, 1960, 388ff.

referring to such aggregates cannot deduce or derive relational properties among them. Thus, the abstraction the "birth rate" is simply a term designating an arithmetically derived statistic based on the sum of all the births in some space over a given period of time. Weber simply glossed this problem and went on with his exposition.

There are other difficulties in Weber's exposition. One of these has to do with the way in which Weber draws out the ramifications of the concept of social action in terms of just what it logically includes and excludes from the domain of sociology. The clear implication of defining social action in terms of subjective meaning in the sense discussed above, as we pointed out earlier, is that there is already in existence an "account" of every culture (or sub-culture, group, etc.) and that this account is itself a form of knowledge, because it is "a complex of subjective meaning which seems to the actor himself or to the observer an adequate ground for the conduct in question." What is the implication of this for social scientists or historians engaged in the process of concept formation rooted in value-relevance?

Oakes argues that Weber's definition of social action implies that the criterion by which the scientific adequacy of any account produced by the social scientist must be judged is its comprehensibility to the *actors*, that is, its necessary comprehensibility in terms of *their* account. This carries with it the extremely stringent test of whether or not the actors "themselves ascribe the identical meaning to their conduct" (Oakes, in Simmel, 1977, "Introduction", 25). If and only if the social scientist's account is comprehensible to the actor or actors, can it be judged scientifically adequate. In and of itself, this seems to impose a severe limitation on social science, namely, that it must logically restrict itself merely to descriptions or reproductions of the "language games," of natural social groupings. This is the position taken by Peter Winch (Winch, 1977). But aside from the more obvious difficulties this stipulation seems to impose (a strict interpretation, for instance, would seem to make impossible all historical research), it could easily be interpreted as a desideratum making the scientific account a duplicate or near-duplicate of the "natural" one, thereby seemingly obviating any need for it. Clearly such a stringent requirement cannot be defended.[37]

Weber's own formulation, "to the actor himself, *or to the observer . . .*" (underlining mine) seems to suggest that some complexes of meaning, at least, might be incomprehensible to the actors involved in them, but nevertheless understood by the observer. It follows that some scientific accounts could have identical status. Repressed experience of ideas, which may be

---

[37] Among several critiques of Winch on this point is that of Habermas, who has argued that in establishing "language games" as the object of social science analysis, Winch fails to explicate the status of the *social science* language game as distinct from all the others, an exercise presuppositional to all social scientific analysis (Habermas, 1979b). In similar vein, Giddens has argued strongly that all social science proceeds in terms of a "double dialectic" in which "sociology, unlike natural science, deals with a preinvented world where the creation and reproduction of meaning-frames is a very condition of that which it seeks to analyze, namely human social conduct." But this requires not a reduction of scientific to lay concepts, or imposition of a rule requiring "rendition in terms of lay concepts," but often just grasping lay concepts, i.e., the form of life whose features the social scientist wishes to explain, "hermeneutically" (Giddens, 1976, 158–159).

driving forces in behavior, the significance of which Weber was evidently aware (having read Freud in 1907), are one case in point. Such behavior, he says, may be comprehensible only to an expert. He may also have had in mind various points touched on elsewhere, such as the idea that the comprehensibility of existing accounts to the actors would more often than not be quite variable, depending on other factors, including the complexity of the account itself, or the fact that actors might not be willing or psychologically capable of recognizing at least certain motivational attributions (especially those perceived as negative), or again, the obvious limitation this criterion places on historical research.

There is another problem related to the one just discussed that we might call the "scope" problem. This has to do with the way in which Weber's stipulations limit the proper or legitimate scope of sociological analysis. The category of traditional action presents one such difficulty. As one of Weber's four pure types of action it must have meaningful content, as in the instance of its application to the deliberate limitation of production in maintaining a given level of consumption, rather than striving to elevate it. But elsewhere Weber virtually places traditional action beyond the legitimate purview of sociology, saying that it is no more than unreflective routine or habit, in which case it is difficult to see how it qualifies as a type of action in the first place.

In this regard Weber's distinction between two types of meaning-interpretation is relevant. He differentiates a rational type which entails "obtaining a completely clear intellectual grasp of the action-elements in their intended context of meaning," from an "empathic or appreciative" form, achieved when, through "sympathetic appreciation, we can adequately grasp the emotional context" of meaning (Weber, 1978b, 5). Here Weber comes close to identifying these two types of meaning interpretation with instrumental and value rationality respectively. His association of meaning with motive or intention has sometimes been interpreted as restricting it to instrumentally rational action, and indeed, Weber does say that "the interpretation of . . . rationally purposeful action possesses, for the understanding choice of means, the highest degree of verifiable certainty," whereas ultimate ends or values, on the other hand, "often cannot be understood completely" (5). But Weber does not on this account exclude such interpretation either in principle, or, very obviously, in his research practice, although he does discuss the difficulties it involves. In some cases it may be necessary to settle for a "purely intellectual" understanding, or failing this, to accept them "as given data" (whatever these are). Furthermore, the degree of susceptibility to emotional states is an important factor in the researcher's ability to achieve an emotional or appreciative interpretation. This is a striking and theoretically significant indication of Weber's distance from the positivists.

Even on the broadest possible interpretation, Weber's definition of social action in terms of meaning, however, seems unnecessarily limiting, as some have remarked (e.g., Winch, 1977; Merquior, 1981). This becomes evident in his substantive work, particularly with respect to traditionalism. Although much traditional action is at best sociologically borderline, major sections of Weber's sociology focus explicitly on traditional types of action: patriarchalism, patrimonialism, feudalism, and so on. Indeed, traditional domination is one of three general ideal types framing the entirety of Weber's political sociology. That Weber was perhaps aware of the overnarrowness of his conception may be seen in remarks immediately following the general discussion of meaning at the beginning of *ES*. Although sociology has been defined two pages earlier as the "science concerning itself with the interpretive understanding of social action and thereby with a causal explanation of its course and consequences" (4), we learn here that "account must be taken of processes and phenomena which are devoid of subjective meaning" (7), in which category Weber includes natural events, physiological states, and the like, but which on his own definition, also encompasses the relatively pure instances of traditionalism as well (although Weber never says as much).

We will here take up one final problem.[38] Do not the doctrines of *Wertbeziehung* and *Verstehen* imply an *unscientific* and incorrigible relativism? This charge has frequently been leveled at Weber. The problem has to be decomposed into at least two distinct questions. First, there is the relatively minor issue of the necessity of separating the impositions of values, or the making of value-judgments, from adducing scientific propositions. Second, there is the problem of the limitations on the scope of analysis attending the doctrines of *Wertbeziehung* and *Verstehen*; specifically, can the process of interpretation be applied to value domains foreign to that of the social scientist? Consider these in turn.

Weber, of course, rejects the first charge. His discussion, however, is unconvincing. He points out, first of all, that any cultural phenomenon may evoke a *non-verstehende* attitude, as for instance, to return to the example above, the rejection of Goethe's love letters to Frau von Stein on the part of "the usual modern sexual philistine" or a Catholic moralist (Weber, 1949, 143–144). Such an "imposition of value," Weber says, is "a task completely transcending the domain of 'interpretation'" (144). "Impositions of value," or value-judgments of this sort may enrich one's "inner life," or "extend one's mental horizons" (144), but there is an important line to be drawn between such renderings and interpretive understandings. The former, Weber says, stands at

> the outermost edge of what can still be called "the elaboration of the empirical by thought"; there is here no longer a concern with "historical work" in the proper and distinctive sense of the word" (145)

In this passage Weber is perhaps appealing implicitly to the court of the scientific collegial community, its accumulated knowledge and methodological practice, although he is nowhere explicit about this. But beyond this, he provides no specific rules that clearly establish ways of distinguishing, and thereby avoiding, the making of value-judgments. Presumably what he has in mind is the entire procedure of type construction and causal analysis, in which "impositions of value" would end up being purged through the application of validity checks inherent in type construction and causal analysis.

Is the social scientific analysis of other value domains precluded by Weber's formulation of social action theory? Does the selection of problems

---

[38] But leave the "rationality" problem until Weber's substantive work has been discussed.

on the basis of value-relevance itself, even apart from employment of *Verstehen* as an investigatory procedure, place analysis of different cultures beyond the purview of science? Weber himself recognizes the *difficulties* involved in this although—given the fact that a good deal of his work *is* an analysis of other cultures remote from the West, particularly India and China—he obviously could not possibly subscribe to any view that in principle made scientific rationality incommensurable with other cultures because it arose in the West. The issue is obviously a fundamental one, which may account for the fact that Weber seems to be on both sides of it.

On the one hand, we may say with some confidence that the main theme of Weber's writings had to do with the unique qualities of Western rationalism, which includes science at its very core, as distinct from the forms of rationality of all other cultures and civilizations. In "Science as a Vocation," for instance, he says that the "concept" and the rational experiment, fundamental to science, are uniquely Western (Gerth and Mills, 1946, 140–141). (We have touched on this earlier and will return to it in Chapter 15.) But against this Weber also asserts the universal validity of science.

> All scientific work presupposes that the rules of logic and method are valid; these are the general foundations of our orientation in the world, and, at least for our special question, these presuppositions are the least problematic aspect of science. (Weber, 1946, 143).

Thus, the rules of logic and method are valid beyond Western culture.

> A systematically correct proof in the social sciences, if it is to achieve its purpose, must be acknowledged as correct even by a Chinese ... (Weber, 1949, 58)[39]

This is so even though the "Chinese" may "lack a 'sense' for our ethical imperative" (the *value* of science), and even though "he can and certainly will deny the ideal itself and the concrete value-judgments derived from it" (58–59). These attitudes, Weber says, cannot "affect the scientific value of the analysis in any way" (59). The logic and method of science must be considered valid even for those for whom they have no value-relevance.

Weber's evident inconsistency on this issue reflects what is perhaps the central dilemma of action, or of any subjectively grounded theory, the problematic status of its validity claims. On the one hand the social scientist is enjoined to grasp the actor's culture on its own terms, in terms of the meanings of the participants in that culture. On the other, he/she must adhere to what is taken to be a basic scientific canon—generalizability. If the concepts of the social scientist are drawn from those of the actors being studied, does this not make it impossible to relate empirical findings to one another, i.e., to generalize about them? This issue, whether the rationality

---

[39] The philosophical remarks at the conclusion of "Objectivity" in Social Science and Social Policy, wherein Weber reflects that as "the light of the great cultural problems moves on, . . . science too prepares to change its standpoint and analytical approaches . . ." (Weber, 1949, 112), may be interpreted as referring to value-relevance and ideal types but *not* to scientific "logic and method."

standards of Western science are to be regarded as universal, and so transcend those of non-Western cultures (or "traditional" regions of Western societies), is no forgotten relic of Weberian sociology; on the contrary, it is today, in myriad forms, a far more important and critical issue than ever.

This concludes our treatment of Weber's philosophical anthropology and methodology. We turn now to his empirical sociology, where these principles may be seen in application.

14

MAX WEBER II
Weber's conceptual scheme and historical sociology

WEBER'S THEORY OF HISTORICAL DEVELOPMENT

Weber's substantive sociology has proven to be an *oeuvre* of substantially greater significance and scope than that of any of the thinkers we have considered up to the present. Even Durkheim's pales by comparison. And it is probably fair to say that nothing on this scale has been achieved since. Weber's work in the sociology of religion alone includes four monographic essays and several other general theoretical works, and his works on political and economic topics, including his sociology of law, comprise another several volumes, including his magnum opus, *Economy and Society* (*ES*), which runs to 1500 pages.[1] Much if not most of this work is still in process of being interpreted and assimilated into sociology. There is thus as yet no truly definitive Weber.

We saw in the previous chapter that Weber was no evolutionist in the sense of Spencer, Durkheim, or the German economic historians he criticized in "Roscher and Knies . . ." (hereafter to be referred to as RK).

---

[1] The monographs in the sociology of religion include *Ancient Judaism* (*AJ*), *The Religion of India* (*RI*), *The Religion of China* (*RC*), and *The Protestant Ethic and the Spirit of Capitalism* (*PE*). Beyond these there is the long essay in *ES* (Chapter 4) entitled "Religious Groups," and the 1913 essay "Religious Rejections of the World," translated by Gerth and Mills (Gerth and Mills, 1946), along with a number of other shorter essays, the best known being "The Protestant Sects and the Spirit of Capitalism" (*SECTS*). The works on economic and political orders appear mainly in *ES*, but also the essay *The Agrarian Sociology of Ancient Civilization* (ASAC), an expanded rewrite of one of his dissertations, the lectures delivered at Munich in 1918–1919 and translated by Frank Knight as *General Economic History*, along with a few additional pieces. There is also the brilliant essay on the sociology of music, translated by Don Martindale, Johannes Riedel, and Gertrude Neuwirth as *The Rational and Social Foundations of Music* (RSM).

Neither, however, was he merely the kind of abstract typologist he has sometimes been charged with being. Whether his sociology should be thought of as a philosophy of history, as Gerth and Mills, among others, have maintained (1946, 51ff.), because of his theory of rationalization, is also questionable,[2] even though Weber himself sometimes employed the term "universal history" (*Universal-Geschichte*), common during the period, in referring not only to the work of others, but to his own as well. But he certainly rejected unequivocally all historical work that tended "to interpret the sequence of types . . . in lawfully determined historical sequence" (1949, 103), and the diversity and uniqueness he finds central to the human social condition (Chapter 13 of this book) imply a historical "openness" foreign to evolutionism. Furthermore, the conception of the ideal types as "fictional" constructions of the researcher employed only for "heuristic" purposes underscores the highly problematic nature of even *known* concrete reality, to say nothing of the future. In his search for "real causes," he was careful in trying to avoid reifying the type into the concrete individual phenomenon or phenomena as causal or caused—a common error of evolutionary thought.

Yet at the same time, Weber did clearly seek to discern tendencies in history. These he described in terms of their variable stability, of their potential for generating conflict, and their "affinity" with other tendencies. The play of these processes results in a kind of dialectic of stability and upheaval, patterns of change that, *in and of themselves* reveal no constant or universal driving agents in history, but that can be comprehended as historical individuals through historical and generalizing ideal types and the genetic processes whereby they come into being. But beyond this, some passages from Weber's works seem to suggest that he claimed to have discovered something approximating an *overall* developmental pattern in the history of the Occident, i.e., the growth or expansion of rationalizing processes in every sphere of social life. If this be evolution, it is evolution along multiple tracks with not only ideological, but materialist "switchmen" as well, stationed all along the line, redirecting events in paradoxical and unintended directions.

In his historical sociology Weber is perhaps best interpreted as having attempted to stake out a position somewhere between evolutionism and purely historicist description, and Schluchter has suggested the term "developmental history" as an appropriate characterization of this.[3] This usage will be followed here.

Weber's sociology, like the sociologies discussed in earlier chapters, may be framed in terms of the way he confronted and worked out the implication of the problematics of social change, individual and society, and theory of science. We have treated the second and third of these in some detail in the previous chapter. But it is the first, the theorization of the social processes that have brought the modern economically developed and developing world into being, that constitutes Weber's central specifically sociolog-

---

[2] In the eyes of antievolutionists, this would, ipso facto, make it evolutionary. See Popper, 1954.

[3] "Weber's sociology offers neither a comprehensive typology nor a universal theory of evolution but a developmental history of the West" (Schluchter, 1981, 24). It ought to be noted that judgments regarding Weber's historical sociology differ greatly. Perry Anderson, for instance, finds his work devoid of any historical theory proper (Anderson, 1974, 410), while it is Randall Collins's judgment, on the other hand, that "Weber's model continues to offer a more sophisticated basis for a theory of capitalism than any of the rival theories of today" (Collins, 1980, 926)—and this would of course include Anderson's.

ical interest. In this respect, it is the connection between his conception of the individual and the modernizing processes of change which define his master problem. Weber thought that the critical feature of western individualism was the historical emergence from the ethics of Protestanism of what we might term a *conscience-driven*, or even conscience-ridden, personality. This individualism has infused western institutions—state, law, economy, religion, broadly conceived, everything connected with the rise of capitalism. By the turn of the century these capitalist social formations had achieved a level of objectification that had rendered them remote from their ethical origins in religion and natural law conceptions. Thus is Weber's problem framed: the fate of the individual personality in a social order which trivializes and deracinates the very individualism from which it has sprung. Weber's sociology, then, as Wilhelm Hennis has recently put it, is an attempt to "discipline" this interest of theorizing the nature of this individual-social order connection as it unfolds in our time (Hennis, 1988).

The main thrust of Weber's scholarship, in consequence, was directed toward accounting for the rise of capitalism in the West, and then more broadly, to explaining the entirety of Western "modernism." We might note in passing that it was probably never his intent to create a sociological *system*, although on occasion such an objective has been attributed to him (by Parsons, for example); the sociological taxonomy at the beginning of Volume 1 of *Economy and Society* was understood as having an entirely heuristic function in relation to problems defined in terms of their value relevance.

The bulk of Weber's scholarly work can be understood in terms of this objective. Both his doctoral dissertations, on medieval trading companies and the agrarian history of the Roman Empire (later in 1908 expanded to include other ancient civilizations) dealt with problems clearly bearing, even if somewhat remotely, on the larger question (Weber, 1924, 313–443; and 1971a). The work that followed, on the displacement of German by Polish workers in the East Elbian region, brought into focus as the central socioeconomic process occurring there, the transformation of the region from a feudal to a capitalist enclave (Weber, 1892). The sociology of religion and of law had as their explicit focus the influence of religious ethics and law systems, respectively, on capitalist development. Beginning especially with *The Protestant Ethic* of 1905, followed by the volumes on ancient Judaism and the Chinese and Indian religions, along with his general essay published as part of *Economy and Society*, Weber's program may be understood as an attempt to adduce the basic contours of the history of Western civilization. He worked out his conceptual scheme in the course of generating his historical works and systematized this scheme only late in life as a step toward a world historical comparative sociology.

Weber's early work was in law and economic history. The methodological essays of the "middle" period were intended, in part, to show how the historical and generalizing disciplines were *related*, rather than merely distinct or even incommensurable disciplines, a project providing the metatheoretical foundations for the work to come. For the most part, Weber's sociological work proper appears only after this. The essay on early capitalism and Protestantism, brought out in 1905 in two parts in the *Archiv*, may fairly be said to mark the beginning of this period. But Weber's *oeuvre* is in part an *integration*, or at least an attempt at integration, of history and sociology. On the basis of these preliminary remarks, I will begin with Weber's general sociology of Western historical development, as the context for discussion of the specific problem of the relation between the Protestant ethic and capitalism, and then go on to a discussion and interpretation of his theory of rationalization.

THE CORE PROBLEM OF WEBER'S SOCIOLOGY: ECONOMIC ETHICS AND THE ORIGINS OF SALVATION RELIGION

Even the most divergent interpretations of capitalism have been in agreement about it being an economic system that, in its motivational force, is in principle nonethical or amoral; the pursuit of gain (along with the survival of the gain-seeking unit) is its only significant driving force. The divergence centers on the consequences: Marxists, of course, hold them to be destructive and anarchic, liberals, that they include productivity, efficiency, growth, and social harmony, at least in the long run, and even though certain social costs must be exacted from other sectors of society.[4] Capitalism has typically been contrasted not only with feudalism, but with practically *all* earlier systems on precisely this point. All other systems, it is held, have been subordinated to institutional control of some sort, be it church, state, kin group, occupational monopoly, or military domination.

Weber's view differs somewhat from both. He finds capitalism—understood in its elementary sense as the pursuit of gain—present in many places and in diverse forms throughout history: "booty capitalism," for example, or the colonial capitalism fostered by control of an administrative apparatus, or the fiscal capitalism made possible by exploiting political position, and so on. In all such cases the "capitalism" is situationally anchored as an element in a larger historical situation, and comprehensible only as such an element. Self-interest, although a universal human tendency, fails to explain not only the diverse types of capitalism appearing in certain historical situations, but its *absence* in others. Weber insisted on understanding the modern form of capitalism, as he did all its earlier manifestations, from a historicist standpoint, i.e., in its unique history and relation to other aspects of society. His thesis is that modern capitalism cannot be understood apart from the specific ethical beliefs and practices of the early Protestant sects, and that this ethic accounts for the historically specific inner nature of the meaning of capitalist activity at least for earlier capitalists (the motivational emancipation of contemporary capitalists from religious ethical norms, Weber was the first to assert, was clearly something else). Weber may have been wrong about this in certain respects, but this is not the issue here. Rather, the point is that his approach to the analysis even of such ostensibly prototypically self-interested and nonethically grounded activity as modern capitalism was to explain it in terms of its *inner meaning* as well as its *external form or functioning* (see Weber, 1948, 64–65). The development of the West, Weber thought, was distinct from other civilizations in large part because of this. Whatever the causes of Western economic development up to around

---

[4] This is obviously a caricature. The actual positions taken by different individuals and groups on this point differ in various important subtle and not-so-subtle ways. The Benthamites, for instance, advocated strong government administration in some areas, on the grounds that in these cases it was the best, or only way, to achieve the *utilitarian* value of the greatest good for the greatest number. On this point they obviously differed from the "Manchesterites."

the sixteenth century, it was Weber's argument that capitalist development could be explained only by incorporating the religious factor into the explanatory equation.

In a parallel fashion Weber examined the major religious of India and China, especially Hinduism and Confucianism. Whereas the ethical orientation and theology of Calvinism and various other Protestant sects fostered economic activity and contributed to economic growth, the opposite was generally true in Asia, where the ethics of these religions, according to Weber, had the effect of impeding economic development.

At this point the reader should recall the discussion of the duality of material and ideal interests in the previous chapter.[5]

If ideas, in addition to material interests, are important—even essential—to a scientific understanding of the human world in the sense of having causal power, then it seemed that an inquiry into what has been historically far and away the most important ideal aspect of human experience—religion—would be the appropriate focus of his research. And if the case for the significant independent effect of religion was to be made, it would be made most powerfully if the effect of religion on economic activity could be shown not in just one, but in a series of historically important societies, or even civilizations. Weber is careful to specify religious *ethics*, not theology, as the principal aspect of religious experience, although theologies, or more broadly, beliefs, are in their significance for social action incorporated into all of his analyses. The influence of the "Protestant ethic" on the development of capitalism in the West is only one case in which the religious ethics-economic action relationship is brought under study.

Now economic and religious activity, of course, take differing organizational forms historically, and these are crucial to all of Weber's sociology. In fact, he may be said to a greater extent than any previous sociologists, to have brought into the center of his sociology an analysis of the organizational structures through which practically all human action takes place. Economic life in antiquity, for instance, was pursued within the organizational framework of the household, organized along kinship lines. Political life thus had no autonomy, even in the enormously expanded households that Weber called patrimonial bureaucracies. It was one of the great critical watersheds in human history when forms of political domination independent of the household began to appear. Organizational forms are likewise crucial to religious action, and the "politics" of religious life cannot be understood apart from them. Indeed, it may be said that one of Weber's conceptual innovations was the expansion of the category of material interest to encompass organization as well as economic considerations.

There are, of course, spheres of ideal meaning other than religion;

[5] Weber arrived at this formulation very late, in 1919–1920, while revising his introduction to the collected essays in the sociology of religion, although the distinction was probably in mind much earlier. In the chapter on "Economic Action" in *ES* he says, for instance, that "all economic activity in a market economy is undertaken and carried through by individuals acting to provide for their own *ideal or material interests*" (202: underlining mine). It is important to keep in mind also that the concepts of ideal and material interest are analytic ones, not tied to specific orders, e.g., economic, political, religious, etc. This was a flexibility Weber needed to undertake analyses of what he regarded as extremely complex interrelations among orders.

literally any human activity can be, and in fact is, constructed in ideal forms: erotic, aesthetic, and a range of leisure activities, for instance, to say nothing of philosophy, understood as an essentially Western intellectual enterprise carried forward mostly independent of control by religious institutions. Weber in various places discussed all of these, and others, in connection with his judgment regarding their significance for economic and political activity. But even philosophy, with a few rather notable exceptions, has generally been the province of a few privileged intellectuals talking among themselves and has rarely penetrated or significantly influenced everyday conduct on a wide scale. Stoicism is a partial exception, because of its importance for the development of Roman law, as are the natural law doctrines of the early modern period. The ideas associated with this—the doctrine of the universality of human reason, and the demands for political rights derived from it—were obviously of great social import, as Roman law and the French Revolution, among other significant historical phenomena, demonstrate.

In Weber's understanding law is in general akin to religion in being a type of normative order. Law, convention, and custom belong to "the same continuum with imperceptible transitions leading from one to the other" (319). Like religion, the sociological significance of law is that it invokes rules of conduct and therefore bears within itself at least a potential for influencing economic action. The growth of the significance of law in the West, central to Weber's sociology, has been a complex and halting process, involving Roman rule and its aftermath, the Catholic church, the emergence of the Western city as an independent contractual association, private and public associations of legal professionals, and most important of all, perhaps, the growth of the modern state. In this process law played a role basic to Western modernization. Like religion, it has an ideal sphere that acquires social significance through its political and organizational vehicles. However, the extent to which Weber considered it to possess the sort of immanent developmental potential that he attributed to religion is uncertain (on this point see Treiber, 1984; also this chapter, 392–93).

Material and ideal interests, then, constitute the parameters of all of social life. Ultimately, all human conduct is scientifically comprehensible only as it is organized to pursue both types of ends, and to pursue them in ways that require analysis of their complex intertwining. The concrete forms of conduct we find in the sociological categories "economic," "political," "religious," "legal," and so on, define the most important dimensions—partial social orders—of society, and their analysis proceeds in terms of the interplay of material and ideal interests within and between them.

"Primitive" Religion and the Transition to Salvation Religion

Unlike the "world religions"—Christianity, Hinduism, Buddhism, Confucionism, Islam, Judaism—early religions were not creators or bearers of ethical codes of conduct. Weber characterizes these as "naturalistic," oriented mainly to spirit worship, largely controlled by magicians manipulating entities—Gods and demons—residing "behind" phenomenal reality. Magicians provide both magical solutions to the problems of individuals and socially organized worship principally in the form of the orgy, "the primordial form of religious association" (Weber, 1978b, 401). The former function is, for Weber, the more important, since it requires the *continuous* profession-alized activity of the magician, as over against the occasional nature of the group ceremony. The magician is the archetypal charismatic, the oldest of all "vocations" (401), whose charisma rests on his ability to achieve extraor-dinary states of ecstasy, often with the aid of drugs or alcohol, or through music and the dance, states only rarely achieved by ordinary beings. The magical powers of magicians are overwhelmingly oriented to the concerns of *this* world: manipulation of the inhabitants of the spirit world addresses the worldly problems of birth and death, sickness and health, the fertility of the harvest, interpersonal conflict, and group unity and knows nothing of the sense and meaningfulness of salvation. In general, Weber emphasizes that societies permeated by magical belief and practice are greatly resistant to change: Magic has a powerful inherent tendency to stereotype relationships of all sorts, including economic ones. This is ordinarily reinforced by the professional material interests of magicians, which rest mainly on the continuing dependence of their clientele for their livelihood, and therefore on the continuing belief in the specific orderliness and predictability of the beings that control nature, along with the magician's own capacity to divine their intentions and manipulate their actions. And this is by no means a phenomenon restricted to the remote past. Weber cites the fact that in nineteenth century China, for instance, the Taoist priests who made a living by divining were able to successfully block the building of railroads and factories (429).

Whether or not there is a significant movement in the direction of religion depends on its importance for the economy and on the power of the magicians' organization (404). Empirically all such movements toward theological and ethical religion are quite complex. What occurs is a dual development, involving the interplay of ideal and material factors. Weber formulates the complex particulars of this within the framework of his concept of rationalization.

Rationalization is doubtless Weber's most general concept and will be discussed in its general sense later. Here we are concerned only with its religious meaning. Weber's clearest and most parsimonious statement is in *RC*.

> To judge the level of rationalization a religion represents we may use two primary yardsticks which are in many ways interrelated. One is the degree to which the religion has divested itself of magic; the other is the degree to which it has systematically unified the relation between God and the world, and therewith its own ethical relativity to the world. (Weber, 1951, 226; see also Weber, 1952, [*AJ*] 425–426, n.1).

The most general relation here is the inverse one between the decline of magic, on the one hand, and on the other, the growth of both a systematically unified relation to God *and* an accompanying expanding suffusion of ethical principles in social action. This relationship, however, is by no means a uniform one. Weber applied this scheme to the relation between religion and economic ethics in China and India (see *RC* and *RI*) emphasizing both the belief and ethical transformations associated with the decline of magic. We shall consider these in turn.

The process of systematizing and making more abstract the elements of magical belief involves a process in which, "magic is transformed from a direct manipulation of forces into a *symbolic* activity" (Weber, 1978b, 403). It has everywhere involved a struggle to transcend various forms of magical and religious heterogeneity or pluralism: the different gods associated with extended kinship groupings, or those of competing political entities, or the fantastic proliferation of deities in ancient Rome. Under most conditions, any movement in the direction of a more rationalized belief system, and certainly achieving the theological culmination of such movements, monotheism, is rather unlikely. The major obstacles to this, as mentioned above, are the interests of magicians, or at various stages of the development, magician-priests (for the dividing line is quite fluid), who monopolize knowledge of and communication with their particular god or gods, on the one hand, and on the other, the traditionalism of the laity, whose lives are organized around and suffused with familiar religious objects and practices.

The shift from magic to religion is thus the work of religious professionals, whose material interests under certain conditions may be served by this development. In general, this has to do with their interest in maintaining and expanding their control over what Weber calls the means of mental production. All such rationalizations presuppose a relatively strong, permanent association of religious professionals eventually coming to function as cult leaders. In this process the transformation of magicians into priests is central. Indeed, Weber defines the priest as a specialist in managing the continuous operation of a cult. Characteristically, he draws out his definition, or *ideal type* of priest, in contrast with the magician. The priest is (1) a cult leader of, (2) a permanently organized enterprise, (3) functioning as an employee or organ "operating in the interests of the organizations' members," (4) engaged in *worship* of the gods (as distinct from their coercion or manipulation), and (5) who possesses as professional equipment "special knowledge, fixed doctrine, and vocational qualifications . . .", in contrast to the ideal-type magician, who is the opposite of all of these (425). The priest, as distinct from the magician, is thus an office holder who claims his authority on the basis of his "service in a sacred tradition," and who "dispenses salvation by virtue of his office" (440). The gradual metamorphosis from tribal or clan magic or cult religion entails the diminution, and perhaps ultimately the rejection of magical manipulation of the spirit world, and the growth of worship. Yet Weber emphasizes the continuities. Prayer and sacrifice, the central practices of religious worship, both have their origins in magic. It can be a fine line indeed between the attempt to manipulate a spirit through the application of certain spells, and the attempt, by sacrifice, to persuade or coerce a god to intercede, or to stay his wrath. The critical factor lies in the shifting of the function of sacrifice (and prayer) to the communal level with its transcendent collective meaning, the function of which then becomes the production and revitalization of community between the sacrificers and the god.

From the standpoint of the social significance of ideas, the main function of priests, then, is to rationalize heterogeneous beliefs into relatively coherent and consistent bodies of doctrine. This process is more or less coterminous with their evolution as professional cult managers. The hardening of what Weber calls "canonical scriptures" into dogmas, the priestly interpretations of the former, gradually supplants the strictly magical forms of propitiation and manipulation of the supernatural. The material and ideal interests of the magician are served by the repeated demonstrations or exhibitions of his charisma, and his ability to evoke the same or lesser variations of these in others. It is this that ties clientele to magician. During the process of the transformation of magicians into priests, this relationship is transformed into one that takes the form of systematic indoctrination centering on sacred texts and their interpretation. Whereas the authority and power of the magician is based on the secrecy of magical knowledge, that of the priest acquires its foundation in the monopoly of authoritative interpretation of sacred texts, on which the meaning of the community's *tradition* is based.

Grounding of the life of the community in such priestly functions tends to encourage closure against new or alien ideas and practices. Other things being equal, the more rationalized the system of belief, the more this is true. Whereas the introduction of new gods or spirits into the heterogeneous pantheon of more or less unconnected deities or spirits, or the casting off of old ones, is relatively easy in societies dominated by magic (witness the Greek or Roman cases, or the early Vedic period of Hinduism), a system based on scriptural interpretation with its tendency toward systematized dogma comes to be a matter of *faith*. Thus, all other beliefs tend to become defined not merely as different, or even incompatible, but as heretical. The implications of this for the nature of the religious life of the community are momentous indeed.

This process does not occur in some sheerly teleological fashion. Weber is clear in arguing that its most important condition is the presence of competing groups and prophesies. In such situations the formal canonization of the scriptures functions as a weapon against the threat of the dissolution of the community. The origin of every great world religion can be traced to this process. Christianity struggled against a variety of sects, particularly the Gnostics, Judaism against apostolic prophesies, Hinduism against certain intellectual as distinct from mystical heterodoxies, Buddhism against the Mahayana movement.[6] In these instances as in others, it is conflict that is the engine of social change. The struggles proceed on both material and ideal planes. From the standpoint of priests, it is *both* their material and ideal interests that are at stake (although the former may be denied on doctrinal or valuational grounds). However, both the weighting or relative significance, and qualitative nature of these, varies greatly from situation to situation. Especially in other-worldly religions, such as Buddhism or Hinduism, and particularly in their "higher" forms, material interests may come to be rejected altogether, in principle, as obstructions to salvation. But even in such cases, where (exemplary) prophecy leads to a total denial of the

---

[6] For more detail in each of these, see, for Christianity, Weber, 1978b, 512, 16; for Judaism, Weber, 1952, 421ff; for Hinduism, Weber, 1958, Chap. 6; for Buddhism, *ibid*, 244ff.

world by the religious professionals or elite, its implications for economic life as practiced among the laity nevertheless remain quite significant, as we shall see.

Throughout this process it is always in the priesthood's material interest to continue its domination of the laity by maintaining whatever rituals to which the latter are tied. The traditionalism of the latter, which priests must always take into account, tends to be an obstacle, as already mentioned, and is the main reason that, even as religious rationalization proceeds, magical elements tend to survive and even to become central to actual religious practice. Weber liked to point out that Catholicism, for example, and Hinduism as well, never were purged of magical elements. He regarded the Catholic sacraments as basically magical and referred in many places to the "Catholic magic."[7]

The second dimension of religous rationalization lies in the realm of ethical conduct, the systematization of which is the distinctive mark of all world religions. Ethical religions, by definition, have some sort of religious *law*, obedience to which is obligatory in order to gain or maintain oneself in God's favor (430).

Originally, there are two methods of influencing the spirits or gods: by magic or by "gratifying their egoistic wishes" (432). The mark of the emergence of ethical religion is the principle of adherence to a *religious law* as a means of obtaining the favors of the gods. In discussing the emergence of this, Weber again emphasizes the continuities with the earlier magical stage. Ethical religion evolves from taboo, which originally sets aside certain aspects of social life as sacred or unclean, ordinarily extraordinary life events such as birth or death, and ritualizes them against intrusion by the unqualified. Such situations are mediated and sustained socially by charismatic powers, especially those of the magician. But such taboos, conceptually unconnected in magical practice, may be rationalized into "a system of norms according to which certain actions are permanently construed as religious abominations subject to sanctions . . ." (433). This may come to take the form of a relatively integrated ethical system, encompassing a great range of the most common and fundamental social practices: Weber specifically mentions such phenomena as dietary restrictions and proscription against work on specific days or against marriage to particular individuals or to members of a specifically defined circle of blood relatives, and so on. The most important institution encouraging an ethical form of religion, Weber says, has been totemism, wherein a rigidly enforced exogamy accompanied by the taboos associated with the totem (its protection and its killing and often feasting on designated times or days) combine to create a tendency toward a powerful system of ethical regulation. The universal application of a religious law applied within a cult commonly comes to take the form of enforced ritual commensalism, which reinforces the bonds among cult members by ritualizing the common meal as worship of the god or gods. In this connection Weber in several places argues that the critical event in the history of Christianity was the feast at Antioch where Peter, after deliberately abrogating the Jewish

---

[7] E.g., "Even the Catholic priest continues to practice something of this magical power in executing the miracle of the mass and in exercising the power of the keys" (Weber, 1978b, 422).

commensalist taboo by eating with the uncircumsized, was reproached by Paul for afterward withdrawing and separating himself from them, thereby setting the cultic particularism of Judaism against the ethical universalism of Christ's message (Weber, 1958, 37).

The rationalization of religious ethics and religious belief tends to occur in somewhat parallel fashion. As Weber puts it, "wherever the coercion of spirits gave way to the worship of the gods who are served by a cult, the magical ethic of the spirit belief underwent a transformation too" (437). The critical transformation involves, first, the idea that the misfortunes befalling the group might be attributable to the wrath of the gods and second, the critical point, that this results from some transgression of his law or laws. The way is here open for a rigorous and systematic application of ethical-legal rules and sanctions, but this makes sense only in the framework of a rationalized religious belief. The "purest" form of this is monotheism, but it may assume other forms, most importantly a systematized dualism, the best example of which is found in Zoroastrianism. In all such developments a principled ethic of conduct is enforced through a range of ritual proceedings that involve a radical transformation of the notions of sin or evil. Whereas in magical systems sin is conceived of as an alien element in the body or soul of the individual which can be exorcised by the appropriate magical procedure, in ethical religion it assumes the radically altered form of *conscience*, in which the possession of the individual by a demon entails a profound struggle within to escape its diabolical power. The Paulinian/Augustinian development of Christianity exemplifies this in its most profound form: It imposes "an ethical sin which burdens the conscience" (437). Even the Zoroastrian dualism tends to externalize this struggle, where it is conceptualized as a battle between cosmic forces. In Christianity it assumes the reality of an *inner* struggle in the soul of the individual. For Weber, this was the most profound aspect of Christianity, not just in the immediate sense of defining the fate of the individual, but in its ultimate economic and social significance for the development of the West.

The cosmic and ethical rationalization of religious experience creates, then, as Weber sums it up, "a unified view of the world derived from a consciously integrated and meaningful attitude toward life" (450). Such conceptions, in their nature, imply the question of just what sort of actual world corresponds to such an ideal. Analysis of this question takes the form of two contrasting sets of ideal types centering on (1) the personal, transcendent, and ethical God of Western religions, especially Judaism, Christianity, and Islam, and (2) the impersonal, pantheistic "gods" of Eastern religions, especially Hinduism and Buddhism. This sets the stage for his analysis of Chinese and Indian religions and of Judiasm and Christianity. Considerations of space necessitate limitations of our discussion only to Judaism and its significance in Weber's analysis of Christianity.

The Historical Significance of Judaism for Christianity and Modern Capitalism

For Weber the most fundamental contrast in religious action is that between the contemplative mysticism of the East and the active inner-worldly asceticism of Christianity. For the former the way to salvation lies in mystical union with the divine or absolute; the world counts for nothing. For the latter, wordly action is invested with religious meaning of a specifically ethical character. The most rationalized form of this is found in Calvinism and its derivatives, most importantly English Puritanism. Weber's analysis of this in *PE* begins with its most important rival reform movement, Lutheranism, along with some observations regarding Catholicism and especially the significance of monasticism,[8] and is essentially restricted to the sixteenth and seventeenth centuries. However, the historical origins of Protestant asceticism go back to the emergent ethical religion that evolved in the course of the history of the ancient Hebrews.

Weber's study of Judaism (*AJ*) was by far his most extensive and complex one, perhaps because, unlike the China and India monographs, it was a study of religious innovation occurring over a protracted period of time,[9] and because of the social and political complexities of the Middle Eastern region, where smaller and weaker peoples found themselves victims of the expansionist policies of great empires on the rise and fall, or caught in the vortex of the struggles between them. The early Hebrews were one such group.[10]

Weber's central thesis in *AJ* is that the historical experience of the Hebrew people constituted a series of recurring conditions that transformed the earlier ritualistic, kinship-based, magic-infused practice into an ethical religion in which conduct was systematically governed by relations with the deity. At the core of the Yahweh religion was the concept of a Covenant (*Berith*), by which the deity as well as the people were bound. This came to mean that the sufferings of the people were a just retribution visited upon them by a stern and wrathful God (e.g., Ezekiel's Lamentations over the destruction of the temple, attributed to God as punishment for Israel's sins). But God was also merciful and held out the promise of a future reign of goodness in *this* world, contingent upon their conduct as a people. It was a contract.

Early Judaism was a religion the "bearers" (*Träger*)[11] of which were

---

[8] Weber had intended to write a major monograph on monasticism.

[9] But not, of course, of economic innovation. There was no particular *economic* consequence of religious rationalization to be found among the ancient Jews (or, for that matter, modern Jewry). Indeed, Weber emphasizes that for the Jews "proving one's piety in practice . . . lay in quite a different area than that of rationally mastering 'the world' and especially the economy," and that those areas in which Jews were "most and longest at home have failed to develop the specific traits of modern capitalism," and that the Jews were perfectly comfortable with precisely those forms of economic acquisitiveness—state- and booty-capitalism, money usury, trade—that "Puritanism abhorred" (Weber, 1952, 345). A dual ethic of economic relations prevailed among the Jews as it did among other premodern peoples, fundamentally distinguishing in-group from out-group relationships.

[10] This account selects the main points of *AJ*. For a short but excellent summary, see Bendix (1960, Chap. 7). Although there are factual errors in Weber's account, due to a large extent to the sources available to him, his analysis in general has evidently been confirmed by later scholarship. See Raphaël (1970).

[11] A very important concept cutting across Weber's theories of religion, stratification, and social movements, even though it does not appear in his exposition of terms in *ES*. *Träger* may be status groups, classes, professional associations or segments of these, that are the critical agencies in perpetuating and sometimes disseminating a cognitive-ethical *Weltanschauung*.

Levite priests, who although Jews, were not full members of the local kinship-based groups. Their practice was heavily oracular, but—very importantly, from Weber's standpoint—employed determination by lot rather than the inspection of entrails and the like, which Weber regarded as being more favorable to intellectual rationalization. Under external conditions of threat and warfare, along with the presence of an already somewhat organized priesthood, Jahweh came, on the one hand, to be a god demanding correct ritual observances, centering especially on circumcision and commensalism, actions revealing continuity with earlier magical practice, but on the other, a remote and wrathful deity in the transcendent image of a warrior exacting draconic punishment for transgressions past and demanding ethically principled conduct as the condition of future salvation—a salvation to be realized in *this* world. In Weber's view this was a movement in the direction of an increasingly intellectual and ethical rationalization.

The emergence of a centralized monarchy in the regimes of Saul, David, and Solomon during the tenth and eleventh centuries, a temporarily successful response to external threats, established the Yahweh religion at the political center of the monarchy, with its priesthood now a temple-based hierarchy, and ensconced as officials of what had become a patrimonial state in the mold of sultanist despotism historically characteristic of the entire region. The consequence—or cost—of this successful struggle was the growth of an increasingly urbanized culture, with its internal stratification, including, most importantly, a charioteering warrior class qualified by property. The other side of this coin was the disarming of the rural peasants and herdsmen, and a monarchy the magnificence and corruption of which (e.g., Bathsheba, Solomon's harem) made it momentarily the political equal of its great rivals (as evidenced in political agreements and intermarriages with them).

The growing despotism of the monarchy, however, led to revolts among the northern Israelite tribes toward the end of the tenth century, resulting in a separation of the kingdoms of Israel and Judah. It was during this period that prophecy—critical to Weber's analysis—became historically significant. Prophets had appeared even before the period of the monarchy, of course, but the later resurgence contained a new element. Now it was the totality of these developments—kingship and its corruptions, injustices connected especially to indebtedness, the presence (even the embracing) of other religions, such as Baal worship. The power of this prophecy lay in the fact that it was grounded in an idealization of the traditionalism of the earlier confederation, with its patriarchial organization, sense of community, and evenhanded if hard justice, a way of life redeemed by the sense of covenant at the core of the old unity. As further disasters overwhelmed the Jewish people, culminating 400 years later in the Babylonian captivity and the Diaspora, the force of prophecy recalling the people to the old ways acquired ever-greater fervor and moral power and fused them into a community that would withstand the bitter trials to which they would be subject for the next 2,500 years. Attempts to resolve it recur repeatedly throughout Western history and take different forms, most importantly: (1) asserting the autonomy of the world, including human nature; (2) declaring the essential goodness of human nature; or (3) at the level of the individual, holding forth the possibility of mystical union with the deity, the highest value of many Eastern religions. But such movements could lead only to charges of heresy or blasphemy. The idea of the autonomy of the world, best exemplified in the claims of science as it emerged from the Middle Ages, denied the significance or even the actuality of the Creation. The idea that human beings are in essence good rather than evil, a position recurrently taken by sectarian groups such as the Pelagians during the Middle Ages (see Chapter 6 of this book) challenges the fundamental doctrine of the Fall and universal guilt. Mysticism, a form of which was created by the Franciscans, approaches the claim that absolute knowledge (although, not of course, rational knowledge) of the deity is possible, and this is inconsistent with Judeo-Christian doctrines of the omniscience of God and the sinful state of mere mortals, and of course—perhaps its greatest offense—bypasses the offices of the priesthood, thereby calling into question their legitimacy, or even their need to exist.

The most important consequence of this paradox came to be the idea that this evil world would sometime in the future be transformed by God into a holy place. It is, again, one of the paradoxes of the Judeo-Christian tradition that a doctrine *logically* seeming to imply a fatalism and worldly passivity in the face of events determined by God, in fact, in its main historical effect, spawned recurring efforts to remake the world in the here and now. It was Weber's perception of this that led him, first, to his analysis of postmedieval Protestantism, and then to his other studies. The question "Under what conditions would religious doctrines turn *toward* the world rather than away from it, as a way of realizing the most desired states of grace?" was set at the core of his study of the relationship between the religious ethics of the early Protestant sects and the rise of capitalism.

Let us now put this account in the framework of the concept of rationalization described earlier.

Described at the most general level, as mentioned earlier, the process of religious rationalization is two-sided: a decline in the power of magic, or "disenchantment," on the one side, and a systematization of religious ideas on the other. As the hold of magic weakens, the demand that the world and the place of human life within it be made intellectually meaningful (and ethically significant) intensifies. The meaning system confronts and explains the evil of the world, and so theodicies constitute the core of religious rationalization. But the *content* of the theodicy is all-important: the Western form, in the very process of its development, exacerbates the tension between this world and the beyond, with its remote and omnicompetent God (for a detailed discussion see Schluchter, 1981). In this sense, an "inner logic of ideas" (Treiber, 1985, 829) drives religious rationalization, but the speed and concrete content of this process depends on external political and economic conditions, in complex interrelationship (with the former usually the more important). We have seen how this worked in the case of the rationalization of ancient Judaism.

Within the domain of ideas we find great variation in the degree to which ideas can acquire an autonomy such that they can exert causal power on human activity and thereby become a driving force for social change and rationalization. Weber represents the two-sided process of disenchantment and rationalization as a matter of degree. The inner core at the one extreme is constituted of disparate, unified magical precepts and practices that are entirely adaptive, or determined by purely external forces, including the interests of the magicians themselves. Under such conditions external factors constitute more or less adequate causes of other aspects of social life. As magic recedes and is displaced by increasingly and systematically formulated ideas about the cosmos and human life, the power of the latter to exert significant causal effect increases—always, it must be remembered, within some specific organizational framework. While always conditioned to one degree or another by externalities, *the meaning system acquires an inner dynamic of its own*: As idea systems are modified and systematized, they themselves tend to create further problems both theological (and eventually philosophical) and ethical, problems that then lead to yet further intellectual modifications and innovations. This process lies at the heart of the relative autonomy of any particular set of ideas.

The core problem of Judaism and Christianity throughout their historical development was a contradiction, originating as the Jewish "theodicy of misfortune," centering on the conception of God as all-knowing and all-powerful confronted by the continuing evil of the world, on the one hand, and the ethically necessary attribution of free will to the individual, on the other. The Calvinist solution to this dilemma was the most radical and extreme ever created, a condition under which the power of religious ideas to have a causal effect on economic life was maximized. It was precisely in this situation that the "inner" dimension of the inner-outer polarity came to exert a powerful transforming effect on economic life during the modernizing of some parts of Europe. It did so, however, in Weber's analysis, only within the broader framework of the complex congeries of causality implicated in the emergence of capitalism in Western Europe to which we turn next.

Weber's analysis of the emergence of modern capitalism can be framed in terms of three foci: (1) its nature; (2) its preconditions, or necessary causes; and (3) the obstacles to the appearance of these preconditions (See Figure 14-1).

Modern Capitalism

Weber approaches modern capitalism by first contrasting it with other types that have appeared throughout history. Even in the short discussion of this in the introduction to *PE*, Weber seems clear enough on this point, although his more expanded discussion of different types of capitalism is not reintroduced here. In *PE* he defines capitalism as such as a system "which rests on the expectation of profit by the utilization of opportunities for exchange, that is on (formally) peaceful chances for profit." Such an enterprise is rational to the extent that "a calculation in terms of money is made, whether by modern book-keeping methods or in any other way, however primitive and crude." Enterprises conducted in this fashion have existed practically everywhere not only in the West in modern times but in China, India, Babylon, Egypt, Mediterranean antiquity, and the Middle Ages. Weber discusses all these premodern forms as essentially one or another variant of opportunities for profit dependent on and conditioned by the nature of political power and administration (Weber, 1950, 334). Typologically, he distinguishes several varieties of political capitalism.[12] Exploitation of profit

---

[12] Here I follow Gerth and Mills's summary account (1946, 66ff.). See also Weber, 1978a, 164–166 and 913–920.

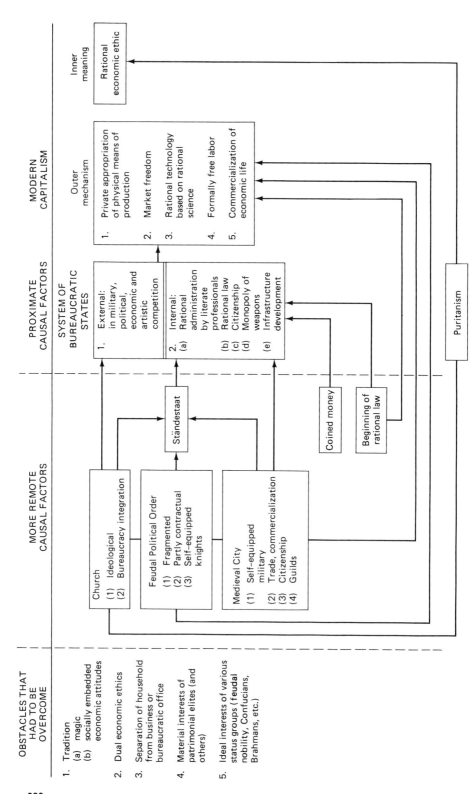

Figure 14-1 Weber's Theory of the Origins of Modern Capitalism

opportunities created by imperialist expansion he refers to as imperialist capitalism. Related to this is colonial capitalism, profit-oriented activity that takes advantage of existing colonial subordination. Wherever particular groups, usually ethnic or racial, such as the Jews throughout much of European history, or the Chinese in parts of southeast Asia, serve important trading interests of the dominant groups as socially marginal traders, Weber speaks of pariah capitalism. Distinct from these is adventure capitalism, typically state-sponsored adventuring in search of treasure, as in the Spanish forays into the New World in the sixteenth and seventeenth centuries. Booty capitalism is a subtype of this in which such expeditions are sporadic or irregular and charismatically led. Finally, fiscal capitalism refers to exploitation of political prerogatives through tax farming, leasing of various activities, or the franchising of war making to specialists like the Italian condottiere.

Modern capitalism differs from all of these, first of all, in that its method of accounting is *rational*. The capitalism of antiquity and the Middle Ages calculated profit and loss in various ways, but none of them had available the methods of modern bookkeeping, which Weber dates to the invention of the balance by Simon Stevin in 1698 (Weber, 1950, 275). This makes possible a precise continuous account of the state of the enterprise, *so long as one fundamental condition is met*: the "battle of man against man on the market" (Weber, 1978b, 93). It is precisely the nature of capitalist economic life as struggle that makes possible its formal rationalization. This is so because the utilities that are the substance of the struggle take the form of market-determined prices, with their market participation impelled or governed by the principle of marginal utility. This seems to imply as a corollary a necessarily lower level of purely *economic* formal rationality under socialism, even though Weber, without explaining himself, thought that interest-based struggles would be as endemic to socialist as to capitalist states (202–206), because of what he regarded as the relative arbitrariness of state pricing procedures.[13] The approximation of the ideal type of formal rationality in modern capitalism, however, has no corollary in its substantive rationality. Indeed, there is a built-in tendency in the direction of the maintenance of and perhaps an increase in economic inequality. Being a "formally rational category," profitability is "indifferent (to) substantive postulates unless these can make themselves felt in the market in the form of purchasing power" (94).

The modern technique of capital accounting becomes critically important because it is implicated in and makes possible the full development of a number of other elements definitive of modern capitalism. These are

1. The appropriation of all physical means of production as disposable property of private companies.

---

[13] Again, Weber's concept and general theory of rationalization will be discussed later. For the moment it is enough to say that economic or market rationality refers to a thoroughgoing means-ends calculative attitude toward economic activity. The relative rationality of capitalist versus socialist price setting has been a controversial issue.

2. Market freedom.
3. A rational technology based on rational science, meaning that its efficiencies are reducible to calculation, thus implying mechanization.
4. Formally free labor, necessary for its rational organization.
5. The commercialization of economic life, i.e., the universal or near-universal use of standardized commercial instruments (contracts of all types, deeds, bonds, credit, etc.).
6. (A calculable law, making possible the legal separation of the household from the workplace, and predictability of adjudication and administration: Weber, 1950, Chap. 22).

The first and second of these, broadly speaking, are what is meant by "free enterprise," i.e., an absence of restrictions on both the organization of production and sale of products for profit. The third shows that Weber, like Marx, regarded the mechanism of production through the application of science-based technology as an essential component of modern capitalism. The fifth is an indispensible technical condition for continuous and predictable functioning on a large scale. The fourth is more or less self-evident, but in the light of the comments of some regarding Weber's differences with Marx, or more broadly, with historical materialism, it is worth quoting him briefly.

> Rational capitalist calculation is possible only on the basis of free labor; only where in consequence of the existence of workers who in the formal sense voluntarily, but actually under the compulsion of the whip of hunger, offer themselves, the costs of products may be unambiguously determined by agreement in advance (277).

The last of these I have placed in parentheses because rational law is as much a precondition of modern capitalism as it is a component of it, as Weber elsewhere clearly indicates. Such seeming inconsistencies in classification probably result from the fact that causal social factors are not usually simple events, but complex social processes occurring over long periods, often continuing on long after having brought their effects into being, and not infrequently being reciprocally influenced by them. The Protestant ethic itself is a good case in point. Also, many historical processes undergo growth or expansion, the development of rational law in Europe being an example. Recall the genetic nature of causal explanation. Historical explanation has to take into account these and other complexities involving the often long-term processes wherein factors interact with one another not only causally, but by "elective affinity" as well.

These elements, embodied in social action at the level of the business organization, are a necessary but not complete account of modern capitalism. Distinct from the form is its "spirit," the critical element of subjective meaning, without which modern capitalism would be a very different kind of economic life. It was precisely this that conventional liberal political economy took for granted. Liberal political economists thought of it either as a universal acquisitive drive (Adam Smith's "propensity to truck, barter, and trade") adequate to account for the productive and expanding nature of modern capitalism, or, in a more behaviorist variant, regarded it as just irrelevant to economic analysis. For Weber, in contrast, it was the most critical question of all.

The spirit of capitalism, Weber says, has to be put together out of the individual parts that are taken from historical reality (Weber, 1948, 47); it is, then, an ideal type. Its essence is the performance of labor "as if it were an end in itself" (62). (Indeed, Weber refers to capitalism in general as "domination of the end by the means" [202]. Empirically, Weber finds the aphorisms of Benjamin Franklin, an ethic that enjoins men to seek profit, "rationally and systematically" representative of the type. Even today everyone is familiar enough with this view of life and the world, which puts aside all else in its total dedication to work (despite the inroads made upon it by accumulation and consumerism). This is not economic action pursued instrumentally to the end of consumption, nor is it in any way hedonistic or performed for one or another sort of glory. These are age-old ends of economic activity, and they are not orientations to economic life adequate to sustain the sort of accumulation that is the essence of modern capitalism. The "summum bonum" of this spirit, Weber says, is the pursuit of ever more money, coupled with an ethical rejection of any form of pleasure experienced spontaneously (53). It is this inner spirit that confers on modern capitalism its dynamic and accumulative character. Weber saw in this ideal type something of a religious quality, akin to the concept of the calling especially as it is understood in Lutheranism. And it was his sense of this, in part, that suggested to him the hypothesis that its origin might lie in Protestantism.[14]

The Causes of Modern Capitalism

The causes of modern capitalism,[15] meaning here the *proximate* causes, in Weber's analysis, were (1) the bureaucratic state, (2) the peculiar nature of Western feudalism, (3) the unique developments associated with the medieval city, and (4) the emergence of a rational form of law. (Figure 14-1 gives a schematic representation of the main elements of Weber's theory.)

The Bureaucratic State

The bureaucratic states that emerged in Europe beginning around the sixteenth century evolved from feudalism, through the state-form called the *Ständestaat*, into *a system of competing states*. Weber's analysis proceeds in terms

[14] The general question of the relationship between religion and economic life was not an entirely novel one early in the twentieth century, having been raised by some earlier historians.

[15] I shall continue to employ the term "modern capitalism" to designate the historical ideal type variously referred to as "modern rational capitalism," "modern bourgeois capitalism," "rationalized capitalism," etc., and reserve the term "rational capitalism" to designate a generic or generalizing ideal type, derived essentially from the historical one, employed mainly in discussions of certain capitalist tendencies appearing elsewhere. For a somewhat similar representation of Weber's theory of the origins of western capitalism see Collins 1980, p. 931, and a revised version of this in Collins, 1986.

of a focus on the more or less independent effects of both its external and internal aspects.

Internally, the bureaucratic state incorporates as its main features the principle of citizenship, a rational law and rational administration (i.e., taking bureaucratic form: to be discussed), and a monopoly, or near-monopoly, over the control of weapons (Figure 14-1). In these respects it differs in principle from the patrimonial state, which is an extension of the principles underlying patriarchal kinship and household management, and does not transcend or eliminate the domain of personal relations. Patrimonialism is not at all conducive to rational capitalism. Patrimonial states may organize various kinds of acquisitive actions, but these literally never become institutionalized as activities independent of the state on a systematic, continuous basis oriented to a concept of growth based on accumulation. Even though certain conditions favorable for the emergence of capitalism may be present, the ties to traditional forms of social organization—clan, village community, etc.—tend to remain intact.

Stating the general state-capitalism relationship in these terms would seem to make the appearance of anything on the order of modern capitalism a most unlikely event. And so Weber considered it to be. However, a number of conditions developing in Europe over centuries created just that concatenation of circumstances necessary for capitalism to become established.

Externally, the more or less centralized European states that began to assume definite form during the sixteenth century brought into being a quite unique form of rule. There had in effect been no European state or states following the fall of Rome; the church provided ideological unity and fostered a fragmented pattern of secular rule. During the Middle Ages the church was generally content to remain remote from the direct exercise of secular authority; maintaining a fragmented political order assured that no challenge to church authority could be mobilized. So the feudal pattern remained for centuries an exceedingly decentralized one. The origin of European feudalism itself Weber attributed to Charles Martel's need for economically expendable but self-equipped knights to displace the peasant militia. This pattern of dispersed control of the means of warfare remained central throughout Europe's history right up to the emergence of the modern state.

The period between late feudalism and the growth of the states was mediated by the *Ständestaat* (polity of estates), in which church, nobles, and the town-dwelling elite collaborated in something on the order of a parliament (Weber, 1978a, 1085–1087). But this mild tendency toward centralization, as was true of many of its later parallels, including those of the present, never had much of a chance of evolving into anything like a European empire. The vested interests of each estate, for a time, worked to check the others, somewhat like the "veto groups" of some modern polities; like so many pluralisms, the power to check exceeded the power of its positive exercise. The feudal "state," then, was an extreme balance of power (which Weber explicitly compared to Montesquieu's treatment of the topic in *Spirit of the Laws*).

It is entirely conceivable that a European patrimonial state and empire could have been brought into being through conquest, but there were too many natural and social obstacles for this to occur. Invaders from the east and north appeared only in the late Middle Ages, when city growth had brought into being a level of wealth great enough to justify the effort and risks involved in raiding or conquering. A concatenation of happy accidents and natural obstacles (e.g., the forests of eastern and central Europe, Swiss archers) combined to thwart barbarian conquest. And the states that did grow up around the fringes of Europe later (Czarist Russia, the Hapsburg Empire, Norman England, and the Swedish Empire at the height of its power under Gustavus Adolphus) either had no interest in empire or were too weak—in the long run, at least—to impose it, despite their ability to mount massively destructive invasions and to rule for a time over one or another part of the area. This relatively stabilized plurality meant that no one power could become strong enough to impose its will over more than a relatively small part of the continent. This basic state competitiveness was a necessary condition for initially state-controlled economic enterprises to eventually disengage themselves from state control. But it was the very *idea* of a state *having* a rational economic policy in the sense of systematically pursuing economic ends in the name and interest of the state and its society that was for Weber the critical thing. And this was a consequence of the fundamentally competitive nature of relations among the states.

We should note that this exemplifies a basic principle of Weber's. Social change occurs partly through the medium of the conflict generated from the tensions occurring within, and often more importantly, between orders. Under some conditions these tensions may be in balance, but all such states are relatively precarious, as history repeatedly shows. The medieval period was a negotiated order in which material, and to some extent ideal, interests were realized by the major parties. The church officialdom came to possess vast sections of the European lands and to retain the religious commitment of the people generally, on whom they imposed religious obligations that met both their material and ideal interests. Secular rulers and their retainers and vassals exercised virtually unrestricted rule in domains defined as nonreligious, generally capitalizing on the legitimacy conferred by the church under the "two swords" doctrine. This balance was finally upset only with the beginnings of the towns and the gradual emergence of an urban mobility that eventually metamorphosed into a revolutionary class of capitalists.

The direction of change, for Weber, depends on a variety of factors that vary from situation to situation. But large-scale social changes in the West have been rationalizing processes occurring within various social orders (or symbol spheres such as music or art [see Gerth and Mills, 1953]). The intellectual rationalization of church theology and ethics, along with the formal rationalization of the organization as an "institutionalization of charisma," generated immense hieratic power that has successfully resisted or accommodated to changes for a thousand years. The rationalizing tendencies in other orders—political and military, in particular—were unable, under the universal hegemony of the church, to generate enough independent ideological or organizational (administrative bureaucracies or military organizations) power to challenge or break away. In this context, the most significant event during the feudal period was the secession of the Eastern Orthodox Church.

The centralized states were ultimately possible only because state makers were able to disarm both the feudal knights and the town burghers. This process was a rather long and complex one, involving many an unholy alliance, but in the long run it simultaneously undercut the independence of both rural landlords and the towns, converting the former into state functionaries dependent on a salary and the latter—ultimately—into an independent bourgeoisie. The main causal factors involved in bringing into being the system of competing states were the nature of feudalism itself, the medieval city, and rational law.

Feudalism

Much of European feudalism came to be organized in fiefs rather than benefices. This is a very important distinction referring to the degree of centralization of political power in so far as it is reflected in specific economic arrangements, especially regarding the rights to the disposal of land. A benefice is a lifelong, nonhereditary office that reverts to the ruler upon the death of its holder; the income from it is not personally owned. A fief, by contrast, designates a grant of rights, especially in land, in exchange for military or administrative service, among members of a stratum standing above other freemen; it is guaranteed contractually. A fief system admits of much less control from the center, or from above, a consequence of its three constitutive components: It is rent-producing, it encourages a code of knightly honor among fief holders, and it is or tends in the direction of becoming hereditary (Weber, 1978b, 1071). Weber distinguished a whole series of variants of fiefs (at one point seven distinct subtypes), the main point of which was to compare the relative power of the center as against the periphery. European feudalism approximated "fully developed feudalism," which Weber referred to as "the most extreme type of systematically decentralized domination" (1078).

In fully developed feudalism, land tenure becomes hereditary and the landlords or vassals retain military autonomy, but provide military services in return for renewal of rights to land on a contractual basis. Unlike modern contracts, however, the services rendered are personal (i.e., not a matter of office incumbency) and rest on vows of fealty. In the extreme form, the lord's authority comes to rest on nothing more than the ritualized status factor embodied in the oath of fealty, meaning that such authority as the king has is based on his position in the status group comprised of lords, vassals, and king. The importance of this lies in the fact that it is the precondition underlying the right to enter into contract. So the contributions of feudalism to the eventual emergence of modern capitalism were two: maintaining a structural barrier to centralization and fostering the principle of contract. These factors made it ultimately possible for other developments, most importantly the emergence of the medieval city and rational law, to eventually take hold and exert a positive influence.

The Medieval City

Weber conducted his analysis of the Western city through a triple comparison: first, between Occidental and Oriental cities; second, between those of Western antiquity and those of the late Middle Ages, and third, between those of southern Europe and those of northern Europe.[16]

He first noted a series of general factors in term of which Occidental and Oriental cities were more or less alike: most of them were both fortresses and markets, seats of administration and law, often the residences of patrician families and of guilds. In size, and in their splendor and magnificence, many Oriental cities completely outshone their Occidental counterparts, especially during the Middle Ages. The Occidental cities, however, came to be organized as independent or autonomous *communes* (*Gemeinde*), in which the general right of political participation, i.e., citizenship, was born. In both the Far and Middle East, the cities never emerged as autonomous political entities, but only as sites for trade, military defense, and administration. Weber's judgment about the evidence regarding Asian and Oriental cities was that it showed quite conclusively the continuing influence of clans or other groups with origins and roots in rural areas, or of occupational associations, business interest groups, military and religious associations, and ward-based political associations, but nowhere anything approximating an independent association of town or city dwellers (1233–1234). A fully developed city, found only in the Occident, is not merely a market, fortress, and administrative center, but takes the form of an independent associational structure and has its own court of law and at least partial autonomy and autocephaly in which the residents participate legally (1226).

Thus, the main factors differentiating the Occidental from the Asian and Oriental cities were the legal status of land and of persons. In the instance of the former, land became alienable, thus providing economic opportunities of varied sorts which strategically situated individuals and groups tended to exploit to their fullest; in the latter, individuals acquired citizenship rights as members of the city corporation, a voluntary association of burghers. In Oriental and Asian cities, the inhabitants remained legally members of rural associations, e.g., the caste in India and clan in China. There are Western parallels: the Russian *mir* association and the slavic *Zadruga*.

Although conditions varied greatly, this was generally a highly conflict-ridden process, for it meant the breaking of the power of landed status groups and rulers, mostly of a feudal nature. Sometimes, as in Genoa and Cologne, it took the form of a "revolutionary usurpation of rights," a defiance of "legitimate powers." Elsewhere it involved a contractual grant of various rights amounting to some degree of autonomy and autocephaly, concessions ceded in the face of the growing strength of city associations

---

[16] The main source is *ES*, Chap. 16. A shorter account appears in *GEH* (Weber, 1950, Chap. 28). In the *GEH* chapter, delivered as a lecture in Munich some years after he had written the *ES* chapter, Weber emphasizes more strongly the military factor and correspondingly tends to play down the economic. The *ES* chapter is a historical-sociological tour de force. According to Anderson, it "remains the best and most original discussion of the question (of ancient and medieval democracy) to this day" (Anderson, 1974, 151n.)

(1250).[17] This revolutionary development was possible in the Occident because of the decentralized character of feudalism in both its economic and military aspects, but especially the latter, for it meant that urban military forces could become strong enough to challenge the knightly armies of feudal lords. Underlying these struggles were the typical commercial interests of the city patricians, which often (but not invariably) diverged from those of the landed nobility. Reinforcing this divergence of economic interests was another rooted in the status ethic of the lords; the low regard in which commercial activity was held tended to push the former in a more egalitarian direction in relation to groups of lower standing in the city, especially artisans and small businessmen. In stark contrast, the great patrimonial empires of the past—and present—in Egypt, China, Russia, and elsewhere made such autonomous urban growth virtually impossible.

Weber thought that there were two primary factors, one material, the other ideal, that were critical for the formation of urban autonomous corporate groups. The first of these was mentioned early—the creation of the self-equipped army of knights, in contrast to the armies of the East, where the soldiers did not possess their own weapons and fought under the command of officers. Here is one of Weber's master themes, the proposition that power is ultimately (and one must emphasize *ultimately*) grounded in control of the means of violence, so that in any analysis of power the question of which group, class, or stratum possesses them is always a critical question.

The second factor was religious. Whereas in the East magical barriers to formation of cities remained in force, in the West the powerful rationalizing forces (in the Jewish prophecy discussed earlier, but in Greek secular culture as well) had destroyed these (Weber, 1950, 322–323).

Within this broad comparative framework, Weber isolated significant differences between Western ancient and medieval cities, differences decisive for the emergence of capitalism. He employs, with some modification, the classical cyclical theory of the city-state of Plato and Aristotle. In the case of each he identifies first, a patrician followed by a plebian form, which in turn devolves into tyranny. The ancient cities grew out of proto-urban monarchies around the Mediterranean coasts as communities of warriors, surrounded by peasants and "barbarians" (Weber, 1978b, 1291). The medieval city, on the other hand, arose in *conflict* with feudal or episcopal lords who were patrimonial officials. In contrast to the ancient patriciate, the economic interests of medieval town dwellers were critical in their struggles against patrimonial constraints. The patricians of the ancient cities were typically rentiers rather than entrepreneurs, whose fundamental class interest rested on exploitation of the rural peasantry and whose knightly style had a *negative* affinity with entrepreneurship. The city of antiquity failed to break the basic class relation of antiquity, in which the landlord extracts his economic support from a mainly rural labor force in one or another form of bondage (tax farming, rent, slavery, etc.). In contrast, the basic economic interests of the

---

[17] It was for this reason that Weber subtitled the earlier editions of *The City* (Non-legitimate Domination). Democracy is self-rule involving struggles among various groups, and in this regard, Collins points out, is not determined by any of the several legitimating principles discussed elsewhere by Weber (see Collins, 1986, 129).

various strata who dominated the medieval cities (the Italian *popolo grosso*, an elite of property and culture, or the guild strata of the northern cities) were centered *in* the city, mainly on guild-based production and trade. This meant that the class conflicts of antiquity remained unresolvable within the urban context, whereas the medieval city displayed a tendency toward "equalization of classes" (Weber, 1950, 330).

In both antiquity and the Middle Ages, the patrician cities were destroyed by revolutions from below. In the former this resulted in the institution of the demos and the ascendency of the ephors in Grece, and the plebs and tribune in Rome; in the latter, in associations of craftsmen like the Italian *capitano del popolo* and the *Zünfte* (guilds) in the north. In both cases democratization gave way to tyranny, although in the medieval period this was confined to Italy. The southern European city in this respect thus stood closer to the ancient city than did the northern European variant. Significantly, the latter became more fully emancipated from the control of kings, notables, and religious hierocrats, and because of this was able to provide a setting more congenial for modern capitalism. This was so despite the fact that the earlier capitalist developments—of types differing critically from the *modern* or *bourgeois* variant—had long been established in Italy.

As Weber repeatedly emphasized, independence from centralized forms of patrimonial domination, while not a sufficient condition for the development of capitalism, has everywhere been a necessary one. Although patrimonial regimes may offer "the whole realm of the ruler's discretion as a hunting ground for accumulating wealth," the result is not more than "great wealth constantly being created and destroyed" (Weber, 1978b, 1099). The great significance of the cities was twofold: They instituted conditions on the basis of which for the first time in human history a rational *economic policy* could be formulated and implemented, even though in content their economic activity was typically rigidly controlled and protectionist; and they constituted a favorable social and political environment for nurture and development of the principle of citizenship, in the sense of the individual possessing a specific legal status and rights of participation in the political sphere. It was critical that the ruling groups—merchant and craft guilds—faced neither overwhelming patrimonial domination from without, nor obstacles to economic activity from within, especially being tarred with the brush of the despised standing of acquisitive activity in the status ethic of the aristocracy. In these circumstances, the guildsmen found themselves with an elective affinity for a practical life ethic such as that which emerged among some of the seventeenth century adherents of Calvinism and its offshoots.

By the seventeenth century the autonomy of the medieval city in every sphere—military, juridical, industrial—had been lost. The decisive fact for the emergence of capitalism, the capacity to form and implement an economic policy, passed now to the centralized monarchies. However, although city autonomy disappeared into the administrative structure of the state, the historically critical institutions that it had nurtured—citizenship and conception of a rational economic policy—survived to play a crucial role in the emergence of modern capitalism.

Table 14-1 Weber's Typology of Law

Theoretical Dimension	RATIONALITY DIMENSION	
	Irrational	Rational

Formal	(A)
	(a) Not controlled by intellect; mainly magical (e.g., oracle)
	(b) Rule-bound by magical formulae
		(C)
		(a) Empirical law finding:
		  (1) controlled by intellect (reasons given)
		  (2) facts considered to have a "tangible" nature (e.g., English common law)
		(b) Logical analysis of meaning:
		  (1) controlled by intellect
		  (2) logically closed system

Substantive	(B) (a) Reasons not given (b) Personalistic, so ruleless (c) Decisions influenced by external considerations of a concrete nature. No boundary between law and extralegal considerations	(D) (a) Facts controlled by intellect (reasons given) (b) Rule-bound law systematized in theoretical casuistry (c) Ethical principles not separated from law, i.e., no boundary between law and extralegal considerations

Law and Modern Capitalism Basic to his sociological analysis of law[18] is Weber's definition of law in terms of the continuous presence of an agency of enforcement, i.e., a staff with powers specifically for this purpose. This definition differs from those of other traditions, both juristic and sociological, juristically, for example, law as the "command of the soveryon," or sociologically, defining law as an expression of the values or norms of the community.

Weber develops his sociology of law on the basis of a typology formulated—inadequately, as we shall see—in two discussions: whether a legal system is relatively rational or irrational, and whether it incorporates mainly substantive or formal principles. This yields a twofold table (Table 14-1). Formally irrational law, its most primitive form, proceeds through consulting oracles or similar magical means. It is irrational in that it adheres to "external characteristics of the facts," by which Weber means that legal determinations are thought to inhere *objectively* in the events of the world rather than being products of the human will and intellect. Such systems are therefore beyond the control of the human intellect. At the same time the magical character of such systems lends them a very strong rule-bound character; the critical aspect of every magical procedure lies in the meticulous exactness with which its rituals are observed.

Although logically one would infer that substantively irrational law would share the property of not being controlled by the intellect with the

---

[18] There are two translations, the earlier by Max Rheinstein (Weber, 1954), and that by Roth and Wittich, in *ES*: Vol 2: Chap. 8. Here I employ the former.

formal irrationality of the oracle, Weber nowhere in his discussion is explicit about this. In fact, it remains unclear from his descriptive passages and examples just what he did intend in this regard. The examplar of this type is the justice administered by the *Khadi*, judges appointed from among the *ulama*, the Muslim priests who codified Islam on the foundation of the original Bedouin ethics and worldview.

The *Khadi* supposedly administer *personalistic* justice; cases are decided on a case-to-case basis and the adjudication incorporates considerations of virtually any sort, legal and extralegal. It is in this sense essentially ruleless. Solomon's decision to award the infant to the woman who was prepared to relinquish it is an example. It appears that Weber here intends to characterize such Solomanic ruleless patterns of adjudication as essentially charismatic in nature. The *legitimation* of the adjudication rests on belief in the extraordinary power attributed to the priest. All well and good. But this, of course, is by no means the same thing as saying that the adjudication is not controlled by the intellect. Indeed an intellectual process of a sort is undeniably present in such adjudications. The crucial point for Weber is that, like charismatic pronouncements in general, such decisions are neither argued nor supported by reasons. It seems probable that Weber saw a parallel, or similarity, in this quality of Khadi justice to the total lack of intellectual control in formally irrational law.

There is one further point of significance. Substantively irrational law has no clear boundary setting it off from the *substantive* forms of ethics, morality, or politics. Even where there is some degree of codified or systematized law, legal determinations reflect such considerations. This is what makes such law *substantive*.

Formally rational law is more complex, consisting of two subtypes. In the first, "facts are considered to have a tangible nature," and adjudication requires systematic *empirical law finding*, of which the English common law is the exemplar. In the second a *logical analysis* of meaning is pursued, legal principles take the form of a logically closed system, and legal determinations are deductions from this.

Weber specifies five "postulates" on which the second of these is based: (1) Every decision is an application of an abstract proposition to a concrete situation; (2) every concrete case can be derived from abstract propositions by means of "legal logic"; (3) the law claims to be a "gapless" system, by which Weber means that all legally bounded conduct is held to be unambiguously subject to adjudication by the application of a set of abstract legal rules; (4) anything not construable rationally is deemed irrelevant, and (5) every social action is visualized as an application or execution of legal propositions, or as an infringement thereof" (Weber, 1954, 64). The systematization of the German civil code by the pandectists[19] in the nineteenth century, involving an extensive "Romanization" of German law, is the best example of this. In general, the civil codes of most European continental countries approximate this subtype.

Finally, substantially rational law refers to *systematically* applied ethical

---

[19] Legal scholars so named because they worked with the Roman pandect, or comprehensive legal code.

principles of whatever type, for example, a conception of distributive justice, or—Weber's examples—the religious law as taught to seminarians (205–206) or the ethically grounded welfare policies of many patrimonial systems (264). The rationality of such law is found in its principled theoretical casuistry that is directed to concrete needs rather than being a deduction from general principles or controlled by a body of precedent. In this sense it is set off from other types by its adherence to "fixed principles" (205–206). It shares with substantively irrational law the principle of a lack of boundary between law and extralegal considerations.

The reader has perhaps noted that in addition to the logical difficulty we noted in connection with Weber's definitions of formally irrational and substantively irrational law, there is a second one implicated in the definitions of the two types of rationality. The problem resides in Weber's use of the concept "formal." We saw that in the case of formally irrational law Weber uses it to designate rule-bound adjudication. However, he also employs it to designate the systematization of legal systems or codes, as in the civil and casuistic systems mentioned above. Kronman has pinpointed the root difficulty of these confusions in the fact that, while Weber formally presents four ideal types of law based on *two* sets of distinctions, in his actual discussions he works with *three*: (1) personal vs. rule-bound, (2) no control by the intellect vs. logical analysis of meaning, and (3) systems in which law is legally distinct from extralegal considerations vs. those in which there is no effective boundary (Kronman, 1983, 79–80). To these a fourth probably should be added: internally logically systematized forms of law vs. those not so systematized. The second type of formally rational law is the only one having this property.

Weber speaks of these types as forms of legal "thought," doubtless reflecting his legal background, but it probably would be sociologically more accurate, and more in line with his conception of social action, to think of them as types of adjudication. This has the advantage of clearly allowing us to distinguish between relatively routinized legal procedures and the process whereby legal systems have come into being, including their causes, discussions of which Weber interlards with those describing adjudication.

The extent to which the law of any particular society actually realizes one or another of these types is, of course, quite variable. Weber seemed to regard the English common law, for instance, as a concatenation of formally rational elements of the empirical type along with a number of substantially irrational components, such as the jury (from the thirteenth century), because it does not indicate the grounds for decision (79), and the day-to-day practice of the justices of the peace (230).

Indeed, the theoretical status of the common law was left quite ambiguous and confused by Weber. He argued that a rationalized legal system was a significant precondition of modern capitalism. Yet he described the common law in the land of the earliest development of modern capitalism mostly, and confusedly, as a code exhibiting a number of important irrational and merely empirically rational features. This theoretical state of affairs has given rise to the "England problem" in Weber's sociology of law (for a discussion, see Newton, 1987).

There is a parallel between Weber's analyses of law and those of religion. The rationalization of law, like that of religion, occurs as magical elements are eliminated, and as legal processes are made increasingly more systematic and intellectually controlled. As with the rationalization of religion, this process is contingent on the presence of legal functionaries of one type or another. What Weber regarded as an immanent presence in any sphere of ideas can be given systematic form only by the appearance of intellectuals who become specialists in the domain in question. And the actions of such legal rationalizers, whether they be legal scholars, corporate groups of practicing lawyers, or even "honoratiores"[20] or priests and prophets, are always, like the priests or prophets engaged in the rationalization of religions, conditioned to one degree or another by their material and ideal interests.[21]

The great watershed in the process of legal development occurs when (if ever) the fundamental principle of jurisprudence moves from law as the personal and arbitrary decision of the soverign, or the judge or charismatic military chief, to the making of legal decisions on the basis of binding legal *rules*. This is a change more or less coterminous with the movement from patrimonial to bureaucratic domination, a process Weber analyzes in some detail in the *Rechtssoziologie* (esp. Chapter 6). The critical empirical issue in this complex process was the creation of *rights*, especially the right to engage in contracts ("the most essential feature of modern subtantive law" [10]). This applies to both individuals and associations of all sorts, but especially businesses. The (more or less) unencumbered right to enter into contracts in any and all areas of human endeavor is a phenomenon of modern times. As late as the eighteenth century even in England, for instance, the rights of English corporations were considered to be nothing more than special privileges granted and revocable by the Crown (183), although in practice they had considerable real freedom, a fact of which Weber was probably aware. The principle of contract was known, of course, but differed from the modern concept in taking the form of a "status contract," to employ Weber's term, doubtless borrowed from Henry Maine's *Ancient Law*.[22] Rather than resting on a concept of rights attached to the individual *qua* individual, the latter stipulates the contractual right as a privilege of one's position in a group, in traditional or legal terms. The modern right of contract takes no account of such qualifications, and this involves a profound change in the legal situations of the individual (105).

In modern times the right to contract is therefore based on the establishment of the concept of the "juristic person" (156), in Weber's judgment rooted in the expansion of markets. Both the principle of contract and of free labor are inconceivable apart from an understanding of what it means to be a person in the legal sense, i.e., to possess the rights of property ownership and free selection of occupation and job. This occurred first and

---

[20] Notables sharing a high status, however legitimated. This may give them the power to influence the legal process.

[21] Whether there are any further parallels between the legal development of the West and the western thrust toward monotheism and related ethically grounded modes of conduct that have constituted the main dimensions of religious rationalization, is not very clear in Weber's writings. For discussions of this point, see Treiber (1984) and Schluchter (1981).

[22] Weber had little to say about civil rights in his writings, a quite characteristic feature of the deteriorating liberalism of the time (see Turner and Factor, 1984, Chap. 1).

most importantly in England; in France, even in the *Code Napoleon*, the embodiment of revolutionary natural law conceptions, it is not to be found.

The rationalization of law in the direction of creation of the juristic person in Western Europe was possible because the form of patrimonialism there was, as Weber puts it, of a "corporate status," rather than just an expansion of the patriarchal principle (185–186). It is here that the *Ständestaat* was important. In this corporative assembly, temporary administrative arrangements tended to become bureaucratic and so relatively permanent because the association itself was entirely distinct from kinship or other particularistic local groups. Also, it was sometimes in the interest of the prince to establish a permanent administrative agency of his own to circumvent the considerable *de facto* economic and political autonomy of the lords. The *Ständestaat* was thus an intermediate (although perhaps not indispensable) political form in the transition to the bureaucratic state. The broad significance of the development of formally rational law for the emergence of modern capitalism, then, rests on the establishment of the juristic individual, a concept essential to the concrete principle and practice of citizenship.

In summary, the bureaucratic state, favorable aspects of feudalism, the medieval city, and rational law, were decisive factors for the emergence of modern capitalism. However, they in turn were possible only with the breaking down of a number of obstacles that in other civilizations remained in place.

Obstacles to Modern Capitalism

The obstacles to the precursors of modern capitalism may be grouped into five sociological categories: (1) basic traditional practices and beliefs, mainly magic and a specific attitude toward the relation between work and income; (2) the structure of economic ethics; (3) separation of household from business or bureaucratic office; (4) the material interests of patrimonial elites; and (5) the ideal interests of a variety of status groups (see Figure 14-1). It is slightly misleading to designate the first as traditional in distinction from the others, since in a larger sense they are all part and parcel of the traditional orders that preceded capitalism. However, so long as this is understood there should be no problem.

We have already discussed magic fairly extensively. Suffice it to say that, in its stereotyping of actions designed to influence events of every sort, magic powerfully institutionalizes irrational means-ends schemata that, for the most part, are incompatible with capitalist rationality. Weber discusses this rather extensively in the cases of India and China, and elsewhere, including his sociology of law (see Table 14-1). The radical opposition of magic not only to science, but to the other forms of rationality in economic life as well, is a central theme running throughout Weber's work.

Related to this is the traditional attitude toward the relation between work and income. The spirit of capitalism is one of maximizing return, whether through investment or labor, exemplified by the modern capitalist entrepreneur or manager, on the one hand, and the worker who performs his work in a systematically routinized way as a duty, "as if it were an absolute end in itself" (Weber, 1948, 62). Precapitalist workers, in contrast, when presented with opportunities to increase income through expanded labor, or because of an increase in wages, typically respond by reducing the hours of work so that the existing level of reward is maintained, but not reduced. In Weber's words, the worker asks not how much can be earned through an expansion of labor, but "how much must I work to earn the wage . . . which I earned before and which takes care of my traditional needs?" (60). Among businessmen relations among competitors were commonly congenial, nested in social circles that constrained naked competitive relations. Working hours were typically restricted so long as earnings were adequate to lead a "respectable" life and perhaps save a bit (66–67). The sheer presence of capitalistic organization, or the "form" of capitalist enterprise, Weber says, is itself not sufficient to overcome these traditional attitudes toward work.

Traditional societies everywhere are organized in terms of a dual economic ethic. The rules of economic activity among members of the family, or clan, or community, or in whatever organizational forms the in-group is defined, are radically different from those governing exchange with outsiders. The contrast is between

> An attachment to traditional and pietistic relations to fellow members of tribe, clan, and house community (oikos) which excludes an attitude of unrestricted gain, and . . . an external orientation encouraging the absolutely unrestricted play of the gain spirit in economic relations (Weber, 1950, 356).

This is extraordinarily difficult. Not only the natural communities themselves, but generally speaking, the world religions, as well, have resisted, denounced, and censured the introduction of impersonal criteria of action into solidary groups. The medieval Catholic principle of the just price is an example. It ought to be said that Weber here is referring to the level of values and norms. History is replete with examples of economic exploitation within solidary groups; the point is that until modern times this has been deviant, and even if carried out successfully, has usually been more or less effectively resisted by the agencies of social control.

The separation of the business enterprise from the household is also, for the most part, a modern innovation, and an essential one for capitalism. One of the conditions necessary to maximize formal rationality in accounting, Weber says, is that enterprise capital be clearly distinguished from the owner's private wealth (Weber, 1978b, 162). This is of great importance, since it is in the nature of the household budget to be oriented to a calculation of needs and the income available for their satisfaction, that is, with the immediate contingencies of consumption, and to be constrained by the traditional norms governing the functioning of the household and the welfare of its members. These constraints are put aside when the entrepreneurial function or bureaucratic office is differentiated from the household, in the case of economic action allowing—although obviously not necessitating—a rationality that finds its most efficient instrument in modern bookkeeping (see Weber's discussion, 1978b, 86–100). Weber opposes "profit-making" to budget management in that whereas the latter is oriented to satisfaction of "fixed wants," the former seeks to produce a surplus and an enhancement of the value of the enterprise, through acquisition of as much control as possible of every market factor. The ideal technical instrument for this is capital accounting.

The material and ideal interests of patrimonial or feudal elites have already been mentioned. In various concrete ways the interests of these elites are usually—but not invariably, of course—tied to the existing order. The material interests of the Brahmans were linked to the kings and other royalty who supported them in return for their services. The Chinese mandarin was forever dependent on his ability to extract surplus from the groups controlling the agricultural output of his district, and so his interests lay with the clan, the organization essential for maintaining this. The material interest of the feudal lords of Europe rested on the manorial system with its peasant labor tied to the land. And the modern class of large corporate capitalists find themselves in the same general position: having an inherent interest in defending their privileges and rights against the incursions of anything "socialistic."

Whether the ideal interests of such groups cohere with their material ones is of course an empirical question, as is the question of whether they typically do possess ideal interests of such significance that they really do become obstacles to change. Weber thought that this was often the case and made much of it in the instances of the aforementioned and other elite status groups. It is here that his concept of status group (to be discussed), with its claims to positive social honor, its movement toward social closure buttressed by internal mechanisms of social control, and its "status ethic," in terms of which the world is made meaningful, comes powerfully into play. Privileged status groups such as those mentioned above not only exercise power partly on the basis of their solidarity, but typically do so, according to Weber, in opposition to legitimacy claims made in the name of economic rationality, especially the elevation of acquisitiveness to some form of value-rationality. The status groups of the Eastern civilizations are certainly Weber's best examples of this, but it can be seen in any traditional society where economic interests as such gain a foothold. The sneering contempt in which French aristocrats looked down on the acquisitiveness of early capitalists, for example, illustrates the point in a particularly pointed fashion.

We conclude this discussion of Weber's overall theory of the origins of the *external* features of modern capitalism with the observation that, in a general way at least, he conformed to the stipulations set forth in his methodological writings: constructing ideal types on the basis of value-relevance along with a loose employment of *Verstehen*, and attempting to show the causal lines among the empirical referents they purport to describe. We turn now to the analysis of the origins of its "spirit" in the religious ethics of the early Protestant sects.

THE PROTESTANT ETHIC AND THE SPIRIT OF CAPITALISM

The essential line of Weber's argument in *PE* (Weber, 1948) and *SECTS* (in Gerth and Mills, 1946, 302–322)[23] is as follows.

[23] There has been some dispute over whether Weber's observations and arguments in his essay "The Protestant Sects and the Spirit of Capitalism" (*SECTS*), written not long after *PE*,

The formation of the many Protestant groups during the early sixteenth century, setting themselves in opposition to the Catholic church on various doctrinal (and other) grounds, encouraged theological and ethical changes that over a period of time produced a radically transformed attitude toward economic activity. These changes were especially pronounced in early Calvinism and its offshoots, especially Puritanism, various Baptist and Pietist sects, and Methodism. Doctrinally, Calvinism prepared the way for a radical reevaluation of acquisitive activity in its reconstruction or radical extension of two Christian principles: (1) a rationalization of the monotheistic principle to the extreme of total remoteness, or "absolute transcendentality," and (2) a powerful reaffirmation of the doctrine of divine election, or predestination. The first makes the Christian God an inscrutable and unapproachable deity who created the world and human life to the end of celebrating his own greater glory. The Original Sin was a lapse from a state of grace whereby the human race brought upon itself everlasting damnation. No acts of human will could ever have the slightest possibility of altering this condition. This is expressed in the Westminster Confession of 1647.

> Man, by his fall into a state of sin, hath wholly lost all ability of will to any spiritual good accompanying salvation so that a natural man, being altogether averse from that good, and in sin, is not able, by his own strength, to correct himself, or to prepare himself therewith (Weber, 1948, 99).

However, in the interest of assuring his glorification, God has made some exceptions.

> By the decree of God, for the manifestation of His glory, some men and angels are predestined unto everlasting life, and others foreordained to everlasting death (100).

No *human* knowledge of one's state of grace is possible, however, because of God's remote and transcendental nature. Belief in election by such a God, it might seem, ought to encourage an acceptance of and resignation to one's fate. Although this sometimes did occur, it is Weber's main argument, as we shall see, that the socially significant consequence was actually in an *inner-worldly* and *activist* direction.

These factors of religious belief were intensified and perpetuated by two others. First, the religious individualism of Protestantism, in reaction against the corruption of Catholicism (originally, mainly the sale of indulgences), generally downplays the significance of ritual, and thus the need for religious professionals or intermediaries as well, casting the individual back on his or her own resources in confronting questions of faith and salvation.

---

constitute an integral part of the Protestant ethic thesis. Weber says that *SECTS* supplements *PE*, but does not amplify this (in Gerth and M:ills, 1946, 450, n.1; also Berger, Stephen, 1971). We shall take the two essays to be complementary sides of Weber's analysis. It has become fairly commonly although not unanimously accepted that the three volumes of the *Religionssoziologie*, treated earlier, are also logically part of the Protestant ethic argument (e.g., Parsons, 1949, Chaps. 14, 15; Salomon, 1935; Aron, 1965), the position accepted here.

Reactions to this differ, but generally it resulted, according to Weber, in a relentless searching of one's conscience and examination of one's motives for hidden or obscure sinful intent and lapses of faith. The typical experience resulting from this, he thought, was a spiritual state of profound loneliness exemplified by the Christian in Bunyan's *Pilgrim's Progress* (107). In this regard Weber contrasts sixteenth and seventeenth century forms of Calvinism with the Catholic confessional, which provides for the individual a psychological release from the sense of sin, that "very human Catholic cycle of sin, repentance, atonement, release, followed by renewed sin" (117). Here we see the enormous social significance that Weber (no less than Durkheim) places on ritual (although its specific theoretical significance is not exactly the same), for it is precisely this—the absence of institutional means of dealing with sin and guilt—that is absent in Calvinism. The repudiation of "all magical means to salvation as superstition and sin" Weber refers to as the "logical conclusion" of the process of the removal of magic, or the "disenchantment of the world" (105). The logical implication of this, in its fully rationalized form, is the effective elimination of the ritual barriers between priesthood and laity, a rejection of the distinction in religious status or qualifications virtually universal in world religions, even to the point, among some sects like the Quakers, of actually abolishing the priesthood. In this respect Lutheranism had taken a decisive step in eliminating the special religious qualifications associated with monastic life. This "other-worldly" asceticism, which has *no* implication for societal economic life, could then later be focused *within* the world—an "inner-worldly asceticism—as an ethical obligation imposed on all.

Second, there is the concept of the calling, which originated in Lutheranism in connection with the doctrine of good works, but which in Calvinism came to acquire an economic interpretation of a very specific sort, conferring on acquisitive economic activity a type of religious sanctification. In Catholic scholastic doctrine, necessary worldly activity such as eating and drinking was morally neutral, and this applied as well to labor. Although he went through several changes in working out his doctrine, Luther ultimately arrived at the position—a radical departure from Catholicism—that, "the fulfillment of worldly duties is under all circumstances the only way to live acceptably to God" (81). This does not mean, however, that Luther expressed anything like the spirit of capitalism. Rather, for him the calling to worldly activity remained essentially traditionalistic, to be accepted as a directive of divine Providence. The individual is enjoined to remain in his proper station and to eschew any thought of engaging in actions that would go beyond this. It was not possible, therefore, for Luther "to establish a new or in any way fundamental connection between worldly activity and religious principles" (85).

The social organizational side of these early sects was analyzed by Weber in *SECTS*. A "sect" is a voluntary religious association of the religiously and morally qualified, as distinct from one that is obligatory, a "church," a "corporation which organizes grace and administers gifts of grace, like an endowed foundation" (in Gerth and Mills, 1946, 305–306), and so implies nothing regarding the moral worth of members.

Now in Calvinism the world exists entirely for the purposes of the glorification of God, and the Christian is placed in this world solely to further this by following God's commandments. Weber asks how it is that such a doctrine, with its peculiar form of radical individualism, could be compatible with the tight sectlike form of organization of these variants of fundamentalist Christianity. Calvinist doctrine and practice resolves this by identifying the fulfillment of worldly tasks with religious *duty*, which "makes labour in the service of impersonal social usefulness appear to promote the glory of God and hence *to be willed by Him*" (109: italics mine). This doctrine is an *ultimate* rationalization, in the sense of being a complete resolution of the theodicy problem (109).

The sect-type organization provided the social *milieu* in which "premiums" placed upon salvation-oriented ethical conduct came to control the actions of the individual. The methodical and rational way of life in terms of which these premiums acquired their meaning took the form of enjoining one to "prove" oneself saved. This had two sides.

> The premiums were placed upon "proving" oneself before God in the sense of attaining salvation—which is found in *all* Puritan denominations—and "proving" oneself before men in the sense of socially holding one's own within the Puritan sects. Both aspects were mutually supplementary and operated in the same direction: they helped to deliver the "spirit" of modern capitalism, its specific *ethos*: the ethos of the modern *bourgeois middle classes* (321).

The sect was thus the organizational vehicle for an individualism in which the believer's every act was not only subject to the monitoring of the conscience, but of a tightly drawn communal social control as well. Weber identified the process by which the sectarian nature of Calvinism intensified the indoctrination of and social control over members: Discipline was vested in the hands of laymen; every individual was required to "hold his or her own" in a competition of piety; and this had the effect of breeding "selected qualities" in them (in Gerth and Mills, 1946, 320).

It was Weber's opinion that these factors, in conjunction, must necessarily have engendered a "salvation anxiety" of unendurable intensity. How could anyone, save perhaps Calvin himself (who was indeed convinced of his election), not experience an overwhelming need to know whether or not one was among the elect? Calvin's doctrine that everyone should simply rest content in the knowledge that God had chosen he regarded as simply beyond the capacity of the average believer to accept. As ultimate rationalization Calvin's doctrine had a "magnificent consistency," but in practice was an "extreme inhumanity" (Weber, 1905, 104). It was inevitable, then, that the question "Am I elect?" arise for every believer with an intensity that would "force all other interests into the background." The consequence, in Weber's view, was an intense pressure to wonder whether there might not be knowable signs of one's state of grace. In so far as Weber is correct about this—and there are legitimate doubts about Weber's judgment regarding the intensity and sociological importance of the salvation anxiety (Zaret, 1985; Parkin, 1982)—one can imagine the mental agony of the dilemma of experiencing the passion to know, yet believing (presumably) that only a few were elect.

   The salvation anxiety Weber thought was engendered by these factors was met by church doctrine that enjoined the believer to believe in his or her election as a religious duty, since self-doubt itself was the temptation of the devil, and lack of self-confidence in the face of self-doubt evidence of a want of faith. And to maintain this self-confidence, engagement with the world is urged on the believer, for in Weber's words, "it alone disperses religious doubts and gives the certainty of grace" (112). It was here that the doctrine of good works had its effect. Although official Calvinist doctrine denies that salvation can be achieved through works, the believer nonetheless could come to believe that these were a sign or indicator of election. Good works cannot purchase salvation, but are a means of ridding one of the fear of being one of the damned (115). Conviction of salvation on this ground, which Lutherans attacked as a doctrine of salvation by works, was supported, Weber thought, by pastoral teachings of divines such as Richard Baxter; in fact, it is such material that constitutes his main evidence.

   The result was a practical religious ethics in which acquisitive economic activity, pursued to the greater glory of God, of course, came to acquire religious meaning as an indicator of one's state of grace. Weber interpreted the religion-economics linkage, in which sect (or church) membership is taken to be a reliable indicator of one's credit rating (about which he obtained first-hand acquaintance during his trip to the United States in 1904), as a survival of this original linking (Weber, in *SECTS*). The critical aspect of this ethic was the systematic and remorseless way in which it had to be applied if it were to serve the function for which it was created. The believer had to "*prove* repeatedly that he was endowed" with the moral qualities of the True Christian, those that qualified him or her for membership (in Gerth and Mills, 1946, 320). This meant not only performing labor as a calling, i.e., as religious duty, but also systematic abstention from all the forms of pleasure whereby the Devil shows his face. This amounted to an infusion of religion into everyday life; indeed, into *each and every act of one's entire life*. In this regard Weber contrasts Calvinist discipline with Hinduism, arguing that the worldly ethic of the latter was *additive*, rather than totalistic or integrated. In Hinduism, the application of "premiums" applied to salvation chances (i.e., one's status upon rebirth) depend on the *sum* of discrete acts consistent with one's dharma. In stark contrast, for the Calvinist, any *single* act had the potential to reveal the absence of grace, with its awful consequence.

   The seemingly paradoxical situation of this religious individualism coupled with sectarian control was manifest in the characteristic formal and unemotional social relations of Puritanism. Puritanism "unwittingly," Weber says, brought about a devaluation of all personal ties, even those of family and neighborhood, in its demand for an unyielding sober and calculative life organization. He portrayed the Puritans as monks now forced into the world, their every action governed by a lifelong asceticism, a constant check on the expression of emotions, a systematic, "destruction of spontaneous, impulsive enjoyment . . ." (Weber, 1905, 119). He even went so far as to trace stereotypical English reserve to Puritanism, contrasting it with a form of what he thought of as its opposite, German *Gemütlichkeit*.

   The historically significant effect of this sober middle-class ethic on the development of modern capitalism lay in its bringing together de facto acquisitive behavior with a principled limitation on consumption. The virtually inevitable consequence was a systematic accumulation of capital (an accumulation that could itself undermine the ascetic practice, as religious leaders like John Wesley understood well [175ff.]), the essential condition of continuous investment and economic growth.

This is not the only time and place, of course, that the spirit of capitalism has arisen but it was, Weber says, the first time that it had assumed such an intense ethically grounded form, and just as important, the first that it has appeared under conditions of relatively high development of the other factors necessary to establish capitalism as an autonomous going concern, and ultimately as the central organizing principle of society.

Throughout his analysis Weber appears to make a double argument, proposing *two* distinct relationships. The first is that between the ethic and the spirit. "The process of sanctifying life could thus almost take on the character of a business enterprise" (124), he says and notes this penetration of Puritan discourse by commercial similes (238, n.102). Here the relation is between two elaborated forms of subjective meaning—ideal, *inner* phenomena—that only gradually became differentiated. But there is a second process going on, also critical to Weber's argument, in which the relationship occurs between the spirit and the *form* of the enterprise. The "capitalistic form of an enterprise and the spirit in which it is generally run," he says, "stand in some sort of adequate relationship to each other . . ." (64). In the one case, an "attitude of mind" finds its most suitable expression in capitalist enterprise"; in the other, "the enterprise has derived its most suitable motive from the spirit of capitalism (124–125). These phenomena can, indeed have, occurred separately. Weber's representation of Benjamin Franklin as an exemplar of the capitalist spirit while running his printing business along strictly handicraft lines in the "backwoods" of Pennsylvania shows one side of this (65). Likewise, a business can be capitalistic in form (see the earlier discussion), yet totally lack the capitalist spirit, as has not uncommonly been the case (65).

The main line of argument in *PE* is clearly an attempt to demonstrate a relationship between "ethic" and "spirit." But the significance of this, assuming for the moment that Weber is correct, depends on the validity of Weber's presupposition that because the capitalism of the sixteenth and seventeenth centuries had not created its own internal ethic, and because it was probably inherently incapable of doing so (Weber's general treatment of market rationality implies this), its legitimizing ethic had to originate elsewhere. But this requires an explanation of just why this particular connection in fact occurred. The first thesis establishes the relationship of the ethic and spirit, the second, of the spirit to the already present form (i.e., those aspects of capitalism included by Weber in his historical ideal type and discussed earlier). *Both* are essential to Weber's argument.

There is a very important aspect of all this that has posed a difficulty for Weber interpreters: namely, the issue of whether Weber intended his argument as a causal one, or as one establishing elective affinity.

Throughout this discussion I have tended to represent Weber's argument as a causal one, rather than one that attempts to establish a relation of "elective affinity." I have done so because, while there is room for dispute on this point, and while it is necessary to recognize a degree of ambiguity in Weber's text, it is nevertheless the case that Weber fairly consistently employs causal language in discussing the ethic-spirit relationship. He says, for instance, that his study treats one side of the "causal chain," then goes on to refer to both this and its reciprocal as being "causal relationships," and asserts that his study attempts a "causal evaluation" (27). Elsewhere, in a short methodological statement reiterating his general methodological position, he says that the explanation of the spirit of capitalism has to be pursued in "concrete genetic sets of relations . . ." (48), and as we saw in the previous chapter, he understood genetic processes as (complex) forms of causality. And at the very end of the study he refers to his study as a "causal interpretation of culture and history" (183). On the other hand, when referring to the "spirit-form" relationship he avoids causal language. He says, for example, that spirit and form

> generally stand in some sort of adequate relationship to each other, but not in one of necessary interdependence (64)

and that it is historical fact that this spirit

> has on the one hand found its most suitable expression in capitalist enterprise, while on the other the enterprise has derived its most suitable motive force from the spirit of capitalism (65).

Is this the language of elective affinity? We suggest that it was Weber's intent, however unclearly rendered, to specify the two relationships as distinct in form, the one as causal, the other as one of elective affinity. Further, we wish to interpret the latter as a sociological rendering of the philosophical inner-outer polarity, illustrating again its significance in Weber's formulation of particular sociological problems. This, it should be noted, is consistent with the "mainstream" understanding of elective affinity as "the decisive connection by which Weber relates class and interests" (in Gerth and Mills, 1946, 62).[24] But it softens or weakens this relation to one of less than causal status, trimming it to fit his non-Marxist insistence upon the relative and varying autonomy of ideal orders or spheres.

Finally, it ought to be noted that the relationship Weber claims to have established is surely one of the great historical ironies, and a double one at that. The first can be nicely stated in terms of Weber's comparison of the Calvinism-capitalism case to the Confucian ethic (Weber, 1951, Chap. 8), which exhalted material well-being as a value, but had no ethical code of conduct comparable to that developed within Calvinism as its practical vehicle. Consequently, Chinese economic policies never achieved their ends of growth and expansion. The Puritans, on the other hand, rejected wealth as an end,

---

[24] Interestingly, the German *Wahlverwandtschaft* in *PE* is *not* translated by Parsons as "elective finity," as Bendix, writing over thirty years later, translated it (from the same passage: Bendix, 1960, 85), but rather as the rather limp "correlation" (91). If this interpretation of Weber's thesis is correct, we suggest that it reflects the historicism-rooted inner-outer frame as an inhospitable context for causal analysis.

yet if Weber is correct, they were instrumental in creating the greatest economic revolution since neolithic times.

The second irony runs even broader and deeper than this. The individualism of Calvinism contributed not only to the inner ethic of capitalism, but more broadly to the larger nature of Western freedom, especially in the sense of the freedom of conscience, in its spread well beyond sheer religious contexts. And this remains a value central to Western society, even if in practice it is often honored more in the breech than in fact. Weber regarded freedom of conscience as "the most basic Right of Man because it comprises all ethically conditioned action and guarantees freedom from compulsion" (Weber, 1978b, 1209). Yet Puritan individualism also left its mark on the larger growth and spread of rationalization in virtually all aspects of life in the West. Of course, since "victorious" capitalism now rests on "mechanical" foundations, as Weber says, it no longer needs—or has— the support of Protestant asceticism. By sometime in the eighteenth century, the spirit of rational accumulation had become strong enough to constitute its own legitimation. But the meaning of this "pursuit of wealth, stripped of its religious and ethical meaning" (182) was for Weber an *absence* of a "way of life" that reduced human existence to a "pure utilitarianism" (183), or stated more abstractly in the language of rationalization, a displacement of ends by means. Capitalism has evolved into an outer shell of a mechanism devoid of inner spirit.

There was a rush to attack Weber's thesis immediately upon its publication, and critical examination of the Protestant thesis continues right up to the present. By and large this criticism has left Weber's thesis damaged but still intact. Much of it has been misplaced, attacking claims Weber never made, or based on misunderstanding of the essentials of his argument.[25]

It has nevertheless become evident that, while much of this criticism of the Protestant ethic thesis is mistaken, misinterprets Weber, or even misses the point entirely, a valid core remains. The main point of this is not really whether Weber was right or that he was wrong, but that his evidence was insubstantial, most importantly on the question of the real beliefs, economic and religious, specifically of seventeenth century Puritans and capitalists, and that the question therefore remains open. The first question regarding his argument, then, must deal with the question of just what sorts of data would be adequate to address this question empirically. It is surprising how few of Weber's critics, whether sympathetic or not, have seen this to be the issue. There has, of course, been an empirical literature that has developed over the years, but until recently research designs adequate to the task of resolving the evidence problem has been lacking.[26]

The historical relationship between the Protestant ethic and the spirit of capitalism, however, remains a controversial issue. Studies such as those

---

[25] A review of the older literature has been compiled by Fischoff, 1944. For some of the more relevant critiques, see Samuelson, 1961; Robertson, 1933; Strauss, 1953; George and George, 1961; Parkin, 1982; Bendix, 1960, 84–85; Tawney, 1938; and Stone, 1967.

[26] Among the few exceptions to this are David Zaret's *The Heavenly Contract: Ideology and Organization in Prerevolutionary Puritanism,* and Gordon Marshall's *Presbyteries and Profits: Calvinism and the Development of Capitalism in Scotland, 1560–1707.*

of Zaret and Marshal (footnote 26) go some distance toward resolving it, perhaps rather surprisingly in favor of Weber, but a definitive statement remains in the province of future research.

We have now discussed the way in which Weber framed his sociology of religion by the concept and theory of rationalization, and looked in some detail at the significance of ascetic Protestantism as a concrete and historically important case of rationalization. We go on now to a discussion of Weber's vision of the unprecedented growth of rationalizing forces in the West.

WEBER'S THEORY OF RATIONALIZATION AND THE RATIONALIZATION OF THE WEST: RATIONALIZATION IN THE SOCIAL ORDERS

In his introduction to *PE* (written very late in his life), Weber says that "very different things" may be understood by "rationalization," and that rationalizations of the most varied character have existed in various departments of life and in all areas of culture, and mentions specifically mystical contemplation, economic life, scientific research, military training, law, and administration (Weber, 1948, 26). But despite the obvious centrality of the idea in his work, he nowhere provides the sort of systematic discussion one would have wished for, so this task has been left to others.[27] Our approach here will be to distinguish: (1) types of rationalities from (2) rationalization processes in different social orders, and then proceed to (3) a general discussion of rationalization in the West.

Types of Rationalities

Among recent treatments of Weber's empirical types of rationality, that of Kalberg (1980) is particularly apropos for our purposes. Kalberg extracts four types of rationality from Weber's texts.[28] Practical rationality (or instrumental rationality: Levine, 1985, 158, n.11) rests on interests and their inherent embeddedness in everyday realities and involves the calculative weighing of means to given ends. As Weber puts it, it is "the type of attitude which sees and judges the world consciously in terms of the worldly interests of the individual ego" (Weber, 1948, 77). Practical rationality is adaptive, and although its anthropological roots must lie in the universal incorrigibility of a certain minimum amount of means-ends calculation in even the simplest or earliest forms of human social organization (e.g., hunting and gathering bands), its developed forms presuppose a diminution of the power of magic (see the discussion in the previous chapter). It has a special affinity for urban business and artisanal strata.

---

[27] See, in particular, Schluchter, 1981; Kalberg, 1980; Brubaker, 1984; Levine, 1985; and Collins, 1986.

[28] There are empirically derived types of action distinct from the abstractly formulated anthropological pure types mentioned in the previous chapter.

Distinct from practical rationality is a theoretical or conceptual[29] type, which "involves a conscious mastery of reality through the construction of increasingly precise abstract concepts . . ." (Kalberg, 1980, 1152). The rationalizations of the world religions, of Western law, philosophy, and science are the preeminent examples. All have in common a quest for meaning by attempting to understand the cosmos, and all are the products of strata of intellectuals. Such rationalities may remain circumscribed by the boundaries of such strata, but under certain conditions may come to exercise an *indirect* but potentially powerful effect on the everyday conduct of others.

Like theoretical rationality, substantive rationality has a theoretical component, but its main thrust is to directly transform or order the world in accord with a more or less systematized complex of values. This is to say that the world comes to be understood and judged against a value standard or standards. All value rationalities, whether religious or secular, are grounded in what is at root an intrinsically irrational standpoint.

Formal rationality has been discussed in the earlier discussion of Weber's sociology of law. A legal system is formally rational if it takes the form of a systematized code consisting of abstract rules in terms of which any legally relevant action can supposedly be adjudicated, or the form of empirical law finding, in which precedents come to function as general rules. Like practical rationality, formal rationality is calculative in means-ends terms, but this process comes to be manifest, as it were, on another plane of abstraction. More generally, formal rationality designates any action that is calculative in terms of abstract rules. The totality of rituals of a preindustrial society, for example, add up to little more than a congeries of disconnected and unrelated magical practices addressed to the manifold of conditions requiring adaptation—an array of practical rationalities. The conduct of the Puritan, on the other hand, goes beyond adaptation in the sense of being an array of practices *integrated* by the application or *imposition* of a formally systematized normative code. For the Puritan, of course, there were very substantial value-rational elements in this, giving it the quality of a powerful substantive rationality, but the systematic and integrated rule-bound character of the code gave it a strong formal character as well. As the former elements weakened, the code survived and spread as an increasingly "purified" formal rationality.

Elsewhere, especially in his discussions of capitalism, Weber says that we may speak of formal rationality where aspects of social action are reduced to or normatively specified in quantitative values. Double-entry bookkeeping with its ramifications is a kind of exemplar of this. The normative control of action in terms of quantitative specifications is easily assimilable to the formalism of rules, and particularly to rules that are intellectually derived or formulated and claim behavioral conformity on the basis of principle. Taylorism in industry, and its offshoots there and elsewhere, which were

---

[29] This term is preferred by Levine as embracing a broader set of phenomena, some of which he regards as, strictly speaking, not theoretical (Levine, 1985). Note also in the same passage some other minor objections to Kalberg's interpretation.

well understood and commented on by Weber, are a good example of this. In our modern world its forms are virtually innumerable.[30]

Because formal rationality appears in social action in connection with purposive, or end-oriented action, but not a value to be achieved in and of itself, yet by definition does set standards to which action must conform, it may be converted from the status of being a *means* to that of an *end*. This aspect of formal rationality played an absolutely decisive role in Weber's general theory of rationalization, as we shall see. In principle, any sphere of society or culture can undergo a transformation in the direction of formal rationalization, but, as we shall discuss shortly, in the West this has been increasingly characteristic of the state and giant corporation.

The concept of "social order" is foundational to Weber's sociology. He defines it as a social relationship in which conduct is, "on the average, oriented toward determinable 'maxims' . . . regarded as obligatory or exemplary [i.e., 'valid'] (Weber, 1978b, 31). Relations between social orders can be characterized in terms of the various rationalities they exhibit, and the causal analysis of historical individuals usually involves transformations of orders and societies that can be analyzed in terms of their changing rationalities. The substantive rationality of the puritans infused economic action with ethical meaning in the seventeenth century and after, but later the typical market orientation of capitalists became divorced from this and devolved into a form of practical means-ends rationality massively intensified by the centrality of the formal elements mentioned above. Any particular form of rationality develops and expands only if some group or stratum becomes its "bearer." The Brahmans, the Confucian literati, and the Pandectists are examples.

When any rationality is normatively established in a social order, that is, has become the legitimate form of social action of the order, it becomes increasingly likely that such a rationality will find itself in relations of conflict with other orders (Collins, 1985, Chap. 4). The extensive formal rationalization of modern state apparatuses, for example, typically becomes the object of attacks from various other societal orders—educational, religious, and so on—the legitimacy of which rests on *different* rationalities, typically of a substantive nature. Such conflicts are the more likely when an order is undergoing a rationality transformation, for instance, in situations where local economies of small scale characterized by substantive rationalities centering around "paternalism" are in process of being transformed into large-scale supracommunal—indeed, supranational—entities wherein the practical and formal rationalities of the market prevail. Or, perhaps, when socialist or social democratic governments shift or seem to shift from the substantive rationality of a practice guided by socialist doctrine to the formal rationality of bureaucratic domination.

Substantive rationalities exert their worldly effects by bringing into being methodical ways of life that can override or influence other rationalities by subjecting them to *ethical* standards. Weber defines an ethical standard as

---

[30] For an analysis of how formal rationality was early introduced into collegiate football in the United States, and ended up shaping the growth of that sport, see Westby and Sack, 1976.

one to which men attribute a certain type of value and which, by virtue of this belief, they treat as a valid norm governing their action (Weber, 1978b, 36)

The extent to which value-rationalization processes may influence a substantive rationality in the direction of internal consistency conforming to an ethical standard is greatly variable. Ethical standards may have an influence on action even in the absence of an "external guarantee," but such instances are historically insignificant. They must become the standards of the community to have significant effects. Even so, ethically infused forms of substantive rationality by no means *necessarily* have the effect of establishing the kinds of systematically ordered ways of life that have significant bearing on economic action. Indeed, the reverse is true. Confucianism and Hinduism were ethical substantive rationalities that for the reasons discussed earlier, failed to exert much influence on economic life. The historically most significant ethical substantive rationalities have, of course, been certain of the world religions, but of great significance in the modern world have been—obviously—such secular ideologies as democracy, liberalism, communism, socialism, and anarchism, as well as others both political and nonpolitical.

Rationalizing processes occur in the social orders of society. In the following section we shall analyze Weber's sociology of rationalization in these orders. We have already dealt in some detail with the religious and legal orders. In the western orders, rationalization meant, first, in the intellectual sphere, a process of clarification and of formulating concepts in an increasingly logical and consistent way; and second, on an ethical plane, the introduction of a consistent and methodical pattern of conduct. In the sociology of law, rationality designates legal processes controlled by the intellect and undergoing increasing internal systematization. Formally rational law is distinguished from the substantively rational type by virtue of its autonomy from ethical claims or codes. Beyond religion and law, however, Weber brings the structures of domination, the market, and administration within the framework of rationalizing processes. Finally, there is the knowledge order, and no discussion of Weber's theory of societal rationalization would be adequate without a treatment of the most significant form of knowledge in the modern world, namely science. We will interpret Weber as asserting that the central rationalizing processes in modern society occur in the orders of knowledge, law, the economy, and state administration,[31]

---

[31] Weber did, of course, treat rationalizing processes in other social orders and symbol spheres. His study of the development of music in the West is arguably the most focused and systematic analysis of rationalizing processes to be found in his work (see Weber, 1969). It is worth mentioning that the idea of rationalization in the cultural sphere derived from Weber became in the post-World War I years a principle focus of members of the Frankfurt school, especially Max Horkeimer, Theodor Adorno, Walter Benjamin, and Herbert Marcuse. With the failure of the international proletariat to demonstrate solidarity during the war and the turn of the Russian Revolution toward Stalinism, the Marxism of the Frankfurt school shifted away from a materialist foundation and analysis of the class struggle to symbolic spheres such as communication in the mass media, language, art, music, and literature. The manifesto of this abandonment of the proletariat as historical agency in the form of a heavily Weber-

discussing each in turn, and then conclude this section with a discussion of the specifically organizational theory of bureaucracy.[32]

Science and Rationalization in Modernizing Societies

Weber's concept of rationalization in the modern capitalist industrialized world may be approached from the standpoint of our earlier discussion of the Enlightenment view of science. From the standpoint of Weber's conceptual scheme of the rationalities, this understanding of science was, *broadly* speaking, an ideal of scientific practice subordinated to and guided by a value-rationality centering on the ideal of "humanity." This idea achieved a philosophical and sociological fusion first, in Condorcet, St. Simon, and Comte, and then, in quite different forms, among many others, in Spencer and Marx. As we tried to show earlier, this grand vision emerged in the form of a revisionist secularized philosophical anthropology that grounded the technical practice of science in the framework of a theory of social change that imagined human history to represent a course of material and ideal progress in the direction of one or another form of utopian ideal. The interplay of these problematics was from the outset a volatile and intellectually explosive one that engendered many intellectual innovations, including the beginnings of sociology.

Weber's conception of rationalizing processes in the continuing development of industrial societies rests on this foundation. Especially in his Munich lecture "Science as a Vocation," he voices a conception of science as it was emerging in the twentieth century at the core of which was the sense that scientific practice was becoming, indeed had already essentially become, divorced from any significant substantive rationality. His argument in that lecture regarding the necessity of divorcing the social sciences from any consideration of the *ends* of action, and limiting their applicability merely to selection of *means* (see Chapter 13), is itself reflective of this development. This seems to convert scientists into technocrats and make of science itself an inherently amoral enterprise. It is not surprising that following Weber's death a protracted debate regarding this understanding of science took place in Germany (see Turner and Factor, 1984, Chapters 4 and 5). In this view the claims of eighteenth and nineteenth century thinkers that science could supplant religion as the substantive rationality not only of the West, but ultimately of humanity, was a short-lived and abortive dream coming at the

---

influenced interment of Enlightenment ideals was Horkeimer and Adorno's *Dialectic of Enlightenment*. But rather than acknowledging him as a major intellectual source of their ideas, most representatives of or identifers with the movement made the self-confessed bourgeois Weber into an intellectual whipping boy. The animus of the members of the school toward Weber was manifested at the 1964 Centenary of Weber's Birth, especially in Marcuse's vitriolic attack on him (Marcuse, in Stammer, 1971, 133–151), which seems to have been motivated, Aron says, "by a kind of fury against Max Weber, as if he was still alive and indomitable" (Aron, 1970, 2, 297). For a good treatment of the critical school's reception of Weber, see Kellner (1985).

[32] Regarding the absence of systematic discourse on Weber's part, it should be remembered that he regarded his own work as only a beginning. At the end of *PE*, he laid out a research agenda to which *PE* was only a preliminary contribution (Weber, 1948, 182–183).

end of the long history of natural law conceptions in the West. The place and nature of science in the modern world, for Weber, rests on a fairly complicated but not always carefully formulated intertwining of theoretical, substantive, formal, and practical rationalities.

We may begin by noting that the theoretical rationalizations of priests and prophets—at least in the West, and especially of the former—have some similarities to scientific rationality, one of them being that both incorporate degrees of formal rationality. But these priestly and prophetic rationalizations were either quite exclusively the preoccupations of religious professionals or became significant in the lives of laity because of their connections to ethical codes that had at least some degree of rationalized form, which is to say that they incorporated substantive rationalities that were capable of investing ordinary life with ultimate meaning.

Science differs fundamentally. Scientists are not today a stratum capable of being bearers and disseminators, let alone creators, of *any* substantive rationality, as the eighteenth and nineteenth century visionaries thought they would become. This is so first of all not in spite of but because of the commonplace that the essential meaning of science is scientific *progress*, understood in a specific sense. Science constantly undermines itself, destroys its own finest truths. It is the "common goal" of scientists that their work be surpassed (Weber, in Gerth and Mills, 1946, 138). But this means that they cannot serve the essentially religious function of providing ultimate values, as Comte and perhaps even Durkheim believed. And it leads to a more fundamental question, the limits of the meaning of science.

Absolutely fundamental to science is its *theoretical* or *conceptual* nature as a belief system comprised of laws or lawlike statements, empirical generalizations, and vast numbers of empirical propositions, to all of which are assigned various truth values. There are also, of course, the technical applications of science, its *practically* rational aspect. In earlier times Weber observes that science was also invested with ultimate meanings (the "path to *true* art" for Leonardo, the demonstration of God's Providence in the workings of nature, etc.), which is to say it constituted a *substantive* rationality. But science today, Weber holds, far from creating meaning, actually engenders a sense of *meaninglessness*, in consequence of its progressive nature. In the stead of a meaningful cosmos, science instantiates a vast causal mechanism, a world ultimately comprised of nothing but an array of natural causal relationships, stripping away every aspect of experience of larger meanings and bringing them under the calculative mentality of means-ends rationality. This is an irony: The instantiation of the formal rationality of means-ends calculation as the methodological norm of science is the (inevitable?) consequence of the pursuit of empirically grounded theoretical knowledge as *rational* knowledge, to the larger or "higher" *substantive* end(s) of revealing the ways of God, nature, or humankind. Any belief in ultimate values is incompatible with both that total relativization of truth which is a necessary corollary of the value of scientific progress, and the instrumentalization of knowledge. Sociologically, the consequence of this "disenchantment of the world" is that "precisely the ultimate and most sublime values have retreated from public life either into the transcendental realm of mystic life or into the brotherliness of direct and personal human relations" (155), or, as Weber implies elsewhere, into absolute skepticism and nihilism. It is perhaps Weber's most devastating critique of modernism, and of science as the intellectual and theoretical core of that modernism, that the formal rationality that he found coming to dominate it, while creating and recreating an array of material forms of progress, simultaneously renders that progress meaningless, especially to the very bearers of its modernizing rationality.

An organizational feature integral to this process is the increasing specialization that is inherent in the growth of science. The modern scientist is a new type of intellectual, one who becomes one of but a few experts in an increasingly narrowly defined area of research. This process displaces the virtually already outmoded cultivated personality, whose intellectual interests and competence spanned all of knowledge in the past and constituted the ground for a personal life style and ethic of conduct. The Chinese Mandarins, the philosophers of Western aniquity, the great figures of the Renaissance, stand as exemplars of the type. But modern science finds in such characters only intellectual anachronisms—"dilettantes" was Weber's term. One of his main generalizations regarding social change was that experts are always superior to dilettantes, and other things being equal (which they sometimes are not), will displace them. This is one of the key internal processes of rationalization.

Weber's analysis unites two distinct critiques having different historical and intellectual geneologies. The sense of the *meaninglessness* of science is a part of, even integral to, the anti-rationalist and tragic outlook of late nineteenth century intellectuals like Nietzsche. The critique of science as destroyer of the ideals and ethical sensibilities of its practicioners (along with those of others) in its very progress, thereby ironically defeating its own historic role, is rooted in the progressive vision of knowledge as the midwife of the new emancipated world. This was a critique already trenchantly stated by Comte. Meaninglessness, we might say, is a consequence immanent in the transformation of the organizational conditions of scientific progress.

Growing meaninglessness and distructiveness, then, results from the spread of formal rationality in both the logic and organization of science. The cosmos is denuded of meaning by related and perhaps mutually reinforcing processes that we call scientific progress. If Weber had lived a few decades longer, he perhaps would have taken note of still another form of the formal rationalizing of science: its growing bureaucratization. Indeed, the pathos of the specialized idiot savant already prefigures and perhaps anticipates such a perception. This view, of course, would situate universities and other science-producing institutions theoretically in a position parallel to the already substantially bureaucratized organizations in the political and economic orders, and further confirmed his diagnosis of modernism as a continuously expanding bureaucratization of all spheres of life. He might also have given some emphasis to the directions in which science was being pressed by these practical rationalizing processes, and to the devastating consequences of this—in particular, to the growing coordination of science with corporate and state interests, especially the military.[33]

---

[33] Although Weber recognized that elements of practical rationality were at work in the evolution of science, he says little about this. Presumably this would include fields such as engineering.

Weber evidently could envision no reprieve from this condition. His advise to young scientists was no more than that stoical minimum he demanded of himself: to "bear the fate of the times like a man" and to insist on the *only* value essential to scientific practice and teaching, "plain intellectual integrity" (156). It is worth noting that this itself was for him enough of a basis on which to reject withdrawal; although he identified with the dillusioned youth of the time, asserting that he hated "intellectualism as the worst devil," he rejected taking flight as a way of settling with this "devil," for "one has to see the devil's ways to the end in order to realize his power and his limitations" (152). Like the Puritans he studied, Weber found his personal salvation, such as it was, in work. The first principle of scholarly integrity he took to be a moral commitment to academic work as a calling, and he came close to making it into an ultimate value, a way of life.

Legal Rationalization in Modern Societies

In his general theoretical formulations, Weber described the development of law as passing through a series of stages from "charismatic law revelation" under conditions of "primitive legal procedure" up to "an increasingly specialized juridical and logical rationality and systematization" . . . administered by "persons who have received their legal training in a learned and formal manner" (Weber, 1987b, 882). This formalization has several historical sources, most importantly, first, in the immanent intellectual thrust toward codification and then logical systematization that appears wherever legally oriented intellectuals acquire some autonomy; and second, in the capitalist imperative of instituting conditions under which reliable and precise calculations can be made, and which assure the future security of enterprise. But this developmental history has been complex and Weber's discussions of the

---

But today, especially in the "great states," we see an increasing coordination of scientific practice with the interests of state and corporate elites. Indeed, institutions central to the political and economic orders are now essential for the very continuation of science, the more so the higher and more expensive the technology. Increasingly such agendas external to science dictate, canalize, or influence the direction and nature of research. In many of the areas of physical science in the United States, the bulk of the support comes from the Department of Defense or related agencies, such as NASA. And these relationships are not, of course, restricted to the physical sciences. Objectively, this can only be described as the turning of scientific practice to these interests, implying a growing de facto identity of scholarly with practical interests and the erosion of autonomous scientific practice, subjectively, as a shrinking of the autonomous scholarly self.

Weber wondered what forces might arise to counter or challenge formal rationalization processes. It is worth noting that among the strongest have perhaps been those arising from within the scientific order itself. The most important of these have challenged precisely the subordination of science to the practical rationalities of state and corporation. The peace and environmental movements, in all their internal complexities, are perhaps the most prominent among these. But on a lesser scale there is also a challenge to the *formal rationality* of science, and one that increasingly comes from within. Here are the small movements of holistic medicine, attempts to wed physics with philosophy, and many others. Do such developments bring into question Weber's categorical insistence that modern science could never transcend its own internal formal rationality, and that it was inherently destructive of substantive rationality? Perhaps. If so, in the terms of Weber's analysis it would be still another irony within an irony.

particulars turn up anything but a uniform process with respect to the growth of formal rationality. To be sure, modern law exhibits high degrees of formal rationality (and we shall return to this), but the differences even now between common law and civil law countries are substantial. Indeed, the bulk of Weber's discussion of formal rationality is given over to a whole series of factors that *oppose* this tendency. And Weber admits that the general theory of rationalization ignores "the fact that in historical reality the theoretically constructed stages of rationalization have not everywhere followed in sequence" (882). And virtually the entire twelve pages of his section entitled "The Formal Qualities of Modern Law" in the *Rechtssoziologie* are given over to *antiformalistic* tendencies.

His analysis of the main aspects of legal development in the modern period illustrates this. Natural law doctrines historically took both formal and substantive forms. Substantive natural law displaced the formally rational variant whenever, as Weber puts it, "the legitimacy of an acquired right comes to be tied up with the substantive economic rather than with the formal modes of acquisition" (870). The abstract formally rational social contract version gave way to a law arising from the particularistic interests leading up to and culminating in the period of the French revolution, the high point of natural law. The Russian Revolution of 1905 was its last socially significant manifestation. Elsewhere, Weber says that rationalizing tendencies in law have often been driven by needs for rational administration of kings or Popes, but these are typically substantive rationalizations (810).

Codifications of law have often been initiated by kings; these are not *formally* rational systematizations (848–850), however, but only compilations. In the high and late Middle Ages of the twelfth century and after, codifications were effected by lawyers trained in Roman law at the universities.[34] Professional lawyers were the most important factor in the influence of Roman law on the European monarchies. Only with the professionalization of law-making is it possible to transcend the particularism of local or national associations. Bourgeois groups of the period, however, were not influenced. Their interests in a calculable law were better served by law merchant and urban real estate law (853). Indeed, more often than not, such needs may be poorly served by logically constructed law in that it may well result in unexpected and irrational legal determinations.

Even the seemingly straightforward and unambiguous need of capitalism for a settled and predictable environment and for procedure and instruments that concretize legal relations, can be met to a considerable extent, at least, by legal forms that are neither formalized nor rational, as was the case in England (see p. 777).

Despite all this, an expansion of formal rationality can be seen in modern legal development. The fundamental rationality of modern law is to be found in both its law-making and law-finding aspects. The procedure

---

[34] It was not that the Roman law was so systematic or abstract: Roman jurists, Weber says, "obviously lacked" abstract conceptions and terms for the most basic legal concepts. It was the late medieval jurists who created civil law jurisprudence, but to do this they had to "tear out of context" various Romanist principles and *create* the sphere of the logically abstract, had to bring into being the doctrine that "what the jurist cannot conceive has no legal existence" (854–855).

of deliberate legislative enactment is a realization of the principle of control by the intellect, and the fact that the process itself is bound by legal norms distinguishes it from the arbitrariness of legal pronouncements of patrimonial princes, charismatic "law prophets" like Moses or Muhammad, and others. The principle of control by the intellect is central also in law finding, in its practice of applying general rules to specific cases, and in introducing specific formal criteria for assessing legal fact. But in addition to this, modern law tends toward high levels of generality and abstractness of formulation and of internal logical consistency (see Brubaker, 1984, 17–19). Legal formal rationality designates an internally consistent system that at its extreme constitutes a "gapless" set of abstract rules (p. 28), i.e., the principle that all legally bounded activity is held to be unambiguously subject to adjudication by the application of such rules, and that this results from their general and abstract character. In theory, this is a condition in which "all conceivable fact situations must be capable of being logically subsumed" (Weber, 1978b, 656).

We may say that modern law acquires some degree of formal rationality through the *theoretical* rationalizations of legal intellectuals. But this does not occur in an organizational vacuum; rather, it is a consequence of the advance of rational administration (although the significance of law in modern society, it must be kept in mind, is obviously not limited to its workings in administrative settings). Weber's central proposition regarding modern legal rationalization, then, is that

> the more rational the administrative machinery of the princes or hierarchs became, that is, the greater the extent to which administrative "officials" were used in the exercise of the power, the greater was the likelihood that the legal procedure would also become "rational" both in form and substance. To the extent to which the rationality of the organization of authority increased, irrational forms of procedure were eliminated and the substantive law was systematized, i.e., the law as a whole was rationalized (Weber, 1978b, 809).

This relationship resulted from the practical needs of administration and is explicit in asserting its relevance for the present as well as the past (809). But especially when law becomes secularized, there develops an administrative interest on the part of those in power in a type of law that achieves a relatively high degree of legal precision and thus calculability of legal decision. This contrasts with the rather typical interests of ecclesiastical authorities in a law that realizes their "expediential and ethical" goals (810). In terms of Weber's typology, we may say that, whereas the rationalization of religious law is for the most part of the substantive type, when it becomes secularized an interest in pure formalism leading to greater calculability is typically introduced.

In the real world a purely formally rationalized law is an impossibility. All legal forms of adjudication are inevitably substantive in some degree. Although the judicial system may approach the formalism of coming to operate like a "technically rational machine" (811), Weber immediately says that such a condition is never anything other than a "specific type of pacified context" (811). Such formalism is always in "inevitable conflict" with the interests of groups of all sorts. And in so far as these interests take legal form, they necessarily involve attempts to introduce *substantively* rational (or conceivably, substantively irrational) law. Such conflicts have occurred in many times and places, but the most important have doubtless been in the modern period because the growth and spread of capitalism has stimulated an unparalled expansion of rational formalism of law that, as we saw earlier, Weber thought to be absolutely necessary for its development.

Rationalizing Processes and the Market Economy

Economic life throughout human history has above all been predominantly practical, i.e., economic activity is carried forward in terms of calculative means-ends schemes more or less adaptive to the circumstances under which a collective subsistance is more or less assured. But this does not mean, as the classical economists liked to think, that such a practical outlook was an anthropological uniformity. Indeed, as we saw earlier, it was one of Weber's cardinal tenents that it surely was not, and his works are replete with examples of two sources of variation in economic life: (1) the group or class situation and (2) the degree and nature of penetration of economic life by ideas, exercise of power, or other influences emanating from other social orders. The "practical rationality" he attributes to urban business and artinsanal strata, as against the "traditionalism" of the peasant (or other workers) is an example of the first, the infusion of economic life by the Protestant ethic, one of the second.

Nowhere is Weber clearer in his application of the concepts of substantive and formal rationality than in his treatment of economic action. The term "formal rationality of economic action," he says, will be used to designate "the extent of qualitative calculation or accounting which is technically possible and which is actually applied" (Weber, 1978a, 85). "Substantive rationality" will be employed to designate "the degree to which the provisioning of given groups of persons . . . with goods is shaped by economically oriented action under some criterion . . . of ultimate values . . ." (85). He goes on to say that while the former concept is unambiguous precisely because of its quantitative expression, the latter "is full of ambiguities" because "there is an infinite number of possible values for this type" (85–86).

The capitalist economy is for Weber distinguished by virtue of its coming to function increasingly as a complex formal rationality. The sluffing off of older value-rational elements within which earlier protocapitalist economic activity was carried on has brought us to a condition in which, stripped of the apologetics of "bourgeois ideologists," capitalism is nothing other than a "loveless and pitilous economic struggle for existence" (quoted from Weber, *Politische Schriften*, by Roth, in Bendix and Roth, 1971, 28). This rationality is comprised of two objective aspects of the workings of the market: money and the money economy, and production.

We have already indicated (Figure 14-1, page 246) the importance of money, specifically coined money, for the emergence of capitalism. Money, more than any other institution, frees economic activity from the constraints of locale, political expediency, and ethically grounded substantive rationalities. An expanding money economy has historically been both the condition and consequence of the breaking down of traditionalistic barriers to economic rationality. The end result of this is a situation in which economic life reaches a level of *objectification* never imagined in times past.

On this issue Weber may have been influenced by Simmel's analysis in his *Philosophy of Money* (see Chap. 11). Simmel argued that establishment of money as the universal medium of exchange has had the effect of radically transforming all spheres of experience and should be thought of as the archetypical form of objectification and the very core of what it means to speak of modernism. Money brings into being an economic process that is *objective* in the sense of being carried forward in near total independence of subjective meaning. The test of whether a relationship is objectified or not thus becomes the extent to which it can be comprehended apart from the intentions of the actors involved. Simmel argues that in becoming objectified in exchange, the validity of economic value comes to transcend the individual, acquiring a value independent of the subjective valuations of any individual (Simmel, 1979). The central idea here is that the money economy—virtually identical with capitalism, for Simmel[35]—acquires a life of its own, becomes so to speak, in familiar terminology, a "mechanism" that functions independent of the wills and sentiments of individuals.

The functioning of the money economy, however, was only one aspect, important though it was, of the capitalist rationalization of economic life. The money economy as given, for Weber, actually served only as the most general condition under which the process of production could be transformed in world-shattering ways. If Weber's reception of Simmel's theory of objectification and the money economy reveal an idealistic influence on his theory of rationalization, his characterization of the transformation of production shows his materialist side, and particularly his debt to the economists and to Marx. Here the central idea is the formal rationality of the *calculability* of every element that enters into production. The calculative means-end relation transcends mere practicality in assuming increasingly sophisticated quantitative form; it brings every function of the enterprise within the framework of quantitative evaluation: the wage and salary scales; costs of materials, services, and transportation; the value of alternative technologies, and more. Framing this process of standardization by means of the budget is the generality of the money economy, but money alone is not the proximate mover of the rationality of the firm. It merely constitutes the essential condition of the maximization of calculability, the sine qua non of capitalist rationality.

To these must be added a third element, the bureaucratic form of organization. Bureaucracy, of course, is not exclusive to economic organizations; indeed, it originated in the dynasties and military orders of antiquity. But the nature of the modern capitalistic enterprise is inconceivable for Weber apart from its internal organization. And here the prime value is control, achieved through rational calculation; thus it is a formal rationality. The objectivity of the money economy and the quantitative standardization made possible by accounting procedures would have no effect on economic life if they were not somehow brought to bear within specific forms of real social relationships. We shall discuss bureaucratization in more detail in the

---

[35] An identification criticized by Weber.

section following. Here it will suffice only to iterate Weber's thesis that bureaucratization makes possible degrees of control and predictability far beyond any level or type of organization known in the past. Bureaucracies as ideal types operate through centralized control, hierarchical ordering of authority and tasks, and the jurisdictional allocation of tasks, usually on the basis of at least some degree of specialization. The money economy is directly implicated, for placing workers on salary makes them (as a group) entirely dependent on the organization, and their actions—supposedly—therefore are more manageable and controllable than has ever been true in the past. Historically, this can be characterized as the transfer of discipline, originating in earlier military spheres, to the organization of the economic sphere (Weber, "Discipline," in Gerth and Mills, 1946, Chap. 10). The essence of the formal rationality of bureaucracy lies in the abstract and depersonalized character of its rules, which make possible its high calculability.

The rationalization of economic life, then, can for Weber be said to involve three interpenetrating forms of formal rationalization: the objectification of the money economy in the form of the capitalist market system, the quantification of the operations of the business organization, and the bureaucratic mode of organization. Taken together, they constitute "the domination of the end by the means" (Weber, 1978b, 202), a powerful trend in which all value rationalities—love, brotherhood, caritas—are consigned to playing mere sideshow roles in the expanding spectacle of the growing formal rationality of capitalism.

Class, Status Group, and Capitalism

The rationalizing processes that have created the modern market economy have a long history the central aspect of which, for Weber, was the displacement of older orders organized principally in terms of status groups and their various political foundations and monopolies. In the description of this process, Weber's distinction between class and status group is indispensable (see Weber, 1978b, Chaps. 4 and 9, p. 6, the latter also appearing as Chapter 7 in the Gerth and Mills translation [1946]).

"Class" designates the sharing of a market position which conditions common "life chances." "Status groups," on the other hand, are associations or communities attempting to usurp, or maintain, a specific degree or level of "status honor," the essential meaning of which is that demands for deference (rituals) from members of other status groups are successfully advanced, and that these rituals define the boundaries of the group with some degree of precision. Status groups attempt to perpetuate their lifestyle, particularly if it is highly valued and the basis of invidious comparisons with other groups and thus a medium of symbolic domination or hegemony. Important empirical relationships between classes and status groups can be identified, the most important of which is probably that, in the long run, status groups must maintain or enhance their economic position either directly or indirectly (as in the instance of impoverished Brahman castes requiring the material support of other castes as a caste (i.e., status group) duty. It is clear throughout Weber's works that he considered *struggles* over status honor and status monopolies to be in many instances as important as or more important than the class conflicts created by differential advantages associated with markets. Both classes and status groups (along with "parties") are to be considered "phenomena of the distribution of power within a community" (Weber, in Gerth and Mills, 1946, 181).

Modern societies exhibit a more differentiated class structure than Marxism allows for. "The social classes," writes Weber, "make up the totality of those class situations within which individual and generational mobility is easy and typical" (Weber, 1978b, 302). The social classes of modern society are four: (1) the privileged, through property and education; (2) the "propertyless intelligentsia and specialists" (white collar workers, civil servants, etc.); (3) the petty bourgeoisie; and (4) the working class *as a whole*, as distinct from any of its fractions (italics mine: DLW), and this last, significantly, "the more so the more automated the work process becomes (305).

These central elements of Weber's concept of class obviously contrast sharply with Marx's concept and were clearly intended to do so in at least three ways. First, Weber's definition is a strictly objective one; he separates all issues of organization, or "action flowing from class interest" from the sheer positioning relative to the market. Weber further distinguishes between the *types* of action that may arise from a class situation: "communal" action, or that "oriented to the feeling of the actors that they belong together," is distinguished from "societal" action, which is oriented to "a rationally motivated adjustment of interests" (Weber, in Gerth and Mills, 1946, 183). Marx, it will be recalled, conflated these (see Chapter 10). Second, Weber defines class in market terms, while Marx did so relative to production. This is obviously a difference with very significant implications for class analysis. Third, Weber extended the idea of class formation beyond its strict Marxian focus, the labor market, to credit and commodity markets as well, claiming that in earlier historical periods the latter had been the decisive forms of class formation and class conflict.[36]

This conceptual elaboration has not gone uncriticized, from various quarters, and perhaps in particular by Marxists. The very category of status group is rejected as a causally autonomous one; as ideal phenomena the actions of status groups are held to be reducible to the interest foundations of classes. Also, shifting the definition of class from production to market, it is argued, misplaces the causal formative dynamic of class and at least implicitly jettisons the Marxian sense of agency. An important attempt to rework these concepts may be found in Pierre Bourdieu's idea of "cultural capital," which applies the market principle to the sphere of status as the latter's central dynamic (Bourdieu, 1977). These and other problems have given rise to a critical literature far too large to be treated further here (but see Giddens, 1975, 78–81, and Jones, 1975).

The class-status group distinction is indispensable to Weber's analysis of the origins of modern capitalism. The long process of the emergence of capitalist societies has been in part the result, in part the condition, of an historic transformation of the closed status groups of the early medieval

---

[36] For an extension of this, see Wiley, 1967. Weber thought class conflict in the credit and commodity markets was mainly a phenomenon of the past. Wiley shows these to be highly salient in U.S. history.

cities into the commercial, then industrial bourgeoisie, or *Bürgertum*. Gianfranco Poggi's reconstruction of Weber's scattered theorization of this movement, and situating of the Protestant ethic-spirit of capitalism thesis in the larger historical context, is an invaluable contribution to a full understanding of Weber's sociology of modern capitalism (Poggi, 1983).

The long-term rationalization of economic life in the West was thus a process in which market processes and the class relations and conflicts produced by these processes destroyed and supplanted the older societies organized mainly round status group relations. Whether Weber envisioned a future in which classes themselves were fated to be displaced by modern party formations is not clear, since he never completed his discussion of "party" in *ES*. He certainly thought of parties in a way parallel to status groups: as formations more or less autonomous from the interest-based formations of the economy. The societally varying strength of the connections between parties and classes in Western societies perhaps suggests the continuing relevance of the main thrust of Weber's conception.

In various ways throughout this exposition, Weber's theoretical focus on relations between and among social orders has been emphasized and described. The ways in which rationalizing processes in economic life and in the legal order are interwined is one very important form of this. A maximum of formal rationality maximizes the calculability of economic action through the market mechanism, which enhances freedom of action. This is reinforced by rationalizing processes in the legal order. The machinelike character of formally rationalized law also moves in the direction of "a relative maximum of freedom" (Weber, 1954, 27), a conception of law resting on the presupposition of the ethical value of the individual and of individual freedom (228). However, this maximization of freedom makes it possible, indeed, virtually inevitable, that those with greater resources will use that freedom to their economic advantage, and to the disadvantage of the already disadvantaged (228–229).There is therefore an irony attending the *affinity* of formal rationalizing processes in the economic and legal orders: As class differences are widened and class conflict exacerbated, the very ideals of justice and freedom supposedly served are undermined.

The rationality of the market, buttressed by that of the legal order, then, has two significant consequences for *substantive* rationalities. The first arises from the inevitable depersonalization and attenuation of human relationships that accompany the working out of the market principle, increasingly overwhelming personal ties and relations of every sort. In our times, Weber says, these are driven into private spheres—artistic and literary circles among the educated, the sociability of club and pub among the working classes—where meanings can be insulated from the ravages of formal rationalities.

The second results from the inequalities created and perpetuated by market and law. It is, of course, mainly the socialist movements that address this condition. Socialist theory and ideals are a substantive rationality. But a socialist economy works on the principle of command, and so in Weber's view, could only foster the expansion of authority in bureaucratic form ("the dictatorship of the official"). Weber preferred the free market as the lesser of two evils.

This brings us to the final type of rationalizing process, the spread of the legal-rational form of legitimacy in the form of bureaucratization. But before we get to this, it is necessary to lay out the broader framing typology of legitimate domination.

The Types of Legitimate Domination

Weber grounds his political sociology in his typology of forms of domination (*Herrschaft*).[37] Rulers *claim* legitimacy on traditional, charismatic or legal-rational grounds, defined as follows:

1. *traditional*: rests on "an established belief in the sanctity of immemorial traditions and the legitimacy of those exercising authority under them"
2. *charismatic*: rests on "devotion to the exceptional sanctity, heroism or exemplary character of an individual person and "of the normative patterns or order revealed or ordained by him"
3. *rational*, or *rational-legal*: rests on "a belief in the legality of enacted rules and the right of those elevated to authority under such rules to issue commands" (Weber, 1978b, 215)

Weber emphasizes that these are, of course, ideal types, to which empirical realities can scarcely be expected to conform with much exactness (216); concrete forms of rule are almost always mixed types (262–266), particularly during transitional periods, as in the "institutionalization" of charisma in a legal-rational or democratic direction.

To these basic definitions a degree of further elaboration may be added. All domination is exercised through organizational means of some sort, and organizations generally have in common a three-tier structure: heads or chiefs, staffs, and the mass of rank-and-file members. This model applies not only to the state, but to all organizations (for a discussion, see Albrow, 1970, Chap. 3). In consideration of the three types of authority, the principle types of each may be given empirical specification. In the instance

---

[37] There has been a dispute over the translation of *Herrschaft* in Weber's works, one that is important for interpreting his intentions. In their 1947 translation of several of the sections of *ES*, Parsons and Henderson rendered *Herrschaft* as "imperative coordination" (Weber, 1947). Later, in his review of Bendix's *Max Weber: An Intellectual Portrait*, Parsons remarked that he now preferred "leadership" on the ground that Weber's emphasis fell on the integrative aspect of *Herrschaft* (despite this, he did employ "authority" in a number of contexts). Albrow suggests that "rule" best captures the German meaning, but in English this is confounded with the very different sense of "rules of the game" (and the like) and so prefers "authority" (Albrow, 1970, 131, n.29). Others, including Bendix (1960, 294–296), Rheinstein and Shils (Weber, 1954, 328), Roth (in Weber, 1978a, 62), and Cohen, Hazelrigg, and Pope (1975, 236–239), have argued that "domination" is a more appropriate translation. Roth points out that because a *Herrschaft* is always a "structure of superordination and subordination, leaders and led, rulers and ruled" (in Weber, 1978b, 62), "domination" is appropriate. Although his usage is admittedly inconsistent, the fact that Weber himself felt it necessary to distinguish between *Herrschaft* and *legitime Herrschaft* (or *Autorität*) surely ought to have some bearing on the issue: Why would he have bothered to distinguish a *legitimate* form of *Herrschaft* if this were already its central meaning? (On this point see also Merquior, 1980, Chap. 6). We will understand the types as forms of *legitimated* domination, i.e., of *authority*.

of traditional authority, we may speak of masters, retainers, or vassals; in that of charismatic authority, leaders, disciples, and followers; and under legal-rational authority, functional superiors, bureaucrats or officials, and individuals defined as legal persons (Merquior, 1980, 101). This is important, for Weber finds major sources of world-historical change in the tensions and conflicts inherent in the relations among these. We have discussed aspects of this earlier. Struggles between kings (or religious heads) and groups emerging from strata subservient to them such as the vassals of the European feudal period were decisive for the social changes leading up to industrialism and capitalism in the West. Weber describes struggles parallel to these elsewhere, particularly in India and China. The main dimension of this is the attempt by the head to maintain subordinates in a condition of dependence. A situation of economic independence is sociologically important mainly because it is one very important factor in conditioning the degree and form of political, or organizational dependence, such as the prebendal system of China, or the fief-type organization of feudal Europe. Whatever the arrangements, they are usually fraught with tension, and potential for actual conflict.

For the most part, Weber thought that the relations between the rulers and their staffs were, historically speaking, much more important than those involving the rank and file. It has long since been conventional wisdom to say that in the West the decisive long-term political event has been the movement of masses into political participation and influence, and in the ideology of democracy, at least, to a state of sovereignty. By and large, Weber was not so impressed. In all his analyses (and polemics) on contemporary politics, he focused on the leadership—of states, parties, and so on—and their relationships with administrative organs, as the decisive actors of the modern period, attributing little causal power to masses.[38] There can be little doubt that his general view of the world, strongly reflected in his philosophical anthropology, profoundly affected the way he worked out his political sociology.

Traditional domination rests on a legitimation in terms of (1) traditions which "themselves determine the content of the command and which are believed to be valid within certain limits . . .", but also in terms of (2) the "master's discretion in that sphere which tradition leaves open to him" (Weber, 1978b, 227). This definition has the consequence of making the analysis of the exercise of traditional domination mainly a matter of attending to the limits of personal discretion on the part of the "master" and his staff, the conditions under which the staff is expanded, and the changing relations between the leader and the staff.

The great historic locus of traditional authority is the patriarchal household. The expansion of the household to encompass a larger territory

---

[38] A view not uncommon in various conservative *fin de siècle* circles. The most important from our standpoint was the Italian School of Pareto and Mosca, both of whom advanced historical analyses as the basis for sociological generalizations demonstrating the practical impossibility of both democracy and socialism. Pareto's "circulation of elites" and Mosca's "political formula" have long since become stock concepts of "elite" schools of social and political analysis. For Pareto, see *The Mind and Society* (1916); for Mosca, *The Ruling Class* (1939). Robert Michels's *Political Parties* may be added to this group. A bit on Michels later.

and discharge economic or military functions may bring into being a "patrimonial" organization, still rooted in tradition and personal relations of patriarchy, but now allowing for greater variation in their exercise. The expansion of the ruler's staff is the critical factor, and the ruler may resort to a variety of expedients to retain control on a personal basis: kinsmen, of course, but slaves, eunuchs, and others with varying types or degrees of vulnerability may be brought in to fulfill administrative functions. In the course of such developments, administration may remain essentially bounded by tradition, in which case Weber labels it "patrimonial," or the element of personal discretion or arbitrariness may predominate, a condition Weber calls "sultanism" (232). The constraints that bound the Chinese emperors to a highly ritualized routine is illustrative of the former, the arbitrariness of Middle Eastern potentates of the latter. Estate systems, fiefs, benefices, and prebendal arrangements are various forms of traditional authority. The main effect of traditional domination in economic matters is to strengthen traditional attitudes. The meaning of this in the orientation to labor was discussed earlier in this chapter.

We have encountered some of the applications of the idea of charisma earlier, particularly in the discussion of religious leadership. In "primitive" religions Weber singles out such types as the "berserk," who experiences "spells of magic passion" (Weber, 1978b, 242), and the shaman, or anyone utilizing his or her capacity for manifesting such extraordinary states for the purpose of controlling or directing the actions of others. In the emergence of the world religions, it is the charismatic leadership of prophets because of their *ethical* orientation; indeed, the Hebrew prophets were Weber's exemplars of the type (and probably partly unconscious role models for his own political activity). Charisma shares with traditional domination the aspect of designating a personal relation between leader and led. The leader represents himself as divinely inspired, capable of heroic deeds, and proclaims a mission that demands the total personal commitment of his followers.

Weber discusses a series of characteristics of charismatic domination. Movements led by charismatic figures are the great historical agencies of revolutionary social change and renewal.

> In a revolutionary and sovereign manner, charismatic domination transforms all values and breaks all traditional and rational norms: It has been written . . . but I say unto you . . ." (1115)

Whereas change effected through bureaucratic rationality proceeds first "from without," by transforming the technical means and economic and social organization, and then *through* these means transforms the people, charismatic belief revolutionizes "from within," as Weber puts it, and then shapes material and social conditions according to its revolutionary will (1116). Here the polarity of inner and outer directly shapes Weber's typology of routes of change under different kinds of legitimate authority.

In the modern world charisma may assume a variety of secular forms, particularly in political leadership, as in the cases of Hitler, Lenin, Mao, and many leaders of Third World liberation movements. Cultural movements of many sorts are charismatically led: Rock musicians, in particular, attract fanatical world-wide followings, in the process mediating cultural changes on a scale probably never envisioned by Weber.

Charismatic ideology generally stands opposed to any routine every-day economic ethic; the cause is always a higher one to which continuous involvement in acquisitive activity is seen as irrelevant or repugnant. Here is an instance of tension and potential conflict—a negative affinity—that increases when rationalization processes in an order expand. This is related to another aspect of charisma: The relation of the followers to the leader becomes a matter of *duty*. Weber emphasizes that it is not merely *recognition* of heroic or magical acts on the part of the leader that constitutes a genuine charismatic relationship, but the creation of a sense of duty to submit to his commands and to follow unquestionably. In this regard, although Weber emphasizes that, while *sociologically* what alone is important is how the individual is actually regarded by his "followers" or "disciples" (242), it is the case that "no prophet has ever regarded his quality as dependent on the attitudes of the masses toward him" (242), a doubtful and empirically unsupported generalization. In other words, although Weber does mention the possibility of charlatans, "genuine" charismatic leaders have belief in their own special nature and use this as the currency to exact obedience from their following.

In this connection Weber also claims that the charismatic relation takes on a communal character in which little or no formal organization is present. All the characteristics of bureaucratic organization, in particular—assigned jurisdictions based on competence, hierarchy, formally designated positions, appointments, dismissals, or careers—are absent. There is only "the call at the insistence of the leader" (243).

Very closely connected with this is the stipulation that the relation between leader and led is unmediated, a *personal* one. This would seem to confine the charismatic relation to small social formations, and it is under such conditions that charisma may be manifest in its closest proximity to its ideal-typical form. But Weber extends his usage to a variety of forms of large-scale social organization: clans, military associations, even empires, as in the case of China. But in such transformations it is unlikely that charismatic domination would function in "pure" form (if indeed it ever would or could).

This brings us to the final, and sociologically of the utmost importance, characteristic of charisma, its inherent instability (1114–1115). For one thing, the leader must live up to his claims or risk the loss of his authority. Even more important is the problem of the transfer of the power upon the leader's death: i.e., the problem of succession. The historically important solutions to this problem Weber calls the "institutionalization" of charisma, to which he devotes a fairly extensive discussion in *ES* (246–254; 1121–1148). Charisma may be institutionalized through kinship, the principle of heredity, or association with an office, as in the case of the Catholic church. Of particular interest is a shift away from the essential authoritarianism of charismatic domination in the direction of a democratic relationship, in which the leader is created by "the grace of those who follow him" (267). This amounts to legitimation by plebiscite and may involve legal-rational elements. We shall return to this matter.

We have earlier discussed legal-rational authority from the standpoint of Weber's substantive sociology of law and the historical significance of the latter in the emergence of capitalism. In his introductory remarks on legal-rational authority in *ES*, he says that the validity of the "pure type" (i.e., ideal type) rests on a set of independent ideas.

1. The legal norm may be established by agreement or *imposition* (italics mine) and on the grounds of expediency *or* value rationality, or both.
2. The body of law is a "consistent system," of abstract rule, intentionally established, itself applied according to "legal precepts."
3. The superior is himself subject to the impersonal order of the law.
4. Compliance is enacted only in one's capacity as a "member" (quotes Weber's) of the organization.
5. Obedience is required only to the impersonal order of the law and not to individuals.

(217–218)

As we saw earlier, legal-rational authority appears in many historical situations, but its overwhelmingly important manifestation appears in the process of bureaucratization, to be discussed shortly.

Weber's typology has been the object of various critiques.[39] One line of criticism is that, like the political theorists of antiquity, he gives only a rationalistic account of forms of rule, and that the actualities of real political behavior, particularly the grounds of obedience, are inadequately conceptualized and theorized. The principle basis of this charge rests on the fact that Weber grounded the typology on "claims" to legitimacy advanced by power holders, claims understood as "ultimate" or irreducible. This does seem nonempirical both in its focus on power wielders to the exclusion of the ruled, and in its assertion regarding the salience of such claims. Regarding the former, it is surely the case, as Parsons puts it, that the range of actual motives involved in conforming to authoritative orders must be distinguished from "the question of the institutional grounding of a system of normative order (Parsons, 1949, 669).

Weber did deal with this question, but in such a way as to residualize such motives. Complying behavior may, and usually does, he says, involve a quite diverse and complex mix, including sheer habit, self-interest, coercion, or "affectual or ideal motives of solidarity" (213). In concrete cases, the orientation of action to an order involves a wide variety of motives" (31; see also 212–215). In his discussions in *ES* (212–215; 31–33), Weber's interest falls on separating such bases of action from those oriented to the "validity" (*Geltung*) of an order. An order is valid insofar as the behavior conforming to its rules and the orders of its representatives are grounded in a belief that the order itself and the commands of its agents are rightful or proper, i.e., *legitimate*. Thus, his concept of authority requires that subordinates act "as if the ruled had made the content of the command the maxim of their conduct for its very own sake" (946). It is of the greatest importance to recognize that, although the attempt to monopolize the means of violence is the one common denominator of all states (Weber, in Gerth and Mills, 1946, 78),

---

[39] See particularly, Wrong, 1970; Merquior, 1980; Bendix, 1960; Dronberger, 1971; and Mommsen, 1984.

and that much behavior is rooted in sheer expedience, the general stability of governments depends on whether they are able to establish their legitimacy claims as "binding," or valid.

Weber's claim, then, is that his typology is based on a recognition of factors lending greater degrees of *stability* to states (or other forms of organization). This is the nub of the problem. Even if Weber's formulation of the typology in terms of power wielders' claims is accepted, it is clear that it is not based on the full empirical range of the ways in which states actually maintain themselves, or even, if we take seriously his statement (above) about habituation to rule being "much the most common attitude," on the *empirically most important* basis of complying behavior, but rather, on one formulated only according to the extent to which power wielders achieve this through the successful establishment of legitimacy claims.

This decision on Weber's part had important consequences for his political sociology. The most obvious is that it biases analysis in the direction of power holders and directs analysis in terms of their view of reality (e.g., Habermas, 1975, Part 3, Chap. 1; Merquior, 1980, 1321; Parkin, 1982, Chap. 3, 2). This in effect seems to imply a limitation of inquiry to situations where legitimation is high and to exclude cases of nonlegitimate rule. Second, there is the matter of whether *claims* to legitimacy are of such import in any case. They probably count for little in the subjective meanings of the ruled, whose compliance is assured to some considerable degree on the various other grounds delineated by Weber himself. But if legitimacy claims are important enough to provide the preeminent typology for political analysis, does this not imply their significance in the subjective meanings of compliers? And conversely, if the real bases of compliance are to be found elsewhere, how do such claims to legitimacy merit the centrality to which they are elevated by Weber?

A closely related problem lies in the fact that many regimes past and present have established and maintained themselves with minimal legitimacy, sometimes over extended periods of time. Although he repeatedly takes account of coercion and utilitarian factors in actual rule, it is noteworthy that Weber almost never speaks of nonlegitimate rule. In fact, the role of force is ubiquitous in Weber's work, and force and legitmation appear together in Weber's (last) definition of the state, in "Politics as a Vocation," in 1918:

> A state is a human community that (successfully) claims the *monopoly* of the legitimate use of physical force within a given territory (Weber, in Gerth and Mills, 1946, 78)

Weber says that one of the strengths of this definition is that it is in accord with popular notions, i.e., the subjective meanings of state "members" (78). And it has become widely accepted and used in the social science disciplines.

Peter Blau has claimed that this combination is paradoxical, because the employment of sanctions reveals that the superior's directives do *not* command the compliance of the subordinates. It is characteristic of all power, he writes, that "its use to coerce others destroys its potential as a source of authority over them" (Blau, "Critical Remarks on Weber's Theory of Au-thority," in Wrong, 1970, 159).

The problem of defining, recognizing, and researching legitimacy is probably the theoretically most difficult one in political sociology. Weber's treatment is fraught with difficulties, yet one can hardly have expected him to have given a thoroughly satisfactory conceptual account of its nature. In fact, despite the problems, his typology proved fruitful not only for his own work, but with various modifications, remains today one of only a very few major conceptual frameworks in political sociology.

In addition to the general difficulties discussed above, Weber's formulations of each of the three types bears with it problems of its own.

Traditional legitimation would seem to be the least troublesome of Weber's types, but it turns out that the principle of "sanctity of tradition" cannot be held logically distinct from charismatic and legal-rational legitimation. Merquior shows that to understand traditionalism as a *type of social action* based on an appeal to the past is to assert legitimation by established precedent, but that this cannot be separated from the legal-rational principle of legitimacy. In effect, traditional authority is reduced to a component of the legal-rational form. Similarly, and perhaps on stronger ground, he maintains that the "sanctity" of tradition is nothing other than charisma in certain of its institutionalized forms (Merquior, 1980, 104–105). On these bases he attempts a reformulation of Weber's types in terms of the logically distinct principles of (1) rule-boundedness, (2) the personalized sacredness of rulers, and (3) observance of rational-legal order. This yields a logically defensible array of three types, as follows:

1. Rule-bound authority exercised under a claim of allegiance to rulers who themselves are literally sacred, in agreement with immemorial usage
2. Rule-bound authority coupled to rational observance of a legal-rational order
3. Rule-free power exercised in personalized fashion (107)

These may be thought of as revised formulations of traditional, legal-rational, and charismatic forms of legitimacy respectively.[40] The heuristic value of this remains open, however, since to the knowledge of the author it has never been employed in research.

In any case, such a revision merely to achieve logical consistency fails to address the other difficulties mentioned, because it remains within the framework of identifying claims to legitimacy as the basis of concept formation. More radical are proposals to incorporate elements other than legitimacy claims into the typology. Parkin, to note just one such example, argues that Weber should have classified authority systems according to the way in which three elements of control—coercion, moral persuasion, and material inducements—were combined, and then approach the question of legitimacy as varying in terms of such different arrangements. With this approach, some regimes would clearly be found to be based on greater degrees of legitimacy than others (Parkin, 1982, 76–77). And such a typology could be combined with one that viewed the legitimacy question from below

---

[40] See Weber's formulation elsewhere, (in *ES*, 954).

as well. Weber's unsystematized remarks in this regard (i.e., his several mentions of moral commitment, habit, fear, and self-interest [Weber, 1986b, 946–947]) lend themselves rather transparently to such an exercise (e.g., Parkin, 1982, 80). Parkin rightly emphasizes that such an approach would also address the critical question, nowhere dealt with by Weber, of the *process* whereby legitimacy comes into being: whether through bona fide spontaneously emerging belief in the rightness of the regime and its agents, or through various forms of manipulation (control of media, disinformation, etc.) producing a "false consciousness."

Weber's concept of charismatic authority has been shown to present a number of conceptual and theoretical difficulties. Despite his insistence on the historical significance of the fundamental difference between personalistic and formalistic relationships, as in the distinction between patrimonial and bureaucratic forms of organization, he has sometimes been charged with dissolving the structural principle of authority into one of personalistic leadership (e.g., Bierstedt, 1954, 70–71). Related to this point is the fact that, while Weber attributes extraordinary power to charismatic leaders and movements, he provides no principled explanation for its occurrence. It seems to be created out of nothing by "great men," or geniuses. The most important source of innovation, he says, is "the influence of individuals who have experienced certain types of abnormal states . . . and hence have been capable of exercising a special influence on others" (Weber, 1954, 22). To the extent that this is so, Weber clearly skirts the edge of a "great man" theory of history, which he otherwise rejected. It is possible that this omission can be attributed to the fact that Weber never got around to the work on sociology of revolution that he intended to write. But it seems more likely, given the "individual-oriented" consistency of his treatment of charisma throughout his works, that it reflects the ontological individualism of his philosophical anthropology.

The emphasis on the universal revolutionary nature of charisma has also sometimes been called into question, especially recently by Schwartz. There are many instances in history where "great men" who satisfy all of Weber's stipulations regarding the possession of charisma and its recognition by followers nevertheless not only do not overthrow tradition, but work to maintain it. This is true, for example, of George Washington, who was heroized in his time (despite the Enlightenment disapproval of this). Schwartz shows that it is necessary to revise Weber's concept of charisma in favor of distinguishing two types of heroic leadership: a republican form in which traditional values are affirmed, along with Weber's charismatic type (Schwartz, 1983, 1987). In Durkheim's terms the whiggish Washington becomes a "symbolic leader."[41]

Schwartz's analysis raises the more general question of the restricted nature of Weber's typology, specifically with reference to the charismatic type. It has been noted that while there are four prime types of action there are only three types of legitimacy (Wrong, 1970; M. Spencer, 1970). Why this seeming discrepancy? In fact, at at least two points Weber distinguished

---

[41] Charisma has often been compared with Durkheim's "sacred," generally with theoretically inconclusive or insignificant results. See, for example, Parsons, 1949, Chap. 17.

a fourth *value-rational* type of legitimacy (Weber, 1978b: 33, 36), one which, however, he never seemed to have employed. Nowhere is he explicit about the reason or reasons for this. Wrong suggests it may be that *all* the forms of legitimacy are in their nature value-rational (Wrong, 1970, 48–49), but this seems to run counter to Weber's explicit characterizations. A clue may be found in a short passage in which Weber identifies natural law as the "purest type of legitimacy" (Weber, 1987b, 37). Perhaps Weber's subsequent deletion of this type from his work had to do with his view that natural law had passed its period of ascendence and had now virtually disappeared. We shall very shortly consider the significance of this view. The larger general point emphasized here is that the nonrecognition of a value-rational type must be regarded as a serious defect of Weber's typology. This seems to rule out value-rationality from political analysis, and indeed, at one point, Weber goes so far as to endorse the extreme but very questionably valid cynically realist position that "the quite different tasks of politics can be solved only by violence" (Gerth and Mills, in Gerth and Mills, 1946, 126).

The concept of charisma became a near staple in a good deal of political sociology since the 1950s. The application of the idea to a wide range of situations of domination or leadership, not just religious and political, but military and broadly cultural as well (Murvar's bibliography (1983) alone lists at least twenty-six items with some reference to charisma in their titles), has occasioned reconsideration of the limits of its validity. Are television personalities, rock musicians like Mick Jagger, politicians like John F. Kennedy, really to be regarded as charismatic? What of the process of image-construction, in which Western political candidates, and socialist and communist leaders present and past are elevated to iconic stature? The appropriateness of applying the concept, at least in Weber's more or less strict sense, has been called in to question. Some have suggested a decomposition of the idea. Bensman and Givant propose that many of the phenomena mentioned above, and many more, are *spurious* forms of charisma in that the relations in question are not *personal* and that they are *staged* to the end of one or another kind of salesmanship (Bensman and Givant, 1975). "A veneer of personality," they write, is merely added to "the *impersonal* (italics mine) social relations that govern urban, market, bureaucratic and mass technological societies" (603). Far from being basically irrational, such events have a high order of rationality in the sense of being calculated and planned (605), which is to say that they constitute an instrumental or practical rationality. (In this connection see Bauer, 1953).

One can perhaps understand Weber's view that a tough-minded appraisal of the practical exercise of state power leads to an appreciation of the stability of tradition and of bureaucratic organization on the one side, and the emotionality and explosiveness of charisma, on the other. The judgment he passes on natural law should be understood in this context: it is an "extreme rationalist fantasy," and the "influence of its logically derived propositions upon actual conduct has lagged far behind its ideal claims." This "influence" can only refer to the dissemination of natural law principles among leaders as legitimacy claims, and among subject populations as the basis of their obedience.[42] If the ideals of democracy are taken to constitute the principal substantive rationality in the political order of the West (and now increasingly elsewhere), Weber's scepticism can be understood. Legitimacy claims of leaders of many Western societies of the time—Germany definitely prominent among them—reveals little talk of democracy as an ultimate legitimation, although it must be granted that this is less true of the leaders of the Western democracies. More to the point is the question of whether much of a democratic substantive rationality was very widely disseminated among the ruled populations. Even today survey research reveals the thinness of this, both as belief and—more importantly—in the actual political actions of the vast majority. In the United States, for example, upward of 95 percent must be regarded as politically passive by virtue of their engaging in no political activity other than voting (although verbal espousal of democratic principles is much higher). And even in the case of voting, virtually all public officials are actually elected by a minority of eligible voters.

Weber treated democracy not as a general type of rule legitimated by value-rationality but as conceptual derivative of other forms of legitimate domination. Three of these are of importance. Direct democracy, in which rulers are held accountable for their actions on a strict basis (Weber, 1978b, 289, 948–952), is possible only in very small communities. And so, except for a few minor instances (e.g., Swiss cantons, U.S. town government, Russian mir), this type is essentially irrelevant (a "marginal type case":949) for the large scale of organization of modern societies and politics (949).

Plebiscitary democracy designates the movement of charismatic domination in a democratic direction, a variant that, in Weber's words, "hides behind a legitimacy that is *formally* (italics mine) derived from the will of the governed" (268). This is *"Führer-Demokratie,"* in Weber's view best seen in American machine politics of the time. For Weber, in either the utilitarian exchange of material benefits for votes, or in the more or less authoritarian administration of the "boss," any sort of democratic value-rationality is conspicuous in its absence.

Western democracy for the most part today takes the form of "free representation," a subcategory of the larger category of "representation" (289–301). Because free representation makes the political actions of representatives matters of their own choice, such representatives, in effect, exercise *authority* over electors (which seems to abuse the concept). They acquire their positions through the actions of parties, whose function is to "present candidates and programs to politically passive citizens" and "create

---

[42] Weber's judgments on natural law should be contextualized in terms of the fate of the *Rechtsstaat*, or law-regulated state. This was a nineteenth century idealization of law as guarantor of the state acting in nonarbitrary ways. For every conflict or problem there is always a higher law to which to appeal. But if the only check on state power is the law, and if laws can be changed, Turner and Factor ask, where is the guarantee against the continued expansion of state legal power? (Turner and Factor, 1984, Chap. 2). At this point the natural law foundations of the state collapse. Weber lived through the period during which the *Rechtstaat* was being displaced by the *Machtstaat*. His theory of legitimacy as the core of state functioning was perhaps an attempt to replace the sociologically unworkable natural law conception of the state (Ibid., Chap. 2).

MAX WEBER II 429

the norms which govern the administrative process" (294). In these and other like characterizations, Weber clearly excludes a democratic substantive rationality from any significant role in parliamentary democracy.

Generally speaking, Weber probably underestimated the significance of democratic growth in the West in the future, and his experience in undemocratic Germany may have been a partial reason for this. On the other hand, if the cacophony of democratic rhetoric—including that emanating from academic circles—is disregarded, Weber's position seems closer to reality than many would care to admit. "Power elite" research beginning at least with C. W. Mills in the 1950s (Mills, 1956) and continuing right up to the present (e.g., Domhoff, 1983) shows that the civics book celebrations of democracy are at best a narrow and partial representation, and quite possibly no more than an ideological fabrication serving legitimation requirements of ruling elites and/or classes.

Despite the fact that much of the criticism of Weber's typology must be accepted, the utility of the typology, not only in Weber's own work, but in that of others, should be recognized. This is perhaps particularly true of those cases where the types were used in conjunction with one another, which is to say, to follow Weber's own strictures. Gerth's analysis of the Nazi regime as a combination of charismatic and bureaucratic elements, is a case in point (Gerth, 1940). More broadly, drawing on a variety of sources, Merquior has advanced an explanation of the vicissitudes of Communist regimes in developing societies in these terms. Revolutionary parties that come to power as bearers of a neo-Marxist modernizing ideology are successful so long as they are able to offer symbolic rewards in lieu of the relative absence of material ones, in so doing blocking the growth of the major obstacle to capital accumulation. The multitude of difficulties that attend development, however, have the effect of making the regime either unwilling or unable to shift to the satisfaction of material needs as a priority. In this process not only the leader but the party advances claims to charismatic legitimation. But the party itself, and the government it creates once in power, are organized bureaucratically. The party is charismatic because of its cultivation of communal action on the basis of ideological elements of Marxism (and perhaps other ideologies, as well), bureaucratic because of the necessity for centralized control over an organization that seeks rational solutions to problems of development (Merquior, 1980, Chap. 7, part 3). The way in which this condition may be maintained in a chronic state even over an extremely long period, but which ultimately turns out to be unworkable, is exemplified not only in the Third World, but in the collapse of the Soviet Union and its Eastern European sattelites.

We may now turn to our discussion of bureaucratization as the decisive empirical form of legal-rational domination.

Legal-Rational Legitimation, Bureaucracy, and Rationalization in the West

Weber virtually identifies bureaucratic organization with legal-rational domination.

The purest type of exercise of legal authority is that which employs a bureaucratic administrative staff (220). Such a staff exhibits the following characteristics, which Weber (in his chapter on bureaucracy in *ES*) divides into structural features of the organization and characteristics of officialdom.

A. Organizational features:
   1. Official jurisdictional areas ordered by rules, so that organizational activities are assigned as official duties delimited in a stable way by rules and continuously fulfilled.
   2. An established hierarchy of authority under a central authority.[43]
   3. Separation of office from private domicile and performance of organizational duties on the basis of written documents maintained in files.[44]
   4. Office management presupposes specialized training as the basis for employment.
   5. Organizational activities become full-time.
   6. Management proceeds according to general rules, the knowledge of which "represents a special technical expertise."
B. Characteristics of officialdom:
   1. The holding of office is a vocation, meaning that incumbency is based on training and evidence of competence, and that the official is oriented to discharge of office as a "duty."
   2. There is a strong relationship between certain organizational characteristics and the extent to which office incumbency determines the status position of the official.
   3. The official is appointed.
   4. Tenure tends to be for life. This has the effect of contributing to the performance of the organization, but may affect the social status of the official and the technical efficiency of the organization negatively.
   5. The official is remunerated by a money salary (and so a money economy is a presupposition of a bureaucracy).
   6. The official moves through a career within the organizational hierarchy. This, along with (4) and (5) contributes to the creation of office sinecures in the form of prebends.

A few points may be added to this. The pure bureaucratic type is contrasted mainly with any and all types of domination based on personal relationships: in terms of authority types, with both (1) the patrimonial, sultanist, and feudal forms of traditionalism (although the latter in some of its forms may be modified by the rational and impersonal principle of contract) and (2) with all forms of charismatic domination. The historical manifestations of bureaucratic domination, prior to the modern period, Weber emphasizes, have nowhere come very close to the ideal types. Patrimonial forms of administration, however, have often acquired bureaucratic characteristics in varying degrees, notably centralized domination, hierarchical structure, defined jurisdictions, and to some degree other of the characteristics listed above. The most critical difference, as Weber saw it, was whether the officials

---

[43] Weber is somewhat ambiguous as to whether centralization (the "monocratic" principle) is to be included in the ideal type. Elements of bureaucratic staff organization may be found, for instance, under the pluralistic collegial form of domination by notables.

[44] These seem rather clearly to be distinct elements. Based on Weber's discussions elsewhere, the former is more fundamental, for bureaucratic administration presupposes the existence of the office. The files contribute to the continuity and rationality of the organization.

remained "unfree" or not; administrative forms in which various of these other aspects became manifest, but in which the officials did not possess "formal" freedom, Weber designated as the subtype "patrimonial bureaucracy" (221).

Perhaps the most important thing about this was that, for the first time, existing ideas about state administration were brought within the purview of social science theory (Albrow, 1970, Chap. 3). Weber took over more or less in toto the already present theory of public administration, which had been a practical discipline taught in universities founded for that purpose (particularly Halle). However, the idea of "bureaucracy" had quite a different meaning: just as in its contemporary popular sense, it designated not the rationality of public administration but its *pathology*. The term itself evidently derives from "bureaumania" coined in France in 1764 to mean an "illness" (19). The idea of the mechanistic quality of state administration as a pathology can be traced in Germany at least to Herder; later, Wilhem von Humboldt in 1792 expressed the fear that "affairs of state were becoming mechanical while men were being transformed into machines" (quoted in Albrow, 1970, 19). Three decades later Freiherr vom Stein, himself a Prussian bureaucrat involved in the reforms following the defeat in 1806 by Napoleon, identified and indicted the officialdom of the time (being salaried, employing book knowledge, being committed to no cause, being propertyless) as a "lifeless governmental machine" (19). Fear of bureaucracy became a powerfully ingrained outlook among liberals.[45] The same attitude acquired some currency in relatively nonbureaucratic England among liberals like Spencer and J. S. Mill.

Interpreters of Weber have commonly attributed to him the intent of advancing the claim that bureaucratization occurs, and bureaucracies exist, because it and they are more "efficient," which is to say, more rational, than alternative forms of administration. But Weber himself doesn't speak of efficiency in this fashion, i.e., as a substantive rationality.[46] A bureaucracy is not rational because it achieves efficiency, but, rather, because it is a form of legal-rational authority. This is to say that the subjective meaning of the social action of its officials (along with others) is oriented around the shared understanding of the appropriateness of such rules and of the particular actions necessitated in following them. All administrative acts are carried forward within the framework of a legal code guaranteeing that they are governed by abstract rules. And as Albrow points out, and as was discussed in the section on Weber's *Rechtssoziologie*, legal rules themselves are rational because they are created by the intellect for the purpose of governing the goal-oriented (i.e., substantive) actions of officials. In the case of bureaucratic administration, this means appointment of officials in accord with criteria of knowledge and expertise as formal qualifications. The rules are rational, then, as Albrow puts it, because "they are a matter for experts" (63).

---

[45] The social change at least partially responsible for the late nineteenth and early twentieth century spread of this view was the rapid proliferation of state bureaucrats, from 700,000 in 1882 to 2,000,000 in 1910 (Green, 7).

[46] Albrow shows that Weber's English language translators incorrectly construe terms like *Zweck* to carry the English language meaning of efficiency (1970, 64–65).

Now every organization has its substantive goals and beneath this its value-rationality, however faintly reflected in its real activities. And organizations of all types seek in varying degrees to achieve these with some quantum of efficiency. This in no way sets bureaucratic administration off from other types of organizations. Another way of saying this is that Weber does not formulate the rationality of bureaucratic administration in terms of efficiency as a *substantive* value, however strongly this value may be manifest in any particular organization, e.g., businesses or armies, or in terms of any other substantive rationality, but rather purely in terms of formal rationality. The legal order of the bureaucracy then makes possible collective concerted action of very high degrees of means-ends *calculability*. The (formally) "rational" (Weber's quotation marks) character of the bureaucracy, Weber says, exhibits a predominance of "rules, means-ends calculus, and matter-of-factness" (Weber, 1978b, 1002).

This is not to say that the question of efficiency is unimportant. Far from this being the case, Weber clearly states that

> The fully developed bureaucratic apparatus compares with other organizations exactly as does the machine with the non-mechanical modes of production. Precision, speed, unambiguity, knowledge of the files, continuity, discretion, unity, strict subordination, reduction of friction and of material and personal costs—these are raised to the optimum point in the strictly bureaucratic administration, and especially in its monocratic form. (973)

In this aspect, bureaucratic organization is found superior to all other forms of administration, by dilettantes, amateurs, part-time notables, all types, in short, that do not bring expert knowledge to the job. It is precisely this technical superiority that is the decisive reason for the spread of bureaucracy. Indeed, "the more complicated and specialized modern culture becomes, the more its external supporting apparatus demands the personally detached and strictly objective expert" (975). Let us look a little more closely at this.

It is perhaps fair, if oversimplified, to sum up the discussion so far by saying that the enhanced calculability and resulting substantive effectiveness of bureaucratic administration results from the application of specialized technical knowledge organized within the framework of a legal order. Bureaucratic administration, Weber says, "means fundamentally domination through knowledge," and this is the feature that makes it "specifically rational" (225). What does Weber mean by this? We shall intrepret him to be proposing that the other essential features of the ideal type of bureaucracy—especially the presence of jurisdictional areas, the hierarchy of authority, and above all, the rules—all in some degree result from or are conditioned by the centrality of scientific and technical knowledge in the exercise of organizational functions and pursuit of organizational goals.

The specialization of knowledge implies the specificity of jurisdictions in its application, although there have always been other bases for this, the need to administer vast areas (e.g., China) and so the necessity of administrative partitioning, for one, or the sheer size of the organization, for another. Even more obviously, authority hierarchies occur at all levels of social development beyond the simplest of societies and are conditioned by a host of factors, but placing the imprimatur of science on organizational authority seemingly establishes a powerful new *legitimation*. Ideally, this would be the concrete realization of the Enlightenment utopian vision: the wedding of knowledge and power, with the former informing and legitimating the exercise of the latter. Impersonal rules defining correct functioning of the office are unquestionably central to Weber's ideal-type bureaucracy. They are in principle absent in charismatic domination, and in patrimonial and feudal forms of organization as well: These and their subtypes are defined by relationships that are with varying emphases personalized and arbitrary. But rules deriving from science can only, like scientific laws, be completely impersonal. In these ways (and some others of less importance), bureaucracies may be thought of as ideal-typically "rational" in terms of the specific effects of knowledge.

But is there not a very basic difficulty here? Weber's ideal type of bureaucracy has often been attacked on the grounds of the defectiveness of his (actual or alleged) claims regarding bureaucratic rationality.[47] Gouldner identifies a contradiction in the ideal type between the principles of expertise and discipline (Gouldner, 1954, 22). And indeed, any tendency toward a conflation of the mindless knee-jerk response of discipline, as Weber characterizes it (Weber, in Gerth and Mills, 1946, Chap. 10), with the reflective, experimental, and problem-solving mentality of scientific and technical knowledge, could only be rejected out of hand. It has sometimes been

---

[47] The centrality of Weber's theory of bureaucracy across an array of disciplines has had the consequence of its having attracted a multitude of critical reviews, in all of its aspects, and from every conceivable standpoint. Much of the earlier critical commentary in sociology centered on Weber's supposed exclusive preoccupation with the "formal system" to the neglect of the "informal," or personal interactional networks found within all organizations (for a discussion see Blau and Scott, 1962, 35). The impetus for this was mainly the discovery that informal groups have a significant impact on production in a number of industrial settings (for a review, see ibid., 89–100). A related line of criticism holds that Weber's analysis was functionalist, and that he ignored organizational dysfunctions (Merton, 1957a, 50–54). In this connection Weber is sometimes said to have made no place for organizational conflict, but this is a misunderstanding (see, in particular, Collins, 1975, Chapter 6, for a convincing refutation). More recently, Weber has been subjected to attacks from the left, in which the theory of bureaucracy is conjoined with the general theory of authority (discussed above) and attacked for its conservatism. Here, in the words of Fischer and Sirianni, characterizing not just Weber but an entire style of analysis, the "bureaucarcy problem" is identified as the "tendency of the executive stratum of power elite of the organization to disengage itself from the interests that initially mandated it . . ." (Fischer and Sirianni, 1984, 13). This is the problem of goal displacement, but Weber was not unaware of it nor did he ignore it in his work. Close to this line of criticism, but more general in focus, is Niklas Luhmann's claim that the "command" model (i.e., bureaucratic organization defined as an especially effective form of domination) is inconsistent with the rationality built into the means-ends schema appropriate for the analysis of rational action at the level of the actor. Luhmann holds that this scheme is inapplicable *at least* to social systems that function by authoritarian processes because such systems encourage the transformation of means into ends (goal displacement) so the very form of the action format is subverted (Luhmann, 1982, Chapter 1). In the language of today's organizational analysis this problem results from Weber's formulation being a *closed system* one, and is solved insofar as the nature of organizational functioning can be described with an *open systems* vocabulary. Anything approximating a thorough review of the full range of criticism of Weber's theory of bureaucracy is quite beyond the scope of this chapter. We confine our discussion to the "rationality problem" in theory, because it is central to Weber's rationalization thesis.

suggested that Weber did not have an understanding of this; however, his very analysis of the exercise of knowledge in bureaucratic administration presupposes a grasp of organizational realities in terms of these "two faces" of bureaucracy, as we will show in the discussion to follow.

We have discussed Weber's approach to scientific knowledge earlier. The issue here is his theorization of its fate under the condition of bureaucratization, and it is worth reading him very carefully on this point because his remarks are very sketchy and we want to be as clear as possible about his views.

Weber's most obvious and often cited remarks regarding the growing indispensibility of technicians is the starting point. Possession of technical knowledge "by itself," he says, "is sufficient to ensure it a position of extraordinary power" (Weber, 1978b, 225). But beyond this,

> bureaucratic organizations, or the holders of power who make use of them, have the tendency to increase their power still further by the knowledge growing out of experience in the service (225).

This comes from day-to-day involvement in the affairs of the organization on a full-time basis, which allows officials to acquire and accumulate "a special knowledge of facts and have available a store of documentary material peculiar to themselves" (225). Weber here appears to describe the tendency to a monopoly of knowledge that goes beyond the sheerly technical rationality already possessed by the specialized official. And this, he says, shades off into the realm of "official secrets" (225), which are "a product of the striving for powers" (225). Elsewhere he is even more explicit. "Expertise alone does not explain the power of bureaucracy." Bureaucrats possess *official information* (italics Weber's) that they transform into official secrets, the latter referred to by Weber as a "notorious concept," the "supreme power instrument" of the bureaucracy (1418).[48]

It is tempting to interpret this as a theory of organization in which, under the ideal-typical characteristics of bureaucracy and of the position of the official, task-relevant knowledge is subverted from its "proper" goals and put to the service of the individual or collective material and ideal interests of officials. And this is clearly not merely a matter of those performing technical tasks needing the power (and rewards) to get on with them, as the naive functionalist interpretation would have it. Purely organizational factors constitute a condition under which power-wielding knowledge bearers increasingly create and make indispensable the knowledge that they monopolize, and in so doing, further buttress their position. As officials pursue their (mainly) material interests, the substantive rationality of science is converted into a formal rationality, and this contributes mightily to that seemingly irresistible expansiveness and fateful permanence Weber attributed to bureaucratic organization. Knowledge becomes power, but this path is, as Eurpídes feared, one "where no man thought . . . so hath it fallen here."

But is this a believable story? Why should any type of social organi-

---

[48] A related point is a "tendency to plutocracy," which Weber says results from the official's interest in lengthy training programs (225).

zation have conferred on it such permanence and inevitability,[49] especially in the case of Weber, whose life work consisted mainly in showing the nature and forms of social change on a world-historical scale? Arguments of no less power could probably be advanced to account for the permanence of different types of organizations throughout history, most of which have since disappeared. We suggest that there is more: specifically, a theory involving the roles played by rationalizing processes within the main social orders. The role of knowledge is only the most obvious of these.

Despite statements to the effect of the superiority of bureaucratic organization resting on technical knowledge, and bureaucracy being fundamentally domination through knowledge, there is reason to regard the real defining feature of bureaucracy as just what the term states: rule through office.

In the detailed listing of the characteristics defining bureaucracy in the chapter-length treatment (*ES*, Chap. 11; this book, 120–121), the theme of "fundamental domination through knowledge" is essentially absent; Weber here mentions only "specialized training" as a prerequisite of office incumbency. It is perhaps of some relevance that his "definition" of socialism, which he thought of mainly as a further intensification of bureaucratic domination was, somewhat polemically, "rule of the official" (rather than the technically correct "rule through office"). No doubt expertise in the discharge of office duties is in all administration a source of legitimate authority. Whether or not this is equivalent to "fundamental domination through knowledge," however, must be regarded as doubtful. On the basis of the general thrust of his writings, including not only the points made above, but also his emphasis on the qualitatively and radically different nature of modern science from older forms of knowledge, we shall maintain that it is not. We shall understand Weber to have considered modern scientific and technical knowledge to be a factor of great causal importance in the expansion of bureaucracy, but a contingent or empirical one *not* included in the *definition* of the ideal type of bureaucracy.

WEBER'S GENERAL THEORY OF RATIONALIZATION

In the preceding section the working of rationalizing processes in the social orders has been described. But analysis of these processes as they work only *within* the orders does not add up to a general theory of societal rationalization. In this section we will suggest that Weber's general theory may be understood as having two parts, one well-known and much debated, the other partly explicit and partly implicit, entailing relationships *among* the orders, a fragmentally articulated theory of *societal* rationalization, which treats of

---

[49] Weber's fatalism about this, reflected in his employment of metaphors such as the "machinelike" nature of bureaucracy, and the "iron cage" awaiting us, is of course, well-known and has come in for plenty of criticism (e.g., Gouldner, 1955). Generally, analysis of the reasons for this are found in Weber's immersion in German fin-de-siècle culture and politics, especially the *Kulturpessimissus* of the educated middle classes clinging to vestiges of the old Romanticism and living in the remnants of past class and status formations. See Ringer, 1969, and for an excellent recent study, Kalberg, 1987.

rationalizing processes that transcend those of any particular order. It should be understood that this discussion is intended only as suggestive.

We have shown the importance Weber attached to scientific knowledge and related technologies which, when grafted onto or incorporated into the processes of organizational functioning, intensify or increase the degree of organizational formal rationality. We may ask just how this occurs.

The sciences are belief systems of high levels of *theoretical* or conceptual rationality, in which elements of *formal* and *practical* rationality may have varying degrees of importance: The abstract logic of explanation is an example of the second; the ties to various "practical" problems the principal mode of the last. Science and related technologies (including the various *social* technologies, especially those employed by management) may enhance the *practical* rationality of an organization, of course, in many generally obvious ways. But science and its technical applications also result in an increase in the intensity of the already existing *formal* rationality. It does so partly by making the requisite knowledge more esoteric, thus increasing the likelihood of a relative few monopolizing it as secret, and perhaps also by constituting a *legitimation* for the exercise of what is defined as a socially necessary function requiring such knowledge.

In the case of the capitalistic economy, the relation to bureaucratization is somewhat different. Capitalism as such is one of two orders in which formal rationality has had its most powerful development. The very elements of the ideal type central to modern capitalism, especially the market principle, make a high level of rational accounting possible, especially in its application to production. But the rationalization of the capitalist economy has gone on apace not only in terms of its internal dynamic. Its historical growth has been tied up intimately with the more or less parallel expansion of bureaucratic organization. "The capitalistic system has undeniably played a major role in the development of bureaucracy," Weber writes, and conversely, without it, "capitalistic production could not continue . . . (Weber, 1978a, 124). The emphasis remains on the reciprocal nature of the relationship.

The description here depicts the specifically economic factors (market relations, budgeting, etc.) and the specifically organizational ones as moving along in a more or less continuously reciprocal fashion, each, as it were, energizing or propelling the development or intensification of the other. Perhaps Weber thought of this relationship as one of elective affinity between formal rationalities, although he never said as much. It is in this context that Weber's assertion of there being "no affinity of capitalism and democracy" should be understood (in *SECTS*: Gerth and Mills, 1946, 60–61).

We saw earlier the complexity of Weber's analysis of rationalizing processes in modern law, and the factors that have opposed the expansion of formal rationality. But all this had to do with internal development and from the standpoint taken here is essentially beside the main point, the relation of the law to bureaucratization. And here Weber is not only clear, but emphatic. "The purest type of exercise of legal authority is that which employs a bureaucratic administrative staff" (220). This appears to be still another affinity, in this instance between the impersonal, rule-grounded, systematic, and calculative nature of legal formal rationality, and the very similar aspects of the ideal-type bureaucracy. Bureaucratic administration is *sine ira et studio*, rule based, and strives to mobilize and take into account every element in calculating its actions. And of course both take the ends or goals of action as given.

In the light of the earlier treatment of Weber's political sociology, the close relation between the modern state and organizational formal rationality is perhaps more than evident. Early in the century Weber, along with a few others, was already emphasizing the *fundamentally* bureaucratic character of the modern state. This formalism overrode the traditional bases of domination in privileged status groups and other feudal and postfeudal formations, to the advantage of groups previously not merely disadvantaged, but completely outside the elitist political process. Weber refers to this as a "leveling" process and maintains that legal equality and protection from arbitrariness in domination demand a formally rational "objectivity of administration" (Weber, 1978b, 979). The great irony of the expansion of the bureaucratic state has been, in Weber's judgment, an emerging rule-based conservatism and rigidity that now threatens to overwhelm the freedom of the individual that it once supported.

We wish to suggest, then, that these ways in which Weber described (1) the incorporation of science and technology into the formal rationality of bureaucratic domination, (2) the way in which capitalism has stimulated bureaucratic development through its need for "stable, strict, intensive and calculable administration" (224); (3) the point-by-point affinity of formally rational law to bureaucratic organizational elements; and (4) the manner in which the formal rationality of bureaucratization has propelled the state to its unprecedented capacity for dominating vast lands and peoples, may be interpreted as a general theory of societal rationalization elucidating, however imprecisely, a series of causal and/or elective factors that have been at work reinforcing and intensifying, perhaps synergistically, the formal rationality of organizations throughout modern societies. This "overdetermined" character of Weber's theory is perhaps at least a plausible factor helping to account for the extreme manner in which Weber sometimes formulates his idea of modernization as rationalization.[50]

All of the foregoing deals with rationalization processes at the social level. But it goes virtually without saying that the implications of the growth and intensification in formal rationality for the individual are immense, and this is, of course, the ultimate concern. Just what did Weber have to say about it?

Little that is systematic, but the big theme, at the core of *Kultur-pessimissus*, is that of the individual lost in the impersonal functioning of society, typically expressed in the metaphors of the machine or the "iron cage." Here formal rationalization saps or destroys any possibility of a life organized through a value-orientation. In the conclusion to *PE*, Weber writes

---

[50] All this, of course, deals only with the conceptual structure of the theory itself and does not address the social conditions contributing to making it seem so reasonable to Weber. Generally, the most convincing of such treatments make a case for the importance of various elements of German society and culture during the Bismarckian and Wilhelmenian period. Most recently, Kalberg's explanation of the *Kulturpessimissus* characteristic of the university-based intellectuals presents just such an analysis (see Kalberg, 1987).

that even as that residue of the Protestant ethic, the sense of duty in one's calling, still "prowls about . . . like the ghost of dead religious beliefs," the pursuit of wealth for its own sake "associated with purely mundane passions, which often give it the character of sport" (182), the consequence of the power of material goods over our lives, comes increasingly to be divorced from any value-rational orientation. Here Weber speculates on a future of "mechanized petrification" in which individuals become caricatures of human beings, "embellished with a sort of convulsive self-importance," "specialists without spirit, sensualists without heart," and a "nullity which imagines that it has attained a level of civilization never before achieved" (182).

In these and other passages, we can perhaps discern three distinct kinds of consequences for the individual. There is the triumph of a purely utilitarian orientation in various walks of life, the "possessive individualism" of McPherson (1962), exhibiting itself particularly in "materialism," or consumer orientation, and in an instrumentalism in social relationships. Distinct from this is what we might call an "automatization" of action as it is structured in an ordered *milieu*. This is the reduction of the consciousness of the individual to an extreme habituation or routinization of action, of which assembly-line work is perhaps the most readily appropriated image. Finally, there is the theme of compartmentalization, in which the actual or potential unity of action is fragmented temporally into a congeries of roles in different action milieux, in such a fashion that the "individual" appears behaviorally as possessing multiple personalities.

Weber himself never theorized this side of formal rationalization in any systematic fashion, and so it is a task that has been left to others, including in particular Karl Mannheim, whose work to a large extent was an attempt to bring together the Weberian and Marxian oeuvres.[51]

Despite the fact that in certain parts of his writings Weber encourages this eschatological interpretation of formal rationality, there have been dissenters. Levine, for one, has attempted to make such a case (Levine, 1985, 162ff.). Others' readings of Weber understand him to be saying that the only hope one can reasonably hold against the ever-greater rationalization of modern life is the possibility of new charismatically led movements of a religious or cultural nature. It is true that in a few terse remarks Weber does speculate in this fashion, but it is a theme nowhere fleshed out. On the other hand, in his 1917 essay "Parliament and Government in a Reconstituted Germany" (in *ES*, App. 2), he did examine the possibilities of democratic limitations on state power in systematic fashion. This essay, written during the war at a moment (in 1917) when hopes for a negotiated peace were at a high point, is an analysis of the political situation in Germany during the Bismarckian and Wilhelmenian periods.

Germany, Weber says, has been ruled by the bureaucracy since Bismarck was forced from office in 1890. This condition he regarded as a legacy of Bismarck himself, who in Machiavellian fashion managed to destroy the foundations of organized political life conceived of loosely along the

---

[51] See, in particular, *Man and Society in an Age of Reconstruction* (1940) and *Ideology and Utopia* (1936).

lines of the Western democracies.[52] In this political situation of an absence of intelligent and inspired leaders (presumably those with an ethic of responsibility), fragmented and self-interested political organizations, and the continued domination of the Junkers, the bureaucracy has become the de facto ruler. To the question, "How can the expansion of this power be checked?", Weber answers, through democracy understood in its parliamentary sense: Parliaments are the means of manifesting the "minimum consent" needed for bureaucratic rule. Indeed, far from going together in some kind of affinity, parliaments have often stood opposed to democracy, and the belief that this was the inherent nature of parliaments was still widespread in Germany.

A parliament can exercise some influence on the bureaucracy, first of all, only if two conditions are met: (1) that parliamentary leaders also serve in the administration (i.e., a parliamentary system), from which vantage point they are in a position to exercise authority over officials (this was not the case in Wilhelmenian Germany) and (2) that they have access to official information (the significance of which is obvious in the light of Weber's estimation of the importance of bureaucratic secrecy). But Weber did not simply conclude the matter in this conventional way. The structural relations between parliament and bureaucracy are themselves not a sufficient condition of parliamentary influence. A parliament is essentially a forum in which political *leaders* emerge, through the hard testing of political competition; in other words, it is the *proving ground* for political leaders. And this occurs mainly through the agency of the political parties. Despite the prevalent fantasizing about government without parties, they are absolutely indispensable organizations for any modern state, increasingly becoming the overwhelmingly dominant forms of wielding power. The nature of parties is critical: Those with differing constituencies or social bases, like the Social Democrats (officially a Marxist party) are a more effective proving ground for the testing and acquiring of leadership capabilities. Indeed, the production of able and committed *party leaders* is, in Weber's view, far and away the most important function of parliament. These are leaders who live "for" politics; others, the drones subsisting off patronage politics, doubtless the greater number by far, live "off" politics. "A parliament composed of those in politics for material interests" (e.g., representatives of interest groups), Weber writes, would be "politically sterile," a collection of purveyors of "political petrification" (1448).

Modern conditions of mass political mobilization are critical for the inner workings of parliament and its capacity to limit bureaucratic rule. This condition fosters two kinds of antidemocratic (in the parliamentary sense) tendencies. The first of these is the bureaucratization of the party apparatus itself. The technical and financial requirements of campaigns, the demands of constant recruitment and ideological work, cannot be met by part-time dilettantes, but require the routinized and remunerated attention of office-holding experts. Weber observed that bureaucratization of the party machines in the United States had not yet occurred, but maintained that it was

---

[52] Weber attributes to Bismarck virtually superhuman powers, an attribution that was probably in part, at least, a reflection of his philosophical individualism.

inevitable. It is at this point that Robert Michels's analysis of the so-called "iron law of oligarchy,"[53] the basic idea of which was evidently suggested to him in the first place by Weber, is relevant.

The second tendency of mass politics that works against the possibility of democratic parliamentary limitation of the bureaucracy is "Caesarism," or more technically, "plebiscitary democracy." This is a concept employed frequently by Weber. Three elements are central: (1) the personal relation of leader and led; (2) the emotionality of the relationship; and (3) in terms of political procedures, the employment of the plebiscite to legitimize rule. The dominant political type here is the demagogue, for mass politics lends itself to demogoguery; Weber might have said that they are brought together by an elective affinity. Needless to say, he thought that this style of leadership, increasingly manifest in Western politics, had an inherent tendency to move outside of the procedural boundaries of formal-legal rationality. And like all forms of charismatic rule, plebiscitary democracy is inherently unstable (there is, as always, the problem of succession, and the complex issues facing the leaders of the modern state cannot possibly be dealt with by the simple "yes" or "no" form of the plebiscite).

To take note of the opposition of mass democracy and its parliamentary form is obviously no novel observation, but a rather hackneyed theme of political writers throughout the nineteenth and twentieth centuries. What is of importance in Weber's treatment, however, is that he did theorize the conditions under which parliamentary democracy might effectively limit bureaucratic authoritarianism. This was at least a partial qualification of his eschatologically inclined understanding of modernization as rationalization.

CONCLUSION: CRITIQUE AND REPRISE

In conclusion to this and the foregoing chapter, we will focus on the most general aspect of Weber's sociology, his theorization of rationality, emphasizing first, the problems attending this, and second, its meaning in the context of the Enlightenment.

Perhaps the main problem of Weber's sociology, to which many of its particular difficulties can be traced, is the way in which Weber formulated his typology of action. Although Weber did assert that an understanding of human *rationality* was *not* adequate ground for the cultural sciences, and that human *irrationality* had to be brought in to the picture, he nevertheless formulated the typology in such a fashion as to seemingly exclude the irrational side of human action from consideration.

Weber generally assumes, and at several points states, that whereas rationality is intrinsically comprehensible (through *Verstehen*), irrationality is not. This is justification for elaborating the typology in the form of the

[53] Michels was for a time one of the younger intellectuals around Weber, and one for whom he sought (unsuccessfully) an academic position. In *Political Parties* (1962) he analyzed mainly the organizational structure and transformations of the Social Democratic party of Germany, of which he had been a member. Evidently his own conclusions about the impossibility of democracy made him so pessimistic that he ended up embracing fascism.

different rationalities, the rationality of each resting on the separation of, and relations between, means and ends that Weber takes to be objectively inherent in purposive behavior. The construction of social action in purposive terms is assumed to make it amenable to rational scientific understanding, whereas nonpurposive action remains (for the most part) inaccessible. Related to this is the fact that although Weber grants emotional behavior the status of a general action type, he employs it virtually nowhere in his empirical work. It is, in effect, collapsed into or incorporated as a component of the value-rational type.

But assigning to purposive, means-ends structured action a status of apprehendibility from the standpoint of the observer fundamentally different from that attributed to nonpurposive, "irrational" action is, at best, problematic. If the test of its validity rests on the *performances* of actors in understanding the actions of others, the unambiguous validity of Weber's claim is by no means clear. There seems to be no a priori reason to think that actors' understandings of emotional, impulsive, or other sorts of behavior considered to be irrational are in principle less intelligible than their purposive, deliberate ones, which seem to involve means-ends relations. Within the *Verstehen* framework, the test of the validity of this would seem to rest on the demonstrated competence of actors, or perhaps their claims regarding their understanding of the actions of others, and the picture here is at best unclear. If interpretation of this proposition is restricted to an application of a strictly "scientific" means-ends causal or explanatory rationality, on the other hand, it either begs the question—insofar as it grounds itself in the putative rationality (or "reasonableness"?) of ordinary behavior—or appeals to some supraempirical or metatheoretical source.

These difficulties lead to a problematic relation between the irrationalities of individuals, on the one hand, and the rationalities on which Weberian sociological analysis must evidently be based, on the other. In so far as human action is not rationally driven (and of course to *some* variable degree it is), this schema appears irrelevant; if human action *is* rational, then how is this reconciled with the irrationality of the individual? Weber appears to want it both ways and ends up sacrificing the irrationalities of action to the utilities of a rationalistic, but far too constricted conceptual scheme. These difficulties resulted in considerable post-Weberian theorizing of the "rationality problem."[54] Of the immediate post-Weberians, Karl Mannheim, for one, and the early figures of the critical school, as well, modified Weber's scheme in important ways. Mannheim distinguished between "substantial" and "functional" rationalities, along with corresponding *irrationalities* (Mannheim, 1940). This solves the problem of the *meaning* of irrationality but does so merely residually, by defining the irrationalities as social actions that challenge existing realities. The critical theorists, Max Horkeimer and

---

[54] The very principle that constructing sociological theory in terms of categories or types of rationality is a fruitful strategy has itself often been rejected. This position, of course, implies the embracing of some fundamentally different strategy of building sociological theory, at least insofar as Weber's expanded conceptual scheme adheres to the assumptions of the basic typology of action. About this there could be endless debate. Many of Weber's lower-level types, e.g., "class," "status," "bureaucracy," "asceticism," and the theories based on incorporating them, have proven to be of great sociological utility.

Theodor Adorno in particular, propose that any workable sense of irrationality must be located in the very workings of organization or culture (see *Dialectic of Enlightenment*). "Instrumental reason" becomes the master principle of modern capitalist culture but the critical school's notion of instrumental reason was, in its basic sense, taken from Weber, and ought to be understood as a derivative (or reincarnation) of Weber's formal rationality type (see footnote 31, this chapter). Although Weber's conceptual scheme includes no types specifically defined by the presence of irrationalism, the *sense* of irrationality in its broadest sense as *constituitive* of the typology itself, specifically of relations between particular *formal* and *substantive* rationalities in which the former displace the latter, is clearly central to his analysis of modernism. Instances of this have been discussed earlier, in connection with Weber's sociologies of religion, law and science.

Weber's attempt to construct modern sociology as the science analyzing the forms of historically manifest reason clearly places him in the tradition of the German Enlightenment and its nineteenth century representatives. Herder's understanding of modern social and cultural forms as mechanisms, Marx's analysis of exchange value and its penetration of culture as a fetishism, and Nietzsche's insights about the ascendence of Appolonian culture, are precursors of Weber's formal rationality, all theorizations of the problematic of knowledge, alternative languages attempting to articulate the nature of the degradation of reason in Western civilization. They are simultaneously ironic inversions of the transformed character of history as progress. This progression moves from metaphorical expression in Herder, to the language of economics in Marx, thence to a generalized depiction of all of Western society and culture in Nietzsche and Weber. All share the sense of the waxing of the calculating mentality and its institutionalization in the various orders and symbol spheres as the central tendency in modernization, a sensibility which may be thought of as becoming the *Weltanschauung* or world hypothesis of this developing stream of social science up to and beyond Weber.

One might speculate that the socio-cultural condition driving this movement is the growing pluralism of and tension between ends. The fragmentation of Western culture is first, a de facto proliferaton of values and value systems, many of which, as Weber insisted—perhaps too dogmatically—are incorrigibly at odds with one another; and second, the ultimate fatalism rooted in this fragmentation, the realization that, short of some near-unimaginable totalitarian order, it is irreversible. The extreme version of this holds out no hope and no salvation. The humanism of the Enlightenment, transformed in the alchemy of modernism, appears now to those with this outlook, as a Faustian bargain with fate, with the triumphant devil leering out at us from within the ever more hegemonic and seemingly unchallengeable forms of the instrumentalizaton of life.

15

SEMINAL CONTRIBUTIONS IN EARLY TWENTIETH CENTURY SOCIOLOGY IN THE U.S.

1) Cooley and Mead
2) Thomas and Znaniecki

Throughout this work the history of sociology has been viewed from the standpoint of the ways in which important earlier thinkers have dealt with the questions framed by problematics that took shape during the seventeenth and eighteenth centuries. Central to this has been the manner in which the seminal sociological theorists of the nineteenth and early twentieth centuries received the reconstructed individualism of the Enlightenment, the ways they found it to be problematic, and the ways—both consciously and unconsciously—it influenced their sociological work. These were quite various. The "French" approach was to deny theoretical status to the individual even as "individualism" was conceived to be the chronic master social problem of French society. Comte banished the individual from any theoretical status in sociology, while Durkheim came close to reducing the socialized individual to a unit devoid of agency merely reflecting the moral reality of the collectivity. Although Durkheim's theorization of ritual in *EF* was a major adumbration of interactionism, it was executed independently of any accompanying attempt to establish the individual consciousness as a theoretically implicated component of this. In *EF* the treatment of the soul is no more than a piecemeal parceling out of the collective moral and cognitive reality. Spencer tried to preserve a sense of the individual beyond the purely utilitarian and hedonistic one attributed to him by Durkheim and others, by reconstituting the eighteenth century theological idea of the moral sense in the nineteenth century dress of both Lamarckian and Darwinist evolution, creating and perpetuating a variety of inconsistencies and contradictions in the process. It is Marx's philosophical anthropology, from among the seminal sociological thinkers of the century considered here, that has in recent times proved to have been the most influential, but only, of course, after the discovery of the early manuscripts in the 1930s and the impetus of the insurgencies of the 1960s. Yet for Marx and Engels as for later Marxists, the social reality is grounded in labor and production, and Marxism has always been hostile to interactionist sociologies (see, for example, Lichtman, 1970).

Although the historicist and romantic traditions provided Weber with a powerfully stated concept of the individual, it was not one readily assimilable to the sociological desideratum of a conception of social structure or social organization conceived of *sui generis*. Weber's variant of the romantic conception of the self, with its Nietzschean insistence on the primacy of the will, blocked both the working out of a theory of how the object world is constructed in consciousness, *and* a theorization of the nature of *intersubjective* meaning that might have informed a more interactionist account of the individual. In this respect Durkheim's theorization of interaction as ritual may now be seen to have been sociologically more fruitful.

For somewhat different reasons deriving at least in part from their philosophical anthropologies, then, neither Weber nor Durkheim ever theorized the nature of the individual in a sociologically adequate way. This was to be the great contribution of American sociology after the turn of the century, especially in the interactionism of Charles H. Cooley and more importantly, G. H. Mead, on the one hand, and in an empirically extended way, the sociology of William I. Thomas and Florian Znaniecki, on the other.[1]

[1] No attempt will be made here to give any extended or systematic treatment to the works of the other founding fathers of American sociology, mainly Ward, Sumner, Giddings, Small, and Ross. Ward and Sumner were older than the others but most of their sociological work appeared during roughly the same period as their younger colleagues. Ward's *Dynamic Sociology*, published in 1883 when he was 42, is the principle exception. Sumner published extensively beginning in the early 1880s but *Folkways*, his first important sociological work, was brought out only in 1906. Sumner was an unreconstructed social Darwinist of the most extreme type, arguing that population pressures created intensities of competition that could not be resolved by intervention of any kind (a doctrine incurring the wrath of businessmen because of his rejection of protectionism and government action against workers in cases of labor unrest: "Industrial war is a sign of vigor".)

Of all the concepts advanced by the early American sociologists (excepting Cooley, Mead and Thomas), Sumner's "folkways" and "mores" and Veblen's "conspicuous consumption" are probably the only ones not long forgotten. Ward was also a Spencerian, but while accepting competition as a natural "genetic" phenomenon, added his own idea of "telesis" in order to provide space for conscious reason-based social reform for which sociology would provide the scientific foundation. Ward developed the more sociological side of Spencer, his analysis of the expansion of the regulating system as differentiation proceeds, to justify state-based rational regulation. The best discussion of this is still by Becker (1968, Chap. 7). Giddings, Small, and Ross were all evolutionists. Indeed, Bierstedt sums up his work on early American sociologists (Sumner, Ward, Cooley, Ross, Znaniecki, McIver, Sorokin, Lundberg, Parsons, and Merton) by maintaining that they all represent a tradition taking "direction from Comte and Spencer and especially the latter . . ." (Bierstedt, 1981, 471). (It could be argued—in fact has been argued—that despite his famous epigram in *The Structure of Social Action* in 1937, "Who Now Reads Spencer?", Parsons could legitimately be included as an evolutionist.) Giddings, Small, and Ross were perhaps more influential in their contributions to developing the sociology departments at Columbia, Chicago, and Wisconsin, respectively. For an excellent study of the growth of American sociology emphasizing the persistence and pervasiveness of its religious roots, including the earliest beginnings in the antebellum proslavery Comtean polemics of Henry Hughes, and its Christian reformist organizational origins in the American Social Science Association of Frank Sanborn, the first vehicle in which the powerful impulse to *professionalize* the discipline appears, see Vidich and Lyman, 1985.

As I suggested in the Preface to Part Three, the central experience of the turn of the century period in the United States was the incredibly rapid industrialization and urbanization, accompanied by massive waves of mostly European immigrants. The availability of land (even well after the "official" closing of the frontier announced by Frederic Jackson Turner as having occurred in 1890) and the absence of a landed aristocracy, along with the relative openness of opportunity resulting from the very pace of development and the presence of a virtually permanent black underclass, both to perform the dirtiest work cheaply and to deflect and absorb much of the class antagonism inevitably generated in the capitalist transition to industrialism, gave the New World experience a cast very different from that of the European societies. Even before the year 1900, these conditions had generated what was by any estimation the most powerful reform movement in American history, the progressive movement.

By and large, progressivism proposed reform on two fronts. First, the virtually unrestrained corporations (symbolized by the formation of the first totally vertically integrated corporation, U.S. Steel, with J. P. Morgan money) would be brought under systematic government regulation. Most importantly, the "trusts" would be broken up and competition restored. Second, through a wide range of organizations and agencies, the very nature of the burgeoning industrial metropolis would be remade, by reforming machine politics; establishing standards for inner-city education, and creating institutions to deal with the welfare issues, such as the settlement houses, special legal status for child criminals, and a general professionalization of the activities defining social assistance or help. After the turn of the century, the progressive outlook came to be powerfully established among the middle classes, and claimed among its adherents many prominent and influential intellectuals such as Woodrow Wilson, William James, and James Hayden Tufts.

With its sense of openness to the future, a powerful carrying forward of the traditional optimism of earlier generations, progressivism came to constitute a social and political environment for which that uniquely American philosophy, pragmatism, had a strong affinity (see, for example, Shalin, 1988, 937–938). Among institutions of higher learning this outlook probably took deepest root at the University of Chicago, in the departments of philosophy and sociology (Westby, 1978). From the standpoint of the growth of sociology, the most important figures there were John Dewey, G. H. Mead, W. I. Thomas, and Robert E. Park. In this chapter we will focus primarily on Mead and Thomas, and to a lesser extent on Dewey, along with Charles Cooley.

G. H. MEAD: INTERACTION AND THE SELF

Mead was born at South Hadley, Massachusetts, in 1863, the son of a Congregationalist minister. The family later moved to Oberlin, Ohio, and Mead attended Oberlin College from 1879 to 1883. Following this he spent a year at Harvard, living in William James's house and serving as tutor to his children. (Although it was evidently the well-known philosopher Josiah

Royce rather than James who at the time most influenced Mead, perhaps because Royce's philosophy was grounded in Christian belief and the Young Mead still carried the residue of his Christian upbringing.) Following this, Mead spent three years studying in Germany, at Leipzig and then Berlin. This was an absolutely critical period in his life for he not only became intimately familiar with the work of Wilhelm Wundt, from whom he drew critical aspects of his later work, especially the concept of the gesture and the social importance of language, and acquired a thorough knowledge of German idealist philosophy, but evidently also divested himself of the religious orientation of his youth. Mead returned to the United States abruptly in 1891 in order to take a position at the University of Michigan, where he evidently first met John Dewey, and where Charles Cooley was at the time a graduate student in economics (Miller, 1982, xix). In 1894 Dewey was called to the philosophy department at the University of Chicago (newly created mainly with Rockefeller money) and Mead accompanied him. There Mead remained until his death in 1931. Along with Dewey, Tufts, and E. S. Ames, he was one of the original creators of pragmatism.

Mead was well-known to faculty members and graduate students in the department of sociology and many of the latter took course work with him, especially after the arrival of Robert E. L. Faris in the department. W. I. Thomas was a graduate student at the time of Mead's arrival, and he became both a student and close friend of Mead's.

Mead published many articles over the course of his career, but no books. The four volumes appearing under his authorship[2] were all compiled posthumously and edited by former students and others. Throughout his life Mead was actively involved in civic and political affairs in Chicago, perhaps most notably with Jane Addams at Hull House, serving for several years as the treasurer of that institution.

SOCIAL INTERACTIONISM: MEAD'S PHILOSOPHICAL ANTHROPOLOGY

In all the sociological conceptions discussed in earlier chapters, either a preexisting self stands outside of and logically prior to the social order, or it is collapsed within that order and so denied any theoretical status.[3] The

[2] *The Philosophy of the Present* (Arthur E. Murphy, ed. with intro.), Chicago: Open Court Publ., 1932; *Mind, Self and Society: From the Standpoint of a Social Behaviorist* (Charles Morris, ed. and intro.), Chicago: U. of Chicago Press, 1934; *Movements of Thought in the Nineteenth Century* (Merritt A. Moore, ed. and intro.), Chicago: U. of Chicago Press, 1936; and *Philosophy of the Act* (Charles Morris, with John M. Brewster, Albert M. Dunham, and David L. Miller, eds. and intro.) Chicago: U. of Chicago Press, 1938. *Mind, Self and Society* will henceforth be referred to as *MSS*. Other works of Mead will be cited as required.

[3] Both philosophical and sociological treatments of the problem of the individual and society tend to polarize between the subjectivity of experience as given and the seeming objective nature of the reality outside of it, and much of the history of social and philosophical thought after the sixteenth century is rendering of different forms of this. Husserl is an outstanding example of the new phenomenological turn in this development at the turn of the century, but his philosophy did not at the time appear to be a promising basis for a sociological

conceptualization of the relation between the self and the interaction process that emerged in the work of Cooley and Mead was foreign to the mainstream of American sociology in the late nineteenth and early twentieth centuries. This can be seen in the work of Franklin Giddings, a more or less representative leader, certainly one of the best known, prolific, frequently read, and influential sociologists of the turn-of-the-century generation. Giddings could perhaps be considered one of these potentially receptive to interactionist ideas because of his concept of "consciousness of kind," which he developed in his *Elements of Sociology* in 1898 (see Chapter 6) in somewhat social or relational terms. Giddings recommends Adam Smith's *Theory of Moral Sentiments* (Giddings, 1902, 75), along with Aristotle and Tarde, as "parallel reading" and makes much of the idea of sympathy as fundamentally constitutive of the consciousness of kind. Twenty-four years later in his *Studies in the Theory of Human Society,* after a goodly amount of interactionist theorizing, Giddings took issue with James Mark Baldwin's theory of the nature of the development of the individual. Baldwin was an "environmentalist," heavily influenced by Gabriel Tarde (as was Giddings) in his emphasis on imitation and suggestion, and who analyzed the emergence of the self in the child in evolutionary and social terms (see Baldwin, 1910; also Richards, 1987, 399). He was one of the first to argue that the moral development of children depends on their social situation, and that the individual self is constituted of "copies" taken in from the external world. It was just this "dialectic of personal growth," as Baldwin put it, with which Giddings took issue. Baldwin had written:

> "My thought of self is in the main, as to its character as a personal self, filled up with my thought of others, distributed variously as individuals; and my thought of others, as . . . the ego and the alter are to our thought one and the same thing" (cited in Giddings, 1922, 162).

Here Baldwin attempts to give a social foundation to the idea of the self. Giddings objected strenuously, arguing that it is inaccurate to say that the thought of one's self is "filled up with my thought of others," that "we must continue to think of the individual as being essentially a natural ego," and along Durkheimian lines, that the *socialized* ego is a product of the pressures emanating from organized society (162–163). Although of course familiar with the works of Cooley and others as well as Baldwin,[4] and even though his own concept of consciousness of kind was inspired by Adam Smith's idea

---

science. It was perhaps Simmel who made the strongest attempt to wed subjectivity and society. But Simmel never transcended the Kantian duality of thought and action. His main influence in American sociology of the period, indeed, up to World War II, was on Robert Park's categorization of the "social processes" competition, conflict, accommodation, and assimilation (see Park and Burgess, 1924), and it is only recently that American interactionist sociology has begun to take his work seriously.

[4] But probably not Mead. Although he could hardly have avoided familiarity with the works of the major figures of the Chicago school—Thomas, Park, and at the time, above all Small—the only reference to any of them in *Studies* . . . is to Small, and to him only as the "interpreter" of Gustav Ratzenhofer to the English-speaking public (267, n.3). Columbia, where Giddings taught, was the leading sociological rival of Chicago at the time.

of sympathy, although the natural law side, Giddings apparently simply did not understand the basic idea of the self as a reflexive entity emergent in the *interactive process*. He was a committed Darwinian/Spencerian evolutionist believing that "consciousness of kind" was an evolutionary emergent, essentially a human mental faculty that *accounted* for human social life, not implicated in the essential nature of the social process itself.

The main influences on Mead's thought were the line of self theory from James through Cooley, the psychologist John Watson's behaviorism, the Germanic idealistic conception of the self, particularly Wundt's concept of the gesture, and the uniquely American philosophy of pragmatism, in its aspect of a theory of knowledge.[5] In the discussion to follow, we shall take up the first three of these, and leave the fourth for later treatment. We may begin with Cooley.

Cooley had become a member of the faculty at the University of Michigan during Mead's tenure there, and the two men remained friends until Cooley's death in 1929. It was specifically Cooley's formulation of the dynamic nature of the self that constituted Mead's point of departure. Although, like virtually everyone else around the turn of the century, Cooley was caught up heavily in evolutionism, and although he kept open a role for heredity and instinct,[6] his work by and large downplays these factors.

Cooley's formulation of the human self in interactional terms is a seminal sociological idea. It has often been noted, and is of course true, that Cooley drew on James's earlier theory of the self, but he gave this a truly distinctive sociological turn. Generally speaking, James's contribution to the Cooley-Mead line of self-interaction theorizing was, first, to detach the metaphysical idea of "consciousness" from its earlier philosophical associations, and locate it in the stream of actual experience, literally a "stream of consciousness," thus making it subjectible to a much more empirical or scientific approach; and second, to derive from this the idea of the multiplicity of selves, along with the terminology of the "I" and the "me" that was later adopted by Mead. (See James, 1948, 152ff., *et passim*). Cooley more or less took over the basic corpus of James's thought, but developed it in an original way. His idea of the "looking-glass self" may be thought of as a partial or incomplete formulation of the nesting of human subjectivity, i.e., the self, in the interaction process. James had perceived and understood in general the

---

[5] Mead was also throughly familiar with the natural science of the time, and developments in physics, along with Alfred North Whitehead's philosophy of science, in particular, are of importance for Mead's later attempt to integrate the philosophies of the natural and social worlds (especially *PA* and *PP*).

[6] He contrasted the role of heredity in animal and human evolution by likening the former to a mechanism like a hand organ on which a few tunes can be played with little or no training over and over, and the latter to a piano, not intended to play just a few tunes, and which cannot be played at all without extensive training, but on which an "infinite variety" of music can be performed (Cooley, 1964, 19). Of instinct in humans he says that he would prefer to avoid the term altogether (24), and although recognizing a limited array of instincts (anger, fear, maternal love, sexual love, and self-assertion or power), he rejected them as having any explanatory relevance for sociology, concluding that the human social or moral progress "consists less in the aggrandizement of particular faculties or instincts . . . than in the discipline of all with reference to a progressive organization of life which we know in thought as conscience" (47).

absolutely central importance of this relationship, but his work is more a description of the various selves ("material" self, various "social" selves, etc.) than it is an *analysis* of the *process* or processes implicated in the *genesis* and *functioning* of the self (or selves). It was Cooley's contribution to theorize this relationship.

The root of Cooley's theory of interaction appears to lie in his interpretation of the growth of sociability in infants and children, and then in adults. His detailed and continuous observations on his own children, in particular, led him to the rather imprecise idea of a "social feeling," which is not an instinct, but a capacity first "indistinguishable from sensuous pleasure," but which then becomes "specialized on persons, and from that time onward (is called out) as a chief aim of . . . life" (Cooley, 1964, 85). Most importantly, social feeling is emotional in nature, and this emotional content is *social* in its genesis. Cooley was very close to the emerging modern view on this point, a considerable achievement considering the prevailing wisdom of the time was quite otherwise, as, for example, in Darwin's theory of facial expressions as instinctively caused expressions of emotion. Against this Cooley asserted that there was *no definite* instinctive capacity to interpret the countenance (101,ff.).[7]

This is important because it seems to have been the basis on which Cooley moved in the direction of a *social* theory of the origin of thought. Thought, he believed, originates in the imaginings of others and discourse with them. It is thus inseparable from communication and takes the form of "personal ideas" of others, others with whom we engage in an *internal discourse* that constitutes the content of the individual consciousness. "The immediate social reality is the idea," and it occurs only "in the mind" (119). "The imaginations which people have of one another are the solid facts of society, and that to observe and interpret these must be a chief aim of sociology" (121). The idea of an internal discourse was to be taken over by Mead and made central to his theory of the self.

Cooley's discussions of the social nature of the self are quite lengthy, and no attempt to reproduce this rich vein of descriptive sociology will be made here. Our discussion will be confined to a characterization of the conceptual apparatus Cooley formulated to frame the reality of self and interaction, the "looking-glass self." The looking-class self consists of three elements: "the imagination of our appearance to the other person; the imagination of his judgement of that appearance, and some sort of self-feeling, such as pride or mortification: (183). In this formulation Cooley wants to emphasize the commonalities that self-acquisition has with all other social learning. "The meaning of 'I' and 'mine' is learned in the same way that the meanings of hope, regret, chagrin, disgust, and thousands of other words of emotion and sentiment are learned" (192). (Note also the emphasis that Cooley here places on the acquisition of language in self-acquisition).

Cooley linked the process of the looking-class self with a particular form of social organization—the primary group. His use of the term "personal idea" is not accidental; it is clear that the social prerequisite of the self-forming process is the close, intimate, and personal set of relationships he

---

[7] Although he made no claim to have disproved Darwin (103).

idealized in his description of the primary group, an idea developed in *Social Organization* (Chap. 3). Cooley actually *defines* the primary group in terms of its function in "forming the social nature and ideals of the individual" (Cooley, 1921, 23). Fundamental to the primary group is its organic "wholeness," and it is only in this *milieu* that the individual is able to have his or her "earliest and completest experience of social unity" (26–27). Humans acquire their nature, their human nature, in the sense of whatever is universal in human experience, in the primary group.

Mead assimilated Cooley's idea of locating the individual self in the same reality as other selves, i.e., the "stream of consciousness".[8] At the hands of Cooley, he says, the self is no longer a "Cartesian presupposition of consciousness" (Mead, 1930, xxix). Establishment of "others" (i.e., any reality not given in the immediacy of experience) is no longer dependent on the prior existence of a self. Cooley has the fundamental idea correct: He breaks down the opposition of subjective and objective, individual and society, self and other. But the metaphor of the looking glass is inadequate to convey the deeper reality of this self-other unity. The unstated presupposition of the notion of "imaginations" as the social reality, Mead says, rests on a prior existence of the "person" or "individual." Cooley bypasses the issue of the status of objective reality. Mead always maintained not only that the objective existence of society was an unavoidable presupposition of any science of society, but that—against phenomenologists and others—it could be established on unassailable grounds. In his short piece both eulogizing and somewhat snidely criticizing Cooley shortly after the latter's death, Mead makes this point by saying that the very recognition of others appearing in our imaginations in some organized fashion implies their having something in common, and therefore, a necessarily objective, i.e., objectively *social*, existence beyond our imaginations (xxvi). The inner experiences we term "psychical" originate in the objective social world of selves and the groups they constitute. Cooley's looking-class self is solipsistic; it collapses all external reality into the subjectivity of the individual (Mead, 1930). Mead's lifework was to build the ground for a science of the social world as *objective*.

Mead's background in German idealistic philosophy was of central importance for his theory of interaction and the self. He assimilated the Hegelian dialectic but also critiqued it (Mead, 1936) in a way rather parallel to that of Marx. Like Marx, he accepted the form of the dialectical process, and like Marx, advanced a critique, one might say, of Hegel's manner of "applying" or interpreting it. Unlike Marx, however, Mead was not interested in refuting idealism in principle, although like Marx, he was committed to developing a theory that could both ground and accommodate progressive change.

Hegel and the other romantics like Fichte and Schelling had the essential idea correct: The self arises in social experience and is at the same time the unity that makes society possible. It is impossible to reduce the world to the self, as Cooley had it, since the organization of the world necessarily comes *from* the self (125). The romantics maintained the inde-

[8] A term Mead employed in a sense that seems fairly close to its usage in the literary movement of James Joyce, Virginia Wolff, and others.

pendence of the self from the world, yet maintained its incorrigible con-nectedness with the world. This separateness within inseparability is described dialectically. We could say that Mead appropriated this core idea and adapted it for his purposes through the idea of "taking the role of the other." Here the self comes back on itself as *object,* more specifically, as an object of *knowledge.* Knowledge of self is the incorrigible mark of selfhood, or better put, the process of self. And further, this knowledge has a status epistemo-logically identical with all other knowledge, since it comes into existence by "looping" through the other. In other words, the self becomes an object to itself only through the route of the other; i.e., it constitutes itself only reflexively. Its nature then, is to be at once an acting unity and an object of knowledge; and this implies the objective presence of other.

The big problem with the romantics was their idealism. Mead wanted to bring the self back to the world, into the real social world of human action, of human behavior. But he wanted to focus *not* on the realm of ideas and their interplay, or on the mind as such, like the idealists, but on actual practical human activity as it appeared in the everyday world, and to formulate the nature and role of mental activity in this setting (see Mead, 1934, Part 1). It is for this reason that Mead appropriated the term *behaviorism* from the famous behaviorist psychologist John B. Watson (creating the "social behaviorism that in today's intellectual climate sounds so anomalous) to describe his position. It is worth noting that this approach has a good deal in common with Weber's focus on behavior defined as social action as the proper object of sociology: Weber—obviously—rejected that central tenet of behaviorism that restricts science to recording and analysis of "observable" behaviors.

We could say that Mead reformulated Cooley's interactionism through appropriating the reflexive principle of the romantics, and in the process resituated the self-as-reflexive as both a product and as an agency constuitive of that process, and by defining the whole conceptual package as "social behavior."

MEAD'S THEORY OF THE SELF AND SOCIAL INTERACTION

In commenting on Mead's intellectual life, John Dewey remarked that practically all of his inquiries developed out of an original haunting problem, "the nature of consciousness as personal and private," or "the role of subjective consciousness in the reconstruction of objects as experienced . . . (Mead, 1932, XXXVI).[9] In developing this Mead introduces the concepts of "mind," "self," and "act" (or "social act").

Mind appears in the course of evolution as a special character of the social act (which we shall shortly consider in detail). It presupposes the social act, but the latter is only a necessary and not a sufficient condition of mind, since its *mechanism* (the mechanism of the act) is present in the life process of lower animal forms as well as of human beings. The concept of the self

---

[9] The most useful general secondary works on Mead are probably Joas (1985) and Miller (1982).

is closely related to that of mind, but is a more "inclusive unity." Both "mind" and "self" are implicated in the idea that can be considered to be Mead's master concept, the "act."

The Act

The concept of the act (Mead, 1938b, esp. Parts 1 and 2) provides a "frame of reference" giving coherence to an array of other concepts which can be fully explicated only as phases or aspects of the act.

Mead distinguishes four stages of the act: (1) impulse, (2) perception, (3) manipulation, and (4) consummation.[10] The beginning of any specific organic activity is the impulse stage. Secretion of the glands and lowering of the level of blood sugar are impulses at the beginning of, in this case, the act of seeking food. The impulse stage is the motive phase of the act. In general, Mead appears to regard such impulses as rooted in the biological nature of the organism. But this does not appear to make them nonsocial or presocial in any intelligible sense. The physiological conditions of social behavior having their ultimate locus in the central nervous system are the "bases" of social behavior, Mead writes, "precisely because they in themselves are also social," by which he means that "they consist in drives or instincts or behavior tendencies . . . which (the individual) cannot carry out or give overt expression and satisfaction to without the cooperative aid of one or more other individuals" (Mead, 1934, 139n.). This seems confused, but it does reveal Mead's insistence on placing the impress of the social on the very roots of behavior.

The succeeding three stages of the act may be thought of as together constituting the response of the organism to the motive introduced in stage 1. Perception, or stage 2 of the act, is the attitude taken toward the impulse stimulation of stage 1. Insofar as response does not issue in some overt activity, we remain in stage 2 of the act. Perception defines the relation between a developed physiological organism and an environmental object from which elements are related. It of course presupposes sense organs, the central nervous system, and a motor apparatus, but is to be understood as socially conditioned.

Stage 3 of the act is the "action" stage. Here, the organism does something about the perception of stage 2, which stands in teleological relation to later phases of the act. It appears that manipulation may refer to either actions (in the overt sense) or symbolic manipulations. It is at this point in the act that the potential for *reflection,* or delayed response, appears, and these terms specifically define what Mead means by mind. Reflection means the symbolic testing of alternative ways of acting, something possible only at the level of human social life.

Stage 4 of the act, the consummatory phase, constitutes the completion of a teleological chain of events in which some kind of "adjustment" occurs. This teleological nature cannot be overemphasized. Mead says that at any point in its unfolding the whole process is present. The future is

---

[10] Compare this to Dewey's stages of "the pattern of inquiry," the form of which is the same in everyday life and science (Dewey, 1938, Chap. 6).

"present" in the sense that the organism, from the inception of the act, *selects* and thus *creates* or modifies its environment. The past lives in a congealed moment of any action, imposing conditions or limits—but also potentialities—for that action (for a good discussion of Mead's concept of time, see Maines, 1983).

Within the manipulatory stage is located the distinguishing character of developed human behavior, *reflection*. It is the symbolic character of human social experience that makes reflection possible, and in turn, reflection serves the function of projecting alternative futures as contingencies of alternative ways of action. It is precisely because of this that human beings may be called rational. Reflection is a way of noting all possible courses of action symbolically. The ends of such courses of action, in the process of reflection, are already at work setting the individual on course.

Mead's idea of mind, then, is situated in the Act, and is a constituent aspect of the process constituting the Act. It is virtually identical to Dewey's; indeed, it is an idea generally shared by all the pragmatists. It can, in fact, be traced to Dewey's article on the reflex arc, in which he criticizes the reflex arc model of behavior on the grounds that its assertion that stimulus and response are discrete events rather than aspects of a human function

> leaves us with a disjointed psychology, whether viewed from the standpoint of development in the individual or in the race, or from that of the analysis of the mature consciousness (Dewey, 1896, 360).

The *continuities* of human experience, which are self-evidently constituitive of that experience, require a conception of consciousness or mind that is located in and conceived of as a part of the process itself.

Meaning, the Self, and the Generalized Other

The concept of the self is intimately related to that of mind. The self is phenomenon possible only because of the peculiar nature of social activity, from whence mind emerges. As mind is the symbolic internalization of the social process, the self is the objectification through language of the attitudes of the "other" whereby the individual becomes an object to himself. There is a sense in which such objectification is an impersonalization, yet it is only through this process that the individual becomes a person. A detailed explanation of the process whereby the self arises is given by Mead in terms of his construction of the nature of *meaning*.

The nature of meaning is found in the peculiar teleological character of a triadic relationship involving the following elements: (1) a gesture as the early phase of the social act (e.g., the barring of fangs by a dog);[11] (2) the response of another organism to the gesture; (3) as it represents the completion of the act of the gesturer. Consciousness, be it noted, is not a

---

[11] Mead drew his concept of the gesture from Wundt. "Wundt isolated a very valuable conception of the gesture as that which becomes later a symbol, but which is to be found in its earlier stages as a part of a social act," he writes (134,42). See the discussion in Part 2, page 7 of *MSS*.

necessary condition of the emergence of meaning for Mead, but is to be found in such situations as the famous "conversation of gestures" present in the dogfight that never becomes bloody. In such instances the second animal responds to the projected completion of the act signaled by the gesture, in this case the barring of the teeth. Whether it runs, feints for an opening, or attacks directly makes no difference: Meaning is, by definition, present, albeit at a relatively primitive level.

The highest development of meaning occurs at the point where a *language of significant symbols* emerges, and is characterized by *self-consciousness*. At this point, "a whole new set of objects appear in nature." Now, a significant symbol, or significant gesture, is distinguished from a nonsignificant one by the fact that in the instance of the former the individual becomes an object to himself. This can be accomplished only through a language of *symbols*. The crucial difference between the conversation of gestures and that of significant symbols lies in the fact that the latter can be extracted and isolated from the social act as a whole. Lower forms of life are incapable of this. The critical feature is that the *same* response is called out in the other. Were the gesture tied incorrigibly to the whole act, this would be impossible. Here we find the key to the *universalization* of meaning. Animals, as it were, live in a world of particulars. The universal in experience is located by Mead in the context of meaning as it appears at the level of symbolic interaction. This was summed up succinctly by Mead: "A person who is saying something is saying to himself what he is saying to others; otherwise he does not know what he is talking about."

Mead details the process of the emergence of the self in his treatment of the generalized biography of the child. In his imaginative conceptualization of mythical companions, for instance, the child is exercising or practicing the capacity to call out in others what is called out in himself. In the now famous phrase, the child "takes the role of the other," playing "house," "cowboys," or "storekeeper." What is involved at this stage of socialization are sets of unorganized self-other symbolizations. Mead contrasts this rather "free" play with the situation present in the organized game. Here, it is necessary for the individual to be prepared to symbolically take the roles of everyone else in the game. The "rules of the game" are attempts to stabilize the organization of roles. Rules are "the set of responses which a particular attitude calls out."

Insofar as an individual "internalizes" such an organization of attitudes, Mead speaks of a "generalized other." "The organized community or social group which gives to the individual his unity of self may be called the 'generalized other'" (Mead, 1934, 154). It is worth nothing that with this Mead established the foundation for a theory of social structure or organization, a task, however, that he barely adumbrated in his section entitled "Society" in *MSS*.[12]

The critical feature of all this is what Mead calls the "internal

---

[12] Probably because he was a philosopher, not a sociologist. He kept fully acquainted however, with the work of sociologists, especially those working within his own general framework. In his 1930 piece on Cooley, he specifically mentions Thomas, Park, Burgess, and Faris in this regard.

conversation," and "internalization and inner dramatization . . . of the external conversation of significant gestures" (173). Mead identifies this— especially against James's and Cooley's emphasis on the affective—as an *intellectual* process. This sounds something like Baldwin's "copies" of external reality, an entity distinct from the *objective* self character as described by Mead. Indeed, Mead is ambiguous on this point. He is careful to distinguish an inner (subjective) region where experiences such as pain or our moods are to be located, but which is unconnected with the conversation of gestures, i.e., stands *outside* of the framework in which the attitudes of others can affect it, is not part of the "internal conversation" and so by his logic, evidently not part of the self. Such experiences are accessible only to the individual. This leaves the inner conversation in an ambiguous status: neither *identifiable* with the *objective* process of mind and self formation, although genetically increasingly an "internalization" of it (1934, 298ff. *et passim*), nor unambiguously subjective. We seem to end up with two versions of the self, one objective, the other "internal" if not "subjective," and sounding not entirely unlike the capacity for reason attributed to the mind in the essentialist view that Mead's entire philosophy is intended to oppose.

There are at least two additional secondary problems that accompany this theorization of the self. One has to do with Mead's overall conception of language as the constituent reality of the self and its emergent nature. Mead's emphasis falls entirely on the essentially liberating nature of this process. What it misses is the potential and often realized *repressive* function of language, the extreme form of this being something like the Newspeak of George Orwell's *Nineteen Eighty Four*. One could perhaps argue that this is somehow *implied* in Mead's theory, but there is little if anything to suggest that he actually had the idea.

Second, the theory of self essentially fails to transcend the Jamesian conclusion that the self is a multiplicity and even goes further than James in disaggegating the latter's "social" self into a fragmented set of *particular* social selves. This has a certain utility of application in modern societies, but it is both philosophically and sociologically incomplete, being self-evidently inadequate from the standpoint of a social theory of the individual, because the particular selves imply some principle of unity to even allow us to speak in these terms. Mead says that such unity of self as may exist is to be located in the social organization, "the unity of which makes us feel a part of society" (142). But this makes the self a mere reflection, or microcosm, of society, thereby canceling the most fundamental sense of the concept, its nature as agency.

"I" and "Me"

The concepts "I" and "me" are a further elaboration of the processive and emergent character of the self.

The self arises through the taking of the attitudes of others. The experience of taking such attitudes Mead terms the "me"; it is the self as a social object. Whatever appears in the immediate experience of the self is the "me." We might say that the "me" is the structuring of attitudes appropriate to a situation at the point of acting in that situation. It is everything given that is presumptively relevant to the action. This suggests that if the self consisted of nothing but "me" roles, the appearance of "anything new under the sun" would be precluded, and any formulation of agency would be absent. The "me" is therefore complemented by the "I."

The "I" is the self as actor, as organizer and interpreter of "me" roles. It is never itself given in experience, for the moment it is actualized it passes from its nature as "I" into the experiential content of the "me." The actual operations that constitute the constructing dimension, the "I," cannot themselves be apprehended (for a discussion, see Joas, 1985, 92ff.).

With its "now you have it, now you don't" character, the "I" is a concept over which more than a few interpreters of Mead have puzzled. It has sometimes been likened to Freud's concept of the Ego, a dubious comparison. Foote and Cottrell confer on it a more complex tripartite content: (1) *health,* or "the ability of the organism to exercise all of its physiological functions and to achieve its maximum of sensory acuity, strength, energy, co-ordination, dexterity, endurance, recuperative power, and immunity"; (2) *autonomy,* or "genuine self government, construed as an ability, not a state of affairs"; (3) *creativity,* or "any demonstrated capacity for innovations in behavior or real reconstruction of any aspect of the social environment" (Foote and Cottrell, 1955).

Extensive exposition of the many interpretations of the "I" and "me" are beyond the scope of this work. The recent work of Stephen Lyng, however, is worth mention both because of its continuity with Foote and Cottrell's formulation, and because of its synthesizing potential of differing paradigms (Lyng, 1990). In the course of his analysis of "edgework," or the deliberate engagement in high risk taking, he interprets Mead's "I" as a self-actualizing experience contingent on the absence or low level of constraint, represented as the "me." He also draws a close parallel between this and Marx's discussions of creativity in the 1844 Manuscripts (see Chapter 10).

> When the "me" is obliterated by fear or the demands of immediate survival, action is no longer constrained by social forces and the individual is left with a sense of self-determination" (879)

Presumably the same distinction would apply in "normal" situations as well as extreme ones; indeed, it would have to, for Mead intended the "I" to be a constituent of all of social life.

As mentioned earlier, Mead made a point of staying abreast of the scientific developments of the time and attempted to synthesize the physical theory of relativity and his own theory of self and society (Mead, 1932, 1938b). The central idea here was what he termed "sociality," which he held to be the common constitutive property of both domains.

> Sociality is the situation in which the novel event is in both the older order and the new which its advent heralds (1932, 49)
>> The novel event must not only be in two systems, it must adjust this plurality of systematic relations in such a fashion that its presence in the later system changes its character in the earlier system or systems to which it belongs while the older relations are reflected in the new system it has entered (69)

. . . There is sociality in nature in so far as the emergence of novelty requires that objects be at once in both the new (and old systems) . . . We find it in teleology in biology and consciousness in psychology (63)

Consider an event that, in one of Mead's phrases, is "poised on a knife-edge of time." Such an event necessarily has a history, and that history consists of a series of event-passages. The event may be a moment of consciousness or of sheer physical inertia: It makes no difference. Now, each event in a given series will have a *different* history, necessarily, since in the case of two events A and B, A being temporally prior to B, A is part of the history of B, but B, in possessing the quality of emergence precisely at that instant on the knife-edge of time, cannot be part of its own history. It becomes history but then it is no longer B, but part of the history of C. B, as the emerging new thing or situation, creates its own history, the history of its singular perspective. It is also at that instant passing into the history of C. Its character of being in both at once is its sociality.

Such is the nature of consciousness, and Mead thought, of the demains of nature as well. The principle of simultaneity is its physical analogue. The world is a unity, and the fundamental nature of that unity is to be found in the human social reality.[13] This is a clear instantiation of the Enlightenment's—and perhaps Hume's in particular—ideal of the grounding of the natural sciences in the human sciences.

MEAD AND PRAGMATISM: THE THEORY OF KNOWLEDGE AND PROGRESS

For the pragmatists—and for the moment I have in mind mainly James and Dewey—knowledge arises in the process of response to blocked habit, that "great flywheel of society," in James's metaphor. Anything interfering with habitual behavior creates a crisis, setting in motion trial-and-error behavior in an attempt to reinstitute the original habitual behavior. The response to blocked habit is emotion; emotion appears in the consciousness of the individual as consciousness of the thwarting of habitual action. But the human species has evolved to the point that unsuccessful trial-and-error behavior may lead to thought, i.e., to reflection on the nature of the situation and the source and nature of its intractability. The essential first step in this is the institution of a problem, or problem definition, which may lead to purely mental or intellectual testing of alternative possible solutions. At a higher level it may involve the abstracting out of elements from the concrete situation and their possible application elsewhere (see Dewey, 1938, Chap. 6, "The Theory of Inquiry," for a discussion). For Mead, this meant that such anticipation of future events had necessarily to be incorporated in the essentials of any conception of social action—as he does in the concept of the act.

The process of problem defining and problem solving is Dewey's paradigm of science and situates scientific activity squarely in the social

---

[13] For a penetrating analysis of this, see Joas, 1985, Chap. 7.

process. The human species shares problem solving as a fundamental activity with animals, but in animal species this does not lead to change; rather, change occurs through unconscious evolutionary processes. In human social life, the more or less rational adaptations that may follow blocked habit bring change in the very course of their realization. When the generalized problem-solving paradigm is formalized as the method of scientific inquiry, it acquires massively enhanced change-inducing powers.

The pragmatists conceived of science as a developed objective, specialized, and rational form of collective adaptation (Dewey, 1938, esp. Chap. 6). Its rationality lies in its enhanced capacity to test out alternative solutions on bases transcending trial and error. Its objectivity is grounded in the universalization of meaning made possible by language. This is exactly what Mead means by "objectivity": the *extractability* of symbolic meanings from the concrete situation and their consequent generalizability.

Scientific activity, then, is fundamentally future-oriented; the testing of its adequacy involves the workability of action alternatives. Its theory of truth—encouraged by Dewey's writings in particular—has because of this often seemed to other professional philosophers to be hopelessly instrumentalized, a bowdlerization of the received scientific canon of truth as a predicate of propositions subjected to certain logical and empirical rules. This is not, it must be said, a matter of "relativizing" truth, for science in general in the twentieth century has without question embraced a relativistic conception of scientific truth (one of Weber's problems). But the received or conventional understanding of this makes the relativity intrinsic to the process of making all previous knowledge obsolescent. It does this by confronting existing knowledge with new facts, formulating hypotheses for test, revising old knowledge, ultimately shifting theories and even paradigms, but all in accord with formal logical and empirical rules as criteria of truth stated in a metalanguage.[14] It is not on the issue of the provisional nature of truth that pragmatism departs from received scientific canon; on this score they are fully compatible. What pragmatism has seemed to want to do has been to replace these tests with one of sheer workability or practicability, to transfer the very concept of truth from the domain of propositions to that of action, thereby reducing the ideal of the true to a mere instrumentalism. For the pragmatists the meanings of scientific concepts lies in their consequences; beliefs having the same consequences have the same meanings. It is this that is, and remains, problematic, for it seems to imply a relativism undermining the very nature of science (see, for example, Russell, 1945, Chaps. 29 and 30).

A related implication of the pragmatist theory of science is that science is historical; the incorrigible emergence of the new produces not a static array of forms that become a positivisticaly conceived of theory or conceptual scheme, but a *history* (Mead, 1906). This implies that the proper scientific object become the narrative. And it means that some kind of

---

[14] But note the problem here. The metalanguage which warrants the rules can itself claim no special warrant, other than by an appeal to even "higher" principles, thereby initiating an infinite regress.

interpretive procedure, never theorized by Mead or the other pragmatists, becomes an essential scientific operation (on this point see Woolwine, 1988).

Yet in spite of these difficulties, the pragmatist theory of science is consistent with its ground, the social theory of the individual-in-interaction, with intellectual activity arising in the process. No conception of science positing mental operations as somehow appearing outside of or prior to this process can stand consistent with it. In fact, the philosophy of science of the pragmatists—certainly of Mead—is fully consistent with what science claims as its most fundamental axiom: the grounding of truth in experience. The relativism of truth that follows from this, the relativism that Kant had tried to transcend, is the incorrigible condition with which science must come to terms. Mead's pragmatism was an attempt to maintain the Enlightenment ideal of science as a liberating enterprise, but to do so while *rejecting* any criterion of truth which asserts itself above competing truth claims, or which legitimizes itself on the basis of standards somehow standing outside the practice itself.

One can say, then, with Joas, that pragmatism is a philosophy that attempts "to abandon the separation between a philosophy that conserves values and an instrumentally curtailed science" (Joas, 1985, 45). Dewey and Mead wanted to democratize science, to make it into a communal activity in which the community both exercised influence over scientific activities and shared in its benefits. Most fundamentally, then, their pragmatism is about the social nature and role of knowledge. Joas sums this up well:

> Knowledge comes from the practical engagement of members of society with an environment they must reshape, and from their communication collaboration and exchange of opinions. Knowledge undergoes development in the process of reaching agreement (47).

It should be clear from the foregoing that the pragmatists' theory of knowledge—and Mead's in particular—is inextricably bound up with the process of change. In their conception, the culture is always open to some extent. And it is science that can make change progressive, against all the irrationalities of the human world—particulars about which Mead says little.[15]

All this is not without problems, particularly the wedding of European romantic idealism to American pragmatism. In order to give the romantic idealistic conception of self a legitimately *scientific* form, Mead brought it, or interpreted it, within the cognitive framework of philosophy. This in a sense created one problem as it solved another. In Dewey's problem-solving model, the core ideas are cognitive: Once habit is broken, the life process is one of recognizing, defining, and solving problems, the more so the higher the evolutionary level. Emotion appears only as an incident, a reaction to blocked habit, and remains an unanalyzed category restricted to the period *prior* to problem solving. It is not part of the woof and warp of *social* life, but conceptualized as restricted to states of the individual, just as in the psycho-

---

[15] A critical point sometimes brought against him. In *MSS,* for instance, he seems to envisage—rather naively—an evolutionary movement toward greater democracy (see Part 4, "Society").

logical theories (the James-Lange theory, in particular) against which Dewey was reacting. This basic model, broadly accepted by Mead despite reservations regarding the centrality of habit), confines the concept of the self appearing in interaction to cognitive processes. Closely related to this is Mead's emphasis not only on the rational aspects of action, but on its instrumental character as well. To depict individuals and collectivities solely as perpetually engaged in problem solving, as forever manipulating or modifying the natural and social environments in goal-seeking activity, approaches a caricaturization of human life.

The generations of sociologists and social psychologists that followed generally regarded Mead as superior to Cooley, as correcting and transcending him. In all this, Cooley's emphasis on the emotional content of interaction was essentially lost. Other influences aside,[16] one important reason for this was probably that the core *problem* Mead addressed was the *genesis* of the self, whereas Cooley, the sociologist working inductively by observing his own children, focused on the nature of the self as a *process*. It is only quite recently that the discipline has begun to move beyond this legacy and frame the analysis of emotions sociologically.[17]

Aside from the restriction to the cognitive, it is clear as well that Mead's formulation was overly simplistic. This was shown with particular force by Goffman, in his analysis of deference and demeanor (Goffman, 1985). For Mead, the individual in quite a simple and straightforward fashion assumes the attitude others take toward him or her. Goffman shows that the self is a continuous product of deference and demeanor rituals. "Deference" is "the appreciation an individual shows of another to that other" (225), and the self requires the social process of deference giving for its reproduction. "Demeanor" designates "that element of the individual's ceremonial behavior typically conveyed through deportment, dress, and bearing, which serves to express to those in his immediate presence that he is a person of certain desirable or undesirable qualities" (225). Everyone is in a moral (i.e., Durkheimian sense of obligation) sense "responsible" for the image others have of themselves; we are likewise responsible for our own demeanor image (229).

> The individual must rely on others to complete the picture of him of which he himself is allowed to paint only certain parts. Each individual is responsible for the demeanor image of himself and the deference image of others, so that for a complete man to be expressed, individuals must hold hands in a chain of ceremony, each giving deferentially with proper demeanor to the one on the right what will be received deferentially from the one on the left. (229)

This is "joint labor," through which "a constant flow of indulgences is spread through society" (229).

---

[16] E.g., the broader social and political emphasis on reason that is part and parcel of left-wing thought, as over against the conservative emphasis on irrationality, in particular its emotional basis.

[17] See, for example, Denzin, 1984.

The actual sociology of organization and change more or less contained in Mead's work, especially in his "generalized other," I would suggest, is to be found elsewhere, and during Mead's time its sociologically most sophisticated, if flawed manifestation, appears in W. I. Thomas's and Florian Znaniecki's monumental *The Polish Peasant in Europe and America.*

THE POLISH PEASANT IN EUROPE AND AMERICA: THEORETICAL AND EMPIRICAL SYNTHESIS IN AMERICAN SOCIOLOGY

W. I. Thomas and Florian Znaniecki's *The Polish Peasant in Europe and America* has been called the greatest work in the history of American sociology.[18] If there is any particular reason for this that should be elevated above all the others, it is probably that the work is the first true, and easily most sophisticated, attempt to meld theory and method. American sociology, as Zaretsky (1984, introduction) points out, had produced plenty of works in the grand nineteenth century tradition of armchair theorizing, and a welter of empirical studies as well, for the most part in the tradition of Christian reform focused on the social problems of the time, particularly immigrant working-class cultural practices and political rebelliousness. *The Polish Peasant in Europe and America* is a systematic attempt to study this problem by expanding the empirical scope to Europe as well as the United States. But more importantly, it is a self-conscious attempt to break with and transcend the tradition of both Christian uplift and the whole mosaic of biology, instinct, and Spencer's evolutionism, and to build on a conception of sociology that took the realm of the collective consciousness (not in Durkheim's sense) or the symbolic as central to understanding human social activity. The work was truly a collaborative one. There is general agreement that had it been authored by either one of its two authors alone—if indeed this would have been possible—it would have been very different and probably very inferior.

W. I. Thomas was a well-published scholar long before the appearance of *The Polish Peasant in Europe and America*[19] (see especially his *Source Book for Social Origins* [1909] and the earlier *Sex and Society* [1907]).[20] He was born in 1863, graduated from the University of Tennessee in literature, and taught there and at Oberlin College. He also studied in Germany during

---

[18] The project began in 1908 when Thomas received a grant for the study from the Helen Culver Fund for Race Psychology. Helen Culver was heir to the same fortune that had funded Hull House, with which Thomas was also regularly involved, and the *The Polish Peasant in Europe and America* is dedicated to her. Zaretsky calls it the single work of "large-scale social theory comparable to those of Max Weber, Emile Durkheim, and Georg Simmel." Like these European counterparts, Thomas and Znaniecki "sought to lay the basis for an empirically-based but non-deterministic sociological theory framed in terms of subjective and purposeful action" (Zaretsky, in Zaretsky, 1984, 1).

[19] Hereafter designated as *PP*.

[20] *Sex and Society* is something of a feminist tract, attempting to account for the inferior position of women in terms of their marginalization in production. The *Source Book* is an anthology of materials drawn from many disciplines that attempts to shed light on human origins. As such it is framed in evolutionary terms.

1888–1889 and thereafter returned frequently to Europe. In 1893 he enrolled in the new doctoral program at the University of Chicago. There he remained until his controversial dismissal in 1918.[21] Although he taught at several institutions in the years following, he never again held a permanent tenured appointment.

Znaniecki was born in Poland in 1882, trained mainly in philosophy, but forced to leave when barred from teaching because of his nationalist convictions (Poland still being partitioned into Russian, German, and Austrian sectors defined at the Congress of Vienna in 1815). He had met Thomas during one of the latter's European trips, and, as the story has it, turned up one day on Thomas's doorstep. About that time Thomas had already decided to focus on a single immigrant group rather than attempt to study several comparatively—his original intent—and to do so using the letters of immigrants as the principal source of data.[22] It would be difficult to imagine a more fortuitously timed collaboration, with Thomas bringing the sociological and theoretical skills, and Znaniecki the philosophical sophistication, knowledge of Poland, and the ability to translate. In later years Znaniecki made important independent contributions to sociology (see Bierstedt, 1981, Chap. 5).

PP is a work that may be thought of as having four interrelated constituent aspects. The first of these is as a study of what we have come to call "ethnic groups." *PP* was a study of *one* such group, originating in Russian Poland and emigrating to the United States. Set in the context of perceiving national groups as social problems, the study stimulated a great outpouring of research on nationality groups of all sorts over the next three decades and after. The work thus contributed decisively to the tradition of social problems study in American sociology, introducing and treating systematically the concept of "social disorganization," an idea that became a virtual domain assumption of American sociology during the depression years. Second, there is the attitudes-values conceptual scheme introduced by Thomas and Znaniecki. This basic conceptual framework was intended to provide the orientation and flexibility that would enable them to frame empirical work that brought together, in the spirit of Mead and the other pragmatists, we shall propose, the polarized foci of the social and the individual. Third, *PP* is a historical work, and although admittedly a historically rather weak one, one that nevertheless-again with the pragmatists—understands social life as a continuous process and transformation that is, in *some* broad and doubtless overly vague sense, evolutionary, although certainly not in the Spencerian sense. Finally, *PP* is self-consciously methodological at a level probably never previously reached in American sociology, a self-consciousness that may be seen, most particularly, in the authors' famous "Methodological Note" to *PP*.

The first of these four characterizations defines the empirical problem dimension of *PP*, the last three the foci of the authors' philosophical anthropology, theory of social change, and conception of the proper nature

---

[21] Thomas was evidently found with the wife of a soldier serving in France, and threatened with prosecution under the Mann act. There were very probably political motives involved as well.

[22] A method he hit upon after spying a trash basket full of them in a Chicago alley.

of sociological knowledge. In the discussion to follow, we shall depart from the format of previous chapters, in which the three problematics have been taken up and given extended discussion in turn. Because the last half of this chapter focuses almost entirely on *PP*, and because it is such a massive work, we shall first provide a descriptive section laying out the essentials of Thomas and Znaniecki's argument and their construction and use of empirical materials. We shall then conclude the chapter with a discussion of the ways the three problematics are implicated in their sociology as it appears in *PP*.

The Polish Peasant

Compared with the elaborate scheme Weber worked out for *ES*, the conceptual framework formulated by Thomas and Znaniecki is one of pristine simplicity, organized in terms of the concepts of "attitude," "values," "social organization," and "disorganization." The first two are fundamental in the sense that they answer to what the authors, in their "Methodological Note" to *PP*, take to be

> the two fundamental, practical problems which have constituted the center of attention of reflective social practice in all times. These are (1) the problem of the dependence of the individual upon social organization and culture, and (2) the problem of the dependence of social organization and culture upon the individual (Zaretsky, 1984, 57).[23]

Note that Thomas and Znaniecki refer to *social practice* as the guiding desideratum of the manner in which they formulate the theoretical task. The point of it all is creation of a social practice that will require a "social technique" to solve the two "problems," and any such social technique requires a theoretical basis. They intend to use the terms "social values" and "attitudes" to designate the "objective cultural elements" and "subjective characteristics of the members of the social group" respectively (57–58). "Social value" refers to

> any datum having an empirical content accessible to the members of some social group and a meaning with regard to which it is or may be an object of activity.

"Attitude" designates

> a process of individual consciousness which determines real or possible activity of the individual in the social world (58)

Thomas and Znaniecki think of these concepts as two sides of the same phenomenon, bonded in action: "The attitude is the individual counterpart

---

[23] Where possible, I will cite from the Zaretsky abridgement of *PP*; otherwise from the 1927 two-volume edition. The earlier Janowicz abridgement (Janowicz, 1966) is also useful.

of the social value" (50).[24] Common to both is the element of meaning. In the case of social values, the meaning is objective, in the sense, for example, of the meaning of foodstuff being its reference to eventual consumption, or of a tool in its reference to the work for which it is designed. In having reference to some meaningful activity, attitudes are conceptually distinct from "psychical states" or "psychological processes," which designate *states of being* abstracted from or considered as independent of the external world. Attitudes are always "toward something" and are not *psychological* data. This is similar to Weber's conception of social action.

Thomas and Znaniecki go on to maintain that in any actual social research it is necessary to make a programmatic decision about the relative importance of attitudes and values: "There is no possibility of giving to attitudes and values the same importance in a methodological scientific investigation: either attitudes must be subordinated to values or the contrary" (60–61). Why this must be so is not entirely clear. What Thomas and Znaniecki seem to have in mind here is a classification of the disciplines on the basis of whether they take one or the other as their primary object of interest. Disciplines dealing with particular domains of culture, art, economics, or language, for example, necessarily take values as their preeminent domain of interest, whereas social attitudes are the focus of social psychology (but not *individual* psychology, which takes as its "central field" universal psychic states, "the most elementary conscious phenomena": 62). In any case, *PP* itself belies the supposed imperative of concentrating on one or the other; its innovativeness lies precisely in its sustained analysis of Polish peasant life at *both* levels, and in showing the relationships between them.

This approach is reflected also in the second pair of concepts central to *PP*, "social organization" and "social disorganization." Social organization designates a condition of congruence or consistency between a society's or group's rules—a form taken by values, on the one hand, and the attitudes of individuals comprising the groups, on the other. Social disorganization refers to a "decrease of the influence of . . . rules on individual behavior" (Thomas and Znaniecki, 1927, 1128). This sounds Durkheimian, but Thomas and Znaniecki hasten to reject any equation of social with personal disorganization. An individual may indeed have a high level of personal life organization, defined as the ability to organize one's life "for efficient, progressive, and continuous realization of his fundamental interests" (1128–1129) under the most disorganized and chaotic of social conditions. (Indeed, this is an essential component of the theory of social change advanced in *PP*, as we shall see).

---

[24] Thomas's sociological social attitude—value polarity as it is worked out by him and Znaniecki in *PP*, is grounded on firm pragmatist foundations. Years earlier, in the introduction to *Source Book for Social Origins*, we find him advancing essential ideas of the pragmatist credo from James and Dewey as the most "serviceable standpoint for the examination of society and social change" (Thomas, 1909, 16). The central idea is "attention," which is "the mental attitude which takes hold of the outside world and manipulates it," and which "is associated with habit on the one hand and with crisis on the other" (17). The disturbance of habits creates crises, bringing attention into play to devise new modes of behavior. This is secured by achieving "control," attention and control being "the objective and subjective sides of the same process" (17).

The Polish Peasant in the Old World

Thomas and Znaniecki follow the Polish immigrants from the old traditional rural peasant society of Eastern Poland and the impact of and reaction to various modernizing and disorganizing forces there to their responses in the New World setting. Documentation in the form of extensive quotations from the peasant letters is presented throughout, and a book-length peasant autobiography is included in Part 4. These documents reveal that peasant life is organized around the family and the local community.

The Polish peasant family as depicted by Thomas and Znaniecki is the sort of solidary corporate group often since described in the literature. The bond between husband and wife is one of "respect" in which love has little or no place; marriages are arranged for economic and social reasons. The peasants in Russian Poland acquired their own land with the abolition of serfdom in 1864, and so many —perhaps most—came to own their own plots. Mostly these were small and passed to the son or sons when the father grew old. The parents had traditional rights of residence in their old age, but the father eventually loses his authority to the sons. The most important thing about the old peasant family is that it constituted a powerful organ of social control, spanning several generations and interlocking with a variety of extended kin groups. It was an adaptation to the economics of smallholding and the political domination of the nobility. Its most important function was probably maintaining a powerful control over the expression of any sort of individualism, by means of a variety of rituals, including gift giving in its Durkheimian-Maussian sense of symbolically representing and reinforcing the moral obligations of social bonds. The church plays an important role: Catholicism is the overall meaning system and the church has both material and ideal interests in maintaining the traditional system.

The disorganization of the family results primarily from the penetration of new economic and economically conditioned factors into the family and community: the position of the Polish economy in the world market, industrialization in Poland, the changing occupational structure, and the migration to urban Poland and elsewhere, including, of course, the United States.

Change occurs as a consequence of social processes that encourage individualistic values. This may be seen in the transformations that exchange processes undergo. Under the condition of family solidarity, in which every action is "merely one moment of this solidarity" (Zaretsky, 1984, 85), the rendering of help "simply strengthens and actualizes the habitual expectation of a general attitude of benevolent solidarity from the other person, which may find its expression at any time in any act of reciprocal help" (86). The weakening of this solidarity allows the act to assume an independent status or meaning, i.e., to acquire a strictly economic meaning. The result is the introduction of the "egotistic" [sic] attitude into economic relations, an attitude destructive of family and communal life. This may be a quite protracted process in which the ultimate point—the quantification of economic value—displaces existing social relations.

At first only family income and its use for collective benefit is affected. For example, an emigrated son at first scrimps and saves and sends the larger part of his earnings home, but in time this becomes onerous, and even unjust. His kin are then perceived as undeserving exploiters, and less money is sent back. The egoistic attitude comes to challenge the values of family and communal solidarity. A further stage occurs with the impact on property; struggles over inheritance may be much more destructive of family solidarity, especially if the point of litigation is reached. However, it is a cardinal point for Thomas and Znaniecki that social disorganization "never goes so far as to destroy entirely the demand for a regulated, organized and harmonious life" (1212). Again, although there is no necessary relationship, personal disorganization may, and often does, accompany social disorganization. Excessive use of alcohol, smoking, crime, sexual promiscuity, and other forms of deviance reflect the individualistic attitude in its "hedonistic" form (1143).

Social disorganization is manifest at first in individualistic *attitudes*, but eventually these begin to assume a collective reality in a new array of *values:* hedonism, vanity, egocentric economic attitudes, new forms of sexual appeal. But the community, in various ways, attempts to reassert its control over the growing individualism by preserving the old system. The church plays a critical role here, and various forms of repression, e.g., lynching, become more common. But disorganization is also the condition of innovation. New methods are introduced: shaming, shunning, and others. The beginning of a new synthesis of regulation occurs: the church, for example, may modify some of its traditional rules, making them more consistent with the changed social behavior.

But such actions are generally unsuccessful. In a sense the struggle is already lost because it is "prevalently retroactive:" attempts to reinforce weakened definitions work against earlier occurring changes. Such attempts reflect naive expectations of social groups regarding traditional definitions that are assumed to endure indefinitely even through periods of rapid change (1248). In Thomas and Znaniecki's view, there is no way of destroying the new attitudes once they have appeared. All attempts at preservation are only delaying actions. Repression, in particular, is ineffective, because it is based on fear. Sooner or later the community must face "the most important and difficult part of its task—the reorganization of attitudes" (1257). This occurs in terms of what Thomas and Znaniecki call "revolutionary attitudes."

Revolutionary attitudes, they argue, are different from those we have described above. The kind of opposition to the rules indicated in "revolt" is individualistic, however many individuals may be involved. A revolutionary tendency may involve demands for the individual, but differs from revolt in being

> "a demand for new values for a whole group—community, class, nation, etc.: each individual acting not only in his own name but also in the name of others" (1265),

and in seeking

> "to abolish the traditional system or at least some of the schemes of behavior which are its parts, to destroy permanently their influence within the given

group, and thus to open the way to a general and permanent satisfaction of those needs which cannot be freely satisfied while the system lasts" (1266)

Thomas and Znaniecki are of the view that revolution is the only "efficient" way of dealing with social disorganization, at least of the type studied in *PP*. Repression or other attempts to preserve or reinstate the traditional system lack the sine qua non of inducing the individual to accept the larger system of emotions and beliefs; only a change in the system itself can bring attitudes and values into congruence. Interestingly, they exclude the actual 1905 political revolution in Russia from their analysis despite the fact that it falls within the period of their data, on their ground that it was more an urban than a rural movement (which was true) and that relevant documents were not available. But they also go beyond these understandable limitations to make a further case on the basis of subject matter being revolutionary *attitudes,* not *acts,* and that the former may be more significant sociologically than the latter (1269, n.). Their focus is therefore restricted to what they call "class" and "religious" revolutionism. Class revolutionism is focused on two points of opposition between peasants and lords: the right of pasturing and access to dry wood on manorial lands, and "land-hunger"; the peasants wish to appropriate government and noble lands to expand their holdings, on the ethical ground that cultivated land is rightfully the property of the cultivator.

Although they introduce the category of revolution into their analysis, Thomas and Znaniecki really have nothing to say about it as a process in and of itself. For reasons about which one can only speculate, in this respect, they quite obviously void their own basic axiom of studying attitudes and values as these are found in action. Instead, the focus shifts to "social reorganization," by which they mean the creation of new schemes of behavior and ultimately a new social system that somehow reconciles the old "absorption of the individual by the group" with "the new self-assertion of the individual against or independently of the group" (1305). They disavow any interest in "the methods by which the social leader discovers the new needs of society and invents new forms of social organization" (1304) and turn to what they consider to be the central aspects of social reorganization: leadership, education, the press, and the role of a variety of new cooperative associations.

Peasant leadership in Poland has come from among four groups: the nobility, urban intellectuals, the clergy, and the peasants themselves. All have faced what we would now call structural barriers to effective leadership. The nobility, obviously, have at least some interests opposed to those of the peasants; the intellectuals are idealists with little actual contact and understanding of peasants and peasant life; the lower clergy are in a very good position to act as leaders, but the church itself has always had a vested interest in maintaining the *status quo* and certainly in discouraging revolution; peasants generally lack the education, perspective, and skills important for leadership. The importance of all of these sources of leadership, Thomas and Znaniecki believe, will increase in the future.

Although they disavow interest in formulating and analyzing *types* of leadership and claim to be concerned only with the "psychology of leadership"

(1311), Thomas and Znaniecki do draw from the letters a typology of leadership having a partial resemblance to Weber's. Leaders exercise leadership through (1) fear or hope, by granting or withholding or withdrawing positive or negative values; (2) prestige, similar to Weber's charismatic leadership, wherein the leader commands by virtue of his personality and the moral significance of his pronouncements and acts; and (3) efficiency, which bears *some* similarity to Weber's legal-rational form, in which the leader's ideas "are judged morally or practically right and are accepted by others on their own merits after reflection or practical test" (1334). The first of these is of little significance for peasant movements because the distribution of already existing resources is not involved in movement leadership. The authors puzzle over the significance of the other two, finally arguing that the intrinsic irrationality of prestige is perhaps a necessary phase in the growth of a peasant movement, but that this gives way to the rationality of efficiency. This process, they observe, occurs more rapidly in some areas than others, particularly in economic life, evidently because of the rationality presumed intrinsic to that domain. The idea of a shift from leadership based on prestige to one based on efficiency is unfortunately not developed by Thomas and Znaniecki (indeed, the data of the letters scarcely seem to support much theorizing on this point at all), but it is important, because it fits in with their view that the movement from traditional peasant life to an urban existence as progressive and driven by rational considerations, and increasingly bringing into being *rationaly* forms of social organization.

The peasant letters present a rich vein of material on the significance of education in reorganization, data that indeed justify the authors' claim that they possess "unparalled sociological interest" (1360). The letters document mainly the consequences of learning to read on the horizons of the peasant consciousness. This stimulates the "desire for new experience," one of the famous four wishes. Some degree of literacy, it appears, was important in that it inculcated a greater receptivity to the claims of the various leaders, and promoted acquisition of a critical perspective on peasant life and society.

The press obviously builds on existing literacy to create some degree of peasant consciousness, seemingly an amalgam of class and national elements. In Poland the press (particularly the *Gazette Swigtezcna*) was of great significance because of the weakness of leadership and because the main links of peasant communities were *vertical*, to church, state, and a few other associations, whereas the press was indispensible in creating a *horizontal* nationwide "social opinion."

Finally, a variety of new and old associations were instrumental in reorganization. As to the latter, there were attempts to reform the local commune into an active political body and to redirect the existing economic organization of the community. But more important were the creation of a host of a new associations: cooperatives, agricultural organizations, savings banks, industrial associations, all voluntary and cooperative in structure. Thomas and Znaniecki place great emphasis on these groups because of their putative level of rationality and the connection of this to individualism: They are *planned,* and this is possible because they are *voluntary* and *participative.* This creates a "harmony of individual and social needs" (1429). The individual becomes oriented to problems of the organization because the organization is *designed,* which is to say, rationally intended to meet the individual's needs. If it were not so, there would be little reason for *most* to participate. But the very existence of such associations—a new level of social organization—creates new problems specifically of the institution: its growth, security, functioning, and so on, problems with which the individual becomes involved simply by virtue of membership. In all this the cooperative method stands in rather stark contrast with coercion: "By starting with individualism it develops a positive interest in fostering social welfare and progress" and although not perfect, is an ideal "enormously capable of becoming the leading principle of a social order whose possibilities of expansion and improvement are practically unlimited" (1431).[25]

The larger significance of all this for Thomas and Znaniecki lies in the *national* significance of the peasant movement. This is essentially a national movement, in which the peasantry is in process of becoming the "future bearer of the economic unity of the nation" (1442–1443). The letters do show a growth of national consciousness, although Thomas and Znaniecki's *interpretation,* that national values encompass all others, is perhaps pressing a reasonable point too far. Theoretically, the movement starts from the isolated and parochial primary group sunk in tradition, with little capacity for rational action, and moves toward a form of social organization based on formal associations that are participative and rational in their approach to the problem of social reconstruction. Modernization proceeds in terms of the sublimation of individualism into cooperative life organized at the national level. This clearly reflects an anticapitalist stance, but Thomas and Znaniecki have little to say about it. Is national cooperation to be socialistic?[26] (Evidently not). What about the tendencies of formal organizations toward bureaucratization and goal displacement? Doesn't class conflict, discussed not at all by the authors, have some significance in this process? And what is the role of the state, which in their account remains untheorized?

Analysis of change in the peasant communities of Russian Poland established the theory of disorganization and reorganization. The conditions faced by the immigrants in the United States provided a radically different social situation to which it could be applied.

The Polish Peasant in the United States

Thomas's and Znaniecki's analysis of the polish peasant in America is predicated on the assumption that Polish-American society can be understood neither as just an extension of traditional Polish peasant life, nor as a process of assimilation, but rather as a complex amalgam of both. The new Polish-American society is a new and quite homogeneous group, partly a

[25] Thomas and Znaniecki here obviously touch on the theory of democracy, without explicitly identifying it as such. In more explicitly political terms, their argument can be construed as asserting that democracy (in being) is the only type of order that is self-legitimating (a point, we might note, that does not seem to have occurred to Weber).

[26] In this regard Zaretsky remarks that Thomas and Znaniecki always described economic rationality individualistically and were therefore unable to identify nonrational economic behavior.

"spontaneous" reproduction of the old, but a reproduction occurring under vastly differing conditions. All the main Polish institutions of social control—family, community, church—become far weaker in the United States than in Poland. The beginnings of reorganization found in Poland have their parallels in the United States, but unfold in a setting in which the various sources of leadership in Poland are absent, thus setting the immigrants on their own and encouraging a much greater independence, for good or ill. Polish-American society has begun, and will inevitably continue, to respond to the challenge of life in the United States by greater conscious reflection and action based on this. But in the process it is experiencing a ravaging social disorganization and individual demoralization.

Two characteristics of Polish emigration to the United States have placed an indelible mark on the resulting Polish-American society. First, this immigration was for the most part a movement of individuals, not families (which was much more the case in the emigration from German and Austrian Poland); second, landless peasants were heavily overrepresented in United States emigration. Both of these features contributed heavily to the disorganization of Polish-American society. In contrast to short-term, usually seasonal emigrants to Germany, whose interest is mainly in supplementing the grudging yield of their small plots by working for a time under relatively high-wage conditions, the emigrants to the United States anticipate a dramatic change in their circumstances. They expect to return to Poland (although far less than half of them do so) considerably advanced materially, with very favorable prospects of buying land and a house.

Thomas and Znaniecki analyze Polish-American society at both local and supra local levels.[27] These institutions achieve some degree of integration of the individual into Polish-American society, but to a far lesser extent than was true in Poland. Early on, Polish settlements in the United States were enclaves grown up through kin and village attachments, and with a good deal of hostility toward and rivalry with other groups. Such a condition tends to perpetuate everything traditional. But the demands of the new situation—particularly the radically different economic system—encourage a degree of collective economic rationality on a larger scale. No longer are the extended kin network, the community, and the somewhat more formal arrangements of the parish available as a traditional "safety net" for people who are unemployed, unemployable, landless, alcoholic, disabled, mentally deficient, and so on. In Poland the individual might be impoverished for any of these reasons and remain so, but would rarely be excluded from the group on moral grounds. In the United States, however, the alternative is an appeal to public charity, an act constituting a "downfall" resulting in disgrace not only for the individual in question, but the larger community as well.[28]

The result was the establishment of various kinds of mutual aid societies, which Thomas and Znaniecki analyze with considerable perspicacity.

---

[27] This discussion is found in *PP*, Part III: Chaps I–III.

[28] A point of some interest on which Thomas and Znaniecki do not expand: One wonders whether this might not be to some extent a reflection of the relief system itself, demanding as it often does that individuals denude themselves of their dignity as a condition of receiving help.

These are, of necessity, large-scale formal organizations embracing virtually all Polish-American communities, but totally unlike conventional insurance companies in having strong participative local branches. The mutual aid society provides first of all for death and sickness benefits that were taken care of in Poland by traditional forms of organization. But its importance to the Polish-American community cannot be accounted for only by the magnitude of the economic benefits. Thomas and Znaniecki analyze these societies in terms of what functionalists have long since labeled a latent function: to become, first, "the social organ of the community," and beyond this, "the source of all initiative and the instrument for the realization of all plans initiated" (1522). The latter replaces the natural spontaneous cooperation of the old village. Thus the society spawns or spins off groups or activities of every sort: intellectual, religious, recreational, and so on. In a sense, the mutual aid society *becomes* Polish-American society. Thomas and Znaniecki see it as embodying a degree of conscious rationality that constitutes a first step, as it were, of a journey that will ultimately end up with the Poles more integrated into American life, although by no means undergoing total assimilation (as other members of the Chicago school, conventional evolutionists mostly, and Robert Park, in particular, envisaged it: see Park and Burgess, 1924). Indeed, the assumption of the indefinite survival of ethnic or national identity runs all through *PP*. The organization provides "a minimum of rational order" for those social relations essential to maintaining a minimum of social cohesion (1590).

Of great importance also is the parish. Just as the mutual aid society has a social significance far beyond its manifest function, so also does the parish transcend its formal nature as a religious association. Thomas and Znaniecki characterize it as "the old community reorganized and concentrated" (1523), combining in its activities the functions of both parish and commune in Poland (the commune being a political-administrative entity). The greater breadth of the parish in the United States, however, by no means enhances its effectiveness. Indeed, its capacity to actually control the life activities of its members is much lower than it was in Poland. This is so partly because of the rapid pace of change, the inability to actually administer a given area, and the absence of legitimate repressive or coercive measures.

Both mutual aid societies and parish reflect an adaptation and modification of old institutions to new conditions; both are creations of Poles and must be thought of as *accomplishments of immigrants,* a *creation* of something new from the old in the presence of specific external challenges, an attempt at *reorganization* (for some reason Thomas and Znaniecki do not employ this term in Part 3). One sees something on the order of the "I" and "me" at work here.

To mutual insurance society and parish must be added the national patriotic organizations, especially the Polish National Alliance and the Polish Roman Catholic Union. These are political organizations that reflect the marginal position of the immigrants. The primary interest of the alliance was to turn Poles into an extension of the Polish nation; the union, reflecting the interests of church and clergy, wanted to create a strong "political idealism," in large degree by promoting the parish as the agency of national preservation. The larger but temporary significance of these is to heighten and intensify the separateness of Poles in the United States whether in terms of Polish nationalism or Polish-American ethnic identity.

Such "supra-territorial" organizations, as Thomas and Znaniecki call them, do, however, give individuals a chance to satisfy their need for both "response" and "recognition."[29] At the local level they are small enough so that the individual knows virtually all others (thus satisfying the need for response), but large enough, being supra-communal, to allow the individual to feel an enhanced sense of identity as a Pole, participation being possible only as a Pole and so building in an inherent *recognition*. But these organizations must be judged only partial successes: On the one hand, they lack the means of *controlling* individualistic behavior; on the other, in important ways they find it in their interest to *encourage* it (e.g., the independent economic activity of the individual). The result is extensive social and personal disorganization.

The conditions of immigrant life are conducive to very far-reaching personal disorganization or demoralization of the immigrant, defined as the "decay of the personal life-organization of an individual member of a social group" (1647). The strength of primary group ties in Poland implies a need for similar ones in the United States, at least in the first and second generations (and there were barely two quantitatively significant adult generations of Poles in the United States by the first decade of the century). The members of the immigrating generation are able to sustain the level of life-organization by reproducing the old life-ways to some extent, but the second generation "degenerates" further. Although "better adapted to the practical conditions of American life their moral horizon grows still narrower . . . and social interests shallower" (1650–1651). Under primary group conditions, such a moral narrowing is not restricted to some particular aspect of life, but, as the very term "life-organization" indicates, affects the entire personality. Its manifestations in behavioral terms occur in many different ways. Thomas and Znaniecki single out what they consider to be the most important of these for analysis: economic dependency, breakdown of married life, and murder, among adults; vagabondage and delinquency among boys; sexual immorality among girls.

The account of economic distress among working-class families could have been written fifty years later with little changed. Reproduction of an ethnically and racially changing underclass has proved to be a chronic condition of American capitalism and its "exceptionalist" welfare state policies. The worker is subject to the vagaries of the market, and depending partly on his or her personal condition (disability, mental condition, skill level, etc.), may cease to produce an income or produce one chronically below the level of subsistence of the family. Before the social legislation of the 1930s, the mutual health insurance organizations, although crucial welfare agencies, were able to deal with the widespread deprivation and disorganization with only extremely limited effectiveness. This was true as well of the social agencies, but in this case the negative effects may very well have outweighed the positive. The agencies assisted those in poverty only by interfering in their lives and creating dependence, thus encouraging the further decay of

---

[29] Technical terms to be discussed in the section following.

their life-organization. The desperation this engendered all too often resulted in total demoralization; prison or asylum were welcomed as forms of relief.

Marriage under conditions of primary group life in Poland was a social institution embedded in and made stable by a set of kin and communal relations. The temperamental fit of husband and wife, whether love, affection, or other emotions were present, was of little importance. In the United States this order of significance is reversed: Marriage rests almost exclusively on the temperamental attitudes of the individuals.[30] Again, much of the description found in the documents could have occurred yesterday. Thomas and Znaniecki say that they show "the cooperation of several causes" (1707), and indeed, although they distinguish "temperamental," "sexual," "economic," and interference by families and state agencies, as types, similar patterns recur throughout all of them. Violence, excessive use of alcohol, suicidal tendencies, economically induced distress, rape, sexual infidelity, and more, appear frequently as syndromes, leading to disruption of the marriage. In many cases—once again thoroughly familiar to sociologists who followed—this demoralization may become very far-reaching without breaching the outer appearances of respectability. As is the case of economic life, when state or private agencies (police, courts, social agencies) enter upon the scene—in *every* case with which they are familiar, say Thomas and Znaniecki— external agencies failed to positively affect the weakened marriage bond and often exacerbated it by converting the situation into one of arbitration, in effect, redefining husband and wife as contesting parties (1748). To cite just one common pattern, in their rather chauvinist view, for the wife to call in the police and have the husband arrested for violent acts against her is an "irreparable act" of interference into conjugal privacy which humiliates the husband by offending his sense of masculine dignity, and which he can therefore never forgive (1750).

Deviant behavior on the part of children, Thomas and Znaniecki believe, cannot strictly be termed "demoralization," since little if any moral influence has been exercised over them in their demoralized families in the first place. Most of the influences present in the old country are absent. Parents, even in homes that are not demoralized, are generally not equipped to effectively educate their children; in urban society this requires special skills and understanding. In the old country more or less effective moral education of young boys required little beyond unreflective but consistent reproduction of the traditional milieu. For girls, loss of virginity in the old society was a disgrace and placed marriage chances in serious jeopardy, sometimes forcing the young woman to leave for the city. In the United States, by contrast, sexual encounters take on the character of a mere incident and are typically just one part of a generally disorganized life pattern. Attempts to exercise parental authority are as likely to provoke revolt as they are to restrain the girl's behavior. In much of this—youth criminality, female promiscuity—the emerging consumer society arching over the consciousness of everyone, plays a major role in enticing the young into behavior that

---

[30] The concept of temperament will be briefly discussed later. Suffice to say at this point that it refers to a level of organization of the individual attitudes independent of social influences.

satisfies the desire for new experience, but that cannot be integrated into the existing life-organization schemes.

Throughout the entire discussion, Thomas and Znaniecki remark repeatedly on what they consider to be the *only* solution to the demoralization of individuals in all its forms. This amounts to a quite "Durkheimian" reorganization of life in terms of a morality like that of the Old World. There will have to be "new ideals" of family life (1752). Economically the Pole needs "an attractive economic aim, or a change in traditional economic attitudes" (i.e., the Poles must enter into the opportunity system). Juvenile delinquents require "strong and positive standards and rules of behavior" (1797). There are scarcely any institutions capable of this in the present situation. The worst possible policy would be further penetration of external institutions into communal life, for they create more demoralization than they alleviate. Whatever the solution, it must come from within, and although Thomas and Znaniecki are not very specific, they seem to envisage a kind of halfway house between strict ethic separatism and assimilation. However, not only the extensiveness of social disorganization in Polish-American society, but the capacity of American institutions to provide a foundation for a reorganized life organization challenge their progressive theorization of this point. Young women, even if they are able to organize their lives in more strictly "American" terms, do so in the framework merely of the "more or less superficial rules of *decorum*" (1821). New ideals of family life are needed, but it is questionable whether the United States has any "really vital family ideals to give" (1752). These and similar observations condemn American society as one characterized by a mass depersonalization that subordinates social life to economic interest and that is capable of intervening to "help" in only the most unintelligent and destructive ways imaginable.

Thomas and Znaniecki end up, however, on an upbeat if vague and ultimately unconvincing note. They speculate very briefly on a future in which the mutual aid societies undergo a further stage of evolution and unite across ethnic or national group lines, incorporating "all the important groups" (1927) and creating a "cooperative society." Such an organization would retain its solidarity-promoting function at the local level, yet be able to represent local interests consciously and rationally at the national level. Thomas and Znaniecki were neither assimilationist nor ethnically particularist; they clearly perceived the pitfalls of either choice as an absolute. One might say that they were "pluralist," but without much clarity about what this might mean concretely, apart from the understanding that an extreme pluralism—i.e., ethnic isolation—implied a future of continuing political irrelevance and powerlessness.

Attitudes, Values, and Personality Types

In their "Methodological Note" Thomas and Znaniecki conceptualized attitudes and values as two sides of the social process, implying, perhaps requiring, that any social action be approached in terms of both attitudes and values (disregarding the homily regarding emphasis). In part 4 of *PP*, after the empirical materials had been analyzed, Thomas and Znaniecki drew out this principle in greater detail. Viewed concretely, human subjectivity has two conceptual components—temperament and character—that in some (varying) degree of integration constitute the "personality." The personality, or individual character, we might say, is the most comprehensive unit in terms of which we may conceptualize the subjective human consciousness. This is never a fixed reality but always a process of development, although of course something that exhibits great variation. These processes Thomas and Znaniecki refer to as "lines of genesis" (1839), and any particular line, they claim, is to be *explained* by application of some "scientific law." Lines of genesis must be formulated in terms of the relation between the particular attitudes defining the main orientation of the personality, on the one hand, and the values present in the milieu, on the other. Thus, a given attitude, a, may become modified as b, and then c, and so on. But this occurs in a fashion that could be interpreted as dialectical (a term avoided by the authors), through the mediation of values:

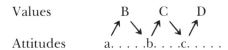

An individual's stock of attitudes may be viewed in terms of its congruence with the values present already in the milieu. Those congruent with his or her attitudes will be accepted, thus probably reinforcing and reproducing them. Those not congruent will probably be rejected. A milieu presenting a limited range of values—such as peasant Poland—is obviously not conducive to the expansion of an individual's attitudes.

Now consider the concepts "temperament" and "character." "Temperament" is defined as

> the fundamental original group of attitudes of the individual as existing independently of any social influences (1844),

"character" as

> the set of organized and fixed groups of attitudes developed by social influences operating upon the temperamental bases (1844).

Temperamental factors are essentially organic, expressed biologically but not given in consciousness. The individual does not consciously organize temperamental attitudes into some sort of meaningful set or harmony. They are just expressed, or inhibited, as such. *Character*-attitudes, in contrast, are expressions of "more or less general tendencies" (1845). Productions of social action are elements of a series, a line of genesis, consciously intended and explicit, at least at times. Attitudes regarding the nature of hunger or sexuality, and for providing their satisfaction, are character-attitudes independent of the temperamental factors themselves. Character-attitudes should not be thought of atomistically; indeed, Thomas and Znaniecki hold that neither attitudes nor values can be understood by "wrenching" them from their broader cultural context. The Puritan's clustering of attitudes regarding sexuality or labor might be a good example (my example: DLW). The relation between these levels of individual experience is perhaps obvious: "An individual with . . . nothing but his temperamental attitudes is not yet a social personality, but is able to become one" (1850). One's temperamental attitudes have implications, one might say, for the sort of social personality one becomes, but for this they must be "reflectively organized." The emergence of some kind of organization of character-attitudes, then, is a kind of "character-building" in that, by definition, it always includes at least some elements of conscious reflective intentional action. It is tempting to understand Thomas and Znaniecki as here having formulated an idea akin to Mead's theory of the reflexive self, but in a concrete form necessary for analysis of empirical materials.

Parallel to the process of character organization is that of life-organization. The character, one might say, is a conscious, more or less intellectual construction, directed inward, perhaps similar to Mead's internal conversation, whereas the life-organization is directed *outward*, a "development of intellectual methods of controlling social reality" (1851). Character organization is an organized response to the imperatives of temperament; life-organization, mastery or control of *social objects*. Thomas and Znaniecki define life-organization as

> the existence, within the sphere of an individual, of a limited number of selected and organized groups of social values which play a predominant part in his life both as partial causes and partial effects of his more or less organized attitudes (1843)

Life-organization may develop in two different ways, as a ready-made scheme imposed on the individual through deliberate education or other forms of learning, or where the individual "works out himself a definition of every new situation in conformity with his existing attitude, which grows in definiteness . . ." (1871–1872). And the mode of acquisition makes a big difference, leading in fact to "opposite" life-organizations. In the first instance the individual will forever remain "dependent on society and its ready schemes," and further development will not occur; in the second, the individual will be able "to construct progressively better schemes to suit his spontaneous evolution" (1879–1880).

The combinations of attitudes comprising the character and life-organization that hypothetically could exist as lines of genesis is virtually infinite, but for scientific purposes it is of course necessary to identify specific constellations. A set of basic distinctions can be made in terms of the relative rigidity or openness of one's character, yielding the famous three character types "Philistine," "Bohemian," and "creative" (1853ff.). The Philistine possesses such a rigid organization of attitudes that receptivity to any new values is virtually precluded; response occurs only to those most permanent influences in the milieu. The Bohemian character is a virtually *unorganized* congeries of attitudes: Some temperamental attitudes may remain in their primary form while others have become intellectualized, for the most part remaining unrelated to one another. Such an individual stands open to "any and all influences." The Philistine is more typical of traditional conditions wherein a limited array of values define the social world; the Bohemian, a denizen of urban worlds where all conceivable values present themselves as a cultural cafeteria, although this is by no means a one-to-one relationship: Bohemians and Philistines appear in all types of societies. The creative individual, in contrast to both, possesses a "settled and organized character," but one that does not exclude the possibility of evolution, since its principle of organization is *productive activity* and it is oriented toward preconceptions of future lines of development of both character and social organization. The creative personality is, however, rather transparently, more of a philosophical ideal than an existing actual personality type; it figures hardly at all in Thomas's and Znaniecki's analysis.

From the standpoint of the evolution of society in a progressive direction, the first two types are exceedingly nonfunctional. The Philistine remains closed to precisely those new values required to transcend the social disorganization of the times; the Bohemian has no sense of inner direction (more or less in David Riesman's sense), and so no criteria for *selecting* among values. The Bohemian adapts easily, but never acquires a systematic life-organization. In a society comprised mostly of Bohemian personalities, both the society and its individuals would evidently just drift along. It is only the creative individual who is fit for the task of remaking society in a humane direction.

The production of Philistine or Bohemian characters occurs through the conflictful struggle of the individual and society. "There is," write Thomas and Znaniecki, "no preexisting harmony between the individual and the social factors of personal evolution. . . . Personal evolution is always a struggle between the individual and society" (1861). The attitudes of the individual—temperamental and characterological—are continuously being suppressed by society's agents; the individual persists in attempting to manifest them, whether impulsively and irrationally or through the rationality of an emerging life-organization. Completely successful suppression produces an individual devoid of problems, with no internal contradictions, no possibility for self-development, a "limited, stable, self-satisfied Philistine" (1871). Completely unsuccessful suppression results in an individual who is incapable of dealing with life situations, is a nonconformist, and who rebels continuously, but in no consistent or organized fashion.

This formulation has *conflict* at its core and in this way departs significantly from Mead's account of self and society, in which conflict is marginalized. It is also without doubt closer to the reality of self and society relations, and consistent with research or personality, development, and related fields. In these aspects of their analysis, it may be Freud, whose popularity in the United States was at the time growing rapidly, whose influence is to be seen.

Philistinism and Bohemianism are part and parcel of any social order, but in today's world of rapid modernization new problems of life-organization are appearing. As the division of labor expands and as individuals require greater and greater specialization not only in occupational life, but in all spheres of experience, Philistinism assumes an increasingly narrow form. This is unlike the typical Philistinism of peasant society, where a more or less common life was led by all, and the development of specialized and separated spheres of experience was held to a minimum (with the peasant class), or, to suggest another example, the medieval guild. Indeed, in somewhat polemical vein, Thomas and Znaniecki assert that the modern professional is "the narrowest type of Philistine the world has ever seen" (1887). In modern urban society, unity of character is achieved at the cost of an unparalleled narrowness of interests. The "new Philistinism" is thus one of dissociated personalities, and this may be the central social problem of the time. Such characters are especially vulnerable to social changes that impact on the social organization of the groups to which their life-organization is adapted. The disruption and decay of intellectual life in American universities with the onset of World War I, when the ability to engage in productive work was lost, is one example (1889). And beyond this, a related problem emerges. The pace of change is becoming so rapid, with group formation and dissolution so common, that it becomes impossible for them to organize and maintain the attitudinal complexes of their members. Society is "losing all its old machinery for the determination and stabilization of individual characters" (1890).

But these conditions cannot continue to exist and deepen. The very nature of this evolution not only creates the crisis but suggests that an emerging definition of the situation (my use of the term: DLW) will lead to a new reorganization. The evolving division of labor creates inefficiencies at both social and individual levels. At the individual level, specialization and the pace of change undercut the effectiveness of individuals in all spheres of activity; at the social level they institute a chronic competitive or conflictful state that becomes increasingly intolerable, Thomas and Znaniecki evidently think, to the actors themselves. There will emerge—indeed, the process has already begun—new demands for efficiency and cooperation. Although associational life must become more cooperative, it will be "more necessary," they say, not unambiguously and begging to question, "to leave to every individual as much freedom as is compatible with efficient cooperation" (1906).

On this issue Thomas and Znaniecki are by no means Durkheimians. They do not imagine that human collective life can be managed only through a common or collective consciousness. Their vision is of a pluralist society, not one in which all groups are assimilated to some dominant set of values and norms. They are perhaps closer to Weber, never imagining that a complex industrial urban society can exorcise conflict from its normal functioning.

However, their view of the engine of change does suggest that, despite the innovativeness of their analysis, they did not, for whatever reason, really come to grips with the problem of the implications of their work for the future. While capitalism is understood to be an exploitative and destructive system, socialism as an alternative is hardly so much as mentioned, despite the fact that the pre-World War I years witnessed the strongest socialist party formation in American history, although only very limited inroads had been made among Polish-Americans. Like Progressives generally, Thomas and Znaniecki wanted some middle road, the early manifestations of which were not obvious anywhere in the Western world in the second decade of the century, and that only in a few path-breaking lands had by the 1930s begun to take the form of social democracy. Social democracy still remains in important respects unestablished in the United States, and one can only speculate whether or not Thomas and Znaniecki's diagnosis of the present would differ greatly from the way they saw it in 1918.

The Four Wishes and the Definition of the Situation

No mention has thus far been made of the well-known four (actually five) wishes: for response, recognition, new experience, security, and mastery (73). The first two are basic to all social life and generally met under primary group conditions by the various forms of social activity in which the worth of the participating individual is manifest, and in realization of one's sexuality. New experience comes into play in situations of change where the individual seeks the new, in many possible ways: sexual, aesthetic, intellectual, travel, adventure, and so on. Mastery is rooted in the emotion of hate, but may be sublimated into socially worthwhile activities. Security is fundamental in some basic sense to all social life.

The wishes thread their way throughout *PP,* ever-present but called to action only here and there, layered over the real analysis of family, community, disorganization, and so on, but adding little to any of it. I suggest that they can be ignored with little loss of content or theoretical power. They are a survival of the instinct theories of the past as these had been incorporated into earlier American sociology,[31] particularly in Small's sociology and Thomas dropped them after *PP.* Such paradigm mixes commonly appear and are common in transitional periods, and particularly in works such as *PP,* and usually take the form of some sort of theoretical eclecticism, the possibly contradictory features of which may become transparent only later, with the advantage of historical perspective. Martindale makes this point apropos of the four wishes.

> The habit of mind associated with instinct theories inclined social scientists to speak as if the various presumed organic motors of conduct (instincts, desires, wishes, interests, or drives) were the direct and primary causes of behavior, even secondary causes of conduct. The new idea was that the organic motor was not the cause of conduct in its raw form but only in the form it assumed as a product of experience (Martindale, 1981, 326, n.26)

The concept for which Thomas is best known, the "definition of the situation," does not appear formally as a theoretically central concept in his work until publication of *The Unadjusted Girl* in 1923 (Thomas, 1923). There, after briefly glossing the *PP* theme that individuals may come to exert some degree of rational determination of their actions only after controlling and inhibiting their maladaptive responses, Thomas goes on to maintain that

> Prior to any self-determined act of behavior there is always a stage of examination and deliberation which we may call *the definition of the situation*

---

[31] Although they perhaps can be reinterpreted as social in nature, (see Wiley, 1986a).

> ... Gradually, a whole life-policy and the personality of the individual
> himself follow from a series of such definitions (Thomas, 1923, 42).

Note the emphasis here on specifically rational processes, "examination" and
"deliberation," and the fact that this rationality may become the all-encom-
passing principle on one's life-organization, a central theme of *PP*. Thomas
then contributes on to recapitulate essentially Meadian themes: the beginning
of the acquisition of the definition of the situation in the family, then a
reaching out to embrace the entire community as a moral code, in effect,
Mead's "generalized other." But they also emphasize the *conflicts* that differing
definitions of the situation inevitably create (42–44). So while it is true that
the idea of the definition of the situation becomes central in *The Unadjusted
Girl* and that the four wishes drop out, it would be incorrect to think that
the basic idea was not of importance in *PP*. The term itself appears in many
places in *PP* (e.g., 1737, 1858, 1875). Thomas did not change his basic
pragmatist understanding of the essential nature of social life; he did drop
a set of concepts reflecting the domain assumption of the instinctive determination of social behavior that was being displaced by the very ideas central
to *PP*.

THE POLISH PEASANT: CONTEXT AND CRITIQUE

In Chapter 10, the centrality of Lamarckianism in Spencer's work, and more
broadly in England, was discussed, but little was said regarding its importance
in the United States. In the case of Spencer, of course, Lamarack stood—
uncomfortably—side by side with Darwin. In the ferment of late nineteenth
century evolutionary theory, with the biological and social sciences still only
partially differentiated, and several major theories—Lamarckism, Darwinism,
Galtonism, and by the turn of the century Weismann's gene theory leading
to the rediscovery of the Mendelian trait—competing with one another, such
combinations were commonplace. This was so in American social and
psychological science in the early decades of the twentieth century.[32] But
Spencer's combination of Lamarck and Darwin was not typical; more commonly Lamarckism was a defense against and counter to Darwinism. As
evolutionary biology Darwinism is determinist, leaving no space for explanations at other levels, and to the extent that it is anything more than a set
of normative prescriptions and proscriptions, *social* Darwinism shares this
deterministic character. Lamarckism was a theory of parallel evolution that
remained attractive to many progressives because it anchored the future in
biology without the pessimistic outlook of Darwinsim, by promising continued
mental evolution. In the absence of a developed and articulated concept of
culture, it was "the mechanism by which man's conscious social activities
affected and effected his further physical evolution"; to abandon it would

---

[32] Especially in psychology. Wiley points out that in cutting its ties to psychology, sociology
turned its back on instinct conceptions (but not necessarily evolutionary ones), leaving the
opened-up space available for nonbiological formulations (Wiley, 1985).

be to do no less than "yield up the social sciences to an unreconstructed biological determinism" (Stocking, 1968, 256).[33]

Furthermore, in its emphasis on the environment, Lamarckism was more congenial to the possibilities of a *social* science. The idea that adaptation to the natural environment could lead to physical and mental changes by no means ruled out the notion that social phenomena—earlier so commonly also thought of as "environmental"—might not have like effects. Darwin himself had toyed with this idea. Lamarckism survived not only after Darwin, but after Weismann as well, but this was often glossed over and obscured by the employment of vocabularies of other paradigms, especially Darwinism. This was generally true of turn-of-the century sociology, but in the decades that followed, some—Giddings being perhaps the most prominent—clung to one or another version of biology, while others like Small and Ellwood moved away from biology—a shift, as Small put it, from "analogical representation of social structures to real analyses of social processes" (Small in 1905, quoted by Stocking, 1968, 263). This drift can be seen clearly in Thomas's work between 1896 and 1909, during which time he shifted from a basically Lamarckian position to the belief, in 1904, that "what have sometimes been regarded as biological differences separating social groups are not really so, and (that) characteristic expressions of the mind are dependent on the social environment" (Thomas quoted by Stocking, 1968, 261), and by 1909, to framing his sociology in terms of "culture" rather than "race" (Stocking, 1968, 263; also Wiley, 1986a). He was thus one of the few who rejected doctrines maintaining that differences in behavior, in putative levels of social organization, in cultural development, in collective achievements, whatever they might be considered to be, were due to biological differences, whatever the mechanism. This process was—and continues to be—an emancipation that cannot, of course, be dated precisely, but the years 1918–1920, just following publication of Alfred Kroeber's "The Superorganic," and just prior to Park and Burgess's *Introduction to the Science of Society*, the first textbook of modern sociology, and the time during which *PP* was brought out, may perhaps reasonably be regarded as the watershed period.[34]

A nonreductionist conception of human nature, i.e., one locating its source in social life, implies a flexible, malleable, and intellectually open human being, if not in fact, at least as potential. Something on this order quite clearly appears to be what Thomas and Znaniecki were trying to formulate in their attitude-value scheme, and to give empirical application in their theory of the personality types. The ways in which they describe the attitude-value relation mirrors Mead's reflexive description of self and society. And the most obvious thing about the personality types is the way in which they build in human agency as a function of the nature of the social order, itself described in dynamic or transformative terms. Personality formation and social change become not just parallel, but interpenetrating *processes*

---

[33] And closely related to this, as Stocking emphasizes, because it supposedly explained the processes of race formation, the problem that became central to evolutionary biology and the emerging social sciences in the late nineteenth century (1968, Chap. 10).

[34] Stocking's view; see 1968, pp. 266–268.

capable of being grasped in their fullness only in relation to one another. This was sociology, in the United States at least, carried out at a new level.

The attitude-value scheme nonetheless proved unsuccessful as an enduring conceptual formula. This was doubtless in part because of the looseness with which these concepts, especially that of "attitude," were formulated. Blumer's judgment that "attitude" was employed as a "blanket term" seemingly for any and all phenomena—appetites, interests, desires, and so on—is certainly right (Blumer, 1939, 20–21). Particularly the fact that the term had a long and well-known pedigree (basically in psychology) of claiming to identify a predisposition to act (given the presentation of a certain stimulus) must have made its radically revised and expanded (and probably unfortunate) use confusing and scientifically questionable. Even the Chicago sociologists of the 1920s, including Thomas himself in later works, abandoned it.

The concept of "value," as noted earlier, was essentially one coming out of the European idealistic tradition and having little currency in American sociological circles (see Wiley, 1986a). The fact that Thomas and Znaniecki's discussion of the concept—notoriously ambiguous and problematic in European social theory and philosophy—was less clear even than that of "attitude" must have added to the readers' difficulties with the work. Furthermore, the somewhat dialectical way in which Thomas and Znaniecki formulated the scheme may have added to the problems of most readers.

Although the attitude-value scheme may be interpreted as a reflection, even to some extent an application, of Mead's reflexive philosophical anthropology, it was only a partial one, and one not very technically elaborated. Most importantly, it failed to build either in or on Mead's *technical* formulation of the interaction process and therefore retained too much of the rigid individual/society polarity Mead had been trying to transcend. Thomas and Znaniecki were working too early, perhaps, to be expected to have assimilated this: it would, of course, have had to have come from a few of Mead's earlier articles and from lectures and the personal relationship between Thomas and Mead. It would, after all, be the better part of two decades before Blumer effected the translation of Mead into "symbolic interactionism." It is reasonably clear, however, that something like this is just what Thomas and Znaniecki needed. Wiley has argued persuasively that they had even greater need for an interactionist conception mediating between the individual and society (or attitudes and values) than Durkheim did, because "they had so much traffic between attitudes and values, and this traffic passes through the missing level" (Wiley, 1986a, 34). And in more specific terms, a firm interactionist conception might have enabled Thomas and Znaniecki to remedy their *underanalysis* of the letters to get down to the "concrete themes" embedded in them (35–36).

One of the great merits of *PP* is its historical dimension. But even though Thomas and Znaniecki theorize the relation between individual and society as a historical one, it cannot be said that they produced anything like a substantively adequate theory of social change. Certainly Weber, and even Durkheim and some of the evolutionists, were clearly superior in this respect. The concepts of social organization and social disorganization were simply too general, and too vague, to adequately carry the historical explanatory load. Closely related is a severe conceptual limitation imposed by the attitude-value scheme: It relegates to the theoretical margin any principled theorization of *social structure*, at times seeming even to collapse structural ideas into those of value. This amounts to saying that Thomas and Znaniecki fail to work out an adequate macrosociology. There is no systematic attempt to state the forms or types of large-scale organization and their modes of coming into being, their functioning, their mechanisms of persistence, the conditions of their decline. There are only ad hoc descriptions of the significance of particular formations or structures at particular times and places working in particular ways, e.g.; the aristocracy, the czarist state, welfare agencies, and so on.[35]

Let us now turn to a consideration of Thomas and Znaniecki's conception of social scientific knowledge. Thomas and Znaniecki in *PP* brought into sociological focus questions that since the 1960s have returned to the center of theoretical debate, questions regarding the distinctive nature of human culture and the possible and proper relation of the social scientist to culture as the object of scientific knowledge.

Spencer and Durkheim had dealt with these problems within the confines of received positivism. Weber had struggled to define a point between that positivism and the historicism of his time at which an interpretive sociology could merit the name of science. Although the sophistication of their argument can in no way be said to match Weber's, Thomas and Znaniecki's methodological declaration has a somewhat similar intent: to establish culture in its then emerging sense as the legitimate object of sociological and social psychological science. It is necessary, they say, to know not only the "objective content" of a "cause," but also the meaning which it has at the given moment for the given conscious beings" (Thomas and Znaniecki, 1927, 1, 38). This formulation attempts to bring into focus the problem of how meaningful phenomena can be approached scientifically. This was Weber's problem.

Thomas and Znaniecki, however, do not pursue this question along Weberian lines. Rather, they understand the problem to be one of assimilating human meaning to causal, or law-grounded explanation. The object of science, they assert, is the identification of causes, and knowledge of causal relations takes the form of laws, or as they put it, "laws of social becoming." They then go on in their "Methodological Note" (and elsewhere) to maintain that the incorrigibility of human subjectivity is not only not an obstacle to this, but that the opposite is the case.

> A nomothetic social science is possible only if all social becoming is viewed as the product of a continual interaction of individual consciousness and objective social reality (1891).

And to this end, of course, individual consciousness, along with "objective social reality, must be subject to causal explanation. This, however, begs the prior question of whether, and by what means, human consiousness can

---

[35] The organizations internal to the Polish communities are partial exceptions to this critique.

properly be an object of science, precisely the issue which Weber took to be the central one in establishing the nature and limits of social science.

We have earlier encountered and discussed the persistent rationale for maintaining the necessity of adducing *laws* in the social sciences: only through laws can social science realize the practical end of *control*. Thomas and Znaniecki identify themselves unequivocally with this position.

> The social technician must find what are the predominant values or the predominant attitudes which determine the situation more than others, and then the question is to modify these values or these attitudes in the desired way by using the knowledge of social causation given by social theory (70).

The lesser problem here is, perhaps, that the question of what the "desired way" might be, and of how it is to be validated, is begged. More important for our purposes is the fact that Thomas and Znaniecki cling to the Comtean formula in order to validate the application of sociological knowledge, for purposes of controlling future development, with all the problems this brings in its train.

At the 1938 Social Science Research Council conference held to reexamine *PP*, Herbert Blumer pointed out that this position clashes with the (Meadian) claim—central to *PP* in its entirety, as we have shown—that social situations must be considered to contain *multiple possiblities* of development, and this is denied by the determinacy of law (Blumer, 1939, 11, 26ff.).[36] Blumer went on to construe the critical issue as being the role of interpretation in social science research. This arises in connection with Thomas's and Znaniecki's contention that the substance of their analysis included "nothing" not essentially contained in the materials (i.e., the peasant letters) themselves (Thomas and Znaniecki, 1927, 76). This appears to be an expression of the correspondence, or mimetic theory of science, in which scientific statements are regarded as being no more and no less than more or less point-for-point reflections of objective reality. Blumer challenged this naive inductionist claim.

> It seems quite clear that, in interpreting the letters, the authors have brought to bear upon them a framework of knowledge, information, and perspective that far transcends the letters themselves. This framework must have been based on an intimate knowledge of Polish peasant life, derived from a wide variety of sources, and on a rich fund of questions, hunches, leads, and ideas which sensitized the authors to special kinds of data and relations (Blumer, 1939, 33).

Blumer's objection goes to essentially the same issue examined so intricately by Weber, albeit from a different perspective and with different— and unfortunately inferior—intellectual resources. The central question in this issue was, as Blumer saw it, "Can social research into subjective experience be made to be scientific?". The answer for Blumer was "yes," as it was for Weber, as well, but with the critical proviso, "only through . . . *"interpretation"*

---

[36] Thomas and Znaniecki accepted this criticism, conceding that they had found so such laws.

and this requires a systematic theorization to establish its precise powers and limits. Weber's methodological writings almost all of which were in print (in German) by 1918, were, of course, just such an inquiry, but evidently unavailable to Blumer as well as to Thomas and Znaniecki.

Why, we may ask, did Thomas and Znaniecki miss so fundamental a theoretical point, while creating the original interpretive *Meisterwerk* of early twentieth century American sociology. Why did they fail to understand their own de facto use of an interpretive method throughout *PP*? One can perhaps only speculate. However, the process of paradigm shift is certainly implicated: the familiar positivist language was still being employed not only by Thomas and Znaniecki, but by Mead, as well. An established social science language capable of expressing the emerging heterodoxy was available in developed form only the Germanic tradition; an American interpretive vocabulary would find a lexicological half-way house in the work of Robert Park, and achieve a full development only with Blumer's symbolic interaction.

CONCLUSION

The decades of the twenties and thirties were not kind to *PP*. The dominant conceptual scheme emerging in the twenties became Robert Park's distinction between the ecological and social (or symbolic) orders. In some ways, this was an advance over *PP,* partly be virtue of its introduction of a materialist category, a major deficiency of *PP*. But in Park's scheme the Meadian reflexivity of self and society, while not entirely lost, became greatly under-stated or underplayed, especially in the "mature" development of the theory when the ecologists took it over. The disorganization scheme, of course, became prominent during the depression years, but for the most part it was simply taken from context and given a range of specific and limited empirical applications with the historical and theoretical richness of *PP* left behind as so much unwanted baggage. But more generally, the 1930s were not kind to theories in which values, culture, status (as against class) and like non-materialist ideas were granted primacy (see Wiley, 1979a, on this point).

That fact that nearly twenty years elapsed between the publication of *PP* and the SSRC conference convened to give it a critical reexamination (Blumer, 1939) suggests that it was a work appearing before its time and so had to be rediscovered—and repromoted. By the 1930s Mead's works had appeared in book form, and Blumer and a few others were at work creating symbolic interactionism. But Blumer's big intellectual debts were to Mead, Faris, and perhaps Park, and symbolic interaction for four decades was unable to shake its sectarian label as a "soft" variant of social psychology. The "decentering" that began in the twenties continued through the war years, up to the ascendency of functionalism around 1950.

Many of the difficulties of *PP* later brought to light—the validity of human documents as scientific data (Blumer, 1939) the seeming overemphasis on *disorganization* (Wiley, 1986a), the absence of major structural categories, class and state in particular (Zaretsky, 1984, introduction), can be framed by this. But whatever its defects, in Zaretsky's judgment—and we must agree—*PP* was a "forerunner to every effort to develop a phenomenological alternative to behaviorist or reductionist principles . . ." (Zaretsky, 1984, 2),

16

CONCLUSION

SOCIOLOGY AFTER 1920

By and large, the growth of sociology in the years after the Great War followed national traditions. Developments in France were heavily influenced by Durkheim, taking the form of a distinctively French structuralism that can be seen in a number of more or less representative works, such as those of Mauss (1967) and LaCombe (1926), and eventually in the massively influential works of Claude Levi-Strauss. Durkheim was known to American sociologists of the 1920s but his influence cannot be said to have been very significant. His real influence on American sociology dates from the 1930s, especially though the interpretation given him by Parsons (1949), and perhaps to a lesser extent by Merton (1934, 1957c). In these works Durkheim's ideas figured strongly in the birth of American functionalism in the late 1940s. This movement, however, certainly did not exhaust Durkheim's influence on American sociology, as later forms of nonfunctionalist theory (e.g., Collins, 1975) clearly show.

Weber's influence on German sociology during the 1920s was less significant than that of Durkheim in France. The young Georg Lukács explicitly recognized a debt to Weber, even though his monumental *History and Class Consciousness,* brought out in 1923, was Marxist to the core (a debt revealed somewhat perversely in his later attack on Weber [Lukács, 1972]). But Lukács ceased sociological work quite early and moved to the field of aesthetics. Karl Mannheim's work, especially *Ideology and Utopia* (1936) along with some of the essays written during the period (e.g., Mannheim, 1968) bear a distinct Weberian influence. And younger scholars such as Heberle, Speier, and Honigsheim were and remained Weberians.

However, Weber's protracted absence from regular university teaching for at least two decades meant that he had virtually no students and so failed to found a school that could think of itself as working within or advancing a tradition. So for a time the influence of Weber's contemporaries such as Tönnies and Leopold von Wiese was perhaps as great as that of Weber. The most significant sociological development in the Germany of the 1920s might well have been Frankfurt School, created largely through the efforts of Max Horkheimer (Tar, 1977; Connerton, 1976). Horkheimer, Adorno, Wilhelm Reich, Walter Benjamin, Erich Fromm, and others attempted to unit Marxian and Freudian ideas in the aftermath of World War I, in part to explain the war itself (particularly Fromm, 1941) and to reorient theoretical attention away from the failure of the international proletariat to unite against the imperial policies of the Great Powers. The Frankfurt critique was a totalistic polemic denouncing bourgeoisie society, in which Hegel and the hegemonic power of ideology and culture replaced Marx and the materialistic doctrine of causation. But its conception of capitalist society as organizationally and ideologically regimented—Marcuse's "one-dimensional society" eventually coming to be the exemplar of this—and rejecting all aspects of liberalism, owes as much to Weber's theory of rationalization as to either Marx or Freud (see Chapter 14).

Weber was also reclaimed by Parsons (Parsons, 1937), who all but ignored his more conflict-oriented, materialistic side, essentially assimilating him to Durkheim as a consensus theorist. However, in the post World War II years German emigré intellectuals such as Mannheim, Hans Gerth, Hans Speier, Paul Honigsheim, and Reinhard Bendix (see, for example, Mannheim, 1936; Gerth and Mills, 1946, 1953; Speier, 1852; Honigsheim, 1968; Bendix, 1956), kept Weber's conflict side very much alive. More recently, from the 1970s on, the recovery and continuing reinterpreting Weber's work has been one of the more important developments in theory. Prominent among those engaged in this have been Anthony Giddens and Randall Collins. Much of the innovating thrust in modern comparative historical sociology has been inspired by Weber.

To some extent the Weber resurgence has occurred in response to the Marxist revival of the 1960s. Recent years have witnessed a lively and increasingly creative confrontation of Weber with Marx, which now appears to be entering a period of rapprochement and possible synthesis (see, for example, Antonio and Glassman, 1985, and Wiley, 1987). (Marxism itself, of course, has since the 1960s entered sociology in a variety of probably enduring, if domesticated forms.)

Other than in France and Germany, sociology in Europe had scarcely taken root. Spencer's followers were almost exclusively American (along with a few Germans and Austrians). In England it was social anthropology rather than sociology that emerged as the ascendent form of distinctively social analysis, a discipline that grew up and that was closely associated with the administration of the empire on a global scale. Much of what was sociological in British thought was to be found in association with social planning (Abrams, 1968). Elsewhere in Europe sociology remained decidedly marginal, represented by a few individuals such as the Italian Pareto (who from the early 1940s on lived in Switzerland and wrote in French), de Greef in Belgium (unjustly ignored), and Westermarck in Finland.

In the United States, of course, the decade of the twenties was a period of exciting growth, particularly at the University of Chicago. Although Mead's influence was important, particularly on Robert E. L. Faris and Herbert Blumer, the dominant figure was Robert Park, who worked out a general social theory that combined a symbolic with an ecological dimension and included a derivative of Simmel's theory of conflict.[1] Park's model of conflict and assimilation (Park and Burgess, 1924) was based mainly on the specific experience of Chicago in the early years of the century although claiming a universal applicability, and ultimately proved much too narrow to serve as a general sociological theory. This weakness was illuminated with the advent of the depression: A theory built up around the actions and experiences of the communal organization of ethnic and other types of status groups (e.g., the rich, hobos, street gangs) proved unadaptable to the problems of *economic* deprivation and political power that became ascendant in the 1930s (Wiley, 1979a).

The growth and institutionalization of sociology virtually everywhere in Europe, of course, was halted with the rise of Nazism in Germany in 1933 and the beginning of the war just a few years later. This hiatus of fifteen years or so meant that the center of gravity of the discipline shifted to the United States, although theoretical developments here, during these years, other than the work of Talcott Parsons (1949) were, at best, exceptionally thin. The "science of leftovers", as the discipline came to be called in some quarters, seized the opportunity to address depression-rooted problems such as the social consequences of unemployment, family disorganization, and related issues within the social disorganization framework, despite its increasingly glaring limitations. In the decade following the war, as Europe recovered, American sociology assumed the clear world leadership of the discipline. But this was essentially a development on two not very closely related tracks: a fetishism of statistical data that C. Wright Mills denounced as "abstracted empiricism," along with the abstractions of Parsonian functionalism. The recovery of the European sociologies contributed very heavily to the eventual challenge to and decline of functionalism during and after the 1960s, and ultimately to the massive diversity that today characterizes sociological theory and sociology itself.

In all of these post-World War II developments, it is fair to say that the directions taken by sociological theory remain focused on topics still framed by the three problematics derived from the Enlightenment. This broad generalization cannot, of course, be proved in detail here; this would require another volume at least as long as this one. But even the most superficial survey of the three or so generations of sociology that have passed since the termination point of this study suggests that it is, in general, a valid judgment.

---

[1] Faris says that although Park and Burgess in their text (1924) supported the theme of human nature "as a product of social living, they also made certain "transitional compromises" (Faris, 1979, 47).

The sociological status of the individual, or of subjectivity and intersubjectivity, however formulated, is far from having been resolved in either the interactionist-constructionist or objectivist sociologies. Symbolic interactionists, phenomenologists, along with those promoting the "rhetorical" or "linguistic" turn, and others, stand on one side; rational choice and exchange theorists, the advocates of artificial intelligence, and at the extreme, the reductionist program of sociobiology, work to establish their very different conceptions of human nature and its relation to the social order, on the other. More generally, the continuing preoccupation with this question on the part of many general theorists, now within the rubric of the "micro-macro" problem, further attests to the continuing significance of the individual-society problematic in framing basic work in sociological theory.

The problem of sociological knowledge, over the same period, but especially in the 1970s and 1980s, has been something of a growth industry in the discipline, despite the fact that most sociologists pay only cursory attention to these developments. This is a literature that, on the one hand, has extended the critique of the positivist foundation of the discipline and by and large found it wanting, and that has attempted to develop theoretically and empirically both the Weberian and Meadian (as well as the phenomenological, dramaturgical, humanist, and other) standpoints. Indeed, one of the important developments here, but no means exclusively the achievement of sociologists, has been a rapprochement or convergence of interactionist-constructionist role theory with Weberian-Husserlian interpretation theory. The issue of the proper form of knowledge in the social sciences, despite the de facto expanding practice mainly along positivist lines, has never been engaged in greater *intellectual* ferment.

Finally, the great questions of social change, of the directions of the world's societies, remain central in sociology and her sister disciplines, if as yet transparently inadequately dealt with. Up through the 1960s, the dominant functionalist school worked with an updated and more sophisticated (and interdisciplinary) version of Spencer's evolutionary theory, which came to be called modernization theory. The increasing inadequacies of this, particularly in its application to the developing world, opened a space for an evolving array first, of Marxist "dependency" theories, beginning with the work of Andrew Gunder Frank (Frank, 1967), then more global-oriented "world-system" theories (e.g., Wallerstein, 1974, 1980) increasingly Weberian in substance (and also generally interdisciplinary). The problematic of social change remains solidly on sociology's agenda.

Is there reason to believe that sociology will ever achieve the condition of being a more or less consensual body of knowledge on the order of physics or other natural sciences, or, more accurately, on the order of what some social scientists imagine them to be? The experience of two hundred years is perhaps beginning to suggest that, as long as the problematics from which the discipline originated remain central in defining the big theoretical issues—which they appear to be continuing to do—it is not reasonable to expect such a state to be reached. Perhaps, as Alexander, only one of the latest following a host of others, has judged,

Social science institutionalizes what is for natural science an aberration, and it does so because the intrinsic possibilities for consensus are strikingly different in the two types of concerns. For reasons related to the nature of the subject matter, disagreement at all levels of the scientific continuum is inherently much more intensive in the social sciences. Proximity of the focus of social scientific analysis to the bases of political and cultural concern in social life heightens the inevitable methodological and substantive barriers to social scientific agreement. (Alexander, 1978–1984, vol. 1, 34).

If this is indeed so, a social science modeled in its essentials after the natural sciences remains more of a dream than ever, even apart from the continuing, if less convincing, claims that cumulation is a substantial reality (e.g., Merton, 1957a; Collins, 1957).[2]

But what does such a judgment imply for that most fundamental aspect of social science, its emancipatory role? Obviously no definitive answer to this question is possible now, nor, one must grant, will perhaps ever be. For one thing the discipline is tied in too many complex ways to its contexts, incorporates too many developmental (and, indeed, retrogressive) "currents" to make such a judgment an easy one. The fact that much, perhaps most, of sociology is now brought into the service of class and elite interests capable of purchasing and directing it, is itself not a coherent ground for the making of such a judgment, for this condition is a continuing one—into which Rousseau had such profound insight—the remaking of which is itself part of the constituitive objective, or the emancipatory interest, as Habermas would say, of any human science. Sociology is a historically evolved creature of its social and political surrounds, that in some of its activities, both intellectual and political, achieves limited autonomy from time to time. If it is to eventually play its emancipatory role on the stage of the world's future, to live up to its charter as, in Bierstedt's estimation (Bierstedt, 1974) the very manifestation of enlightenment, it follows that its practicioners must place first and foremost on the agenda the issues of the nature and conditions of that autonomy.

[2] For a persuasive argument rejecting the science as cumulation argument as appropriate for the social sciences. See Willer, 1971, 131.

BIBLIOGRAPHY

ABEL, THEODORE, "The Operation Called Verstehen," *American Journal of Sociology*, 54, no. 3 (November 1948), 211–218.
———, *Systematic Sociology in Germany*. New York: Columbia University Press, 1929.
ABRAMS, PHILIP, *Historical Sociology*. Ithaca, New York: Cornell University Press, 1982.
———, *The Origins of British Sociology*. Chicago: University of Chicago Press, 1968.
AHO, JAMES, *German Realpolitik and American Sociology*. Cranbury, N.J.: Associated University Presses, 1975.
ALBROW, MARTIN, "Legal Positivism and Bourgeois Materialism: Max Weber's View of the Sociology of Law," *British Journal of Law and Society*, 2, no. 1 (Summer 1975), 14–31.
———, *Bureaucracy*. London: Pall Mall, 1970.
ALEXANDER, JEFFREY C., *Theoretical Logic in Sociology* (4 vols.). Berkeley and Los Angeles: University of California Press, 1978–1984.
———, and BERNHARD GIESEN, "From Reduction to Linkage: The Long View of the Macro-Micro Debate," in *The Micro-Macro Link*, eds. Jeffrey Alexander *et al*. Berkeley: University of California Press, 1987.
———, BERNHARD GIESEN, RICHARD MÜNCH and N. SMELSER, Eds., *The Micro-Macro Link*. Berkeley: University of California Press, 1987.
ALLCOCK, JOHN B., "Emile Durkheim's Encounter with Pragmatism," *Journal of the History of Sociology*, 4, no. 1 (Spring 1982), 27–51.
ALPERT, HARRY, *Emile Durkheim and his Sociology*. New York: Columbia University Press, 1939.
ALTHUSSER, LOUIS, *Lenin and Philosophy and Other Essays*. London: New Left Books, 1971.
———, *For Marx*, tr. B. Brewster. London: Allen Lane (Penguin Books), 1969.
———, and E. BALIBAR, *Reading Capital*, tr. B. Brewster. New York: Pantheon Books, 1970.
AMES, VAN METER, "Mead and Husserl on the Self," *Philosophy and Phenomenological Research*, 15, no. 3 (March 1955), 320–331.
ANCHOR, ROBERT, "Heinrich Rickert," in *The Encyclopedia of Philosophy*, ed. Paul Edwards, 7, 192–194. New York: MacMillan and Free Press, 1967.
ANDERSON, EVELYN, *Hammer or Anvil: The Story of the German Working Class Movement*. London: V. Gollancz, 1945.
ANDERSON, PERRY, *Considerations on Western Marxism*. London: New Left Books, 1976.
———, *Lineages of the Absolutist State*. London: New Left Books, 1974.
ANDRESKI, STANISLAV, *Max Weber: Capitalism, Religion and Bureaucracy*. London: Allen and Unwin, 1983.
———, *The Essential Comte*. New York: Barnes and Noble, 1974.
———, *Herbert Spencer: Structure, Function and Evolution*. New York: Joseph, 1971.
———, "Method and Substantive Theory in Max Weber," *British Journal of Sociology*, 15, no. 1 (March 1964), 1–18.

ANTONI, CARLO, *From History to Sociology: The Transition in German Historical Thinking.* Detroit: Wayne State University Press, 1959.

ANTONIO, ROBERT J., "Values, History, and Science: The Meta-Theoretic Foundations of the Weber-Marx Dialogue," in *A Marx-Weber Dialogue,* eds. Robert Antonio and Ronald Glassman. Lawrence, Kansas: University of Kansas Press, 1985.

————, and RONALD GLASSMAN, *A Weber-Marx Dialogue.* Lawrence, Kansas: University of Kansas Press, 1985.

APEL, KARL-OTTO, "Das Verstehen," *Archiv für Begriffsgeschichte,* Vol. 1, 142–199. Bonn: Bouvier, 1955.

APPLEBAUM, RICHARD P., "Marx's Theory of the Falling Rate of Profit," *American Sociological Review,* 43, no. 1 (February 1978), 67–80.

AQUINAS, ST. THOMAS OF, *Summa Theologica,* ed. A. C. Pegis. New York: Random House, 1945.

ARBLASTER, ANTHONY, *The Rise and Decline of Western Liberalism.* London: Basil Blackwell, 1984.

ARISTOTLE, *Politics,* tr. B. Jowett, intro. R. McKeon. New York: Modern Library, 1941.

ARJOMAND, SAID AMIR, *The Shadow of God and the Hidden Imam.* Chicago: University of Chicago Press, 1984.

ARON, RAYMOND, *Main Currents in Sociological Thought,* Vol. 2. Garden City, New York: Doubleday Anchor, 1970.

————, *Main Currents in Sociological Thought,* Vol. 1. New York: Basic Books, Inc., 1965.

ASHCRAFT, RICHARD, "Marx and Weber on Liberalism as Bourgeois Ideology," *Comparative Studies in Society and History,* 14 (1972), 130–168.

AUGUSTINE, SAINT, *The City of God,* tr. Marcus Dods. New York: Random House (Modern Library), 1950.

————, *Confessions.* New York: Random House, 1949.

AVINERI, SHLOMO, *The Social and Political Thought of Karl Marx.* Cambridge: Cambridge University Press, 1968.

BACON, FRANCIS, *Novum Organum.* Oxford: Clarendon Press, 1889.

————, *New Atlantis.*

BADIE, BERTRAND, and PIERRE BIRNBAUM, *The Sociology of the State,* tr. Arthur Goldhammer. Chicago and London: University of Chicago Press, 1983.

BALDWIN, JAMES MARK, *The Story of the Mind.* New York: Appleton Century Crofts, 1910.

BALDWIN, JOHN D., *George Herbert Mead.* Beverly Hills, California: Sage Publications, 1986.

BARAN, PAUL, and PAUL SWEEZY, *Monopoly Capital.* London: Penguin Books, 1966.

BARKER, ERNEST, ed., *Social Contract.* New York: Oxford University Press, 1962.

BARKER, MARTIN, "Kant as a Problem to Weber," *British Journal of Sociology,* 31, no. 2 (June 1980), 224–245.

BARNARD, F. M., ed., *Herder on Political and Social Culture.* Cambridge: Cambridge University Press, 1969.

BARNES, HARRY ELMER, ed., *An Introduction to the History of Sociology.* Chicago: University of Chicago Press, 1948.

BARNES, J. A., "Durkheim's Division of Labor in Society," *Man,* 1 (New Series), no. 2 (June 1966), 158–175.

BAUER, RAYMOND A., "The Pseudo-Charismatic Leadership in Soviet Society," *Problems of Communism,* 2 (1953), 11–14.

BAUMGARTEN, E., *Max Weber: Werk und Person.* Tübingen: J.C.B. Mohr, 1964.

BAYLE, PIERRE, *Selections from Bayle's Dictionary,* eds. E. A. Bellen and M. duP. Lee, Jr. Princeton, New Jersey: Princeton University Press, 1952.

BECKER, ERNEST, *The Structure of Evil.* New York: Free Press, 1968.

BECKER, HOWARD P., *Through Values to Social Interpretation.* Durham, North Carolina: Duke University Press, 1950.

————, and HARRY ELMER BARNES, *Social Thought from Lore to Science* (3 Vols.). New York: Dover Publications, Inc., 1961.

BEETHAM, DAVID, *Bureaucracy.* Minneapolis: University of Minnesota Press, 1987.

BELLAH, ROBERT N., *Habits of the Heart.* Berkeley: University of California Press, 1985.

————, ed., *Emile Durkheim: On Morality and Society.* Chicago: University of Chicago Press, 1973.

BENDIX, REINHARD, *Force, Fate and Freedom.* Berkeley: University of California Press, 1984.

————, *Kings or People.* Berkeley: University of California Press, 1978.

————, "Max Weber and Jacob Burckhardt," *American Sociological Review,* 30, no. 2 (April 1965), 176–184.

————, *Max Weber: An Intellectual Portrait.* New York: Doubleday, 1960.

————, *Work and Authority in Industry.* New York: Wiley, 1956.

————, and GUENTHER ROTH, *Scholarship and Partisanship: Essays on Max Weber.* Berkeley: University of California Press, 1971.

BENSMAN, JOSEPH, and MICHAEL GIVANT, "Charisma and Modernity," *Social Research,* 42, no. 4 (1975), 570–614.

BENSMAN, JOSEPH, ARTHUR VIDICH, and NOBUKO GERTH, *Politics, Character and Culture: Perspectives from Hans Gerth.* Westport, Connecticut: Greenwood Press, 1982.

BENTHAM, JEREMY, and JOHN STUART MILL, *The Utilitarians.* New York: Doubleday and Company, Dolphin Books, 1961. Includes Bentham's *Principles of Morals and Legislation* and Mill's *Utilitarianism* and *On Liberty.*

BENTON, TED, *Philosophical Foundations of the Three Sociologies.* London: Routledge and Kegan Paul, 1977.

BERGER, STEPHEN, "The Sects and the Breakthrough into the Modern World," *Sociological Quarterly,* 12, no. 4 (Autumn 1971), 486–499.

BERGSTRÄASSER, Arnold, "Wilhelm Dilthey and Max Weber: An Empirical Approach to Historical Syntheses," *Ethics,* 57, no. 1 (October 1946), 92–110.

BERKELEY, GEORGE, *A Treatise Concerning the Principles of Human Knowledge.*

BERLIN, ISAIAH, *Vico and Herder,* London: Hogarth Press, 1976.

————, *The Enlightenment.* New York: Mentor Books, 1956.

BERNERT, CHRIS, "From Cameralism to Sociology with Albion Small," *Journal of the History of Sociology*, 4, no. 2 (Fall 1982), 32–63.

BESNARD, PHILLIPPE, *The Sociological Domain: The Durkheimians and the Founding of French Sociology.* Cambridge: Cambridge University Press, 1983.

BIERSTEDT, ROBERT, *American Sociological Theory, a Critical History.* New York: Academic Press, 1981.

————, "Social Thought in the Eighteenth Century," in *A History of Sociological Analysis*, eds.Tom Bottomore and Robert Nisbet. New York: Basic Books, 1978, 3–28.

————, "Once More the Idea of Progress," in *Power and Progress: Essays on Sociological Theory*, ed. Robert Bierstedt. New York: McGraw Hill, 1974, pp. 279–294.

————, ed., *Florian Znaniecki on Humanistic Sociology.* Chicago: University of Chicago Press, 1969.

————, *Emile Durkheim.* New York: Dell Books, 1966.

BLAU, PETER, *Exchange and Power in Social Life.* New York: Wiley, 1964.

————, *Bureaucracy in Modern Society.* New York: Random House, 1956.

————, and ROBERT K. MERTON, eds., *Continuities in Structural Inquiry.* Beverly Hills, California: Sage Publications, 1981.

————, and W. RICHARD SCOTT, *Formal Organizations.* San Francisco: Chandler, 1962.

BLOCH, ERNST, *Natural Law and Human Dignity.* Cambridge: Massachusetts Institute of Technology Press, 1986.

BLOCH, MARC, *Feudal Society.* Chicago: University of Chicago Press, 1961.

BLUMER, HERBERT, *Symbolic Interaction.* Englewood Cliffs, N.J.: Prentice Hall, Inc., 1969.

————, An Appraisal of Thomas and Znaniecki's *The Polish Peasant in Europe and America*, New York: Social Science Research Council, 1939, Bulletin no. 44.

BOCK, KENNETH, "Theories of Progress, Development, Evolution," in *A History of Sociological Analysis*, eds. Tom Bottomore and Robert Nisbet. New York: Basic Books, 1978, pp. 80–117.

————, *The Acceptance of Histories*, Berkeley: University of Calfornia Press, 1956.

BODIN, JEAN, *Six Books Concerning a Republic* (facsimile). Cambridge: Harvard University Press, 1962.

BOLIN, ROBERT, and SUSAN BOLTON BOLIN, "Sociobiology and Paradigms in Evolutionary Theory" (Comment on Quadagno), *American Sociological Review*, February 1979, and "Reply" by Quadagno, *American Sociological Review*, 1980) 45, no. 1 (February 1979), 154–162.

BONALD, LOUIS DE, *Théorie du pouvoir politique et religieux dans la société civil.* Paris: Libraire Bloud et Barral, 1880.

BOTTOMORE, TOM, "A Marxist Consideration of Durkheim," *Social Forces*, 59, no. 4 (July 1981), 902–917.

————, ed., *Karl Marx: Early Writings.* New York: McGraw-Hill, 1964.

————, ed., *Selected Writings in Sociology and Social Philosophy.* New York: McGraw-Hill, 1956.

————, and ROBERT NISBET, *A History of Sociological Analysis.* New York: Basic Books, 1978.

BOURDIEU, PIERRE, *Distinction: A Social Critique of the Judgment of Taste.* Cambridge: Harvard University Press, 1987.

————, *Outline of a Theory of Practice.* New York: Cambridge University Press, 1977.

BOWLES, SAM and HERBERT GINTIS, *Democracy and Capitalism: Property, Community and the Contradictions of Modern Social Thought.* New York: Basic Books, 1987.

BOYD, WILLIAM, *The Educational Theory of Jean-Jacques Rousseau.* New York: Russell and Russell, 1963.

BRADLEY, RAYMOND, *Charisma and Social Structure.* New York: Random House, 1987.

BRAUDEL, FERNAND, *Civilization and Capitalism: 15th–18th Century* (3 vols.). New York: Harper and Row, 1981–1984.

BRINTON, CRANE, *The Shaping of the Modern Mind.* New York: Mentor Books, 1953.

BROWN, RICHARD HARVEY, *Society as Text.* Chicago: University of Chicago Press, 1987a.

————, "Theories of Rhetoric and the Rhetoric of Theories: Emile Durkheim and the Political Symbology of Sociological Truth," in *Society as Text*, ed. Richard Harvey Brown. Chicago: University of Chicago Press, 1987b.

————, "History and Hermeneutics: Wilhelm Dilthey and the Dialectics of Interpretive Method," in *Structure, Consciousness and History*, eds. Richard Harvey Brown and Stanford M. Lyman. Cambridge: Cambridge University Press, 1978.

————, and STANFORD M. LYMAN, eds., *Structure, Consciousness, and History.* Cambridge: Cambridge University Press, 1978.

BRUBAKER, ROGERS, *The Limits of Rationality.* London: Allen and Unwin, 1984.

BRUNN, HANS HENRIK, *Science, Values and Politics in Max Weber's Methodology.* Copenhagen: Munksgaard, 1972.

BRYANT, CHRISTOPHER G. A., *Positivism in Social Theory and Research.* London: Macmillan, 1985.

BRYSON, GLADYS, *Man and Society, the Scottish Inquiry of the Eighteenth Century.* Princeton: Princeton University Press, 1945.

BUFFON, GEORGE LOUIS LE CLERC, COMTE DE, *De l'homme.* Paris: F. Maspero, 1971.

BULMER, MARTIN, "The Chicago School of Sociology: What Made It a 'School'?" *The History of Sociology: An International Review*, 5, no. 1 (Spring 1985), 61–77.

————, *The Chicago School of Sociology: Institutionalization, Diversity, and the Rise of Sociological Research.* Chicago: University of Chicago Press, 1984.

————, "The Polish Peasant in Europe and America," *New Community*, 10 (1983), 470–476.

BURCKHARDT, JACOB, *The Civilization of the Renaissance*. New York: Oxford University Press, 1945.
BURGER, THOMAS, *Max Weber's Theory of Concept Formation, History, Laws and Ideal Types*. Durham, North Carolina: University of North Carolina Press, 1976.
BURKE, EDMUND, *Works*. London: Oxford University Press, 1906.
————, *Reflections on the Revolution in France*. New Rochelle, New York: Arlington House, undated [1790].
BURROW, J. W., *Evolution and Society: A Study in Victorian Social Theory*. Cambridge: Cambridge University Press, 1970.
BURY, J. B., *The Idea of Progress*. New York: Dover Books, 1955.
BUTLER, ELIZA M., *The Saint-Simonian Religion in Germany*. Cambridge: Cambridge University Press, 1926.
CAMIC, CHARLES, *Experience and Enlightenment: Socialization for Cultural Change in Eighteenth-Century Scotland*. Chicago: University of Chicago Press, 1983.
————, "Charisma: Its Varieties, Preconditions, and Consequences," *Sociological Inquiry*, 50, no. 1 (1980), 5–23.
————, "The Utilitarians Revisited," *American Journal of Sociology*, 85, no. 3 (November 1979), 516–550.
CARNIERO, ROBERT L., ed., *The Evolution of Society: Selections from Herbert Spencer's Principles of Sociology*. Chicago: University of Chicago Press, 1967.
CASANOVA, JOSE V., "Interpretations and Misinterpretations of Max Weber: The Problem of Rationalization," in *Max Weber's Political Sociology*, eds. Ronald Glassman and Vatro Murvar. Westport, Connecticut: Greenwood Press, 1984, pp. 141–153.
CASSIRER, ERNST, *The Individual and the Cosmos in Renaissance Philosophy*. Philadelphia: University of Pennsylvania Press, 1963a.
————, *The Question of Jean-Jacques Rousseau*, tr. P. Gay. Bloomington, Indiana: University of Indiana Press, 1963b.
————, *The Enlightenment*, tr. Fritz Koelln and James Pettegrove. Boston: Beacon Publishing Company, 1955.
————, P. O. KRISTELLER, and J. H., RANDALL, eds., *The Renaissance Philosophy of Man*. Chicago: University of Chicago Press, 1948.
CASTIGLIONE, BALDESAR, *Book of the Courtier*, tr. L. E. Opdyke. New York: Scribners, 1903.
CIPRIANI, ROBERTO, "The Sociology of Legitimation: An Introduction," *Current Sociology*, 35, no. 2 (Summer 1987), 1–20.
CLARK, TERRY N., *Prophets and Patrons: The French University and the Emergence of the Social Sciences*. Cambridge: Harvard University Press, 1973.
————, *On Communication and Social Influence: Selected Papers* (on G. Tarde). Chicago: University of Chicago Press, 1969.
————, "Emile Durkheim and the Institutionalization of Sociology in the French University System," *European Journal of Sociology*, 9, no. 1 (Summer 1968), 37–71.
COHEN, IRA, "The Underemphasis on Democracy in Marx and Weber," in *A Marx-Weber Dialogue*, eds. Robert Antonio and Ronald Glassman. Lawrence, Kansas: University of Kansas Press, 1985, pp. 274–299.
COHEN, JERE, "Reply to Holton," *American Journal of Sociology*, 89, no. 1 (November 1983), 181–187.
————, "Rational Capitalism in Renaissance Italy," *American Journal of Sociology*, 85, no. 6 (May 1980), 1,340–1,355.
————, LAWRENCE E. HAZELRIGG, and WHITNEY POPE, "De-Parsonizing Weber: A Critique of Parsons' Interpretation of Weber's Sociology," *American Sociological Review*, 40, no. 2 (April 1975), 229–241.
COHEN, MORRIS R., and ERNEST NAGEL, *An Introduction to Logic and Scientific Method*. New York: Harcourt Brace, 1934.
COLLINGWOOD, R. G., *Essays in the Philosophy of History*. Austin, Texas: University of Texas Press, 1965.
————, *The Idea of History*. London: Oxford University Press, 1946.
COLLINI, STEFAN, *Liberalism and Sociology: L. T. Hobhouse and Political Argument in England 1880–1914*. Cambridge: Cambridge University Press, 1979.
COLLINS, RANDALL, *Max Weber: A Skeleton Key*. Beverly Hills, California: Sage Publications, 1986.
————, *Three Sociological Traditions*. New York: Oxford University Press, 1985.
————, "The Weberian Revolution of the High Middle Ages," in *Crises in the World System*, ed. A. J. Bergesen. Beverly Hills, California: Sage Publications, 1983, pp. 205–226.
————, "A Theory of Ritual Interaction," *American Journal of Sociology*, 86, no. 5 (March 1981), 984–1014.
————, "Weber's Last Theory of Capitalism: A Systematization," *American Sociological Review*, 45, no. 6 (December 1980), 925–942.
————, *Conflict Sociology*. New York: Academic Press, 1975.
————, "A Comparative Approach to Political Sociology," in *State and Society*, ed. Reinhard Bendix. Boston: Little Brown, 1968, pp. 42–64.
COMTE, AUGUSTE, *A General View of Positivism*. New York: Robert Speller and Sons, 1957 [1848].
————, *The Positive Philosophy*, tr. Harriet Mortineau (3 vols.). London: George Bell and Sons, 1896.
————, *System of Positive Polity*, tr. John H. Bridges. London: Longmans Green, 1875–1877 [1830–1842].
———— , "Discours sur l'esprit positif," tr. M. Goldman. Unpublished, undated [1844].
CONDILLAC, ETIENNE BONNOT DE, *Treatise on the Sensations*, tr. Geraldine Carr. Los Angeles: University of Southern California School of Philosophy, 1930.
CONDORCET, MARIE JEAN ANTOINE NICOLAS CARITAT, MARQUIS DE, *Sketch for a Historical Picture of the Progress of the Human Mind*. New York: Noonday Press, 1955.
CONNERTON, PAUL., ed., *Critical Sociology*. New York: Penguin Books, 1976.

CONSTAS, HELEN, "Max Weber's Two Conceptions of Bureaucracy," *American Journal of Sociology*, 63, no. 4 (January 1958), 400–409.

COOLEY, CHARLES H., *Social Process* (introduction by Roscoe C. Hinkle). Carbondale, Illinois: University of Southern Illinois Press, 1966.

———, *Human Nature and the Social Order* (introduction by Philip Reiff; forward by George Herbert Mead). New York: Shocken, 1964.

———, *Social Organization*. New York: Scribners, 1921.

COPPENS, PETER ROCHE DE, *Ideal Man in Classical Sociology*. University Park, Pennsylvania: The Pennsylvania State University Press, 1976.

CORRIGAN, PHILIP, HARVEY RAMSEY, and DEREK SAYER, *Socialist Construction and Marxist Theory*. New York: Monthly Review Press, 1978.

COSER, LEWIS A., *Masters of Sociological Thought*. New York: Harcourt Bracc Jovanovich, Inc., 1971.

COSER, ROSE, "The Complexity of Rules as Seedbed of Individual Autonomy," in *The Idea of Social Structure: Essays in Honor of Robert Merton*, ed. Lewis A. Coser. New York: Harcourt Brace Jovanovich, Inc., 1975.

CRANSTON, MAURICE, and RICHARD S. PETERS, eds., *Hobbes and Rousseau*. Garden City, New York: Doubleday Anchor, 1972.

CROCE, BENEDETTO, *The Philosophy of Giambattista Vico*, tr. R. G. Collingwood. New York: Russell and Russell, 1964 [1913].

CROCKER, LESTER G., *Diderot: The Embattled Philosopher*. New York: Free Press, 1954.

CUSHING, FRANK H., "Zuñi Fetishes." Annual Report of the Bureau of Ethnology. Washington, D.C., 1883.

DAHRENDORF, RALF, *Life Chances: Approaches to Social and Political Theory*. Chicago: University of Chicago Press, 1979.

———, *Class and Class Conflict in Industrial Society*. Berkeley: University of California Press, 1959.

DALLMAYR, FRED R., and THOMAS A. MCCARTHY, *Understanding and Social Inquiry*. Notre Dame, Indiana: Notre Dame University Press, 1977.

DANIELS, ROBERT V., "Fate and Will in the Marxian Philosophy of History," *Journal of the History of Ideas*, 21, no. 4 (October/December 1960), 538–552.

DANTO, ARTHUR C., *Analytical Philosophy of History*. Cambridge: Cambridge University Press, 1965.

DARWIN, CHARLES, *The Origin of Species and the Descent of Man* (6th and 2d eds). New York: Modern Library, 1936 [1859; 1871].

———, *The LIfe and Letters of Charles Darwin*. London: Murray, 1888.

DAVIS, KINGSLEY, and WILBERT MOORE, *Human Society*. New York: Macmillan, 1949.

DAVY, GEORGES, "Emile Durkheim," *Revue de métaphysique et de morale*, 26 (1919), 181–198.

DAWE, ALAN, "Theories of Social Action," in *A History of Sociological Analysis*, eds. Tom Bottomore and Robert Nisbet. New York: Basic Books, 1978, pp. 362–414.

———, "Theory and the Social Order," *British Journal of Sociology*, 21, no. 2 (June 1970), 207–218.

DEEGAN, MARY JO, "Women in Sociology: 1892–1920," *Journal of the History of Sociology*, 1, no. 1 (Fall 1978), 11–34.

———, and JOHN S. BURGER, "W. I. Thomas and Social Reform," *Journal of the History of the Behavioral Sciences*, 17, no. 1 (January 1981), 114–125.

———, and JOHN S. BURGER, "George Herbert Mead and Social Reform," *Journal of the History of the Behavioral Sciences*, 14, no. 2 (October 1978), 362–372.

DENZIN, NORMAN, *On Understanding Emotion*. San Francisco: Jossey-Bass, Inc., 1984.

DERRIDA, JACQUES, *Of Grammatology*. Baltimore: John Hopkins University Press, 1976.

DEWEY, JOHN, *Logic: The Theory of Inquiry*. New York: Henry Holt and Company, 1938.

———, *Experience and Nature*. New York: Dover Books, 1929.

———, "Interpretation of the Savage Mind," in *Source Book for Social Origins*, ed. W. I. Thomas. Chicago: University of Chicago Press, 1909, pp. 173–185.

———, "The Reflex Arc Concept in Psychology," *The Psychological Review*, 3, no. 4 (July 1896), 357–370.

DIDEROT, DENIS, and JEAN DE ROND D'ALLEMBERT, *Encyclopédie ou, Dictionnaire raisonée des sciences*, eds. N. S. Hoyt and Ernst Cassirer. Indianapolis: Bobbs-Merrill, 1965 [1751–1765].

DILTHEY, WILHELM, *Selected Writings*, ed. H. P. Rickman. New York: Cambridge University Press, 1976.

———, *Pattern and Meaning in History*, ed. H. P. Rickman. New York: Harper Torchbooks, 1961.

DINER, S. J., "Department and Discipline: The Department of Sociology at the University of Chicago, 1892–1920," *Minerva*, 13, no. 4 (Winter 1975), 514–553.

DOMHOFF, G. WILLIAM, *Who Rules America Now? A View for the Eighties*. Englewood Cliffs, New Jersey: Prentice Hall, 1983.

DONDO, MATHURIN, *The French Faust, Henri de Saint-Simon*. New York: Philosophical Library, 1955.

DOUGLAS, JACK, *The Social Meanings of Suicide*. Princeton: Princeton University Press, 1967.

DOW, THOMAS, "The Theory of Charisma," *Sociological Quarterly*, 10, no. 3 (Summer 1969), 306–318.

DOWRENWEND, B. P., "Egoism, Altruism, Anomie and Fatalism: A Conceptual Analysis of Durkheim's Types," *American Sociological Review*, 24, no. 4 (August 1959), 466–473.

DRAPER, HAL, *Karl Marx's Theory of Revolution* (2 vols.). New York: Monthly Review Press, 1977.

DRONBERGER, ILSE, *The Political Thought of Max Weber*. New York: Appleton-Century-Crofts, 1971.

DROYSEN, JOHANN GUSTAV, *Outline of the Principles of History*, tr. E. B. Andrews. Boston: Ginn and Company, 1893.

DUNCAN, DAVID, *Life and Letters of Herbert Spencer*. London: Methuen and Company, 1908.

DURKHEIM, EMILE, "Childhood," in *Durkheim: Essays in Morals and Education*, ed. W. S. F. Pickering. London: Routledge and Kegan Paul, 1979a.

———, "A Discussion on the Boarding School and the New School," in *Durkheim: Essays on Morals and Education*. ed. W. S. F. Pickering. London: Routledge and Kegan Paul, 1979b, pp. 155–159.

———, "A Discussion on Positive Morality: The Issue of Rationality in Ethics," in *Durkheim: Essays on Morals and Education*. ed. W. S. F. Pickering. London: Routledge and Kegan Paul, 1979c, pp. 52–64.

———, "Rousseau on Educational Theory," in *Durkheim: Essays on Morals and Education*. ed. W. S. F. Pickering. London: Routledge and Kegal Paul, 1979d, pp. 52–64.

———, *The Evolution of Educational Thought: Lectures on the Formation and Development of Secondary Education in France*, tr. P. Collins. London: Routledge and Kegan Paul, 1977.

———, "The Dualism of Human Nature and Its Social Condition," in *Emile Durkheim, On Morality and Society*, ed. Robert Bellah. Chicago: University of Chicago Press, 1973a, [1914] pp. 149–163.

———, "Individualism and the Intellectuals," in *On Morality and Society, Selected Writings*, ed. Robert Bellah. Chicago: University of Chicago Press, 1973b, pp. 43–57.

———, *The Division of Labor in Society*, tr. G. Simpson. Glencoe, Illinois: Free Press, 1964 [1893].

———, *Socialism and Saint-Simon*, tr. C. Suttler. London: Routledge and Kegan Paul, 1959.

———, *Rules of Sociological Method*. New York: Free Press, 1958 [1895].

———, *The Elementary Forms of the Religious Life*. London: Allen and Unwin, 1957a [1915].

———, *Professional Ethics and Civic Morals*, tr. C. Brookfield. London: Routledge and Kegan Paul, 1957b [originally publ. 1950 from lecture notes].

———, *Education and Sociology*, tr. S. D. Fox. Glencoe, Illinois: The Free Press, 1956 [originally publ. between 1902 and 1911].

———, *Pragmatisme et sociologie*. Paris: Libraire Philosophique J. Vrin, 1955.

———, "Individual and Collective Representations," in *Emile Durkheim Sociology and Philosophy*, tr. D. F. Pocock. London: Cohen and West, 1953a, 1–34.

———, *Sociology and Philosophy*, tr. D. F. Pocock. London: Cohen and West, 1953b.

———, "Value Judgements and Judgements of Reality," in *Emile Durkheim Sociology and Philosophy*, tr. D. F. Pocock. London: Cohen and West, 1953c, pp. 80–97.

———, *Suicide*, trs. John A. Spaulding and George Simpson. Glencoe, Illinois: The Free Press, 1951 [1897].

———, "Deux lois de l'évolution pénale," *L'année sociologique*, 4 (1900), 65–95.

———, "De la définition des phénomènes religieuses," *L'année sociologique*, 11 (1899), 1–28.

———, La philosophie dans les universités allemandes," *Revue internationale de l'enseignement*, 13 (1887a), 313–338, 423–440.

———, "La science positive de la morale en Allemagne," *Revue Philosophique*, 24 (1887b), 33–58.

———, and MARCEL MAUSS, "Primitive Classification," tr. R. Needham. Chicago: University of Chicago Press, 1963.

EASTON, LLOYD D., and KURT H. GUDDAT, eds. and trs., *Writings of the Young Marx on Philosophy and Society*. New York: Doubleday, 1967.

EDEN, ROBERT, *Political Leadership and Nihilism: Weber and Nietzsche*. Tampa: University of South Florida Press, 1983.

———, "Doing Without Liberalism: Weber's Regime Politics," *Political Theory*, 10, no. 3 (August 1982), 379–408.

EISEN, ARNOLD, "The Meanings and Confusions of Weberian 'Rationality,'" *British Journal of Sociology*, 29, no. 1 (March 1978), 57–90.

ELDRIDGE, J. E. T., *Max Weber: The Interpretation of Social Reality*. New York: Scribner's, 1971a.

———, "Weber's Approach to the Sociological Study of Industrial Workers," in *Max Weber and Modern Sociology*, ed. Arun Sahay. London: Routledge and Kegan Paul, 1971b, pp. 97–111.

ELLIS, DESMOND P., "The Hobbesian Problem of Order," *American Sociological Review*, 36, no. 4 (August 1971), 692–773.

ELTON, G. R., *Reformation in Europe*. London: Fontana, 1963.

ENGELS, FRIEDRICH, "Letter to Joseph Bloch," in *The Marx-Engels Reader*, ed. Robert C. Tucker. New York: Norton, 1972, pp. 760–765.

———, *The Peasant War in Germany*, tr. J. Moissaye. New York: International Publishers, 1966 [c. 1926].

———, "On Authority," in *Marx and Engels: Basic Writings on Politics and Philosophy*, ed. Lewis Feuer. Garden City, New York: Doubleday Anchor, 1959, pp. 481–485.

———, *Herr Eugen Dühring's Revolution in Science*. New York: International Publishers, 1939.

———, "The Role of Labor in Ape's Evolution into Man," tr. M. Goldenburg, with assistance of Leonard Mims, in *Dialectics: A Marxist Literary Journal*, 8 (1876), 1–14.

ERMARTH, MICHAEL, *Wilhelm Dilthey: The Critique of Historical Reason*. Chicago: University of Chicago Press, 1978.

EURIPIDES, *The Bacchae*.

FANFANI, AMINTORE, *Catholicism, Protestantism and Capitalism*. New York: Sheed and Ward, 1955.

FARIS, ROBERT E. L., *Chicago Sociology, 1920–1932*. Chicago: University of Chicago Press, 1970.

FENTON, STEVE (with R. REINER and I. HAMNET), *Durkheim and Modern Sociology*. Cambridge: Cambridge University Press, 1984.

FERGUSON, ADAM, *Principles of Morals and Political Science* (2 vols.). New York: Garland, 1978.

———, *An Essay on the History of Civil Society*. Edinburgh: Kincaid and Bell, (facsimile) 1971 [1767].

FERNBACH, DAVID, ed., *Karl Marx: The Revolutions of 1848: Political Writings* (2 vols.). New York: Random House Vintage, 1974.

FERRAROTTI, FRANCO, *Max Weber and the Destiny of Reason*. New York: Sharpe Publishers, 1982.

——, *Toward the Social Production of the Sacred: Durkheim, Weber, Freud*. La Jolla, California: Essay Press, Inc., 1977.

FEUER, LEWIS S., *Marx and Engels: Basic Writings on Politics and Philosophy*. Garden City, New York: Doubleday Anchor, 1959.

FEUERBACH, LUDWIG, *The Essence of Christianity*, tr. Marian Evans. London: Paul, Trench and Trubner, 1893.

FICHTE, JOHANN GOTTLIEB, *The Vocation of Man*, tr. P. Preuss. Indianapolis: Hackett Publishing Co., 1987.

FINE, GARY ALAN, and SHERRYL KLEINMAN, "Interpreting the Sociological Classics: Can There Be a True Meaning of Mead?" *Symbolic Interaction*, 9, no. 1 (Spring 1986), 129–146.

FISCH, M. H., and T. G. BERGIN, eds. and tr., *The Autobiography of Giambattista Vico*. Ithaca, New York: Cornell University Press, 1944.

FISCHER, FRANK, and CARMEN SIRIANNI, eds., *Critical Studies in Organization and Bureaucracy*. Philadelphia: Temple University Press, 1984.

FISCHOFF, EPHRAIM, "The Protestant Ethic and the Spirit of Capitalism—the History of a Controversy," *Social Research*, 11, no. 1 (February 1944), 53–77.

FLETCHER, RONALD, "Frederic Le Play," in *The Founding Fathers of Social Science*, ed. Timothy Raison. London: Penguin Books, 1979, pp. 64–71.

FLEW, ANTONY, *David Hume: Philosopher of Moral Science*. New York: Basil Blackwell, 1986.

FLINT, ROBERT, *History of the Philosophy of History*. New York: Scribner's, 1894.

FONTENELLE, BERNARD DE BOUVIER, "On the Ancients and Moderns," in *The Idea of Progress; a Collection of Readings*, ed. Frederick Teggart. Berkeley: University of California Press, 1949, pp. 176–187.

——, *Dialogues of the Dead*.

FOOTE, NELSON, and L. S. COTTRELL, *Identity and Interpersonal Competence*. Chicago: University of Chicago Press, 1955.

FREEDMAN, ROBERT, *Marx on Economics*. New York: Harcourt Brace, 1961.

FREEMAN, DEREK, "The Evolutionary Theories of Charles Darwin and Herbert Spencer," *Current Anthropology*, 15, no. 3 (September 1974), 211–237.

FREUND, JULIEN, "German Sociology in the Time of Max Weber," in *A History of Sociological Analysis*. eds. Tom Bottomore and Robert Nisbet. New York: Basic Books, 1978, pp. 149–186.

——, *The Sociology of Max Weber*, tr. M. Ilfort. New York: Vinatage Books, 1969.

FREYER, HANS, *Soziologie als Wirklichkeitswissenschaft*. Darmstadt: Wissenschaftliche Buchgesellschaft, 1964.

FRIED, MORTON H., *The Evolution of Political Society*. New York: Random House, 1967.

FRIEDELL, EGON, *A Cultural History of the Modern Age*, tr. Charles F. Atkinson. New York: A. A. Knopf, 1932.

FRIEDRICH, CARL, "Some Observations on Weber's Analysis of Bureaucracy," in *Reader in Bureaucracy*, ed. Robert K. Merton et al. Glencoe, Illinois: The Free Press, 1952, pp. 27–33.

FROMM, ERIC, *Socialist Humanism: An International Symposium*. Garden City, New York: Doubleday, 1966.

——, *Escape from Freedom*. New York: Farrar and Rinehart, 1941.

FUHRMAN, ELLSWORTH, "Morality, Self and Society: The Loss and Recapture of the Moral Self," in *Sociological Theory in Transition*, eds. Mark Wardell and Steven Turner. Winchester, Massachusetts: Allan and Unwin, 1986.

FULLER, B. A. G., *A History of Modern Philosophy*. New York: Henry Holt and Co., 1938.

GADAMER, HANS-GEORG, *Reason in the Age of Science*. Cambridge: M.I.T. Press, 1982.

GAY, PETER, *The Enlightenment: An Interpretation* (2 vols.). New York: Alfred A. Knopf, 1966.

GELLNER, DAVID N., "Weber, Capitalism, and the Religion of India," *Sociology*, 16, no. 4 (November 1982), 526–543.

GELLNER, ERNEST, *Relativism in the Social Sciences*. New York: Cambridge University Press, 1985.

——, "Concepts and Society," in *Rationality*, ed. Bryan Wilson. Oxford: Basil Blackwell, 1974, pp. 18–49.

GEORGE, C. H., and K. GEORGE, *The Protestant Mind of the English Reformation*. London: Methuen, 1961.

GERAS, NORMAN, "Marx and the Critique of Political Economy," in *Ideology in Social Science*, ed. Robin Blackburn. New York: Random House (Pantheon Books), 1972, pp. 284–305.

GERTH, H. H., "The Nazi Party: Its Leadership and Composition," *American Journal of Sociology*, 45, no. 4 (January 1940), 517–541.

——, and C. WRIGHT MILLS, *Character and Social Structure*. New York: Harcourt Brace and Company, 1953.

——, and C. WRIGHT MILLS, eds., *From Max Weber: Essays in Sociology*. New York: Oxford University Press, 1946.

GIBBON, EDWARD, *The Decline and Fall of the Roman Empire* (abr.). New York: Harcourt Brace, 1960 [1776–1788: 3 vols.].

GIDDENS, ANTHONY, *The Nation State and Violence*, Vol. 2 of *A Contemporary Critique of Historical Materialism*. Berkeley: University of California Press, 1985.

——, *The Constitution of Society: Outline of the Theory of Structuration*. Berkeley and Los Angeles: University of California Press, 1984.

——, *Central Problems in Social Theory*. London and Basingstoke: MacMillan Press, Ltd., 1982.

——, *Power, Property and the State*, Vol. 1 of *A Contemporary Critique of Historical Materialism*. Berkeley and Los Angeles: University of California Press, 1981.

——, *Durkheim*. London: Fontana Modern Masters, 1978.

————, *New Rules of Sociological Method*. New York: Basic Books, 1976.
————, *The Class Structures of the Advanced Societies*. New York: Harper and Row Torchbooks, 1975 (1973).
————, *Politics and Sociology in the Thought of Max Weber*. London: MacMillan, 1972.
————, *Capitalism and Modern Social Theory*. London: Cambridge University Press, 1971a.
————, "Durkheim's Political Sociology," *Sociological Review*, 19, no. 4 (November 1971b), 477–519.
————, "The Suicide Problem in French Sociology," *British Journal of Sociology*, 16, no. 1 (March 1965), 3–18.
GIDDINGS, FRANKLIN, *Studies in the Theory of Human Society*. New York: MacMillan, 1922.
————, *The Elements of Sociology*. New York: MacMillan, 1902 [1898].
GLASSMAN, RONALD, "Legitimacy and Manufactured Charisma," *Social Research*, 42, no. 4 (Winter 1975) 615–636.
————, and VATRO MURVAR eds., *Max Weber's Political Sociology*. Westport, Connecticut: Greenwood Press, 1984.
GODWIN, WILLIAM, *Enquiry Concerning Political Justice* (2 vols.). Toronto: University of Toronto Press, 1946.
GOFFMAN, ERVING, "The Nature of Deference and Demeanor," in *Three Sociological Traditions: Selected Readings*, ed. Randall Collins. New York: Oxford University Press, 1985 (orig. publ. in *American Anthropologist*, 58, no. 3 (1956), 473–499.
GOLDMANN, LUCIEN, *The Philosophy of the Enlightenment*. London: Routledge and Kegan Paul, 1973.
GOODMAN, MARK JOSEPH, "Type Methodology and Type Myth: Some Antecedents of Max Weber's Approach," *Sociological Inquiry*, 45, no. 1 (1975), 45–58.
GOUDSBLOM, JOHAN, *Sociology in the Balance: A Critical Essay*. Oxford: Basil Blackwell, 1977.
GOUHIER, HENRI, *La jeunesse d' Auguste Comte et la formation du positivism* (3 vols.). Paris: J. Vrin, 1933.
GOULDNER, ALVIN, *The Two Marxisms*. New York: Oxford University Press, 1980.
————, *The Dialectic of Ideology and Technology*. New York: Seabury Press, 1976.
————, "Anti-Minotaur: The Myth of a Value-Free Sociology," in *The New Sociology*, ed. Irving Horowitz. New York: Oxford University Press, 1964, pp. 196–217.
————, "Metaphysical Pathos and the Theory of Bureaucracy," *American Political Science Review*, 49, no. 2 (June 1955), 496–507.
————, *Patterns of Industrial Bureaucracy*. Glencoe, Illinois: The Free Press, 1954.
GRAFSTEIN, ROBERT, "The Institutional Resolution of the Fact-Value Dilemma," *Philosophy of the Social Sciences*, 11, no. 1 (March 1981), 1–14.
GRAÑA, CESAR, *Modernity and Its Discontents*. New York: Harper and Row, 1967.
GRANET, MARCEL, *La pensée chinoise*. Paris: La Renaissance du Libre, 1934.
GREEN, MARTIN, *The von Richtofen Sisters*. New York: Basic Books, 1974.
GREEN, ROBERT, ed., *Protestantism and Capitalism: The Weber Thesis and Its Critics*. Boston: Heath, 1965.
GROTIUS, HUGO, *The Rights of War and Peace*. New York: Oceana, 1964 [1675].
GUENÉE E BERNARD, *States and Rulers in Later Medieval Europe*, tr. J. Vale. London: Basil Blackwell, 1985.
HABERMAS, JÜRGEN, *The Theory of Communicative Action, Vol. 2: The Lifeworld and System: A Critique of Functionalist Reason*, tr. T. McCarthy. Boston: Beacon Press, 1987.
HABERMAS, JÜRGEN, *The Theory of Communicative Action*, Vol. 1: *Reason and the Rationalization of Society*, tr. T. McCarthy. Boston: Beacon Press, 1984.
————, *Communication and the Evolution of Society*. London: Heinemann, 1979.
————, *Legitimation Crisis*. Boston: Beacon Press, 1975.
————, *Theory and Practice*, tr. J. Viertel. Boston: Beacon Press, 1973.
HAGSTROM, WARREN, *The Scientific Community*. New York: Basic Books, 1965.
HAINES, VALERIE A., "Is Spencer's Theory an Evolutionary Theory?" *American Journal of Sociology*, 93, no. 4 (March 1988), 1200–1223.
HALFPENNY, PETER, *Positivism and Sociology*. London: Allen and Unwin, 1982.
HALL, JOHN A., *The Causes and Consequences of the Rise of the West*. Berkeley: University of California Press, 1986.
————, *Powers and Liberties*. New York: Viking Penguin, 1985.
HALLER, WILLIAM, *The Rise of Puritanism*. New York: Columbia University Press, 1938.
HAMLYN, D. W., "Causality and Human Behavior," in *Readings in the Theory of Action*, eds. Norman Case and Charles Landsmann. Bloomington, Indiana: University of Indiana Press, 1968, pp. 48–67.
HARRIS, C. T., and C. SANDUSKY, "Love and Death in Classical Music," *Symbolic Interaction*, 8, no. 2 (Fall 1985), 291–310.
HASKELL, THOMAS, *The Emergence of Professional Social Science: The American Social Science Association and the Nineteenth Century Crisis of Authority*. Urbana, Illinois: University of Illinois Press, 1977.
HAWTHORNE, GEOFFREY, *Enlightenment and Despair*. Cambridge: Cambridge University Press, 1976.
HAYEK, F. A., *The Counterrevolution of Science*. New York: Free Press, 1952.
HEAP, JAMES L., "Verstehen, Language and Warrants," *Sociological Quarterly*, 18, no. 1 (Spring 1977), 177–184.
HECHTER, MICHAEL, ed., *The Microfoundations of Macrosociology*. Philadelphia: Temple University Press, 1983.
HEGEL, G. F. W., *Philosophy of Right*, tr. T. M. Knox. London, New York: Oxford University Press, 1978 [1821].
————, *Hegel's Philosophy of Mind* (including *Zuzätze* in Baumann's text), tr. A. V. Miller. Oxford: Clarendon Press, 1971 [1908].

————, *The Philosophy of History*, tr. J. Sibree. New York: Dover Publications, 1956.

————, *Science of Logic* (2 vols.), trs. H. W. Johnston and L. G. Struthers. New York: MacMillan, 1929.

HEKMAN, SUSAN, *Weber, The Ideal Type, and Contemporary Social Theory*. Notre Dame: University of Notre Dame Press, 1983.

HELLER, AGNES, *The Theory of Need in Marx*. New York: St. Martin's, 1976.

HELVETIUS, CLAUDE ADRIEN, *A Treatise on Man: His Intellectual Faculties and His Education*, tr. W. Hooper. London: Albion Press, 1810 [1773].

HENNIS, WILHELM, *Max Weber: Essays in Reconstruction*. London: Allen and Unwin, 1988.

HENRICH, DIETER, *Die Einheit der Wissenschaftslehre Max Webers*. Tübingen: J. C. B. Mohr, 1953.

HERBST, JURGEN, *The German Historical School in American Scholarship*. Ithaca, New York: Cornell University Press, 1965.

HERDER, JOHANN GOTTFRIED VON, *Reflections on the Philosophy of the History of Mankind* (abridged and with an introduction by Frank Manuel). Chicago: University of Chicago Press, 1968 [1784–1791].

HEUSS, THEODORE, "Max Weber in seiner Gegenwart," in Max Weber, *Gesamelte Politische Schriften*, 7–31. Tübingen: J. C. B. Mohr, 1971 [1920].

HILBERT, RICHARD A., "Anomie and the Moral Regulation of Reality: The Durkheimian Tradition in Modern Relief," *Sociological Theory*, 4, no. 1 (Spring 1986), 1–19.

HILFERDING, RUDOLF, *Das Finanzkapital*. Frankfurt: Europäische Verlagsanstadt, 1968.

HILL, CHRISTOPHER, *Society and Puritanism in Pre-Revolutionary England*, 2d edition. New York: Schocken Books, 1967.

————, "Protestantism and the Rise of Capitalism," in *The Economic and Social History of Tudor and Stuart England in Honor of R. H. Tawney*, ed. F. J. Fisher. Cambridge: Cambridge University Press, 1961, pp. 15–39.

HINKLE, GISELA, "Rejoinder to Volkart," *Social Research*, 20, no. 4 (Winter 1953), 473–477.

HINKLE, ROSCOE, "Charles Horton Cooley's General Sociological Orientation," *Sociological Quarterly*, 8, no. 1 (Winter 1967), 5–20.

HINTZE, OTTO, *The Historical Essays of Otto Hintze*, ed. Felix Gilbert. New York: Oxford University Press, 1975.

HIRSCHMAN, ALBERT O., *The Passions and the Interests: Political Arguments for Capitalism Before Its Triumph*. Princeton: Princeton University Press, 1977.

HIRST, PAUL Q., *Social Evolution and Sociological Categories*. London: Allen and Unwin, 1976.

————, *Durkheim, Bernard, and Epistemology*. London and Boston: Routledge and Kegan Paul, 1975.

HOBBES, THOMAS, *English Works*. London: William Molesworth, 1839–1845.

————, *Leviathan*.

HOBSBAWM, E. J., "Karl Marx's Contribution to Historiography," in *Ideology in Social Science*, ed. Robin Blackburn. New York: Random House (Pantheon Books), 1972, 265–283.

————, *Primitive Rebels*. New York: Norton, 1965.

HOBSON, JOHN A., *Imperialism*. Ann Arbor: University of Michigan Press, 1971 [1902].

————, *The Evolution of Modern Capitalism*. New York: Scribner's, 1926.

HOLBACH, PAUL HENRI THIRY, BARON D', *Système de la nature, ou, des lois du monde physique et du mond moral*. Hildesheim: G. Ohms, 1966.

HOLLANDER, PAUL, *The Many Faces of Socialism*. New Brunswick, New Jersey: Transaction Books, 1983.

HOLTON, R. J., "Max Weber, 'Rational Capitalism,' and Renaissance Italy: A Critique of Cohen," *American Journal of Sociology*, 89, no. 1 (July 1983), 166–180.

HOMANS, GEORGE, *Social Behavior: Its Elementary Forms*. New York: Harcourt Brace, 1961.

HONIGSHEIM, PAUL, *On Max Weber*, tr. Joan Rytina. New York: The Free Press, 1968.

HOOK, SIDNEY, *From Hegel to Marx*. New York: Humanities Press, 1950.

HORKEIMER, MAX, and THEODOR ADORNO, *Dialectic of Enlightenment*. London: Allen and Unwin, 1973.

HORNE, THOMAS A., *The Social Thought of Bernard Mandeville*. New York: Columbia University Press, 1978.

HORTON, JOHN, "The Dehumanisation of Anomie and Alienation," *British Journal of Sociology*, 15, no. 4 (December 1964), 283–300.

HOWE, RICHARD H., "Max Weber's Elective Affinities: Sociology Within the Bounds of Pure Reason," *American Journal of Sociology*, 84, no. 2 (September 1978), 366–385.

HUFF, DOUGLAS, and STEPHEN P. TURNER, "Rationalizations and the Application of Causal Explanations of Human Action," *American Philosophical Quarterly*, 18 (1981), 213–220.

HUGHES, H., STUART, *Consciousness and Society*. New York: Random House (Vintage), 1958.

HUGHEY, MICHAEL W., "The Idea of Secularization in the Works of Max Weber: A Theoretical Outline," *Qualitative Sociology*, 2, no. 1 (May 1979), 85–111.

HULL, DAVID L., *Darwin and His Critics*. Chicago: University of Chicago Press, 1973.

HUME, DAVID, *Writings on Economics*, ed. E. Rotwein. Freeport, New York: Books for Libraries Press, 1972.

————, *Essays Moral, Political and Literary*. London: Oxford University Press, 1963a.

————, "Of Refinement in the Arts," in *Essays Moral, Political and Literary*. London: Oxford University Press, 1963b [1748], pp. 159–167.

————, "Of the Original Contract," in *Social Contract*, ed. Ernest Barker. New York: Oxford University Press, 1962, pp. 147–166.

————, *A Treatise of Human Nature*. Oxford: Clarendon Press, 1949 [1739].

————, *Enquiry Concerning Human Understanding*. Chicago: Open Court Publishing Company, 1912 [1748].

HUNT, A., *The Sociological Movement in Law*. Philadelphia: Temple University Press, 1978.

HUSSERL, EDMUND, *Ideas: General Introduction to Pure Phenomonology*, tr. R. W. Boyce Gibson. New York: MacMillan, 1931.

HUTCHESON, FRANCIS, *Illustrations on the Moral Sense*. Cambridge: Harvard University Press, 1971 [1728].

———, *A System of Moral Philosophy*. New York: A. M. Kelley, 1968 [1755: posthumous edition].

HUXLEY, THOMAS, "The Struggle for Existence in Human Society," in *Collected Essays*, Vol. 9. New York: D. Appleton, 1896–1902, pp. 195–236.

HYNES, EUGENE, "Suicide and Homo Duplex," *Sociological Quarterly*, 16, no. 1 (Winter 1975), 87–104.

IBN KHALDOUN, ABU ZAID 'ABDAL-RAHMAN, *The Muquddimah: An Introduction to History*, 3 Vols., New York: Pantheon, 1958.

IGGERS, GEORGE, *The German Conception of History*. Middletown, Connecticut: Wesleyan University Press, 1968.

———, *The Doctrine of Saint-Simon: An Exposition*, tr. and with introduction by Iggers. Boston: Beacon Press, 1958.

ISRAEL, JOACHIM, *Alienation: From Marx to Modern Sociology, a Macrosociological Analysis*. Boston: Allyn and Bacon, 1971.

IZZO, ALBERTO, "Legitimation and Society: A Critical Review," *Current Sociology*, 35, no. 2 (Summer 1987), 41–56.

JAMES, WILLIAM, *Essays in Radical Empiricism and a Pluralistic Universe*, ed. Ralph B. Perry. New York: E. P. Dutton, 1971.

———, *Pragmatism*. New York: Meridan Books, 1970.

———, *The Principles of Psychology*, 2 Vols. New York: Dover Publications, 1950.

———, *Psychology* (abridgement by James of *Principles of Psychology*. New York: Henry Holt, 1890). Cleveland: World Publishing Company, 1948 [1892].

———, "Does 'Consciousness' Exist?" *Journal of Philosophy, Psychology and Scientific Methods*, 1, no. 18 (September 1, 1904), 477–491.

JAMESON, FREDRIC, "The Vanishing Mediator: Narrative Structure in Max Weber," *New German Critique*, 1, no. 1 (Winter 1974), 52–89.

JANOWICZ, MORRIS, ed., *W. I. Thomas on Social Organization and Social Personality: Selected Papers*. Chicago: University of Chicago Press, 1966.

JASPERS, KARL, *Leonardo, Descartes, and Max Weber*, tr. R. Mannheim. London: Routledge and Kegan Paul, 1963.

JOAS, HANS, *G. H. Mead: A Contemporary Re-examination of His Thought*. Cambridge: M.I.T. Press, 1985.

JOHN OF SALISBURY, *Polycraticus*, abr. and ed. M. Markland. New York: Frederick Ungar Publishing Company, 1979.

JONES, BRYN, "Max Weber and the Concept of Social Class," *Sociological Review*, 23, no. 4 (November 1975), 729–758.

JONES, W.T., *A History of Western Philosophy*. New York: Harcourt Brace, 1952.

KALBERG, STEPHEN, "The Origin and Expansion of *Kulturpessimismus*: The Relationship Between Private and Public Spheres in Early Twentieth Century Germany," *Social Theory*, 5, no. 2 (Fall 1987), 150–164.

———, "The Role of Ideal Interests in Max Weber's Comparative Historical Sociology," in *A Marx-Weber Dialogue*, eds. Robert Antonio and Ronald Glassman. Lawrence, Kansas: University of Kansas Press, 1985, pp. 46–67.

———, "Max Weber's Types of Rationality: Cornerstones for the Analysis of Rationalization Processes in History," *American Journal of Sociology*, 85, no. 5 (March 1980), 1145–1179.

KAMES, HENRY HOME, LORD, *Sketches of the History of Man*. Edinburgh: W. Creech, 1774.

KANT, IMMANUEL, *On the Old Saw: That It May Be Right in Theory But It Won't Work in Practice*, tr. E. B. Ashton. Philadelphia: University of Pennsylvania Press, 1974 [1773].

———, *Critique of Pure Reason*.

———, *Critique of Practical Reason*.

KAPSIS, ROBERT E., "Weber, Durkheim and the Comparative Method," *Journal of the History of the Behavioral Sciences*, 13, no. 4 (October 1977), 354–368.

KATOVICH, MICHAEL, "Durkheim's Macrofoundations of Time: An Assessment and Critique," *Sociological Quarterly*, 28, no. 3 (Fall 1987), 367–385.

KEAT, RUSSELL, and JOHN URRY, *Social Theory as Science*. London: Routledge and Kegan Paul, 1975.

KELLNER, DOUGLAS, "Critical Theory, Max Weber, and the Dialectics of Domination," in *A Marx-Weber Dialogue*, eds. Robert Antonio and Ronald Glassman. Lawrence, Kansas: University of Kansas Press, 1985.

KLOSS, ROBERT MARSH, and RON E. ROBERTS, *Social Movements, Between the Balcony and the Barricade*. St. Louis: Mosby, 1974.

KNORR-CETINA, KARIN, "The Micro-Sociological Challenge of Macro-Sociology: Towards a Reconstruction of Social Theory and Methodology," in *Advances in Social Theory and Methodology: Toward an Integration of Micro- and Macro-Sociologies*, eds. Karin Knorr-Cetina and Aaron V. Cicourel. London: Routledge and Kegan Paul, 1981.

———, and AARON CICOUREL, eds., *Advances in Social Theory and Methodology: Toward An Integration of Micro- and Macro-Sociologies*. London: Routledge and Kegan Paul, 1981.

KOLAKOWSKI, LESZEK, *Main Currents of Marxism: Its Rise, Growth, and Dissolution*, 3 Vols. Oxford: Clarendon Press, 1978.

———, *The Alienation of Reason: A History of Positivist Thought*, tr. N. Guterman. Garden City, New York: Doubleday, 1968.

KORSCH, KARL, *Karl Marx*. New York: Russell and Russell, 1963.

KROHN, MARVIN D., "A Durkheimian Analysis of International Crime Rates," *Social Forces*, 57, no. 2 (December 1978), 654–670.

KRONMAN, ANTHONY T., *Max Weber*. Stanford, California: Stanford University Press, 1983.

KUHN, THOMAS S., *The Structure of Scientific Revolutions*. Chicago: University of Chicago Press, 1970 [1962].

LACOMBE, ROGER, *La méthode sociologique de durkheim*. Paris: Librarie F. Alcan, 1926.

LA METTRIE, JULIAN OFFRAY DE, *L'homme machine: A Study in the Origins of an Idea*, ed. and intro. Aram Vartanian. Princeton, New Jersey: Princeton University Press, 1960.

LANGTON, JOHN, "Darwinism and the Behavioral Theory of Sociocultural Evolution: An Analysis," *American Journal of Sociology*, 85, no. 2 (September 1979), 288–309.

LASCH, SCOTT, and SAM WHIMSTER, eds., *Max Weber, Rationality and Modernity*. Winchester, Massachusetts: Allen and Unwin, 1987.

LASSWELL, HAROLD, "The Garrison State," in *War: Studies from Psychology, Sociology, Anthropology*, eds. L. Bramson and G. Goethals (rev. ed.). New York: Basic Books, 1968.

LAZARSFELD, PAUL, and ANTHONY R. OBERSCHALL, "Max Weber and Empirical Social Research," *American Sociological Review*, 30, no. 2 (April 1965), 185–199.

LE BON, GUSTAVE, *The Psychology of Peoples: Its Influence on their Evolution*. New York: MacMillan, 1898. [1984]

———, *The Crowd*. New York: MacMillan, 1894.

LEFEBVRE, HENRI, *The Sociology of Marx*. New York: Random House, 1969.

LEHMANN, WILLIAM C., *John Millar of Glasgow*. Cambridge: Cambridge University Press, 1960.

LEMERT, CHARLES C., *French Sociology: Rupture and Renewal Since 1968*. New York: Columbia University Press, 1981.

LENIN, V. I., *Imperialism: The Highest Stage of Capitalism*.

———, *The State and Revolution*.

LENSKI, GERHARD, "History and Social Change," *American Journal of Sociology*, 82, no. 3 (November 1977), 548–564.

———, *Power and Privilege: A Theory of Stratification*. New York: McGraw Hill, 1966.

LENZER, GERTRUD, ed., *Auguste Comte and Positivism: The Essential Writings*. New York: Harper Torchbooks, 1975.

LEPENIES, WOLF, *Between Literature and Science: The Rise of Sociology*. New York: Cambridge University Press, 1988.

LE PLAY, FRÉDÉRIC, *On Family, Work and Social Change*, ed. and tr. Catherine Bodard Silver. Chicago: University of Chicago Press, 1982.

LEVINE, DONALD N., *The Flight from Ambiguity*. Chicago: University of Chicago Press, 1985.

———, "Rationality and Freedom: Weber and Beyond," *Sociological Inquiry*, 51, no. 1 (1981), 5–25.

———, *Georg Simmel on Individuality and Social Form*. Chicago: University of Chicago Press, 1971.

LEVINE, NORMAN, *The Tragic Deception: Marx Contra Engels*. Santa Barbara: Clio Books, 1975.

LEVISON, ARNOLD B., *Knowledge and Society: An Introduction to the Philosophy of the Social Sciences*. Indianapolis: Bobbs-Merrill, 1974.

LEVI-STRAUSS, CLAUDE, *The Elementary Structures of Kinship*. Boston: Beacon Press, 1969 [1949].

LEWIS, J. DAVID, "The Classic American Pragmatists as Forerunners to Symbolic Interactionism," *Sociological Quarterly*, 17, no. 3 (Summer 1976), 347–359.

———, and RICHARD L. SMITH, *American Sociology and Pragmatism*. Chicago: University of Chicago Press, 1980.

LICHTHEIM, GEORGE, *From Marx to Hegel*. New York: Herder and Herder, 1971a.

———, *The Origins of Socialism*. New York: Praeger, 1971b [1969].

———, *Marxism* (2d edition). London: Routledge and Kegan Paul, 1964.

LICHTMAN, R., "Symbolic Interactionism and Social Reality: Some Marxist Queries," *Berkeley Journal of Sociology*, 6 (1970), 75–94.

LITTLE, DAVID, *Religion, Order, and Law: A Study in Pre-Revolutionary England*. New York: Harper and Row, 1969.

LOCKE, JOHN, *The Second Treatise on Government*.

———, *An Essay Concerning Human Understanding*. Oxford: Clarendon Press, 1894 [1690].

LOEWENSTEIN, KARL, *Max Weber's Political Ideas in the Perspective of Our Time*, trs. Richard and Clara Winston. Amherst: University of Massachusetts Press, 1965.

LOVEJOY, ARTHUR O., *The Great Chain of Being*. Cambridge: Harvard University Press, 1964 [1936].

———, *Reflections on Human Nature*. Baltimore: Johns Hopkins University Press, 1961.

LÖWITH, KARL, *Hegel to Nietzsche*. New York: Garland Publishers, 1984.

———, *Max Weber and Karl Marx*. London: Allen and Unwin, 1982.

———, *Meaning in History*. Chicago: University of Chicago Press, 1949.

LUHMANN, NIKLAS, *The Differentiation of Society*. New York: Columbia University Press, 1982.

LUKÁCS, GEORG, *The Destruction of Reason*. London: Merlin, 1980.

———, "Max Weber and German Sociology," tr. A. Cutler, *Economy and Society*, 1 (November 1972), 386–398.

LUKES, STEVEN, *Emile Durkheim: His Life and Work.* London: Allen and Lane, 1973a.
————, *Individualism.* New York: Harper and Row, 1973b.
————, "Methodological Individualism Reconsidered," *British Journal of Sociology*, 21, no. 2 (June 1968), 119–129.
LÜSCHER, KURT, "The Relevance of G. H. Mead for the Comparative Analysis of Contemporary Societies," presented at the 82nd Annual Meeting of the American Sociological Association. Chicago, 1987.
LYMAN, STANFORD M., "The Acceptance, Rejection, and Reconstruction of Histories: On Some Controversies in the Study of Social and Cultural Change," in *Structure, Consciousness and History*, eds. Richard Harvey Brown and Stanford Lyman. Cambridge: Cambridge University Press, 1978, pp. 53–105.
LYNG, STEPHEN, "Edgework: A Social Psychological Analysis of Voluntary Risk Taking," *American Journal of Sociology*, 95, no. 4 (January 1990), 851–886.
MCLELLAN, DAVID, *Karl Marx: His Life and Thought.* New York: Harper and Row, 1973.
MCCLOSKEY, ROBERT C., *American Conservatism in the Age of Enterprise*, 1865–1910. New York: Harper and Row, 1951.
MacFarlane, Alan, *The Origins of English Individualism.* London: Basil Blackwell, 1978.
MACFIE, A. L., *The Individual and Society.* London: George Allen and Unwin, 1967.
MCGUINNESS, ARTHUR E., *Henry Home, Lord Kames.* New York: Twayne Publishers, Inc., 1970.
MACHIAVELLI, NICCOLÒ, *The Prince.*
————, *The Discourses.*
MCINTOSH, DONALD, "Weber and Freud: On the Nature and Sources of Authority," *American Sociological Review*, 35, no. 5 (October 1970), 901–911.
MCPHAIL, CLARK, and CYNTHIA REXROUT, "Mead vs. Blumer: The Divergent Methodological Perspectives of Social Behaviorism," *American Sociological Review*, 44, no. 3 (June 1979), 449–467.
MCPHERSON, CRAWFORD B., *The Political Theory of Possessive Individualism.* Oxford: Clarendon Press, 1962.
MACY, MICHAEL, "Value Theory and the 'Golden Eggs': Appropriating the Magic of Accumulation," *Sociological Theory*, 6, no. 2 (Fall 1988), 131–152.
MAINES, DAVID, "Social Organization and Social Structure in Symbolic Interaction," *Annual Review of Sociology* (Vol. 3). Palo Alto: Annual Reviews, 1977, pp. 235–260.
————, NOREEN M. SUGRUE, and MICHAEL A. KATOVICH, "The Sociological Impact of G. H. Mead's Theory of the Past," *American Sociological Review*, 48, no. 2 (April 1983), 161–173.
MAISTRE, JOSEPH DE, *The Works of Joseph de Maistre*, ed. Jack Lively. New York: MacMillan, 1964.
MAKKREEL, RUDOLF A., *Dilthey, Philosopher of the Human Studies.* Princeton: Princeton University Press, 1975.
————, "Wilhelm Dilthey and the Neo-Kantians: The Distinction of the *Geisteswisenschaften* and the *Kultur-wissenschaften*," *Journal of the History of Philosophy*, 7 (1969), 423–440.
MANDEL, ERNEST, *Marxist Economic Theory* (2 vols.). New York: Monthly Review Press, 1968.
————, and GEORGE NOVACK, *The Marxist Theory of Alienation.* New York: Pathfinder Press, 1970.
MANDEVILLE, BERNARD DE, *The Fable of the Bees.* London: J. Tonson, (6th ed.), 1729.
MANN, MICHAEL, *The Sources of Social Power,Vol. 1: A History of Power from, the Beginning to A.D. 1760.* Cambridge: Cambridge University Press, 1986.
MANNHEIM, KARL, "Historicism," in Karl Mannheim's *Essays on the Sociology of Knowledge* (4th ed.), ed. Paul Kecskemeti. London: Routledge and Kegan Paul, 1968, 84–133.
————, "Conservative Thought," in Karl Mannheim's *Essays on Sociology and Social Psychology*. London: Routledge and Kegan Paul, 1953.
————, *Man and Society in an Age of Reconstruction*, tr. E. Shils (enlarged edition). New York: Harcourt Brace, 1940.
————, *Idealogy and Utopia*, trs. L. Wirth and E. Shils. New York: Harcourt Brace and World, Inc., 1936 [1929].
MANUEL, FRANK, *Shapes of Philosophical History.* Stanford, California: Stanford University Press, 1965.
————, *The Prophets of Paris.* Cambridge: Harvard University Press, 1962.
————, *The New World of Henri Saint-Simon.* Cambridge: Harvard University Press, 1956.
MARCUS, STEVEN, *Engels, Manchester and the Working Class.* New York: Random House, 1974.
MARCUSE, HERBERT, *Negations.* London: Allen Lane, 1968.
————, *Reason and Revolution.* New York: Oxford University Press, 1941.
MARGLIN, STEPHEN, "What do Bosses Do? The Origins of Capitalist Production," *The Review of Radical Economics*, 6 (Summer 1974), 33–60.
MARGOLIS, JOSEPH, *Pragmatism Without Foundations.* New York: Basil Blackwell, 1989.
MARSHALL, GORDON, *In Search of the Spirit of Capitalism: An Essay on Max Weber's Protestant Ethic Thesis.* New York: Columbia University Press, 1982.
————, *Presbyteries and Profits: Calvinism and the Development of Capitalism in Scotland, 1560–1707.* Oxford: Clarendon Press, 1980.
MARSILIUS OF PADUA, *Defensor Pacis*, tr. Alan Gewirth. New York: Columbia University Press, 1956.
MARTINDALE, DON, *The Nature and Types of Sociological Theory* (2d rev. ed.). Boston: Houghton Mifflin, 1981.
————, "Verstehen," in *International Encyclopedia of the Social Sciences* (1968), 16, New York: MacMillan and Free Press, 308–312.
————, *Social Life and Cultural Change.* New York: Van Nostrand, 1962.
————, *The Nature and Types of Sociological Theory.* Boston: Houghton Mifflin, 1960.
MARVIN, F. S., *Comte: The Founder of Sociology.* New York: Russell and Russell, 1965.

MARX, KARL, *Grundrisse*, tr. and ed. David McLellan. London: Penguin Books, 1973.
——, *Capital: A Critique of Political Economy* (Vols. 2 and 3). New York: International Publishers, 1967 [1885, 1894].
——, "Contribution to the Critique of Hegel's Philosophy of Right," in *Karl Marx: Early Writings*, tr. and ed. Tom Bottomore. New York: McGraw-Hill, 1964 [1843], pp. 43–53.
——, *The Poverty of Philosophy*. New York: International Publishers, 1963.
——, *Capital, A Critique of Political Economy*, Vol. 1. New York: Random House, Modern Library, 1906 [1867].
——, and FRIEDRICH ENGELS, *The German Ideology*. London: Lawrence and Wishart, 1965 [1845–1846].
——, and FRIEDRICH ENGELS, *The Holy Family, or Critique of Critical Critique*, tr. R. Dixon. Moscow: Foreign Languages Publishing House, 1956.
——, FRIEDRICH ENGELS, and V. I. LENIN, *The Essential Left*. New York: Barnes and Noble, 1961.
MATHESON, CRAIG, "Weber and the Classification of Forms of Legitimacy," *British Journal of Sociology*, 38, no. 2 (June 1987), 199–215.
MATHEWS, FRED H., *Quest for an American Sociology: Robert E. Park and the Chicago School*. Montreal and London: McGill-Queen University Press, 1977.
MAUPERTUIS, PIERRE LOUIS MOREAU DE, "Système de la nature," in *Oeuvres*, Vol. 2. Hildesheim and New York: George Ohms Verlag, 1974, pp. 135–216.
MAUSS, MARCEL, *The Gift*. New York: Norton, 1967.
MAWSON, A. R., "Durkheim and Contemporary Social Pathology," *British Journal of Sociology*, 21, no. 3 (September 1970), 298–313.
MAYER, CARL, "Max Weber's Interpretation of Karl Marx," *Social Research*, 42, no. 4 (Winter 1975), 701–719.
MAYR, E., *The Growth of Biological Thought*. Cambridge, Massachusetts: Belknap, 1982.
MEAD, GEORGE HERBERT, "The Genesis of the Self and Social Control," in *George Herbert Mead: Selected Writings*, ed. Andrew Reck. Indianapolis: Bobbs-Merrill, 1964, pp. 251–277.
——, "The Nature of Scientific Knowledge," in George Herbert Mead's *Philosophy of the Act*, ed. C. W. Morris. Chicago: University of Chicago Press, 1938a, pp. 45–61.
——, *Philosophy of the Act*, ed. C. W. Morris. Chicago: University of Chicago Press, 1938b.
——, *Movements of Thought in the Nineteenth Century*, ed. M. H. Moore. Chicago: University of Chicago Press, 1936.
——, *Mind, Self and Society*, ed. C. W. Morris. Chicago: University of Chicago Press, 1934.
——, *Philosophy of the Present*, ed. Arthur E. Murphy. Chicago: Open Court Publishers, 1932.
——, "Cooley's Contribution to American Social Thought," *American Journal of Sociology*, 35, no. 5 (March 1930). Reprinted as "Foreward" in Cooley's *Human Nature and the Social Order*. New York: Shocken, 1964, pp. xxi–xxxviii.
——, "The Teaching of Science in College," *Science*, 24 (September 28, 1906), 290–397.
MENGER, KARL, *Principles of Economics*, trs. and eds. J. Dingwell and B. F. Hoselitz. Glencoe, Illinois: Free Press, 1950.
MERQUIOR, J. G., *Rousseau and Weber: Two Studies in the Theory of Legitimacy*. London: Routledge and Kegan Paul, 1980.
MERTON, ROBERT K., *Social Theory and Social Structure* (2d ed). Glencoe, Illinois: The Free Press, 1957a.
——, "Manifest and Latent Functions," in Robert K. Merton's *Social Theory and Social Structure*. Glencoe, Illinois: Free Press, 1957b, pp. 19–84.
——, "Social Structure and Anomie," in Robert K. Merton's *Social Theory and Social Structure*. Glencoe, Illinois: Free Press, 1957c, pp. 131–160.
——, "Bureaucratic Structure and Personality," in *Reader in Bureaucracy*, eds. Robert K. Merton and others. Glencoe, Illinois: The Free Press, 1952a, 361–371.
——, et al., *Reader in Bureaucracy*. Glencoe, Illinois: The Free Press, 1952b.
——, "Durkheim's Division of Labor in Society," *American Journal of Sociology*, 40, no. 3 (November 1934), 319–328.
MERZ, JOHN THEODORE, *A History of European Thought in the Nineteenth Century*, 4 Vols. New York: Dover, 1965 [First publ. 1904–1912 by Wm. Blackwell and Sons].
MESSNER, STEVEN F., "Societal Development, Social Equality, and Homicide: A Cross-National Test of a Durkheim Model," *Social Forces*, 61, no. 1 (September 1982), 225–240.
MICHELS, ROBERT, *Political Parties*. New York: Collier, 1962.
MIDGLEY, E. B. F., *The Ideology of Max Weber, A Thomist Critique*. Aldershot, England: Gower, 1983.
MILL, JOHN S., *Philosophy of Scientific Method*. New York: Hafner, 1974 [1850].
——, *Auguste Comte and Positivism*. Ann Arbor, Michigan: University of Michigan Press, 1961 [1865].
——, *Utilitarianism* and *On Liberty*, in *The Utilitarians*. New York: Doubleday and Company, Dolphin Books, 1961.
MILLAR, JOHN, *The Origin of the Distinction of Ranks*. London: Longman, Hunt, Rees and Orme, 1806.
——, *An Historical View of the English Government from the Settlement of the Saxons in Britain to the Accession of the House of Stuart* (4 vols.). London: Mawman, 1803.
MILLER, DAVID L., ed., *The Individual and the Social Self, Unpublished Work of George Herbert Mead*. Chicago: University of Chicago Press, 1982.
MILLS, C. WRIGHT, *The Power Elite*. New York: Oxford University Press, 1956.

MITZMAN, ARTHUR, *The Iron Cage: An Historical Interpretation of Max Weber.* New York: Knopf, 1970.

MOERS, ELLEN, *The Dandy: Brummell to Beerbohm.* New York: Viking, 1960.

MOLLOY, STEPHEN, "Max Weber and the Religions of China: Any Way Out of the Maze," *British Journal of Sociology*, 31, no. 3 (September 1980), 377–400.

MOMMSEN, WOLFGANG J., *Max Weber and German Politics 1890–1920*, tr. Michael S. Steinberg. Chicago and London: University of Chicago Press, 1984.

———, *The Age of Bureaucracy.* Oxford: Basil Blackwell, 1974.

MONBODDO, LORD (JAMES BURNET), *Of the Origin and Progress of Language.* New York: Garland Publishers, 1970 [1792].

MONTESQUIEU, CHARLES DE SECONDAT, *The Spirit of the Laws*, tr. Thomas Nugent, with intro. by Franz Neumann. New York: Hafner Publishing Co., 1966 [1748].

———, *Persian Letters.* Washington and London: M. Walter Dunne, 1901 [1739].

MOONEY, M., *Vico in the Tradition of Rhetoric.* Princeton, New Jersey: Princeton University Press, 1985.

MOORE, BARRINGTON, JR., *Social Origins of Dictatorship and Democracy.* Boston: Beacon Press, 1966.

MORGAN, LEWIS H., *Ancient Society.* New York: Holt, Rinehard and Winston, 1877.

MORROW, GLEN, *The Ethical and Economic Theories of Adam Smith.* New York: Longmans Green, 1922.

MOSCA, GAETANO, *The Ruling Class*, tr. Hannah D. Kahn, ed. and rev. Arthur Livingston. New York: McGraw-Hill, 1939.

MOSSNER, ERNEST CAMPBELL, *The Life of David Hume.* Austin: University of Texas Press, 1954.

MUNCH, PETER, "Empirical Science and Max Weber's Verstehende Soziologie," *American Sociological Review*, 22, no. 1 (February 1957), 26–32.

———, "'Sense' and 'Intention' in Max Weber's Theory of Social Action," *Sociological Inquiry*, 45, no. 4 (1875), 59–65.

MURPHY, RAYMOND, "Exploitation or Exclusion?" *Sociology*, 19, no. 2 (May 1985), 225–243.

MURVAR, VATRO, *Max Weber Today: An Introduction to a Living Legacy: Selected Bibliography.* Brookfield, Wisconsin: University of Wisconsin-Milwaukee, 1983.

NAGEL, ERNEST, "The Logic of Historical Inquiry," in *Readings in the Philosophy of Science*, eds. Herbert Feigl and May Brodbeck. New York: Appleton-Century-Crofts, 1953a, 688–700.

———, "Teleological Explanation and Teleological Systems," in *Readings in the Philosophy of Science*, eds. Herbert Feigl and May Brodbeck. New York: Appleton-Century-Crofts, 1953b.

NANDAN, YASH, *Emile Durkheim: Contributions to L'Année sociologique.* New York: MacMillan, 1980.

NELSON, BENJAMIN, *On the Roads to Modernity: Conscience, Science and Civilization.* Totowa, New Jersey: Rowman and Littlefield, 1981.

———, "On Orient and Occident in Max Weber," *Social Research* 43, no. 1 (Spring 1976), 114–129.

———, "Max Weber's 'Author's Introduction' (1920): A Master Clue to His Main Aims," *Social Inquiry*, 44, no. 4 (1974), 269–278.

———, "Weber's Protestant Ethic," in *Beyond the Classes?* eds. Charles Glock and Phillip E. Hammond. New York: Harper and Row, 1973, pp. 71–130.

———, "Comments" (on Herbert Marcuse), in *Max Weber and Sociology Today*, ed. Otto Stammer. New York: Harper and Row, 1971.

NEWTON, JANET, *The English Legal Profession and Early Law Reform: A Weberian Analysis.* Ph.D. Dissertation, Department of Sociology, Pennsylvania State University, 1987.

NIEBUHR, H. RICHARD, *The Social Sources of Denominationalism.* New York: Henry Holt and Company, 1929.

NISBET, H. B., *Herder and the Philosophy and History of Science.* Cambridge, England: Modern Humanities Research Association, 1970.

NISBET, ROBERT, "Conservatism," in *A History of Sociological Analysis*, eds. Tom Bottomore and Robert Nisbet. New York: Basic Books, 1978, 80–117.

———, *The Sociology of Emile Durkheim.* New York: Oxford University Press, 1974.

———, *Social Change and History.* New York: Oxford University Press, 1969.

———, *The Sociological Tradition.* New York; Basic Books, 1966.

———, ed. and contributor. *Emile Durkheim.* Englewood Cliffs, New Jersey: Prentice Hall, 1965.

NORTHRUP, F. S. C., *The Meeting of East and West: An Inquiry Concerning World Understanding.* New York: MacMillan, 1945.

OBERSCHALL, ANTHONY, *Empirical Research in Germany, 1848–1914.* Paris: Mouton, 1965.

O'LEARY, BRENDAN, *The Asiatic Mode of Production.* New York: Basic Blackwell, 1989.

OLLMAN, BERTELL, *Social and Sexual Revolution: Essays on Marx and Reich.* Boston: South End Press, 1979.

———, *Alienation: Marx's Conception of Man in Capitalist Society* (2d ed.). New York and Cambridge: Cambridge University Press, 1976.

ORTONY, ANDREW, *Metaphor and Thought.* Cambridge: Cambridge University Press, 1979.

OUTHWAITE, W., *Understanding Social Life: The Method Called Verstehen.* London: Allen and Unwin, 1975.

PAGE, CHARLES H., *Class and American Sociology.* New York: Shocken, 1969.

PARETO, VILFREDO, *The Mind and Society*, 4 vols., trs. Andre Bongiorno and Arthur Livingston. New York: Harcourt Brace, 1935 [1916].

PARK, ROBERT E., and ERNEST BURGESS, *Introduction to the Science of Sociology.* Chicago: University of Chicago Press, 1924.

———, and HERBERT A. MILLER, *Old World Traits Transplanted.* New York: Harper and Brothers, 1921.

PARKIN, FRANK, *Max Weber.* New York: Tavistock Publishers and Ellis Harwood, Ltd., 1982.

————, *Marxism and Class Theory: A Bourgeois Critique*. New York: Columbia University Press, 1979.

PARSONS, TALCOTT, "Emile Durkheim," *International Encyclopedia of the Social Sciences* (1968a), 4, 311–320.

————, "Order as a Sociological Problem," in *The Concept of Order*, ed. Howard Buckle. Seattle: University of Washington Press, 1968b, pp. 373–384.

————, *Societies: Evolutionary and Comparative*. Englewood Cliffs, New Jersey: Prentice Hall, 1966.

————, "An Analytical Approacy to the Theory of Social Stratification," in Talcott Parsons, *Essays in Sociological Theory* (rev. ed.). Glencoe, Illinois: The Free Press, 1954 [1949].

————, *The Social System*. Glencoe, Illinois: The Free Press, 1951.

————, *The Structure of Social Action*. Glencoe, Illnois: The Free Press, 1949.

PAYNE, HARRY C., *The Philosophes and the People*. New Haven: Yale University Press, 1976.

PEEL, JOHN DAVID, *Herbert Spencer, the Evolution of a Sociologist*. New York: Basic Books, 1971.

PEIRCE, CHARLES SANDERS, *Collected Papers of Charles Sanders Peirce*, eds. Charles Hartshorne and Paul Weiss. Cambridge: Harvard University Press, 1931–1958.

PEPPER, STEPHEN C., *World Hypotheses*. Berkeley: University of California Press, 1970.

PEREZ-DIAZ, VICTOR M., *State, Bureaucracy and Civil Society: A Critical Discussion of the Political Theory of Karl Marx*. London: MacMillan, 1978.

PERKINS, MERLE L., *Jean-Jacques Rousseau: On the Individual and Society*. Lexington, Kentucky: University of Kentucky Press, 1974.

PERRAULT, CHARLES, "A Comparison of the Ancients and Moderns," in *The Idea of Progress: A Collection of Readings*, ed. Frederick J. Teggart. Berkeley and Los Angeles: University of California Press, 1949, pp. 188–194.

PERRIN, ROBERT G., "Herbert Spencer's Four Theories of Social Evolution," *American Journal of Sociology*, 81, no. 6 (May 1976), 1, 339–359.

PETRAS, JOHN W., "Changes of Emphasis in the Sociology of W. I. Thomas," *Journal of the History of the Behavioral Sciences*, 6 (January 1970), 70–79.

PICKERING, W. S. F., *Durkheim: Essays on Morals and Education*. London and Boston: Routledge and Kegan Paul, 1979.

————, *Durkheim on Religion: A Selection of Readings with Bibliographies*. London: Routledge and Kegan Paul, 1975.

PIRENNE, HENRI, *Economic and Social History of Europe*. London: Routledge and Kegan Paul, 1936.

PLAMENATZ, JOHN, *Karl Marx's Philosophy of Man*. London: Oxford University Press, 1975.

————, *Man and Society*, 2 vols. New York: McGraw-Hill, 1963.

POGGI, GIANFRANCO, *Calvinism and the Capitalist Spirit: Max Weber's Protestant Ethic*. Amherst: University of Massachusetts Press, 1983.

————, *The Development of the Modern State: A Sociological Introduction*. Stanford: Stanford University Press, 1978.

POLANYI, KARL, *The Great Transformation*. New York: Rinehart, 1944.

POPE, ALEXANDER, "An Essay on Man," in *The Literature of England* (3d ed.), Vol. 1, eds. George Woods, Homer Watt, and George Anderson. New York: Scott, Foresman & Co., 1947, pp. 995–1,004.

POPE, WHITNEY, "Classic on Classic: Parson's Interpretation of Durkheim," *American Sociological Review*, 38, no. 4 (August 1973), 399–415.

————, and BARCLAY JOHNSON, "Inside Organic Solidarity," *American Sociological Review*, 48, no. 5 (October 1983), 681–692.

POPPER, KARL, *The Poverty of Historicism*. London: Routledge and Kegan Paul, 1954.

PORTIS, EDWARD BRYAN, "Max Weber's Theory of Personality," *Sociological Inquiry*, 48, no. 2 (1978), 113–120.

POULANTZAS, NICOS, *Classes in Contemporary Capitalism*. London: New Left Books, 1975.

PRIESTLY, JOSEPH, *A Description of a New Chart of History* (11th ed.). London: J. Johnson, 1801.

QUADAGNO, JILL S., "Paradigms in Evolutionary Theory: The Sociobiological Model of Natural Selection," *American Sociological Review*, 44, no. 1 (February 1979), 110–119.

RAISON, TIMOTHY, ed., *The Founding Fathers of Social Science, A Series from New Society*. London: Scolar Press, 1979.

RAPHAËL, FREDDY, "Max Weber et la Judaïsme antique," *Archives européenes de sociologie*, 11, no. 1 (1970), 297–336.

RECK, ANDREW, ed., *George Herbert Mead: Selected Writings*. Indianapolis: Bobbs-Merrill, 1964.

REICH, WILHELM, *People in Trouble*. London: Rangeley, 1953.

REISMAN, D. A., *Adam Smith's Sociological Economics*. New York: Barnes and Noble, 1976.

REX, JOHN, *Sociology and the Demystification of the Modern World*. London: Routledge and Kegan Paul, 1974.

————, "Ideal Types and the Comparative Study of Social Structures," in John Rex's *Discovering Sociology*. London: Routledge and Kegan Paul, 1973, pp. 192–211.

RICHARDS, ROBERT J., *Darwin and the Emergence of Evolutionary Theories of Mind and Behavior*. Chicago: University of Chicago Press, 1987.

RICKERT, HEINRICH, *The Limits of Concept Formation in Natural Science: A Logical Introduction to the Historical Sciences*, tr. and ed. G. Oakes. Cambridge: Cambridge University Press, 1986 [1896–1902].

————, *Science and History, A Critique of Positivist Epistemology*, ed. A. Goddard, tr. George Reisman. New York: Van Nostrand, 1962.

RINGER, FRITZ, *The Decline of the German Mandarins*. Cambridge: Harvard University Press, 1969.

RITSERT, J., *Social Classes, Action, and Historical Materialism.* Amsterdam: Hague Press, 1982.

RITZER, GEORGE, *Sociology: A Multiple Paradigm Science.* Boston: Allyn and Bacon, 1975.

ROBERTSON, H. W., *Aspects of the Rise of Economic Individualism: A Criticism of Max Weber and His School.* Cambridge: Cambridge University Press, 1933.

RORTY, RICHARD, *Consequences of Pragmatism.* Minneapolis: University of Minnesota Press, 1982.

ROSSIDES, DANIEL W., *The History and Nature of Sociological Theory.* Boston: Houghton Mifflin, 1975.

ROTH, GUENTHER, "Marx and Weber on the United States—Today," in *A Marx-Weber Dialogue*, eds. Robert Antonio and Ronald Glassman. Lawrence, Kansas: University of Kansas Press, 1985, pp. 215–233.

———, "Socio-Historical Model and Developmental Theory: Charismatic Community, Charisma of Reason and the Counterculture," *American Sociological Review*, 40, no. 2 (April 1975), 148–157.

———, "Political Critiques of Max Weber: Some Implications for Political Sociology," *American Sociological Review*, 30, no. 2 (April 1965), 213–223.

———, and WOLFGANG SCHLUCHTER, *Max Weber's Vision of History: Ethics and Methods.* Berkeley: University of California Press, 1979.

ROUSSEAU, JEAN-JACQUES, *Emile*, tr. Allan Bloom. New York: Basic Books, 1979.

———, *The First and Second Discourses*, ed. R. D. Masters, trs. R. D. Masters and J. R. Masters. New York: St. Martin's, 1964.

———, *The Social Contract*, tr. Charles Frankel. New York: Hafner Publishing Co., 1947.

———, *The Confessions of Jean-Jacques Rousseau*, tr. W. C. Mallory. New York: Tudor Publishing Co., 1936.

RUESCHEMAYER, DIETRICH, "On Durkheim's Explanation of the Division of Labor," *American Journal of Sociology*, 88, no. 3 (November 1982), 579–589.

RUGGIERO, GUIDO DE, "Positivism," *Encyclopedia of the Social Sciences* (1938), Vol. 12, 260.

RUMNEY, JAY, *Herbert Spencer's Sociology, a Study in the History of Social Theory.* New York: Atherton Press, 1965 [1937].

RUNCIMAN, WALTER G., ed., *Weber: Selections in Translation*, tr. E. Mathews. Cambridge: Cambridge University Press, 1978.

RUSSELL, BERTRAND, *History of Western Philosophy.* New York: Simon and Schuster, 1972 [1945].

SAHAY, ARUN, ed., *Max Weber and Modern Sociology.* London: Routledge and Kegan Paul, 1971.

———, *Hindu Reformist Ethics and the Weber Thesis: An Application of Max Weber's Methodology.* London University Ph.D. Thesis, 1969.

SALOMON, ALBERT, "German Sociology," in *Twentieth Century Sociology*, eds. George Gurvitch and Wilbert Moore. New York: Philosophical Library, 1945, pp. 596–620.

———, "Max Weber's Sociology," *Social Research*, 2 (February 1935), 60–73.

SAMUELSSON, KURT, *Religion and Economic Action.* New York: Basic Books, 1961.

SAUSSURE, FERDINAND DE, *Course in General Linguistics.* London, Peter Owen, 1960.

SCAFF, LAWRENCE, "Max Weber and Robert Michels," *American Journal of Sociology*, 86, no. 6 (May 1981), 1269–1286.

SCHAFF, ADAM, *Marxism and the Human Individual.* New York: McGraw-Hill, 1970.

SCHEFFLER, ISRAEL, "Prospects of a Modest Empiricism," *Review of Metaphysics*, 10, no. 1 (March 1957), 383–400; and 10, no. 2 (June 1957), 602–625.

SCHELTING, ALEXANDER VON, *Max Weber's Wissenschaftslehre.* Tübingen: J. C. B. Mohr, 1934.

SCHLEIERMACHER, FRIEDRICH, *On Religion: Speeches to Its Cultured Despisers.* New York: Harper and Row, 1958 [1799].

SCHLUCHTER, WOLFGANG, *The Rise of Western Rationalism: Max Weber's Developmental History.* Berkeley: University of California Press, 1981.

SCHNEIDER, LOUIS, *The Scottish Moralists on Human Nature and Society.* Chicago: University of Chicago Press, 1967.

SCHROETER, GERD, "Dialogue, Debate, or Dissent? The Difficulties of Assessing Max Weber's Relation to Marx," in *A Marx-Weber Dialogue*, eds. Robert Antonio and Ronald Glassman. Lawrence, Kansas: University of Kansas Press, 1985, pp. 2–19.

SCHUMPETER, JOSEPH, *Capitalism, Socialism and Democracy.* New York: Harper, 1950.

SCHUTZ, ALFRED, *The Phenomenology of the Social World*, trs. G. Walsch and F. Lehnert. Evanston, Illinois: Northwestern University Press, 1967.

SCHWARTZ, BARRY, *George Washington: The Making of an American Symbol.* New York: Free Press, 1987.

———, "Emerson, Cooley and the American Heroic Vision," *Symbolic Interaction*, 8, no. 1 (Spring 1985), 103–120.

———, "George Washington and the Whig Conception of Heroic Leadership," *American Sociological Review*, 48, no. 1 (February 1983), 18–33.

SCHWARTZ, R. D., AND J. C. MILLER, "Legal Evolution and Societal Complexity," *American Journal of Sociology*, 70, no. 2 (September 1964), 159–69.

SCHWENDINGER, HERMAN, and JULIA R. SCHWENDINGER, *The Sociologists of the Chair.* New York: Basic Books, 1974.

SEE, HENRI, *Modern Capitalism: Its Origins and Evolution.* New York: Adelphi Press, 1928.

SENNOTT, ROGER S., and RICHARD V. TRAVISANO, "Puritanism and Rationality: The Socially Impossible Consciousness," *Humanity and Society*, 9, no. 1 (February 1985), 29–47.

SETH, JAMES, *English Philosophers and Schools of Philosophy.* London: E. P. Dutton, 1925.

SEWART, JOHN, "Verstehen and Dialectic: Epistemology and Methodology in Weber and Lukács," *Philosophy and Social Criticism*, 5, no. 3 and no. 4 (July and October 1978), 319–366.

SHAFTSBURY, ANTHONY (ANTHONY ASHLEY COOPER, 3RD EARL), *Characteristicks of Men, Manners, Opinions* (3 vols.) corrected ed. Indianapolis: Bobbs-Merrill 1964 [1714].

SHALIN, DMITRI N., "G. H. Mead, Socialism, and the Progressive Agenda, *American Journal of Sociology*, 93, no. 4 (January 1988), 913–951.

———, "Pragmatism and Social Interactionism," *American Journal of Sociology*, 91, no. 1 (February 1986), 9–29.

———, "The Romantic Antecedents of Meadian Social Psychology," *Symbolic Interaction*, 7 (Spring 1984), 43–65.

SHELLING, THOMAS, "On the Ecology of Micromotives," in *The Corporate Society*, ed. R. Morris. London: MacMillan, 1974, pp. 19–64.

SHILS, EDWARD, "Charisma, Order, and Status," *American Sociological Review*, 30, no. 2 (April 1965), 199–213.

SICA, ALAN, *Weber, Irrationality, and Social Order*. Berkeley: University of California Press, 1988.

———, "Reasonable Science, Unreasonable Life: The Happy Fictions of Marx, Weber, and Social Theory," in *A Marx-Weber Dialogue*, eds. Robert Antonio and Ronald Glassman. Lawrence, Kansas: University of Kansas Press, 1985, pp. 68–88.

———, "The Unknown Max Weber: A Note on Missing Translations," *Mid-American Review of Sociology*, 9, no. 2 (1984), 3–25.

SIMIRENKO, ALEX, "Ersatz Charisma: Sociological Interpetation of Socialist Countries," *Newsletter on Comparative Studies of Communism*, 4, no. 1 (1971), 3–15.

SIMMEL, GEORG, *Essays on Interpretation in Social Science*, tr., ed., and intro. Guy Oakes. Totowa, New Jersey: Rowman and Littlefield, 1980.

———, *The Philosophy of Money*. Boston: Routledge and Kegan Paul, 1979 [1899].

———, *The Problems of the Philosophy of History*, ed. and tr. Guy Oakes. New York: Free Press, 1977.

———, *The Sociology of Georg Simmel*, ed. K. Wolff. Glencoe, Illinois: Free Press, 1950.

SIMON, W. M., *European Positivism in the Nineteenth Century: An Essay in Intellectual History*. Ithaca, New York: Cornell University Press, 1963.

SIMPSON, GEORGE, *Auguste Comte: Sire of Sociology*. New York: Crowell, 1969.

SKOCPOL, THEDA, *States and Social Revolutions*. New York: Academic Press, 1979.

SMALL, ALBION, *General Sociology: An Exposition of the Main Development in Sociological Theory from Spencer to Ratzenhofer*. Chicago: University of Chicago Press, 1925.

———, "Fifty Years of Sociology in the United States (1865–1915)," *American Journal of Sociology*, 21, no. 6 (May 1916), 721–864.

———, *Adam Smith and Modern Sociology*. Chicago: University of Chicago Press, 1907.

———, and GEORGE VINCENT, *An Introduction to the Study of Society*. New York: American Book Co., 1894.

SMITH, ADAM, *Lectures on Jurisprudence*, eds. R. L. Meek, D. D. Raphael, and P. G. Stein (Glasgow ed.). Oxford: The Clarendon Press, 1978 [Reports of 1762 and 1766 first published 1896].

———, *The Theory of Moral Sentiments*. New York: Augustus Kelly, 1966 [1759].

———, *An Inquiry into the Nature and Causes of the Wealth of Nations*, 2 vols. Homewood, Illinois: Richard Irwin, 1963 [1776].

SOHM, RUDOLF, *Outlines of Church History*, tr. May Sinclair. Boston: Beacon Press, 1958.

SOMBART, WERNER, *The Jews and Modern Capitalism*, tr. M. Epstein. Glencoe, Illinois: Free Press, 1951 [1911].

———, *The Quintessence of Capitalism*. London: T. F. Unwin, 1915.

SOREL, GEORGES, *Reflections on Violence*. New York: Collier Books, 1961 [1908].

SOROKIN, PITIRIM, *Contemporary Sociological Theories*. New York: Harper, 1928.

SPEIER, HANS, *Social Order and the Risks of War*. New York: Stewart, 1952.

SPENCE, LARRY D., *The Politics of Social Knowledge*. University Park, Pennsylvania: The Pennsylvania State University Press, 1978.

SPENCER, HERBERT, *The Study of Sociology*. New York: Appleton-Century Crofts, 1961 [1873].

———, *Descriptive Sociology, or Groups of Sociological Facts*, eds. Donald Duncan and others (13 vols). London and elsewhere: 1873–1934.

———, *Principles of Ethics*. New York: D. Appleton and Company, 1904 [1879–1893].

———, *Principles of Sociology*, 2 vols. London: Williams and Nagate, 1898 [1876–1896].

———, *Social Statics* (abr. and rev.), together with *The Man and the State*. New York: Appleton, 1896 [1850 and 1884].

———, *Principles of Biology*. New York: Appleton, 1884 [1866].

———, *First Principles*. New York: A. L. Burt, 1880 [1862].

———, "Progress: Its Law and Cause," *Westminster and Foreign Quarterly Review*, 67, article 5 (April 1857), 244–267.

———, *Principles of Psychology*. London: Longmans Green, 1855.

———, "A Theory of Population, Deduced from the General Law of Animal Fertility," *Westminster and Foreign Quarterly Review*, 57, article 4 (April 1852), 250–268.

SPENCER, MARTIN E., "Weber on Legitimate Norms and Authority," *British Journal of Sociology*, 21, no. 2 (June 1970), 123–134.

SPENGLER, OSWALD, *Decline of the West*, tr. C.F. Atkinson. New York: Alfred A. Knopf, 1926.

SPINOZA, BENEDICT, *Ethics*.

SPRONDEL, WALTER M., and CONSTANS SEYFARTH, eds., *Max Weber und die Rationalisierung sozialen Handelns*. Stuttgart: Ferdinand Enke, 1981.

STAMMER, OTTO ed., *Max Weber and Sociology Today*. New York: Harper and Row, 1971.

STANDLEY, ARLINE, *Auguste Comte*. Boston: Twayne Publishers, 1981.

STARK, WERNER, *The Sociology of Knowledge*. London: Routledge and Kegan Paul, 1958.

STEIN, LORENZ VON, *History of the Social Movement in France*, tr. and ed. Kaethe Mergelberg. Totowa, New Jersey: Bedminster Press, 1850.

STEPHENS, JOHN D., *The Transition from Capitalism to Socialism*. Urbana and Chicago: University of Illinois Press, 1986.

STEWART, JOHN B., *The Moral and Political Philosophy of David Hume*. New York and London: Columbia University Press, 1963.

STOCKING, GEORGE W., *Race, Culture and Evolution: Essays in the History of Anthropology*. New York: The Free Press, 1968.

STONE, GREGORY, and HARVEY FARBERMAN, "On the Edge of Rapprochment: Was Durkheim Moving Towards Symbolic Interactionism?" *Sociological Quarterly*, 8, no. 2 (Spring 1967), 149–164.

STONE, LAWRENCE, *The Crisis of Aristocracy*. New York: Oxford University Press, 1967.

STRAUSS, DAVID F., *The Life of Jesus*, tr. Marian Evans. St. Claire Shores, Michigan: Scholarly Press, 1970 [1835].

STRAUSS, LEO, *Natural Right and History*. Chicago: University of Chicago Press, 1953.

STRYKER, SHELDON, *Symbolic Interactionism: A Social Structural Version*. Menlo Park, California: Benjamin Cummings, 1980.

SUMNER, WILLIAM GRAHAM, *Folkways*. Boston: Ginn Publishers, 1906.

SWANSON, GUY, *The Birth of the Gods*. Ann Arbor: University of Michigan Press, 1960.

SWEEZY, PAUL, "Some Problems in the Theory of Capitalist Accumulation," *Monthly Review*, 26, no. 1 (May 1974), 38–55.

SWIDLER, ANN, "The Concept of Rationality in the Work of Max Weber," *Sociological Inquiry*, 43, no. 1 (1973), 35–42.

SWINGEWOOD, ALAN, "Origins of Sociology: The Case of the Scottish Enlightenment," *British Journal of Sociology*, 21, no. 2 (June 1970), 164–181.

SZACKI, JERZY, *History of Sociological Thought*. Westport, Connecticut: Greenwood, 1979.

TALMON, JACOB, *The Origins of Totalitarianian Democracy*. London: Secker and Warburg, 1952.

TAR, ZOLTAN, *The Frankfurt School*. New York: Wiley, 1977.

TAWNEY, R. H., *Religion and the Rise of Capitalism*. Baltimore: Penguin, 1938.

———, *The Agrarian Problem in the Sixteenth Century*. London: Longmans Green, 1912.

TAYLOR, KEITH, *Henri Saint-Simon*. New York: Holmes and Meier, 1975.

TAYLOR, STEVE, *Durkheim and Suicide*. New York: MacMillan, 1982.

TEGGART, FREDERICK J., *The Idea of Progress: A Collection of Readings*, rev. and intro. George H. Hildebrand. Berkeley and Los Angeles: University of California Press, 1949.

———, *Theory and Processes in History*. Berkeley: University of California Press, 1941.

TENBRUCK, FRIEDRICH H., "The Problem of Thematic Unity in the Works of Max Weber," *British Journal of Sociology*, 31, no. 3 (1980), 313–351.

THERBORN, GÖRAN, *Science, Class, and Society*. London: New Left Books, 1976.

THOMAS, PAUL, *Karl Marx and the Anarchists*. London: Routledge and Kegan Paul, 1985.

THOMAS, W. I., *On Social Organization and Social Responsibility*, ed. M. Janowitz. Chicago: University of Chicago Press, 1966.

———, *Social Behavior and Personality*. New York: Social Science Research Council, 1951.

———, *The Unadjusted Girl*. Boston: Little, Brown, 1923.

———, *Source Book for Social Origins*. Chicago: University of Chicago Press, 1909.

———, and FLORIAN ZNANIECKI, *The Polish Peasant in Europe and America*, 2 vols. New York: Knopf, 1927 [1918–1920].

THOMPSON, KENNETH, ed., *Readings from Emile Durkheim*. New York: Tavistock, 1985.

———, *Auguste Comte: The Foundation of Sociology*. London: Thomas Nelson and Sons, Ltd., 1976.

THRUPP, SYLVIA L., "The Role of Comparison in the Development of Economic History," in *Society and History: Essays by Sylvia L. Thrupp*. Ann Arbor: University of Michigan Press, 1977, pp. 274–292.

TIRYAKIAN, EDWARD, "Emile Durkheim," in *A History of Sociological Analysis*, eds. Tom Bottomore and Robert Nisbet. New York: Basic Books, 1978, pp. 187–236.

TOCQUEVILLE, ALEXIS DE, *Democracy in America*, tr. Henry Reeve. London: Oxford University Press, 1946 [1835].

TODD, ARTHUR JAMES, *Theories of Social Progress*. New York: MacMillan, 1918.

TÖNNIES, FERDINAND, *Community and Society*, tr. Charles Loomis. New York: Harper and Row, 1963 [1887].

TRAUGOTT, MARK, ed., *Emile Durkheim on Institutional Analysis*. Chicago: University of Chicago Press, 1978.

TREIBER, HUBERT, "Criticism as a Vocation: Theory and Practice in a Disenchanted World: A Review Essay" (A Review of Anthony Kronman's *Max Weber*) *Contemporary Crises*, 9, no. 4 (December 1985), pp. 375–386.

———, "'Elective Affinities' Between Weber's Sociology of Religion and Sociology of Law," *Philosophy and Social Criticism: International Quarterly Journal*, 10, nos. 3 and 4 (1984), 809–861.

TREITSCHKE, HEINRICH VON, *Politics*, abr. and ed. Hans Kohn. New York: Harcourt Brace, 1963 [1896–1897].

TREVOR-ROPER, HUGH, *Religion, the Reformation and Social Change.* New York: MacMillan, 1967.
TRUZZI, MARCELLO, ed., *Verstehen: Subjective Understanding in the Social Sciences.* Reading, Massachusetts, and elsewhere: Addison-Wesley Publishing Co., 1974.
TUCKER, ROBERT C., *The Marx-Engels Reader.* New York: Norton, 1972.
TUCKER, WILLIAM, "Max Weber's *Verstehen*," *Sociological Quarterly*, 6, no. 1 (Winter 1965), 157–165.
TURGOT, ANNE ROBERT JACQUES, *On the Progress of the Human Mind*, tr. M. de Grange. Hanover, New Hampshire: The Sociological Press, 1929.
TURNER, BRYAN S., *For Weber: Essays on the Sociology of Fate.* London: Routledge and Kegan Paul, 1981.
———, "The Structuralist Critique of Weber's Sociology," *British Journal of Sociology*, 28, no. 1 (March 1977), 1–16.
———, *Weber and Islam.* London: Routledge and Kegan Paul, 1974.
TURNER, JONATHAN, *Herbert Spencer: A Renewed Appreciation.* Beverly Hills, California: Sage Publications, 1985.
TURNER, STEPHEN P., "Weber on Action," *American Sociological Review*, 48, no. 4 (August 1983), 506–519.
———, "Interpretive Charity, Durkheim, and the 'Strong Programme' in the Sociology of Sciences," *Philosophy of the Social Sciences*, 11, no. 2 (June 1981), 231–243.
———, and REGIS A. FACTOR, *Max Weber and the Dispute over Reason and Value.* London: Routledge and Kegan Paul, 1984.
TYLOR, EDWARD B., *Primitive Culture.* New York: Harper, 1958 [1851].
VAN DER SPRENKEL, OTTO, "Max Weber on China," *History and Theory*, 3 (1963), 348–370.
VEBLEN, THORSTEIN, *The Theory of the Leisure Class.* New York: MacMillan, 1899.
VICO, GIAMBATTISTA, *The New Science of Giambattista Vico*, tr. Thomas G. Bergin and Max Fisch. Ithaca, New York: Cornell University Press, 1948 [1725, expanded version 1731].
VIDICH, ARTHUR, and STANLEY LYMAN, *American Sociology: Worldly Rejections of Religion and Their Directions.* New Haven, Connecticut: Yale University Press, 1985.
VINER, JACOB, "Adam Smith and Laissez-Faire," in Jacob Viner's *The Long View and the Short.* Glencoe, Illinois: Free Press, 1927, pp. 213–245.
VOLKART, EDMUND H., *Social Behavior and Personality: Contributions of W. I. Thomas to Theory and Social Research.* New York: Social Science Research Council, 1951.
VOLPE, GALVANO DELLA, *Rousseau and Marx*, tr. J. Fraser. Atlantic Highlands, New Jersey: Humanities Press, 1979.
WADE, IRA O., *The Intellectual Origins of the French Enlightenment.* Princeton, New Jersey: Princeton University Press, 1971.
———, *The Structure and Form of the French Enlightenment*, 2 vols. Princeton, New Jersey: Princeton University Press, 1977.
WALLERSTEIN, IMMANUEL, *The Modern World System*, Vols. 1 and 2. New York: Academic Press, 1974 and 1980.
WALLIMAN, ISIDOR, *Estrangement: Marx's Conception of Human Nature and the Division of Labor.* Westport, Connecticut: Greenwood Press, 1981.
WALLWORK, ERNEST, *Durkheim: Morality and Milieu.* Cambridge: Harvard University Press, 1972.
WARD, LESTER FRANK, *Dynamic Sociology*, 2 vols. New York: Appleton and Company, 1883.
WARNER, R. STEPHEN, "Max Weber: Analysis of Rationalization," in *Sociological Theory: Historical and Formal*, eds. N. J. Smelser and R. Stephen Warner. Morristown, New Jersey: General Learning Press, 1976.
WARRINER, CHARLES K., "Social Action, Behavior and *Verstehen*," *Sociological Quarterly*, 10, no. 4 (Fall 1969), 501–511.
WATERS, MALCOM, "Collegiality, Bureaucratization, and Professionalization: A Weberian Analysis," *American Sociological Review* 94, no. 5 (March, 1989), p. 945–972.
WAX, MURRAY, "On Misunderstanding Verstehen: A Reply to Abel," *Sociology and Social Research*, 51, no. 3 (April 1967), 323–333; and Theodore Abel's "Reply," pp. 334–336.
WEBER, MARIANNE, *Max Weber: A Biography*, tr. and ed. H. Zohn. New York: Wiley, 1975.
WEBER, MAX, "Some Categories of Interpretive Sociology," tr. E. Graber, *Sociological Quarterly*, 22, no. 2 (Spring 1981), [1913] 151–180.
———, "The National State and Economic Policy," *Economy and Society*, 9, (November 1980), 428–449 [1895].
———, "Anticritical Last Word on *The Spirit of Capitalism*," tr. Wallace Davis, *American Journal of Sociology*, 83, no. 5 (March 1978a), [1910] 105–131.
———, *Economy and Society*, 2 vols. Berkeley: University of California Press, 1978b (orig. publ. posthumously. See 1964 Winckelman edition. First English complete translation 1968).
———, *Critique of Stammler*, tr. Guy Oakes. New York: Free Press, 1977 [1907].
———, *Roscher and Knies: The Logical Problems of Historical Economies*, tr. Guy Oakes. New York: Free Press, 1975.
———, "Georg Simmel as a Sociologist," *Social Research*, 39, no. 1 (Spring 1972), 155–163.
———, *The Agrarian Sociology of Ancient Civilization*, tr. R. I. Frank. Atlantic Highlands, New Jersey: Humanities Press, 1971a.
———, "Socialism," tr. D. Hytch, in J. E. T. Eldridge's *Max Weber: The Interpretation of Social Reality.* New York: Scribner's, 1971b, pp. 191–219.
———, *The Rational and Social Foundations of Music*, tr. Don Martindale et al. Carbondale and Edwardsville: Southern Illinois University Press, 1969.
———, *Gesammelte Aufsätze zur Wissenschaftslehre*, ed. J. Winckelman. Tübingen: J. C. B. Mohr, 1968.

————, *The Religion of India*, trs. H. H. Gerth and Don Martindale. Glencoe, Illinois: The Free Press, 1958.
————, *Max Weber on Law and Economy in Society*, trs. Max Rheinstein and Edward Shils. Cambridge: Cambridge University Press, 1954.
————, *Ancient Judaism*, tr. H. H. Gerth and Don Martindale. Glencoe, Illinois: The Free Press, 1952 [1917–1919].
————, *The Religion of China*, tr. H. H. Gerth. Glencoe, Illinois: The Free Press, 1951.
————, *General Economic History*. Glencoe, Illinois: The Free Press, 1950 (orig. publ. 1923 from lectures given in 1919–1920. Orig. English publ. 1927).
————, *The Methodology of the Social Sciences*, trs. E. Shils and H.Finch. Glencoe, Illinois: The Free Press, 1949.
————, *The Protestant Ethic and the Spirit of Capitalism*. London: Allen and Unwin, 1948 [1905].
————, *The Theory of Social and Economic Organization*, trs. Talcott Parsons and Charles Henderson. New York: Oxford University Press, 1947.
————, *Gesammelte Aufsätze zur Sozial- und Wirtschaftsgeschichte*. Tübingen: J. C. B. Mohr (Paul Siebeck), 1924.
————, *Die Verhältnisse der Landarbeiter im ostelbischen Deutschland, Vol. 55* (Schriften des Vereins für Sozialpolitik). Berlin: Duncker and Humboldt, 1892.
WEBER, WILLIAM, *Music and the Middle Class: The Social Structure of Concert Life in London, Paris and Vienna*. New York: Holmes and Meyer, 1975.
WEISMANN, AUGUST, *Essays Upon Heredity*, 2 vols., 2d ed.; ed. E. Poulton et al. Oxford: Clarendon Press, 1891.
WEISS, JOHANNES, *Weber and the Marxist World*. London and New York: Routledge and Kegan Paul, 1981.
WESSELL, LEONARD P., JR., *Prometheus Bound: The Mythic Structure of Karl Marx's Scientific Thinking*. Baton Rouge, Louisiana: Louisiana State University Press, 1984.
WESTBY, DAVID L., "The Chicago School and American Sociology," *Journal of the History of Sociology*, 1, no. 1 :(Fall 1978), 120–131.
————, "Max Weber," *American Academic Encyclopedia*.
————, "A Typology of Authority in Complex Organizations," *Social Forces*, 44, no. 4 (June 1966), 484–491.
————, and ALLAN SACK, "The Functional Rationalization and Commercialization of College Football: Its Origins," *Journal of Higher Education*, 47, no. 6 (November and December 1976), 625–647.
WHITEHEAD, A. N., *Adventures of Ideas*. New York: Mentor, 1955.
WHORF, BENJAMIN, and EDWARD SAPIR, *Language, Thought and Reality: Selected Writings*, ed. John B. Carrol. Boston: M.I.T. Press, 1956.
WICKWAR, W. H., *Baron D'Holbach: A Prelude to the French Revolution*. New York: Augustus Kelley, 1968.
WILEY, NORBERT, "Pierce, Mead, and the Internal Conversation," presented at the annual meetings of the American Sociological Association, San Francisco. August 1989.
————, "The Micro-Macro Problem in Social Theory," *Sociological Theory*, 6, no. 2 (Fall 1988), 254–260.
————, ed., *The Marx-Weber Debate*. Washington,D.C.: Sage Publications, 1987.
————, "Early American Sociology and the Polish Peasant," *Sociological Theory*, 4, no. 1 (Spring 1986a), 20–40.
————, "The Genesis of Human Nature in the Primates," presented to the German-American Theory Conference, Berkeley, California, August 1986b.
————, "The Sacred Self: Anomalies in Durkheim's Treatment," paper presented at the annual meeting of the American Sociological Association, New York, 1986c.
————, "The Current Interregnum in American Sociology," *Social Research*, 52, no. 1 (Spring 1985), 179–207.
————, "The Rise and Fall of Dominating Theories in American Sociology," *Contemporary Issues in American Sociology*, eds. W. Snizek, E. Fuhrman, and M. Miller. Westport, Connecticut: Greenwood Press, 1979a.
————, "Notes on Self Genesis: From Me to We to I," *Symbolic Interaction*, 2, no. 2 (Fall 1979b), 87–105.
————, "America's Unique Class Politics: The Interplay of the Labor, Credit and Commodity Markets," *American Sociological Review*, 32, no. 4 (August 1967), 531–541.
WILLER, JUDITH, *The Social Determination of Knowledge*. Englewood Cliffs, New Jersey: Prentice Hall, 1971.
WILSON, EDMUND, *To the Finland Station*. Garden City, New York: Doubleday, 1940.
WILSON, EDWARD O., *Sociobiology: The New Synthesis*. Cambridge, Massachusetts: Belknap, 1975.
WILSON, JOHN, *Social Theory*. Englewood Cliffs, New Jersey: Prentice Hall, Inc., 1983.
WILTSHIRE, DAVID, *The Social and Political Thought of Herbert Spencer*. New York: Oxford University Press, 1978.
WINCH, PETER, *The Idea of a Social Science*. London: Routledge and Kegan Paul, 1977.
————, "Man and Society in Hobbes and Rousseau," in *Hobbes and Rousseau*, eds. Maurice Cranston and Richard S. Peters. Garden City, New York: Doubleday Anchor, 1972, pp. 233–253.
WOLFE, ALAN, *The Limits of Legitimacy*. New York: The Free Press, 1975.
WOLFF, KURT, ed., *Emile Durkheim 1858–1917*. Columbus: Ohio State University Press, 1960.
WOLIN, SHELDON, *Politics and Vision: Continuity and Innovation in Western Political Thought*. Boston: Little, Brown, 1960.
WOOLWINE, DAVID E., "Meaning in Science and History in George Herbert Mead," unpublished manuscript, 1988.
WORSLEY, PETER, *Marx and Marxism*. New York: Tavistock, 1982.

WRIGHT, ERIC O., *Class, Crisis and the State.* New York: New Left Books, 1978.

WRONG, DENNIS, ed., *Max Weber.* Englewood Cliffs, New Jersey: Prentice Hall, 1970.

WUNDT, WILHELM, *Elements of Folk Psychology,* tr. E. L. Schaub. New York: MacMillan, 1915.

WYNNE-EDWARDS, V. C., *Animal Dispersion in Relation to Social Behavior.* Edinburgh: Oliver and Boyd, 1962.

ZARET, DAVID, "Religion and the Rise of Liberal-Democratic Ideology in 16th and 17th-Century England and France," *American Sociological Review,* 54, no. 2 (April 1989), 163–179.

———, *The Heavenly Contract: Ideology and Organization in Pre-Revolutionary Puritanism.* Chicago: University of Chicago Press, 1985.

———, "From Weber to Parsons and Schutz: The Eclipse of History in Modern Social Theory," *American Journal of Sociology,* 85, no. 5 (March 1980), 1180–1201.

———, "Sociological Theory and Historical Scholarship," *American Sociology,* 13, no. 2 (May 1978), 114–121.

ZARETSKY, ELI, ed., *The Polish Peasant in Europe and America: William I. Thomas and Florian Znaniecki.* Chicago: University of Chicago Press, 1984.

ZEITLIN, IRVING M., *Ideology and the Development of Sociological Theory* (2d ed.). Englewood Cliffs, New Jersey: Prentice Hall, 1981.

———, *Rethinking Sociology.* Englewood Cliffs, New Jersey: Prentice Hall, 1973.

———, *Marxism: A Reexamination.* New York: Van Nostrand, 1967.

ZNANIECKI, FLORIAN, *The Method of Sociology.* New York: Farrar and Rinehart, 1934.

———, *Cultural Reality.* Chicago: University of Chicago Press, 1919.

ZOHN, HARRY, *Max Weber: A Biography.* New York: Wiley, 1975.

NAME INDEX

Abel, Theodore, 353
Abrams, Philip, 487
Addams, Jane, 446
Adorno, Theodore, 53, 407, 442, 486, 487
Aho, James, 190
Alaric, 97
Albrow, Martin, 100, 101, 122, 123, 419, 431
Althusser, Louis, 181, 185, 197, 201
Ambrose, Saint, 98
Ames, van Meter, 446
Anderson, Evelyn, 320
Anderson, Perry, 197, 366, 387
Andreski, Stanislav, 131, 147
Anselm, Saint, 68
Antonio, Robert, 487
Applebaum, Richard P., 227
Aquinas, Saint Thomas, 7, 34, 52, 96
Aristotle, 8, 16, 51, 105, 138, 141, 447
Aron, Raymond, 2, 7, 11, 13, 132, 143, 265, 290, 397, 408
Augustine, Saint, 18, 31, 96, 97–101
Avenari, Schlomo, 213

Bacon, Francis, 12, 21, 55–56, 57, 71, 266
Babeuf, Francois, 38
Badie, Bertrand, 330
Baldwin, James Mark, 21, 81, 447
Baran, Paul, 215
Barker, Ernest, 324
Barnard, F. M., 110, 111, 113, 115, 116
Barnes, Harry Elmer, 9, 11, 36, 98, 118
Bathsheba (of the Old Testament), 377

Baudelaire, Charles, 285
Bauer, Bruno, 169, 182, 183
Bauer, Raymond, 427
Baxter, Richard, 400
Becker, Howard P., 9, 11, 36, 98, 118, 121, 132
Becker, Ernest, 53, 132, 444
Becket, Thomas, 100
Beckman, Max, 323
Beerbohm, Max, 285
Bellah, Robert, 243, 261
Bendix, Reinhard, 323, 324, 326, 330, 345, 403, 414, 419, 423, 487
Benjamin, Walter, 407, 487
Bensman, Joseph, 116, 427
Bentham, Jeremy, 168, 243, 249, 356
Benton, Ted, 353, 356
Berger, Peter, 347
Berger, Stephen, 397
Bergson, Henri, 240
Berkeley, Bishop, 54, 59
Berlin, Isaiah, 54, 103, 106, 109, 112, 114, 119, 123
Bierstedt, Robert, 102, 426, 444, 462
Bismarck, Otto von, 237, 333, 438–439
Birnbaum, Pierre, 330
Blanc, Louis, 236
Blau, Peter, 424, 425, 433
Blaug, M., 94
Bloom, Allan, 44
Blum, Leon, 240
Blumer, Herbert, 482, 484, 485, 487
Bock, Kenneth, 10, 109
Bodin, Jean, 18, 37
Bonaparte, Louis, 59, 73, 209, 223, 225
Bonaparte, Napoleon, 237

Bottomore, Tom, 182, 190, 194, 198, 227, 229
Bougle, Celestin, 240
Boulanger, General, 238
Boulton, Matthew, 146
Bourdieu, Pierre, 417
Bourgeois, Leon, 291
Boutroux, Emile, 240
Boyle, Robert, 54
Brahe, Tycho, 140
Brewster, John M., 446
Brinton, Crane, 15
Brown, Richard Harvey, 335
Brubaker, Robert, 319, 324, 327, 404, 413
Brummel, Beau, 285
Brunetiere, Frederick, 283
Brunn, Hans Henrik, 324
Bryan, William Jennings, 237
Bryce, James, 261
Bryson, Gladys, 63, 73
Buffon, George Lous le Clerc, comte de, 21
Buonratti, Michelangelo, 38
Bunyan, John, 62
Burckhart, Jacob, 326, 328
Burger, Thomas, 324, 337, 338, 342
Burgess, Ernest, 447, 454, 471, 481, 487
Burke, Edmund, 36, 96, 101, 116, 119, 120, 121, 123
Bury, J. B., 8

Calvin, John, 131
Campanella, Tomasso, 102
Carlyle, Thomas, 220
Carniero, Robert L., 159, 160, 162, 163, 165
Cassirer, Ernst, 8, 11, 12, 15, 20, 22, 38, 43, 113, 295
Catherine the Great, 13
Cellini, Benvenuto, 16
Charlemagne, 128
Christ (Jesus), 375
Clark, Terry N., 284
Clemeneau, Georges, 291
Cohen, Morris, 19
Cohen, 419
Colletti, Lucio, 88
Collingwood, R. G., 18, 33, 105
Collins, Randall, 192, 193, 309, 366, 383, 388, 406, 433, 486, 487
Comte, Auguste, 8, 10, 15, 25, 30, 60, 64, 70, 97, 101, 116, 124, 125, 126–145, 148, 149, 153, 175, 177, 188, 189, 190, 193, 230, 240, 242, 243, 248, 272, 292, 408, 409, 443
Condillac, Etienne Bonnet de, 54, 66–67, 71, 179, 180
Condorcet, Marquis de, 4, 9, 10, 14, 29, 30, 128, 138
Connerton, Paul, 487
Constantine (Emperor), 97
Constas, Helen, 132
Cooley, Charles H., 79, 81, 239, 240, 310, 444, 445, 446, 448–51, 454, 455, 460
Copernicus, 101
Coppens, Roche de, 132
Coser, Lewis, 147
Cottrell, Leonard, 456
Coulanges, Fustel de, 240

Croce, Benedetto, 105, 324
Cromwell, Oliver, 23
Crusoe, Robinson (fictional character), 53
Culver, Helen, 461
Cushing, Frank H., 304
Cyrus, King, 118

Dahrendorf, Ralf, 225, 227
D'Alembert, Jean Le Rond, 8, 13
Dallmayr, Fred, 334
Danto, Arthur C., 356
Darwin, Charles, 109, 145, 146, 148, 150, 158, 231, 286, 443, 448, 480, 481
Darwin, Erasmus, 146
Davis, Kingsley, 87
Davy, Georges, 292
de Bonald, Louis, 7, 97, 118, 120, 122, 123, 132, 143, 290
Debs, Eugene, 237
Decius, King, 97
de Mably, Abbe Bonnet, 43
De Maillet, Benoit de, 20
de Maistre, Joseph, 7, 96, 118, 119, 120, 122–24, 290, 321
de Meux, Madame, 13
de Greef, Guillaume, 488
Democritus, 192
Denzin, Norman, 460
DesCartes, Rene, 4, 21, 128, 131, 174, 450
de Stael, Madame, 128
de Vaux, Clothilde, 130
Dewey, John, 62, 445, 446, 451, 452, 453, 457–59
Diderot, Denis, 13, 15, 40, 117
Dilthey, Wilhelm, 321, 322, 334, 335, 336
Djilas, Milovan, 222
Duncan, David, 157
Domhoff, William, 429
Dondo, Mathurin, 128
Douglas, Jack, 294, 301
Draper, Hal, 223
Dreyfus, Captain, 236, 238, 241, 283
Dronberger, Ilse, 319, 320
Droyson, Johann, 321, 328
Dunham, Albert M., 446
Durkheim, Emile, 3, 7, 8, 38, 133, 151, 156, 160, 167, 236–317, 345, 365, 409, 443, 441, 447, 460, 461, 464, 465, 474, 482–83, 486, 487

Easton, Lloyd, 178, 179
Eisen, Arnold, 324
Eldredge, J. E. T., 325
Engels, Fredrich, 50, 167, 178, 179, 183, 188–235, 444
Epicurus, 192
Erasmus, 16
Euripides, 39
Ezekiel, The Prophet, 376

Factor, Regis, 325, 393, 428
Farberman, Harvey, 310
Faris, Ellsworth, 446, 454, 485

Faris, Robert E. L., 488
Fenton, Steve, 238, 247
Ferguson, Adam, 13, 14, 18, 26, 30, 73, 74, 80, 83,
    85, 86–87, 88, 90, 120, 164, 166, 168, 175
Fernbach, David, 218, 225, 226
Feuer, Lewis, 200, 202, 221, 222
Feuerbach, Ludwig, 180, 181–87
Fichte, Johann Gottlieb, 327, 328
Finch, Henry, 319
Fisch, M. H., 105
Fischer, Frank, 433
Fishoff, Ephriam, 403
Flint, John, 110
Fontenelle, Bernard de Bouvier, 4
Foote, Nelson, 456
Frank Andrew Gunder, 489
Franklin, Benjamin, 8, 383, 401
Frazer, James, 305
Frederick II, 13, 29
Freud, Sigmund, 238, 332, 456, 477, 487
Fried, Morton, 222
Fromm, Eric, 185, 487
Fuller, B. A. G., 20

Galileo, 54, 101, 137
Gall, Franz Josef, 139
Galton, Samuel, 126, 146
Gay, Peter, 8, 13, 15, 22, 36, 43, 81
George, C. H., 403
George, K., 403
Gerth, Hans, 319, 328, 330, 331, 365
Gibbon, Edward, 71, 81, 84, 88, 97
Giddens, Anthony, 67, 227, 247, 253, 255, 264,
    287, 293, 299, 360, 417, 487
Giddings, Franklin, 81, 239, 240, 444, 447, 481
Givant, Michael, 427
Glassman, Ronald, 487
Godwin, William, 19, 36, 37, 50, 117
Goethe, Johann Wolfgang von, 332
Goffman, Erving, 309, 313
Goodman, Mark, Joseph, 335
Gottl-Ottlilienfeld, Friedrich von, 336
Goudsblom, Johann, 142
Gouldner, Alvin, 7, 130, 189, 190, 204, 218, 227,
    233, 435
Graña, Cesar, 92, 127, 285
Green, Robert W., 431
Grotius, Hugo, 25, 34
Guddat, Kurt H., 178, 179
Gumplowicz, Ludwig, 240
Gustavus, Adolphus, 385

Habermas, Juergen, 326, 360, 424
Halbwachs, Maurice, 298
Hamlyn, G. W., 354
Hankins, Frank, 130
Hartley, David, 65
Hawthorne, Geoffrey, 52, 74, 149, 163, 167, 169,
    255, 299, 322
Haym, R., 109
Hazelrigg, Larry, 100, 419
Hazlitt, Robert W., 36
Heberle, Rudolph, 486

Hegel, G. F. W., 5, 120, 125, 169, 170–78, 179,
    181–87, 192, 227, 229, 230–31, 292, 322,
    327, 328, 332, 450, 487
Hekman, Susan, 337, 342, 359
Heller, Agnes, 187, 201
Helvetius, Claude Adrien, 28–29, 54
Hennis, Wilhelm, 367
Henrich, Dieter, 319, 324, 326
Herbst, Jurgen, 321, 329, 333, 334
Herder, Johann Gottfried von, 7, 8, 68, 96, 101,
    109–18, 119, 122, 123, 124, 137, 143, 321,
    329, 431, 442
Herodotus, 103
Hess, Moses, 169
Hilbert, Richard A., 295
Hilferding, Rudolf, 237
Hirschman, Albert O., 15, 331
Hirst, Paul Q., 278, 279
Hobbes, Thomas, 4, 22, 23–31, 33, 35, 41, 54, 238,
    242, 243, 246, 317, 330
Hobsbawm, Eric, 205
Hobson, John A., 237, 240
Holbach, Paul Henri Thiry, Baron d', 20, 65
Homer, 103
Honigsheim, Paul, 318, 319, 328, 486, 487
Hook, Sidney, 178, 183
Horkheimer, Max, 53, 407, 442, 486
Horne, Thomas, A., 35
Hughes, H. Stuart, 236, 334, 444
Hugo, Victor, 285
Hume, David, 8, 13, 15, 20, 21, 52, 53, 54, 57, 63,
    67–71, 73, 74, 75–78, 79–81, 82, 89–90,
    126, 265, 332, 457
Hunt, J., 293
Husserl, Edmund, 80, 174, 359, 446, 489
Hutcheson, Francis, 22, 73
Huxley, Thomas, 137, 149
Hymes, Eugene, 299

Iggers, George, 128, 321, 322
Irenaeus (Christian Church Father), 98
Israel, Joachim, 195

Jagger, Mick, 427
James, William, 240, 445, 448, 455, 457, 460
Jameson, Frederic, 286
Janowicz, Morris, 463
Jaspers, Karl, 319, 325
Jaures, Jean, 240
Jefferson, Thomas, 74
Joachim, the Abbot, 102
Joas, Hans, 19, 451, 456, 457, 459
John of Salisbury, 100
Johnson, Samuel, 13
Jones, Bryn, 328
Jones, W. T., 31, 55, 56
Joyce, James, 450
Justin Martyr, Saint, 98

Kalberg, Stephen, 66, 404, 405, 435, 436
Kames, Henry Home, 21, 68, 73

Kant, Immanuel, 8, 11, 15, 42, 74, 115, 120, 169, 173, 174, 242, 243, 283, 313, 327, 332
Keat, Russell, 141
Kellner, Douglas, 408
Kennedy, John, 427
Kepler, Johannes, 150
Khaldoun, Ibn, 143
Kloss, Robert, 144
Knies, Karl, 248, 319, 324, 329, 333, 346
Knox, John, 32
Kolakowski, Leszek, 185
Kokoschka, Oskar, 323
Korsch, Karl K., 189, 233
Kroeber, Alfred, 481
Kronman, Anthony T., 324, 332

La Combe, Roger, 480
Lamarck, Jean Baptiste Pierre Antoine de Monet de, 30, 145, 149, 158, 442, 480, 481
Lamenais, Felicite Robert de, 291
La Mettrie, Julan Offray de la, 20, 65
LaPlace, Pierre Simon, 140
La Salle, Ferdinand, 236
Lasswell, Harold, 164
Le Bon, Gustave, 240
Lefebvre, Henri, 190, 224
Leibnitz, Gottfried Wilhelm von, 21, 53, 68, 131, 179
Lenin, V. I., 180, 222, 237
Lenski, Gerhard, 193
Lenzer, Gertrude, 136
Le Play, Frederick, 41, 118, 120
Lessing, Gothold, 8
Levi-Bruhl, Lucien, 303
Levi-Strauss, Claude, 87, 486
Levine, Donald, 284, 324, 404, 405, 438
Levy-Bruhl, Lucien, 240, 303
Lichtheim, George, 38, 178, 190, 206, 227
Lifshitz, M., 106
Lippman, Walter, 261
Littré, Emile, 143
Locke, John, 4, 15, 20, 29, 44, 54, 55, 56–64
Loewenstein, Karl, 319
Lorenzo the Magnificent, 51
Lovejoy, Arthur O., 11, 19, 21
Lowie, Robert, 271
Löwith, Karl, 106, 107, 319, 324
Lukács, Georg, 486
Lukes, Steven, 238, 240, 248, 272, 295, 305, 356
Lyman, Stanford, M., 444
Lyng, Stephen, 456

Mably, Gabriel, 50
Machiavelli, Nicolo, 51, 88, 103, 120
Macy, Michael W., 207
Maine, Henry, 163, 251, 393
Maines, David, 453
Makkreel, Rudolf, 338
Malthus, Thomas, 150
Mandel, Charles, 210
Mandeville, Bernard, 13, 22, 32–33, 71
Mannheim, Karl, 438, 441, 486, 487
Manuel, Frank, 9, 13, 14, 102, 127

Mao Tse Tung, 180
Marcuse, Herbert, 407, 487
Marshall, Gordon, 73, 403
Marsilius of Padua, 100
Martell, Charles, 384
Martindale, Don, 101, 162, 163, 189, 248, 359, 379
Martineau, Harriet, 130
Marvin, F. S., 133
Marx, Karl, 8, 41, 50, 60, 70, 101, 106, 125, 131, 145, 166, 169, 177, 178, 179–87, 188–235, 239, 250, 259, 332, 408, 415, 417, 438, 442, 443, 450, 486, 487
Matthews, Fred, 189
Maupertuis, Pierre Louis Moureau de, 21, 65
Mauss, Marcel, 294, 303, 313
McCarthy, Thomas A., 334
McLellan, David, 192, 198, 201, 231
McPherson, Crawford B., 4, 282
Mead, G. H., 21, 81, 178, 239, 240, 310, 327, 445–61, 476, 482, 485
Meinecke, Friedrich, 321
Mendel, Gregor, 153
Menger, Carl, 332, 333
Merquoir, J. G., 319, 322, 337, 349, 361, 419, 423, 424, 425, 429
Merton, Robert, 276, 433, 444, 486
Merz, John Theodore, 237, 260
Meyer, Eduard, 346, 356, 357
Michels, Robert, 240, 420, 440
Mill, John Stuart, 131, 142, 143, 243, 248, 273, 274, 431
Millar, John, 73, 82, 84
Miller, David L., 446, 451
Mills, C. Wright, 168, 227, 319, 328, 330, 331, 365
Milne–Edwards, Henri, 260
Mitzman, Arthur, ch. 13, p. 318
Moers, Ellen, 285
Mommsen, Wolfgang J., 319, 328, 423
Monboddo, Lord (James Burnet), 73, 83, 112
Montesquieu, Charles de Secondat, 13, 15, 18, 22, 27–28, 30, 60, 81, 84, 113, 127, 138, 143
Mooney, M., 108
Moore, Wilbert, 43
Moore, Merritt A., 446
Morelly, Thomas, 43
Morgan, J. P., 445
Morgan, Lewis Henry, 197
Morris, Charles, 446
Mosca, Gaetano, 102
Mueller, Adam, 244
Munch, Peter, 354
Munsterberg, Hugo, 324
Murphy, Arthur, E., 210, 446
Murphy, Raymond, 210
Murvar, Vatro, 319, 427

Nagel, Ernest, 342
Nandan, Yash, 284
Napoleon, Louis, 209, 223, 225
Nelson, Lord, 324
Newton, Isaac, 12, 51, 54, 140, 141, 392
Nicolini, Fausto, 102
Niebuhr, H. Richard, 147
Nietzsche, Friederick, 99, 326, 332, 410, 442, 444
Nisbet, Robert, 97, 118, 247

Northrup, F. S. C., 114
Novak, Robert, 201

Oakes, Guy, 324, 333, 360
Odo, Abbot, 68
Ollman, Bertell, 226, 227, 228
Oppenheimer, Franz, 240
Orwell, George, 455
Outhwaite, W., 356
Owen, Robert, 36, 50

Paine, Tom, 36
Pareto, Vilfredo, 332, 420, 488
Park Robert, 240, 445, 447, 454, 471, 481, 485, 487
Parkin, Frank, 353, 399, 424, 425, 426
Parsons, Talcott, 43, 160, 262, 265, 270, 276, 299,
    320, 334, 367, 397, 419, 426, 444, 486, 487,
    488
Pascal, Blaise, 246
Paul, Saint, 96, 98
Peel, John David, 143, 147, 168
Peirce, Charles, 21
Pepper, Stephen, 331
Perkins, Merle L., 40, 43
Peter, Saint, 374
Petty, William, 206
Pickering, W. S. F., 292
Plamenatz, John, 194, 195
Plato, 43, 322
Poggi, Gianfranco, 357, 418
Polanyi, Karl, 3
Polybius, 13
Pompanozzi, 16
Pope, Alexander, 21, 31, 299
Popper, Karl, 322
Portis, Edward Bryan, 324
Postelthwayt, Malachi, 13
Priestly, Joseph, 146
Proudhon, Pierre-Joseph, 39, 202
Prometheus, 204

Quadagno, Jill, 149
Quetelet, Adolphe, 130

Rabelais, Francois, 16
Ranke, Leopold, 321, 328, 329, 332
Raphael, Freddy, 376
Ratzenhofer, Gustav, 240, 447
Reich, Wilhelm, 239, 487
Renouvier, Charles, 240
Rheinstein, Max, 419
Ricardo, David, 175, 195, 249
Richards, Robert J., 149, 150, 447
Rickert, Heinrich, 330, 335, 337, 338
Rickman, H. P., 356
Riesman, David, 261
Ringer, Fritz, 320, 325, 333
Ritzer, George, 189
Roberts, Ron E., 144

Robertson, H. W., 72
Robinet, A., 20
Roscher, Wilhelm, 248, 319, 324, 329, 333, 334,
    336, 346
Ross, E. A., 239, 240, 444
Rossides, Daniel W., 147, 163
Roth, Guenther, 318, 330, 419
Rousseau, Jean-Jacques, 8, 11, 12, 38, 39–50, 64,
    71, 73, 117, 127, 185, 243, 244, 283, 317
Royce, Josiah, 445, 446
Ruge, Arnold, 169
Rumney, Jay, 147
Runciman, Walter G., 330
Ruskin, John, 73, 94
Russell, Bertrand, 239

Sack, Allan, 406
Saint-Simon, Claude Henri de Rouvroy, Comte de,
    127, 128–129, 130, 141, 249
Salisbury, John of, 100–101
Salomon, Albert, 397
Samuelson, Kurt, 403
Sanborn, Frank, 444
Scaff, Lawrence A., 321
Schäffle, Albert, 244, 248
Schaff, Adam, 185, 321
Scheffler, Israel, 60
Schelling, Friedrich, 12
Schelting, Alexander von, 342
Schluchter, Wolfgang, 330, 366, 378, 393, 404
Schmoller, Gustav, 248, 332, 333
Schneider, Louis, 12
Schopenhauer, Arthur, 326, 332
Schumpeter, Joseph, 4
Schutz, Alfred, 324
Schwartz, Barry, 426
Scotus, Duns, 68
Seneca, 98
Sewart, John, 358
Shaftesbury, Anthony, 34–36, 50
Shaw, George Bernard, 237
Shils, Eduard, 236, 319
Sica, Alan, 319
Simmel, Georg, 240, 284, 285, 286, 324, 415, 447
Stevin, Simon, 381
Simpson, George 129, 131, 139, 244
Sirianni, Carmen, 433
Small, Albion, 81, 240, 444, 447, 479, 481
Smith, Adam, 10, 15, 33, 68, 73, 74, 78–81, 82, 83,
    86, 88, 90–94, 95, 116, 127, 132, 158, 164,
    166, 168, 175, 195, 208, 305, 446
Solnay, Sarah, 244
Solomon, King (Old Testament), 24, 48
Sombart, Werner, 240, 333, 349
Sorel, Georges, 236, 238
Sorokin, Pitirim, 444
Southey, Robert, 37
Spence, Larry, 57
Spencer, Herbert, 10, 30, 123, 125, 131, 145,
    146–68, 178, 188, 189, 190, 193, 230, 240,
    242, 243, 248, 270, 286, 408, 431, 448, 461,
    480, 483, 487
Spencer, Thomas 426
Speier, Hans, 486, 487
Spinoza, Benedict, 21

Spock, Doctor Benjamin, 44
Stammer, Otto, 330
Stammler, Rudolf, 68
Steward, Dugald, 8, 12, 73, 74
Stewart, John B., 63, 73, 74, 75
Stirner, Max, 169
Stocking, George, 65, 66, 67, 481
Stone, Gregory, 310, 453
Straus, David, 182–83
Strauss, Leo, 403
Sumner, William Graham, 239, 240, 444
Swain, Joseph Ward, 244
Sweezy, Paul, 210
Swidler, Ann, 324
Sybel, Heinrich, 321

Talmon, Keith, 38
Tarde, Gabriel, 240, 295, 447
Tawney, R. H., 403
Taylor, Keith, 128, 129
Tenbruck, Friedrich H., 330
Therborn, Goran, 2, 18, 26
Thierry, Auguste, 128
Thomas, W. I., 239, 240, 443, 444, 454, 461–85
Thompson, Kenneth, 38, 57
Thucidides, 10
Tiryakian, Edward, 241
Tocqueville, Alexis de, 118, 220, 286, 290, 291
Todd, Arthur James, 8
Tönnies, Ferdinand, 49, 240, 323, 326, 329, 333, 486
Toynbee, Arnold, 9
Traugott, Mark, 244, 245
Treiber, Hubert, 378, 393
Treitschke, Heinrich, 321, 328, 329
Troeltsch, Ernst, 330
Tufts, James Hayden, 445, 446
Turgot, Anne Robert Jacques, 8, 9, 10, 13, 14, 15; 30
Turner, Frederic Jackson, 445
Turner, Johnathan, 147, 162–63
Turner, Stephen, 325, 348, 393, 428
Tylor, Eduard P., 305

Urry, John, 141

Veblen, Thorstein, 10, 92, 216, 444
Vico, Giambattista, 7, 13, 14, 52, 54, 68, 96, 101–09, 110, 111, 112, 113, 118, 119, 122, 123, 124, 137, 175, 232
Vidich, Arthur, 444

Voltaire, 6, 8, 11, 12, 13, 14, 15, 21, 26, 81, 117
vom Stein, Freiherr, 431
von Below, Georg, 348
von Humboldt, Alexander, 321, 328, 431
von Humboldt, Wilhelm, 328
von Savigny, Friedrich Karl, 96
von Weise, Leopold, 240, 486
Wagner, Adolf, 333
Wagner, Richard, 285
Wallace, Alfred Russel, 150
Wallas, Graham, 237
Wallenstein, Immanuel, 489
Walliman, Isador, 184, 185, 197, 201
Wallwork, Ernest, 243
Ward, Lester, 239, 240, 444
Warriner, Charles K., 353
Washington, George, 426
Watson, John, 448, 451
Watt, James, 146
Weber, Marianne, 318, 320
Weber, Max, 7, 30, 52, 87, 92, 116, 147, 164, 240, 260, 286, 316, 318–442, 444, 458, 461, 463, 468, 478, 482, 483, 484–87, 489
Wedgewood, Josiah, 146
Weismann, August, 480, 481
Wessell, Leonard P., 204
Wesley, John, 401
Westby, David L., 319, 406, 445
Westermarck, Edward, 488
Whitehead, Alfred North, 58, 62, 74
Whitman, Walt, 285
Whyte, William H., 261
Wilburforce, Bishop, 149
Wiley, Norbert, 19, 310, 417, 479, 480, 481, 485, 487, 488
Wilhelm, Kaiser, 237, 322
Wilson, Woodrow, 445
Wiltshire, David, 147, 163
Winch, Peter, 42, 353, 360, 361
Winckelman, Johannes, 319
Wittich, Claus, 390
Wolfe, Alan, 237
Wolff, Virginia, 450
Woolwine, David E., 459
Wordsworth, William, 36
Worsley, Peter, 12
Wrong, Dennis, 423, 425, 426, 427
Wundt, Wilhelm, 241, 446
Wynne-Edwards, V. C., 150

Zaret, David, 201, 340
Zaretski, Eli, 461, 463, 465, 469, 485
Zeitlin, Irving M., 191, 214
Znaniecki, Florian, 240, 443, 444, 461–85
Zohn, Harry, 318

SUBJECT
INDEX

Alienation
  Augustine, 181
  and estrangement (Marx), 184 *fn*, 196–205
  Feuerbach, 182–4
    Marx's critique of, 184, 196
  Hegel, 181
    Marx's critique of, 102
  of proletariat, 202–5
Anarchism, 211 *fn*, 236
  anarcho-syndicalism, 236 *fn*, 291 *fn*
  Sorel, 236
Arts, the (Art)
  compared to div., of Labor (Durkheim), 249
  historicism expressed in, 323
  in progress, Turgot's view of, 13 *fn*
Attitude–value scheme (Thomas and Znaniecki),
    463–64 *et passim*
Authority, concept of
  Augustine, 98–99
  centralization of, in Spencer's political sociology,
    163–64
  Comte, 133
  Führerprinzip, 320
  John of Salisbury, 100
  reactionary conservatives, 121
  in Renaissance, 101
  Weber, defined (*see* also Domination), 419

Bildung, concept of
  in German culture, 325–26
  Rousseau's influence on, 38 *fn*
Bureaucracy (bureaucratic administration)
  discussed, 429–35

Durkheim, 248
  critique of, 433 *fn et passim*
  and knowledge, 431–5
  Marx, 221–2
  as pathology, 431
  Weber, defined, 429–31
Bourgeoisie
  and destruction of the family, Marx's and
    Engels's view, 200 *fn*
  French, compared with English, by Marx and
    Engels, 179
  German, 320–21

Calling, doctrine of the, 398
Capitalism
  Comte, 136
  constraints on, 218–19
  critical Marxist view of, 487
  culture of, 220–21
  Durkheim, 249–50, 261, 278–87, 316–17
  Hegel, 175, 177 *fn*
  Marx, 184 *passim*
    and precapitalist society, 197–200
  United States, 139, 445
  Weber
    causes of, 383–94
    master problem for, 367–68
    modern (modern bourgeois), 379–83
    obstacles to, 394–96
    Protestant ethic, and spirit of, discussed,
      396–404
    rationalizing processes in, 414–6
    spirit of, 382–83, 396
    types of, 379–81

Catholicism,
  in capitalist development, 385–86
  Comte, 137
  and concept of community, 96
  and the confessional, 398
  philosophes, view of, 15–16
Cause, concept of,
  Comte, 141–42
  Durkheim, 272–76, 277
    as morphological, 252–53, 331–32
  Hegel, 181
  Hume, 58–60
  Weber, 346–49, 382
Charisma, 371, 373, 374, 421–22, 426–27
  institutionalization of (Weber), 385
  law prophets (Weber), 413
Christianity, (*see also* Catholicism, Protestantism,
    Religion)
  and alienation, 181
  Augustine, 98–101
  early, 97–98
  Feuerbach, 182–4
  and philosophes, 15
  among Polish peasantry, 461
  reactionary conservatives, 119, 120, 124
  Spencer's milieu, 146–47
  Vico, 104
  Weber (*see also* Economic ethics, Interests,
    Rationalization), sects, 397–99
Citizenship (Weber), 384, 387, 389
Class (social class), 48
  bias (Spencer), 155
  conflict, in United States, 445
  consciousness, in Marx, 203 *passim*, 224–9
  and ethnic conflict, in United States, 239
  Hegel, 176–77
  Marxist theory of, 185, 224–229
    critian Marxists' theory of, 407 *fn*
  Smith, A., 93–94
  Weber
    and class conflict in ancient and medieval cities,
      387–89
    contrasted with Marx, 417
    defined, 416
    Marxist critique of, 417
    and rationalization of capitalist economy,
      416–19
Class struggle (*see Class*; conflict)
Commerce
  and dependency, A. Smith's view, 85 *fn*
  philosophes' view, 13 *fn*
Concepts, Weber's types of, 340–42, 344
Conflict (*see also* Class)
  class, Marx and Engels, 197–205
  and div. of labor (Durkheim), 246–47, 252
  ethnic, 239
  "Faustian", among capitalists, 216 *fn*
  Hegel, 171–73
  Hobbes, 24
  Rousseau, 41, 42
  Scots, 88–90
  Spencer, 161, 162, 164–65
  Weber
    and creativity in romanticism, 325
    and individual, conception of, 328–32
    and law, 428 *fn*
    in medieval and ancient cities, 387–89

  organizational, 433 *fn*
  and social change, theory of, 385–86
Consciousness
  collective, Durkheim's concept of, 244–45 *et
    passim*
  Dewey's concept of, 451
  false, Marx's concept of, 224, 228 *fn*
  individual, Durkheim's concept of, 244–45 *et
    passim*
  of kind, Giddings' theory of, 81 *fn*, 447–48
  self-, (Hegel), 327, *passim*
Conservatism, political, 5, 118
  Comte, 137–38, 144–45
  Durkheim, 247 *fn*
  Hegel, 169
  Spencer, 167–68
  Vico, 108
  Young Hegelians', Marx's and Engels's view, 178
Contradiction
  Hegel, 173–75, 177, 181
  Marx, 217 *passim*
Crime
  Durkheim's theory of, 277–79
  and punishment, 268, 277–79
  Smith, A., 85 *fn*
Critical Marxism (critical theory)
  Frankfurt school, 332, 407 *fn*, 487,
  Marx, 182
Culture
  Appolonian, 442
  German, 323, 325, 329
  Greek, 321
  knowledge of, from standpoint of value
    relevance, 338–39
  national intellectual, 238–40
  Thomas's concept of, 481
  Western, and science, 363–64
"Currents", Durkheim's concept of, 257, 268, 269,
    279–80, 297, 301
Cyclical theories
  in Middle Ages, 102 *fn*
  Vico, 102–5

Dandy (dandyism), 285 *fn*
Darwinism, 148–49
  in Spencer, 151–52 *et passim*, 443, 480–81
Deference and demeanor, Goffman's theory of, 460
Democracy (*see also* Authority, Domination, State),
    320
  Durkheim, 292
  Weber, 428–29
Definition of the situation (Thomas), 479–80
Dialectic
  Hegel, 170–73 *passim*
  Marx, 214
Division of labor
  Comte, 133–34
  Durkheim
    and anomie, 259
    causes of, 251
    and the dualism of human nature, 260–61
    forced, 259–60
    and society, 252 *ff*
    theory and types of, 248–62
  Hegel, 176–77

Marx, 185, 202, 210–11, 228–29
Rousseau, 42
Scots' theory of role in development, 84–85
Spencer, as model for theory of biological
evolution, 151
Diversity, human
in eighteenth century social thought, 25–31
and the individual as meaning-constructor, 324
Domination, legitimate, Weber's ideal type of (*see
also* Authority),
defined, 419–20
discussed, 420–29 *et passim*
charismatic, 421–22
critiques of, 423–29
legal-rational, 422–23
partrimonial, 389
traditional, 420–21
Dualism of human nature (*homo duplex*)
Augustine, 97–99
challenges to, 377–78
Christian, 31 *fn*
Comte, 134
Durkheim's conception of, 246–247
Manicheanism, 31 *fn*
Dynamic density, Durkheim's concept of, 25

Economic ethics, Weber's concept of
and Buddhism, 373
and Calvinism, 369
and Confucianism, 369
and Hinduism, 369
and Judaism, 375–79
and salvation religions, 368–79
Education
Comte, 133
Durkheim, 243–4, 291–2
Hegel, 173
Helvetius, 28–9
Rousseau, 433 *ff*
Smith, A., 92–93
Elective affinity, Weber's concept of, 255, 345, 366,
401–2, 418, 440
Elite(s)
in England, modernizing, 146–47
power, and democracy, 429
theories of, Pareto and Mosca, 420 *fn*
Emergence, 19 *fn*
Empiricism
Durkheim, 262 *ff*
Herder, 114 *fn*
Hume, 61–64
Spencer, 157
Thomas and Znaniecki, 461
Weber, 339
Emotion
Cooley, 449, 460
in pragmatist theory of knowledge, 457–59
Enlightenment, the
and Christian doctrine, 19–33
Comte, 134, 193
Durkheim, 241–42
and theory of Suicide, 296–97
and education, 29
and evil, problem of, 31–37

Frankfurt school, critique of, 332, 407–8 *fn*
and the Greeks, 13
Hegel, 230
and human diversity, 25–31
and human nature, conception of, *Chapter Three*
and knowledge, 72
Marx, 193–94
and modernization in England, 146–48
and opposition to historicism, 321–22
and the (three) problematics, in post-World War
II sociology, 488–89
and Rousseau's theory of, 43–48
Spencer, 151–52, 159, 166, 168, 193
and technology, 13
and travel, 26
Environmentalism, 148
Giddings, 447
Helvetius, 28–29
implications of, for sociology, 30
Montesquieu, 27–28
Epistemological Protestantism
in Bacon's philosophy, 56
Durkheim, 267
Ethics, Weber's two types of, 326 *fn*
Evil, problem of
in Comte, 136–7
in eighteenth-century thought, 317–37
among Israelites, 378–79
in Marx, 235
in Spencer, 148, 151
in Zoroastrianism, 375
Evolution, theory or theories of
American sociologists, 444 *fn*
Comte, 60
Darwin, 149, 150, 155, 480
Durkheim, 251, 255, 270–72 *et passim*
in eighteenth century, 20–21
Lamarck, 149, 150, 155, 480
and the moral sense, in Spencer, 151
and natural selection, 151
in *Polish Peasant* (Thomas and Znaniecki), 461 *fn*,
477
and population pressures, 151 *fn*
and race, 481 *fn*
and religion, 149–50
Spencer, 60, 148, 150–63
Weber, 330 *fn* 365–66
rejection of, 329–32
Exchange-value (*see* Use-value)
Exploitation, Marx's theory of, 209–17

Family
Comte, 132–33
Hegel, 175
Marx and Engels, 200, 204
Fetishism of commodities (Marx), 200, 202, 220–22
Feudalism, 386–9
Folkways (and mores), 444 *fn*
Freedom (*see* Individual, concept of; Human
agency; Philosophical anthropology)
Functionalism
Spencer, 160–62
Durkheim, 272–79

Geisteswissenschaften, 334, 338
  Vico, 107
Gemeinschaft, Tönnies's concept of, 323, 329
General will, 38 *fn*
German expressionism, 323
Gesselschaft, Tönnies concept of, 323
Gesture, 448
Great chain of being, 21 *fn*
  Hobbes, 23
  Vico, 108
Guilds
  Durkheim, 288–90
  Weber, in ancient and medieval cities, 387–89

Habit, Dewey's concept of, 457
Heroic genius, 285 *fn*
Hierarchy of the sciences
  Comte, 138–43
  Saint-Simon, 129
Historical materialism (*see* Marxism)
Historicism, 321–23 *et passim*, 444
History
  Burke, 119–20
  Comte, 135, 137, 181
  Dilthey, 334–36
  Durkheim, 273–79
  Hegel, 177 *fn*
  de Maistre, 119
  Marx and Engels, 197, *passim*
  Thomas and Znaniecki, in *Polish Peasant*, 482–3
  Vico, 102 *ff*
  Weber, 328–32, 365–68
    developmental, 366 *fn*
Human agency
  Durkheim, 245–47, 265 *fn*, 269
  Giddens (structuration), 68 *fn*
  Marx and Engels, 180, 200, 235
  Thomas and Znaniecki, 481–82
  Weber (*see* Philosophical anthropology)
Human nature (*see also* Individual and Society;
    Philosophical Anthropology)
  Christian concept of, *Chapter Three*
  Comte, 131–32, 138
  dualism of (*see* Dualism of human nature)
  Durkheim, 242–8
  and Enlightenment, 19 *ff*
  Hegel, 171
  Hobbes, 23–25
  Spencer, 148–54
Humanism
  Feuerbach, 183, 184, 185
  Marx, 185 *fn*

Ideal types, Weber's
  critique of, 355–56
  discussed, 342–46
  historical, 340, 343–45
  "pure", of action, 351–52
  quasi-generic, 344–45
  and subjective meaning, 358–60
Idealism
  Durkheim's method, opposed to, 267
  German, 327–28

Hegel's, 169–77
  Marx's critique of Hegel's, 178
  romantic concept of self in, 451
  Weber's, 330–32
Ideology
  imperialist, 237
  of Junkers, 320
  Marx's concept of, 221, 224, 226
  Neo-marxist modernizing, 429
  and state, in Durkheim, 290–93
  unified, in Middle Ages, 384
Idols, Bacon's, 55–56
Immiseration of working class, Marx's theory of,
    203, 214–17
Imperialism, 237
  Hobson, 237
  Lenin, 237
  Weber, 320
Individual and society, concept of
  Comte, 131–32 *et passim*
  Durkheim, 244 *passim*
  and emergence of sociology in the eighteenth
    and nineteenth centuries, 18
  in Greek and Judeo-Christian culture, 17–18
  Hobbes, 23–25
  reactionary conservatives, 122
  Vico, 113
  Weber, 324–28
    and history, 329–32
    and natural selection, 331 *fn*
    and "personality", 325
    and romanticism, 325–28
Individualism
  anarchistic, 285 *fn*
  Bellah, 261 *fn*
  Comte, 136
  Durkheim,
    and "cult of individual", 283–84, 286
    and progress, 247
    and social solidarity, 253–57
  in interpretations of American culture, 261 *fn*
  Kant, 283
  possessive, 284
  Rousseau, 283
  Simmel, 284–6
  in sociologies of sociological theorists, 443
  Tocqueville, 206 *fn*, 261 *fn*
  Weber, 286
  Whyte, Wm., 261 *fn*
Industrialization (industrialism)
  Comte and Saint-Simon, 127
  English, 240 *fn*
  French, 238
  German, 237, 320, 323
  Spencer, 146–48
  United States, 445
Interactionism, 444
  American sociology, 239
  Cooley, 448–50
  Durkheim,
    religion, sociology of, 308–9, 312–13
    suicide, sociology of, 302–3
  Hume, 76–77
  Mead, 450–57
    the act, 452–53
    critique of, 455, 460–61
    generalized other, 454–55

I and me, 455–57
  internal conversation, 454–55
  meaning, 453–54
  sociality, 456–57
Inequality (*see also* Class; Social stratification)
  Durkheim, 259–60
  Rousseau, 40–42
  Smith, A., 90–94
Inner-outer polarity
  in German historicism, 238, 322–23
  in Herder, 118
  in Weber, 368, 378–79, 421
Instincts,
  Comte's sociology, 131, *et passim*
  Cooley's sociology, 448 *fn*
  Weber's rejection of, 324–25
Intellectuals
  alienated, 127
  "free-floating" (Mannheim), 127
  role of, in eighteenth-century social thought, 13
  Weber
    legal, 413
    priestly, theory of, in religious rationalization, 372–75
Interests, category of
  and class, 417
  in eighteenth century thought, 15 *fn*
  in Marx and Marxism, 228 *fn*, 331–32
  among Catholic church officialdom, 385
  Weber
    capitalist, 379 *passim*
    among Catholic church officialdom, 385
    material and ideal, discussed, 331
    in organizations, 369
    among priests and magicians, 371 *et passim*
Interpretation (*see also Verstehen*)
  Thomas and Znaniecki, 484–85
  and values in Weber's sociology, 362
  Vico, 107–8
Iron cage, 436 *fn*
Irony
  Durkheim
    functionalism, 27 *fn*
    suicide, theory of, 3
  Marx, 204
  Scots, 85–88
  Spencer, 168
  Vico, 104
  Weber, in spirit of capitalism-Protestant ethic theory, 402–3
Irrationality
  in critical Marxism, 442
  in critique of Enlightenment, 332
  in Mannheim's sociology, 441–42
  Weber
    ideal types, absence of in, 440–41
    and law, 390–94
    and magic, 394
    in philosophical and anthropology, 332

Joint labor, 460
Judaism
  ancient, Weber's study of, 319, 375–79
  and suicide, Durkheim's theory of, 296

Justice,
  Hegel, 175–76
  Khadi, 391
  and personal rights, Spencer's theory of, 158–59

Knowledge
  as adaptive, 51
  Baconian conception of, 51
  in Enlightenment, primacy of, 52–54
  and faith, 52
  Hume's theory of, 61–64
  premodern conceptions of, 51–52
  and reason, 52 *ff*
  Weber
    and bureaucracy, 431–35
    and rationalization, 408–11
Knowledge, theory of social,
  Comte, 138–43
  Dewey, 457, 459–60
  Durkheim, 262–79
  Hegel, 173–75
  Herder, 113–15
  Marx, 229–34
  Mead, 457–59
  reactionary conservatives, 123
  Saint-Simon, 128–29
  Spencer, 154–56
  Thomas and Znaniecki, 483–85
  Vico, 106–8
  Weber, 332 *ff*
Kulturpessimus, 326, 435 *fn*, 437
Kulturwissenschaften, 338

Labor
  aristocracy, Lenin's theory of, 257
  theory of value (Marx), 206–9
  unions (Durkheim), 294
Lamarckism
  in American sociology, 480–81
  in Spencer's sociology, 149–50, 158–59 *passim*, 443, 480–81
Language
  in work of eighteenth-century thinkers, 68 *fn*
  Herder, 112, 114
  in nominalist-realist controversy, 68 *fn*
  reactionary conservatives, 122
  Rousseau, 41
Law, scientific
  of the changing organic composition of capital, Marx's, 211–13
  Comte's, of the three stages, 134–38, 141, 144–45
  of the falling rate of profit, Marx's, 211–13
  and ideal of freedom, 64–70
  Marx, 232
  natural, doctrine of
    Vico, 104–5
    Weber, judgement on, 427–28
    Whitehead, distinctions regarding, 58 *fn*
  and scientific empiricism, 54–61
  Thomas and Znaniecki, 484
  Weber, 340–1, 347 *fn*

Law, sociology of
  Durkheim, types of, 258–59
  Weber, 370, 436–37
    and capitalism, modern, 390–94
    and common, in England, 392
    and juristic person, creation of, 383–84
    and religious development, 392–93
Liberal market society, Scot's theory of, 81–90
liberalism, 5
  Comte, 137, 144
  and critical Marxism, 487
  Durkheim, 247 *fn*
    classical, rejection of, 248
  European, 236
  Hobbes, 25
  weakness of, in Germany, 320–21
  Weber's, 320–21
Life-organization (Thomas and Znaniecki), 472
Lutheranism, 322–23, 383

Machinery, role of, in Marx's theory of surplus
    value, 213 *fn*
Magic, in Weber's sociology of religion, 371–74 *et
    passim*
Marxism, (*see* Chapter Ten)
  and Durkheim's forced division of labor, 261
  "nightmare", 222 *fn*
  and sociology, 188–91
  Weber's
    critique of, 407 *fn*, 442
    judgement on, 330–32
    similar view of capitalism, 382
Master-slave relationship
  Hegel, 172–73
  Herder, 115
  Marx, 229
Materialism
  French, 179–81
  historical, 197
  Marx's and Engels's, 179–81
  Weber's, 330–31
Meaninglessness
  in Weber's philosophical anthropology, 324
  in Weber's understanding of science, 410–11
Mechanical solidarity (*see* Social solidarity)
Mechanism, concept of
  in eighteenth-century thought, 20, 431
  in French materialism, 321
  in German historicism, 321, 323
  in German romanticism, 238
  Herder, 115–8
  Weber
    sociology, 438
    theory of bureaucracy, 431 *et passim*
Method
  Durkheim's, 262–79
    comparative, 253, 275–76
    use of law as indicator in, 258–59
  Weber's
    comparative, 348
    Verstehen in, 335–36, 349–52, 355, 396
Methodenstreit, 332–34
Military society, Spencer's concept of (*see* also
    Societal types), 163–6
Mind, concept of,

Bacon's, 55–56
Comte's, 135, 145
in eighteenth-century social thought,
    transformation of, 8–11, 13–15
Hume's, 58–60
Locke's, 56–57
Mead's, 451–52, 457–58
in doctrine of parallelism, 54–55
Mode of reproduction (Marx and Engels), 180, 197,
    217
Modernism
  Communist ideology of, 429
  of culture in U.S., 469
  Rousseau's critique of, 39–42
  Weber's understanding of (*see also*
    Rationalization), 442
Money
  Marx, 220–21
  Simmel, 415
  Weber, 414–15
Moral sense
  Shaftesbury's philosophy of, 33–36
  Spencer's theory of, 148, 151, 155, 157
Moral sentiments
  Ferguson's theory of, 80
  and Giddings's concept of consciousness of kind,
    81 *fn*
  Smith's, A., theory of, 78–81
Morality, importance of, in Durkheim's sociology,
    242 *et passim*
Motives, in Weber's sociology, 352–54
Mysticism (Weber), 378

Natural selection
  Darwin, 149 *fn*, 150
  Spencer, 152 (*see also* Social Darwinism)
  Weber's view of, in sociology, 331 *fn*
natural socialbility, as Shaftesbury's solution to
    problem of evil, 33–36
Naturwissenschaften, 334
  Vico, 107

Occupational groups, Durkheim's theorization of,
    288–90, 293–94
Organic conception of society
  Durkheim, 252, *passim*
  German historicism, 321, 322
  Hegel, 175
  John of Salisbury, 100
  reactionary conservatives, 120–21
  Spencer, 161–62
    critique of, 162–63
  Vico, 105
  Weber's rejection of, 329
Organic solidarity (*see* social solidarity)
Original sin, doctrine of
  in Enlightenment, 20
  in Paul of the Epistles, 98

Parties, political, 439–40
  Durkheim's theory of the state, absence of in, 293

German, Weber's estimation of, 320–21
Michels's analysis of, 440 *fn*
Passions, 8
  Comte, 145
  Durkheim, 247
  Hume
    theory of knowledge and, 63
    theory of personal relationships and, 75 *ff*
  and material progress, Millar's theory of, 86–87
  rehabilitation of, in Enlightenment, 22–23
  Weber, 326
Penalty of taking the lead (Veblen), 10
Personality types, Thomas's and Znaniecki's theory
  of, 474–79
  Bohemian, 476–77
  character-attitudes in, 475–77
  Creative, 477, 478
  life-organization in, 476–77
  Philistine, 476–78
  temperamental factors in, 475–76
Phenomenology
  Hegel, 172, 173, 174
  Husserl, 446
Philosophes, 8 *et passim*
Philosophical anthropology, 4–5
  Comte, 131–32
  defined, 4–5
  Durkheim, 242–48
  Enlightenment, types of in, 25–50
  Herder, 113
  Hobbes, 23–25
  Marx, 185–87, 193–96
  Spencer, 148–54
  Vico, 105–6
  Weber, 324–32
Polish peasantry
  in New World, 469–74
    mutual aid societies among, 470–71
    social disorganization among, 472–74
    supra-territorial org's among, 472
  in Old World, 465–69
    associations among, 468–69
    class revolution, absence among, 467
    family organization among, 463–66
    individualism among, 466–69
    leadership among, 467–68
    revolutionary attitudes among, 466
    social disorganization among, 466
    social reorganization among, 467
Politics
  Comte's view of, 144
  Durkheim's view of, 241–42, 283, 292
  German, 320–21
  Weber's, 320–21
Population pressures
  and division of labor, Durkheim's analysis,
    251–52
  Marx, 215–16
  Spencer, 151
  Sumner, 444 *fn*
Populism, 236, 237
Positivism
  Bacon, 55–56
  Comte, 132, 134, 136, 141, 144
  Durkheim, 262–79 *et passim*
  during the Enlightenment, 72
  in Hume's epistemology, 64, 69–70

Spencer, 156
Thomas and Znaniecki, 484–85
Power
  Comte, 133
  Durkheim, 293
  Weber (*see* Authority; Domination)
Pragmatism, 446 *et passim*
Praxis
  Comte, 143–44
  Durkheim, 241–42
  Fichte, 327
  Hegel, 230–31
  Marx, 232–34
  Spencer, 167–68
  Weber, 319–21, 362–64, 440–42
Primary group (Cooley), 449–50
Problematics (three)
  defined, 2–3
    human nature, 4–5
    social change, 3–4
    social knowledge, 5–6
  interrelations, 126–27
  Rousseau, 48–49
  Spencer, 166–68
Progress, doctrine or theory of
  and alienation, in Smith's and Ferguson's theory
    of liberal market society, 85–86
  in Aristotle's philosophy, 10 *fn*
  Comte, 134–38
  Condorcet, 9–10
  and evil, problem of, 11
  and Greek though, 15–16
  as growth of mind, 15
  Herder's inconsistency regarding, 109–10
  ironic consequences of, in Scots' theory of liberal
    market society, 85–90
  and knowledge, 10–11
    two aspects of, 11–16
  and natural law, 11–14
  and the natural order, 14 *ff*
  philosophes' skepticism about, 10–11
  and religion, 15
  Rousseau's critique of, 39–43
  Saint-Simon, 128
  Turgot, 8–9
  Vico, 104
  Weber's rejection of, 328–32
Progressivism, 190, 445, 448
Proletariat, 12
  Comte, 134
  critical Marxism, 407 *fn*
  and imperialism, 237
  Marx's theory of, 180, 202–5
Protestant ethic, 340, 396–404
  and spirit of capitalism, 348–49
Protestantism, 319
  in Durkheim's theory of suicide, 299
  sects (Weber), 369, 396
Puritanism (*see also* Protestantism; Protestant ethic),
  376, 411
  and Confucianism, 402–3
  ahd Hinduism, 400

Rationality, concept of
  Durkheim, 266, 272

Rationality, concept of (*cont.*)
  Mannheim, 441–42
  Weber
    and the individual, 326
    in law, 390–92
    state economic policy and, 385, 389
    types, pure, 351–52 *et passim*
    types, empirical, 404–8 *et passim*
      formal, 381, 395, 405–6 *passim*
      intellectual, 377–79
      practical, 404
      substantive, 381, 405, 406–7
Rationalization, Weber's concept of
  in capitalist development, 381, 382, 392–94,
    414–18
  and disenchantment, 378
  in law, 390–94, 411–14
  in religion, 370–79
  in science, 408–11
  types
    formal, 403–7 *et passim*
    intellectual, 390, 377–79
    substantive, 406 *et passim*
Rationalization, Weber's general theory of, 435–40
Reason (*see also* Rationality)
  and authority, 21
  Comte, 134–45, 137, 145
  as a critical capacity, 21
  degradation of, 442
  Durkheim, 242, 293
  Herder, 111–12
  Kant, 174
  and progress, 12, 21, 332
  and public opinion, 12
  Rousseau's critique, 43
  Scots
    and the passions, 74 *passim*
    role in progress, 83
  Weber, 325
Relations of production (*see* Mode of production)
Religion (*see also* Catholicism; Protestantism;
    Puritanism)
  Durkheim, 253, 255 *fn*, 267 *fn*
    beliefs, 305, 310–13
    defined, 305–6
    ritual, 307–9, 312–13
    and science, 313–16
    theory of, 303–13
    totemic, 305–6
    clans, 304–5
  Hindu, 400
  of Humanity
    Comte, 131, 134, 136
    Durkheim, 284
  in military society, role of, Spencer's theory of,
    164
  Weber, 370, *passim*
  Zoroastrianism, 375
Reserve army of proletariat (labor reserve), Marx's
    theory of
  categories, Marx's 214–15
  function, 213
Revolution,
  France, 238
  Marx, 2–4, 227 *fn*
  medieval cities, 387–89
  modernizing, 429

Ritual, 265 *fn*, 267 *fn*, 280
  in Durkheim's sociology of religion, 306 *et passim*
  in Weber's sociology of religion, 368–79, *passim*,
    396–404
Romanticism (Romantic movement), 38 *fn*, 127, 178
  German, 238–39
  Hegel, 169, 178
  Mead, 450–51
  Weber, 325–26
Rules of sociological method, Durkheim's, 262–79

Salvation anxiety, 397–98
Science of ethics, Durkheim's idea of, 242, 317
Self, idea of the
  Baldwin, 447
  Hegel, 327 *passim*
  Hume, 64 *fn*
  looking-glass (Cooley), 448
    Mead's critique of, 450
  Marx, 196 *fn*
  and rationalization, Weber's analysis, 437–38
  Romantic idea of, 327–28, 444, 450–51
  Smith, A., 79–80
Social action, Weber's sociology of
  critique of, 352–64
  discussed, 336–52
Social class (*see* Class; Social stratification)
Social Darwinism, 147, 152
  struggle for existence (Spencer), 152
  in Sumner's sociology, 444 *fn*
Social disorganization (*see also* Polish peasantry),
    462, 464
Social facts, Durkheim's concept of, 242
  and causality, 279–81
  classified, 268–70
  constraining nature of, 263–67
  crystallized and uncrystallized, 268–70 *passim*
  defined as things, 265
  externality of, 263–67
  generality of, 264
  morphological, 268 *et passim*
  pathological, 258, 271–72, 278
Social level(s), problem of
  Durkheim, 263 *ff passim*
  Hobbes, 250
  and the level of the individual, 356–58
Social mobility
  Comte, 136
  Durkheim, 259–60
Social order(s), Weber's concept of
  defined, 406
  discussed, 406
  interrelations among, 418
Social problem the, 237
Social solidarity, Durkheim's concept of
  and individualism, 253–57
  types, 252 *passim*
Social statics, Comte's concept of, 131–34
Social stratification (*see also* Class),
  Comte, 133–34
  Millar, 82
  Smith, A., 91–92
  Weber
    class and status group, 416
    among Israelites, 377

Socialism, 236, 237
  of the chair (*Kathedersozialismus*), 332–33 *fn*
    Durkheim's similarity to, 288 *fn*
  Debs, 237
  Durkheim's view of, 286–88
  Fabian, 236–37
  guild, 291 *fn*
  Marx's conception of, 228–9
  and sociology, 237
  utiopian, Marx's and Engels's critique of, 221
  Weber's view of, 418
Societal types, Spencer's theory of, 163–66
Sociological explanation, conditions of, 18–19
Sociology
  American, 444, 488 *passim*
  and Christian belief, 19
  double dialectic of (Giddens), 360 *fn*
  English, 240 *fn*
  European, and Naziism, 488
  German, 323, 327
  and human nature, 19
  and individual-society polarity, 17–18
  and language games, as object of, 360–61
  and levels of reality, 19 *fn*
  and Marxism, 188–91
  national contexts of, 237–40
  as a science of ethics (Durkheim), 242, 263
  as a scientific discipline, 17–19
Species being (Marx), 194, 199
Spectator, the (Smith, A.), 79
Sponteneity
  Durkheim's concept of, 245–46, 257
    discussed, 261, 265 *fn*, 270, 279
    and forced division of labor, 260
    and mechanism, 238–39
Status (Weber)
  ethic, 396
  group
    defined, 416
    obstacle to capitalism, 396
    in rationalization of capitalist economy, 416–19
State
  Comte, 133
  Durkheim, 248, 288, 291–14
  Hegel, 177
  Hobbes, 24
  and inequality, in Scots' sociology, 89–90
  Marx, 222–24
  reactionary conservatives, 121–22
  Smith, A., 94, 84 *fn*
  Weber
    defined, 424
    centralization of in Europe, 385–86
    Machtstaat, 322, 428 *fn*
    patrimonial, 384–85
    Rechtstaat, 322, 428 *fn*
    Ständestaat, 383, 384, 394, 428 *fn*
Struggle for existence (*see also* Natural selection)

Darwin, 149
  Durkheim, 251
  Spencer, 152
Subjective meaning (Weber), 301, 345, 349–52
  — and ideal type construction, 358–59
  and social relationship, concept of, 358–59
Suicide, Durkheim's theory of
  causes, 296–97
  critique of, 298–302
  defined, 296
  and dualism of human nature, 299–300
  and Enlightenment, 303
  normality or abnormality of, 297–98
  types, 295
Surplus value, Marx's theory of, 210–14
Symbol (*see* Interactionism)
Sympathetic imagination (Herder), 113–15
Sympathy, concept of
  Hume, 63, 74–78
  Smith, A., 78–81

Tableau cérébrale (Comte), 131–32, 135
Technology, 13
Theodicy (Weber), 378, 379
Theses on Feuerbach, Marx's, 185–87
Traditionalism (Weber), 394–95

Unity of the sciences, Comte's theory of, 139–43
Use-value (and exchange-value), Marx's theory of,
  198, 205–9
Utilitarianism
  Benthamites, 368 *fn*
  Condillac, 66–67
  Durkheim, 272
    rejection of, 243
  and evil, problem of, Mandeville's solution of,
    32–3
  in Hume's theory of societal relations, 77–78
  Smith, A., 33

Verstehen (*see also* Interpretation)
  Dilthey, 334–35
  Herder, 118
  Vico, 107–08
  Weber, 335–36, 349–52, 355, 396
Volk, concept of
  in German historicism, 322, 329
  Herder, 110, 112, 115
Volkswirtschaft school of economics, 329, 332–33 *fn*

Young Hegelians, 169, 178